Biomimetic Humanoid Robots with Human Consciousness

Biomimetic Humanoid Robots with Human Consciousness

Mohsen Shahinpoor

JENNY STANFORD
PUBLISHING

Published by

Jenny Stanford Publishing Pte. Ltd.
101 Thomson Road
#06-01, United Square
Singapore 307591

Email: editorial@jennystanford.com
Web: www.jennystanford.com

British Library Cataloguing-in-Publication Data
A catalogue record for this book is available from the British Library.

Biomimetic Humanoid Robots with Human Consciousness

ISBN 978-981-5129-87-8 (Hardcover)
ISBN 978-1-003-71373-9 (eBook)
DOI 10.1201/9781003713739

Contents

Vision of This Book xiii
Preface xxv
Acknowledgment xxvii
Prologue xxix
Chapter Summaries xxxv

1. Evolution of Consciousness in the Universe **1**
1.1 Introduction 1
1.1.1 Why Should We Develop Humanoids? 18
1.2 Life and Universe 19
1.3 Evolution and Integration of Life and Consciousness 21
1.4 Modeling the Consciousness in the Universe 25
1.5 The Living World 26
1.6 Life and Information 26
1.7 Biological Information 29
1.8 Exploring the Nervous System in the Context of Consciousness 31
1.9 Exploring the Nervous System and Consciousness 32
1.10 Informational Hierarchy and Integration 33
1.11 Life and Evolution 36
1.12 Group Approach 37
1.13 Intelligence and Living System 41
1.14 Intelligence of the Home Environment 42
1.15 Social Intelligence, Consciousness, and Language 45
1.16 Life, Intelligence, and Consciousness beyond Matter Fields 47
1.17 The Biological Field 50
1.18 Etheric Theory 53
1.19 Etheric Theory and Consciousness 55
1.20 Consciousness beyond Death 56

1.21 Energy Review 56
1.22 Biocommunication 60
1.23 New Developed Theories 62
1.24 Entropy and Information 63
1.25 Plants and Their Thoughts 67
1.26 Universe of the Thinking 72
1.27 Brain Waves 76
1.28 Intelligence and Consciousness of Nonliving Matter 80

2. Possible Scenario to Make Intelligent Biomimetic Humanoid Robots with Comparable Human Consciousness 93
2.1 Introduction 93
2.2 Associative Neural Architecture or ANR 95

3. Mathematics of Consciousness Using Integrated Information Theory (IIT) Originated by Guiliu Tononi and the Role of Universal Numbers and Data Toward the Evolution of Consciousness and Intelligence in the Entire Universe 107
3.1 Introduction 107
3.2 Transition Probability Matrices (P_{ij}) 110
3.3 From Phenomenal Axioms to Physical Postulates 116
3.3.1 Axioms of Phenomenal Existence 116
3.3.2 Postulates of Physical Existence 117
3.4 Explanatory Identity between Experiences and Φ-Structures 118
3.5 Operational Physicalism 119
3.6 Operational Reductionism ("Atomism") 120
3.7 Intrinsic Perspective 120
3.8 Overview of IIT's Framework 121
3.9 Implementing the Postulates 122
3.9.1 Existence 122
3.9.2 Intrinsicality 122
3.9.3 Information 123
3.9.4 Integration 123
3.9.5 Exclusion 124
3.9.6 Composition 124

3.10 Ontological Principles of IIT 125
3.10.1 Principle of Being 125
3.10.2 Principle of Maximal Existence 125
3.10.3 Principle of Minimal Existence 126
3.11 Identifying Substrates of Consciousness 126
3.12 System Intrinsic Information 128
3.13 Informativeness (Over Chance) 129
3.14 Selectivity (Over States) 129
3.15 Maximal Cause–Effect State 130
3.16 Intrinsic Difference 131
3.17 Directional System Partitions 132
3.18 System-Integrated Information (φ_s) 133
3.19 Results and Discussion 135

4. Evolution of Universal Numbers and Data Toward the Evolution of Universal Consciousness and Intelligence in the Universe 143
4.1 Introduction 143
4.2 Representative Smart and Intelligent Nonliving Materials 145
4.3 MicroRNAs: 2024 Nobel Prize in Physiology and Medicine 146
4.4 Ionic Crystals 148
4.5 Ionic Polymeric Gels 148
4.6 Shape-Memory Alloys 149
4.7 Shape-Memory Polymers 150
4.8 Piezoelectric and Piezoresistive Materials 151
4.9 Piezoresistive Effect 152
4.10 Electrorheological Materials 152
4.11 Magnetorheological Materials 153
4.12 Electro- and Magnetostrictive Materials 154
4.13 Common Intelligent Materials 154
4.14 Smart and Intelligent Structures 155
4.15 Determining Smartness and Intelligence Quotients 157
4.16 Representative Smart and Intelligent Nonliving Materials 159
4.17 Artificial Smart Materials and Structures 159
4.18 Intelligent Distribution of Matter 165

4.19 Role of Geometry in the Evolution of Matter, Intelligence, Life, and Consciousness 171
4.19.1 Basic Shapes 171
4.19.2 The Pi Number 175
4.19.3 The Phi Number φ 177
4.20 Variable Minds Variable 187

5. Design, Development, and Construction of Biomimetic Humanoid Robots 191
5.1 Introduction 191
5.2 A Brief History of Electroactive Polymers and Artificial/Synthetic Muscles 193
5.2.1 Electrically Conductive and Photonic Polymers 195
5.2.2 Magnetically Activated Polymer Gels and Polymers 195
5.2.3 Electronic EAPs/Ferroelectric Polymers 196
5.2.4 Electrets and Piezoelectric Polymers 197
5.2.5 Dielectric Elastomer EAPs 197
5.2.6 Liquid Crystal Elastomer Materials 198
5.2.7 Ionic EAPs/Ionic Polymer Gels (IPGs) 199
5.2.8 Nonionic Polymer Gels/EAPs 200
5.2.9 Ionic Polymer–Metal Composites 200
5.2.10 Conductive Polymers or Synthetic Metals 201
5.2.11 Shape-Memory Alloys and Shape-Memory Polymers 202
5.2.12 Metal Hydride Artificial Muscle Systems 203
5.2.13 Electrorheological Fluids Smart Materials 203
5.2.14 Magnetorheological Fluids Smart Materials 204
5.2.15 Magnetic Shape-Memory Smart Materials 205
5.2.16 Giant Magnetostrictive Materials 206
5.2.17 Fibrous Ionic Polyacrylonitrile Gel (PAN, PANG) as Artificial Muscles 207
5.2.18 Piezoresistivity 207
5.2.19 Electrostrictive Materials as Smart Actuators and Sensors 208
5.2.20 Hydrogels and Nanogels as Smart Actuators and Sensors 208

5.2.21 New Stimuli-Responsive Smart Materials Actuators and Sensors 209
5.2.21.1 Giant Magnetoresistive Materials 209
5.2.21.2 Mechanochromic Smart Materials and Mechanical Metamaterials 210
5.2.21.3 Smart Nanogels for Biomedical Applications 210
5.3 A Brief History of Electromotive Polymers 210
5.3.1 Contraction 216
5.3.2 Mechanisms 217
5.4 Role of Microparticles in Contraction of Gels 217

6. Fundamentals of Robotics Toward Design and Development of the Robotic Part of the Humanoid Robot 253
6.1 Introduction 253
6.2 Introduction to Humanoid Robots: General Configurations 258
6.2.1 History of Robotics 258
6.3 Fundamentals of Robotics 262
6.3.1 Kinematics of Robotic Manipulators 262
6.3.1.1 Introduction to kinematics of robotic manipulators 262
6.3.1.2 General description of robotic manipulators 263
6.3.1.3 Brief description of mathematical notations 265
6.3.1.4 Mathematical preliminaries on vectors and matrices 266
6.3.1.5 Homogenous representation of points and objects 266
6.3.1.6 Homogenous transformations 269
6.3.1.7 Robotic manipulator joint coordinate systems 272
6.3.1.8 Denavit–Hartenberg (D–H) representations 273
6.3.1.9 Direct and inverse kinematics in robotics 279
6.3.1.10 Robotic workspace 285

7. Development of a Portable Small Nuclear Battery for Biomimetic Humanoid **297**
7.1 Introduction 297
7.2 What Happens in Radioactive Decay? 299
7.3 Beginnings of Atomic Batteries 301
7.4 Nanotechnology for the General-Purpose Atomic Battery 302
7.5 What Is a Nuclear Battery? 304
7.6 How Are Nuclear Batteries Different? 304
7.7 How Do Atomic Batteries Work? 304
7.8 Types of Nuclear Batteries 305
7.9 Nuclear Diamond Batteries 305
7.10 Breakdown of Radioactive Elements for Battery Usage 306
7.10.1 Uranium Power 306
7.10.2 Plutonium Batteries 306
7.11 Nuclear Battery Applications 306
7.12 Nuclear Battery Lifespan 307
7.13 Disadvantages of Nuclear Batteries: Do Batteries Give Off Radiation? 307
7.14 Nuclear Battery Cost 307
7.15 Ongoing Research and Development of City Labs' Batteries (NanoTritium™ Technology) 308
7.16 The Road Ahead 309

8. Design and Development of Advanced Intelligent AI Computers **311**
8.1 Introduction 311
8.2 Anesthesiology and Consciousness 313
8.3 Roger Penrose's Mind-Bending Theory of Reality 316

9. Steps Toward Designing and Developing Biomimetic Humanoid Robots **319**
9.1 Introduction 319
9.2 Actuation and Sensing Configurations 322
9.3 Novel Family of IPMCs as Active Robotic Surface Mask 327
9.4 IPMC Modeling and Simulation 328

9.5 Applications of IPMCs to Humanoid Robots 331
9.5.1 Brief Introduction to IPMCs as Multifunctional Materials 331
9.6 Feasibility of Providing Kinesthetic Force Feedback to Humanoid Robots by Electroactive Polymeric Sensors (IPMCs) 336
9.7 Integrating IPMCs with Robotic End-Effectors for Kinesthetic Force Feedback to Humanoid Robots in Touching and Contacting Human Flesh or Organs by Electroactive Polymeric Sensors 341
9.8 Help for the Robotic Surgery 348

10. Quantum Fields and Quantum Entanglement 351
10.1 Introduction 351
10.2 Quantum Entanglement 355
10.3 Exploiting Entanglement: Quantum Teleportation 356
10.4 Quantum Information 356
10.5 Quantum Cryptography 358
10.6 Introduction to Multiple Quantum Entanglement 361
10.6.1 Entropy 361
10.6.2 Testing a System for Entanglement 363
10.6.3 Entanglement of Macroscopic Objects 363
10.7 Conclusion 364

11. Development and Promotion of Artificial Intelligence (AI) Software and Hardware for Advanced Computers 373

12. Development of Advanced Software to Understand IA Consciousness 387

13. Emergence of Machine Consciousness to Replace or Mimic Human Consciousness 397
13.1 Introduction 397
13.2 Can a Machine Be Conscious? What Is "Consciousness"? 400
13.3 Types of Consciousness 400

13.4 Understanding Consciousness is Needed First Before Realizing Artificial Consciousness 401
13.5 Identifying Artificial Consciousness 401
13.5.1 What Does It Mean for a Machine to Act Intelligently? 402
13.5.2 The Turing Test 402
13.5.3 The Chinese Room Argument 403
13.6 Are Human and Machine Intelligence the Same? 403
13.7 Philosophy of Artificial Intelligence and Artificial Consciousness 404
13.7.1 Can a Machine Have Emotions? 404
13.7.2 Can a Machine Be Self-Aware? 405
13.7.3 Can a Machine Be Original or Creative? 405
13.7.4 Can a Machine Be Benevolent or Hostile? 405
13.8 Creating Artificial Consciousness: Could You Give a Robot a Soul? 406
13.9 Ethics of Exploiting Artificial Consciousness 407
13.9.1 Robot Slaves 407

14. Concluding Remarks **415**
14.1 Introduction 415
14.2 Steven Dick: Why Aren't Aliens Already Here? 417

Bibliography 423

Appendix A: Complete List of References 425

Index 479

Vision of This Book

The vision of this book is designing and developing biomimetic humanoids (robots) with human consciousness. This vision is to lay the foundation for humanity's eventual survival and sustenance in the entire universe and potentially the survival of some related biosystems.

It underscores the book's main goal and the potential impact of the proposed technology. As emphasized before, this book's fundamental idea is to develop robots with the consciousness of a human master, which can be a companion to the human master for several years. The human master plays a crucial role in the humanoid's life, providing the necessary resources and maintenance for survival.

Upon exiting the human master, the humanoid robot takes over under the name of the human master, replaces him as a substitute, and, with his or her consciousness, lives immortally, can space travel in the Universe, and becomes an alien from Earth. The humanoid robot will not need air (oxygen), water, or food, but only energy like a long-lasting replaceable battery.

Of course, the humanoid must be maintained in terms of its electromechanical sensors and actuator systems, as well as any other biomimetic wearing or physical structures or body muscles. Regular and timely maintenance is necessary. It must also be emphasized that the humanoid will also need enough resources to be left behind by its human master for it to be able to continuously have energy or long-lasting batteries to provide energy for its dynamics and motions. It should also be mentioned that the knowledge and technology available to create look-alike smart functioning robots are currently very advanced (see Boston Dynamics, Atlases I and II, Hyundai Robotics in Korea, US Companies, Sophia (David Hanson), US Universities, Japanese entities, Asimov, Grace, Nadine, AI-DA, Jia Jia, Chinese entities, Navigator-Alpha, Jia Jia, French entities, Aldebaran's NAO, Pepper, Romeo and Plato, British humanoids, AMECO, Germany, BMW automation robot Figure-02, Italy, automation robot RO-BEE, and also other European countries humanoids, for example). It will be quite possible to design and fabricate a humanoid robot and equip it with the consciousness of a human master. The book hopes to describe how humanity can survive the Universe despite the biological, medical, and time limitations, and how our humanoids left behind can carry us forward, serve us, explore space, and become space aliens for other planets.

Humanity proposes to create humanoids, transforming from organics-based life to silicon-based and possibly lithium-based living systems as humanoid robots. As Captain James T. Kirk (William Shatner) and the crew of the Starship Enterprise have emphasized, one wonders if a human could ever be out there in deep space to live and survive.

Figure V.1 USS Enterprise crew members.

This book presents the possibility of human survival in the Universe through its humanoid robots with human consciousness, traveling in deep space, and possibly living forever (immortality of humans by its humanoid robots). Just imagine the immortal humanoid named Captain Kirk in the Universe. This book presents the possibilities of doing so.

Depending on the source (as the number varied between some episodes), 350–450 crewmen were aboard the original USS Enterprise. Figure V.1 depicts some of the main crew members.

The book introduces advanced, smart, stimuli-responsive, intelligent wearable materials and their possible use for designing and developing biomimetic humanoid robots with human consciousness. It then introduces possible scenarios to make intelligent, sustaining robots with human consciousness.

The book introduces the concept of identity-vita-assigned consciousness (IVA-consciousness) to help the humanoid robot learn, memorize, and understand that its master is a human with a name, address, and vita about his or her life so far. It is important to make the robot understand that it is a humanoid of a particular human; it is unique and cannot be duplicated, reborn, or reproduced similarly.

The present book is about the frontiers of consciousness research. It maintains that machine consciousness is meaningless because machines have no conscious identity.

Captain Kirk's humanoid robot belongs to the human master Captain Kirk. Similarly, a larger version of the humanoid robot can still be reproduced as humanoid 2 under the same human master, Captain Kirk, called Captain Kirk humanoid robot 2. Figure V.2 depicts such an arrangement.

This will enable humans to fabricate not exactly look-alike humanoid robots but much larger monster humanoid robots for more complex and hard operations, as well as possible space travel like the Star Trek series, and visiting other planets as aliens from planet Earth of our solar system.

The present book maintains that machine consciousness is meaningless because machines have no conscious identity. How could you expect a machine or AI (artificial intelligence) computer to gain consciousness if it does not know who or what it is? Machine consciousness should evolve in a machine; every consciousness has its own identity. The book presents a unique idea, never stated before, of IVA-consciousness. That is why the book presents a scenario to embed an intelligent computer equipped with AI in a person early in anyone's life to record, see, sense, smell, feel, and comprehend all events in one's life, second by second, thus building an IVA-consciousness in the embedded resident intelligent computer over time. This procedure or approach also includes sentient feelings and emotions. This AI computer will be called the *consciousness-building computer*. The memory of this computer will eventually be transferred to the biomimetic humanoid robot in time.

Figure V.2 Look-alike humanoid robots with possible, much larger dimensions for the bigger robot.

The book is also revolutionary for changing humanity's future. It is well-known that humans and biosystems all have to eventually leave Earth and move on to other planets to live immortally, particularly without needing water, food, air, or other bio-organics to survive. The book's proposal on biomimetic humanoids will create a biomimetic humanoid robot similar to a human, which looks like a human wearing soft, stimuli-responsive clothing. It will look very similar to the actual person whose IVA-consciousness is transferred to it from an individually embedded consciousness computer to create IVA-consciousness in the humanoid.

The humanoid will start to live next to and be a collaborator and companion for several years to the corresponding human master upon realization. The human will transfer the story of his life and various individual life events to the humanoid robot gradually over time and make the robot understand that a human is its boss and should learn to follow his or her life and increase its consciousness resources. It will represent the human from here on and always be aware of who it is. The companionship will end when the individual human reaches the end of his or her life (sickness, age, etc.) and decides to leave the humanoid robot to stay on as a replacement for himself or herself. Humans will transfer as much consciousness and awareness as possible during collaboration and companionship to biomimetic humanoid robots.

The book proposes research on how to transfer IVA-consciousness to biomimetic humanoid robots. They will interact regarding the transferred consciousness as described in the book. Patience and perseverance are the key. When the time arrives, the corresponding human needs to exit (due to old age or terminal sickness) to complete his or her life by cremation or burial. Then, the humanoid robot with human consciousness will live immortally and can travel into deep space without needing air, water, food, or whatever is needed on Earth to stay alive during normal life. However, it will have a nuclear battery to have energy for a long time before charging or replacing it.

Research on machine consciousness, which is entirely non-organic, also clearly shows that humanoids could go from organic-based life to non-organic and silicone-based life. Discussing the preservation of humanity through machine consciousness seems doable, and creating immortality in humanoids is a philosophical issue.

Further, the human master will not become redundant. He or she will live as long as possible and continue interaction and companionship with his or her humanoid robot with the transferred consciousness. Of course, anybody's human life will eventually end, and the person can leave the world by either cremation or burial. The humanoid robot will live on with the transferred and improved human IVA-consciousness.

We are always exploring these capabilities in ourselves and sometimes need help from a council. A robot does not know what kind of robot it is and what it can do. Robot inverse kinematics and inverse dynamics software can instruct it to move in certain ways or configurations, perform complicated maneuvers and motions, translate to any language, recognize the music and its creator and composer, and provide safety help and perform stimuli-responsive reactions (see Atlas 1 robot maneuvers and flipping from Boston Dynamics).

The human IA consciousness recorded in the embedded consciousness computer will be transferred to the robot's memory bank as IVA-consciousness. After the transfer, the human and the humanoid robot start to interact and communicate with each other and become companions. They learn about the IVA-consciousness software to communicate with the humanoid robot.

In this final interaction between the human and the humanoid robot, the human consciousness can be transferred by cognition, logical explanations, and analysis. The book proposes this interaction as an *oral cognitive consciousness transfer* from a human to a humanoid robot. The humanoid robot will not reproduce itself because it has its own identity and personality. These humanoids do not need to reproduce; they only live on and can travel to other planets and deep space on interplanetary ships similar to the Enterprise in the Star Trek episodes. As described before, humanoid robots can be much larger than normal humans if desired and needed.

The book also describes how the quantum theories of Roger Penrose and Stuart Hameroff address the fundamental problems of consciousness, namely the inner phenomenal appearance of the mental content and the qualia. In the philosophy of mind, qualia are defined as instances of subjective, conscious experience. The term qualia derives from the Latin neuter plural form. The book tries to explain cognition, i.e., how the brain understands and produces meaningful thoughts. The proposed book also discusses the connection between the brain and consciousness and the role of microtubules in storing conscious understandings and awareness. The book also briefly discusses microtubules and how they control and interact with IA consciousness. A highly disputed theory in the mid-1990s by Stuart Hameroff and Roger Penrose states that consciousness is based on quantum vibrations in tubulin/microtubules inside brain neurons. These are explained in Chapter 8.

Another theory, "orchestrated objective reduction" ("Orch OR"), was first put forward in the mid-1990s by the eminent mathematical physicist Roger Penrose and prominent anesthesiologist Stuart Hameroff. They suggested that quantum vibrational computations in microtubules were "orchestrated" ("Orch") by synaptic inputs and memory stored in microtubules and designated by Penrose as "objective reduction" ("OR"), hence "Orch OR." Microtubules are major components of the cell's structural skeleton. Orch OR was harshly criticized, as the brain was considered too "warm, wet, and noisy" for seemingly delicate quantum processes. However, evidence has shown warm quantum coherence in plant photosynthesis, bird brain navigation, sense of smell, and brain microtubules.

Quantum consciousness is also important (Smith, 2018). Alternate realities using quantum physics can increase our understanding of awareness with quantum consciousness. The book invites the reader to see alternate realities, parallel lives, interdimensional consciousness, the eternal state, and even the very fabric of the Universe.

Four aspects of quantum consciousness—the creator effect, entanglement, everywhereness, and holographic healing—are especially emphasized. The book also explores the various realms of consciousness, including stored, alternate, parallel, and interdimensional consciousness.

The book describes the design and development of biomimetic soft wearable robotic structures equipped with stimuli-responsive ionic polymeric nanocomposites and shape-memory alloy (SMA) artificial muscles with deformation sensing and actuation capabilities. The book will also discuss and further explore the possibility of making these materials sentient. The next detailed topic is the development of strategies and methods to transfer human knowledge, understanding, and consciousness to an advanced intelligent computer with AI capabilities. The book also presents the development of AI software and hardware for advanced computers. Captain Kirk's neuralink approach for brain-interfacing and remote communications is a good beginning toward making intelligent computers.

The book also looks into developing advanced software to understand consciousness and how to transfer the software to selected individual volunteers to transfer their consciousness to an intelligent (AI-based) computer. In this discussion, the book will present a brief review of the human brain and its major components, such as the cerebellum and cerebral cortex, as well as the miracle of neurons and associated axons, dendrites, synapses, and electrical and chemical synapses, action and sensing potentials, microtubulins and microtubule interactions and quantum oscillations, interactions, and collaborations.

The basic strategy to transfer consciousness to human beings may start after the human being is born and can be started as a child or an individual to enter the program of eventually making the humanoid robot become a non-organic biomimetic robot with the IVA-consciousness. It is important to assign an identity to a person before his or her consciousness is transferred to an intelligent AI computer. At that junction, he or she is embedded with an AI-based advanced computer integrated with the individual's neural brain (neurons, axons, dendrites, and synapses) to record the human's movement and sensing capabilities and even possibly sentient feelings or emotions. Thus, a strategy is needed for the individual to express these feelings to the resident intelligent computer with IVA-consciousness. Here, the smart computers equipped with IVA-consciousness observe and record all events as the child or individual observes and responds to them. This computer will be called the consciousness storage computer. The book also introduces and promotes *oral transfer and oral cognition of consciousness* to humanoid robots. The humanoid robot will always be instructed to know that it is a humanoid robot of a human and to generate some self-awareness of its own identity and its model human.

This may also be interpreted as a cognitive oral consciousness transfer from one brain to another. As the child grows, the embedded computer will record everything observed, heard, or experienced. The book also considers the description of sentient feelings and their feedback on the resident IA consciousness. The only catch is that the emotional effects and feelings regarding love, hate, like, dislike, jealousy, anger, regrets, music enjoyment, sex enjoyment, vengeance/retaliation, worry, etc. are included.

The book will describe how feelings and emotions are transferred to consciousness by describing or experiencing them (cognitive transfer). The individual will continuously communicate with an embedded AI computer to describe feelings and emotions and include them in the IVA-consciousness. Here, the strategy can be for any human to create a humanoid robot and transfer the IA consciousness to the robot during their life and companionship before the end of the human's life. A humanoid robot can be designed and fabricated for any human at any age, rather than at a very young age. Humanoid robots and humans will become friends and companions from here on until the end of life for humans. The human will also describe his or her life story, related events, and important phases to the humanoid robot during their companionship. This is how the humanoid robot gradually accepts its own new identity as the humanoid of a human master.

Developing methodologies, strategies, and consciousness for individuals with their humanoid robot is essential in this phase. The book also suggests that humans who have completed their life cycle and have created their corresponding biomimetic humanoid robot with human IA consciousness will be free to complete their lives.

The transfer will occur in special AI computer laboratories. Facilities will be available in these laboratories for individuals ready to design, fabricate, and make operational biomimetic humanoid robots with IVA-consciousness. These AI laboratories can also convert animals into biomimetic robots with consciousness and sentience.

The book further discusses the design and development of moving capabilities (walking, running, flying, jetting, jumping, swimming, etc.) and sensing capabilities such as love, hate, like, dislike, jealousy, anger, regrets, music enjoyment, sex enjoyment, vengeance/retaliation, and worry. This will enable humans to fabricate robots that are not exactly look-alike humanoids but with much larger dimensions for special applications such as space travel and visiting other planets as aliens from the planet Earth of our solar system.

Further Readings

Alpher, R. A., and Herman, R. (1948). Evolution of the universe. *Nature*, **162**:774–777.

Chalmers, D. (2010). *The Character of Consciousness (Philosophy of Mind)*. Oxford University Press.

Dunai, T. J., and Finlay, S. M. (2009). Reporting of cosmogenic nuclide data for exposure age and erosion rate determinations. *Quaternary Geochronology*, **4**(6):437–440.

Erhard, M., Krenn, M., and Zeilinger, A. (2020). Advances in high-dimensional quantum entanglement. *Nature Reviews Physics*, **2**:365–381.

Gamow, G. (1946). Expanding universe and the origin of elements. *Physical Review*, **70**:572.

Guth, A. (2004). Inflation, In *Carnegie Observatories Astrophysics Series*, Vol. 2: *Measuring and Modeling the Universe*, ed. W. L. Freedman. Cambridge: Cambridge University Press.

Haikonen, P. O. (2003). *The Cognitive Approach to Conscious Machines*. Imprint Academic.

Haikonen, P. O. (2022). *Existence, Origin, and Weird Technology: Exploring Humanity's Ultimate Questions*. World Scientific Publishing Company.

Hubble, E. (1929). Extra-galactic nebulae. *Proceedings of the National Academy of Sciences*, **15**(3):168–173.

Merleau-Ponty, M. *Phénoménologie de la perception, 1945 (French), 1962 (English)*, English translation from French by Colin Smith (first English translation), Donald Landes (second English translation), Éditions Gallimard, Routledge & Kegan Paul, 1945, English translation (1962), 466 (1965 Routledge edition), ISBN, 978-0415834339 (2012 Routledge edition).

Shahinpoor, M. (2024). Immortal biomimetic humanoid robots with a human consciousness. *International Journal of Robotics and Automation*, **10**(3):70–71.

Shahinpoor, M., and Gheshmi, S. (2015). *Robotic Surgery*. Singapore: Jenny Stanford Publishing.

Smith, P. (2018). *Quantum Consciousness: Journey Through Other Realms*. Llewellyn Publications.

Preface

The objective of the recent book is to describe a non-fiction scenario in which humanity will survive the universe immortally by the creation of look-alike biomimetic humanoid robots with a special consciousness. The humanoid robot will know that it represents a human master (owner) with an *identity and a life vita* (resume, life story, and memories) and that it will have a consciousness or self-awareness of itself and will be staying in this universe even after the human master has left. The newly developed humanoid robots will stay around for several years as the human masters' companions and best friends and will gradually learn and understand the consciousness of their human masters.

Thus, the idea is to enable humans to create and develop look-alike biomimetic humanoid robots to survive the universe immortally and be able to travel in space to other planets and galaxies using the quantum entanglement phenomenon and artificial intelligence. Thus, humanity and its influence and culture will remain in the universe and will not be terminated by environmental threats and the non-possibility of life to survive the future changes to planet Earth.

Regarding the Kardeshev Scale, I believe we are moving toward a type III civilization and will have access to the energy resources of galaxies.

It should also be noted that much bigger humanoid robots (monsters) with human consciousness (IVA-consciousness) can also be created and possibly used for larger tasks, interplanetary transport, or visiting other planets as space aliens from Earth.

Mohsen Shahinpoor

Acknowledgment

I thank my former doctoral student Dr. Morteza Seidi, currently Professor of Mechanical Engineering at the University of Texas, San Antonio, for his help with various parts of this book, especially creating the images of humanoid robots. I have included a lot of references for the material the book presents. I have given appropriate references to all of them. I would also like to apologize for any repetitions or overlaps, which I have tried to minimize.

Prologue

The average lifetime of a human being (about 70 years) is very short when viewed in the context of the whole of human history (more than 10,000 years). However, compared with the age of the Universe, humankind's existence represents just a blink in time. In this short period, humankind has accomplished amazing things. Men/women have always tried to discover more about their environment, striving to go beyond their natural limits. This could be considered a means of ensuring their survival. Still, it can also be viewed as a search for answers to questions on the purpose and origin of life, the nature of the Universe, intelligence, and consciousness.

The first considerable answers were given thousands of years ago in ancient India and Persia's wild but secure caves. These ancient cultures made profound observations that remain a model of wisdom for the ancient world until today. Many documents inherited from the Indo-Arians and Asyro-Babylonians also reveal advanced cosmogenic concepts and theories characteristic of the ancient world (predating ancient Greece). All these emphasize the idea of universal unity and integrity. However, even if they were the result of intuitive thinking, their theories were later confirmed by the writings of the ancient Greeks. Today, humans can formulate answers based on scientific data regarding their origins and the Universe's origins—initially, two main cosmogenic theories.

The first cosmogenic theory (Dunai and Finlay, 2009) presupposes that the Universe did not have an initial moment of apparition. Therefore, accordingly, it has always existed and does not expand. However, this theory was dropped when the Universe's expansion was accurately demonstrated (Hubble's law, 1929, also known as the Hubble–Lemaître law). The second cosmogenic theory (Gamow, 1946) presumes that the Universe has a certain age and is continuously expanding. The age of the Universe is determined by an initial moment called the Big Bang (Merleau-Ponty, 1945, 1962). However, both theories consider the existence of fundamental cosmic noise and isotropic cosmic radiation, which were discovered in 1964 by Penzias and Wilson. It is worth mentioning that Gamow, Alpher, and Herman (1946) proposed the existence of this cosmic radiation when they elaborated on the theory of Big Bang in 1949 (Taille, 1977).

The Big Bang is a physical theory describing how the Universe expanded from an initial high density and high temperature state. It was first proposed in 1931 by a Roman Catholic priest and physicist, Georges Lemaître, when he suggested the Universe emerged from a "primeval atom." British astronomer Fred Hoyle coined the term "Big Bang" during a 1949 BBC radio broadcast. The Big Bang occurred some 13.7 billion years ago, when the Universe began as a tiny, dense fireball that inflated (Guth, 1981). In a 1948 paper, Gamow (1948) argued that the Big Bang universe would first be dominated by radiation—a raging sea of energy. As this expanded, the energy would mostly be converted to matter. Alpher and Herman (1948) predicted that a remnant of the radiation would remain—a cosmic background radiation permeating all space. Accepting the expansion/inflation theory of the Universe and the theory of Big Bang, it can be supposed that in the beginning, there was only an energetic field creating or penetrating a Guth cosmic vacuum. The initial Big Bang, which led to the Universe's inflation (Guth, 1981), probably happened about 13.7 billion years ago. It is presumed to have produced temperatures up to 1 trillion degrees (10^{12}°C). This would have created a highly agitated and chaotic state unfavorable for matter formation. However, the Universe's expansion, combined with the cooling of the hot Universe, allowed the formation of unstructured nuclei of matter (i.e., elementary particles such as quarks and electrons). A few millionths of a second later, quarks aggregated to produce protons and neutrons. Within minutes, these protons and neutrons combined into nuclei, and the master molecule, hydrogen, was created. Thus, the cooling of the Universe began the intelligent evolution of the whole universal structure, including the formation of the first master molecule, hydrogen (H), and subsequently universal consciousness because it was hydrogen that led to the formation of stars, such as our sun, and the entire galaxies and matter in the Universe, using gravitational force. Thus, it could be claimed that hydrogen was the first element with some inherent consciousness.

Recall that consciousness was created by the material world, which is based on the master molecule hydrogen and gravity. Combining one electron with one proton led to the first element, hydrogen, the master molecule. Whatever the beginning would have been—an expanding Universe, a pulsating one, or even a Universe with no beginning—the evolution of matter remains the same, moving from chaos to organization. This phenomenon is related to the *second arrow of time* (Robert Hazen), which will be discussed in later chapters. There is also the *first arrow of time,* which is related to the second law of thermodynamics and the increase in entropy in isolated systems and the Universe. We will present these topics in more detail later in this book. However, it should be emphasized that human error in understanding the Universe occurs not because of our limitations but because of how humans think and question existence. This recognition of our fallibility keeps us open-minded and constantly seeking new answers. Various theories are presented in this book that might shed a little light on these questions. The Universe's expansion is also accelerating. The 2011 Nobel Prize in Physics was awarded to Saul Perlmutter from the Lawrence Berkeley National Lab, Brian Schmidt from the Australian National Lab, and Adam Reiss from Johns Hopkins University for their discovery of the Universe's accelerating expansion.

Note that the Universe appears to have about 73% of invisible dark energy and about 23% of invisible dark matter, which only shows its gravitational influence in keeping the galaxies together. In contrast, ordinary matter is only 4% visible, of which less than 2% accounts for all galaxies. Figure P.1 shows approximately the material structure of the Universe as depicted earlier.

Astronomical studies have determined that the cosmic bodies in the Universe have different ages. This proves that the Universe was not created at once and that matter was and is subjected to continuous transformation and evolution. Thus, all the structural elements in the Universe seem to have their history: they appear, evolve, and then disappear by transformation into something else. From elementary particles, one gets to hydrogen, then to higher chemical elements, and finally to life, intelligence, consciousness, and the human being, which is also an integrated system of matter and energy. What, then, can one say about the role of consciousness and intelligence? Is it intelligence that determines the system, or is intelligence determined by the system? These questions will be addressed later when the deterministic way of thinking of humans is emphasized.

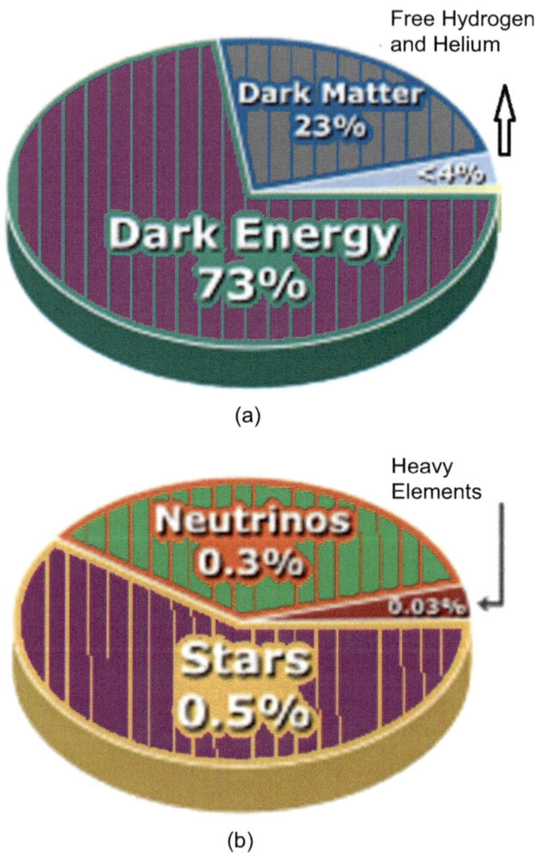

Figure P.1 The distribution of matter in the Universe.

The ultimate goal of this book is to describe a realistic future in which humanity will survive through collaboration and companionship with humanoid robots. This notion is not science fiction, but about how humanity and life and associated intellectual properties can survive immortally by creating humanoid robots from humans, with consciousness similar, as much as possible, to that of humans. The biomimetic humanoid robots would serve as companions to their masters/owners and learn almost everything about human consciousness. The humanoids will take over and live immortally once the lives of their human masters are close to being over (by age or sickness). The robots will replace the master humans in the Universe and continue to live and carry over the responsibilities and possibilities of the human masters. Most importantly, such humanoid robots will create the possibility of living elsewhere in the Universe and transferring and storing away the intellectual properties and assets of the entire humanity, which cannot be saved on Earth in time. Note that humanoid robots can stay alive if they have the necessary energy to live on and travel through space to other planets. They can live there forever and help the local entities as aliens from Earth.

These humanoids can benefit from *quantum entanglement* to immediately move through universal space to any cosmic destination. This book fully describes the essential steps to get there in Chapter 10. Interestingly, the vision here is that the humanoids can become aliens visiting other planets using quantum entanglement, which means fast (no time) travel from one part of the Universe to another.

Another exciting possibility is the technology of designing and developing humanoid robots with identity-vita-assigned consciousness (IVA-consciousness). This means that a robot can not only be instructed that it is a humanoid of a human master with his or her identity, but also can possess a vita (resume) of the human master. Note that it is possible to make humanoid robots quite large compared to an average human being, like a giant robotic monster with a human master consciousness, especially for space travel and special needs.

Humanoid robots could be quite massive and strong. Furthermore, they can help human masters in any professional activity and even sports, and they can learn all that through training and instructions. Please note that technology can make humanoid robots much more capable and flexible in moving their joints. They can easily bend their fingers, elbows, and knees forward and backward or turn their necks backward if necessary.

References and Further Readings

Alpher, R. A., and Herman, R. (1948). Evolution of the universe. *Nature*, **162**:774–779.

Dunai, T. J., and Finlay, S. M. (2009). Reporting of cosmogenic nuclide data for exposure age and erosion rate determinations. *Quaternary Geochronology*, **4**(6):437–440.

Gamow, G. (1946). Expanding universe and the origin of elements. *Physical Review*, **70**:572.

Gamow, G. (1948). The evolution of the universe. *Nature*, **162**:680–682.

Guth, A. H. (1981). Cosmic inflation. *Physical Review D*, **23**:347.

Merleau-Ponty, M. (1945). Phénoménologie de la perception, 1945 (French), 1962 (English), English translation from French by Colin Smith (1st English translation), Donald Landes (2nd English translation), Éditions Gallimard, Routledge & Kegan Paul, 1945, English translation (1962), 466 (1965 Routledge edition), ISBN, 978-0415834339 (2012 Routledge edition).

Chapter Summaries

The Fundamental Idea

This book's fundamental idea is to present a plan to design and develop biomimetic humanoid robots with the consciousness of a human master. After the human leaves, the humanoid robot takes over, lives immortally, and can space travel in the Universe, and become an alien visiting other planets from Earth. The humanoid robot will not need air (oxygen), water, or food, but only a source of energy like a long-lasting replaceable battery, such as the diamond battery.

This book presents a non-fictional possibility for human beings to develop intelligent biomimetic humanoid robots that could represent them after they leave human life. To live in the Universe immorally and continue representing their human master forever, they must have enough energy. For this, they can have long-lasting nuclear batteries.

The book first summarizes 14 chapters and then describes them in more detail later in the book.

Summary of Chapter 1

This chapter discusses the evolution of consciousness in the Universe, starting with the Big Bang. The master molecule hydrogen, H, is the beginning of consciousness in the Universe. Recall that hydrogen enabled the formation and creation of stars, galaxies, materials, and the current universe. The consciousness emanates from the material world anyway. Also recall that consciousness starts with maintaining that all living systems are conscious, particularly our solar system's Sun and stars, which are alive, dynamic, intelligent, and possess consciousness.[1]

Definition of consciousness: "The ability to be aware of and to be able to have a relationship between oneself and one's environment." The most basic definition, however, is "*awareness*." Another

[1]See Dr. Steven Greer's Conscious Universe—the Holographic Conscious Universe Breakdown. (https://www.youtube.com/watch?v=mgfJP8-IowM)

definition suitable for more complex organizations of matter, such as animals with a brain, includes a description that contains some of the following ideas: "thoughts, sensations, hate, jealousy, vengeance/retaliation, perceptions, anger, tastes, moods, emotions, sexual desires, love, dreams, worry and awareness of self." Like life, consciousness is easy to recognize but very difficult to define.

Summary of Chapter 2

In this chapter, we discuss the possible scenarios for designing, fabricating, and operating intelligent biomimetic humanoid robots with human consciousness. Let us call the generic human master Captain Kirk, so that the robot will be called Captain Kirk's humanoid robot. This is the first awareness instruction to the humanoid robot that it is a substitute for Captain Kirk, and its name is Captain Kirk's humanoid robot. This robot will be aware of its identity and designation. It will also possess a complete vita of the human master and the details of his or her life. The humanoid robot will become a companion of the human and live with the master for several years. Thus, the humanoid robot will become more conscious and aware of its master and mimic the master easily. It can help humans master any professional activities and even sports activities, and it can learn all that through training and instructions.

Note that the current technology can make sophisticated humanoid robots much more flexible in moving their joints. They can easily bend their fingers, elbows, and knees forward and backward or turn their necks around.

The basic strategy for transferring consciousness to a humanoid robot may start after the human being is born and grows to be an individual, entering the program of eventually creating a non-organic biomimetic humanoid robot with human identity and vita-assigned consciousness. The humanoid robot is initially instructed to have the identity of its master human. It is extremely important to make the humanoid robot's memory accept that it is a humanoid of a human master and knows about the master's life and activities through knowledge of the master's detailed vita. The humanoid robot will be equipped with identity-vita-assigned consciousness (IVA-consciousness) and a particular and unique identity of the human master.

Summary of Chapter 3

This chapter delves into the current mathematical theories of consciousness, focusing on the groundbreaking Integrated Information Theory (IIT) and originating from the scientific endeavors of Giuolo Tononi, Professor, Department of Psychiatry, University of Wisconsin, Madison, United States of America, and his colleagues.[2]

IIT has emerged as one of the most influential and captivating theories of human consciousness mathematics. In its latest iteration (IIT 4.0), the theory takes on a metaphysical aspect known as *idealistic ontology*. Ontology and idealism assert that the existence of all things depends upon the state of the mind; thus, ontological idealism rejects the perspectives of physicalism and dualism. IIT is also supported by Christof Koch, Chief Scientific Officer, Allen Institute for Brain Science, Seattle, Washington, USA.

Giulio Tononi's IIT starts from a conscious experience via five phenomenological axioms: *existence, composition, information, integration, and exclusion*. From these axioms, five postulates are derived about the properties of physical mechanisms required to support consciousness. The theory provides a principled account of both the quantity and the quality of an individual experience and a calculus to evaluate whether or not a particular system of mechanisms is conscious and of what.

Summary of Chapter 4

Evolution of universal numbers and data toward the evolution of universal consciousness and intelligence in the Universe: Mathematical modeling of universal consciousness and the role of MAGIC numbers such as π, φ, and quantum field ϕ: Representative smart and intelligent nonliving materials as well as Fibonacci numbers, golden ratio φ, magical frequencies,[3] and the universal constant $\alpha = 1/137$. The mysterious number $\alpha = 0.00729735256$ is dimensionless and is called the *fine structure constant*. It appears

[2]https://doi.org/10.1371/journal.pcbi.1011465

[3]639 Hz, 528 Hz (DNA repair), 888 Hz (resonates with the highest realms of consciousness and spiritual elevation, abundance, and prosperity), 963 Hz (connected to consciousness; believed (Nikola Tesla) to be the frequency of God to attract blessings, love, and miracles)

everywhere in our equations of quantum physics and the splitting of electron waves, and scientists are still trying to figure out why.

The evolution of fundamental particles, molecules, material, and universal numbers, as well as data on the evolution of universal consciousness and intelligence in the entire universe, is presented in this chapter. The roles of MAGIC numbers such as π, the golden ratio φ, and the quantum field ϕ are also discussed. First, a review of smart, stimuli-responsive, electrically controllable materials is given. In the first moments after the Big Bang, the Universe was extremely hot and dense. As the Universe cooled, conditions became just right to give rise to the building blocks of matter—the quarks and electrons. A few millionths of a second later, quarks aggregated to produce protons and neutrons. Within minutes, these protons and neutrons combine, and the master molecule *hydrogen* is created. The reader is referred to the research on quarks and electrons to learn about the evolution of initial fundamental particles.[4]

Thus, the cooling of the Universe began the intelligent evolution of the whole universal structure, including the formation of the first master molecule hydrogen (H) and subsequently universal consciousness, because it was the hydrogen that led to the formation of stars like our own Sun and the entire galaxies and matter in the Universe. So, it could be claimed that the master molecule hydrogen was the first element with some inherent intelligence and consciousness. Recall that consciousness has been created by the material world, which is based on the master molecule hydrogen. It combined one electron with one proton, which led to the formation of the first element—hydrogen, the master molecule.

Hubble's discovery was the first observational support for Georges Lemaître's Big Bang theory of the Universe, proposed in 1927. Lemaître proposed that the Universe expanded explosively from an extremely dense and hot state and continues to expand today. Subsequent calculations have dated this Big Bang to approximately 13.7 billion years ago. In 1998, two teams of astronomers working independently at Berkeley, California, observed that supernovae—exploding stars—were moving away from Earth at an accelerating rate. This earned them the Nobel Prize in Physics in 2011. The prize was divided: one-half awarded to Saul Perlmutter, and the other half

[4]The early universe, CERN. https://home.cern/science/physics/early-universe#:~:text=Origins,which%20we%20are%20all%20made.

jointly to Brian P. Schmidt and Adam G. Riess "for the discovery of the accelerating expansion of the Universe through observations of distant supernovae."

As described before, the Universe was extremely hot and dense after the Big Bang. It gave rise to the building blocks of matter—the quarks and electrons. A few millionths of a second later, quarks aggregated to produce protons and neutrons. Within minutes, these protons and neutrons combined into nuclei. As the Universe expanded and cooled, things began to happen more slowly. It took about 380,000 years for electrons to be trapped in orbits around nuclei, forming the first atoms. These were mainly hydrogen, which is still the most abundant element in the Universe. Present observations suggest that the first stars formed from clouds of gas around 150–200 million years after the Big Bang. Heavier atoms, such as carbon, oxygen, and iron, have since been continuously produced in the hearts of stars and catapulted throughout the Universe in spectacular stellar explosions called supernovae.

Summary of Chapter 5

This chapter introduces the design, development, and construction of biomimetic humanoid robots and teaches them the human consciousness of their master owner, a human, who gets help and support from stimuli-responsive, smart, wearable intelligent materials and artificial muscles.

This chapter also introduces stimuli-responsive, smart, intelligent materials and artificial muscles to design, develop, fabricate, and construct biomimetic humanoid robots with human consciousness. It is important to assign an identity to the individual humanoid, which will have consciousness with the identity and vita of its human master, called IVA-consciousness.

Having more than just an IVA-intelligent computer or robot is important. It is important to have consciousness with identity and vita for a humanoid robot. Under these circumstances, the humanoid robot with no identity in consciousness may become out of control because of a lack of identity and develop undesirable scenarios.

This is the beginning of imparting some consciousness to a humanoid robot. It informs and alerts the robot that it will be assigned the identity of its human master/owner and will be given some details about his or her vita and background. Thus, anytime the humanoid robot and its intelligent computer are on with power, the robot knows that it has the same identity as the human master. This is the beginning of self-awareness for the humanoid robot, always knowing that it has an identity and a past story (vita) and corresponds to the human master.

The humanoid robot now needs to be wearing clothing. The clothing should look the same, and it may be identical to the clothing worn by the human master. Smart, intelligent, stimuli-responsive electroactive polymers are the clothing fabrics to be tailored and worn by the humanoid robots. Of course, the humanoid robot should look like the master human, possibly in regular clothing. Giant humanoid robots (number 2, Captain Kirk's humanoid robot 2) can also be fabricated with the same IVA-consciousness, as will be discussed later with pictures.

As described before, humanoid robots can help humans master professional and even sports activities. They can learn all that through training and instructions. Note that current robot technologies can make humanoid robots much more capable and flexible in moving their joints. They can easily bend their fingers, elbows, and knees forward and backward or turn their necks backward if necessary.

Summary of Chapter 6

This chapter presents some fundamental aspects of robotic transformations, inverse kinematics, and inverse dynamics. Of course, the position is that this technology is now well-developed in humanoid robots, except that the associated consciousness is not fully implemented.

In this chapter, we address the fundamental ideas behind intelligent robots and biomimetic robotics, as well as the design and development of the robotic part. The humanoid robot will be designed and constructed to resemble the intended human. The humanoid robot will have an embedded smart computer with a microprocessor that records all events in its and its human master's lives. The humanoid robot will live with its owner (man or woman), gradually learn or become aware and knowledgeable of its owner's consciousness, and transform into the consciousness of its owner, a human. The proposed book presents some fundamental aspects of robotic transformations, inverse kinematics, and inverse dynamics. Some of the materials in this chapter are also covered in the book *Robotic Surgery* (M. Shahinpoor and S. Gheshmi, 2015). Of course, moving toward biomimetic soft robots and humanoid consciousness has a good connection here in robotic surgery.

Future humanoid robots will also be able to perform robotic surgery like surgeons. The current advanced robotic applications, such as surgical systems, evolved from the laparoscopic advanced robotic applications, such as surgical procedures, and made it possible for surgeons to perform surgery away from the patient with much more concentration and ease. However, what the surgeons lost in this transition was the sensation of tissues and organs and kinesthetic force feedback during surgery.

It is interesting to note that even during laparoscopic surgery, surgeons can still feel and sense the tissues and organs they are handling and operating on with laparoscopic/endoscopic tools and feel the kinesthetic forces at work. However, the kinesthetic force feedback was replaced with visual feedback during normal robotic surgery. It is to be noted that some of this kinesthetic force feedback was lost in the transition from open to laparoscopic surgery due to trocar friction and varying lever arms, anyway.

However, using smart materials such as ionic polymer metal composites (IPMCs) and appropriate calibration and tuning, one may recover the kinesthetic force feedback during surgery. IPMCs are great for robotic force feedback applications because they work perfectly well in the wet human body environment and generate millivolt-level sensing signals for kinesthetic force feedback.

Summary of Chapter 7

This chapter deals with the development of a portable small nuclear battery to provide energy for the activities of a biomimetic humanoid robot (human or animal) for a long time. Nuclear batteries are the portable power of the future. These portable power supplies will be replaceable if needed. Note that the humanoid robot will have no internal organs like a normal human being. All movements are electromechanical, and sensory and motor neurons are replaced by adjoining smart (intelligent) stimuli-responsive materials worn by biomimetic humanoid robots. The humanoid robot with human consciousness will be entirely electromechanical and capable of surviving immortally in time. See Chapters 5 and 6 for a description of wearable stimuli-responsive smart materials, robotic manipulators, and humanoid robots. As described in Chapters 5 and 6, the humanoid robots will need energy to operate their various electromechanical actuators, sensors, related instrumentation, and the resident IVA-conscious computers. The solution appears to be nuclear batteries, which are discussed in this chapter. It has been reported that some nuclear batteries can last for up to 28,000 years.[5]

In 2024, the Chinese company Betavolt announced a coin-sized nuclear battery using radioactive nickel sandwiched between thin layers of diamond, which acts as a semiconductor.[6] The battery could power devices such as mobile phones, laptops, and drones for half a century, with an energy density 10 times higher than the current most powerful lithium-ion batteries.

Summary of Chapter 8

This chapter describes research on the design and development of advanced intelligent artificial intelligence (AI) computers and software that can learn to think like humans at any age and take related actions like humans. This chapter briefly describes the brain anatomy, including major parts such as the cerebellum and cerebral cortex, and the adjoining more than 100 billion neurons and associated axons, neurons, dendrites, synapses, and their collaborative interactions. It also discusses the connection between the brain and consciousness and the role of microtubules in storing conscious understandings and awareness. The chapter also briefly discusses how microtubules control and interact with IA consciousness. Stuart Hameroff and Roger Penrose's highly disputed theory, first proposed in the mid-1990s, describes consciousness as based on *quantum vibrations in tubulin/microtubules* inside brain neurons.

---

[5]Nuclear Batteries, the Portable Power of the Future? https://www.bbvaopenmind.com/en/technology/innovation/nuclear-batteries-portable-power-of-the-future/#:~:text=In%202024%2C%20the%20Chinese%20company%20Betavolt%20announced%20a%20coin%2Dsized,times%20higher%20than%20our%20current| OpenMind (bbvaopenmind.com))

[6]Nuclear Battery Betavolt's BV100 to last 50 years (youtube.com)

Another theory, called "orchestrated objective reduction" ("Orch OR"), was first put forward in the mid-1990s by eminent mathematical physicist Sir Roger Penrose and prominent anesthesiologist Stuart Hameroff.

They suggested that quantum vibrational computations in microtubules were "orchestrated" ("Orch") by synaptic inputs and memory stored in microtubules by Penrose's "objective reduction" ("OR"), hence "Orch OR." Microtubules are major components of the cell's structural skeleton. Orch OR was harshly criticized, as the brain was considered too "warm, wet, and noisy" for seemingly delicate quantum processes. However, evidence has shown warm quantum coherence in plant photosynthesis, bird brain navigation, sense of smell, and brain microtubules.

Justin Riddle describes how microtubule operation is similar to a universal quantum computer that acts as a single executive unit in single cells. First, computer scientists are trying to model human behavior using neural networks that treat individual neurons as the base unit. But unicellular organisms can do many of the things that we consider to be human behavior! How does a single-cell life form perform this complex behavior? Let us look inside a cell; what makes it tick? Many think that DNA holds some secret code or algorithm that executes the decision-making process of the cell. However, the microscope reveals a different story where the microtubules are performing a vast array of complex behaviors: swimming toward food, away from predators, and coordinating protein delivery and creation within the cell. This begs the question: how do microtubules work? Well, they are single proteins organized into helical cylinders. What is going on here? Typically, we think of a protein's function as being determined by its structure, but the function of a single protein repeated into tubes is tough to unravel. Stuart Hameroff proposed that perhaps these tubulin proteins act as bits of information, and the whole tube works as a universal computer that can be programmed to fit any situation. Given the limitations of digital computation, Roger Penrose was looking for a quantum computer in biology, and Stuart Hameroff was looking for more than a digital computation explanation.

Hence, the Hameroff–Penrose (1995, 1996) model of microtubules as quantum computers was born. Chapter 8 further describes these phenomena.

Summary of Chapter 9

This chapter addresses the steps toward designing and developing biomimetic humanoid robots, making them look very much like normal human beings. This means soft movement of arms, legs, fingers, neck, waist, and other body parts. Obviously, one must also design and develop clothing and soft wearable braces and suits. The design and development of biomimetic soft wearable robotic structures equipped with artificial muscles, such as ionic polymeric nanocomposites, shape-memory alloy (SMA) artificial muscles, piezoelectric muscles, dielectric elastomer muscles, metal hydride muscles, electrostrictive and magneto-restrictive muscles, plus many more, have been discussed in this chapter. These muscles will also have deformation sensing and activation capabilities. This chapter also discusses the possible design of biomimetic humanoid robots equipped with polymeric artificial muscles for facial expressions using IPMCs.

This chapter also covers the possible design of the facial expressions of biomimetic humanoid robots using IPMCs as artificial robotic bodies and face skin.

An important area of biomimetic robotics is creating facial expressions by moving various parts of the robot's facial muscles. This process is quite complicated but creates more human-like facial expressions. This chapter proposes a novel design of a facial mask using IPMCs.

A new family of IPMC sensors and actuators has been proposed as a flexible surface mask to form a biomimetic, flexible, soft sensor and actuator system. The surface mask made with IPMCs will be experimentally capable of bending, rolling, turning, twisting, and simultaneous sensing. However, their sensing characteristics as a soft biomimetic surface actuator and sensor are shown to have great potential for ubiquitous robot–human interactions.

Upon various types of deformation, they are shown to generate unique output voltage signals and transient currents to be correlated to the surface mask feedback force. Furthermore, a flexible sheet of IPMC can be actuated simultaneously on the fly by a small power supply embedded in the humanoid robot. The active surface mask version of IPMC can be applied as smart skin for all body parts of the humanoid robot to develop human-like dexterous and soft manipulation. This chapter introduces a possible design for an IPMC robotic surface mask or muscles with soft actuation and sensing in a flexible surface configuration.

The human face possesses a maximum of 43 muscles and over 24 individual muscles on each side, possibly 30, depending on how they are counted. It takes 12 muscles to smile and 43 muscles to frown.

Summary of Chapter 10

Having completed the development of humanoid robots and getting them ready to start their immortal lives in the Universe, one needs to develop strategies for spatial travel in this huge universe. Here is when the quantum fields and effects could be of enormous value, and in particular, the notion and properties of *quantum entanglement* will be of great value. This chapter discusses these issues for humanoid robots.

Using quantum entanglement will enable humanoid robots to travel through space. They must develop quick displacement and relocation systems using their IVA-consciousness toward the collapse of the wave function and produce the entanglement effect to transport the humanoid from one part of the Universe to another part and possibly another time.

This is quite an exciting notion for the future of humanity. In fact, the 2022 Nobel Prize in Physics was awarded to the researchers Alain Aspect, John Clauser, and Anton Zeilinger for their research work on the foundation of quantum entanglement. The Nobel Prize in Physics is typically awarded to scientists. However, in 2022, the Nobel Prize was awarded to three physicists who revealed that the Universe is even stranger than we know due to quantum entanglement.

In short, researchers Alain Aspect, John Clauser, and Anton Zeilinger have discovered that entangled particles behave like a single unit even when separated far away.

Wireless technologies will be employed for this phase. Strategies and methods will be developed to transfer human knowledge, understanding, and consciousness to advanced intelligent computers with AI capabilities. In this chapter, the quantum effects of moving from one part of the Universe to another at a distance are related to quantum entanglement. When humanoid robots with IVA-consciousness travel through space, they must develop quick displacement and relocation systems.

Summary of Chapter 11

This chapter delves into the development of AI software and hardware for advanced computers, along with energy, matter intelligence, life, and consciousness (EMILC), and the evolution of EMILC. The development of strategies and methods to transfer human knowledge, understanding, and consciousness to advanced intelligent computers with AI capabilities has been discussed. Does consciousness collapse the quantum wave function? This idea was taken seriously by John von Neumann and Eugene Wigner but is now widely dismissed. We develop the idea by combining a mathematical theory of consciousness (IIT) with an account of quantum collapse dynamics (continuous spontaneous localization).

The idea of combining a mathematical theory of consciousness (IIT, Giulio Tonini) with an account of quantum collapse dynamics (continuous spontaneous localization) has been developed here. The quantum Zeno effect falsifies simple versions of the theory, but more complex versions remain compatible with empirical evidence. The *quantum Zeno effect* is a phenomenon in quantum physics where observing a particle prevents it from decaying as it would in the absence of the observation. In principle, versions of the theory can be tested by experiments with quantum computers.

Summary of Chapter 12

Advanced software was developed to understand IA consciousness. The software was then transferred to selected volunteers so that their IA consciousness could be transferred to an intelligent (AI-based) computer.

The development of methodologies, strategies, and paradigms to consider the transferred individuals as they complete training their humanoid robots through long-term companionship is also discussed. The human master will continuously teach the human robots about consciousness, especially the complex consciousness on love, hate, jealousy, anger, regrets, music enjoyment, sex enjoyment, vengeance/retaliation, worry, and anxiety. Thus, the humanoid robots will eventually acquire consciousness from the master human and develop their communication skills. Here, the biomimetic humanoid robot with human consciousness starts to live independently but under the human master's identity and consciousness. Essentially, the transfer of consciousness to humanoid robots starts with identifying the transferring consciousness. In other words, as discussed in Chapters 1 and 2, this was designed and created with an onboard set of microprocessors, computing instructions, storage, and onboard intelligent computers, which may also be AI computers.

Programming a humanoid robot, say Captain Kirk's humanoid robot, to identify itself as Captain Kirk's humanoid will enable the human master (Captain Kirk) to transfer all the consciousness issues and knowledge gradually to the onboard computers, both with the human master as well as the humanoid robots. The human master and the humanoid will then treat each other as companions and communicate about the master's consciousness for several years.

Summary of Chapter 13

This chapter discusses the emergence of machine consciousness to replace or mimic human consciousness. Artificial consciousness (also known as machine consciousness, synthetic consciousness, or IVA-consciousness) refers to a non-biological, human-created machine that is aware of its existence as well as the resume of the human master it represents.

Machine consciousness will help the design, development, fabrication, and operation of the humanoid robot in moving capabilities (walking, running, flying, jumping, skiing, swimming, jetting, etc.). Here, the book covers robotic fundamentals (robotic surgery, smart materials, robotic structures, and artificial muscles), such as homogeneous transformations, Denavit–Hartenberg transformations, and direct and inverse kinematics.

The basic strategy to transfer consciousness to human beings starts after the human being is born as an individual and grows up. It is later embedded with an AI-based, advanced computer. The embedded AI smart computer observes and records all events as the individual observes and reacts to them. As the individual grows, the embedded computer using IVA-consciousness will record and may recall everything observed, heard, or experienced. There will be laboratory research facilities for the individuals ready to design, develop, fabricate, and make operational the humanoid biomimetic robot and transfer consciousness and life vita (resume) from humans. When the transferred individuals are ready to exit for whatever reason (sickness or old age), they will be accordingly cremated or buried. At the same time, their corresponding biomimetic humanoid robot will emerge to lead a new life. These laboratory chambers can also convert animals into biomimetic robots with consciousness and sentience.

The only catch is that emotional effects and feelings, such as love, hate, like, dislike, jealousy, anger, regrets, music enjoyment, sex enjoyment, vengeance/retaliation, worry, and anxiety, are included. These issues will be discussed in Chapter 13.

Summary of Chapter 14

This chapter maintains that humanity should move toward designing, developing, fabricating, and operating silicon-enabled or lithium-enabled humanoid robots with IVA-consciousness and away from organic life, which will not survive in time. This book presents a non-fiction possibility for human beings to develop operational, intelligent biomimetic humanoid robots that could represent them after they leave human life to live in the Universe immorally and continue representing their human master forever, as long as they have enough energy to do so.

However, they can have long-lasting nuclear batteries. Thus, this could be the beginning of biomimetic humanoid robots for all human beings to stay on and be able to live immorally and travel in space to other planets as space aliens from Earth.

The basic strategy to transfer consciousness to human beings starts after the human being is born as an individual and grows up. It is later embedded with an AI-based advanced computer.

The embedded AI smart computer observes and records all events as the individual observes and reacts to them. As the individual grows, the embedded computer using IVA-consciousness will record and may recall everything observed, heard, sensed, or experienced. There will be laboratory facilities for the individuals ready to fabricate the humanoid biomimetic robot, start training it, and transfer some consciousness to it.

The transfer of consciousness from humans to a biomimetic humanoid robot then starts. The vision is for these human robots to serve humanity in the future with their learned consciousness. The first thing to do is to instruct the humanoid robot that he or she has a master human with an identity, say Captain Kirk's humanoid. Thus, the humanoid robot will have what we have described as IVA-consciousness and the humanoid AI computer's initial memory and knowledge transfer. When the transferred individuals are ready to exit human life for whatever reason (sickness or old age), they will exit and be accordingly cremated or buried.

At the same time, their corresponding biomimetic humanoid robot will emerge to represent the human Captain Kirk and lead a new life as Captain Kirk's humanoid robot with almost Captain Kirk's consciousness. These laboratory facilities can also convert animals into biomimetic robots with consciousness and sentience. The humanoid robot of Captain Kirk can now travel in space and essentially move to any other planet as it will not need air, water, food, and only a long-lasting nuclear battery, which will also be replaceable. Thus, human beings will be able to survive in this vast universe.

The ultimate goal of this book is to describe a realistic future, and not science fiction, about how humanity and life can survive immortally by creating humanoid robots with the consciousness of humans. The humanoid will take over once human life is close to being over (age or sickness). It can stay alive if it has the necessary energy to live on and even travel through space and other planets. It can live there forever and help local entities.

These humanoids can benefit from quantum entanglement to immediately move through universal space to any cosmic destination. This book fully describes the essential steps to get there in Chapter 10. Interestingly, the additional vision here is that the humanoids can become space aliens visiting other planets using quantum entanglement, a concept that should intrigue the audience.

Furthermore, humanoid robots can be made larger than normal human beings. This may be beneficial for special applications, such as when humanoids travel through space by quantum entanglement, control the travel of a space vehicle, and visit other planets as aliens from Earth.

Chapter 1

Evolution of Consciousness in the Universe

1.1 Introduction

In this chapter, we discuss the evolution of consciousness in the Universe, starting with the Big Bang. We maintain that all living, dynamic systems are conscious; in particular, our solar system's star, the Sun, is alive, dynamic, intelligent, and possesses consciousness. Note that there are an estimated 300 billion stars in our own Milky Way Galaxy, and there are an estimated 200 billion or more, possibly 1 trillion galaxies in the Universe.

It is maintained here that the *master molecule*, hydrogen H, is the initial force for the beginning of consciousness in the Universe! Recall that gravitational forces and attractions caused the formation and creation of stars, galaxies, and materials, enabling the master molecule hydrogen H to create the material universe. Consciousness emanates from the material world anyway! Recall that consciousness starts with the master molecule hydrogen.

Biomimetic Humanoid Robots with Human Consciousness
Mohsen Shahinpoor

ISBN 978-981-5129-87-8 (Hardcover), 978-1-003-71373-9 (eBook)
www.jennystanford.com

DOI: 10.1201/9781003713739-1

It is maintained here that all living systems are conscious, particularly our solar system's Sun and stars, which are alive, dynamic, intelligent, and possess consciousness.[1]

Definition of consciousness: "The ability to be aware of and to be able to have a relationship between oneself and one's environment." The most basic definition, however, is "awareness." Another definition suitable for more complex organizations of matter, such as animals with a brain, includes a description that contains some of the following ideas: "thoughts, sensations, love and affection, regrets, perceptions, hate, like, jealousy, dislike, tastes, moods, vengeance/retaliation, emotions, dreams, love, like, enjoyment of food, sex, music, motivations, hate, worry, anxiety, and awareness of self." Just like life itself, consciousness is one of those things that is easy to recognize but very difficult to define.

Figure 1.1 Professor John Hopfield, left, of Princeton University, and Professor Geoffrey Hinton, of the University of Toronto, the 2024 Nobel Prize winners in Physics (Associated Press).

We can assume that all stars are alive, dynamic, intelligent, and conscious. Thus, it appears that the Universe is conscious dynamically. We maintain that all living systems are conscious, particularly our

[1]See Dr. Steven Greer's Conscious Universe (The Holographic Conscious Universe Breakdown). https://www.youtube.com/watch?v=mgfJP8-IowM

solar system's Sun and stars, which are alive, dynamic, intelligent, and possess consciousness.[2]

Incidentally, the 2024 Nobel Prize in Physics for discoveries and inventions that enable machine learning within artificial neural networks was awarded to Geoffrey Hinton, a British Canadian computer scientist at the University of Toronto, and John Hopfield of Princeton University (Fig. 1.1).[3]

The development of machine learning has expanded over the past 20 years and benefits from structures such as artificial neural networks (ANNs), which are modeled after the dynamics and reconfiguration of 10 billion neurons in the human brain. Nowadays, when we talk about *artificial intelligence*, ANN is often the type of technology we mean.

Figure 1.2 shows an example of ANN with permission from Johan Jarnestad/The Royal Swedish Academy of Sciences.

Figure 1.2 An example of an ANN. © The Royal Swedish Academy of Sciences.

[2]Ibid. On the other hand, one can recite the vision of the Godfathers of AI, John Hopfield and Geoffrey Hinton, who believe that "machines will also have consciousness in time." https://www.youtube.com/watch?v=qrvK_KuIeJk

[3]Read more at http://www.cbc.ca/news. Former Caltech and Google scientists win Physics Nobel for pioneering artificial intelligence

We elaborate on the evolution of consciousness in the Universe, starting with the Big Bang some 13.7 billion years ago. A recent book by Popa and Shahinpoor titled *Energy, Mass, Intelligence, and Life* (EMIL) (Popa and Shahinpoor, 2000) fully describes and maintains that after the Big Bang, the released energy started to convert to mass, which subsequently was converted to intelligent molecular structures such as DNA (deoxyribonucleic acid) and RNA (ribonucleic acid). RNA differs from DNA chemically because the nucleotides in RNA are ribonucleotides and contain ribose (hence the name ribonucleic acid). RNA contains the bases adenine (A), guanine (G), and cytosine (C); it contains the base uracil (U) instead of the thymine (T) in DNA.

The biological systems gradually developed intelligence to replicate, survive, and create life. However, the aforementioned book did not cover the evolution of universal consciousness after the evolution of life and intelligence. Thus, EMIL has been converted to EMILC (energy, mass, intelligence, life, and consciousness) in this book. In the following paragraphs, we present a summary of the evolution of consciousness from the Big Bang time.

Popa and Shahinpoor (2000) maintain that it was first the energy partially converted to matter, which ultimately became intelligent enough (RNA, DNA) to reproduce itself, survive, and create life and, subsequently, consciousness in the biological systems. The humanoid robot will be built to look similar to the human individual it is modeling and representing. It will have moving actuators and sensors to move all joints and sense any skin contact and move a bunch of surface mask IPMC muscles. The present book will also prepare a special chapter on the design and creation of a humanoid robot. As described before, the humanoid robot can be much bigger or smaller than normal humans and can be trained and used similarly.

Figures 1.3–1.5 show the similarity between a human and his/her humanoid robots. Of course, humanoid robots will not have any biological organs such as the heart, lungs, kidneys, and digestive systems.

Figure 1.3 Some humanoid robots. *Source*: FastCompany.

(a)

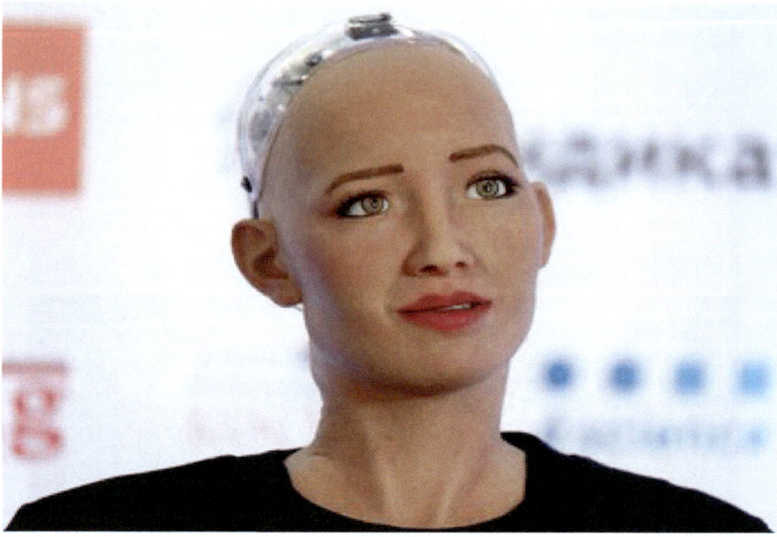

(b)

Figure 1.4 (a) Sophia (Hanson Robotics). (b) Sophia, with Cloud Technology Controls.

Figure 1.5 Sophia with David Hanson.

Sophia is considered the most advanced humanoid robot (2016) designed and built by David Hanson. She is the world's first robot citizen and the first robot innovation ambassador for the United Nations Development Program. She is one of a kind, and her interaction with people is the most unlikely thing you can ever see in a machine. A Hong Kong-based company, Hanson Robotics, designed her. She was created to look like Audrey Hepburn, a famous Hollywood actress, because the creators aimed to fit her as an old age companion in nursing homes or a crowd manager at events.

The purpose of creating Sophia was to make a robot capable of gaining social skills. Sophia has been embedded with *neural networks* and *artificial intelligence* to recognize human faces and understand their gestures and emotions. She can also interact with different people and respond appropriately.

Figure 1.6 shows how David Hanson, CEO of Hanson Robotics, reacts to "Han the Robot" and "Sophia the Robot" during a demonstration at the RISE Technology Conference in Hong Kong in July 2017. Figures 1.7 to 1.16 show additional humanoid robots from various international sources with appropriate descriptions.

Figure 1.6 Sophia, Dave Hanson, and Isaac Lawrence (AFP/Getty Images).

Figure 1.7 A humanoid robot being trained.

Figure 1.8 A lookalike humanoid robot called Geminoid-F (Getty Images).

Figure 1.9 This robot "Actroid Repliee" looks exactly like a TV newscaster (Yoshikazu Tsuno/AFP/Getty Images).

Figure 1.10 Former astronaut Mamoru Mori and Osaka University professor Hiroshi Ishiguro posing with female humanoid robots "Otonaroid" and "Kodomoroid" at the National Museum of Emerging Science and Technology in Tokyo in June 2014 (Yoshikazu Tsuno/AFP/Getty Images).

Figure 1.11 Osaka University professor Hiroshi Ishiguro displaying his latest humanoid robot "Ononaroid" in June 2014 (Yoshikazu Tsuno/AFP/Getty Images).

Figure 1.12 Japanese actor Ken Matsudaira, clad in a robot suit, smiling next to an android robot made in his likeness, called "Real Android Matsuken," in November 2013 (Ken Matsudaira/AFP/Getty Images).

In Japan, the human population is shrinking and robots are on the rise.[4] The concept of lifelike *sex robots* (x-robots) will get one step closer to reality. That is when a San Marcos company unveiled "Harmony," an anatomically correct sex doll with a patented animatronic talking head with programmable personality and memory. Here are the top five humanoid sex robots:

1. **Erica:** This humanoid robot combines impeccable dexterity with advanced machine learning, making it an ideal assistant in industrial settings.
2. **Junko Chihira:** The cutting-edge features of this humanoid robot are designed to assist medical professionals in performing delicate surgeries with unparalleled precision and efficiency.
3. **Jia Jia:** The extraordinary capabilities of this humanoid robot are specifically designed to provide personalized care and support to individuals with disabilities.
4. **Ocean One:** This robot displays the seamless integration of humanoid robots in the entertainment industry.

[4]Find out more on CBSN On Assignment.

5. **Gita Bot:** In the world of household robotics, this humanoid robot acts as a multifunctional assistant, helping with daily tasks and creating a smart living environment.

Figure 1.13 Realbotix CEO/creative director Matt McMullen standing with the doll Harmony, which has a robotic head. McMullen is also the founder of Abyss Creations, which makes the Real Doll. Eduardo Contreras / San Diego Union-Tribune.

Figure 1.14 Humanoid woman (Getty Images).

Figure 1.15 The Chloe Automation humanoid robot from AI Robots.

There is also the development of a new humanoid robot, Chloe, for the Detroit car companies and automation.

The present book further discusses the use of nuclear batteries to provide long-term energy for the activities of a biomimetic robot (humanoid or animal) as needed. Solar energy is another means of charging batteries. These portable power supplies will be replaceable if desired or needed. The possible creation of a safe and small nuclear source for energy production is also briefly discussed. The book then uses the available knowledge, technology, and software to design and develop advanced intelligent AI computers and software that can learn to think like humans at any age and take possible related actions like humans.

Figure 1.16 Visitors taking photographs of a humanoid robot (Jia Jia) (Tomohiro Ohsumi/Getty Images).

The book emphasizes the importance and necessity of assigning an identity to the consciousness being generated, recorded, and recalled. The individual will have a consciousness with an identity. These will be called identity-vita-assigned consciousness (IVA-consciousness). Note that the humanoid robot will become a companion of its human master for several years as it learns more about the human master's consciousness and possibly experiences the human master's feelings and interactions.

It is important not to have just an AI intelligent computer or robot with consciousness without identity. Under these circumstances, the robot with consciousness may develop ideas, become out of control because of a lack of identity, and develop undesirable scenarios.

The basic strategy to transfer consciousness to human beings may start after the human being is born and can even be started for a grown-up individual entering the program of eventually developing a non-organic biomimetic humanoid robot companion with the identity assigned consciousness of the human master. It is important again to realize that the human master has an identity to be assigned to the humanoid robot before his or her consciousness is transferred to an intelligent IA computer. At that junction, he or she is embedded with an advanced computer integrated with the individual's neural brain (neurons, axons, dendrites, and synapses) to record all human beings' actions, movements, sensing capabilities, and even possibly sentient feelings and emotions. Thus, a strategy is developed for the individual to express these feelings to the resident intelligent computer with IVA-consciousness. The smart embedded consciousness computers equipped with IVA-consciousness will observe and record all events as the individual observes and reacts to them. As the individual ages, the embedded consciousness computer will also grow in memory and record everything observed, heard, felt, enjoyed, involved, or experienced.

The book also considers the description of sentient feelings and their feedback to the resident consciousness. The book will describe how feelings and emotions are transferred to consciousness by describing them cognitively or experiencing them and describing them to the humanoid robot. Oral transfer of consciousness will also play an important role in transferring consciousness to the humanoid. The book also emphasizes that normally the humanoid robot will have no sexual activities because it does not need to do so. Recall that it does not reproduce exactly, either. However, it can repair itself if its electro-magneto-mechanical structures, microprocessors, and systems malfunction. Humanoid robots can also be fabricated to be much bigger than normal humans.

As indicated earlier, it should be emphasized that this book does not cover the hard design and fabrication of electromechanical sensors and actuators in humanoid robots. These details are essentially available off the technical shelves. However, the book does involve smart/intelligent materials and artificial muscles to provide novel dynamic maneuverability and intelligence for humanoid robots.[5]

---

[5]Note that the descriptions and design of hard electromechanical sensors and actuators are fully described in the author's other books on robotics:

M. Shahinpoor, *Intelligent Robotic Systems: Modeling & Simulation*, ERI Press, Albuquerque, New Mexico, second edition (2011)

M. Jamshidi, R. Lumia, J. Mullins, and M. Shahinpoor, Robotics and Manufacturing: Recent Trends in Research, Education, and Applications, ASME Press Series, New York, New York, vol. 4, pp. 11–12, New York (1993)

M. Shahinpoor, *A Robot Engineering Text Book*, Harper and Row Publishers, New York and London (1987)

M. Shahinpoor, *Kypc Robototexhnkny* (Kypc Robot Technology), in Russian, MIR Publishers, Moscow, Former Soviet Union, (1990). Russian Translation of *A Robot Engineering Text Book*, Harper and Row, New York (1987).

M. Jamshidi, J.Y.S. Lu, and M. Shahinpoor, *Recent Trends in Robotics: Modeling, Control and Education*, North-Holland Publishing Corp., New York, and Amsterdam, November (1986)

M. Shahinpoor and S. Gheshmi, *Robotic Surgery: With Smart Materials, Robotic Structures, and Artificial Muscles*, Jenny Stanford Publishing, Singapore (2014)

The basic strategy to create a humanoid robot and transfer IVA-consciousness to it will start after the human finishes the design, development, fabrication, electromechanical operations, and creation of his or her humanoid robot. The humanoid will eventually become a non-organic biomimetic humanoid robot. Initially, upon design and fabrication, software installation, and electromechanical operations, including widespread sensing by smart materials, the humanoid robot will also be equipped with an AI smart computer and memory processor and will have plenty of software and programs to communicate with its human master as well as other people and can act like an intelligent robot, as well. It is essential to assign an identity to the humanoid robot right off the bat, as emphasized before. At that junction, the owner of the humanoid robot equips it with an AI-based advanced computer and will have a host of intelligent dynamic stimuli-responsive sensors and actuators and possibly in contact with the owner's neural brain (neurons, axons, dendrites, and synapses) to record all human actions, movements, and sensing capabilities and even possibly conscious feelings and emotions and save all the information in the humanoid's memory banks. Thus, a strategy is also developed for the individual to express these feelings to the humanoid resident intelligent computer with IVA-consciousness. The humanoid robot will first become aware of who it is (for example, Captain Kirk's humanoid robot). The smart embedded consciousness computers equipped with IVA-consciousness will observe and record all events as the individual observes and reacts to them while growing older. The humanoid robot will become a longtime companion and friend of its owner for several years and gradually familiarize itself with the consciousness of its human master/owner. As the person and the humanoid robot grow older together, the embedded consciousness computer will also grow in memory and record everything observed, heard, felt, enjoyed, involved, or experienced. The only catch here is the recording of emotional effects and feelings regarding love, hate, likes, anger, dislikes, jealousy, fascination, admiration, respect, regrets, music enjoyment, sex enjoyment, vengeance/retaliation, worry, anxiety, etc. The oral transfer of consciousness will also play an important role in transferring consciousness to the humanoid robot.

The book also emphasizes that humanoid robots will not normally have sexual activities because they do not need to do so. However, such desirable activities may also be taught to them to make them aware of such feelings. However, sex humanoid robots are quite a possibility and are currently an expanding market. Recall that it does not reproduce itself exactly. However, it can repair itself in case of any malfunction of its electro-magneto-mechanical units and structures. Furthermore, as described before, it can be fabricated in a much larger (monster-like) body, as shown in Fig. V.2 in Vision of This Book.

The book describes the fundamental idea of designing and developing biomimetic humanoids (robots) with a human master's consciousness. The book will lay the foundation for the eventual survival of human beings in time in the entire universe and possibly even apply to all biomimetic humans, animals, and related biosystems. Essentially, creating organics-based creatures (humanoids) to become silicon-based or lithium-based creatures should be based on a long-term companionship plan with the humanoid robots. The book first introduces advanced, smart, stimuli-responsive intelligent materials and their possible use for designing and developing biomimetic humanoid robots with human consciousness. It then introduces possible scenarios to make intelligent humanoid robots with a human master's consciousness.

David Chalmers maintains that consciousness is what we can know best and explain least.[6] It is the inner subjective experience of what it feels like to see red, smell garlic, or hear Beethoven. Consciousness has intrigued and baffled philosophers. To begin with, we must define and describe consciousness. What should be included in a complete definition and description of consciousness? It is the ability to be aware of and to be able to have a relationship between oneself and one's environment. The most basic definition, however, is "awareness." Another definition suitable for more complex organizations of matter, such as animals with a brain, includes a description that contains some of the following ideas: "thoughts, sensations, hate, jealousy, perceptions, admirations, amazement, tastes, moods, emotions, dreams, vengeance/retaliation, musical enjoyment, and awareness of self." Just like life itself, consciousness is one of those things that is easy to recognize but very difficult to define.

---

[6]*The Character of Consciousness, Philosophy of Mind*, Oxford University Press (Oct 28, 2010)

1.1.1 Why Should We Develop Humanoids?

The Earth is in a precarious and dangerous phase. Icebergs may melt in about 100 years, and many cities will be underwater. Professors Lenore and Manuel Blum of the Computer Science Department at Carnegie Mellon University (Lenore and Manuel Blum 2023) maintain that it may take less than 500 years to end living on Earth.[7]

Dangerous atmospheric conditions may also arise, and hurricanes and tornados may make Earth unlivable. Furthermore, the Sun will run out of hydrogen energy and continue to expand and increase its brightness, drastically altering the solar system. Oceans will be baked dry, and the entire planet will be consumed.

Life on the planet will run into trouble well before it disintegrates. Even before the Sun burns most of its hydrogen, it will have changed from its present state to a life and biology-damaging state. The Sun has been increasing its brightness by about 10%; every billion years, it burns hydrogen. Increased brightness means an increase in the heat that our planet receives. As the planet heats up, the water on the surface will begin to evaporate.

An increase in the Sun's luminosity by 10% over the current level does not sound like a lot, but this small change in our star's brightness will be catastrophic for our planet. This change is a sufficient increase in energy to change the location of the habitable zone around our star. The habitable zone is defined as the range of distances away from any given star where liquid water can be stable on the surface of a planet. With a 10% increase in brightness, the Earth will no longer be within the habitable zone. This will mark the beginning of the evaporation of our oceans. The Earth will be too hot to maintain water on its surface.

This 10% increase in the Sun's brightness, triggering the evaporation of our oceans, will occur over the next billion years or so. Most models suggest that as the oceans evaporate, more and more water will be in the atmosphere instead of on the surface. This will act as a *greenhouse gas*, trapping even more heat and causing more and more oceans to evaporate until the ground is mostly dry and the atmosphere holds the water, but at an extremely high temperature.

As the atmosphere saturates with water, the water held in the highest parts of our atmosphere will be bombarded by high-energy

---

[7]Coding Consciousness: An Algorithm for Awareness? (youtube.com)

light from the Sun, splitting apart the molecules and allowing the water to escape as hydrogen and oxygen, eventually bleeding the Earth dry of water. The Sun's death could mean new life in the outer solar system. What will happen to the solar system when the Sun starts to die? As this book describes, it might be the end of planet Earth, but life could still find a way. We will all be long gone, and the Earth will not be habitable. The only chance for survival would be for an advanced civilization to migrate to a new planetary home. The book describes an alternative for humanity to survive and enter interplanetary and deep space exploration. Our star, the Sun, is powered by nuclear fusion, and it turns hydrogen into helium in a process that converts mass into energy. Once the fuel supply is gone, the Sun will start growing dramatically. Its outer layers will expand until they engulf much of the solar system, as it becomes what astronomers call a *Red Giant*. The slow death will kill off life on the Earth, but it may also create habitable worlds in the solar system's coldest reaches. Any humans left around might find refuge on Pluto and other distant dwarf planets out in the Kuiper Belt, a region past Neptune packed with icy space rocks.

1.2 Life and Universe

As emphasized, the average lifetime of a human being is very short when viewed in the context of human history. However, compared with the age of the Universe, humankind's existence represents just a blink in time. Humans have always tried to discover more about their environment, striving to go beyond their natural limits. This could be considered a means of ensuring their survival, but it can also be viewed as a search for answers on the purpose and origin of life, the nature of the Universe, and the human future.

The first considerable answers were given thousands of years ago in ancient India and Persia's wild but secure caves. The ancient Hindus and Persian cultures made profound observations, and their artwork remains a model of wisdom for the ancient world. Many documents inherited from Indo-Arians and Asyro-Babylonians reveal advanced cosmogenic concepts and theories characteristic of the ancient world (predating ancient Greece). All these emphasize the idea of universal unity and integrity. However, even if they were the result of intuitive thinking, their theories were later confirmed by the writings of the ancient Greeks. Today, humans can formulate answers based on scientific data regarding their origin and the Universe's origin—initially two main cosmogenic theories (Merleau-Ponty, 1945–1962). The first one presupposes that the Universe did not have an initial moment of apparition. Therefore, it was believed that it has always existed and is unexplainable. However, when Edwin Hubble (Hubble's law) accurately demonstrated the expansion of the Universe, this theory was dropped. The second theory (Gamow, 1946) presumes that the Universe has a certain age and is continuously expanding. Its age is determined by an initial moment called the Big Bang (Merleau-Ponty, 1945–1962). However, both theories consider the existence of fundamental cosmic noise and isotropic cosmic radiation, which were discovered in 1964 by Penzias and Wilson. It is worth mentioning that Gamow, Alpher, and Herman proposed in 1946 the existence of this cosmic radiation when they elaborated on the theory of the Big Bang in 1949 (Smith, 2018; Taille, 1977).[8]

Georges Lemaître (1894–1966) was a Belgian cosmologist, Catholic priest, and father of the Big Bang theory.

By accepting the Universe's expansion theory and the Big Bang theory, it can be supposed that initially there was only an energetic field penetrating a cosmic vacuum. The initial inflation (Guth, 1981) probably happened about 13.7 billion years ago. It is presumed to produce temperatures up to 1 trillion degrees (10^{12} °C), which would have created a highly agitated and chaotic state unfavorable for matter formation. However, the expansion of the Universe, combined with the cooling of the hot universe, allowed the formation of unstructured nuclei of matter (i.e., the elementary particles, quarks, electrons, protons, and neutrons). Thus, the cooling of the Universe was the beginning of the intelligent evolution of the universal structure. Even though quarks are believed to be the smallest fundamental particles, there is also the Higgs boson, which may be even smaller. The Higgs boson is the fundamental force-carrying particle of the Higgs field, which is responsible for granting other particles their mass. Peter Higgs (1955) first proposed this field in the mid-1960s.

[8]Dr. Steven Greer's Conscious Universe (The Holographic Conscious Universe Breakdown). https://www.youtube.com/watch?v=mgfJP8-IowM.

Combining one electron with one proton formed the first element: hydrogen (*master molecule*). Whatever the beginning would have been—an expanding universe, a pulsating one, or even a universe with no beginning—the evolution of matter remains the same, moving from chaos to organization. It should be emphasized that human error in understanding the Universe occurs because of how humans think and question existence. Various theories are presented in a book that might shed light on these questions.

Astronomic studies have determined that the cosmic bodies in the Universe have different ages. This proves that the Universe was not created at once and that matter was and is subjected to continuous transformation and evolution. Thus, all the structural elements of the Universe seem to have their history: they appear, evolve, and then disappear by transformation into something else. From elementary particles, one gets to hydrogen, higher chemical elements, and finally to life, consciousness, and the human being or an integrated system of matter and energy. What, then, can we say about the role of intelligence and consciousness? Do they determine the system, or does the system determine intelligence and consciousness? These questions will be partially addressed later when the deterministic way of thinking of humans will be emphasized. Here, we describe various aspects of the evolution and emergence of consciousness in the Universe.

1.3 Evolution and Integration of Life and Consciousness

Humans have always wanted to know how life appeared on the Earth and if other living systems are outside our planet. Because of the lack of scientific proof, various theories have developed according to the level of knowledge acquired during each period of human existence. The universal theory of creation states that God created life and everything else. It was not until the beginning of the 20th century when Oparin (1924) and Haldane (1929) developed a theory that postulated that life on the Earth appeared 5 billion years ago in a so-called "primordial soup" from which sprang the formation of the first organic molecules (amino acids). It took about 1 billion years for the organic molecules to evolve into living cells, and the evolution from living cells to humans took 2.7 billion years more. If one accepts that the first organic molecules appeared on the Earth 3 billion years ago, a question still lingers. What happened in the rest of the Universe? Did life appear somewhere else, too? As long as the components of living bodies can be found anywhere in the Universe, then from a materialistic point of view, it is possible that life also appeared on other planets. What is the relationship between energy, intelligence, and consciousness? Even if one accepts Einstein's relation between mass and energy, a living body still needs an intelligent system to maintain a continuous energy exchange between the living body and its environment to survive.

This system must ensure the capture, transformation, and management of energy. In its evolution from simple to complex, life appeared by organizing matter hierarchically. These levels of conversion to elementary particles to atoms to molecules to molecular aggregates to cells to tissues to organs to organ systems to bodies to species to bio systems to the living world appears to be the normal operation in nature and universe. It is still difficult to understand perfectly how this evolution took place. However, classical physical principles could be applied (e.g., minimum energy principle). Despite nonliving matter, living matter seems to contradict the second and third laws of thermodynamics regarding entropy, which states that the entropy of a closed system is continuously increasing (second law) and that the entropy of a system is determined by its temperature (third law). Thus, while common matter tends to increase entropy, living bodies tend to gain negentropy, as Schrödinger (Schrödinger, What is Life? 1967) called it, to maintain or even reduce their entropy. This seems to fit Weisz's theory because reduced entropy means increased organization. Thus, the living body fights to increase its organization by gaining more negentropy. However, can one define negentropy? This can be defined simply as highly organized matter. The organization can be considered an elementary form of intelligence.[9]

Dr. Robert Hazen, a staff scientist at the Earth and Planets Laboratory of Carnegie Science in Washington, DC, thinks that a

---

[9]This notion is also discussed regarding the first and second arrows of time in this reference. This interview is an episode from@The-Well, https://bit.ly/thewell-youtube. You may be familiar with the "arrow of time."

single arrow of time may be too limiting. A second arrow, which he has dubbed "the law of increasing functional information," considers evolution. Specifically, Hazen explains that evolution seems to not only have time but also function and purpose.

Hazen explains that it appears the Universe uses a similar way of evolving biology and other complex systems throughout the cosmos. This idea suggests that as the Universe ages and expands, it becomes more organized and functional, nearly opposite to theories surrounding increasing cosmological disorder. Hazen suggests that these two "arrows"—entropy and organized information—could run parallel.

The four fundamental elements of living matter are carbon, hydrogen, oxygen, and nitrogen (CHON). Carbon, a tetravalent element, is perhaps the most important because it allows the formation of organic combinations (note the valence of carbon; its importance will be discussed later). Some organic combinations store a considerable amount of energy in the form of sugars, whose molecular structures are well known. This energy is released to the organism by a metabolic process (sugars act as energy storage devices).

Lipids are another category of substances required by living bodies. Carbon is linked to hydrogen, oxygen, nitrogen, or phosphorus in the composition of lipids. However, the organic substances fundamentally required by living organisms are proteins. They contain about 24 amino acids and form life's structural and functional framework. Because the carbon atom can saturate its four valences with different radicals, it forms energetically asymmetric structures. This molecular asymmetry of proteins could be the main reason for the reactivity of living bodies.

The formation of organic molecules from the corresponding atoms could be possible in certain conditions such as atmospheric lightning or intense ultraviolet radiation, which are the hypothesized conditions during which the Earth was formed. However, similar conditions can also be found in other places in the Universe. This, once again, does not exclude the possibility of the appearance of life on other planets. Whatever the birthplace of organic substances, their evolution was mainly chemical. It is well supported that the Cambrian age seawater was quite different from today's seawater. It contained a wide range of organic substances, which determined its nutritional properties. That is why it is often called "*primordial soup*." The first organisms to appear in this medium were spherical and fed themselves with the abundant organic nutrients from the primordial soup—the so-called autotrophic feeding. Later, this was replaced by photosynthesis—the so-called heterotrophic feeding. The organisms that made this transition were quite possibly from the group of *Euglena viridis*, which can feed both autotrophic and heterotrophic.

Photosynthesis represents a very important step in the evolution of life. During photosynthesis, oxygen is released into the atmosphere, which other organisms can use later. This was the first step in the hierarchic organization of a biosystem. It represents the first trophic chain. Oxygen release also led to the formation of the ozone layer, which acts as a protective shield against ultraviolet radiation. Using photosynthesis, plants transform inorganic matter into organic matter and oxygen, providing food and oxygen for the animal kingdom. Carbon's organic combinations ensured both the energetic source (sugars and lipids) and the structural elements of the living systems (amino acids $R\text{-}R'NH_2\text{-}COOH$). However, deoxyribonucleic acid (or DNA) is the key element that forms intelligent structures (dynamic and alive). DNA can be undoubtedly considered the most intelligent form of matter. Its appearance was the most important moment in biological (especially human) evolution. It allowed organisms to reproduce by mutation and selection, leading to the wide range (micro to macro) of living organisms today.

However, how did DNA develop? The 1965 Nobel Prize laureate Jacques Monod states that DNA was developed by pure chance (Monod, 1971). He considers that chance is responsible for evolution. However, this would mean, citing Waddington, that we can compare evolution with throwing many bricks together and hoping that they will fall and be arranged in a recognizable structure, like a house. In the meantime, Prigogine (1973) theorized the probability of life appearing by chance to be about $1/10^{10}$. Thus, instead of chance, we should consider that life appeared as a logical requirement, an intelligent evolution of matter based mainly on natural selection and survival strategies. According to the systems theory (von Bertalanffy, General Systems Theory, 1968), an assembly of elements in reciprocal interaction exhibits properties that the sum of the properties of the individual elements cannot express. In a living system, each component presents its condition of survival, simultaneously both the cause and the effect. Consequently, we can suppose that the combinations between elements were initially based solely on their chemical affinities.

When organic structures appeared, however, they were capable of metabolism and reproduction, and their evolution, and especially the evolution of consciousness, may have been based on different laws and principles. Therefore, life and consciousness are part of the evolutionary laws of the Universe, as matter and energy are always changing and always maintaining a dynamic equilibrium.

1.4 Modeling the Consciousness in the Universe

The intelligent structures that determined the evolution of matter, intelligence, life, and consciousness imposed rules applicable to all organized systems. Thus, these rules can lead to the main principle of universal coherence. Each system is hierarchically dependent on a superior one and is part of the main system: the Universe. For example, the Earth would not exist if it were not a part of the galaxy, and life would not exist on the Earth if the Sun did not exist.

Dr. Rupert Sheldrake of the Weekend University maintains that the Universe is conscious and humans, animals, and plants have souls.[10] Shelldrake believes that the cosmos is like a developing organism, and so is our planet, Gaia. Recall the hard problem of finding space for human consciousness in the Universe. Note that some form of mind, experience, or consciousness is associated with all self-organizing systems, including atoms, molecules, and plants. The Sun and other stars and the entire galaxies are conscious. If so, what about the mind of the Universe as a whole?[11]

Note that the cooling of the Universe began the intelligent evolution of the whole universal structure, including the formation of the first master molecule, *Hydrogen H*, and subsequently universal consciousness because it was the hydrogen gas and gravity that led to the formation of the stars, such as our own Sun and the entire galaxies (milky way of ours) and matter in the Universe, using gravitational forces. Thus, it could be claimed that the master molecule hydrogen was the first element with some inherent consciousness.

---

[10]https://www.youtube.com/watch?v=XqWbIVlnmNM&t=12s

[11]You can keep Rupert Sheldrake's work updated on his website: www.sheldrake.org. Links: Rupert's website is http://sheldrake.org/

1.5 The Living World

On Earth, all living structures are based on geometrical combinations of a certain number of amino acids. The huge diversity of living systems is thus the result of an intelligent arrangement of these amino acids (which form proteins with different structures). This arrangement, or sequence, is dictated by the genetic code encrypted in the DNA. Therefore, DNA, which can be found in every cell, serves as a program with rules of organization for the living system. How could matter evolve to such a superior form of intelligence? In this book, we will explore some theories that go a little beyond the limits of our current level of knowledge.

The "fuel" of living systems is mostly sugar, which is produced by plants from carbon dioxide, water, and solar radiation. Sugar is stored in all living systems as tropospheric acid (TPA). From this, it can be observed that the fundamental dependence on the Sun is common to all the living systems on Earth. However, besides needing fuel, a living system also needs information, intelligence, and consciousness. Consequently, to survive, living systems also need specialized information-processing devices. All living cells must be able to receive (release) information from (to) their environment, whatever their structure and organization level.

Inside a biosystem is a tightly woven dependence among all the living organisms forming the system. For example, animals depend on plants because plants provide oxygen and sugar, essential to the life and health of living animals and plants.

In the same way, humans, possibly the most complex organism on Earth, live in tight dependence on other organisms. Therefore, the existence of a biological system is conditioned by the existence of other systems, which themselves are conditioned by systems like the Earth, the Sun, galaxies, and the Universe.

1.6 Life and Information

Information plays a fundamental role in the evolution and organization of material species. Monod (1971) states that "living bodies are strange things" because their existence ignores some fundamental principles of modern physics, like the second law of thermodynamics. On the other hand, Prigogine (1973) has said that only some of the properties of a living system can be deducted from the laws of thermodynamics and statistical mechanics (Prigogine, 1973). However, some basic terms must be described to understand better the relations between matter, energy, and information.

It was previously mentioned that matter is organized into hierarchic systems. Consequently, the properties of a subsystem belonging to a certain system are determined by considering the cumulative properties of a hierarchy and, therefore, by integrating the properties of all the elements in that subsystem with the interactions between the system and its environment (other subsystems). Systems can be classified analytically into closed (isolated) and open systems. This classification is according to the relations of given subsystems with their environment in connection with the exchange of matter, energy, or information. However, all living systems are considered open. They continuously exchange matter, energy, and information with their environment, as they are completely integrated within their environment. They are hierarchically organized, and the links between different hierarchical subsystems could be considered informational links since each link carries a package of information that identifies it within the hierarchy. The reason could reside in the hierarchic classification of links between systems. Thus, the primary link could be the physical one. The chemical link follows this, and the most advanced link could be considered the informational link. However, it is unclear that this is the order of the link hierarchy and that all the substances in the Universe must have a similar hierarchy. The most probable explanation is that these links are deeply integrated, each determining the others. There may be a connection between this notion of consciousness and the integrated information theory (IIT) of Giulio Tononi (2015).

The degree of complexity of a systemic hierarchy is given by the number of levels and by the degree of interaction between the subsystems contained in the hierarchy. In addition, the order is the result of intelligent action. Therefore, the more ordered a system is, the more intelligent it is. On the one hand, the more complex a system is, the more ordered it is as a survival strategy that ensures its stability. Also, according to its definition, any material system with a temperature greater than 0°K (−273°C) tends to decompose due to the increased Brownian movement. Thus, any nonliving system at a temperature higher than 0°K tends to increase its disorder (and entropy). This leads to different disintegration temperatures based on the properties and bonds of various materials. There are also positive and negative arrows of time, which will be discussed later in the book. On the other hand, as open systems, biological systems tend to oppose the disintegration trend, their entropy variation being generally negative (often called negentropy). In other words, a biological system follows the natural trend of creating disorder. Still, at the same time, this trend is compensated for through a complementary trend by creating negentropy, which annihilates the entropic trend. This dynamic organization equilibrium can be maintained in biological systems only because of the exchange of matter, energy, and information with the environment. But how could non-biological systems maintain their organization? Even if it sounds strange, they could do it in the same way but on a different scale. One should not forget that matter formation resulted from the "environment" and its dynamic conditions. Therefore, matter appeared due to interactions between energetic and informational systems (natural law). So, did energy and information exist before matter appeared? This is another mystery because "matter is energy" and is organized in a way that evolves information. However, to get organized, the matter needs an informational impulse. Again, the most reasonable explanation seems to be the dynamic interaction between systems. Therefore, we could define living systems as dissipative, having a continuous oscillation about a point of equilibrium.

Self-controlling characteristics condition the functionality of such a system based on feedback mechanisms. The main difference between a living system and a nonliving one is the ability of a living system to exercise self-control, self-regulation, and self-organization, ensured by antientropic devices.

The feedback mechanisms are based on information processing. One can even say that any system that does not perceive its environment is a nonliving system. It is clear that during the evolution of the biosystem, its ability to process information increased along with its complexity of organization. The greater the ability to process information, the greater the possibilities for adaptation of a living system, leading to increased autonomy in its environment.

1.7 Biological Information

Information can be defined as a discreet or continuous sequence of measurable events distributed over a certain period. It can also be considered a message or a series of messages about the variations of a system's internal or external environment. However, a message consisting of signals becomes information after a system receives and decodes it. Any living system is a source of information and a sink of information. These properties can be extended with some limitations to nonliving systems. Therefore, we can say that, generally, matter is both a source and a sink of information. However, the difference between a living and a nonliving system is that a living one has informational filters, which allow the system to sort out the information and receive only the information that has a certain meaning for the system. A system to receive filtered information requires specialized devices capable of receiving certain types and amounts of information.

After the information is received and decoded, it must be processed. For this task, a living system develops several processing rules or algorithms. Algorithms form a processing program that determines the functionality and self-conservation of the system. However, information requires energy to circulate inside or outside a system. Despite the physical matter, where causes are usually of the same order of magnitude as their effects, in biological systems, very small variations in the informational flux can lead to considerable effects. As a relevant example, one can recall the effects of enzymes or hormones on an organism and how minute changes in them can result in the life or death of a living system.

Thus, we can deduce that information plays a very important role in intelligent systems like biological ones. However, the information considered thus far has been dynamic information that circulates. Both living and nonliving systems have static information, too, which is stored by more or less specialized devices. Unfortunately, static information is more difficult to define and control. For example, we mention human memory, stored at a neocortex or paleocortex level. Even if the chemical reactions that take place in the neocortex or paleocortex can be identified and explained, the content of the information stored there is not accessible to "intruders."

A new theory might introduce the term *information field*. According to this theory, information can be considered a special field. The classical definition for a field is that it represents a form of existence of matter. We already know about the dualism of matter–energy, where matter can be in both a physical state and a field state (energy). Can we include *information* in this relation and form a triad? To answer this question, we must first consider the memory and intelligence of biological systems.

It is generally accepted that any biological system is based on two main informational processes: inherited and those acquired during life. Inherited information includes the experience of the species. Its genesis can be explained by admitting that it appears with the species as an expression of certain repeatable environmental conditions. This inherited informational package has the role of conservation and perpetuation of the species. These programs are responsible for instincts, and the organism executes them automatically regardless of obstacles. These "inherited programs" are highly intelligent with logical sequences. Their exact genesis, however, is quite difficult to explain.

Acquired information affects only the particular system that acquires it, unlike inherited information, which affects the whole species. Of course, the two types interact during a system's life. In higher-organized systems, such as the human body, other informational processes, such as mental ones, also influence them. Less organized biological systems process information by simple logic: "yes" or "no." This behavior could also be partially extended to nonliving systems based on the action–reaction principle.

A human being has a more complex device for processing information. Their logic is not only "yes" or "no." It can also include "some yes" and "some no." In this sense, they use *fuzzy logic*. This means that information received and decisions made become more quantified as information and decision that are more complex. All these determine a person's level of intelligence. This process also includes emotions. Indeed, the phrase "I like it" cannot express the whole meaning of the statement because it does not convey the intensity of the feeling. You can like something more or less, and in the meantime, you can dislike or hate more or less that same something. However, this fuzzy logic type can be considered a degree of freedom of affectivity or an increased desire for more options.

1.8 Exploring the Nervous System in the Context of Consciousness

For superior organized biological systems, information is mainly processed by the nervous system, whose activity is purely informational (but with electrochemical support). Consciousness may also play an important role here. However, protozoa have no nervous system even if they perform several vital processes. Therefore, their breathing is performed by direct oxygen diffusion inside the cell's cytoplasm. Digestion is performed by including food (bacteria) within cytoplasmic spacing, while food is digested inside digestive vacuoles. On the other hand, in more complex multicellular systems, cells became more specialized within the system, finally forming organs and internal systems.

Superior organisms, having more specialized organs and subsystems, require a structure able to coordinate the biological system to achieve its main goal: the survival of the body and the species. This coordinating structure is the nervous system. Protozoa have no nervous system in their anatomic structure and, consequently, no material evidence of a coordinating structure. This does not mean protozoa are not coordinated; it simply means they are coordinated energetically.

The evolution of the nervous system, as a material structure, starts with a single double-circuit neuron that appears at coelenterates. Two neurons, a sensory one and a motor one, form the first nervous circuit. In the following steps, other association neurons are added. These added neurons intermediate the information transfer between the receptor circuit and the effector circuit. Then, neurons gathered in nervous centers and ganglions evolve to the highest level, the brain.

In this later step of evolution, the nervous system is divided into two main parts: the vegetative nervous system and the conscience. The vegetative nervous system is responsible for vital functions that are performed automatically, i.e., they are not controlled rationally. Conscience, on the other hand, is mainly a function of the organism and its relation with the environment and society, determining the behavior of the organism. It is interesting to note here that the survival program of any superior organism is dictated by the vegetative system, an intelligent measure designed to ensure the perpetuation of the species.

However, even inferior systems, such as plants, can "memorize" their own experience and act accordingly. Even if their behavior might seem strange, as they do not possess nervous systems, it is proven that they promptly react in the presence of a person who periodically cuts a leaf (Baxter). How can that plant "see" the person? Well, one may say that the plant does not see but feels the energetic field surrounding another organism. But how can one distinguish between "good vibes" and bad ones?" Obviously, feeling only the energetic field is not enough; there must also be some informational interactions.

Suppose the vegetative nervous system controls all the vital functions of the organism and ensures the propagation of the species. In that case, you might wonder why it is necessary to have a conscience. Well, consciousness is a step in evolution that improves the activity of the vegetative nervous system. Due to the influence of consciousness, the organism's physiology is not strictly conditioned by the environment, as the organism tries to improve its living conditions consciously. For humans, behavior is not determined strictly by the survival program but is the result of physiological, social, moral, and cultural determinations.

1.9 Exploring the Nervous System and Consciousness

Taking into account the above arguments for nervous system evolution, and evolution of consciousness, life might appear very complicated. However, coming back to magnocellular systems, we can reconsider their functionality. Therefore, as they are open systems, they must be integrated into their environment. This involves information exchange in addition to the exchange of matter and energy. Being a simple system, a nervous system is not necessary for survival. However, the question here is how to process information using simple systems. The associated chemical reactions alone would not be able to do this because it would be impossible to process information by just chemical interaction with the environment and fulfill the survival conditions required by a living system. Is it energy that supports the information processing of simple living systems? Well, energy must be intelligently coordinated, but by whom or what? Consciousness plays an important role here. Another important question is whether matter can think independently or is designed by some external Universal Intelligence and consciousness to think and process information.

1.10 Informational Hierarchy and Integration

A simple analysis of the types of matter known so far reveals many similarities at any scale, from atomic to galactic and from living to nonliving systems. Whatever the beginning, whether the Big Bang, Creation, or both, matter evolved from simple to complex with different informational models for organizing and operating the material world.

The geometry of different material structures presents many similarities. Therefore, if we consider the logarithmic spiral, one can observe that it can be found in various places within the Universe. Thus, we find it in the shape of galaxies, DNA, plant seeds that have to grow spirally in the soil to germinate, or in the shape of the shells of some marine and terrestrial animals, and many, many other examples. Even the evolution of civilization or the life cycle (from cradle to grave) can be metaphorically considered a spiral, too. Of course, geometry plays a very important role in the evolution and organization of matter. From ancient times, the unexplainable occurrence of a certain number called the Golden Number, or the Golden Section, which can be found in almost any form of matter, has been reported. These numeric topics will be discussed in more detail later.

Most of the things that humans invented during their evolution were already "invented" and used by nature before. So, if humans are the most sophisticated example of the intelligent structure of matter, can humans only invent things that already exist in nature? What is more intelligent than the human species?

One could say that any piece of matter follows a certain model and that the synergy of all material models results in a universal model of matter and life. Indeed, it is understood how cells are formed and how they work. Still, it is not understood yet how identical cells, having identical genetic codes, present different evolution, leading to the formation of different organs. In addition, it has yet to be completely understood how an amino acid or a protein is sent exactly to the cell that needs it. However, as we will see later, one possible mechanism might be the one that develops informational integration, where proteins are assigned so-called "zip codes" or information sequences (Gunter Blobel, 1999 Nobel Prize Laureate in Medicine).

Another example involves the cell's adaptation to the requirements of the system. Thus, we can consider the following experiment: If a cell from the eye of a frog embryo is taken and transplanted into another tissue (e.g., in a leg), the cell will lead to the formation of a tissue similar to the one where it was transplanted. The frog will not have eyes on the leg, as one might expect. In the same way, if some human cells are isolated and kept in neutral, artificial tissue cultures, in time they lose their identity.

In other words, they lose the informational model of the organism that produced them. If then some horse serum is added to the culture, the development of the cells will be similar to the one of regular horse cells. If these "horse cells" are reintroduced into the human body, however, they will recover their initial model (Watson, 1974). Therefore, we can conclude that matter can memorize, forget, adapt, and think.

These observations lead to the unique existence of an informational model of living matter. This model offers a structural and functional program specific to any living system, a program that is not identifiable with the genetic code but is transmitted by it.

The organization of matter, from elementary particles to the enormity of the Universe, represents information found in all structures of matter, be it alive or not. This informational structure appears together with the organization of matter in its evolution from simple to complex. Organization *means* information since the material system appears to be filled with an informational field that contains all the elements required by the organization and functionality of the system.

Information must be highly organized within a super-intelligent system, like a living system. Thus, information, like matter, is organized hierarchically into interdependent classes or subsystems. Biorhythms are a good example of the integration of the informational structure of a living system within the main system represented by the Universe. A marine worm called the Eunice worm, living in the Atlantic Ocean, detaches a part of its body containing its reproductive elements at 2:00 am on the eighth night after the first full moon occurring after the beginning of fall (Pora, 1978). Because of highly intelligent informational organization and integration, living systems, such as the Eunice worm, can perform tasks that seem unimaginably complex for a simple system. The informational pattern is another element that determines the informational structure of living systems. It may be hard to understand and believe that the nervous system controls all the reactions in a living system without an informational system. Like matter and energy, which are organized hierarchically, information is organized hierarchically, in addition to forming an informational model or pattern of the system, and it also contains more sub-models within its hierarchy.

By acknowledging the existence of a hierarchical informational structure, we can better understand and explain the peculiar phenomena encountered in living systems. For instance, consider a person who has had an arm amputated but still "feels" the arm. This phenomenon suggests that even though the material part of the arm no longer exists, the system's informational structure retains its information. As the brain processes this information, it generates the sensation of "feeling" the arm, highlighting the urgent need to understand the influence of the hierarchical informational structure.

Thus far, we have discussed the informational structure within a living system. We also observed that information is organized on hierarchic levels or classes and is well integrated within the other structures of living systems. Therefore, since matter and energy are integrated in hierarchical structures, from simple to complex, their structure has influenced the formation of the Universe.

It seems logical that information should be hierarchically organized in the Universe. However, at the current level of scientific achievements, this can be only hypothesized, as information cannot be measured directly; we cannot identify its universal structure. Based on this supposition, the material world may result from an informational field or structure. It should comprise its pattern in material structure as one of the primordial "substances" that led to matter formation. In addition, going further, we can deduce that living systems possess, besides a nervous system, an informational field associated with the material structure and is, therefore, integrated within it.

1.11 Life and Evolution

As we already have mentioned, many theories regarding the creation or evolution of life have been developed throughout history. Even if most of them agree that evolution is responsible for the development of living systems from simple to complex forms, theories on the causes of evolution vary greatly. Initially, humans thought that the creation of the species was an act of God or other supernatural forces. Then, the famous theory of Darwin gained support, which stated that the whole process of the evolution of living organisms is the result of natural selection.

More recent theories (e.g., Monod's theory, 1949) claim that natural evolution is based on the interplay between chance and necessity, bringing about adaptive evolutionary change, a mathematical model for the growth of microorganisms. The Monod equation is a mathematical model for the growth of microorganisms. Jacques Monod (1910–76, a French biochemist, Nobel Prize in Physiology or Medicine in 1965) proposed using an equation of this form to relate microbial growth rates in an aqueous environment to the concentration of a limiting nutrient.[12] Monod suggests that evolution happened due to chance. It is known that non-reversible changes in a species can take place only by altering its genetic code, i.e., by mutations. Genetic mutations may happen at times, especially in the presence of radiation. However, the results can be favorable or unfavorable to the evolution of living systems. Furthermore, by considering only mutations, the theory of natural selection might be discounted, although it has been proven to exist. It is a long way from random "accidents" to the evolution of a whole species. Suggesting that human evolution happened only by chance seems unlikely.

To develop an accurate theory on the evolution of life, we must first understand and define life. Only with this knowledge can a model of life be developed. From the point of view of universal integration, defining life is a difficult task since, as human beings, we are part of a living system. In other words, we are inside the system,

[12]This publication briefly describes Monod's theory. Monod, Jacques (1949). "The growth of bacterial cultures". *Annual Review of Microbiology,* 3: 371–394.

and a system is best examined from the outside. However, given that we still need precious initial information, the only solution is to start from a simple concept and develop more complex theories based on observations and deductions.

1.12 Group Approach

The simplest model from which one may consider life is the sum of two basic elements: birth and death. Thus, a cell has just two states: it is either alive or dead. Determining this, we observe that between birth and death, a cell must survive. This is a very important pattern of any living system and is directly related to intelligence.

Furthermore, the theory of the survival of a cell can be expanded to encompass the survival of a species, which involves a more complex survival strategy that includes reproduction. Reproduction is associated with growth and stasis. However, specialized devices must carefully control growth because endless growth would negatively influence the evolution and survival of the species. Growth limitation results from integrating the living system within its environment and the Universe. Thus, we can observe the importance of communication between systems in the mechanism of universal integration—also, a living system's intelligence results from external informational influence and internal organization.

This dualism leads to various behavior patterns and different paths of organization and evolution. For a comprehensive approach, we should take a group approach to life and its evolution, depicting a living environment (multilevel hierarchical system) as "moduli" formed by specific subsystems.

The Russian scientist V.L. Kalmykov described the relationship between these subsystems as a set of mutually opposite functions (Table 1.1).

Therefore, self-organization is mainly an informational process based on the informational links between the subsystem and its environment. Based on the elements considered thus far in our model, the most important feature of an intelligent structure can be explained. The organizational ability of living systems can be thermodynamically described as the product of an assembly of structures that are thermodynamically unstable but kinetically stable. Self-organization emerges from the Universe's hierarchical structure and the need for the system comprising it to ensure survival.

Table 1.1 Ten pairs of functions characterizing the inter-system relations

Direct function reverse function	Right-hand mirror reflection Left-hand mirror reflection
Identification	Identification ion
Right-hand mirror reflection	Left-hand mirror reflection
Change of position in space	Reversion of position in space
Transformation of configuration	Restoration of configuration
Increase in the number of elements	Decrease in the number of elements
Provision of inlet Provision of outlet	Connection isolation
Switch-on (mediation) Switch-off	Switch-on
Switch-on (mediation)	Switch-off
Inflow Outflow	Outflow
Concentrating Scattering	Scattering

Here, we mention Dr. Robert Hazen's *Second Arrow of Time*. He believes that some mysterious power in nature wrote the software for such design and amazing color arrangements and beauty. This is an increase in the order and beauty of nature.[13] Hazen, a staff scientist at the Earth and Planets Laboratory of Carnegie Science in Washington, DC, thinks that a single arrow of time may be too limiting. A second arrow of time, which he has dubbed "the law of increasing functional information," considers the evolution and the emergence of new organized configurations, say an orchid flower design. Specifically, Hazen explains that evolution seems to have time, function, and purpose.

Hazen explains that it appears the Universe uses a similar way of evolving biology and other complex systems throughout the cosmos. This idea suggests that as the Universe ages and expands, it becomes more organized and functional, nearly opposite to theories

[13]This interview is an episode from @The-Well, https://bit.ly/thewell-youtube

surrounding increasing cosmological disorder. Hazen suggests that these two "arrows"—entropy and organized information—could run parallel.

Opposed to self-organization is entropy, which has the role of keeping the system away from a stable equilibrium and favoring, thus, its evolution. It must also be mentioned that entropy is also responsible for the beauty of design and organizations in the world, such as the fantastic design of flowers such as orchids Angle and Dove, and similar ones, as shown in Fig. 1.17.

Figure 1.17 Beautiful orchid flowers Angle and White Dove.

The relationship between entropy and self-organization can be mathematically modeled if the living system is considered a dynamic system of interacting parts, entropies, with conditions. Another approach might use the game theory on living systems, as with dynamic systems. This theory is mainly a probabilistic method that develops a mathematical model starting from a set of "games" initially defined and considering various finite strategy spaces.

The term "game" in this theory refers to a strategy adopted by a system, which can be defined as a sequence of actions and properties that a system might follow during its evolution. Practically speaking, living systems do not require finite strategy spaces since they limit their strategy spaces according to interactions with their environment. Therefore, the game theory could be applied here by considering the case of infinite strategy spaces. One of the most important features of the evolutionary games theory is replicator dynamics based on the evolutionary strategy of a dynamic system increasing in frequency only if it is a successful and beneficial strategy for the system's survival. Therefore, this strategy will be applied more and more until a better one replaces it. Mathematically, the relative increment in the frequency of a set of strategies is given exactly by the success of that set.

Whatever the correct theory of evolution might be, one thing is true: Living matter continuously adapts to its environmental conditions. However, in accepting this fact, another question is raised regarding the adaptation mechanism. This mechanism seems to be an intelligent informational structure able to store and analyze information about the environment or certain repeatable events. Eventually, the information is used to predict these conditions' evolution and adapt the living system to them. There is a continuous exchange of matter, energy, and information between the system and its environment in any living system, being an open system. Therefore, could adaptation be considered an intelligent answer to environmental stimuli? If evolution happened by chance, intelligence cannot evolve only by chance and errors. We should cite Einstein here, who said, "God does not play dice with the Universe."

In the living world, the common element of a living system, whatever its level of evolution, is its communication ability. This is the result of the mechanism for processing information found in any living system to facilitate its relationships with other systems from the environment and to facilitate these relationships between the internal subsystems of the living system. Therefore, any cell from an organism continuously communicates with others in the organism. As a whole, the organism is continuously communicating with its environment. Without this ability to communicate, life would not be possible.

However, one might ask what the limits of the environment are and if the environment is communicating with other superior systems as well. We could define the "environment" as the set of systems immediately surrounding a given system. In this case, the environment continuously communicates with the other systems that form the Universe. We could also define the "environment" as the whole universe, which hosts all living systems. If this is the case, we can suppose that the environment has nothing above it in the hierarchy and only communicates with other systems placed on a lower level of the hierarchy.

1.13 Intelligence and Living System

The intelligence of any living system is mainly characterized by a main goal—the perpetuation of the species. This involves complex feedback mechanisms that help the living system remain integrated and stable in the hierarchy. In this case, the intelligence of the system is defined as the behavior or the set of actions performed by the system according to the indefinite laws of integration. An organism is integrated within its environment in much the same way as a cell is integrated within its organism (the cell's environment). However, a cell can live independently as well, as in the case of protozoa. Therefore, we will attempt to define intelligence starting at the cellular level with the premise that intelligence is more than the sum of mental processes.

The intelligence of any living system is mainly characterized by a main goal—the perpetuation of the species. This involves complex feedback mechanisms that help the living system remain integrated and stable in the hierarchy. In this case, the system's intelligence is defined as the behavior or the set of actions performed by the system according to the indefinite integration laws. An organism is integrated within its environment in much the same way as a cell is integrated within its organism (the cell's environment). However, a cell can also live independently, as in the case of protozoa. Therefore, we will attempt to define intelligence starting at the cellular level with the premise that intelligence is more than the sum of mental processes and tends to move toward consciousness.

If we analyze the Universe, we might easily observe its full coherence. The Universe contains a set of strictly dependent relations between all its elements, exhibiting a form of highly intelligent organization. One of the main mechanisms of the organization of matter seems to be the feedback mechanism, which determines the stability and functionality of all forms of matter. The feed-before (feed-forward) mechanism might explain the matter's evolution. Thus, we could consider life as continuity on a higher level in its evolution.

The Universe cannot be imagined as a chaotic system, even if it is supposed to have started with chaos. Chaos directly results in instability. Although order might be created out of chaos, it has its own rules (more or less known to science). However, these rules appear to follow the movement of matter. However, if matter appears because of organization, and organization appears because of matter's movement, then how did the movement of matter appear? There must be a primordial intelligence that is still not understood. This could be called the intelligence or the consciousness of the matter itself, its presence is anywhere, and that is why it has been ignored thus far. Therefore, considering the intelligence of matter, we could deduce that one of the main properties of intelligence is the ability to exchange and generate information and evolve consciousness. More than that, being able to generate information, matter also can self-model and, for superior living forms, replicate itself.

One might ask a question with deep implications: Is there a God who created the world? The true answer might never be known, as everybody has a different understanding of God. For children, God can be something that keeps bad dreams away from them at night. For adults, depending on their religion, God might represent the Creator and the universal ruler. However, we could define God through God's powerful assistants and as possessing "Universal Intelligence" whose presence is observed in every tiny place within the Universe. This Universal Intelligence also generated and has maintained the universal rules that, among other things, created human beings and other living systems. Thus, God's powerful assistants, through the Universal Intelligence, are the intrinsic parts of energy, matter, intelligence, life, and consciousness. Therefore, a human is a tiny part of the Universe, while God's powerful assistants can be manifested inside everybody and everything.

1.14 Intelligence of the Home Environment

As mentioned previously, the animal world strictly depends on nature, and its intelligence reflects nature's intelligence. This might be one of the prerequisites of equilibrium. Animals have to adapt their behavior to their environment to survive. That is why animals present two types of adaptive behavior: *automatic*, based on instincts, and *rational*, an act of will and a conscious decision.

Instincts are based on the individual's experience and comprise information transmitted by the genetic code from one generation to another. This information helps predict the environmental conditions the individual will be exposed to during his life and prepares reactions accordingly. However, some individual experiences often do not fit those from the instincts "database." In this case, to adapt, the animal must make rational decisions to ensure survival. This kind of intelligent system proves to be extremely complex. In addition to the inherited program, the individual has the complementary possibility to survive. Universal Intelligence designed the human body so complexly that it can defend itself in almost any situation. However, when it voluntarily ignores and suppresses some of its natural control, it adapts to certain conditions not covered by the basic program. This second step of decision-making represents a very important step in the evolution of intelligence, as the system is synergetic and not necessarily hierarchic. Nature's variability and unpredictability can explain the requirements for such a synergetic system. It involves a huge set of factors. That is why no intelligent program can predict the exact conditions of the environment. Therefore, the most effective approach seems to be chosen by nature, i.e., a basic program that includes general conditions that could occur during an individual's life and a complementary program that consciously analyzes all the details of any prevailing condition and decides accordingly. However, besides the synergy of the two intelligent programs, the animal response to any natural condition is also based on the strength of the influence of each factor determining a specified condition. Thus, if an animal is exposed to a certain condition mainly covered by the inherited program and has to deal with conditions not covered by this program, then his reaction will be instinctual and automatic if they do not threaten the animal's life. But if the strength of the factors not covered by the basic program is greater than the one it covers, then the reaction has to be rational.

Another type of intelligence in the animal world is social intelligence. It is impossible to decide if this intelligence is mainly instinctive or rational. However, one of its goals is to ensure the species' survival. That is why certain insects, for example, gather in colonies and form a social environment where every individual has a certain task and belongs to a certain hierarchical level within the community. This behavior evolved as a necessity because these insects might have had difficulty surviving when environmental conditions were too harsh for that individual. That is why, by forming colonies, they also invoke an intelligent survival strategy. Some individuals are responsible for gathering food, some are responsible for defending their territory, others are responsible for maintaining and improving their living territory, and still others are used for reproduction and the perpetuation of the species. Interestingly, such an organization can be easily compared with human society. This might lead to an interesting conclusion: If insects formed colonies because they could not survive as individuals, why did humans do the same? Human supremacy on Earth results from collective intelligence, which explains human society's amazing progress and evolution. As a back reaction, it has also determined the evolution of intelligence. So, human society's development was determined by intelligence, while its evolution influenced the evolution of intelligence.

Another interesting observation regarding the intelligence of nature is that any system in the Universe possesses the exact amount of intelligence necessary for survival. Of course, it might be difficult to measure or quantify this intelligence. It is also difficult to predict whether a certain system could be more adaptable (intelligent) in different circumstances than in existing ones. However, if this is true, it can be considered another step in understanding the complex intelligence of the Universe and represents a mechanism capable of making available to the system as much intelligence as needed. What are the criteria on which this decision is based? What are the properties of the intelligence of a system that leads to perfect integration of the system within the Universe by using the minimum effort? These questions cannot be answered now because the integration and adaptation mechanisms are still incomplete.

One of the main difficulties in understanding intelligence and consciousness is the continuously variable strength of the inherited intelligence—rational intelligence ratio found in the Universe. In the living world, for example, a human being cannot "feel" an impending storm as well as an octopus, even if the human being can be considered more "intelligent" than the octopus. However, as the human's life is not in danger from the storm, his inherited intelligence does not react to the stimuli that could predict it. Therefore, the human reaction in this case is mainly rational. A human being confronted with the storm would seek shelter to protect himself. However, using his specialized sensitive devices, the octopus would "feel" the approaching storm well before that time. This warning system allows the octopus to get to the bottom of the ocean in time (Pora, 1978). Otherwise, the octopus would not have enough time to get to the bottom and avoid being crushed on the rocks by the big waves during a storm.

1.15 Social Intelligence, Consciousness, and Language

To account for the social evolution of different species, we must consider another factor that spurs development: speech communication. It was mentioned before that an open system performs a continuous exchange of information (among others). In nonliving systems or living systems with no social organization, the transmission of information is different from that of living systems, which form communities and communicate with one another. The principal form of communication is performed by emitting and receiving certain sounds that, taken together, comprise a language. Therefore, the members of any community can emit sounds that have a certain meaning for the other members. In this way, they can coordinate their joint activities. A language is shaped by the anatomy of each species and the structure of its environment. For a long time, it was believed that fish do not "speak." They are quite communicative, and their ultrasound signals travel faster in water (about 1500 m/s) than in air (about 340 m/s) as human sounds have to do.

The human ear is normally able to perceive sound waves with a frequency between 16,000 and 20,000 Hz. In contrast, bats communicate with each other by emitting sounds in frequencies up to 150,000 Hz, which is well into the range of ultrasounds. It is in this higher frequency that dolphins and other fish communicate. However, the principle of ultrasound communication is based on the reflection of such waves. Underwater, this mechanism enables dolphins to sense the presence of very small objects. Insects also use infrasounds to communicate. They create so much "noise" that it would be intolerable to most human beings if the human ear could perceive infrasounds. What happens when more species communicate in the same range of sound? Well, not much, as each species has its language that cannot be totally understood by other species. However, language is also an intelligent manifestation because, besides communicating inside a community, it conveys a certain meaning to other species. Of course, other species cannot understand the meaning of all the sounds, but some vital sounds (that express danger, territory delimitation, etc.) are understood. So, how do members of a species recognize each other by such signals? This is a very interesting phenomenon called imprinting related to consciousness. Every sound emitted by an animal has a certain pattern that differs from the patterns of the other members of that species. So, in time, the members of a community become accustomed to the patterns of their "neighbors," and thus, they can differentiate them. Of course, all the patterns might sound the same for someone outside the community. The songs of the birds are also interesting to consider. What sounds like "music" to us may be a bird calling to its partner, establishing its territory, or performing a mating ritual.

Another type of "language" in living systems is bioluminescence. This is the property of all living systems that emit light radiation in different ranges. While some organisms (e.g., certain organisms living in the oceans) emit in the visible spectra, humans emit radiation below the limit of visual perception. Although a few highly sensitive people can see human emissions, we must rely on special tools that record human emissions.

We have noted thus far a whole set of intelligent devices that living systems possess and use to survive. These natural devices are used to find food, identify friends from foes, or defend against enemies. The sexual instinct appears to be as necessary for survival as other instincts. If there were no deaths, there would be no need for reproduction. To ensure the survival of the species, reproduction is needed, too. This might explain the lack of reproduction in nonliving systems: It is not required (because death does not exist in a nonliving system except that it radiates away). We can go further and deduce that any system, living or nonliving, has a certain level of intelligence, which is naturally imposed by the universal system requirements. Thus, a rock would never talk since language is not required for its survival. A rock survives if it is strong enough to face environmental conditions (rain, wind, pressure from other rocks, etc.). On the other hand, a human does not need the resilience of a rock because his normal condition does not require such an exterior hardness. However, the parts of the human body that require extra strength or protection are provided with proper "hardeners," such as bones, nails, or hair. This is an intelligent adaptation of the human (or animal) body to its environment.

1.16 Life, Intelligence, and Consciousness beyond Matter Fields

As we have already observed, matter adapts continuously to its existing conditions. Many intelligent devices are involved in this task. One might ask what constitutes intelligent support for these devices. Is there a basic intelligence that determines the rest of the intelligence hierarchy? If so, how does it work, and what is its support?

This question can only be partially answered based on the current scientific achievements. To understand a system completely, one must be able also to examine the system from the outside. Therefore, to understand the Universe completely, one must be able to go outside the Universe, which is impossible. All we can do is hypothesize and then verify our hypothesis using well-defined situations. This is how science evolved, motivated by a need to understand and control the immediate environment and to embrace the bigger challenge of understanding and exploring the Universe.

De Broglie's theory (1924) is one of the most important discoveries in the science of matter, which associates every tiny piece of matter with a wave. In 1924, Louis de Broglie introduced the idea that particles, such as electrons, could be described not only as particles but also as waves. Prince Louis-Victor Pierre Raymond de Broglie of Sorbonne University, Institut Henri Poincaré, Paris, France, won the Nobel Prize in Physics in 1929 "for his discovery of the wave nature of electrons."

This was substantiated by the way streams of electrons were reflected against crystals and spread through thin metal foils. Matter vibrates and exists as both a solid state and as a wave. We can observe that the waves associated with matter form a field surrounding the matter. Some scientists consider this field as electromagnetic. We would rather consider it as simply energetic since the electromagnetic nature of the field surrounding the matter might be a particular case.

An electromagnetic field covers living systems. It has been observed that other energetic fields cover living bodies as well. These fields could be pictured as layers that surround the body. Valentina and Simeon Kirlian first discovered this property of matter in 1939. They accidentally recorded this field in a photographic film. It began one of the biggest controversies in the physics of living systems. Their technique was based on photographically recording an object exposed to an electromagnetic field and high frequency. Russian researchers intensively analyzed this phenomenon, which spread to the rest of the world (Czechoslovakia, Italy, the USA, and Romania). Initially, this procedure was used to identify neoplasm early or to record the biological field of plants. As each scientist tried to identify his own improvement in the procedure, the process acquired different names: electrography, electromyography, or the corona effect. However, this field has been known for a long time under the name of "aura." It is quite interesting how people have learned about it, and they even cover the walls of churches with pictures of saints whose heads are surrounded by aura. When these representations were drawn or painted, no device could visualize the aura surrounding a human being. Could it be that saints and other divine individuals were blessed with stronger body corona effect visible to the naked eye? Inorganic structures give an image that is static, monochromatic, and reproducible.

Organic living structures give dynamic, colorful images that reflect the organism's physiology at that particular moment. Variations in the Kirlian image of living structures are caused by the dynamic equilibrium that characterizes life. However, it has been proven experimentally that many factors influence the Kirlian image (Celan, 1994). This suggests that, since the biological field determines the oscillations in a living system, it must represent the biological field since the Kirlian image is dynamic. The biological field must determine the factors influencing it. Figure 1.18 depicts a few Kirlian light images and photography.

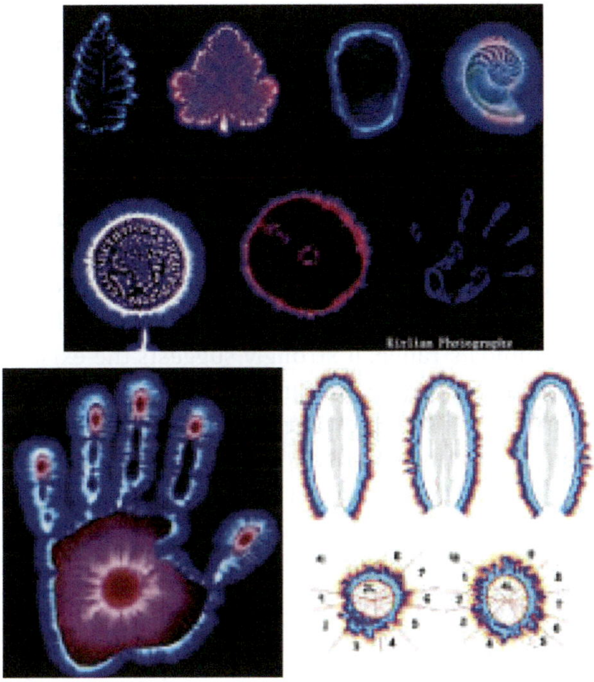

Figure 1.18 Kirlian photographs of some leaves and a human hand.

In the USA, Thelma Moss (1974) and her team performed interesting experiments at the UCLA regarding the biological field of plants and humans. They observed that the colors appearing in a biological field are red, white, and blue. In addition, she observed a tight dependence between the shape and color of a subject's biological field and response. More than that, she observed for the first time in the history of science a specific Kirlian light for the "shape" of love. Thus, lovers embracing each other create a single biological field from their fields. It is very interesting how feelings can unite two fields belonging to separate material entities.

In addition, emotions affect the color of the biological field. Thus, a state of anxiety or depression is reflected by a "cloudy" image of the biological field. The color of the image, in this case, is predominantly red. On the other hand, a state of relaxation or happiness is reflected by a larger, shinier image of the biological field. The color of this image is a combination of white and blue. It has also been observed (Moss, 1974) that some rare individuals do not change the image of their field regardless of their emotional state, and others present no image at all (Moss, 1974). This might be explained as a dysfunction or lack of vitality.

Going deeper into the world of shapes and colors of the biological field, it has been observed that any particular thought, desire, idea, and feeling can be reflected in the shape and color of the biological field. Thus, if somebody is moving toward a particular location, the shape of his biological field is somehow elongated toward that location. Therefore, the person reaches the location energetically before he or she reaches there normally, as a material entity. Even though this sounds strange, it strongly suggests the existence of an influential force that can be identified as the power of the mind. If this biological field is so important, why cannot humans see or feel it more readily? Well, as we mentioned earlier, it is simply because humans do not need that ability for survival.

Every system gets the minimum amount of capabilities necessary for survival. However, in plants and animals, where language is lacking, this form of communication is a necessity.

Incidentally, alcohol is another factor that influences the biological field. The effects of alcohol on a person's physical and mental abilities are well known. This change in the image of the biological field could lead to new interpretations of how changes in blood chemistry affect body and brain function.

1.17 The Biological Field

To further our understanding of biological fields, examining a therapeutic method of traditional Chinese medicine called acupuncture may be helpful. Acupuncture utilizes certain vortices related to points of reduced resistance in the body's tissues (this phenomenon can also be found in plants). These areas ensure the stability of the organism's energetic structure. Together, matter and energy form a very intelligent feedback mechanism that maintains the vital energetic-material equilibrium of the organism. In other words, the biological field determines the vitality of the organism, while the structure's continuous evolution is coordinated by the energy to ensure its survival. There are some 361 acupoints such as lungs, large intestine, stomach (ST), spleen (SP), heart (HT), small meridian (SI), bladder (BL), kidney (KI), pericardium (PC), triple energizer (TE), gall bladder M (GB), liver (LR), governor vessel (GV), and conception vessel (CV).

To gain a broader perspective of this biological field, we must also analyze its role and influence on living systems. However, nonliving matter is still matter, which means it has a field associated with it. Are there any differences between the fields of living bodies and nonliving bodies? In addition, if so, how is it explained? Perhaps the best way to answer this question is to look at these fields' roles.

First, fields interact between themselves to facilitate communication. Since communication with the environment is a vital requirement for open systems, communication with the biological field is also a requirement. Even if terms like information and intelligence are not fully understood, a field can be considered a medium for information transfer. We already know that information can be found either in motion when communicated or static when it is held in memory. Since associated fields are important for information transport, intelligence must be important for information storage. Thus, the more intelligent a system is, the more organized its stored information will be, and the more sophisticated the connection between the levels of stored information will be.

Going deeper into the world of biological fields, one could compare these with fingerprints, as each biological system has its specific biological field. A biological field is determined and influenced by internal factors (physiological rhythms and mental conditions) and external factors (such as temperature, interaction with other biological and non-biological fields, or environmental factors). On the other hand, the nature of the biological field is both energetic and informational. The energetic nature of the field is evident since it can be visualized. However, the informational nature could be clearer to demonstrate. The best demonstration uses photography of a green leaf from a tree. If the leaf is photographed after its top cut, the resulting image shows that its biological field remains intact. The leaf's biological field preserves the leaf's initial shape, though the intensity of the cut zone may be diminished. This means that the biological field has a kind of field memory.

The properties of the biological field might be considerably more than those already discussed. It is still not clear how this field is produced and how it interacts, so it is quite difficult to offer a complete characterization. Many experiments have been performed on the reactions of the biological field to different stimuli. The results are, to date, mainly empirical. As another example, we can observe that the interaction between two systems occurs first at the biological field level and only later at a physical level. Thus, when a microorganism enters an organism, the two fields interact without any physical effect on the organism. However, if the field of the microorganism proves to be stronger than that of the organism, the organism initiates a physical defense by its regular means. Therefore, "illness" appears sometime after the microbial attack. The basis of the field is not completely understood, so it is still hard to talk about a mathematical model. However, it can be undoubtedly stated that the biological field is an intelligent entity with its own shape, which does not necessarily correspond to the shape of the associated solid body.

Another experiment that explains the role biological fields play in living systems involved the measurement of an egg's biological field before the beginning of embryo differentiation (Burr, in Watson, 1974). Even though the nervous system is not yet formed, the intensity of the biological field is markedly increased at the location where the nervous system will form. This leads us to conclude that living systems are formed on an energetic matrix. Thus, the biological field can be considered a field of forces that organize the matter in a living system. Because order is closely related to intelligence, we can state that intelligence and the shape and properties of a biological field determine the appearance and evolution of a living system. Another hypothesis might be that a field is more easily ordered and intelligently organized than matter, which already has its energetic organization. Thus, an energetic field must interact with matter's energetic structure to organize matter, leading to the desired order at a material level.

This new approach has already found interesting applications, particularly in agriculture. Researchers can determine which will germinate by analyzing the biological field of a set of seeds. What about the role of DNA? Isn't it important anymore? Well, of course, DNA is still the most organized and intelligent form of matter known. It is the most important factor in cell division and evolution.

However, as the biological field is not a material entity, we can deduce that the evolution of living systems might result from the synergy of the DNA material and the non-material biological field. Going further, we can also suppose that, as any tiny, nonliving piece of matter has an associated wave field, in a like manner, any living system (material) has a biological field associated with it. This biological field differs from the wave field associated with regular matter because it is much more ordered and intelligent. Therefore, the energetic matrix that forms the biological field represents the evolution of the primordial wave field and can be associated with the evolution of intelligence and consciousness.

Another issue regarding the biological field is the way information is transmitted. It is well known that to be transmitted, information needs a support infrastructure, like an electromagnetic wave. Considering that, some experiments were performed where a subject was completely screened so that no electromagnetic wave could break the shield. The subject could still send information outside the shield by using telepathy (Vasiliev, 1963). This suggests that information is not transmitted by electromagnetic waves alone. So, what other form of energy could support transmitting information?

1.18 Etheric Theory

Scientists have developed various theories regarding the medium in which everything is contained. This ubiquitous, continuous field is called ether. Although it does not represent a particular form of energy, ether may be important in explaining some of our unknowns. It is well known that all material is composed of atoms. An atom comprises a nucleus and one or more electrons that orbit around the nucleus at different energy levels. This concept prompts an interesting question: What is the nature of the medium between the electrons and the nucleus, and what are the properties of that "something"? Some supposed it to be ether. Unfortunately, no measure is possible for the properties of ether aside from its dimension. Different hypotheses and models have been developed, however. Even if one calls it nothing, this "nothing" exists between atomic particles and is found throughout the Universe. It cannot be ignored since it represents the only continuum in the Universe.

This medium could have many implications for the transmission of information, too. First, since its existence cannot be measured, neither can its resistance. If we presume its resistance is close or equal to zero, it would represent an ideal support for transmissions. What are its energetic properties that support transmitting information? Does it have its own energetic field, or is there only an energetic interaction between atomic particles? Taking this to a macromolecular scale, we can compare this structure with a composite material, whose continuum phase is represented by ether, and the atomic particles represent inclusions. Scientists have defined and measured the permittivity of free space as

$$€_0 = 8.854187817 \times 10^{-12}\ C^2/Jm$$

and its permeability or its magnetic susceptibility as

$$\mu_0 = 12.566370614 \times 10^{-7}\ T^2m^3/J.$$

The permeability constant is given by $\mu_0 = 4\pi \times 10^{-7}$ H/m. The permittivity of free space, ϵ_0, possesses the value 8.85×10^{-12} F/m. The field in permeability is the magnetic field, while the field in permittivity is the electric field.

This ether theory is primarily applied to non-equilibrium thermodynamics phenomena. However, its properties affect microphysics and space theories. The main property of ether is presumed to be diffusivity. This is determined by the ether concentration, which fluctuates according to environmental conditions. Since it is a variable continuum, omnipresent in the Universe, the ether could be considered an etheric field of points. In a steady state (i.e., without any material or energetic influence), an etheric field is assumed to be homogenous. However, this homogeneity is based on average values since the etheric field presents frequent fluctuations. A model is required to use the etheric field in different applications. The minimum requirement of such a model would be a reaction system based on two coupled elements and a nonlinear reaction step.

To describe the energetic properties of the ether, one may assume it contains potential energy fields of a very low magnitude. Therefore, at larger concentrations, one would have a higher magnitude, which implies a higher reactivity. This potential field determines motion within the ether. Based on this notion, one could further deduce the polar nature of the etheric structure and its directional motion based on the direction of the potential gradients. From here, several implications become evident. Thus, organized ether increases communication abilities, forming real communication channels.

1.19 Etheric Theory and Consciousness

This theory could easily explain many strange, unexplained phenomena such as telepathy, paranormal activity, and plant communication, which would no longer be mysteries. As with any theory, however, this one must first be proven. Thus far, the only method to prove it is the empirical one. Maybe later, a mathematical model would be possible after many experiments have been performed in various fields of interest (so that the theory could be generalized). The impact of this theory on modern science would be considerable since it would introduce new concepts. For example, in addition to the evolution of matter from nonliving systems to living systems, the perpetuation of life should be considered not only by cell perpetuation but also by energy perpetuation.

Studying the properties of a biological field, Celan (1994) observed that it interacts with biological and electromagnetic fields. The result of this interaction can be more or less controlled, depending on the level of interaction. Thus, an induced electromagnetic field could influence the permeability of cell membranes, sugar metabolism, and the neurological–endocrine equilibrium. Furthermore, induced electromagnetic fields could be used to treat certain conditions.

If every atom is composed of moving charges, it means that the completely material world is supported by many energetic fields. The big challenge is to demonstrate that these fields together form a whole, an energetic macrocosmos. What are the consequences of this energetic whole? First, it would enable extremely fast information transfers since the energetic macrocosmos would form an infinite network of informational channels. This would lead to an increased ability to process information and, therefore, to a higher degree of order. We can further deduce that this order determines (or is determined by) a higher level of intelligence.

Consider that this means of communication is highly integrated within the informational structure of the Universe. As we mentioned, individuals from the same species have their own language. Thus, information can be transmitted by using a language or a coding–decoding communication system. This is time consuming but normally would not affect the individual's life. Information transmitted through a biological field seems to be uncoded; therefore, its perception is faster. Information involves more than language because it can be understood by any living system that receives it. On the other hand, what would life be for any living system if it continuously received immense amounts of information from other living systems?

The system would eventually become saturated and overwhelmed. Thus, the Universal Intelligence field is again proved by the ability to create a filter for this kind of information. Even if we do not yet fully understand how it works, the existence of this filtering mechanism is very important for survival and the evolution of living matter. It should be mentioned here that a suggested system for filtering out parasitic information is the brain's use of fuzzy logic algorithms (Zadeh, 1973).

1.20 Consciousness beyond Death

Cardiologist Dr. Pim van Lommel became internationally known after his groundbreaking study on near-death experiences (NDEs) was published in the respected medical journal *The Lancet* in 2001. The study was remarkable in that it was prospective: conditions were set and ready before patients underwent cardiac arrest. The results showed that merely physiological explanations for NDEs were inadequate, raising profound questions about the nature of consciousness and its relation to brain function.

1.21 Energy Review

The fundamentals of energy should be reviewed since energy is a key factor in matter's structure and evolution. Energy can be found in different forms. Thus, we can speak about potential energy, kinetic energy, electric energy, thermal energy, wind energy, atomic energy, nuclear energy, etc. Anything that produces any kind of force is considered energy. However, it is not always possible to identify the true energy source, which can lead to confusion.

We can divide all energy into static and dynamic. The difference between the two is that static energy is embedded within a geometric structure and does not directly influence its environment. Dynamic energy exists mainly as a field with dynamic geometry according to its environmental interactions. We should note the presence of dualism here. Static energy (also called potential energy) is mainly stored energy, which could become dynamic under certain conditions. In addition, static energy can be associated with the overall equilibrium (mostly unstable) of the structure embedding the energy.

There are different means to measure the properties according to each type of energy. We will not detail these properties since we are mainly interested in energy. Therefore, we will only consider energy in its primordial form, which evolved and developed the forms known today. From this perspective, we can refer to energy as power, a rate of energy transfer.

First, let us address a more advanced topic: the energy involved in mental processes and interactions. Many specialists in the medical field would say that any mental process has at its foundation a set of chemical reactions leading to the secretion of various hormones, stimulants, or inhibitors of a certain process. We could go further by saying that the energy that supports a mental process is chemical. On the other hand, a mental process is initiated by an informational stimulus (even if this might be temporarily converted into a chemical support). We know the input information and chemical energy. However, what is the output? The result is nothing more than a conscious thought. How should we consider a thought from an energetic point of view? Is it chemical? Not directly. The term best describes it as "the power of the mind." Is this a form of energy? It has to be. We have an energetic input that can be transformed but never lost.

A good example of the "power of the mind" is telekinesis. Even though telekinesis cases are rare, they still exist and demonstrate how a person can move an object by thinking about moving it (without touching it). We should note the demonstration of telekinesis presented by Uri Geller of Israel here.

An object can only be moved if it experiences a physical force produced by an energy source. We must consider that the energy that moves the object comes from pure thought. We can hypothesize that the power of the mind exists because a simple chemical reaction could not possibly move an object that it does not contact (except for magnetic reactions). The invention of Popa and Shahinpoor (remotely biologically triggered sensor and switch) shows evidence of the effect of a biological field on bio-switches.

As previously noted, at least a part of the energy required for the motion should come from the mental process commanding the motion. You might wonder now, "Where does the rest of the energy come from?" Here, we should remember the theory of the ether, particularly the various potentials randomly distributed within the etheric field. We supposed that the "power of the mind" determines the organization of the randomly distributed energetic potentials within the range covered by the two elements (mental source and target object). Thus, the etheric field acts as an amplifier (and, therefore, energy source), as well as a communication channel and active interface with the material structure. Now, based on this new view of ether, we could go further and look for any connections between ether and intelligence and, ultimately, between ether and Universal Intelligence. These connections might very well exist. If they do, they could explain the structure of Universal Intelligence. However, since we cannot explain the properties of ether yet, we cannot speculate further.

As was mentioned earlier, life is not possible within a perfect equilibrium because a perfect equilibrium would not permit the rapid changes needed to allow adaptation to ever-changing environmental conditions. A perfectly stable equilibrium would not permit motion either, since no active resultant force determines the motion. Variation is necessary to support life. However, if everything in the Universe varied randomly, this would not support life either because of the lack of order and, consequently, the lack of intelligence would not allow any survival strategy to develop. Thus, the only way to maintain life is through the presence of an intelligent, periodic variation. How periodicity appeared and it replaced randomness is a question that nobody can answer. Even though we cannot answer this question, we still ask about the hows and whys of evolution and progress.

Rhythms exist everywhere, in both microcosmos and macrocosmos. If a rhythm characterizes a living system, it is called a biorhythm. However, biorhythms integrate perfectly within the Universe and the universal rhythms. Thus, biorhythms depend on the variation in cosmic radiation of a low frequency, on the variation in the gravitational field, or on the rotation of the planet (which determines days and nights). This may be primarily influenced at the level of the biological field.

Another material that plays a very important role in the evolution of life is water. Of course, the fundamental elements of life are carbon (C), hydrogen (H), oxygen (O), and nitrogen (N), or simply CHONs. We know that water has a high ability to form unstable colloidal systems. Therefore, as water is the main component of living systems, one could infer that this is one of the principal components that led to the big step from nonliving systems to living systems by ensuring the proper environment for unstable equilibrium that favors periodic variations. This idea could lead one to develop a theory about living systems on other planets. Water has a great combination of properties, from the ability to form unstable colloidal solutions to changing structure orientation between right-handed and left-handed. Any planet in the Universe must have water in its composition (or another substance not known on Earth but with similar properties) to permit the appearance of living systems. This theory might lead one to understand the energy of the pyramids, a strange phenomenon strongly linked to water's properties. The aspects involving the influence of geometrical shapes on the evolution of matter and intelligence will be treated in later chapters.

Other biorhythms include respiration, heartbeat, brain activity (sleeping and waking), stomach and liver functions, etc. Any physiological activity is periodic. Even at social levels, everything occurs in regular cycles. Somebody is born as somebody else dies; somebody sleeps as somebody else is awakened; we all grow up, mature, and die. The natural cycle of cradle to grave is well planned. However, a better understanding of biorhythms can be extremely beneficial, not only for known organisms but also for understanding the possibility of regression. Eventually, we may find new meanings in biorhythms for nonliving systems.

Whatever the approach of science will be in the future, the basis of matter formation and evolution, up to the appearance of living systems, must have started because of periodic variations. This requirement comes from the condition of evolution of intelligence, which, in turn, is based on order and dynamic equilibrium. A system must be neither static nor chaotic to have a progressive and intelligent evolution. It must be in dynamic equilibrium.

1.22 Biocommunication

As mentioned in previous passages, communication is one of the keys to integration. Therefore, analyzing how an open system (e.g., biological) communicates might be interesting. Thus far, one has observed how living systems communicate through language. A language is essentially a code. Thus, if a system wants to transmit information to another system, it must first encode it in a conventional language code and then transmit it. The other system must perceive and decode it to get the meaning of the information. There are other means of communication besides this. For example, in certain conditions, cells communicate with each other even if they are separated. If a glass wall isolates two identical cell cultures and one of the cultures is infected with a virus, there is no influence on the second culture. However, if a quartz wall separates the cells, the symptoms of the first culture (the infested one) also appear in the second. The main difference between the two substances is their permeability; quartz is not opaque to ultraviolet. This means that information from one cell culture is transmitted to another by radiation in the ultraviolet spectrum. Thus, scientists are starting to believe that communication between living systems (also called biocommunication) is performed through waves of ultraviolet radiation (wavelengths 10^{15}–10^{17} Hz). However, this conclusion came after the hypothesis that information is transmitted using electromagnetic waves. The biological field is still not completely understood, and it might be possible that other forms of energy are supporting information transmission.

Humans can hear a spectrum of frequencies between 20 Hz and 20,000 Hz, the perceptible range of human hearing. This facilitates fast communication. To be transmitted, the informational patterns must be synthesized as a sequence of coded signals, which must be amplified and transmitted. Water is supposed to play an important role in this step for living systems. Water may be the prime element that permitted living systems to evolve as dynamic systems. Nonliving systems, which contain less water than the living ones, are more rigid. However, they may have developed a subatomic informational structure using the etheric field as an amplifier.

It can be easily observed that all phenomena involving matter, energy, and intelligence require an interdisciplinary approach. A mathematician will only observe all these from a mathematical point of view, a biologist from a biological one, and the same for a physicist or an engineer. They could create a more accurate or detailed picture by combining their expertise. Another obstacle to assessing phenomena that are not quite common (e.g., telepathy or telekinesis) is that their occurrence is rare, and thus, the ability to analyze them is quite constrained.

We might ask why such phenomena rarely occur because they result from common, natural properties of matter. The answer may lie in the adaptability of intelligent systems. Why would a person use telepathy to transmit a message to someone in front of him if he could communicate by simply talking? Or if the message has to travel a distance, he could call the other person on the telephone or write a letter.

Nature commonly chooses the most efficient way (from an energetic point of view) of doing everything with minimal resources. Therefore, if talking is more efficient than telepathy, then humans use talking. Telepathy must be a skill inherited from our ancestors who did not have a properly developed language or other efficient communication abilities. As language skills developed, however, telepathy became less and less useful. Nowadays, only a few people still can use these skills. Living systems are adaptive, however, and with practice and adequate training, anybody should be able to recover this lost (or latent) ability.

One might speculate whether telepathic abilities are also available to animals. According to many experiments performed in specialized research centers worldwide, the answer is positive. Even though it is quite hard to identify a telepathic process directly, the experiments showed definite reactions of animals to strong stimuli transmitted telepathically. What is not yet established is the level of development at which telepathy can be used, i.e., how developed an animal must be to use telepathy. We consider that the answer to this question can be found by simply analyzing the need for and the utility of telepathy in a living system.

Thus, telepathy could work somehow even for plants because they do not have any other means of communication among themselves. Of course, some people might say that plants simply exchange information between them, in close range, which cannot be considered telepathy.

In addition, as we consider normality at Earth's level, we might extend the concept to the whole Universe. Therefore, we discover that the biggest barrier for scientists to understand the Universe and its evolution is their "filtering" of results through their common senses, which are "normal" for the time and location. More and more, scientists have started to pass this barrier because, as was mentioned earlier in this book, the best way to analyze a system is to do it from outside the system, where a more comprehensive perception is possible. Thus, since most measuring devices are based on the human senses, it has been quite difficult to record signals that belong to a class not covered by "common" human senses.

With the discovery of electricity, though, different devices produced that extended range of measurable phenomena. So, the human body was analyzed using these new types of devices. It has been proven that different electric signals within the human body can be easily recorded.

Thus, electric signals can monitor and even control certain body activities. The question is whether or not the human organism is an electric network. If yes, this would mean that only matter and electricity could produce and maintain life, which is not true. What is that "something extra" that is characteristic of life?

1.23 New Developed Theories

Well, even if it still cannot be mathematically modeled, the existence of a not-yet-defined form of energy has been proven experimentally. We still do not know the laws of this form of energy; it cannot be controlled or reproduced. However, we cannot ignore the phenomena caused by this energy just because we also cannot explain it. The reason seems beyond our "common sense," as discussed earlier.

We must also consider that a system needs the influence of another, more advanced system that has evolved beyond its own level of sophistication to evolve. This resembles the famous principle of physics, which states that heat always passes from a warm body to a cold one until the two bodies reach equilibrium.

Newly developed theories might shed more light on this field. Shannon's theory of information and communication, the theory of the quanta, or the recent data from neurophysiology could help us understand the modeling of biological communications.

1.24 Entropy and Information

In 1948, Claude Shannon developed the first truly mathematical model for the transmission of information. He was investigating the efficiency of transmitting information over a noisy communication channel, but his theory brought a revolutionary perspective to all information-related fields.

He considered a basic communication system comprising an information source, a transmitter, a communication channel, a receiver, and a destination. To characterize information by a mathematical model, Shannon considered all the elements involved in communication as discrete elements. Statistical computations determine the communication capability of each element. In addition, a noise source was considered, which induces perturbations during communication (Fig. 1.19).

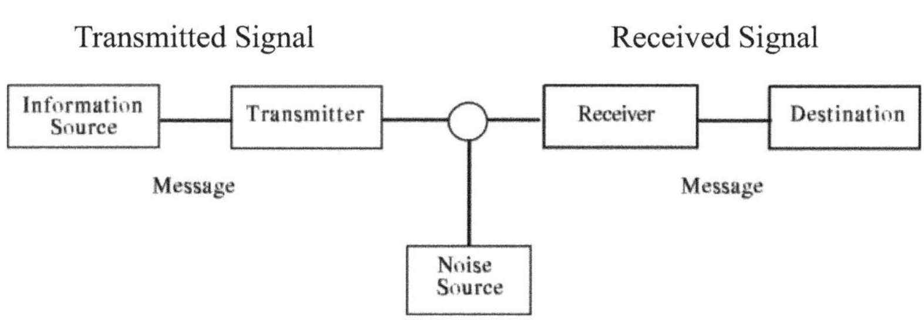

Figure 1.19 A basic communication system.

He concluded that the process of transmitting and processing information is stochastic since it produces a sequence of symbols governed by a set of probabilities. In addition, it can be said that the number of possible states of the system is determined by the set of symbols contained within the system, which is a finite number. This number can be determined from the probabilities of the sequencing of symbols. There is also a set of transition probabilities that describe the state a particular system will follow its current state.

This type of stochastic process is known as the "discrete Markov process." Figure 1.20 contains a simple example Shannon offers, based on five symbols (letters A, B, C, D, and E) with probabilities of 0.4, 0.1, 0.2, 0.2, and 0.1.

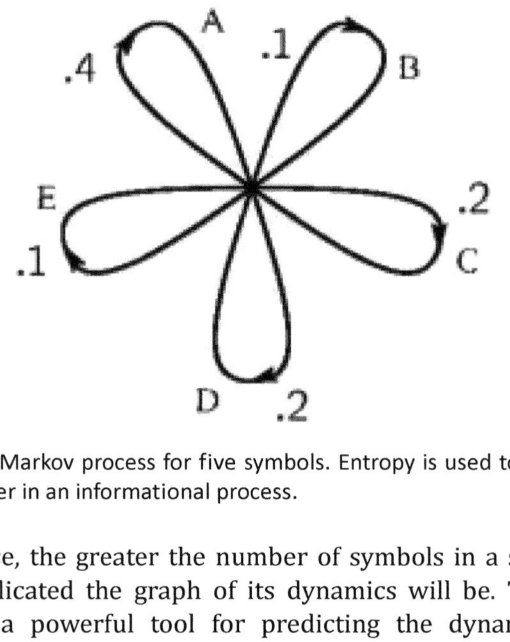

Figure 1.20 Markov process for five symbols. Entropy is used to analyze the degree of order in an informational process.

Of course, the greater the number of symbols in a system, the more complicated the graph of its dynamics will be. This model represents a powerful tool for predicting the dynamics of an informational system.

However, since the communication model is based on probabilities, the entropy here could be defined as the uncertainty with which the system will follow a specific path.

Boltzmann introduced the entropy formula, which refers to the number of microscopic states of a system. This equation reads as follows:

$$S = k_{\mathrm{B}} \ln W \tag{1.1}$$

where k_{B} is the *Boltzmann constant* (also written as simply k) and equals to 1.380649×10^{-23} J/K, and is a *natural logarithm* function. W can be counted using the formula for permutations:

$$W = \frac{N!}{\prod_i N_i!} \tag{1.2}$$

where i ranges over all possible molecular conditions and "!" denotes *factorial.* The restriction that must be applied here is that entropy cannot exceed the channel capacity and, therefore, is directly dependent on the number of elements within the informational system. This restriction applies only to the ideal case of an isolated informational system.

In real systems, when perturbations appear, the probability that a system will evolve toward a particular state decreases with the increased intensity of the perturbations. Each perturbation adds a specific number of symbols to the system, which affects the final state of the evolving process. In other words, it induces new states that are incompatible with the system's trend.

An intelligent system would have to initiate action to compensate for the effects of the perturbations. One immediate solution would be to increase the number of its own symbols. However, this would also increase the volume of the system and the processing time of any information. A more advanced solution would be to develop hierarchical structures, thus increasing the level of order within the system.

This process would create a network of multiple communication channels together with a multilevel feedback device, which would lead to considerably decreased uncertainty. This is obtained by a correction performed at multiple hierarchic levels of differing intensities.

Therefore, a correcting signal is more powerful when it comes from a superior level, but, sometimes, it might not be necessary to go up to that level since a correcting signal from a lower level would do the task properly. An energetic optimization of internal resources would be created. The sketch of such a correction mechanism in an informational system is presented in Fig. 1.21.

This hierarchical structure of an informational system is constructed by the system's self-organization ability. Therefore, like any other type of system within the Universe, an informational system develops its survival strategy by self-organization, based on unfavorable environmental influences. As the informational system evolves, its hierarchic structure evolves too. First, it consolidates its current levels and then expands with a new branch, either on the same level or by adding new levels. The criteria taken into account in the organization of an informational system are quite complex and lead to complicated mathematical models. We should remember that any evolution of such a system follows the universal rules of survival, which are based on commonly recognized principles. One of these is the principle of minimum energy. According to this principle, systems will evolve toward a state characterized by the minimum level of energy. In this manner, a system can easily control and "defend" its stable state and, therefore, its survival. This can be considered a dissipative system, which means that energy must be expended to create order out of chaos.

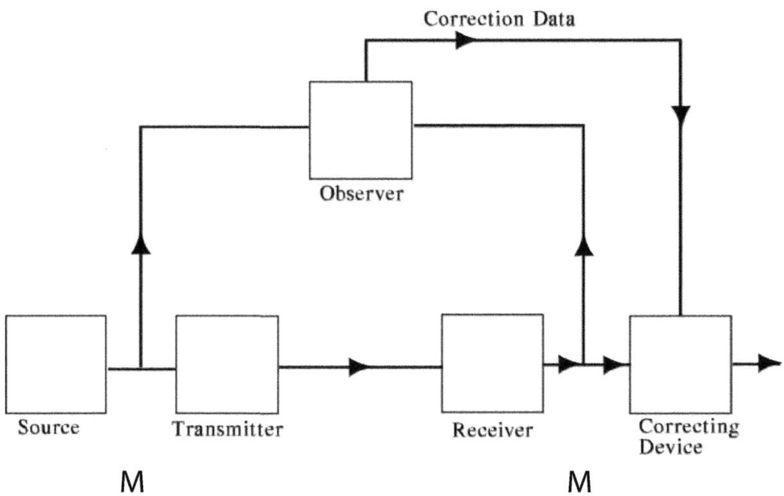

Figure 1.21 Sketch of a correction mechanism.

A dissipative system fits very well the principle of the minimum energy as applied to ordered systems. Thus, an intelligent or "smart" system expends the minimum required for its existence, conserving energy for creating the internal order that ensures the survival of the system. This model was constructed on an informational system with a discrete distribution of elements. Increasing the number of elements infinitely will result in the behavioral characteristics of a continuous system.

Therefore, considering the universal hierarchy, we could deduce that a subsystem's evolution primarily depends on the system above it since the system tends to reach equilibrium within the system hierarchy. In addition, the superior system tends to reach equilibrium with the system below it and, eventually, with those of the same level. If the system above it is static, equilibrium of the whole structure should be reached easily. However, if the system above it evolves too, and our system evolves in response, it will produce a dynamic change in the lower system. In fact, we could describe the Universe as a huge hierarchy of dynamically interdependent systems evolving according to universal law or Universal Intelligence. Since we need both a starting point and a reference point to analyze any evolutionary process, one could consider Universal Intelligence in this theory to have no beginning and no end.

The completely hierarchical system must have something at its top to influence the other hierarchy levels. If we consider the top-level static, the whole structure is evolving toward a universal equilibrium, which could be reached on time. This would also mean that the Universe has a beginning and will have an end. The Universe then could be considered eternal. An important point for this argument is the well-known fact that energy can be transferred but never destroyed. It is eternal. So, if the Universe has an end, when everything will be in equilibrium, what will be the role of energy? It would probably exist only as latent energy, available to be used if an external source disturbs the perfect equilibrium.

1.25 Plants and Their Thoughts

So far, we have focused mainly on intelligent material structures and communications at the animal and human levels. However, as mentioned, communication as biocommunication is possible in a very broad area, between materials and structures and other species. Plants are also living systems, so they should be able to communicate. If they communicate, can they also think?

Recently, numerous sets of experiments have been performed to answer this question (Backster, 1972). The principal method of investigation has involved measuring the resistivity at the surface of the plant. It has been observed that plants, like any other dynamic system, have a variable resistivity on their surface. It has also been observed that the resistance varies in response to their environment and, mainly, to other living systems in their environment. Thus, when a person who usually takes care of a plant comes close to it, the variations in resistance are not considerable, which suggests a state of calm or relaxation (or even security). However, if another person, who usually tortures the plant, comes close, sudden variations of the resistivity of the plant are seen. Moreover, if a person stands near a plant to harm it, the same large variations are recorded (Backster, 1973).

These phenomena can be interpreted only by accepting that a plant, even if it cannot see, "feels" its environment and even our thoughts. Feeling the field of a person that usually harms the plant could be explained by pattern recognition since every living system has a unique energetic "fingerprint." Even in this case, however, the plant should have some memory so that it can recognize the pattern of the "aggressor." If this phenomenon were automatic, what could we say about understanding a plant's thoughts and reacting to them accordingly? It simply means that plants can receive and process information, which places them on a superior level of intelligence.

More than that, some experiments indicate much higher possibilities of plant reaction to events in their environment. Thus, if a bowl of boiling water is placed in a room that contains a few plants and a device randomly throws shrimps into the bowl of boiling water, the plants "feel" the deadly event and suddenly become very agitated (Backster, 1973). This phenomenon was observed and analyzed during a procedure that connected each plant to an individual measuring device. It was noted that the plants' reaction was violent and started simultaneously with all other plants in the room the moment the shrimps were thrown into the boiling water (Backster, 1973). These experiments suggest that a primordial mechanism for perceiving and processing information exists in plants. We might even call it "cellular conscience."

This theory could be used in several ways. First, one could theorize that this informational device represents the primordial nervous system. It is still difficult to determine the evolutionary path that different systems followed. Second, we do not even know how plants perceive this type of information or how they can process it, understand its meaning, or react accordingly. However, it might be possible that certain living systems developed their informational capabilities toward a more interactive process, which formed the nervous system during evolution.

One might ask if any cell of a superior living system, like an animal, has the same property as the plants. If they do, then why is it necessary to have two parallel "devices" for perceiving and processing information? It is simply because both "devices" are specialized, i.e., they perceive and process certain types of information. This means that the "cellular conscience" and the nervous system are complementary. This complementarity creates a dualism, which might play an important role in maintaining vital dynamic equilibrium.

The truth may be somewhere in the middle. It seems plants use this informational device as their main nervous system. This means that plants evolved so that this device could fulfill their need to perceive and process information. One cannot consider this device inferior to the nervous system, as it performs a quite similar task adapted to the local specific requirements. However, we could consider the nervous system more complex since it controls a system that is indeed more complex than the system inherent in plants. Going deeper into the world of plants, it might be useful to approach their system from the point of view of "intelligence." The plant's system depends on a biological rhythm. By using artificial life, which reproduces the solar light continuously over a longer period (a few days), it was observed that plants get tired. Like any living system, they need to alternate activity and relaxation. Therefore, the intelligent structure of plants produces a state of tiredness when the system attains a certain level of exhaustion because of continuous activity. In this way, plants, like animals, continuously perform alternating cycles of consuming and recharging.

We might wonder why plants and animals did not adapt their systems in such a way that the so-called "recharging" takes place during consumption. In this way, the efficiency of the system would be greater. If a plant or animal could perform these two processes simultaneously, the resulting "design" would be inappropriate. We mentioned before the intelligent way all systems in the Universe are designed. Each system processes only the minimum amount of resources it needs. Of course, in addition to continuous energy consumption, every living system, which is an open system, has also continuous "input." Plants also have specific sensitivity. It was observed that some plants react quickly when they are touched. As an example, we can offer the Venus flytrap, as a carnivorous plant, which has the advanced ability to count, through its sensory hairs, the number of touches that an insect makes inside its lobes so it can trap the insect by closing its lobes quickly (see Shahinpoor, 1995 and Shahinpoor and Thompson, 1995). Plants are also very receptive to music. Music waves can favor or inhibit a plant's activity. Classical music seems to enhance the living processes of plants greatly. This was observed mainly at the level of cytoplasm, which moves faster when classical music is played in the neighborhood of a plant (Tompkins and Bird, 1975). Conversely, rock music seems to inhibit plant growth. If exposed for a prolonged period, the plant eventually dies. We should consider this a group reaction of all cells within the plant because plants do not have a centralized unit capable of processing information. Therefore, they are capable of intracellular and intercellular processing of information. How can plants survive as a unified system and what ensures the unity of the system? Apparently, there are only two options. The first is a field covering the plant that energetically keeps all the cells together and distributes all information. The second is an external influence that is corroborated with intercellular communication.

Again, one finds two complementary devices ensuring a dynamic equilibrium in the living organism. Some scientists and even ancient papers consider that biological fields also have a kind of dualism. This was interpreted as polarity, but it is still difficult to define polarity in this case. What is certain is the fact that a biological field has at least two components that act in a complementary manner. Because of this dualism, a person might appear sympathetic, apathetic, or antipathetic at first sight. Maybe that is why some authors consider this dualism as a mixture of "positive" and "negative" or "good" and "bad." However, we would rather consider this dualism as "one half" and "the other half." The two halves continuously interact to ensure the dynamic equilibrium of the system.

Studies have shown that plants also have short-term and long-term memories (Backster, 1973). As we have mentioned previously, a plant reacts when a person who has harmed it comes near. If that person approaches the plant without doing anything to it, the plant still acts defensively, as if that person was actually inflicting, because it can remember its previous experience. Moreover, after repeatedly stimulating a plant with an electric impulse anytime a particular rock was placed near the plant, the plant reacted to that rock anytime it was placed near the plant, even when no electric impulses were sent. Thus far, we have only analyzed the reaction between plants and other living systems. This last experiment implies an interaction between plants and nonliving systems. We have observed that a plant can recognize another living system and that biocommunication between the two systems can be established. However, as a rock is not like a normal living system, how could it affect the plant? Plants may not see or recognize shapes. There must be something that causes a nonliving system to influence the perception mechanism of plants. Again, the theory of energetic fields might give us a reasonable answer. By using Kirlian photography, it was demonstrated that nonliving matter is also covered by a field, which is static. A field with a static shape should be more easily identified than a dynamic one. On the other hand, the field of a piece of nonliving matter mainly reflects the elements composing that piece of matter. How could a plant differentiate two similar pieces of matter and associate one of them with a certain event (e.g., electric stimulation)? Things here get a little more complicated as we introduce a new term: the "associated informational field." The person who repeatedly placed the rock near the plant knew that the placing would be associated with the electric stimulation. This thought, this package of information, became associated with the static field of the rock.

This theory goes well beyond the limits of the current level of science because it suggests the existence of active memory in nonliving matter. Is that possible? For now, we can only presume this, to explain the outcome of certain experiments. A mathematical model or a scientific explanation of this kind of memory is not available yet. However, we can extend our thinking about the static memory of nonliving materials by noting that shape-memory alloys have evolved fairly plausible mathematical modeling in recent years (Wang and Shahinpoor, 1995, 1997), as well as a reasonable scientific explanation of resident thermal memory at the solid–solid phase transformation from martensite to austenite. In summary, we can conclude that plants, like other living systems, continuously communicate with their environment. Thermal, electrical, or chemical stimuli have direct, explainable impacts on plant activity, but other means of communication have not yet been completely understood. It is difficult to identify and understand them, as their nature is not known yet. One must note that the complete integration of plants within the Universe would only be possible through advanced mechanisms, which would be more complex than those involved in the reactions to physical–chemical stimuli.

Plants are integrated into their environment and, further, into the Universe. They grow and evolve according to the synergy of factors of any nature that influence them. Growth in plants appears to be an intelligent process, which could be compared with the forwarding of a military troop on a battlefield. Thus, it has been observed that plants grow systematically and, after each step of growth, immediately grow backward for a quarter of the length of the step, as if they were analyzing their evolution and consolidating their new position. From an artistic perspective, we could compare this growth with a rhythmic dance: a long step forward followed by a short step backward. It must be noted that only intelligent structures could control and consolidate each position gained on the scale of evolution. This is one of the major differences between self-controlled living systems and machines. A machine can perform specific tasks, according to the commands given to it. These commands come from an intelligent system able to control and predict who a human being is; ultimately, therefore, even the most advanced machines have a very limited range of decisions, and even this is determined by human intelligence. Thus, a machine can only be considered a smart effector, not an intelligent entity.

1.26 Universe of the Thinking

Thinking and consciousness present a superior, intelligent form of information processing, which helps a system integrate within its external hierarchy and control its internal hierarchy. Survival strategies, of course, achieve the goal of integration.

The universe of "thinking" still presents a vast unknown for modern science. We only know what we have observed and deduced from various perceptions. Since there are so many phenomena that are common to us and are still unexplained, we cannot give a complete explanation of the process of thinking and consciousness.

The primary reason for being unable to explain "thinking and consciousness" might reside in the deep background of matter itself. The matter has evolved together with intelligence and consciousness. At the same time, the evolution of intelligence and consciousness is reflected by the evolution of the ability to integrate and process information. The ultimate step in this continuous process of evolution might be the super-specialized mechanism of processing information that we call "thinking and consciousness."

However, we must make the distinction between "thinking, consciousness" and the "brain." Thinking is a complex informational process. The brain represents only the material support that mediates this process. From a strictly material point of view, phosphorus is the principal element that allows the existence and evolution of thinking. A recent theory asserts that the brain receives information from its environment with the help of a noise background called *vigil tonus* (Bremer, Moruzzi, and Magoun, in Sager, 1965). A network of nervous fibers infiltrating the cerebral structures through the dorsal spine maintains the tonus.

The brain receives information through a specific path and a non-specific path. The specific path is formed by a few neurons with long fibers, which collect information from all the sense organs and transmit it to the cortex. The non-specific path transmits the same information to the reticulate formation using neurons with short fibers. These transmissions of information within the organism are supposed to take place at the nervous system level and are based on the synaptic mechanism.

The dual process of transmitting information through the neuronal channels involves excitation and inhibition. These processes are periodic and not in phase. Thus, they create a continuous oscillation whose limits vary according to the system's state.

The non-specific paths send impulses to the reticulate formations, which determine the *vigil tonus* of the cortex. This *vigil tonus* is required by perception and is normally called consciousness. It maintains continuous communication between the cortex and the reticulate formations. It also represents the background noise that helps decode the various information received from the sense organs. Therefore, the state of consciousness depends strictly on the state of communication between the cortex and the reticulate formations. At the same time, the tonus of the reticulate formations is maintained by the stimuli arriving from the outer and inner worlds. Sleeping partially disconnects the reticulate formations from the sense organs. In fact, we prefer to consider this partial disconnection as a temporary increase in the limiting of information filtration and integration. The cortex is not completely disconnected from the outer and/or inner worlds. Thus, a more intense impulse can reactivate the connection and recover consciousness. As mentioned before, the brain is not just the center of consciousness. It also coordinates many vital functions of the organisms without any conscious interference. For example, heartbeat. It performs these tasks automatically since they are part of the genetically inherited program. Consciousness can enhance the organism's ability to adapt when this is required. This must be why nonliving matter has no consciousness; its system is static, and its evolution is performed automatically by preprogrammed intelligent mechanisms.

Another aspect of consciousness is based on the so-called "hunger for information" principle. A conscious organism continuously searches for information to keep its consciousness active. While the mechanism of consciousness is genetically inherited, its function is based exclusively on conditions particular to each moment and each spatial location. Thus, if an organism is isolated from any source of information, certain physiological dysfunctions will gradually appear. In these conditions, consciousness and thinking could easily be shaped by supplying only one type of information containing a controlled meaning. This procedure is called "brainwashing."

Going a little deeper into the world of thinking, we can state that even the cells have their consciousness, which we might call microthinking. Every cell reproduces the tasks of an organism but at a molecular level. It receives information from its outer and inner environments and reacts accordingly. Thus, cells can communicate, process information, memorize, and learn. Moreover, all the cells from a piece of tissue work together to facilitate the tissue's performance. The cellular micro-conscience is the basis for the most fundamental level of integration within a living system. Therefore, it has been suggested that even biocompatibility may be coordinated by this micro-consciousness. If this is true, future studies might be able to use the intelligence of matter to affect certain properties of a living system by influencing the micro-consciousness of its cells.

It has been popularly accepted that the brain uses only 10–20% of its total capacity for processing for conscious operation. The discovery of this phenomenon has led to the development of various theories. Why doesn't the brain use a higher percentage of its ability to process information? What happens in the 80–90% that is not used?

As mentioned in a previous chapter, the brain of a human being uses only a small fraction of its capacity to process conscious information simply because it does not need more. The intelligent structure of the brain allows this extra capacity so that, in certain critical conditions, it can "awake" abilities that are currently in a latent state. Thus, telepathy and other paranormal abilities could represent abilities of the brain that are normally in a latent state but can be activated in certain conditions, such as life-threatening situations or intense specialized training. Hypnosis allows access to some of these latent resources. Through hypnosis, artistic potential can be revealed, or certain artistic abilities can be considerably improved after a few sessions. Foreign languages can be learned much more easily by using hypnosis. How can hypnosis produce results that are normally impossible? In fact, hypnosis represents a particular state of the human mind. In ancient times, it was used in limited religious communities. Today, hypnosis is mainly used for therapeutic purposes. Its mechanism is not completely understood, and its use is mainly based on previous empirical results.

Hypnosis can remove many barriers imposed by the nervous system. Thus, a hypnotized person can accept uncommon situations. He can "view," by suggestion, persons or things that are not present. Consequently, hypnosis could play an important role in gaining greater knowledge of the brain's abilities. Another application of hypnosis is "age regression," in which the hypnotized person can, through suggestion, recall memories from the past. Thus, a person may remember the events that occurred long ago and would be forgotten otherwise. Scientists think this is interesting because it indicates how the brain processes and stores information. Hypnosis could lead us to redefine terms such as "to forget" and "to remember." It may be supposed that forgotten information is, in fact, information that is not accessed for a long period and, to avoid overloading the active system is encrypted and stored at deeper, less accessible levels. This structure proves, once again, the intelligent structure and organization of matter.

Another theory of how hypnosis works suggests that it is a direct connection to the inherited program of the organism, with its link with the conscious world disconnected. Thus, if something is suggested to a hypnotized person, he reacts immediately to it because the real world cannot otherwise inform him. The suggested information cannot be verified and is immediately accepted as true. This leads to a theory of the synergy of information. Anything has a sum of properties that cannot be perceived by one organ of perception alone; it requires synergetic processing of information from different organs of perception to obtain a realistic comprehension of that thing at a conscious level. Human consciousness has three states we know: the state of awakening (which includes thinking), the state of sleep, and the state of dreams. There is another state, however, that lies between waking and sleeping and has raised many controversies. As this state is mainly an interface state, it is quite difficult to analyze, but it possesses some interesting properties. It apparently leads to an extension of human thinking, since the levels of filtration are lower in this state.

Another interesting property of the living systems that confirms their fantastic intelligence regards time. Everybody is familiar with the astronomic time of seconds, minutes, hours, days, and years. However, there is also biological time, which is specific to each living individual. Some living systems can stop their biological time if their life is threatened by environmental conditions. Thus, certain organisms (small, indeed) can be preserved at very low temperatures for a long period (astronomic). When the organism is brought back to normal temperature, it can resume its activity at the point at which it was suspended. The freezing process causes an automatic reaction within the organism that stops its biological clock. This process was determined by an inherited program, which could not distinguish if only the individual was in danger or the whole species.

1.27 Brain Waves

From what we have deduced thus far, we can conclude that conscious intelligence controls the mental activity of the organism. We already know that the brain extends its activity outside its material limits. In addition to its energetic field, the brain also emits specific waves.

Brain waves are sinusoidal and, based on their frequency, are classified into the following:

- Delta waves (frequency between 0.5 and 4 cycles/second)
- Theta waves (frequency between 4 and 7 cycles/second)
- Alpha waves (frequency between 8 and 13 cycles/second)
- Beta wave (frequency between 13 and 40 cycles/second)

All the above can be recorded by using a special device called an electroencephalograph (EEG). The following section describes some characteristics of these brain waves.

Delta waves are characteristic of the immature brain, the deepest stages of sleep, and certain altered cerebral conditions. Theta waves are generally present in human brains until age 14 and in certain abnormal cerebral conditions. They are also characteristic of light sleep and drowsiness. It must be noted here that the seven-cycles-per-scan waves relate to the ability of certain organisms to predict unusual phenomena, such as earthquakes. The exact mechanism used for this prediction ability is still under investigation and is still not completely understood.

Beta waves are characteristic of intense cerebral activity. These waves are quite rapid and reflect the conscious state of mind, mainly the wakening state. Thus, if a person is completely relaxed, with eyes closed, an EEG shows beta waves that are quite low. If the person suddenly opens his or her eyes, the beta waves immediately become the most prominent waves in the EEG.

Alpha waves were discovered first around 1908. That is why they are named for the first Greek letter. They are characteristic of psychosensitive relaxation states: a wakeful state when no stimuli get past the filtration barriers. Alpha waves appear and disappear; they are not present during deep sleep or in high arousal (fear, anger). Coincidentally, the frequency of alpha waves is quite similar to the mean variation of a geomagnetic field.

Alpha waves are very important because they characterize a state where consciousness can go deeper within the body. This is called "passive thinking" and is known as a highly creative power. Because no external influences enter during this state, the conscious can work constructively based on available information. It enables people to reach the hidden chambers of the unconscious. A self-induced alpha state has been observed to lead to a strong reverie sensation. This state could be voluntarily reached after intensive training. This represents a gate opening into the voluntary evolution of mind and intelligence.

Practically, anybody can enter the alpha state simply by relaxing. This relaxation is associated with a decrease in heartbeat, respiratory rhythm, and a slight decrease in blood pressure. These effects are well known, having been thoroughly analyzed by scientists. Uncommon results occur when the alpha state becomes more pronounced.

The EEG changes considerably as the alpha waves are mixed with theta waves. Some scientists call this the alpha–theta state. This state is associated with a decrease in the amount of oxygen and lactic acid in the blood. Oxygen concentration in the blood decreases after the diminished metabolism occurs, while lactic acid directly influences relaxation and anxiety. The higher the content of lactic acid, the higher the anxiety.

Lactic acid is a product of the anaerobe metabolism. This leads to the observation that lactic acid in the blood is decreased by the increase in aerobic metabolism. Therefore, it is not the relaxation state alone that determines the decrease in lactic acid in the blood. Rather, it is controlled by certain hormones (e.g., noradrenaline), which regulate the hypothalamus hyperphysical–cortical suprarenal mechanism. We might conclude that during the alpha–theta state, the nervous parasympathetic system takes over the sympathetic nervous system, which demonstrates a decrease in the number of catecholamines in the blood. This effect leads to an increased storage of energy.

These effects are very beneficial for the organism since the resulting necrobiosis relieves many conditions. Then, why does one have to self-induce this state? Why is it not spontaneous? Well, in a certain manner, it is spontaneous and usually appears during the early stages of sleep. However, the self-induced alpha–theta state enables an individual to consciously push the capabilities of this state and develop new senses and knowledge. One should note, however, that this procedure is not suitable for individuals suffering from psychiatric disorders.

To better understand the four main brain waves, we could compare them to the four gears on a standard transmission automobile. If delta waves represent the first gear, which is the slowest, theta waves would correspond to the second gear, with alpha and beta waves representing the third and fourth gears, respectively. However, what would happen if we started the car in first gear and then shifted directly into fourth? Obviously, the life of the gearbox would be considerably decreased.

Something similar happens in the brain. Take the following example. After a deep sleep (characterized by delta waves), a person is awakened suddenly by the ringing of an alarm clock. He gets out of bed immediately and hurries to get ready for work, anxious about being late. This reaction produces a full spectrum of beta waves. He might even drink coffee to stimulate his wakefulness, which promotes beta waves while suppressing the alpha and theta waves.

Then, he works continuously during the day, without taking time to relax or contemplate. This state continues until night-time when exhaustion sets in, and he falls deep asleep. The daily average balance of brain waves for people in modem society consists mainly of delta and beta waves; most alpha and theta waves are almost nonexistent.

Like the transmission in a standard automobile, when only the two extreme limits are used (first and fourth gears), it causes undue stress on the system because the proper sequence of "gears" has been violated. Therefore, the individual's capacity to process information decreases, as does the general control and efficiency of the living system. Some subsystems (for example, certain organs) begin to function improperly, causing various physical/mental conditions.

Mechanisms (which are very important for the proper operation of the whole system) may become defective and, in time, break down. System failures accumulate and eventually lead to the system's general and final failure. This behavior contradicts the survival strategy all living systems developed and demonstrates a lack of intelligent organization. This is mainly a social phenomenon, which unfortunately characterizes modern civilized society.

Along with so many wonderful achievements in social evolution, we should not ignore this negative aspect. We should act promptly and responsibly to maintain the quality and survival of our species.

Even with this short description of brain waves, the significance of the self-induced alpha state in the control of the organism can be readily seen. First, self-inducing the alpha state represents a control of the brain waves. In the alpha state, an individual can "feel" his organs and functions and influence them. The "controls" of the organism are taken over by the conscious. However, all actions are strictly supervised by the intelligent structure of a higher level represented in this state by the subconscious.

If one explores this problem more deeply and analyzes the next level, the subconscious, one discovers integration issues. One also reaches, ultimately, what we have termed the Universal Intelligence. Therefore, the control of an organism seems to be much more complicated than initially perceived. One can never define the "something" that completely controls the organism. Is it the consciousness? Definitely not, because the organism's vital functions exist whether we consciously control them or not. Is it God's powerful assistants or the Universal Intelligence? Not quite, since other specific devices mainly control the molecular activity. Consequently, we prefer to consider an integrated, multilevel control structure as the most accurate definition for the "control" of a living system.

Humans have enhanced their capabilities through the procedures acquired from evolution, civilization, culture, and education. These procedures have taught us to defend ourselves from environmental threats and to increase our comfort by creating tools that replace physical labor and maximize efficiency. However, this artificial evolution has also increased physical stress and sedentary lifestyles. Today, stress is a pervasive factor in our lives. Every aspect of our society is stressful, and we must carefully consider the evolution of our species compared to the evolution of matter, energy, intelligence, life, and consciousness.

We cannot push beyond certain limits without consequences. It would be unwise to allow technology and society to evolve at the expense of human life and the continuity of our species.

1.28 Intelligence and Consciousness of Nonliving Matter

We have analyzed different aspects of consciousness, intelligence, and information processing of biological systems. However, one cannot ignore nonliving matter because it presents some very interesting cases that identify it within the Universe. In fact, there is no nonliving matter in the Universe. The master molecule hydrogen was described as having its own consciousness because it created the material universe from which consciousness emerged.

It is not consciousness that humans can understand. Note that humans cannot even recognize and understand another human's consciousness. Regarding material smartness and intelligence, one can define the type of intelligence according to how the information is organized.

Refer to Chapter 4 for the definitions of various material smartness quotients (MSQs) and material intelligence quotients (MIQs), as well as structural smartness quotients (SSQs) and structural intelligence quotients (SIQs). As will be shown later, materials can be considered smart or intelligent, as can material structures or systems. One must, therefore, introduce a SSQ and a SIQ. To classify materials based on the above quotients of smartness and intelligence, some reference values related to MIQ are needed. The family of amino acid sequences and structures has been chosen as a reference for smartness and structural smartness assigned the MSQ value of 1000.

As working objects of engineers and scientists, materials are conventionally classified into two main categories: smart and intelligent materials. Smart materials can automatically and inherently sense or detect changes in their environment. They respond to those changes with some actuation or action.

In addition, intelligent materials possess or show a survival strategy that prompts appropriate actions or actuations from sensed or detected environmental change. Recall that one must first determine all the hierarchical structures involved in the evolution of each material. At each level of the hierarchy, associated smartness and intelligence must be numerically computed.

These computations, even if they seem difficult to perform because of a lack of data, are much simpler than one thinks. Starting from the concept of intelligence, one realizes that a system's intelligence and adaptation are directly related to its ability to continuously exchange information with its environment. If it also reacts to environmental changes, it is a dynamic and conscious system.

The ability of a system to perceive changes in its environment can be called "sensing." As previously seen, sensing is directly related to smartness and, if associated with a set of reactions, to intelligence.

In an open system, one must develop a specialized informational system based on codes to exchange information with the environment. If one can identify a survival code for a material system, then one can consider that system intelligent and conscious.

Depending on the complexity of the survival code, one can assign to that material system an intelligent quotient or a smartness quotient (if only sensing is present, with no survival strategy). A model code must be created to identify the reaction codes of materials. We assume that sensing and reaction can be performed by eight separate means. Table 1.2 shows that each has an associated model and reaction plan.

Table 1.2 Reaction codes and the associated plans of reaction

Sense	Model	Plan	ACT
Electromagnetic	Code No. 1	Plan No. 1	Electromagnetic
Gravitational	Code No. 2	Plan No. 2	Gravitational
Thermal	Code No. 3	Plan No. 3	Thermal
Mechanical	Code No. 4	Plan No. 4	Mechanical
Chemical	Code No. 5	Plan No. 5	Chemical
Molecular	Code No. 6	Plan No. 6	Molecular
	Code No. 7	Plan No. 7	Ionic
Other	Code No. 8	Plan No. 8	Other

As we have already considered material systems and dynamic systems, we can visualize the reciprocal interactions between four fundamental elements of intelligence in the form of a tetrahedron (Fig. 1.22).

Figure 1.22 shows the tetrahedron of adaptive or learnable intelligence as the simplest 3D geometry. The fundamental relationship between geometry and intelligence starts here.

After analyzing the adaptive intelligence of material systems, the next step is to assess their ability to learn from their environment. Learning in nonliving systems is much simpler than in living systems. It does not involve language or other forms of coded information.

Physicist John Bell describes the Einstein camp in this debate on "Bertelsmann's socks and the nature of reality," Speakable and Unspeakable in quantum mechanics. Einstein-Podolsk-Rosen (EPR) paradoxes in mixed states that accurately represent the output of physical systems that generate squeezing and entanglement of space. The paradox of macroscopic entanglement occurs when we have a quantum superposition of two macroscopically distinguishable, for EPR, that would be an unthinkable 'spooky action at a distance. To avoid such action at a distance, they have to attribute real properties before observation to the space–time regions in question and correlated properties, which predetermine the outcomes of these particular observations. Since these real properties, fixed in advance of observation, are not contained in quantum formalism, that formalism for EPR is incomplete. It may be correct, as far as it goes, but the usual quantum formalism cannot be the whole story.

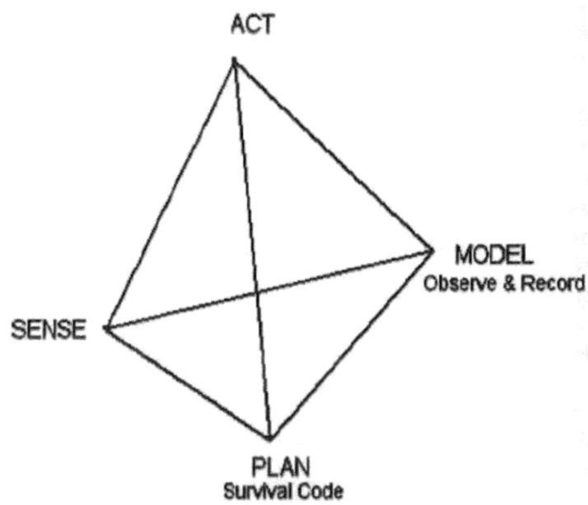

Figure 1.22 The tetrahedron of adaptive intelligence.

References

Backster, C. (2003). Primary perception: Biocommunication with plants, *Living Foods and Human Cells*. California, USA: White Rose Millennium Press.

Backster, C., and White, S. G. (1985) Biocommunications capability: Human donors and in vitro leukocytes. *International Journal of Biosocial Research,* **7**(2), 132–146.

Blum, L., and Blum, M. A. (2023). Theoretical computer science perspective on consciousness and artificial general intelligence. *Engineering,* **25**(1).

Bremer, F. (1965). Existence of a mutual tonic inhibitory interaction between the preoptic hypnogenic structure and the midbrain reticular formation. *Brain Res.* **96**, 71–75. doi: 10.1016/0006-8993(75)90573-9, he also collaborated with Bremer, Moruzzi, and Magoun, in Sager.

Celan, E. (1997). *Biofield and Bioradiation*, Teora, Bucharest (ed.), p. 139.

Georgie, D. D., and Gadder, S. P. (2022). Sensitivity of entanglement measures in bipartite pure quantum states. *Modern Physics Letters B*, **36**(22): 2501012250255.

Guth, A. H. (1981). Cosmic inflation. *Phys. Rev. D*, **23**, 347.

Guth, A. H. (2004). Inflation, In *Carnegie Observatories Astrophysics Series, Vol. 2: Measuring and Modeling the Universe*, W. L. Freedman (ed.), Cambridge: Cambridge Univ. Press.

Hazen, R., has discussed the Second Arrow of Time in Well, Is there a second arrow of time? New research says yes, Leading mineralogist Dr. Robert Hazen on the missing law of nature that could explain why life emerges in addition to all other amazingly complex and beautiful evolutionary outcomes.

Higgs, P. (1955). The Higgs boson is the fundamental force-carrying particle of the Higgs field, which is responsible for granting other particles their mass. Peter Higgs(1955) first proposed this field in the mid-sixties.

Lavallette, P. (1994). Diffusivity.

Lemaître, G. (1894–1966) was a Belgian cosmologist, Catholic priest, and father of the Big Bang theory—photo courtesy of AIP Emilio Segré Visual Archives, Dorothy Davis Locanthi Collection.

Merleau-Ponty, M. (1962). *Phénoménologie de la perception, 1945 (French), 1962 (English)*, English translation from French by Colin Smith (1st English translation), Donald Landes (2nd English translation), Éditions Gallimard, Routledge, & Kegan Paul, 1945, English translation, 466 (1965 Routledge edition), ISBN 978-0415834339 (2012 edition).

Moss, T. (1979). *The Body Electric: A Personal Journey into the Mysteries of Parapsychological Research, Bioenergy, and Kirlian Photography*. J. P. Tarcher. ISBN 978-0-312-90437-1.

Oparin, A. I. (1924). *The Origin of Life, Translation of Ann Synge*, from Russian.

Popa, S., and Shahinpoor, M. (2000). *Energy, Matter, Intelligence and Life (EMIL)*, Book by ERI Press, Albuquerque, NM, 2000.

Pora, E. A., and Precup, O. (1971). Contribution to de l'excretion azote chez les poissons. VIII. Action des hormones corticodes et de l'ACTH (journal article), *Marine Biology*, **11**(1), 77–81., DOI: 10.1007/BF00348023.

Prigogine, I. (1973). The statistical interpretation of non-equilibrium entropy. In: Cohen, E. G. D., Thirring, W. (eds.) *The Boltzmann Equation. Acta Physica Austriaca*, **10**. Springer, Vienna. https://doi.org/10.1007/978-3-7091-8336-6_18

Schrödinger, E. (1967). *"What is Life"? Mind and Matter*, combined reprint 1967 Edition by Cambridge University Press.

Shahinpoor, M. (1987). *A Robot Engineering Text Book*, Harper and Row Publishers, New York and London.

Shahinpoor, M. (1991). *Robot Technology*, in Russian, MIR Publishers, Moscow, Former Soviet Union, Russian Translation & Extension of Reference 4 by Harper and Row Publishers, *A Robot Engineering Text Book*.

Shahinpoor, M. (1997). Intelligent civil engineering materials, and structures revisited, In *Intelligent Civil Engineering Materials and Structures*, F. Ansari, A. K. Maji and C. Leung (eds.), Engineering Mechanics Division/ ASCE, pp. 44–61.

Shahinpoor, M. (2011). *Intelligent Robotic Systems: Modeling & Simulation*, ERI Press, Albuquerque, New Mexico, second edition.

Shahinpoor, M., and Thompson, M. S. (1995). The Venus flytrap as a model for biomimetic material with built-in sensors and actuators, *J. Materials Science & Engineering*, **C2**, 229–233.

Shahinpoor, M., and Wang, G. (1995). Electro-thermo-mechanics of SMA fiber bundles embedded in an elastic medium, In *Active Materials and Smart Structures*, G. L. Anderson and D. C. Lagoudas (eds.), SPIE Publication, **2427**, 272–382.

Tirard, S. (2017). J. B. S. Haldane and the origin of life. J Genet, 96, 735–739. https://doi.org/10.1007/s12041-017-0831-6.

Tompkins, C. and Peter, B. (1975). The Secret Life of Plants. Penguin Books.

Vasiliev, L. L. (1964). Mysterious phenomena of the human psyche. *The Journal of Parapsychology*, **28**(1), 56.

von Bertalanffy, L. (1968). *General System Theory: Foundations, Development, Applications*. George Braziller Publishers, New York, 295 pages.

Wang, G., and Shahinpoor, M. (1997). A new design for a rotatory joint actuator made with shape memory alloy contractile wire, *J. Intelligent Materials Systems & Structures*, **8**(3), 191–279.

Wang, G., and Shahinpoor, M. (1997). Design for shape memory alloy rotatory joint actuators using shape memory effect and pseudo elastic effect, *Smart Materials Technologies*, **3040**, 23–30.

Wang, G., and Shahinpoor, M. (1997). Design, prototyping and computer simulation of a novel large bending actuator made with a shape memory alloy contractile wire, *Smart Materials and Structures Journal*, **6**(2), 214–221.

Watson, L., Barker, N. P., and Jacobs, S. W. L. (1974). Amphipogon (Gramineae) does have microhairs. *Telopea*, **8**, 155–156.

Zadeh, L. A. (1973). Introduction of the concepts of a linguistic variable and fuzzy if-then rules.

Further Readings

Akopian, N. (2006). Entangled photon pairs from semiconductor quantum dots. *Phys. Rev. Lett.* **96**(2), 130501.

Aspect, A. Dalibard, J., and Roger, G. (1982). Experimental test of Bell's inequalities using time-varying analyzers, *Phys. Rev. Lett.* **49**, 1804.

Augusiak, R., Demianowicz, M., Tura, J., and Acín, A. (2015). Entanglement and nonlocality are inequivalent for any number of parties. *Phys. Rev. Lett.* **115**(3), 30404.

Bell, J. S. (1964). On the Einstein Podolsky Rosen paradox. *Phys. Physique Fizika.* **1**, 195.

Bhaskara, V. S. and Panigrahi, P. K. (2017). Generalized concurrence measure for faithful multiparticle pure state entanglement quantification using Lagrange's identity and wedge product. *Quantum Inf. Process.* **16**(5), 118.

Blum, L., and Blum, M. (2023). A theoretical computer science perspective on consciousness and artificial general intelligence. *Engineering.* **25**(1), 12–16.

Boerkamp, M. (2023). Quantum entanglement observed in top quarks. *Physics World*, **36**(12).

Boette, A., Rossignoli, R., Gigena, N., and Cerezo, M. (2016). System-time entanglement in a discrete-time model. *Phys. Rev. A.* **93**(6), 062127.

Bokulich, A., and Jaeger, G. (2010). *Philosophy of Quantum Information and Entanglement*, Cambridge University Press.

Bub, J. (2019). *Quantum Entanglement and Information. Stanford Encyclopedia of Philosophy*. Stanford, California: Stanford University.

Clauser, J. F., Horne, M. A., Shimony, A., and Holt, R. A. (1969). Proposed experiment to test local hidden-variable theories. *Phys. Rev. Lett.* **23**, 880.

Cramer, J. G. (2015). *The Quantum Handshake: Entanglement, Nonlocality and Transactions*. Springer, Verlag, International.

Duarte, F. J. (2019). *Fundamentals of Quantum Entanglement*. Bristol, UK: Institute of Physics.

Dunai, T. J., and Finlay, S. M. (2009). Reporting of cosmogenic nuclide data for exposure age and erosion rate determinations. *Quater. Geochronol.*, 437–440.

Einstein, A., Podolsky, B., and Rosen, N. (1935). Can quantum-mechanical description of physical reality be considered complete? *Phys. Rev. Lett.* **47**, 777.

Freedman, S. J., and Clauser, J. F. (1972). Experimental test of local hidden-variable theories. *Phys. Rev. Lett.* **28**, 938.

Fries, N., Vitagliano, G., Malik, M., and Huber, M. (2019). Entanglement certification from theory to experiment. *Nat. Rev. Phys.* **1**, 72–87.

Gamow, G. (1946). Expanding universe and the origin of elements. *Phys. Rev.* **70**, 572.

Georgie, D. D., and Gadder, S. P. (2022). Sensitivity of entanglement measures in bipartite pure quantum states. *Modern Phys. Lett. B.* **36**(22), 22501012250255.

Georgie, D., and Cohen, E. (2022). Entanglement measures for two-particle quantum histories. *Phys. Rev. A.* **106**(6), 062437.

Gibney, E. (2014). Entangled photons make a picture from a paradox. *Nature.* https://doi:10.1038/nature.2014.15781.

Gour, G., and Wallach, N. R. (2013). Classification of multipartite entanglement of all finite dimensionality. *Phys. Rev. Lett.* **111**(6), 060502.

Grassl, M., Rötteler, M., and Beth, T. (1998). Computing local invariants of quantum-bit systems. *Phys. Rev. A.* **58**(3), 1833–1839.

Gühne, O. (2004). Characterizing entanglement via uncertainty relations. *Phys. Rev. Lett.* **92**(11), 117903.

Gühne, O., and Lewenstein, M. (2004). Entropic uncertainty relations and entanglement. *Phys. Rev. A.* **70**(2), 022316.

Gühne, O., and Tóth, G. (2009). Entanglement detection. *Phys. Rep.* **474**(1–6), 75.

Gurvits, L. (2003). Classical deterministic complexity of Edmonds' problem and quantum entanglement. *Proceedings of the Thirty-Fifth Annual ACM Symposium on Theory of Computing*, San Diego, CA, USA, June 9–11, 2003. New York: ACM Press.

Hardy, L. (1992). Quantum mechanics, local realistic theories, and Lorentz-invariant realistic theories. *Phys. Rev. Lett.* **68**(20), 2981–2984.

Hillery, M., and Zubairy, M. S. (2006). Entanglement conditions for two-mode states. *Phys. Rev. Lett.* **96**(5), 050503.

Hofmann, H. F., and Takeuchi, S. (2003). Violation of local uncertainty relations as a signature of entanglement. *Phys. Rev. A.* **68**(3), 032103.

Holland, M. J., and Burnett, K. (1993). Interferometric detection of optical phase shifts at the Heisenberg limit. *Phys. Rev. Lett.* **71**(9), 1355–1358.

Holodeck, M., Holodeck, P., and Holodeck, R. (1998). Mixed-state entanglement and distillation: Is there a bound entanglement in nature? *Phys. Rev. Lett.* **80**(1998), 5239–5242.

Horodecki, R., Horodecki, P., Horodecki, M., and Horodecki, K. (2009). Quantum entanglement. *Rev. Modern Phys.* **81**(2), 865–942.

Huang, Y. (2010). Entanglement criteria via concave-function uncertainty relations. *Phys. Rev. A.* **82**(1), 012335.

Huang, Y. (2013). Entanglement detection: Complexity and Shannon entropic criteria. *IEEE Trans. Inf. Theory.* **59**(10), 6774.

Hubble, E. (1929). Extra-galactic nebulae. *Proc. Natl. Acad. Sci.* **15**(3), 168–173.

Jaeger, G. (2009). *Entanglement, Information, and the Interpretation of Quantum Mechanics.* Heidelberg: Springer.

Jozsa, R., and Linden, N. (2002). On the role of entanglement in quantum computational speed-up. *Proc. Royal Society A: Math., Phys. Eng. Sci.* **459**(2036), 2011–2032.

Kitagawa, M., and Ueda, M. (1993). *Squeezed spin states. Phys. Rev. A.* **47**(6), 5138–5143.

Kocher, C. A. (1971). Time correlations in the detection of successively emitted photons. *Ann. Phys.* **65**(1), 1–18.

Kotler, S., Peterson, G. A., Shojaee, E., Lecocq, F., Cicak, K., Kwiatkowski, A., Geller, S., Glancy, S., Knill, E., Simmonds, R. W., Aumentado, J., and Teufel, J. D. (2021). Direct observation of deterministic macroscopic entanglement. *Science.* **372**(6542), 622–625.

Lami, L., and Regula, B. (2023). No second law of entanglement manipulation after all. *Nat. Phys.* **19**(2), 184–189.

Leinaas, J. M., Myrheim, J., and Ovrum, E. (2006). Geometrical aspects of entanglement. *Phys. Rev. A.* **74**(1), 012313.

Lo Franco, R., and Compagno, G. (2018). Indistinguishability of elementary systems as a resource for quantum information processing. *Phys. Rev. Lett.* **120**(24), 240403.

Ma, X.-S., Zotter, S., Kofler, J., Ursin, R., Jennewein, T., Brukner, Č., Zeilinger, A. (2012). Experimental delayed-choice entanglement swapping. *Nat. Phys.* **8**(6), 480485.

Markoff, J. (2015). Sorry, Einstein. Quantum Study Suggests 'Spooky Action' Is Real. *The New York Times*. Retrieved October 21, 2015.

Marletto, C., Coles, D. M., Farrow, T., and Vedral, V. (2018). Entanglement between living bacteria and quantized light witnessed by Rabi splitting. *J. Phys. Commun.* **2**(10), 101001.

Merleau-Ponty, M. *Phénoménologie de la perception, 1945 (French), 1962 (English)*, English translation from French by Colin Smith (1st English translation), Donald Landes (2nd English translation), Éditions Gallimard, Routledge & Kegan Paul, 1945, English translation (1962), 466 (1965 Routledge edition), ISBN, 978-0415834339 (2012 edition).

Monod, J. (1971). *Chance and Necessity: An Essay on the Natural Philosophy of Modern Biology*. New York: Vintage Books.

Monod, J., and Bornek, E. (Eds.) (1971). *Of Microbes and Life*. New York: Columbia University Press.

Monod, J. (2010). The Nobel Prize in Physiology or Medicine 1965, François Jacob, André Lwoff. *Nobelprize.org*. Retrieved June 30, 2010.

Moreva, E. (2014). Time from quantum entanglement: An experimental illustration. *Phys. Rev. A*. **89**(5), 052122.

Nielsen, M. A. (1999). Conditions for a class of entanglement transformations. *Phys. Rev. Lett.* **83**(2), 436.

Nielsen, M. A., and Chuang, I. L. (2000). *Quantum Computation and Quantum Information*. Cambridge University Press, pp. 112–113.

Pan, J. W. (1998). Experimental entanglement swapping: Entangling photons that never interacted. *Phys. Rev. Lett.* **80**, 3891.

Pirandola, S., Andersen, U. L., Banchi, L., Berta, M., Bunandar, D., Colbeck, R., Englund, D., Gehring, T., Lupo, C., Ottaviani, C., Pereira, J. L., Razavi, M., Shamsul Shaari, J., Tomamichel, M., Usenko, V. C., Vallone, G., Villoresi, P., and Wallden, P. (2020). Advances in quantum cryptography. *Adv. Opt. Photon.* **12**(4), 10121236.

Plenio, M. B., and Virmani, S. (2007). An introduction to entanglement measures. *Quant. Inf. Comp.* **1**, 1–51.

Prigogine, I. (1973). Irreversibility as a symmetry-breaking process. *Nature* **246**, 67–71.

Renner, R., Gisin, N., and Kraus, B. (2005). An information-theoretic security proof for QKD protocols. *Phys. Rev. A*. **72**, 012332.

Rozatkar, G. (2018). *Demonstration of Quantum Entanglement*. OSF.

Sakurai, J. J., and Napolitano, J. J. (2010). *Modern Quantum Mechanics* (2 edn.). Pearson.

Schrödinger, E. (1935). Discussion of probability relations between separated systems. *Math. Proc. Camb. Philos. Soc.* **31**(4), 555–563.

Schrödinger, E. (1936). Probability relations between separated systems. *Math. Proc. Camb. Philos. Soc.* **32**(3), 452–446.

Shadbolt, P. J., Verde, M. R., Peruzzo, A., Politi, A., Laing, A., Lobino, M., Matthews, J. C. F., Thompson, M. G., and O'Brien, J. L. (2012). Generating, manipulating and measuring entanglement and mixture with a reconfigurable photonic circuit. *Nat. Photon.* **6**(1), 45–59.

Shahinpoor, M., and Gheshmi, S. (2015). *Robotic Surgery.* Singapore: Jenny Stanford Publishing.

Siegel, E. (2023). No, we still can't use quantum entanglement to communicate faster than light. *Forbes.* Retrieved January 6, 2023.

Smith, P. (2018). *Quantum Consciousness: Journey Through Other Realms.* Llewellyn Publications.

Steward, E. G. (2008). *Quantum Mechanics: Its Early Development and the Road to Entanglement.* Imperial College Press.

Swain, S. N., Bhaskara, V. S., and Panigrahi, P. K. (2022). Generalized entanglement measure for continuous-variable systems. *Phys. Rev. A.* **105**(5), 052441.

Swingle, B., and van Raamsdonk, M. (2014). Universality of gravity from entanglement. https://inspirehep.net/literature/1295886.

Thomas, R. A., Parniak, M., Østfeldt, C., Møller, C. B., Bærentsen, C., Tsaturyan, Y., Schliesser, A., Appel, J., Zeuthen, E., and Polzik, E. S. (2020). Entanglement between distant macroscopic mechanical and spin systems. *Nat. Phys.* **17**(2), 228–233.

Tononi, G., and Koch, C. (2015). Consciousness: Here, there and everywhere? *Phil. Trans. Royal Soc.*, **370**(1668).Van Raamsdonk, M. (2010). Building up spacetime with quantum entanglement. *Gen. Relativ. Gravit.* **42**(10), 2323–2329.

Vértesi, T., and Brunner, N. (2014). Disproving the Peres conjecture by showing Bell nonlocality from bound entanglement. *Nat. Commun.* **5**(1), 5297.

Walborn, S., Taketani, B., Salles, A., Toscano, F., and de Matos Filho, R. (2009). Entropic entanglement criteria for continuous variables. *Phys. Rev. Lett.* **103**(16), 160–505.

Werner, R. F., and Wolf, M. M. (2001). Bound entangled Gaussian states. *Phys. Rev. Lett.* **86**(16), 3658–3661.

Wineland, D. J., Bollinger, J. J., Itano, W. M., Moore, F. L., and Heinzen, D. J. (1992). Spin squeezing and reduced quantum noise in spectroscopy. *Phys. Rev. A.* **46**(11).

Wiseman, H. M., Jones, S. J., and Doherty, A. C. (2007). Steering, entanglement, nonlocality, and the Einstein–Podolsky–Rosen paradox. *Phys. Rev. Lett.* **98**(14), 140402.

Wogan, T. (2021). Vibrating drumheads are entangled quantum mechanically. *Physics World*. Retrieved June 14, 2021.

Yin, J., Cao, Y., Li, Y.-H., Liao, S.-K., Zhang, L., Ren, J. G., Cai, W. Q., Liu, W. Y., Li, B., Dai, H., Li, G. B., Lu, Q. M., Gong, Y. H., Xu, Y., Li, S. L., Li, F. Z., Yin, Y. Y., Jiang, Z. Q., Li, M., Jia, J. J., Ren, G., He, D., Zhou, Y. L., Zhang, X. X., Wang, N., Chang, X., Zhu, Z. C., Liu, N. L., Chen, Y. A., Lu, C. Y., Shu, R., Peng, C. Z., Wang, J. Y., and Pan, J. W. (2017). Satellite-based entanglement distribution over 1200 kilometers. *Science*. **356**(6343), 1140–1144.

Yin, J., Cao, Y., Yong, H.-L., Ren, J.-G., Liang, H., Liao, S.-K., Zhou, F., Liu, C., Wu, Y.-P., Pan, G.-S., Zhang, Q., Peng, C.-Z., and Pan, J.-W. (2013). Bounding the speed of 'spooky action at a distance'. *Phys. Rev. Lett.* **110**(26), 260407.

Yin, J., Li, Y.-H., Liao, S.-K., Yang, M., Cao, Y., Zhang, L., Ren, J.-G., Cai, W.-Q., Liu, W.-Y., Li, S.-L., Shu, R., Huang, Y.-M., Deng, L., Li, L., Zhang, Q., Liu, N.-L., Chen, Y.-A., Lu, C.-Y., Wang, X.-B., Xu, F., Wang, J.-Y., Peng, C.-Z., Ekert, A. K., and Pan, J.-W. (2020). Entanglement-based secure quantum cryptography over 1,120 kilometers. *Nature*. **582**(7813), 501–505.

Zadeh, L. A. (1973). Introduction of the concepts of a linguistic variable and fuzzy if-then rules.

Chapter 2

Possible Scenario to Make Intelligent Biomimetic Humanoid Robots with Comparable Human Consciousness

2.1 Introduction

The basic strategy to transfer consciousness to humanoid robots may start after the human is born. It can be started when a person is young or growing. The individual entering the program eventually creates a corresponding non-organic biomimetic humanoid robot with the "assigned consciousness and vita of the corresponding human whom we call the human master." Non-organic means that the humanoid robot will not have any organic biological organs such as the heart, kidneys, lungs, or digestive system. Instead, it will be entirely electro-magneto chemical. The preferred age to enter the program is middle age, but any other age will also work. An individual willing to enter the program must set aside enough resources, assets, expertise, and software collection first to initiate the humanoid robot's design, development, fabrication, programming, and operation. Once the humanoid robot of an individual is ready for operation, the process of injecting consciousness into it will start. It is important to use a human's identity and vita (resume) before

Biomimetic Humanoid Robots with Human Consciousness
Mohsen Shahinpoor

ISBN 978-981-5129-87-8 (Hardcover), 978-1-003-71373-9 (eBook)
www.jennystanford.com

DOI: 10.1201/9781003713739-2

their consciousness is transferred to an intelligent biomimetic look-alike humanoid robot and its corresponding embedded artificial intelligence (AI) computer. From here on, the humanoid robot is self-aware and conscious of its identity and a short resume of its life (human master's life) assigned to it.

The humanoid robot will have electromagnetic mechanical systems (sensors and actuators) and software to move, operate, and sense. At that junction, the robot is embedded with an AI-based advanced computer possibly integrated with the individual's neural brain (neurons, axons, dendrites, and synapses) to record the human's movement and sensing capabilities and even possibly sentient feelings or sentience. A strategy will be developed for the individual to express these feelings to the resident intelligent computer in the humanoid with identity-vita-assigned consciousness (IVA-consciousness). It is essential to initially make the humanoid robot accept and understand that it has an identity and the vita of the human master/owner it represents. This is the first step in self-awareness. It will adopt the intellectual position that it represents a human being with a name, identity, and partial life story, and people should always be aware of that fact. This is the beginning of awareness and consciousness for the humanoid robot. The smart computers equipped with IVA-consciousness observe and record all events as the individual observes and reacts to them. As humans grow, embedded computers also grow in memory and intelligence to record everything observed, heard, or experienced.

The proposed design and development also consider the description of conscious, sentient feelings, and their feedback to the resident consciousness. The humanoid robot is then instructed to accept and understand that there is always an environment in which it operates. The only catch here is the emotional effects and feelings regarding love, hate, like, dislike, anger, jealousy, regrets, music enjoyment, sex enjoyment, respect, admiration, vengeance/retaliation, worry, anxiety, etc. The book will describe how feelings and emotions are transferred to the consciousness by describing or experiencing them through oral transfer of cognition and consciousness. In this regard, the individual human will continuously communicate with an AI computer onboard to describe feelings and emotions and include them in the IVA-consciousness of the humanoid robot.

2.2 Associative Neural Architecture or ANR

As discussed earlier, the basic strategy to transfer consciousness to human beings may start after the human being has grown up to be a middle-aged individual or younger to enter the program of eventually creating (designing, developing, fabricating, and operating) a non-organic biomimetic humanoid robot with the identity assigned consciousness of the master. It is important again to emphasize the need to assign the identity of a human master to a humanoid robot, familiarize the robot with a summary of his or her vita, and transfer consciousness into an intelligent AI computer in the humanoid robot before.

At that junction, he or she is embedded with an AI-based-Advanced computer integrated with the individual's neural brain (neurons, axons, dendrites, and synapses) to record all human beings' actions, movements, and sensing capabilities and even possibly sentient feelings and emotions. Thus, a strategy is developed for the individual to express these feelings to the humanoid robot resident intelligent computer with IVA-consciousness. The identity of the human master may be a summary of his or her vitae to enable the humanoid robot to have a better awareness and understanding of the human master's identity and consciousness. The smart embedded consciousness computers equipped with IVA-consciousness will observe and record all events as individuals observe and react to them. As the individual grows, the embedded consciousness computer will also grow in memory and record everything observed, heard, felt, enjoyed, involved, or experienced. The book proposal also considers the description of sentient feelings and their feedback to the resident consciousness. The only catch here is the emotional effects and feelings regarding love, hate, like, anger, dislike, hate, jealousy, fascination, admiration, respect, regrets, music enjoyment, sex enjoyment, vengeance/retaliation, worry, anxiety, etc. The proposed plan will describe how feelings and emotions are transferred to consciousness by simply describing them cognitively or experiencing them.

Oral consciousness transfer will also play an important role in transferring consciousness to the humanoid. The book also emphasizes that the humanoid robot will have no sexual activities because it does not need to do so. Recall that it does not reproduce either. However, it can repair itself if its electro-magneto-mechanical structures, microprocessors, and systems malfunction.

It is important to assign an identity to a person before his or her consciousness is transferred to an intelligent IVA computer. Thus, a strategy is developed for the individual to express these feelings to the resident intelligent computer with IVA-consciousness. The smart embedded consciousness computers equipped with IVA-consciousness will observe and record all events as the individual observes and reacts to them. As the individual and the humanoid robot grow and be in continuous companionship, the embedded consciousness computer will also grow in memory and record everything observed, heard, felt, enjoyed, involved, or experienced. The book also considers the description of conscious feelings and their feedback to the resident consciousness.

The book will describe how feelings and emotions are transferred to consciousness by describing them cognitively or experiencing them during the human and humanoid robot's companionship. Oral transfer of consciousness will also play an important role in transferring consciousness to the humanoid. The book also emphasizes that the humanoid robot will normally have no sexual activities or desires because it does not need to do so. Even though it may be possible to instill and teach sexual desires in a humanoid robot, recall that it does not reproduce either. However, it can repair itself in case of any malfunction of its electro-magneto-mechanical structure.

The fundamental idea of this book is to present a plan to design and develop biomimetic humanoids (robots) with a human consciousness. This will lay the foundation for humanity's eventual survival and sustenance in the entire universe in time and possibly the survival of some related biosystems. Humanity is proposing to design, fabricate, and operate specific humanoid robots with the identity of their human masters to transform from organic-based life to silicon-based and possibly lithium-based living systems. Captain James T. Kirk (William Shatner) and the crew of the Starship Enterprise need space to live and survive. This proposed R&D plan presents the possibility of human survival in the universe, traveling in deep space benefiting from *quantum entanglement possibilities* for long-distance transportation. Quantum entanglement will be discussed later in Chapters 7, 9, and 10. The humanoid robots will possibly live forever (immortality of humans by their humanoid robots). Just imagine the immortal humanoid motion in the universe. The book introduces advanced, smart, stimuli-responsive, intelligent wearable materials and their possible use for designing and developing biomimetic humanoid robots with human consciousness. It then introduces possible scenarios to make intelligent, sustaining robots with a human consciousness. The book introduces the concept of IVA-consciousness to make the humanoid robot understand that its master is a human. It is important to make the humanoid understand that it is a humanoid of a particular human master; it is unique and cannot be reproduced. This will be the first step in creating self-knowledge and self-awareness for the humanoid robot to know that its master is a human with consciousness and identity, kind of transferred to it, as well.

The book is about frontiers of consciousness research. It maintains that machine consciousness is meaningless because machines have no consciousness identity. How could you expect a machine or AI computer to gain consciousness if it does not know who or what it is? Machine consciousness should evolve in a machine; every consciousness has its own identity. This book presents a unique idea, never stated before, of IVA-consciousness. That is why it presents a scenario to embed an intelligent computer equipped with AI in a person early in life to record, see, sense, smell, feel, and comprehend all events, second by second, thus building an IVA-consciousness over time to communicate wirelessly with the humanoid resident's AI computers. This AI computer will be called the consciousness-building computer. Note that humans will also be equipped with smart AI computers to communicate wirelessly with the humanoid resident's AI computers, transferring any consciousness scenarios and activities to the humanoid's computers.

The book also proposes revolutionary directions for changing humanity's future. It is well known that humans and biosystems all have to eventually leave Earth and move on to other planets to live on immortally, particularly without needing water, food, air, or other bio-organics to survive. The book's proposal on biomimetic humanoids will create a biomimetic humanoid robot similar to a human, which looks like a human wearing soft stimuli-responsive clothing. It will look very similar to the person whose AI-consciousness has been partially transferred to it from a human master companion or an individually embedded consciousness computer to create IVA-consciousness in the humanoid, which will be a companion to the corresponding human upon realization. The human will transfer the story of his or her life and various life events to the humanoid robot and make the robot understand that a human is its boss. It will represent the human and always be aware of who it is. The companionship will end when the individual human reaches the end of his or her life and decides to leave the humanoid robot to stay on as himself or herself. Humans will transfer as much consciousness and awareness as possible to the biomimetic humanoid robots during companionship.

The book proposes a detailed research plan for transferring IVA-consciousness to the biomimetic humanoid robot. This process involves a series of interactions between humans and robots, as described in the book. Eventually, the human master of a humanoid robot needs to leave due to sickness or old age. When that time arrives, the corresponding human master will need to exit or complete his or her life through cremation or burial. At this point, the humanoid robot with human consciousness will take over and continue to exist indefinitely. It will be capable of deep space travel, free from the need for air, water, or food. Instead, a nuclear battery, providing energy for an extended period before requiring recharging or battery replacement, will power it.

Research on machine consciousness, which is entirely non-organic, also clearly shows that we could go from organic to non-organic and silicone-based life. Discussing the preservation of humanity through machine consciousness seems doable, and creating immortality in humanoids is possible and is a philosophical question.

Further, humans will not become redundant. They will live as long as possible for the humans and continue interaction and companionship with their humanoid robot with the transferred consciousness. The humanoid robot will live on with the transferred and improved human consciousness. Further, there will be enough resources and support left for it to support the humanoid for a long time and further equip it with the consciousness of the original human master.

We are always exploring these capabilities in ourselves and sometimes need help from a council. A robot does not know what kind of robot it is and what it can do. Robot inverse kinematics and inverse dynamics software can instruct it to move in certain ways or configurations, perform complicated maneuvers and motions, and perform stimuli-responsive reactions (see the Atlas 1 robot maneuvers and flipping from Boston Dynamics). Figure 2.1 depicts the amazing Atlas 1 robot from Boston Dynamics.

Figure 2.1 Atlas I from Boston Dynamics/Hyundai.

The humanoid robot will be designed and constructed to look exactly like the human master it is modeling. Note that we can teach robots to move in any legal way and perform in machine learning and consciousness.

The human IVA-consciousness recorded in the embedded consciousness computer will be transferred to the robot's memory bank as IVA-consciousness. After the transfer, the human and the humanoid robot start to interact and communicate with each other and become companions and friends and try to interact by teaching the humanoid robot regarding the IVA-consciousness software to communicate with the humanoid robot. In this final interaction between the human and the humanoid robot, the human consciousness can be transferred by cognition, logical explanations, and analysis to the humanoid robot. The book proposes this interaction as an *oral cognitive consciousness transfer* from a human to a humanoid robot. The humanoid robot will not reproduce itself because it has its identity and personality. These humanoids do not need to reproduce; they only live on and can travel to other planets and deep space on interplanetary ships similar to the Enterprise in the Star Trek episodes.

The book also describes how the theories of Roger Penrose and Stuart Sameroff address the fundamental problems of consciousness, namely the inner phenomenal appearance of the mental content and the qualia. The book tries to explain cognition, i.e., how the brain understands and produces meaningful thoughts. The book also discusses the connection between the brain and consciousness and the role of microtubules in storing conscious understandings and awareness. The book also discusses briefly the microtubules and how they control and interact with IVA-consciousness. A highly disputed theory in the mid-1990s by Stuart Hameroff and Roger Penrose describes that consciousness is based on quantum vibrations in tubulin/microtubules inside brain neurons.

Another theory, "orchestrated objective reduction" (Orch OR), was first put forward in the mid-1990s by the eminent mathematical physicist Roger Penrose and prominent anesthesiologist Stuart Hameroff, MD. They suggested that quantum vibrational computations in microtubules were "orchestrated" (Orch) by synaptic inputs and memory stored in microtubules and designated by Penrose as "objective reduction" (OR), hence "Orch OR." Microtubules are major components of the cell's structural skeleton. Orch OR was harshly criticized, as the brain was considered too "warm, wet, and noisy" for seemingly delicate quantum processes. However, evidence has shown warm quantum coherence in plant photosynthesis, birdbrain navigation, sense of smell, and brain microtubules. Quantum consciousness[1] is also important. Alternate realities using quantum physics can increase our understanding of awareness with quantum

[1]Peter Smith, *Quantum Consciousness: Journey through Other Realms*, Llewellyn Publications, 2018.

consciousness. This book invites the reader to see alternate realities, parallel lives, interdimensional consciousness, the eternal state, and even the very fabric of the universe.

Physicist John Bell depicts the Einstein camp[2] as follows: "For EPR that would be an unthinkable 'spooky action at a distance.' To avoid such action at a distance they have to attribute, to the space-time regions in question, real properties in advance of observation, correlated properties, which predetermine the outcomes of these particular observations. Since these real properties, fixed in advance of observation, are not contained in quantum formalism, that formalism for EPR is incomplete. It may be correct, as far as it goes, but the usual quantum formalism cannot be the whole story."

Four aspects of quantum consciousness—the creator effect, entanglement, everywhereness, and holographic healing—are especially emphasized. The book also explores the various realms of consciousness, including stored, alternate, parallel, and interdimensional consciousness.

The book describes the design and development of biomimetic soft wearable robotic structures equipped with stimuli-responsive ionic polymeric nanocomposites (IPMCs) and shape-memory alloy (SMA) artificial muscles with deformation sensing and actuation capabilities. The proposed book will also discuss and further explore the possibility of making these materials sentient.

The next detailed topic is the development of strategies and methods to transfer a human's knowledge, understanding, and consciousness to an advanced intelligent computer with AI capabilities. The book also presents the development of AI software and hardware for advanced computers. Captain Kirk's neural ink approach for brain-interfacing and remote communications is a good beginning toward making intelligent computers.

The book also looks into developing advanced software to understand consciousness and how to transfer the software to selected individual volunteers to transfer their consciousness to an intelligent (AI-based) computer. In this discussion, the book will present a brief review of the human brain and its major components, such as the cerebellum and cerebral cortex, as well as the miracle of neurons and associated axons, dendrites, synapses, and electrical

[2]In his article "Bertelsmann's socks and the nature of reality," p. 143 of *Speakable and Unspeakable in Quantum Mechanics.*

and chemical synapses, action and sensing potentials, micro-tubulins and microtubule interactions and quantum oscillations, interactions and collaborations.

The basic strategy to transfer consciousness to human beings may start after the human being is born and can be started as a child or an individual to enter the program of eventually making the humanoid robot become a non-organic biomimetic robot with the *identity-assigned consciousness*. It is important to assign an identity to a person before his or her consciousness is transferred to an intelligent AI computer. At that junction, he or she is embedded with an AI-based advanced computer integrated with the individual's neural brain (neurons, axons, dendrites, and synapses) to record all movement and sensing capabilities of the human and even possibly sentient feelings and emotions. Thus, a strategy is needed for the individual to express these feelings to the resident intelligent computer with IVA-consciousness. Here, the smart computers equipped with IVA-consciousness observe and record all events as the child or individual observes them, reacts, and responds to them. This computer will be called the consciousness storage computer. The book also introduces and promotes *oral transfer and oral cognition of consciousness* to the humanoid robots. The robot will always be instructed to know that it is a humanoid robot of a human and generate some self-awareness of its own identity and model human.

This may also be interpreted as a cognitive oral consciousness transfer from one brain to another. Embedded computers record everything they observe, hear, or experience as humans grow. The book also considers the description of sentient feelings and their feedback on the resident IVA-consciousness. The only catch here is the emotional effects and feelings regarding love, hate, like, dislike, jealousy, regrets, anger, admiration enjoyment, sex enjoyment, vengeance /retaliation, worry, anxiety, etc. The book will describe how feelings and emotions are transferred to consciousness by describing oration and experiencing them (cognitive transfer). The individual will continuously communicate with an AI smart, intelligent embedded consciousness computer to describe feelings and emotions and include them in the IVA-consciousness.

Pentti Haikonen has discussed the cognitive transfer of consciousness in *The Cognitive Approach to Conscious Machines* and *Existence, Origin, and Weird Technology* (World Scientific 2022).

Here, the strategy can be for any human to create the humanoid robot and transfer the IVA-consciousness to the realized humanoid robot during human life and companionship with the humanoid robot before the end of life for the human. A humanoid robot can be designed and fabricated for any human at any age rather than very young. Humanoid robots and humans will become friends and companions from here on until the end of life for the master human. The human will also describe his/her life story, related events, and important phases to the humanoid robot during companionship. This is how the humanoid robot gradually accepts its own new identity as a humanoid of a human.

Developing methodologies, strategies, and consciousness for individuals with their humanoid robot is essential in this phase. The proposed book also suggests that humans who have completed their human life cycle and have created their corresponding biomimetic humanoid robot with human IVA-consciousness will be free to complete their lives. Here, the strategy may be to create a humanoid robot and start to interact with it. Here, the human waits for the individual to be close to the end of life and then decides to have his/her humanoid robot eventually replace the human. Before the end of individual life, the transfer will occur in special laboratory chambers. There will be laboratory chambers for the individuals ready to transfer from human life to become biomimetic humanoid robots with IVA-consciousness.

Naturally, when a person is close to dying for whatever reason (sickness or old age), they will be ready to be replaced by their humanoid robot transferred to become a humanoid with IVA-consciousness if they have not already done so. The transferred individuals will eventually be ready to exit. They will be either cremated or buried, while their corresponding biomimetic humanoid robot will continue to lead a new long life forever under the identity of the corresponding human. These laboratory facilities can also convert animals into biomimetic robots with consciousness and sentience.

The book further discusses the design and development of moving capabilities (walking, running, flying, jetting, jumping, swimming, etc.) for the biomimetic humanoid robot with human consciousness. The humanoid robot will be built to be similar to the human individual it is modeling. It will have moving actuators and sensors to move all joints. The book will also present a special chapter on the design and creation of a humanoid robot. As the book emphasizes, one wonders if a human could ever be in space.

References and Further Readings

Aspect, A., Dalibard, J., and Roger, G. (1982). Experimental test of Bell's inequalities using time-varying analyzers. *Phys. Rev. Lett.* **49**, 1804.

Bell, J. S. (1964). On the Einstein–Podolsky–Rosen paradox. *Physics* **1**, 195.

Clauser, J. F., Horne, M. A., Shimony, A., and Holt, R. A. (1969). Proposed experiment to test local hidden-variable theories. *Phys. Rev. Lett.* **23**, 880.

Einstein A., Podolsky, B., and Rosen, N. (1935). Can quantum-mechanical description of physical reality be considered complete? *Phys. Rev.* **47**, 777.

Freedman, S. J., and Clauser, J. F. (1972). Experimental test of local hidden-variable theories. *Phys. Rev. Lett.* **28**, 938.

Haikonen, P. (2011). XCR-1: An experimental cognitive robot based on an associative neural architecture. *Cogn. Comput.* **3**(2), 360–366.

Hameroff, S. R. (1994). Quantum coherence in microtubules: A neural basis for emergent consciousness. *J. Consc. Stud.* **1**, 91–118.

Hameroff, S. R. (2006). The entwined mysteries of anesthesia and consciousness: Is there a common underlying mechanism? *Anesthesiology* **105**, 400–412.

Hameroff, S. R. (2021). 'Orch OR' is the most complete, and most easily falsifiable theory of consciousness. *Cogn. Neurosci.* **12**(2), 74–76.

Hameroff, S. R. (2022). Consciousness, cognition and the neuronal cytoskeleton: A new paradigm needed in neuroscience. *Front. Mol. Neurosci.*, **15**, 869935.

Pan, J. W. (1998). Experimental entanglement swapping: Entangling photons that never interacted. *Phys. Rev. Lett.* **80**, 3891.

Penrose, R. (1989). *The Emperor's New Mind: Concerning Computers, Minds, and the Laws of Physics.* Oxford: Oxford University Press.

Penrose, R. (1996). On gravity's role in quantum state reduction. *Gen. Rel. Grav.* 28, 581–600.

Penrose, R. (2022). New physics for the Orch OR consciousness proposal, in *Consciousness and Quantum Mechanics*, S. Gao (ed.). Oxford: Oxford University Press.

Penrose, R., and Hameroff, S. (1995). What gaps? Reply to Grush and Churchland. *J. Conscious. Stud.* **2**(2), 98–112.

Prigogine, I. (1973). Irreversibility as a symmetry-breaking process. *Nature* **246**, 67–71.

Prigogine, I., and Lefever, R. (1973). Theory of dissipative structures, in *Synergetics*, H. Haken (ed.). Wiesbaden: Vieweg+Teubner Verlag.

Rasmussen, S., Karampurwala, H., Vaidyanath, R., Jensen, K. S., and Hameroff, S. (1990). Computational connectionism within neurons: A model of cytoskeletal automata subserving neural networks. *Phys. D Nonlinear Phenomena* **42**, 428–449.

Schrödinger, E. (1935). Discussion of probability relations between separated systems. *Math. Proc. Camb. Philos. Soc.* **31**(4), 555–563.

Schrödinger, E. (1936). Probability relations between separated systems. *Math. Proc. Camb. Philos. Soc.* **32**(3), 446452.

Smith, P. (2018). *Quantum Consciousness: Journey through Other Realms.* Llewellyn Publications.

Chapter 3

Mathematics of Consciousness Using Integrated Information Theory (IIT) Originated by Guiliu Tononi and the Role of Universal Numbers and Data Toward the Evolution of Consciousness and Intelligence in the Entire Universe

3.1 Introduction

This chapter discusses the mathematics of consciousness using the groundbreaking integrated information theory (IIT 4.0), originating from the scientific endeavors of Prof. Giulio Tononi, Department of Psychiatry, University of Wisconsin, USA, and his colleagues.[1]

It delves into the current mathematical theories of consciousness, focusing on the IIT, the symbol of which is Phi Φ. It has emerged as one of the most influential and captivating theories of human consciousness mathematics. In its latest iteration (IIT 4.0), the theory takes on a metaphysical aspect, known as *idealistic ontology*.

[1]Professor Giulio Tononi and his co-researchers inspire this chapter. This chapter is also dedicated to the Mathematics of Consciousness, particularly using Integrated Information Theory (IIT, 4, Φ) originated by Professor Giulio Tononi and his co-researchers.

Biomimetic Humanoid Robots with Human Consciousness
Mohsen Shahinpoor

ISBN 978-981-5129-87-8 (Hardcover), 978-1-003-71373-9 (eBook)
www.jennystanford.com

DOI: 10.1201/9781003713739-3

Ontology and idealism assert that the existence of all things depends upon the state of the mind; thus, ontological idealism rejects the perspectives of physicalism and dualism. Christof Koch, Chief Scientific Officer, Allen Institute, also supports IIT for brain science.[2]

Tononi's IIT starts from conscious experience via five phenomenological axioms: *existence*, *composition*, *information*, *integration*, and *exclusion*. From these axioms, five postulates are derived about the properties required by physical mechanisms to support consciousness. The theory provides a principled account of both the quantity and the quality of an individual experience and a calculus to evaluate whether or not a particular system of mechanisms is conscious and of what.

Tononi emphasizes that we must understand no matter how intelligent computers and machines may be, they can write, move actuators, sense stimuli, translate languages, play music, etc., but they exist only as tools. His research maintains that it is about being rather than doing and to be meant to be conscious. We may argue that intelligent computers may be taught to understand that being in (power) means being in this universe. A smart computer may be instructed to announce that I am not on and possibly my energy source is turned off. This kind of self-awareness aims to provide some consciousness for intelligent AI computers.

According to IIT 4, we need a theory of consciousness that says what experience is and what type of physical systems can have it to address these issues. Tononi and IIT 4 aim to account for the properties of experience in physical (operational) terms. It identifies the essential properties of experience (axioms), infers the necessary and sufficient properties that its substrate must satisfy (postulates), and expresses them in mathematical terms.

In this chapter, a summary of IIT 4 is presented, and the mathematical theories of consciousness inspired by Albantakis et al. (2023) are discussed. This chapter is comprehensive. According to Albantakis et al. (2023), IIT discusses empirical evidence, makes testable predictions concerning the presence and quality of experience, and permits inferences and extrapolations. IIT 4.0 incorporates several developments of the past 10 years, including

---

[2]See Tononi, G., and Koch, C. (2015). The mathematics of consciousness (integrated information theory). *Philosophical Transactions of the Royal Society*, **370**(1668).

a more accurate formulation of the hypotheses. By fully unfolding a system's fundamental cause–effect power, distinctions, and relations, a substrate can account for the quality of experience.

As a theory of consciousness, IIT aims to answer two questions: (1) Why is experience present or absent? (2) Why do specific experiences feel the way they do? The theory's starting point is the existence of experience. IIT then aims to account for phenomenal existence and its essential properties in physical terms. It concludes that a substrate—a set of interacting units—can support consciousness if it can take and make a difference for itself (intrinsically), select a specific cause and effect as a fundamental with a definite border and grain, and specify a structure of causes and effects through subsets of its units.

To that end, IIT provides a mathematical formalism that can be employed to "unfold" the substrate's cause–effect structure. This allows IIT to answer the two questions:

1. Experience is present for any substrate that fulfills the essential properties of existence.
2. Specific experiences feel the way they do because of the specific cause–effect structure specified by their substrates.

According to Albantakis et al. (2023), IIT attempts to account for the presence and quality of consciousness in physical terms. It starts from the existence of experience as an axiom and proceeds by characterizing its essential properties—those that are immediate and irrefutably true of every conceivable experience (axioms). These are then formulated as essential properties of physical existence (postulates). A substrate must satisfy the necessary and sufficient conditions to support an experience. Note that "substrate" is purely operational—a set of units that a conscious observer can observe and manipulate.

In addition, the postulates can be assessed based purely on a substrate's transition probability matrix, as illustrated by a few idealized causal models. Thus, a substrate of consciousness must be able to take and make a difference upon itself (existence and intrinsicality), specify a cause and effect state that is highly informative and selective (information), and do so in a way that is both fundamental (integration) and definite (exclusion).

Finally, it must specify its cause and effect in a structured manner (composition), where the causal powers of its subsets over its subsets compose a cause–effect structure of distinctions and relations—a Φ-structure. Thus, a complex does not exist as such but only "unfolded" as a Φ-structure—an *intrinsic entity* that exists for itself, absolutely, rather than relative to an external observer.

3.2 Transition Probability Matrices (P_{ij})

In transition probability, P_{ij} is defined as the probability of a property or experience in state j that will occur next time, given that the property in state i has occurred at this time. For a property of m finite states, P_{ij} is a conditional transition probability of the property going from one state i at time r to property $V_{\tau+1}$, of state i at hour $\tau + 1$ or $P_{ij} = P\ (V\tau_{+1} = j | V\tau = i)$ with m states determined. An $m \times m$ transition probability matrix PM can be determined as PM = $[P_{ij}]$ for $i, j = 1, 2, ..., m$ in which, P_{ij} have the following properties:

- $\sum j = 1, mP_{ij} = 1, f$ or $i = 1, 2, ..., m$
- $P_{ij} \geq 0$, for all i and j.

A typical transition probability matrix for a given period r and season s can be expressed as

PM(s, r) = [Pi,js,r], where s = 1, 2, ..., S, and r = 1, 2, ..., R.

A computer program called WTPM was developed to calculate the PM(s,r).

As shown above (Albantakis et al., 2023), these requirements constrain what substrates can and cannot support consciousness. Substrates that lack specificity due to indeterminism and degeneracy cannot grow to be large complexes. Due to architectural or functional fault lines in their interactions, weakly integrated substrates are less integrated than some of their subsets. Because they are not maximally irreducible, they do not qualify as complexes.

This is the case even though they may "hang together" well enough from an extrinsic perspective. Furthermore, even maximally integrated substrates may support Φ-structures that are extremely sparse, as in the case of directed cycles. Based on the postulates of IIT, a universal substrate ultimately "condenses" into a set of disjoint (non-overlapping) complexes, each constituted of a set of macro- or micro-units. The importance of intrinsic existence (of experience) in IIT contrasts with standard attempts to account for consciousness as something "generated by" or "emerging from" a substrate constituted of matter, energy, and physical laws.

Each experience corresponds to a Φ-structure, not a set of functions, processes, or computations. Said otherwise, consciousness is about being, not doing (Albantakis et al., 2023). This means that systems with different architectures may be functionally equivalent—in terms of both global input–output functions and global intrinsic dynamics—but they will not be phenomenally equivalent.

Accordingly, artificial systems powered by super-intelligent computer programs but implemented by feed-forward hardware or encompassing critical bottlenecks would experience nothing (or nearly nothing) because they have the wrong kind of physical architecture, even though they may be behaviorally indistinguishable from human beings (Findlay et al., 2019).

Even though the entire framework of IIT is based on just a few *axioms and postulates*, it is impossible to exhaustively apply the postulates to unfold the cause–effect power of realistic systems (Barrett and Mediano, 2019; Moyal et al., 2020). It is not feasible to perform all possible observations and manipulations to characterize a universal total productive maintenance (TPM) fully or to perform all calculations on the TPM necessary to condense it exhaustively into complexes and unfold their cause–effect power in full. The number of possible systems, system partitions, and candidate distinctions—each with its partitions and relations—results from multiple, nested combinatorial explosions. Moreover, these observations, manipulations, and calculations would need to be repeated at many different grains, with many rounds of maximizations. For these reasons, a full analysis of complexes and their cause–effect structure can only be performed on idealized systems of a few units (Mayner et al., 2018). On the other hand, we can simplify the computation considerably by using various assumptions and approximations, as with the "cut one" approximation described by Mayner et al. (2018). In addition, while the number of relations vastly exceeds the number of units and distinctions (the upper bound for a system of n units is $2^{(2^n-1)}-1$), it can be determined analytically, and so can Φ be for a given set of distinctions. Developing tight approximations and bounded estimates of a system's integrated information is one of the main areas of ongoing research related to IIT (Tononi and Sporns, 2003).

Despite the infeasibility of an exhaustive calculation of the relevant quantities and structures for a realistic system, IIT already provides considerable explanatory and predictive power in many real-world situations, making it eminently testable (Melloni et al., 2008). A fundamental prediction is that Φ should be high in conscious states, such as wakefulness and dreaming, and low in unconscious states, such as dreamless sleep and anesthesia. This prediction has already found substantial support in human studies that have applied measures of complexity inspired by IIT to classify subjects as conscious versus unconscious successfully (Casarotto et al., 2016; Massimini et al., 2005; Melloni et al., 2008). IIT can also account mechanistically for the loss of consciousness in deep sleep and anesthesia (Pigorini et al., 2015). Furthermore, it can provide a principled account of why certain portions of the brain may constitute an ideal substrate of consciousness and others may not, why the borders of the main complex in the brain should be where they are, and why the units of the complex should have a particular grain (the one that yields a maximum of Φ). A stringent prediction is that the location of the main complex, as determined by the overall maximum of Φ within the brain, should correspond to its location as determined through clinical and experimental evidence. Another prediction that follows from the first principles is that constituents of the main complex can support conscious contents even if they are mostly inactive, but not if they are inactivated (Haun et al., 2016). Yet another prediction is that the complete inactivation of constituents of the main complex should lead to absolute agnosia (unawareness that anything is missing).

IIT further predicts that the quality of experience should be accounted for by the way the Φ-structure is composed, which in turn depends on the architecture of the substrate specifying it. This was demonstrated in a recent paper showing how the fundamental properties of spatial experiences—those that make space feel "extended"—can be accounted for by those of Φ-structures specified by 2D grids of units, such as those found in much of the posterior cortex (Haun et al., 2016). This prediction aligns with neurological evidence of their role in supporting the experience of space (Haun et al, 2016). Ongoing work aims to account for the quality of experienced time and that of experienced objects.

A related prediction is that changes in the strength of connections within the neural substrate of consciousness should be associated with changes in experience, even if neural activity does not change (Song et al., 2017). Also, similarities and dissimilarities in the structure of experience should be accounted for by similarities and dissimilarities among Φ-structures and Φ-folds specified by the neural substrate of consciousness.

More generally, further validation of IIT will depend on a systematic back-and-forth between phenomenology, theoretical inferences, and neuroscientific evidence.

In addition to empirical work to validate the theory, much remains to be done at the theoretical level. According to IIT, the meaning of an experience is its feeling—whether of spatial extendedness, temporal flow, or objects, to name a few ("the meaning is feeling"). This means that every meaning is identical to a sub-structure within a current Φ-structure—a content of experience—whether extrinsic inputs trigger it or occur spontaneously during a dream. Therefore, all meaning is ultimately intrinsic. Ongoing work aims to explain how intrinsic meanings can capture relevant features of causal processes in the environment. It will also be important to explain how intersubjectively validated knowledge can be obtained despite the intrinsic and partially idiosyncratic nature of meaning.

To the extent that the theory is validated through empirical evidence from the human brain, IIT can offer a plausible inferential basis for addressing several questions that depend on an explicit theory of consciousness.

As indicated in the section on phenomenal and functional equivalence and argued in ongoing work, one consequence of IIT is that typical computer architecture is unsuitable for supporting consciousness, regardless of whether their behavior may resemble ours. It can be inferred from IIT that animal species that may look and behave quite differently from us may be highly conscious as long as their brains have a compatible architecture.

As recently argued, IIT implies that we have true free will—that we have true alternatives, make true decisions, and truly cause. Because only what truly exists (intrinsically, for itself) can truly cause, we, rather than our neurons, cause our willed actions and are responsible for their consequences (Tononi et al., 2022).

Even so, there are many ways in which IIT may turn out to be inadequate or wrong. Are its axiomatic basis and the formulation of axioms as postulates sound and unique? In addition, most critically, can IIT survive the results of empirical investigations assessing the relationship between the quantity and quality of consciousness and its substrate in the brain?

A scientific theory of consciousness should account for experience, which is subjective, in objective terms (Ellia et al., 2021). Being conscious—having an experience—is understood to mean that "there is something it is like to be": something it is like to see a blue sky, hear the ocean roar, dream of a friend's face, imagine a melody flow, contemplate a choice, or reflect on the experience one is having.

In physical terms, IIT aims to account for phenomenal properties—the properties of experience. IIT's starting point is the experience rather than its behavioral, functional, or neural correlates. Furthermore, in IIT, "physical" is meant in a strictly operational sense—in terms of what can be observed and manipulated.

The starting point of IIT is the existence of an immediate and irrefutable experience. From this "zeroth" axiom, IIT sets out to identify the essential properties of consciousness—those that are immediate and irrefutably true of every conceivable experience. These are IIT's five axioms of phenomenal existence: every experience is for the experiencer (intrinsicality), specific (information), unitary (integration), definite (exclusion), and structured (composition).

The next step of IIT is to formulate the essential phenomenal properties (the axioms) in terms of corresponding physical properties (the postulates). This formulation is an "inference to a good explanation" and rests on basic assumptions such as realism, physicalism, and atomism: methodological guidelines of IIT. If IIT is correct, the substrate of consciousness, beyond having cause–effect power (existence), must satisfy all five essential phenomenal properties in physical terms: Its cause–effect power must be for itself (intrinsicality), specific (information), unitary (integration), definite (exclusion), and structured (composition).

On this basis, IIT proposes a fundamental explanatory identity: An experience is identical to the cause–effect structure unfolded from a maximal substrate (defined below). Accordingly, any experience's specific phenomenal properties must be explained well regarding the specific physical properties of the corresponding cause–effect structure, with no additional ingredients.

Based again on "inferences to a good explanation," IIT formulates the postulates in a mathematical framework that is, in principle, applicable to general models of interacting units. A mathematical framework is needed (1) to evaluate whether the theory is self-consistent and compatible with our overall knowledge about the world, (2) to make specific predictions regarding the quality and quantity of our experiences and their substrate within the brain, and (3) to extrapolate from our consciousness to infer the presence (or absence) and nature of consciousness in beings different from ourselves (Albantakis et al., 2023).

Ultimately, the theory should account for why our consciousness depends on certain portions of the world and their state, such as certain regions of the brain and not others, and why it fades during dreamless sleep, even though the brain remains active. It should also account for why an experience feels the way it does—why the sky feels extended, why a melody flows in time, and so on. Moreover, the theory makes several predictions concerning the presence and the quality of experience, some of which have been and are being tested empirically.

While the theory's main tenets have remained the same, its formal framework has been progressively refined and extended. Compared to IIT 1.0, 2.0, and 3.0, IIT 4.0 presents a more complete, self-consistent formulation and incorporates several recent advances. Chief among them is a more accurate formulation of the axioms as postulates and mathematical expressions, introducing an intrinsic difference (ID) measure that is uniquely consistent with IIT's postulates, and explicitly assessing causal relations.

After introducing IIT's axioms and postulates (Albantakis et al., 2023), what follows in its updated mathematical formalism? In the "Results and Discussion" section, we apply the mathematical framework of IIT to representative examples and discuss some of their implications. The article is meant to reference the theory's mathematical formalism, concisely demonstrate its internal consistency, and illustrate how a substrate's cause–effect structure is unfolded computationally.

3.3 From Phenomenal Axioms to Physical Postulates

3.3.1 Axioms of Phenomenal Existence

Traditionally, an axiom is a statement that is assumed true, cannot be inferred from any other statement, and can serve as a starting point for inferences. The existence of experience is the ultimate axiom—the starting point for everything, including logic and physics (Albantakis et al., 2023).

On this basis, IIT proceeds by considering whether experience—phenomenal existence—has some axiomatic or essential properties that are immediate and irrefutably true of every conceivable experience. Drawing on introspection and reason, IIT identifies the following five:

1. Intrinsicality experience is *intrinsic*: it exists *for itself.*
2. Information experience is *specific*: it is *this one.*
3. Integration experience is *unitary*: it is *a whole*, irreducible to separate experiences.
4. Exclusion experience is *definite*: it is *this whole.*
5. Composition experience is *structured*: it is composed of *distinctions* and the *relations* that bind them together, yielding a *phenomenal structure* that feels *the way it feels.*

IIT takes the above axioms to be complete: No further properties of experience are essential. Other properties that might be considered as candidates for axiomatic status include space (experience typically takes place in some spatial frame), time (an experience usually feels like it flows from a past to a future), change (an experience usually transitions or flows into another), subject–object distinction (an experience seems to involve both a subject and an object), and intentionality (experiences usually refer to something in the world, or at least to something other than the subject).

These include a sense of self (many experiences include a reference to one's body or even to one's narrative self), figure–ground segregation (an experience usually includes some object and some background, often bound to a time and a place), will (experience offers the opportunity for action), and affect (some mood often colors experience).

However, experiences lacking each candidate's properties are conceivable; conceiving them does not lead to self-contradiction or absurdity. They are also achievable, as revealed by altered states of consciousness reached through dreaming, meditative practices, or drugs.

3.3.2 Postulates of Physical Existence

To account for the many regularities of experience, it is a good inference to assume the existence of a world that persists independently of one's experience (*realism*). From within consciousness, we can operationally probe the physical existence of things outside of our experience through observations and manipulations. To be granted physical existence, something should have the power to "take a difference" (be affected) and "make a difference" (produce effects) in a reliable way (*physicalism*). IIT also assumes "operational reductionism," which means that, ideally, to establish what exists in physical terms, one would start from the smallest units that can take and make a difference so that nothing is left out (*atomism*) (Albantakis et al., 2023).

By characterizing physical existence operationally as cause–effect power, IIT can formulate the axioms of phenomenal existence as postulates of physical existence. This establishes the requirements for the *substrate of consciousness*, where "substrate" is meant operationally as a set of units that can be observed and manipulated. The substrate of consciousness can be characterized operationally by cause–effect *power*. Its units must *take and make a difference.*

Building from this "zeroth" postulate, IIT formulates the five axioms in terms of postulates of physical existence that must be satisfied by the substrate of consciousness:

- **Intrinsicality:** Its cause–effect power must be *intrinsic*. It must take and make a difference *within itself.*
- **Information:** Its cause–effect power must be specific. It must be in this state and select this cause–effect *state*. This state has maximal *intrinsic information* (*ii*), a measure of the difference a system takes or makes over itself for a given cause state and effect state.
- **Integration:** Its cause–effect power must be unitary. It must specify its cause–effect state as *a whole set* of units, irreducible

to separate subsets of units. Irreducibility is measured by *integrated information* (φ) over the substrate's minimum partition.

- **Exclusion:** Its cause–effect power must be *definite*. It must specify its cause–effect state as *this whole set* of units.
- **Composition:** Its cause–effect power must be structured. Subsets of its units must specify cause–effect states over subsets of units (distinctions) that can overlap with one another (relations), yielding a cause–effect *structure* or *Φ-structure* ("Phi-structure") that is *the way it is*.

Distinctions and relations, in turn, must also satisfy the postulates of physical existence: They must have cause–effect power within the substrate of consciousness in a specific, unitary, and definite way (they do not have components, being components themselves). They thus have an associated φ value. The Φ-structure unfolded from a complex corresponds to the quality of consciousness. The total of the φ values of the distinctions and relations that compose the Φ-structure measures its *structure-integrated information* Φ ("big Phi," "structure Phi") and corresponds to the quantity of consciousness.

According to IIT, the physical properties characterized by the postulates are necessary and sufficient for an entity to be conscious. They are necessary because they account for the essential properties of experience in that it is inconceivable for an experience to lack any of them. They are also sufficient because no additional property of experience is essential in the sense that it is conceivable for an experience to lack that property. Thus, no additional physical property is required to be a substrate of consciousness.

The postulates of IIT have been and are being applied to account for the location of the brain's consciousness substrate and its loss and recovery in physiological and pathological conditions.

3.4 Explanatory Identity between Experiences and Φ-Structures

Having determined the necessary and sufficient conditions for a substrate to support consciousness, IIT proposes an explanatory identity: Every property of an experience is accounted for in full by the physical properties of the Φ-structure unfolded from a maximal substrate (a complex) in its current state, with no further or "ad hoc" ingredients. That is, there must be a one-to-one correspondence between how the experience feels and how distinctions and relations are structured. Importantly, the identity is not a correspondence between the properties of two separate things. Instead, the identity should be understood in an explanatory sense: The intrinsic (subjective) feeling of the experience can be explained extrinsically (objectively, i.e., operationally or physically) in terms of cause–effect power.

The explanatory identity has been applied to account for how space feels (spatial extendedness) and which neural substrates may account for it.

We should generally assume that an explanation is good if it can account for a broad set of facts (*scope*), does so in a unified manner (*synthesis*), can explain facts precisely (*specificity*), is internally coherent (*self-consistency*), is coherent with our overall understanding of things (*system consistency*), is simpler than alternatives (*simplicity*), and can make testable predictions (*scientific validation*). For example, IIT 4.0 aims at expressing the postulates of intrinsicality, information, integration, and exclusion in a self-consistent manner when applied to systems, causal distinctions, and relations (see formulas).

We should assume that something exists (and persists) independently of our experience. This hypothesis is much better than solipsism, which explains and predicts nothing. Although IIT starts from our phenomenology, it aims to account for the many regularities of experience in a way that is fully consistent with realism.

3.5 Operational Physicalism

To assess what exists independently of our own experience, we should employ an operational criterion: systematically observe and manipulate a substrate's units and determine that they can indeed take and make a difference reliably. Doing so demonstrates a substrate's cause–effect power—the signature of physical existence.

Ideally, the cause–effect power is fully captured by a substrate's transition probability matrix TPM). This assumption is embedded in IIT's zeroth postulate.

3.6 Operational Reductionism ("Atomism")

Ideally, we should account for what exists physically in terms of the smallest units we can observe and manipulate, as captured by unit TPMs. Doing so would leave nothing unaccounted for. IIT assumes that, in principle, it should be possible to account for everything purely in terms of the cause–effect power—cause–effect power "down" to conditional probabilities between atomic units. Eventually, this would leave neither room nor need to assume intrinsic properties or laws.

3.7 Intrinsic Perspective

When accounting for experience itself in physical terms, existence should be evaluated from the intrinsic perspective of an entity—what exists for the entity itself—not from the perspective of an external observer. This assumption is embedded in IIT's postulate of intrinsicality and has several consequences. One is that, from the intrinsic perspective, the quality and quantity of existence must be observer independent and cannot be arbitrary. For instance, information in IIT must be relative to the specific state the entity is in, rather than an average of states as assessed by an external observer. Similarly, it should be evaluated based on the uniform distribution of possible states, as captured by the entity's TPM, rather than on an observed probability distribution. Units outside the entity should be treated as background conditions that do not contribute directly to what the system is. The intrinsic perspective also imposes a tension between expansion and dilution (Barbosa et al., 2020, 2021). From the intrinsic perspective of a system (or a mechanism within the system), having more units may increase its informativeness (cause–effect power measured as deviation from chance), while at the same time diluting its selectivity (ability to concentrate cause–effect power over a specific state).

3.8 Overview of IIT's Framework

IIT 4.0 aims to provide a formal framework for characterizing the cause–effect structure of a substrate in a given state by expressing IIT's postulates in mathematical terms. In line with operational physicalism, we characterize a substrate by the transition probability function of its constituting units.

On this basis, the IIT formalism first identifies sets of units that fulfill all required properties of a substrate of consciousness according to the postulates of physical existence. First, for a candidate system, we determine a maximal cause–effect state based on the intrinsic information (*ii*) that the system in its current state specifies over its possible cause states and effect states. We then determine the maximal substrate based on the integrated information (φ_s, "system Phi") of the maximal cause–effect state. To qualify as a substrate of consciousness, a candidate system must specify a maximum of integrated information (φ_s^*) compared to all competing candidate systems with overlapping units.

The second part of the IIT formalism *unfolds* the cause–effect structure specified by a maximal substrate in its current state, its Φ-structure. To that end, we determine the distinctions and relations specified by the substrate's subsets according to the postulates of physical existence. Distinctions are cause–effect states specified over subsets of substrate units (*purviews*) by subsets of substrate units (*mechanisms*). Relations are congruent overlaps among the cause and effect states of distinctions. Distinctions and relations are also characterized by their integrated information (φ_d, φ_r). The Φ-structure they compose corresponds to the quality of the experience specified by the substrate; the sum of their $a_{d/r}$ values corresponds to its quantity (Φ).

While IIT must still be considered a work in progress, having undergone successive refinements, IIT 4.0 is the first formulation of IIT that strives to characterize Φ-structures completely and to do so based on measures that satisfy the postulates uniquely. IIT considers physical existence synonymous with having cause–effect power, the ability to take and make a difference.

Consequently, a substrate U with state space Ω_U is operationally defined by its potential interactions, assessed in conditional probabilities (physicalism). We denote the complete transition probability function of a substrate U over a system update as

$$As\, u \rightarrow \bar{u}$$

$$\mathcal{T}_U \equiv p(\bar{u}|u), u, \bar{u} \in \Omega_U \tag{3.1}$$

A substrate in IIT can be described as a stochastic system $U = \{U_1, U_2, U_n\}$ of n interacting units with state space.

$$\Omega_U = \Pi_i \Omega_{U_j} \tag{3.2}$$

In addition, the current state $u \in \Omega_U$.

We assume that the system updates in discrete steps, that the state space Ω_U is finite, and that the individual random variables $U_{ri} \in U$ are conditionally independent of each other given the preceding state of U:

$$p(\bar{u} \mid u) = \prod_{i=1}^{n} p(\bar{u}_i \mid u). \tag{3.3}$$

3.9 Implementing the Postulates

In what follows, our goal is to evaluate whether a hypothetical substrate (also called "system") satisfies all the postulates of IIT. To that end, we must verify whether the system has cause–effect power that is intrinsic, specific, integrated, definite, and structured.

3.9.1 Existence

According to IIT, existence, understood as cause–effect power, requires the capacity to both make *and* make a difference. Based on a complete description of the system in terms of interventional conditional probabilities $\mathcal{T}_U$, cause–effect power can be quantified as causal *informativeness*.

3.9.2 Intrinsicality

Building upon the existence postulate, the intrinsicality postulate further requires that a system exerts cause–effect power *within itself.* In general, the systems we want to evaluate are open systems

$S \subseteq U$ that are part of a larger "universe" U. From the intrinsic perspective of a system S, the set of the remaining units, W, merely acts as background conditions that do not contribute directly to cause–effect power. To enforce this, we causally marginalize the background units, conditional on the universe's current state, rendering them causally inert (see Section 3.11 for details).

3.9.3 Information

The information postulate requires a system's cause–effect power to be specific: The system in its current state must select a specific cause–effect state for its units. Based on the *principle of maximal existence*, this is the state for which intrinsic information is maximal—the *maximal cause–effect state*. *Intrinsic information* (*ii*) measures the difference a system takes or makes over itself for a given cause and effect state as the product of informativeness and selectivity. As we have seen (existence), *informativeness* quantifies the causal power of a system in its current state as a reduction of uncertainty concerning chance. *Selectivity* measures how much cause–effect power is concentrated over that specific cause or effect state. Uncertain uncertainty in the cause or effect state reduces selectivity concerning other potential cause and effect states.

3.9.4 Integration

By the integration postulate, it is not sufficient for a system to have cause–effect power within itself and select a specific cause–effect state; it must also specify its maximal cause–effect state in an irreducible way. This can be assessed by *partitioning* the set of units that constitute the system into separate parts. The system-integrated information (i_s) then quantifies how much the intrinsic information specified by the maximal state is reduced due to the partition. Integrated information is evaluated over the partition that makes the least difference, the *minimum partition* (MIP), by the *principle of minimal existence*. Integrated information is highly sensitive to the presence of *fault lines*—partitions that separate parts of a system that interact weakly or directionally.

3.9.5 Exclusion

Many overlapping sets of units may have a positive value of integrated information (φ_S). However, the exclusion postulate requires that the substrate of consciousness must be constituted of a definite set of units, neither less nor more. Moreover, units, updates, and states must have a definite grain. Operationally, the exclusion postulate is enforced by selecting the set of units that maximizes integrated information over itself (φ_s^*), based again on the principle of maximal existence. That set of units is called a *maximal substrate* or *complex*. Over a universal substrate, sets of units for which integrated information is maximal compared to all competing candidate systems with overlapping units can be assessed recursively (by identifying the first complex, then the second complex, and so on).

3.9.6 Composition

Once a complex has been identified, composition requires that we characterize its *cause–effect structure by considering all its subsets and fully unfolding its cause–effect* power.

Usually, causal models are conceived in holistic terms, as state transitions of the system as a whole, or in reductionist terms, as a description of the individual units of the system and their interactions. However, to account for the structure of experience, considering only the cause–effect power of the individual units or the system, as a whole would be insufficient. Instead, by the composition postulate, we have to evaluate the system's cause–effect structure by considering the cause–effect power of its subsets and their causal relations.

In the following, we will provide a formal account of the IIT analysis. The first part demonstrates how to identify complexes. This requires that we (a) determine the cause–effect of the state of a system in its current state, (b) evaluate the system-integrated information (φ_S) over that cause–effect state, and (c) search iteratively for maxima of integrated information (φ_S^*) within a universe. The second part describes how the postulates of IIT are applied to unfold the cause–effect structure of a complex.

This requires we identify the causal distinctions specified by subsets of units within the complex and the causal relations determined by how distinctions overlap, yielding the system's Φ-structure and structure-integrated information (Φ).

3.10 Ontological Principles of IIT

3.10.1 Principle of Being

The *principle of being* states that *to be is to have cause–effect power*. In other words, in physical and operational terms, to exist requires taking and making a difference. The principle is closely related to the so-called Eleatic principle, as found in Plato's Sophist dialogue (Cooper, 1997): "I say that everything possessing any kind of power, either to do anything to something else or to be affected to the smallest extent by the slightest cause, even on a single occasion, has real existence: for I claim that entities are nothing else but power." A similar principle can be found in the work of the Buddhist philosopher Dharmakīrti: "Whatever has causal powers, that exists" (Tillemans, 2021). Note that the Eleatic principle is enunciated as a disjunction (either to do something... *or* to be affected...). In contrast, IIT's principle of being is presented as a conjunction (take *and* make a difference).

3.10.2 Principle of Maximal Existence

The *principle of maximal existence* states that what exists is what exists the most when it comes to a requirement for existence. The principle is offered by IIT as a good explanation for why the system state specified by the complex and the cause–effect states specified by its mechanisms are what they are. It also provides a criterion for determining the set of units constituting a complex—the one with maximally irreducible cause–effect power—for determining the subsets of units constituting the distinctions and relations that compose its cause–effect structure and for determining the units' grain. To exemplify, consider a set of candidate complexes overlapping over the same substrate. By the postulates of integration and exclusion, a complex must be both unitary and definite. By the maximal existence principle, the complex should be the one that lays the greatest claim to existence as *one* entity, as measured by system-integrated information (φ_S). For the same reason, candidate complexes that overlap over the same substrate but have a lower value of φ_S are excluded.

In other words, if having maximal φ_S is the reason for assigning existence as a unitary complex to a set of units, it is also the reason to exclude from existence any overlapping set not having maximal φ_S.

3.10.3 Principle of Minimal Existence

Another key principle of IIT is the *principle of minimal existence*, which complements maximal existence. The principle states that when it comes to a requirement for existence, *nothing exists more than the least it exists.* IIT offers the principle as a good explanation for why a system can only exist as one system if it is irreducible; its degree of irreducibility should be assessed over the partition across which it is least irreducible (the MIP). Similarly, a distinction within a system can only exist as one distinction to the extent that it is irreducible, and its degree of irreducibility should be assessed over the partition across which it is least irreducible. Moreover, a set of units can only exist as a system or as a distinction within the system if it specifies both a fundamental cause and an irreducible effect, so its degree of irreducibility should be the minimum between the irreducibility on the cause side and the effect side.

3.11 Identifying Substrates of Consciousness

Our starting point is a substrate U in its current state u with TPM $\mathcal{T}_U$. We consider any subset $s \subseteq u$ as a possible complex and refer to a set of units $S \subseteq U$ as a candidate system. (Note that s and u are sets of tuples containing both the units and their states.)

By the intrinsicality postulate, the units $W = U/S$ are background conditions and do not contribute directly to the cause–effect power of the system. They are causally marginalized to discount the contribution of background units, conditional on the universe's current state. This means the background units are marginalized based on a uniform marginal distribution, updated by conditioning. The process is repeated separately for each unit in the system, and they are then combined using a product (in line with conditional independence), eliminating any residual correlations due to the background units. Accordingly, we obtain two TPMs $\mathcal{T}_e$ and $\mathcal{T}_c$ (for evaluating effects and causes, respectively) for the candidate system *S*. For evaluating effects, the state of the background units is fully determined by the universe's current state. The corresponding TPM, $\mathcal{T}_e$, is used to identify the effect of the current state:

$$\mathcal{T}_e = \mathcal{T}_e(\mathcal{T}_{U,u,w}) \equiv p_e(\bar{s} \mid s) = p(\bar{s} \mid s, w), \quad s, \bar{s} \in \Omega_s \tag{3.4}$$

where $w = u/s$. For evaluating causes, knowledge of the current state is used to compute the probability distribution over potential prior states of the background units, which is not necessarily uniform or deterministic. The corresponding TPM $\mathcal{T}_c$ is used to evaluate the cause of the current state:

$$\mathcal{T}_c = \mathcal{T}_c(\mathcal{T}_{U,u,w}) \equiv p_c(s \mid \bar{s}) = \prod_{i=1}^{|S|} \sum_{\bar{w}} p(s_i \mid \bar{s}, \bar{w}) \left(\frac{\Sigma_{\hat{s}} p(u \mid \hat{s}, \bar{w})}{\Sigma_{\hat{u}} p(u \mid \hat{u})} \right), \quad s, \bar{s} \in \Omega_S. \tag{3.5}$$

In both TPMs, the background units *W* are rendered causally inert so that causes and effects are evaluated from the intrinsic perspective of the system.

The intrinsic information $ii_{c/e}$ is a measure of the intrinsic cause or effect power exerted by a system *S* in its current state over itself by selecting a specific cause or effect state $\bar{s}$. The cause–effect state for which intrinsic information (ii_c and ic_e) is maximal is called the maximal cause–effect state:

$$S' = \{S'_c, S'_e\} \tag{3.6}$$

The integrated information φ_S measures the irreducibility of a cause–effect state, compared to the directional system partition θ' that affects the maximal cause–effect state the least (MIP). Systems for which integrated information is maximal (φ_S^*) compared to any competing candidate system with overlapping units are called maximal substrates or complexes.

The IIT 4.0 formalism to measure a system's integrated information φ_S and to identify maximal substrates was first presented by Marshall et al. (2023).

Given a causal model with corresponding TPMs $\mathcal{T}_e$ and $\mathcal{T}_c$, we wish to identify the maximal cause–effect state specified by a system in its current state over itself and to quantify the causal power with which it does so. In this way, we quantify the cause–effect power of a system from its intrinsic perspective rather than from the perspective of an outside observer.

3.12 System Intrinsic Information

Intrinsic information $ii(S,\bar{S})$ measures the causal power of a system S over itself, for its current state s, over a specific cause or effect state $\bar{s}$. Intrinsic information depends on interventional conditional probabilities and unconstrained probabilities of cause or effect states and is the product of selectivity and informativeness. On the effect side, intrinsic effect information of the current states over a possible effect state $\bar{s}$ is defined as:

$$ii_e(s,\bar{s}) = p_e(\bar{s}\mid s)\log\left(\frac{p_e(\bar{s}\mid s)}{p_e(\bar{s})}\right), \tag{3.7}$$

where $p_e(\bar{s}\mid s)$ is the interventional conditional probability that the current states produce the effect state $\bar{s}$, as indicated by T_e.

$$p_e(\bar{s}) = |\Omega_S|^{-1}\sum_{s\in\Omega_S} p_e(\bar{s}\mid s), \tag{3.8}$$

The interventional unconstrained probability $p_e(\bar{s})$ is defined as the marginal probability of $\bar{s}$, averaged across all possible current states of S with equal probability (where $|\Omega_S|$ denotes the cardinality of the state space Ω_S).

On the cause side, the intrinsic cause information ii_c of the current states over a possible cause state $\bar{s}$ is defined as:

$$ii_c(s,\bar{s}) = p_c^{\leftarrow}(\bar{s}\mid s)\log\left(\frac{p_c(s\mid \bar{s})}{p_c(s)}\right), \tag{3.9}$$

where $p_c(s,\bar{s})$ is the interventional conditional probability that the cause state $\bar{s}$ produces the current state, as indicated by $\mathcal{T}_c$, and the interventional unconstrained probability is again defined as the marginal probability of s, averaged across all possible cause states of S with equal probability,

$$p_c(s) = |\Omega_S|^{-1}\sum_{\bar{s}\in\Omega_S} p_c(s\mid \bar{s}). \tag{3.10}$$

Moreover, $p_c^{\leftarrow}(\bar{s} \mid s)$ is the interventional conditional probability that the current state's $s \in \Omega_S$ was produced by $\bar{s}$; it is derived from $\mathcal{T}_c$ using Bayes' rule, where we again assign a uniform prior to the possible cause states $\bar{s}$,

$$p_c^{\leftarrow}(\bar{s} \mid s) = \frac{p_c(s \mid \bar{s}) \cdot |\Omega_S|^{-1}}{p_c(s)} = \frac{p_c(s \mid \bar{s})}{\sum_{\hat{s} \in \Omega_S} p_c(s \mid \hat{s})}. \quad (3.11)$$

3.13 Informativeness (Over Chance)

The logarithmic term (in base 2 throughout) is called *informativeness.* Note that informativeness is expressed in terms of "forward" probabilities (probability of a subsequent state given the current state) for both ii_e and ic_e. However, ii_e evaluates the increase in the probability of the effect state due to the current state based on $\mathcal{T}_e$, while ii_c evaluates the increase in the probability of the current state due to the cause state based on $\mathcal{T}_c$.

Informativeness is additive over the number of units: If a system specifies a cause or effect state with probability $p = 1$, its causal power increases additively with the number of units whose states it fully specifies (*expansion*), given that the chance probability of all states decreases exponentially.

3.14 Selectivity (Over States)

From the intrinsic perspective of a system, cause–effect power over a specific cause or effect state depends not only on the deviation from chance it produces but also on how its probability is concentrated in that state rather than being diluted over other states. This is measured by the *selectivity* term in front of the logarithmic term, corresponding to the conditional probability of that specific cause or effect state. Note that here, on the cause side, we use the "backward" probability (probability of a prior state given the current state) obtained through Bayes' rule, while we use the "forward" probability of the effect state $\bar{s}$ given s on the effect side. Selectivity means that if $p < 1$, the system's causal power becomes subadditive (*dilution*).

For example, as shown by Barbosa et al. (2021), if an unconstrained unit is added to a fully specified unit, intrinsic information does not just stay the same but decreases exponentially. From the intrinsic perspective of the system, the informativeness of a specific cause or effect state is diluted because it is spread over multiple possible states. Yet, the system must select only one state.

Altogether, taking the product of informativeness and selectivity leads to a tension between expansion and dilution: A larger system will tend to have higher informativeness than a smaller system because it will deviate more from chance, but it will also tend to have lower selectivity because it will have a larger repertoire of states to select from.

Because of the selectivity term, indeterminism and degeneracy reduce intrinsic information. As shown by Marshall et al. (2023), indeterminism decreases the probability of the selected effect state because it implies that the same state can lead to multiple states. In turn, degeneracy decreases the probability of the selected cause state because it implies that multiple states can lead to the same state, even in a deterministic system.

The intrinsic information *ii* is quantified in units of *intrinsic bits*, or *ibits*, to distinguish it from standard information-theoretic measures (typically additive). Formally, the *ibit* corresponds to a point-wise information value (measured in bits) weighted by a probability.

3.15 Maximal Cause–Effect State

Taking the product of informativeness and selectivity on the system's cause and effect sides captures the postulates of existence (taking and making a difference) and intrinsicality (taking and making a difference over itself) for each possible cause or effect state, as measured by intrinsic information. However, the information postulate further requires that the system select a specific cause or effect state. The principle of maximal existence determines the selection: The cause or effect specified by the system should be the one that maximizes intrinsic information. On the effect side (and similarly for the cause side),

$$s'_e(\mathcal{T}_e, s) = \underset{\bar{s}\in\Omega_S}{\operatorname{argmax}}\ ii_e(s, \bar{s})$$
$$= \underset{\bar{s}\in\Omega_S}{\operatorname{argmax}}\ p_e(\bar{s} \mid s)\log\left(\frac{p_e(\bar{s} \mid s)}{p_e(\bar{s})}\right). \quad (3.12)$$

The system's intrinsic effect information is the value of ii_e for its maximal effect state:

$$ii_e(\mathcal{T}_e, s) := ii_e(s, s'_e) = \max_{\bar{s}\in\Omega_S} p_e(\bar{s} \mid s)\log\left(\frac{p_e(\bar{s} \mid s)}{p_e(\bar{s})}\right). \quad (3.13)$$

We have made the dependency of s' and ii_e on $\mathcal{T}_e$. For intrinsic information to properly assess the cause–effect power, all probabilities must be derived from the system's interventional transition probability function while imposing a uniform prior distribution over all possible system states. If $ii_e(\mathcal{T}_e, s) = 0$, the system S in states has no causal power. This is the case if and only if $p_e(\bar{s} \mid s) = p_e(\bar{s})$ for every $\bar{s}$. (Likewise, it can be shown that $ii_c(\mathcal{T}_c, s) = 0$ if and only if $p_c(s \mid \bar{s}) = p_c(s)$ for every $\bar{s}$.) It is worthwhile to mention that when $ii_e(\mathcal{T}_e, s) \neq 0$, the system state always increases the probability of the intrinsic effect state compared to chance. Similarly, when $ii_c(\mathcal{T}_c, s) \neq 0$, the intrinsic cause state increases the probability of the system state. Note also that a system's intrinsic cause–effect state does not necessarily correspond to the actual cause and effect states (what happened before/will happen after) in the system's dynamical evolution, which typically also depends on extrinsic influences. (For an account of actual causation according to the causal principles of IIT, see Albantakis et al. (2019).)

3.16 Intrinsic Difference

Because consciousness is the way it is, the formulation of its properties in physical, operational terms should be unique and based on quantities that uniquely satisfy the postulates. Intrinsic information is formulated as a product of selectivity and informativeness based on the ID (Barbosa et al., 2020).

This is a measure of the difference between two probability distributions that uniquely satisfy three properties (causality, intrinsicality, and specificity) that align with the postulates of IIT (but also have independent justification):

1. **Causality (existence):** The measure is zero if and only if the system does not make a difference.
2. **Intrinsicality (intrinsicality):** The measure increases if the system is expanded without noise (expansion) and decreases if the system is expanded without signal (dilution).
3. **Specificity (information):** The measure reflects the cause–effect power of a specific state over a specific cause and effect state.

The properties uniquely satisfied by the ID are described in a general mathematical context, and some additional discussion is provided by Albantakis et al. (2023).

Note that, on the effect side, ice is formally equivalent to the ID between the constrained and unconstrained effect repertoire $p_e(\bar{s})$. On the cause side, applying Bayes' rule to compute the selectivity term means that it is not strictly equivalent to the ID between two probability distributions. However, analogously to the effect formulation, it is defined as the product of selectivity and informativeness of causes.

3.17 Directional System Partitions

To that end, we define a set of *directional* system partitions $\Theta(S)$ that divide S into $k \geq 2$ parts $\{S^{(i)}\}_{i=1}^{k}$, such that

$$S^{(i)} \neq \phi, S^{(i)} \cap S^{(j)} = \phi, \text{ and } \bigcup_{i=1}^{k} S^{(i)} = S. \tag{3.14}$$

In other words, each part $S^{(i)}$ must contain at least one unit, there must be no overlap between any two parts $S^{(i)}$ and $S^{(j)}$, and every unit of the system must appear in exactly one part. For each part $S^{(i)}$, the partition removes the causal connections of that part with the rest of the system in a directional manner: either the part's inputs, outputs, or both are replaced by independent "noise" (they are "cut" by the partition in the sense that their causal powers are substituted by chance). Directional partitions are necessary because, from the intrinsic perspective of a system, a subset of units that cannot affect the rest of the system or cannot be affected by it cannot truly be a part of the system. In other words, to be a part of a system, a subset of units must be able to interact with the rest of the system in both directions (cause and effect).

A partition $\theta \in \Theta(S)$ thus has the form

$$\theta = \{S^{(1)}_{\delta_1}, S^{(2)}_{\delta_2}, \ldots, S^{(k)}_{\delta_k}\}, \tag{3.15}$$

where $\delta_i \in \{\leftarrow, \rightarrow, \leftrightarrow\}$ indicates whether the inputs ($\leftarrow$), outputs ($\rightarrow$), or both ($\leftrightarrow$) are cut for a given part. For each part $S^{(i)}$, we can then identify a set of units $X^{(i)} \subseteq S$ whose inputs to $S^{(i)}$ have been cut by the partition, and the complementary set $Y^{(i)} = S/X^{(i)}$ whose inputs to $S^{(i)}$ are left intact.

$$X^{(i)} = \begin{cases} S \setminus S^{(i)} & \text{if } \delta_i \in \{\leftarrow, \leftrightarrow\} \\ \bigcup\limits_{\substack{j \neq i: \\ \delta_j \in \{\rightarrow, \leftrightarrow\}}} S^{(j)} & \text{if } \delta_i \in \{\rightarrow\}. \end{cases} \tag{3.16}$$

In the first case, if $\delta_i \in \{\leftarrow, \leftrightarrow\}$, all inputs to $S^{(i)}$ from $S/S^{(i)}$ are cut. In the second case, if $\delta_i \in \{\rightarrow\}$, there may still be inputs to $S^{(i)}$ that are cut, which correspond to the outputs of all $S^{(j)}$ with $\delta_j \in \{\rightarrow, \leftrightarrow\}$.

Given a partition $\theta \in \Theta(S)$, we define partitioned transition probability matrices $\mathcal{T}_e^{\theta}$ and $\mathcal{T}_c^{\theta}$, in which all connections affected by the partition are "noised." This is done by combining the independent contributions of each unit $S_j \in S$ in line with the conditional independence assumption. For the effect of TPM (and analogously for the cause),

$$\mathcal{T}_e^{\theta} \equiv p_e^{\theta}(\bar{s} \mid s) = \prod_{j=1}^{n} p_e^{\theta}(\bar{s}_j \mid s), \bar{s}, s \in \Omega_S, \tag{3.17}$$

where the partitioned probability of a unit $S_j \in S^{(i)}$ is defined as

$$p_e^{\theta}(\bar{s}_j \mid s) = \left|\Omega_{X^{(i)}}\right|^{-1} \sum_{x^{(i)} \in \Omega_{X^{(i)}}} p_e(\bar{s}_j \mid x^{(i)}, y^{(i)}), \tag{3.18}$$

In addition, $y^{(i)} = s/x^{(i)}$. This means that all connections to unit S_j affected by the partition are *causally marginalized* (replaced by independent noise).

3.18 System-Integrated Information (φ_s)

The integrated effect information φ_e measures how much the partition $\theta \in \Theta_S$ reduces the probability with which a system S in state $s \in \Omega_S$ specifies its effect state s'_e:

$$\varphi_e(\mathcal{T}_e, s, \theta) = p_e(s'_e \mid s) \left| \log \left(\frac{p_e(s'_e \mid s)}{p_e^{\theta}(s'_e \mid s)} \right) \right|_+ . \tag{3.19}$$

Note that φ_e has the same form as the intrinsic information $ii_e(s, \bar{s})$, with the partitioned effect probability taking the place of the unconstrained (marginal) probability. Here, $|.|_+$ represents the positive part operator, which sets the negative values to zero. This ensures that the system as a whole raises the probability of the effect state compared to the partitioned probability. Likewise, the integrated cause information φ_c is defined as

$$\varphi_c(T_c, s, \theta) = p_c^{\leftarrow}(s'_c \mid s) \left| \log \left(\frac{p_c(s \mid s'_c)}{p_c^{\theta}(s \mid s'_c)} \right) \right|_+ . \tag{3.20}$$

By the principle of maximal existence, if two or more cause–effect states are tied for maximal intrinsic information, the system specifies the one that maximizes $\varphi_{c/e}$. By the zeroth postulate, existence requires cause and effect power, and the integration postulate requires that its cause–effect power be irreducible. By the principle of minimal existence, then, system-integrated information for a given partition is the minimum of its irreducibility on the cause and effect sides:

$$\varphi_s(\mathcal{T}_e, \mathcal{T}_c, s, \theta) = \min\{\varphi_c(\mathcal{T}_c, s, \theta), \varphi_e(\mathcal{T}_e, s, \theta)\}. \tag{3.21}$$

Moreover, again by the principle of minimal existence, the integrated information of a system is given by its irreducibility over its MIP $\theta' \in \Theta_S$, such that

$$\varphi_s(\mathcal{T}_e, \mathcal{T}_c, s) := \varphi_s(\mathcal{T}_e, \mathcal{T}_c, s, \theta'). \tag{3.22}$$

The MIP is defined as the partition $\theta \in \Theta_S$ that minimizes the system's integrated information relative to the maximum possible value it could take for arbitrary TPMs T_e', T_c' over the units of system S.

$$\theta' = \underset{\theta \in \Theta(S)}{\operatorname{argmin}} \frac{\varphi_s(\mathcal{T}_e, \mathcal{T}_c, s, \theta)}{\max\limits_{T_e', T_c'} \varphi_s(\mathcal{T}_e', \mathcal{T}_c', s, \theta)}. \tag{3.23}$$

Accordingly, the system is reducible if at least one partition $\theta \in \Theta_S$ makes no difference to the cause or effect probability. The normalization term in the denominator of Eq. 3.23 ensures that $\varphi_s(\mathcal{T}_e, \mathcal{T}_c, s)$ is evaluated fairly over a system's fault lines by assessing integration relative to its maximum possible value over a given partition. Using the *relative* integrated information quantifies the strength of the interactions between parts in a way that does not depend on the number of parts and their size. As proven by Marshall et al. (2023), the maximal value of $\varphi_s(\mathcal{T}_e, \mathcal{T}_c, s, \theta)$ for a given partition θ is the normalization

$$\max_{T_e', T_c'} \varphi_s(T_e', T_c', s, \theta) = \sum_{i=1}^{k} |S^{(i)}||X^{(i)}| \tag{3.24}$$

The factor that corresponds to the maximal possible number of "connections" (pairwise interactions) affected by θ. For example, as shown by Marshall et al. (2023), the MIP will correctly identify the faultline dividing a system into two large subsets of units linked through a few interconnected units (a "bridge"), rather than defaulting to partitions between individual units and the rest of the system. Once the MIP has been identified, the integrated information across it is an *absolute* quantity, quantifying the loss of intrinsic information due to cutting the MIP of the system.

In general, multiple candidate systems with overlapping units may have positive values of $\varphi_s(\mathcal{T}_e, \mathcal{T}_c, s)$. By the exclusion postulate, the substrate of consciousness must be definite; that is, it must comprise a definite set of units. But which one? Once again, we employ the principle of maximal existence: Among candidate systems competing over the same substrate concerning an essential requirement for existence, in this case, irreducibility, the one that exists is the one that exists the most. Accordingly, the maximal substrate, or complex, is the candidate substrate with the maximum value of system-integrated information (φ_s^*), and overlapping substrates with lower φ_s are thus excluded from existence. We are determining maximal substrates recursively. Here, we refer the reader to the complete paper by Albantakis et al. (2023).

3.19 Results and Discussion

In this section, Albantakis et al. (2023) apply the mathematical framework of IIT 4.0 to several example systems. The goal is to illustrate three critical implications of IIT's postulates:

1. **Consciousness and connectivity:** How units interact determines whether a substrate can support an Φ-structure of high Φ.
2. **Consciousness and activity:** How changes in the state of a substrate's units change Φ-structures.
3. **Consciousness and functional equivalence:** How functionally equivalent substrates may not be equivalent in terms of their Φ-structures, and thus in terms of consciousness.

The following examples will feature very simple networks constituted of binary units $U_i \in U$ with $\Omega_{U_i} = \{-1,1\}$ for all U_i and a logistic (sigmoidal) activation function

$$p(U_{i,t} = 1 \mid u_{t-1}) = \frac{1}{1+\exp\left(-k\sum_{j=1}^{n} w_{j,i}u_{j,t-1}\right)}, \tag{3.25}$$

where $k > 0$.

In the above equations, the parameter k defines the slope of the logistic function and allows one to adjust the amount of noise or determinism in the activation function (higher values signify a steeper slope and, thus, more determinism). The units U_i can thus be viewed as noisy linear threshold units with weighted connections, where k determines the connection strength. Please note that this chapter on the mathematics of consciousness is inspired by Albantakis et al. (2023).

The bottom line is that one needs to collect all the information based on various experiences and even imaginative experiences and integrate (total summation) all of it to answer the question of the emergence of consciousness. The information is too huge for normal computations. The over 10 billion neurons in the brain can easily handle such a huge integration or summation of all information.

References and Further Readings

Albantakis, L. (2020). Integrated information theory. In: Overgaard, M., Mogensen, J., and Kirkeby-Hinrup, A. (Eds), *Beyond Neural Correlates of Consciousness*. Routledge, pp. 87–103.

Albantakis, L., and Tononi, G. (2015). The intrinsic cause-effect power of discrete dynamical systems: From elementary cellular automata to adapting animats. *Entropy*, **17**(8), 5472–5502.

Albantakis, L., and Tononi, G. (2019). Causal composition: Structural differences among dynamically equivalent systems. *Entropy*, **21**(10), 989.

Albantakis, L., Barbosa, L., Findlay, G., Grasso, M., Haun, A. M., Marshall, W., et al. (2023). Integrated information theory (IIT) 4.0: Formulating the properties of phenomenal existence in physical terms. *PLoS Computational Biology*, **19**(10), e1011465.

Albantakis, L., Hintze, A., Koch, C., Adami, C., and Tononi, G. (2014). Evolution of integrated causal structures in animats exposed to environments of increasing complexity. *PloS Computational Biology*, **10**(12), e1003966.

Albantakis, L., Marshall, W., Hoel, E., and Tononi, G. (2019). What caused what? A quantitative account of actual causation using dynamical causal networks. *Entropy*, **21**(5), 459.

Albantakis, L., Prentner, R., and Durham, I. (2023). Measuring the integrated information of a quantum mechanism. *Entropy*, 25.

Ay, N., and Polani, D. (2008). Information flows in causal networks. *Advances in Complex Systems*, **11**(01), 17–41.

Balduzzi, D., and Tononi, G. (2008). Integrated information in discrete dynamical systems: Motivation and theoretical framework. *PLoS Computational Biology*, **4**(6), e1000091.

Balduzzi, D., and Tononi, G. (2009). Qualia: The geometry of integrated information. *PLoS Computational Biology*, **5**(8), e1000462.

Barbosa, L. S., Marshall, W., Albantakis, L., and Tononi, G. (2021). Mechanism integrated information. *Entropy*, **23**(3), 362.

Barbosa, L. S., Marshall, W., Streipert, S., Albantakis, L., and Tononi, G. (2020). A measure for intrinsic information. *Scientific Reports*, **10**(1), 18803.

Barrett, A. B., and Mediano, P. A. M. (2019). The phi measure of integrated information is not well defined for general physical systems. *Journal of Consciousness Studies*, **26**(1–2), 11–20.

Boly, M., Massimini, M., Tsuchiya, N., Postle, B. R., Koch, C., and Tononi, G. (2017). Are the neural correlates of consciousness in the front or in the back of the cerebral cortex? Clinical and neuroimaging evidence. *Journal of Neuroscience*, **37**(40), 9603–9613.

Brooks, M. (2022). Roger Penrose: "Consciousness must be beyond computable physics." *NewScientist*, 14 November 2022.

Carroll, S. (2021). Consciousness and the laws of physics. *Journal of Consciousness Studies*, **28**(9), 16–31.

Casarotto, S., Comanducci, A., Rosanova, M., Sarasso, S., Fecchio, M., Napolitani, M., et al. (2016). Stratification of unresponsive patients by an independently validated index of brain complexity. *Annals of Neurology*, **80**(5), 718–729.

Chalmers, D. (2010). *The Character of Consciousness, Philosophy of Mind*, Oxford University Press.

Cooper, J. (1997). *Plato: Complete Works*. Hackett.

Dunai, T. J., and Finlay, S. M. (2009). Reporting of cosmogenic nuclide data for exposure age and erosion rate determinations. *Quaternary Geochronology*, **4**(6), 437–440.

Ellia, F., Hendren, J., Grasso, M., Kozma, C., Mindt, G., Lang, J. P., et al. (2021). Consciousness and the fallacy of misplaced objectivity. *Neuroscience of Consciousness*, **21**(2), 1–12.

Erhard, M., Krenn, M., and Zeilinger, A. (2020). Advances in high-dimensional quantum entanglement. *Nature Review Physics*, **2**, 365–381.

Esteban, F. J., Galadí, J. A., Langa, J. A., Portillo, J. R., and Soler-Toscano, F. (2018). Informational structures: A dynamical system approach for integrated information. *PLOS Computational Biology*, **14**(9), e1006154.

Findlay, G., Marshall, W., Albantakis, L., Mainer. W. G. P., Koch, C., and Tononi, G. Dissociating intelligence from consciousness in artificial systems: Implications of integrated information theory. In: *Proceedings of the 2019 Towards Conscious AI Systems Symposium*, AAAI SSS19; 2019 and forthcoming.

Foster, N. N., Barry, J., Korobkova, L., Garcia, L., Gao, L., Becerra, M., et al. (2021). The mouse cortical–basal ganglia–thalamic network. *Nature*, **598**(7879), 188–194.

Froes, M. M., Correia, A. H. P., Garcia-Abreu, J., Spray, D. C., Campos De Carvalho, A. C., and Neto, V. M. (1999). Gap-junctional coupling between neurons and astrocytes in primary central nervous system cultures. *Proceedings of the National Academy of Sciences*, **96**(13), 7541–7546.

Gamow, G. (1946). Expanding universe and the origin of elements. *Physical Review*, **70**, 572.

Grasso, M., Albantakis, L., Lang, J. P., and Tononi, G. (2021). Causal reductionism and causal structures. *Nature Neuroscience*, **24**(10), 1348–1355.

Guth, A. H. (1981). Cosmic inflation. *Physical Review D*, **23**, 347.

Guth, A. H. (2004). Inflation. In: Freedman, W. L. (Ed), *Measuring and Modeling the Universe, Carnegie Observatories Astrophysics Series*, Vol. 2. Cambridge: Cambridge University Press.

Hameroff, S. (2022). Consciousness, cognition and the neuronal cytoskeleton: A new paradigm needed in neuroscience. *Frontiers in Molecular Neuroscience*, **15**, 869935.

Hameroff, S. R. (1994). Quantum coherence in microtubules: A neural basis for emergent consciousness. *Journal of Consciousness Studies*, **1**, 91–118.

Hameroff, S. R. (2006). The entwined mysteries of anesthesia and consciousness: Is there a common underlying Mechanism? *Anesthesiology*, **105**(2), 400–412.

Hameroff, S. R. (2021). "Orchy OR" is the most complete, and most easily falsifiable theory of consciousness. *Cognitive Neuroscience*, **12**(2), 74–76.

Hanson, J. R., and Walker, S. I. (2021). Formalizing falsification for theories of consciousness across computational hierarchies. *Neuroscience of Consciousness*, **21**(2).

Haun, A. M., and Tononi, G. (2019). Why does space feel the way it does? Towards a principled account of spatial experience. *Entropy*, **21**(12), 1160.

Haun, M. (2016) *Cognitive Organisation*, Book published by Springer-Verlag.

Hires, S. A., Gutnisky, D. A., Yu, J., O'Connor, D. H., and Svoboda, K. (2015). Low-noise encoding of active touch by layer 4 in the somatosensory cortex. *eLife*, **4**, e06619.

Hoel, E. P., Albantakis, L., and Tononi, G. (2013). Quantifying causal emergence shows that macro can beat micro. *PNAS*, **110**(49), 19790–19795.

Hoel, E. P., Albantakis, L., Marshall, W., and Tononi, G. (2016). Can the macro beat the micro? Integrated information across spatiotemporal scales. *Neuroscience of Consciousness*, **2016**(1).

Hubble, E. (1929). Extra-galactic nebulae. *Proceedings of the National Academy of Sciences*, **15**(3), 168–173.

Intrinsic Ontology Wiki; Available from: https://centerforsleepandconsciousness.psychiatry.wisc.edu/intrinsic-ontology-wiki/.

Janzing, D., Balduzzi, D., Grosse-Wentrup, M., and Schölkopf B. (2013). Quantifying causal influences. *The Annals of Statistics*, **41**(5), 2324–2358.

Kalita, P., Langa, J. A., and Soler-Toscano, F. (2019). Informational structures and informational fields as a prototype for the description of postulates of the integrated information theory. *Entropy*, **21**(5), 493.

Kanwisher, N. (2010). Functional specificity in the human brain: A window into the functional architecture of the mind. *Proceedings of the National Academy of Sciences*, **107**(25), 11163–11170.

Kastrup, B. (2023). Your Consciousness is Not in Your Head. Interview with Bernardo Kastrup, PhD.

Khosla, M., and Wehbe, L. (2022). High-level visual areas act like domain-general filters with strong selectivity and functional specialization. *bioRxiv*. doi: https://doi.org/10.1101/2022.03.16.484578.

Kleiner, J., and Tull, S. (2021). The mathematical structure of integrated information theory. *Frontiers in Applied Mathematics and Statistics*, **6**, 74.

Krohn, K., and Rhodes, J. (1965). Algebraic theory of machines. I. Prime decomposition theorem for finite semigroups and machines. *Transactions of the American Mathematical Society*, **116**, 450.

Krohn, S., and Ostwald, D. (2017). Computing integrated information. *Neuroscience of Consciousness*, **2017**(1).

Lemon, R., and Edgley, S. (2010). Life without a cerebellum. *Brain*, **133**(3), 652–654.

Mainen, Z. F., and Sejnowski, T. J. (1995). Reliability of spike timing in neocortical neurons. *Science*, **268**(5216), 1503–1506.

Marshall, W., Albantakis, L., and Tononi, G. (2018). Black-boxing and cause-effect power. *PLOS Computational Biology*, **14**(4), e1006114.

Marshall, W., Grasso, M., Mayner, W. G., Zaeemzadeh, A., Barbosa, L. S., Chastain, E., et al. (2023). System integrated information. *Entropy*, **25**.

Massimini, M., Ferrarelli, F., Huber, R., Esser, S. K., Singh, H., and Tononi, G. (2005). Breakdown of cortical effective connectivity during sleep. *Science*, **309**(5744), 2228–2232.

Mayner, W. G. P., Marshall, W., Albantakis, L., Findlay, G., Marchman, R., and Tononi, G. (2018). PyPhi: A toolbox for integrated information theory. *PLoS Computational Biology*, **14**(7), e1006343.

Melloni, L., Mudrik, L., Pitts, M., and Koch, C. (2021). Making the hard problem of consciousness easier. *Science*, **372**(6545), 911–912.

Melloni, L., Schwiedrzik, C. M., Rodriguez, E., and Singer, W. (2009) (Micro) Saccades, corollary activity and cortical oscillations. *Trends in Cognitive Sciences*, **13**(06), 239–245.

Merleau-Ponty, M. (2012). *Phénoménologie de la perception, 1945 (French), 1962 (English)* English translation from French by Colin Smith (1st

English translation), Donald Landes (2nd English translation), Éditions Gallimard, Routledge & Kegan Paul, 1945, English translation (1962), 466 (1965 Routledge edition).

Middleton, F. A., and Strick, P. L. (2000). Basal ganglia and cerebellar loops: Motor and cognitive circuits. *Brain Research Reviews*, **31**(2–3), 236–250.

Moyal, R., Fekete, T., and Edelman, S. (2020). Dynamical emergence theory (DET): A computational account of phenomenal consciousness. *Minds and Machines*, **30**(1), 1–21.

Nagel, T. (1974). What is it like to be a bat? *The Philosophical Review*, **83**(4), 435–450.

Nolte, M., Reimann, M. W., King, J. G., Markram, H., and Muller, E. B. (2019). Cortical reliability amid noise and chaos. *Nature Communications*, **10**(1), 1–15.

Oizumi, M., Albantakis, L., and Tononi, G. (2014). From the phenomenology to the mechanisms of consciousness: Integrated information theory 3.0. *PLoS Computational Biology*, **10**(5), e1003588.

Pearl, J. (2000). *Causality: Models, Reasoning and Inference*, Vol. 29. Cambridge: Cambridge University Press.

Penrose, R. (1989). *The Emperor's New Mind: Concerning Computers, Minds, and the Laws of Physics*. Oxford: Oxford University Press.

Penrose, R. (1996). On gravity's role in quantum state reduction. *General Relativity and Gravitation*, **28**, 581–600.

Penrose, R. (2022). New physics for the Orch OR consciousness proposal. In: Gao, S. (Ed), *Consciousness and Quantum Mechanics*. Oxford: Oxford University Press.

Penrose, R., and Hameroff, S. (1995). What gaps? Reply to Grush and Churchland. *Journal of Consciousness Studies*, **2**, 98–112.

Pigorini, A., Sarasso, S., Proserpio, P., Szymanski, C., Arnulfo, G., Casarotto, S., et al. (2015). Bistability breaks-off deterministic responses to intracortical stimulation during non-REM sleep. *Neuroimage*, **112**, 105–113.

Ponce, C. R., Xiao, W., Schade, P. F., Hartmann, T. S., Kreiman, G., and Livingstone, M. S. (2019). Evolving images for visual neurons using a deep generative network reveals coding principles and neuronal preferences. *Cell*, **177**(4), 999–1009.

Rasmussen, S., Karampurwala, H., Vaidyanath, R., Jensen, K. S., and Hameroff, S. (1990). Computational connectionism within neurons: A model of cytoskeletal automata subserving neural networks. *Physica D: Nonlinear Phenomena*, **42**, 428–449.

Sarasso, S., Casali, A. G., Casarotto, S., Rosanova, M., Sinigaglia, C., Massimini, M., et al. (2021). Consciousness and complexity: A consilience of evidence. *Neuroscience of Consciousness*, **7**(2), 1–24.

Sarasso, S., D'Ambrosio, S., Fecchio, M., Casarotto, S., Viganò, A., Landi, C., et al. (2020). Local sleep-like cortical reactivity in the awake brain after focal injury. *Brain*, **143**(12), 3672–3684.

Shahinpoor, M., and Gheshmi, S. (2015), *Robotic Surgery*. Singapore: Jenny Stanford Publishing.

Song, C., Haun, A. M., and Tononi, G. (2017). Plasticity in the structure of visual space. *Eneuro*, **4**(3).

Steriade, M., Nunez, A., and Amzica, F. (1993). A novel slow (<1 Hz) oscillation of neocortical neurons in vivo: Depolarizing and hyperpolarizing components. *Journal of Neuroscience*, **13**(8), 3252–3265.

Tillemans, T. (2021). Dharmakīrti. In: Zalta, E. N. (Ed), *The Stanford Encyclopedia of Philosophy*. Stanford University Press.

Tononi, G. (2004). An information integration theory of consciousness. *BMC Neuroscience*, 5, 42.

Tononi, G. (2015). Integrated information theory. *Scholarpedia*, **10**(1), 4164.

Tononi, G., Albantakis, L., Boly, M., Cirelli, C., and Koch, C. (2022). Only what exists can cause An intrinsic view of free will. *arXiv*, 2206.02069.

Tononi, G., and Koch, C. (2015). Consciousness: Here, there, and everywhere? *Philosophical Transactions of the Royal Society B*, **370**(1668), 20140167.

Tononi, G., and Sporns, O. (2003). Measuring information integration. *BMC Neuroscience*, **4**(31), 1–20.

Tononi, G., Boly, M., Massimini, M., and Koch, C. (2016). Integrated information theory: From consciousness to its physical substrate. *Nature Reviews Neuroscience*, **17**(7), 450–461.

Watakabe, A., Skibbe, H., Nakae, K., Abe, H., Ichinohe, N., Rachmadi, M. F., et al. (2022). Local and long-distance organization of prefrontal cortex circuits in the marmoset brain. *Neuron*, **111**(14), 2258–2273.

Yu, F., Jiang, Q.-J., Sun, X.-Y., and Zhang, R.-W. (2015). A new case of complete primary cerebellar agenesis: Clinical and imaging findings in a living patient. *Brain*, **138**(6), e353–e353.

Zanardi, P., Tomka, M., and Venuti, L. C. (2018). Towards quantum integrated information theory. *arXiv*, 1806.01421.

Chapter 4

Evolution of Universal Numbers and Data Toward the Evolution of Universal Consciousness and Intelligence in the Universe

4.1 Introduction

The evolution of fundamental particles, molecules, materials, and universal numbers, as well as data toward the evolution of universal consciousness and intelligence in the entire universe, is presented in this chapter. The roles of MAGIC numbers such as Pi (π), Fibonacci numbers, gravitational constant (G),[1] Golden Ratio,[2] and quantum field (ϕ) and quantum ratio (α)[3] (fine structure constant) are also discussed. These mysterious universal numbers, including the magic frequencies 639 Hz, 528 Hz, 777 Hz, 888 Hz, and 963 Hz introduced by Nikola Tesla, are entangled with the evolution and appearance of

[1] $G = 6.67430(15) \times 10^{-11}$ m^3/kgs^2 = $6.67430(15) \times 10^{-11}$ Nm^2/kg^2
[2] $\varphi = 1.6234...$
[3] $\alpha = 1/137$ or $\alpha = 0.00729735256$

Biomimetic Humanoid Robots with Human Consciousness
Mohsen Shahinpoor

ISBN 978-981-5129-87-8 (Hardcover), 978-1-003-71373-9 (eBook)
www.jennystanford.com

DOI: 10.1201/9781003713739-4

consciousness in the Universe. The frequency of 963 Hz is considered the frequency of God, which supposedly attracts blessings, love, and miracles.

The transformative frequencies of 963 Hz present a profound connection with your inner divine power. This powerful frequency is believed to activate the pineal gland, enhance intuition, and facilitate spiritual growth. In this soothing and meditative composition, we have carefully curated a blend of harmonious sounds and frequencies to guide you on self-discovery and spiritual awakening. As you listen, allow the healing vibrations of 963 Hz to resonate through your being, helping you align with the higher realms of consciousness.

The mysterious number α = 0.00729735256 is dimensionless and is called the *fine structure constant*. It appears everywhere in our equations of quantum physics and the splitting of electron waves, and scientists are still trying to figure out why. It originated from electrons transiting from one object to the next and releasing energy from electrons and light photons. They can be found in quantum mechanics equations, such as:

$\alpha = (e^2/4\pi€_0hc) = (1.602711 \times 10^{-19}\ C)^2/4\pi\ (8.954 \times 10^{-12}\ C^7/Nm^2)\ (6.626^{-34}\ Nms))\ (3 \times 10^8\ m/s\ ) = 1/137$, where e is the electron charge in Coulombs, h is the Planck constant, and c is the speed of light (c = 299792458 m/s).

According to Wikipedia, some important constants are as follows:

- The 9 *Yukawa couplings* for the quarks and leptons (equivalent to specifying the *rest mass* of these *elementary particles*)
- Two parameters of the *Higgs field* potential
- Four parameters for the *quark mixing matrix*
- Three coupling constants for the *gauge groups* SU(3) × SU(2) × U(1) (or equivalently, two coupling constants and the *Weinberg angle*)
- A phase for the *quantum chromodynamics vacuum*

The number of 19 independent fundamental physical constants is subject to change under possible *extensions of the standard model*, notably by the introduction of *neutrino mass* (equivalent to seven additional constants, i.e., three Yukawa couplings and four *lepton mixing* parameters).

Wikipedia lists the following fundamental universal constants:

- Electron charge: $1.602176634 \times 10^{-19}$ C
- Newtonian gravitational constant G: $6.67430(15) \times 10^{-11}$ m^3/kgs^2
- Planck constant h: $6.62607015 \times 10^{-34}$ J/Hz
- Speed of light c: 299,792,458 m/s
- Vacuum electric permittivity ε_0: $8.8541878188(14) \times 10^{-12}$ F/m
- Vacuum magnetic permeability μ_0: $1.25663706127(20) \times 10^{-6}$ N/A^2
- Electron mass m_e: $9.1093837139(28) \times 10^{-31}$ kg
- Fine structure constant α: 0.0072973525643
- Josephson tunneling constant KJ = 2e/h (=483597.8484...$\times 10^9$ Hz/V)
- Rydberg constant R∞ = α2mec/2h (= 10973731.568157(12) m^{-1})
- von Klitzing constant RK = h/e2 (25812.80745... Ω)

First, a review of smart, stimuli-responsive, electrically controllable materials is given. The Universe was extremely hot and dense in the first moments after the Big Bang. As the Universe cooled, conditions became just right to give rise to the building blocks of matter—the quarks and electrons. A few millionths of a second later, quarks aggregated to produce protons and neutrons. Within minutes, these protons and neutrons combined into nuclei. The reader is referred to the work of quarks and electrons (CERN, home.cern) to learn about the evolution of initial fundamental particles. Pease see Refs. (Benveniste, 1998; Shahinpoor and Thompson, 1995).

4.2 Representative Smart and Intelligent Nonliving Materials

Like smart materials, intelligent materials can automatically and inherently sense or detect environmental changes and respond to them with some actuation or sensing action. Intelligent materials possess or show a survival strategy that prompts appropriate actions or actions from sensed or detected environmental influences.

If one takes an engineering approach to the classification of materials mentioned above, one must assign certain quotients to each material to quantitatively characterize them. Therefore, one would conventionally introduce the terms of the material smartness quotient (MSQ) and the material intelligence quotient (MIQ) (see Shahinpoor and Wang, 1995; Shahinpoor, 1997). As will be shown later, materials can be considered smart or intelligent, as can material structures or systems. One must, therefore, introduce a structure or system smartness quotient (SSQ) and a structure or system intelligence quotient (SIQ). To classify materials based on the above quotients of smartness and intelligence, some reference values related to MIQ are needed. The family of amino acid sequences and structures has been chosen as a reference for smartness, and structural smartness has been assigned the MSQ value of 1000. The family of ribonucleic acid sequences, such as RNA, microRNA, or miRNA, and DNA, is chosen as a reference for intelligence and assigned the MIQ value of 1000. These references have been arbitrarily chosen based on the materials and structures currently known.

4.3 MicroRNAs: 2024 Nobel Prize in Physiology and Medicine

This year's Nobel Prize honored two scientists for discovering a fundamental principle governing gene regulations. The 2024 Nobel Prize in Physiology or Medicine was awarded jointly to Professor Victor Ambros of the University of Massachusetts Medical School and Gary Ruvkun, professor of genetics at Harvard Medical School, for their ground-breaking discovery of microRNA and its crucial role in post-transcriptional gene regulation.

As the Universe expanded and cooled, things began to happen more slowly. It took 380,000 years for electrons to be trapped in orbits around nuclei, forming the first atoms. These were mainly hydrogen and helium, which are still by far the most abundant elements in the Universe.

Present observations suggest that the first stars formed from clouds of gas around 150–200 million years after the Big Bang. Heavier atoms, such as carbon, oxygen, and iron, have since been continuously produced in the hearts of stars and catapulted throughout the Universe in spectacular stellar explosions called supernovae.

But stars and galaxies do not tell the whole story. Astronomical and physical calculations suggest that the visible universe is only a tiny amount (4%) of what the Universe is made of. A large fraction, 23%, is made of an unknown type of matter called "dark matter." Unlike stars and galaxies, dark matter does not emit any light or electromagnetic radiation, so we can detect it only through its gravitational effects and power as it holds the galaxies together.

An even more mysterious form called "dark energy" accounts for about 73% of the Universe's mass–energy content. Even less is known about it than dark matter. This idea stems from the observation that all galaxies seem to be receding from each other at an accelerating pace, implying that some invisible extra energy is at work.

Note that the Universe appears to have about 73% or so of non-visible dark energy and about 23% or so of non-visible dark matter, which only shows its gravitational influence in keeping the galaxies together. In contrast, ordinary matter is only 4% visible, of which only less than 2% account for all galaxies.

We must emphasize that materials are ranked differently according to the classification scale used. For example, proteins, with an MSQ of 1000, have a rating of about 700 on the materials intelligence scale (MIQ). This difference occurs because a particular material can have a certain level of smartness, based on its sensing response and reaction capabilities, yet has a survival strategy at a lower level.

This would give it a higher rank on the materials smartness scale and a lower rank on the materials intelligence scale. Because of its environmental integration, another material could possess a highly advanced survival strategy for its internal structure but present a lower sensitivity and reactivity. This would earn it a lower position on the MSQ scale than the MIQ scale.

One can also analyze a material's intelligence based on its adaptability. Materials exist in the same environment as living matter and are exposed to dynamic changes. This leads to the theory that materials evolve. However, the evolution of materials must be treated on a different scale and with a different approach than that of living matter. To analyze materials from the perspective of evolution (which also involves survival), one must first determine all the hierarchical structures involved in the evolution of each material. At each level of the hierarchy, associated smartness and intelligence must be numerically computed. These computations, even if they seem difficult to perform because of a lack of data, are much simpler than one thinks. Starting from the concept of intelligence, one realizes that both intelligence and adaptation of a system are directly related to the ability of the system to exchange information with its environment continuously and gradually start to be conscious about is environment. This makes it an open system. If it also reacts to environmental changes, it is a dynamic system. Now, one can discuss nonorganic evolution and intelligent materials.

From an intelligence and smartness point of view, the important nonliving materials are ionic crystals, ionic polymeric gels, shape-memory alloys and polymers, piezoelectric, electrostrictive, magnetostrictive, electrorheological, and magnetorheological materials. In the following sections, these are briefly introduced and discussed.

4.4 Ionic Crystals

While the topic of ionic crystals is vast and complex, it is important to highlight their role in the evolution of artificial intelligence and consciousness. Take, for instance, the semiconductor silicon, a relevant example of ionic crystals. The embedded positive–negative (P-N) nodes in such crystals have revolutionized the field of computer chips, computers, and microprocessors. This evolution mirrors the development of artificial intelligence, making ionic crystals a fundamental part of manufacturing AI systems toward consciousness.

4.5 Ionic Polymeric Gels

Ionic polymeric gels are polymeric materials whose characteristics of self-organization and responses to dynamic environments are similar to those of proteins, collagen, DNA, or RNA. Therefore, ionic polymeric gels can be considered materials with high smartness and intelligence. An ionic polymeric gel structure comprises a three-dimensional network formed by cross-linked macromolecular polyelectrolytes. The ionic structure of these gels contains several fixed ions and mobile ions. The fixed ions relate to sites of various polymer cross-links and segments. This structure causes the ionic polymeric gel to swell or shrink in aqueous solutions with chemical or electrical stimuli. Suppose such a gel is exposed to an electric field. In that case, the electrophoretic migration of mobile ions and water molecules attached to them causes differential osmotic pressure in material deformation. If the gel is deformed, an electric field is generated. Thus, these materials both sense and actuate. Based on the properties mentioned above, it can be concluded that ionic polymeric gels have a highly developed response to electrochemical stimuli. They are conventionally assigned an MIQ of 400 (Shahinpoor, 1995, 1996). The synergistic effect of the gel's internal ionic structure, which takes over the individual properties of each gel component, should also be noted. Smartness is implied here by the material structure or organization rather than by the matter alone. The structure's geometry plays an important role, too, since the structure's geometry responds predictably to a given stimulus. The gel deformation could be interpreted as the structure's attempt to reach the geometry that would ensure equilibrium under those conditions. As the given conditions change, the geometry of the structure changes accordingly.

4.6 Shape-Memory Alloys

Shape-memory alloys (SMAs) are considered smart materials with embedded crystalline memory. They can react to temperature differences with shape changes memorized by the materials. They were assigned an MIQ of 400 (Shahinpoor, 1995, 1996) and an MSQ of 100. The most widely used SMA is a nickel–titanium alloy called nitinol. If deformed during a certain range of temperature (in the martensitic phase), this type of alloy "remembers" its initial shape; when heated above the transition temperature (in the austenitic phase), it recovers its initial shape.

The recovery can be partial or total, depending on the initial plastic deformation strain. Usually, initial deformation strains as high as 6–8% can be completely recovered by heating the nitinol alloy. This response to thermal stimuli suggests many interesting applications. The most important application would be to employ the alloy to transform thermal energy into mechanical energy (i.e., work). For example, a wire of nitinol, initially plastically elongated, in the martensitic phase. If the wire is placed vertically, with one end fixed while the other is attached to a hanging weight, it is heated above the transition temperature. It will recover its initial shape, shrinking and thus lifting the weight. Then, by cooling the wire material, a transition to a martensitic phase will occur, and the wire will soften significantly. A resilient structure can use this softness to bring the structure back to its initial deformed shape. To be considered an SMA, a material must have a transformation temperature range low enough to be easily reached by common means.

Heating an SMA is usually performed by passing an electric current through a wire, which leads to the Joule effect (heating), or by placing the wire in a hot environment (e.g., hot liquid). Even though NiTi alloy is the most widely used SMA, other alloys exhibit this same property, such as AgCd, AuCd, CuAlNi, CuSn, CuZn, CuZnSi, CuZnAl, CuZnSn, InTi, NiAl, FePt, MnCu, and FeMnSi.

Later in this chapter, aluminum and silicon present high levels of intelligence as pure matter alone, without being combined with other materials. Although the elements in the above enumeration do not have a high level of intelligence, they possess an intelligent structure due to the synergy between the elements composing the alloy.

4.7 Shape-Memory Polymers

In addition to metals, some polymers possess a shape-memory effect. This is found in block co-polymers, where polymer chains contain alternating homo-polymer segments. Despite the lower force of the polymeric shape-memory alloy, it can still be useful in medical applications.

The smartness of SMA and polymer structures resides in the prompt response to the stimuli. However, their intelligence is calculated based on their natural ability to diminish internal energetic load. This is done by modifying its geometry to a previous state characterized by a lower energetic load. In other words, a shape-memory alloy or polymer does not directly "remember" its initial shape but rather its initial energetic shape, which was dictated by the minimum energy principle.

Therefore, after a plastic deformation, thermal energy helps a heated SMA recover its low-level energetic state. Most of the time, this state coincides with the geometric shape before the plastic deformation.

4.8 Piezoelectric and Piezoresistive Materials

The piezoelectric and piezoresistive effects consist of solid motions that may impose an electric field in a material with enabled dipoles. The inverse is also true; the deformation of this type of material produces a small electric charge. If a voltage is applied across certain solid surfaces exhibiting the piezoelectric effect, the solid will undergo a mechanical distortion. Pierre Curie discovered this piezoelectric effect in 1883. It can be found naturally, especially in certain crystals (e.g., quartz and Rochelle salt) and ceramic materials such as PZT (lead zirconate titanate piezo).

Because of the dualism of the piezoelectric effect, piezoelectric materials can be used for both sensing and actuation. Many materials are used today in piezoelectric applications since piezoelectric ceramics are fragile, difficult to fabricate in complicated shapes, and have high acoustic impedance. Therefore, it seems more sensible to create composite piezoceramic-piezopolymers.

The most useful polymers in such applications are the PVDF (polyvinylidene-difluoride) and the co-polymer P(VDF-TrFE) with approximately 25% trifluoro ethylene. One must also consider that PVDF can be prepared in four morphological phases. However, only two present a perfect piezoelectric effect, and only one can be used for orientation in a strong electric field. It should be noted that because they are light and adaptable, piezoelectric materials could be used for active shape, vibration, and acoustic control of various structures. Easily integrated into structures, they are very attractive in structural control. They eliminate the need for moving parts, which conventional actuators require. Structural control with piezoelectric materials is achieved by embedding them in the structure or bonding them to its surface.

Regarding the smartness and intelligence of piezoelectric materials, one can easily observe their ability to respond to electrical or mechanical stimuli. This behavior automatically confers piezoelectric materials with a high degree of smartness. However, even if the survival strategies of these elements are present, they are difficult to explain and interpret because of their complex nature.

In other words, one can observe the rapid response of the piezoelectric materials to electric and mechanical stimuli, but this ability cannot be associated with a survival strategy.

It is interesting to recognize here the ability of piezoelectric materials to convert electrical energy into mechanical energy and mechanical energy into electrical energy. One could expand on their unique properties by considering the magnetic field, which occurs with a variable electric field.

4.9 Piezoresistive Effect

Their resistance changes when pressure or straining is applied to certain semiconductors or metals. This is called the piezoresistive effect, yet the defining factor here is the resistance change of the piezo property. Changes in the resistance of materials mark the piezoresistive effect because of pressure or deformation. In both cases, pressure plays a key role in the effects that surround piezo properties. Piezo resistors are the most fundamental devices that run on the piezoresistive effect.

Irish physicist Lord Kelvin, who noted a phenomenon in metal devices that fits the basic description of the effect, recognized the piezoresistive effect in 1856.

4.10 Electrorheological Materials

Electrorheological fluids are smart materials that can undergo a rapid and reversible change in their rheological behavior when an electric field is applied. This effect can be induced in two-phase liquids (liquid dispersions) with a dispersed solid phase in a non-conducting liquid. Usually, the liquid phase is based on mineral and paraffin oils, while the solid phase is formed from spherical particles, which can be polymers. It should be noted that water or any other polar liquid is very important for the electrorheological effect.

In the absence of an electric field, most electrorheological materials behave Newtonian. However, when an electric field is applied, they assume the characteristics of a Bingham plastic fluid: The viscosity of the electrorheological material is highly increased and no longer a linear variable.

The electrorheological effect (i.e., the viscosity of the electrorheological material) depends on the strength of the electric field, not on the frequency of the field's current production. The typical response time of electrorheological fluids is within a few milliseconds.

Various theories have been developed to explain electrorheological behavior. Most focus on the influence of the solid phase on the liquid phase during exposure to an electric field. This effect develops linear clusters of spheres that lead to percolating fibrils. As the strength of the electric field increases, these fibrils produce an increase in viscosity, which, in turn, leads to the solidifying of the material.

Electrorheological materials have different applications for actuators, sensors, valves, brakes, and clutches. However, a better understanding of the electrorheological effect could broaden their applications. From the point of view of smartness, we are dealing with materials that "sense" an exterior stimulus (electric field) and react immediately to the intensity of the specific stress. Consequently, they are cataloged as materials with a high degree of smartness. They are also intelligent since they possess a certain degree of self-control.

4.11 Magnetorheological Materials

Magnetorheological materials are quite similar to electrorheological materials. The only difference is that the change in rheological properties occurs in a magnetic field.

The composition of the magnetorheological materials differs from the electrorheological materials by their solid phase, which consists of magnetizable particles. The solid phase most commonly used consists of iron ore. They are 20–50 times stronger than the electrorheological materials.

Magnetorheological materials are less sensitive to temperature variation and can be operated at lower energy sources. When a magnetic field is applied, the response time of the magnetorheological materials is about milliseconds and can generate a yield stress from zero to 90 kPa. Magnetorheological materials have applications similar to electrorheological materials: actuators, brakes, dampers, valves, etc. Like electrorheological materials, magnetorheological materials are intelligent materials with a high degree of smartness.

4.12 Electro- and Magnetostrictive Materials

Electro- and magnetostrictive materials (ferromagnetic metals, ferrites, certain alloys, Terfenol, or composites) can change their dimensions (geometry) if exposed to an electric or magnetic field. Similar to piezoelectric materials, these materials generate an electric field when stressed.

Even if magnetostrictive materials present a high degree of smartness, their application is somewhat limited because of high energy consumption and their nonlinear response. On the other hand, electrostrictive materials generally develop higher strain and forces and use less power. Their main fields of application are in the actuators and certain types of sensors (force and torque sensors).

4.13 Common Intelligent Materials

Two very common materials represent smart, even intelligent, materials. These are aluminum and silicon. Both aluminum and silicon are the most abundant metallic and semiconductor materials and non-conductive oxides on the Earth (aluminum is abundant even on the moon). Their oxides are the most abundant insulators in nature. In addition, the very quick formation of an aluminum oxide layer on any aluminum surface in an oxidizing environment could be considered a survival strategy.

Its goal is to protect the non-oxidized material, which is a conductor of electromagnetic waves. Silicon shows a similar reaction. Another example of aluminum's smartness is that it can convert normal water to pure hydrogen by forming aluminum hydroxide. On the other hand, silicon is the most used material in the computer industry. It plays a fundamental role in VLSI and semiconductor fabrication processes.

4.14 Smart and Intelligent Structures

If the smartness and intelligence of materials can be discussed, one should also be able to consider smart and intelligent structures. These structures are found in one or more material constituents that, individually, would not attain the level of smartness or intelligence reached by the structure. We find a more important element in smart and intelligent structures besides a hierarchic summation of the properties of the structure's constituents. This is the geometry of the structure. Of course, geometry also plays an important role in materials, intelligence, and consciousness, but its importance is greatly increased for structures.

Structures can be divided between nonliving and living structures (also called living systems). Aspects of living systems have been described in the previous chapters. We must emphasize that even the common cell from a living system would be considered a highly intelligent structure. It comprises all the mechanisms and components that allow it to survive alone and replicate. However, as a survival strategy, most cells are part of a larger living structure called an organism.

Note that one does not normally consider plant organisms. As long as they are formed by cells and represent intelligent structures, they can be included in the same category as organisms.

We will present the hierarchic structure of a bacteriophage as an example of an intelligent structure. First, note that this structure fulfills the three criteria of intelligent structuring: the existence of subassemblies, the minimization of free energy, and sequential assembly and conformational switching. Subassemblies are normal for any hierarchical structure since they divide it into specific levels.

Minimizing free energy is very important in the bacteriophage structure since it optimizes a certain basic property of the system, which, in this case, is thermodynamic free energy.

This could be explained by the bacteriophage containing proteins capable of polymorphic assembly into almost equal thermodynamic stability configurations.

This complex structure of bacteriophage gives one a brief example of intelligent organization at a structural level. Many more examples could be presented from both living and nonliving worlds.

Bacteriophage is any of a group of viruses that infect bacteria. Bacteriophages were discovered independently by Frederick W. Twort in Great Britain (1915) and Félix d'Hérelle in France (1917). D'Hérelle coined the term *bacteriophage*, meaning "bacteria eater," to describe the agent's bacteriocidal ability. Figure 4.1 depicts the operation of the T4 virus.

However, one should note a very important aspect of intelligent structures: A structure is generally a complementary form of organization for a system that enables its evolution to advance beyond the capabilities of its components.

Recent efforts have been made to create artificial structures with a high degree of smartness and intelligence.

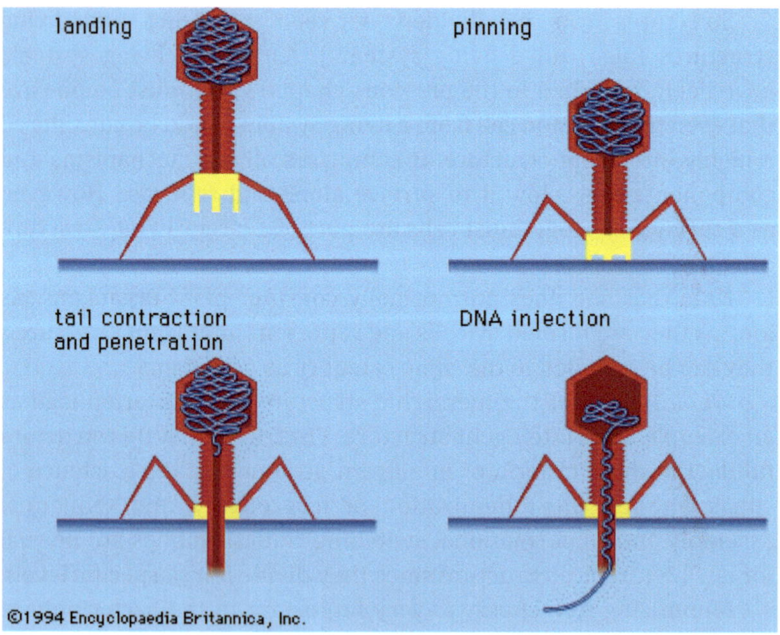

Figure 4.1 Bacteriophage: General structure of T4 bacteriophage and a model of its mode of attachment to, and injection of its DNA into, a bacterial cell.

These attempts have used common materials that possess a lower level of smartness. The applications of these structures cover a broad range, including MEMS, nanotechnology (NEMS), robotics, medicine, and hard-to-reach locations (such as hazardous spatial or deep-ocean missions).

4.15 Determining Smartness and Intelligence Quotients

Now that we have seen the main aspects involved in smart and intelligent materials and smart and intelligent structures, it would be interesting to develop a general method for establishing smartness and intelligence quotients. We should begin by tabulating all the properties of a certain material or structure.

Then, we could determine a weighting function for relative smartness and intelligence. However, determining the function is still quite difficult, as there might still be properties of a material or structure that were not included in the properties table, and they might have quite an important role in that material's or structure's smartness or intelligence.

The four main properties of aluminum are that it has low density (2.7 g/cm^3), is nontoxic, has high thermal conductivity and excellent corrosion resistance, and is easily cast, machined, and formed. It is also nonmagnetic and nonsparking.

However, as we will see in the following chapter, the geometrical aspects must be more detailed. Another important property of a material is its adaptability. Like living matter, materials must adapt to their environment to survive. Table 4.1 gives some properties of aluminum.

However, as we will see in the following chapter, the geometrical aspects must be more detailed. Another important property of a material is its adaptability. Like living matter, materials must adapt to their environment to survive.

Therefore, the better the adapted materials, the higher their intelligence or smartness quotient. Of course, environmental conditions are the chief factors that determine a material's existence.

That is why a material that might seem well adapted in a more static environment could quickly deteriorate if exposed to a more aggressive or dynamic environment.

Table 4.1 Physical and chemical properties of aluminum

Property Number (P)	Property	Value	Weighting Function (W)
P1	Atomic number	13	W1
P2	Atomic weight	26.98154	W2
P3	Crystal structure	FCC; Ill	W3
P4	Density	2.698	W4
P5	Melting point	660.37°C	W5
P6	Boiling point	2494°C	W6
P7	Latent heat of fusion	94.9 cal/g	W7
P8	Latent heat of vaporization	2576 cal/g	W8
P9	Heat of combustion	7420 cal/g at 25°C	W9
P10	Specific heat	0.215 cal/g °C at 25 °C	W10
P11	Thermal conductivity	0.566 cal/g °C at 25°C	W11
PI2	Coefficient of thermal expansion	23×10^{-6}/°C	W12
PI3	Thermal diffusivity	0.969 cm/s at 25°C	W13
P14	Electrical resistivity	2.7×10^{-8} at 25°C	W14
P15	Hardness	2–2.9 MPa	W15
P16	Reflectivity	85–90%	W16

However, this exposure could be considered sudden since each material was formed over a long period, and violent nuclear reactions in the Universe determined its formation. From formation to adaptation, it took a much longer time. If we try to study a material's ability to adapt, we should wait a similar period. Since this is neither practical nor possible, we can only analyze the material's ability to adapt shortly after its formation or after certain known environmental variations.

For example, during the glacial period, all the materials on the Earth's crust were exposed to a constant low temperature. This affected the thermal properties of certain materials. Other materials and structures had to adapt to windy conditions, for example. In this case, geometry played a very important role in intelligence.

4.16 Representative Smart and Intelligent Nonliving Materials

For example, in Egypt, Giza has two very important and famous monuments (in fact, there are four, but only two categories). One is the Sphinx, and the other is the Great Pyramid of Cheops (along with the pyramids of Kefren and Mikerinos). All these monuments were presumably built in the same period, about 5000 years ago (the accepted building date is 2700 B.C., although some scientists consider the Great Pyramid much older). While the pyramids are well-preserved, the Sphinx had to be renewed because of erosion. Besides the materials' quality, the structure's geometry proved to be an important factor in erosion. For better understanding, we will discuss the influences of geometry in much more detail in the following chapter.

4.17 Artificial Smart Materials and Structures

As we have already seen, many naturally available materials and structures present a high level of smartness and intelligence. However, these do not always fit the particular needs of humans. That is why humans tried to mimic nature to create smart and intelligent structures capable of helping them and their society. Consequently, researchers started to draw natural models into their practical applications from various fields such as civil engineering, nanotechnology, military applications, and many others. They produced actuators and motors that behave like muscles, sensors used as nerves or memory, and networks that represent the brain and the spine. These new intelligent structures usually have substantial advantages over traditional products because they present a higher level of control and increased feasibility and sustainability.

One such application could be a robotic hand with skin made from piezoelectric polymers. This type of skin induces a voltage between the electrodes. When under pressure, it could be used as a fine sensing device. The sensing accuracy of such a device is so high that it can even be used to read Braille pads for blind people. Another application would be the use of actuators as a rotor control. The actuators would act like flaps and would eliminate the need for a swash-plate mechanism, which has a control function over the entire rotor blade. In addition, a ladder could be equipped with smart sensing devices that would promptly react in the case of an overload, thus reducing the risk of failures and accidents. This device could also monitor the state of the ladder and its aging. This way, it offers a tool to help users better control maintenance operations. Furthermore, SMA can counteract strain in concrete infrastructures. At the same time, sensors placed within them could monitor the presence of cracks in cement and/or corrosion in the steel reinforcing rods. A thin layer of actuators and fiber optic sensors could alert the pilot of subtle physical and chemical changes, presaging failure and monitoring (and compensating for) aircraft body fatigue.

Another novel application involves magnetostrictive materials. Currently, the most commonly used magnetostrictive material is Terfenol-D, which has properties far more advanced than other magnetostrictive materials. Terfenol-D is mainly used as small rods (several centimeters long), acting as actuators and sensors.

Using a large number of actuators and sensors in a particular design, however, would increase the price of the final product and may require the integration of all the sensors within a central command unit. Comparing this structure with the nervous system or any informational structure in the informational hierarchy, we should observe that the most viable design involves hierarchical levels that determine modules. These modules perform local tasks (e.g., sensing and control) synergistically integrated within the system.

We also know that any piece of matter has an energetic component that allows it to exist in a given form. However, little is known about the information carried and processed by matter or how matter appeared in the Universe. We will deal with these problems in this chapter. A good example is water in the ocean. How could molecules of H_2 bind together so nicely and formally to create liquid water massively? Does that mean the ocean also has consciousness to maintain its integrity?

If we accept the validity of the Big Bang theory, it helps explain matter formation and evolution. According to this theory, the Universe was initially a very concentrated mass. One might say that the Universe had mass and was composed of matter. This is quite possible, but there is a so-called "horizon" that limits our "view" of the past 15 billion light years. This "horizon" is the result of the expanding universe. The more time passes, the larger the horizon becomes. However, the starting point remains the same. We can only assume what happened immediately after the Big Bang some 13.7 billion years ago.

After the huge explosion and subsequent inflation, the matter would have been very hot and consisted of charged subatomic particles known as plasma. These particles were electrons, positrons, and neutrinos, to which were added photons. One could briefly describe the Universe at that time as being formed out of matter (as neutrinos and electrons), antimatter (as positrons), and energy (as photons and other forms of energy). It is already supposed that matter and antimatter equals energy (as photons). It would be interesting to know how the matter–antimatter–energy cycle worked. How did matter and antimatter appear? Were they derived directly from energy? It is quite likely. However, with the available data, it is still impossible to know exactly what happened.

After the Big Bang, the Universe began to expand and inflate (Guth, 1981). As particles departed from the explosion core, they cooled. As would be expected, the first element was the master molecule, *hydrogen*. It consists only of a proton and an electron. However, as the process of cooling continued, neutrons combined with protons to make heavier nuclei (e.g., *helium*). Most of the electrons were annihilated by positrons (their antimatter), which generated photons (light). In other words, matter had to lose some of its energy to self-organize and form different elements. Because of the elements' high energy (manifested as thermal energy), matter could not form. No linkage could take place between particles.

Considering this and recalling Brownian motion, which increases with the increase in temperature, the concept of "entropy" was developed. Entropy characterizes disorder: The higher the temperature, the higher the entropy.

Over many thousands of years, as both expansion and cooling continued, electrons gradually reduced their speed and were finally captured by heavier nuclei. Thus, the first hydrogen and helium atoms were formed, together with the commonly known isotopes deuterium and tritium. It is supposed that the first lithium atoms were formed during this period. The first nuclear reactions that occurred after the Big Bang are depicted below:

$$^2H + n \rightarrow {}^3H + \text{energy}$$
$$^2H + p \rightarrow {}^3He + \text{energy}$$
$$^2H + {}^2H \rightarrow {}^4He + \text{energy}$$
$$^3He + {}^2H \rightarrow {}^4He + p$$
$$^3H + {}^2H \rightarrow {}^4He + n$$

The matter started to become organized. Minute energy conglomerates are organized into a small space while traveling in four-dimensional space at high speed. Thus, photons (light) were born, followed by electrons, protons, neutrons, and mesons. On the other hand, there may have been, initially, only energy in the form of photons, namely:

$$E = \sum_i^{\infty} hni\, v_i \rightarrow hn_i\, v_i$$

where h is the Planck constant, n is the number of photons with frequency v; over the whole spectrum of creation. Note that the Planck constant relates photon energy to its frequency such that energy $e = hv$, where $h = 6.62607015 \times 10^{-34}$ J/Hz is the Planck constant, as shown in Fig. 4.2.

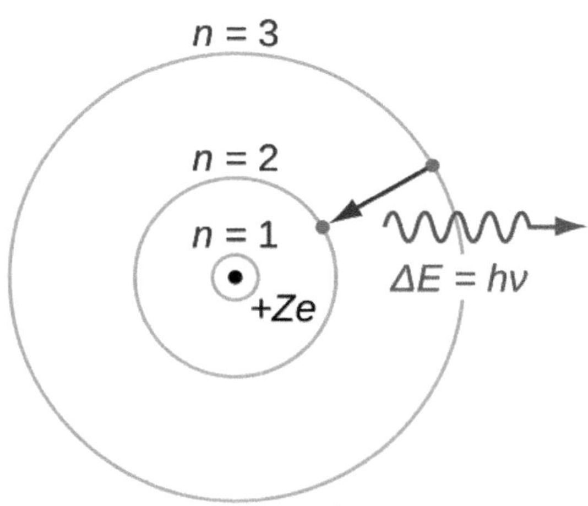

Figure 4.2 As electrons jump from an outer orbit to lower orbits, they radiate photon energy (light) as they transit.

One might wonder why the electrons had to be captured by heavier nuclei. The answer seems evident: It offered more stability and order since it was more organized. Why should there have been a tendency for dynamic systems to gravitate toward more stable configurations? Suppose one accepts this unproven model for the time being. In that case, it is not hard to believe that the original Universal Intelligence was a systematic mass/charge distribution at the earliest stage of evolving intelligence. Should this be claimed as the beginning of intelligence? One might consider it so because up to this point, energy was the most predominant element in the Universe.

However, one type of anything can never form a stable, durable configuration. Energy had to transform itself partially into matter and information. Information generated intelligence, while matter (together with energy and information) generated geometrical configurations.

All the known elements were gradually synthesized through a thermonuclear reaction. Heavier elements were synthesized in so-called "stellar ovens," which provided enough thermal energy for the nuclear reactions. Our sun, for example, is still producing helium from hydrogen through nuclear fusion. It is like an exploding hydrogen bomb. Other stars with lower, or even absent, resources of hydrogen burn helium to synthesize carbon, oxygen, etc. Having the whole spectrum of elements, one can start studying their evolution. This can be done by analyzing their density and abundance at any location in the Universe. Based on these factors, the history of the material location can be calculated.

Today, astrophysicists calculate that matter is much more abundant in the Universe than antimatter. This raises an important question. According to the initial conditions, the ratio of these two should not be so large. The answer to this question is a supposition: Matter also occurs due to specific interactions that do not follow the basic conservation laws.

This suggests an interesting idea. In a closed system, everything is conserved within the system. However, if more subsystems form that closed system, some of them open systems, the conservation laws no longer apply to the open subsystems but to the whole system.

To continue our discussion of the Universe, we should consider it a closed system since we cannot imagine something beyond the Universe. If the Universe is a closed system, everything should be conserved. By conservation, we do not mean preservation, which involves conserving an item in a certain form, condition, etc. Thus, the Universe appears to have been conserved, while everything inside the Universe is in continuous transformation: energy transforms into matter, matter into energy, and so on. Energy was involved in the creation and perpetuation of matter. But, if it is supposed that matter also occurred due to certain non-conservative reactions, this would mean that the particular form of energy we considered is only a part, or a subsystem of a bigger, conservative energetic system. What would that mean? Some scientists have called this the Great Unification Theory (a continuation of Einstein's work).

This theory introduces a unified force most prominent in the Universe immediately after the Big Bang. At that time, all the strong, weak, and electromagnetic forces acted as one unified force that would have had various effects on the evolution of matter. However, this theory supposes that energy might also exist in certain forms that are yet unknown (or did not exist at that time).

As the Universe is a closed system, a unified force or energy would mean something conservative, representing a hierarchically superior level of existence. In the meantime, the existence of a hierarchy requires the existence of an order, which implies the existence of information about smart and intelligent structures.

This makes sense if one remembers the barriers we discovered in understanding living systems, particularly the energetic issues related to biological fields, communication, etc. On the other hand, if immediately after the Big Bang, the Universe was already organized as a primordial, smart/intelligent structure, then what determined the appearance and evolution of intelligence? All that one can say is that intelligence existed forever and will never disappear. This notion can be stated as a universal theorem:

Theorem 1: The Big Bang created an expanding assembly of energy and matter, and a field of intelligence and consciousness simultaneously presented with energy and primordial matter. Therefore, intelligence plays an important role in this dynamic process, as it leads to the decrease in universal entropy, increasing the order.

You might ask now how this could affect the evolution of the Universe. Well, as the Universe continuously expands and inflates (or even temporarily, according to some theories), the links between its components become weaker. This could finally lead to a break. To avoid this, Universal Intelligence had to decrease the entropy of the Universe, thus giving it more stability. The more stable any system is, the less chances there will be for a break to occur. It turns out that there is also a positive axis of time toward organization and structures away from disorder.

Step by step, as temperatures continued to drop after the Big Bang, more and more elements were formed. Keep in mind that the number of the elements formed was not infinite. Only 99 elements have been found on the Earth; we list them in the Periodic Table of Elements. This does not mean that there are no other elements in the Universe. However, considering the energetic limitations, one could say that their number is relatively small even if other elements exist in the Universe. We can be relatively certain that with the creation of the elements, matter started to group itself over many millions of years to form what we see today: stars, galaxies, meteors, comets, cosmic radiation, etc. Rather, we are interested in the abundance and properties of material elements resulting from intelligent evolution.

4.18 Intelligent Distribution of Matter

As the first step in estimating the abundance of elements, we should consider the Earth's tertial structure. It is assumed that the Earth was formed as a cold body and, later, its interior heated due to gravitational contraction and radioactive activity. Thus, the Earth's core became a furnace with a melted mixture of elements. The composition and distribution of elements in the Earth's core are not a function of each element's density but of their geochemical affinity. For example, elements with a strong affinity for oxygen or sulfur tend to be concentrated in the outer limits of the core, where oxygen is more abundant.

These are followed by titanium, phosphorus, hydrogen, and manganese, which cover about 1.4% of the Earth's crust. All the other elements cover only 0.6% of the Earth's crust (Tables 4.2 and 4.3). Things are more complicated on the Earth's crust. More data and factors are available and should be considered in the analysis.

For example, isotope abundance is of great interest because it provides precious data concerning the Earth and the solar system (by comparing the ratios).

Table 4.2 Logarithmic abundance of elements in the Earth's crust (percent by weight): After Brian H. Mason (1971)

Element	Atomic Number (Z)	Logarithmic Abundance (Si = lOb)
Li	3	470
Be	4	22.4
B	5	28.1
C	6	2710
N	7	108
0	8	2,960,000
F	9	3750
Ne	10	0.00036
Na	11	125,000
Mg	12	87,300
Al	13	306,000
Si	14	1,000,000
P	15	3860
s	16	1640
Cl	17	430
Ar	18	0.100
K	19	67,100
Ca	20	91,700
Sc	21	45
Ti	22	9310
V	23	240
Cr	24	195
Mn	25	1850
Fe	26	91,000
Co	27	34.6
Ni	28	60.5

Element	Atomic Number (Z)	Logarithmic Abundance (Si = lOb)
Cu	29	88.0
Zn	30	62.0
Ga	31	27.4
Ge	32	1.55
As	33	2.70
Se	34	0.11
Br	35	3.94
Rb	37	137
Sr	38	520
Y	39	32.1
Zr	40	173
Nb	41	26.2
Mo	42	1.02
Ru	44	0.0010
Rh	45	0.0010
Pd	46	0.036
Ag	47	0.094
Cd	48	0.135
In	49	0.098
Sn	50	1.70

Table 4.3 Approximate composition of the Earth (Brian H. Mason)

Element	Percentage	Element	Percentage
Fe	38.80	Na	0.51
0	27.17	Co	0.20
Si	13.84	Cr	0.19
Mg	11.25	Mn	0.13
s	2.74	P	0.08
Ni	2.70	K	0.06
Al	1.07	Ti	0.06
Ca	1.07		

One can explain the differences between the composition of the Earth's crust and the general composition of the Earth by the factors we enumerated earlier, mainly in connection with the geochemical affinity of each element.

However, terrestrial data seems to differ from cosmic data regarding the abundance of volatile elements or permanent gases on the Earth. Hydrogen can be found combined with oxygen, such as water. Also, the carbon and nitrogen content is altered by forming volatile gases such as NH_3 and CH_4, which escaped the Earth while it was hot. We have briefly described the abundance of elements on the Earth and deduced only data that would be more or less accurate according to the specific influence of the Earth's conditions. For a thorough analysis of matter evolution at the level of the Universe, we need to analyze the composition of other cosmic bodies and the abundance of elements in each of these periods. This task is complicated by the need for more devices to perform these measurements. Thus, we cannot obtain data about the planetary magnetism or seismic waves of other planets. However, we can analyze their gross composition, which could be relevant. The analysis of meteorites is a good alternative until we can completely analyze the composition of other planets.

Meteorites are small cosmic bodies presumed to originate from a planet that "died" and decomposed. They can be observed in space by using a regular telescope. They produce a "fireball" appearance from friction with the atmospheres they pass through. Some have fallen on the Earth and been analyzed, but most meteorites rarely reach the Earth's surface. Their substance usually dissipates when it meets the resistance of the Earth's atmosphere, and they eventually reach the ground as meteoritic dust. In our galaxy, most meteorites are found between Mars and Jupiter.

Earth is believed to have collided with such meteorites, as evidenced by the Barringer "meteor" crater near Winslow, Arizona, and a crater in Quebec, Canada. Meteorites can be classified into three main classes: irons (siderites), stony irons (siderolites), and stones (aerolites). The iron meteorites are composed mostly of nickel and iron, having an average composition of 90% Fe, 8.5% Ni, 0.6% Co, and less than 0.01% Si. Even if this composition does not offer a wide variety, iron meteorites are important from a geometrical point of view.

As already mentioned, iron ranks low on the smartness/intelligence scale based on its geochemical affinity. However, its geometrical configuration compensates for this. Most of the siderites are octahedrites, meaning they display an octahedral structure called the Widmanstätten figure when cut, polished, and etched.

On the other hand, about 8% of iron meteorites consist of kamacite crystals, which exhibit a cubic cleavage and so-called "Neumann lines." Only about 12% of the siderites (represented by ataxites) do not exhibit the two geometrical configurations described above, being mainly granular. Stony irons, or siderolites, are formed by near equal volumes of stony and nickel–iron constituents. In contrast, stony meteorites, or aerolites, contain chiefly silicates and small amounts of sulfides, nickel, and iron. So far, all cosmic data comes from direct measurements. To study the composition of the stars, which are too far from the Earth for measurement, we can obtain data only by analyzing their emission spectra. Whatever the investigation method, we can estimate the difference in composition between the different cosmic bodies.

Based on these values, we can further determine the planet's history and the evolution of matter in its circumstances. As in any hierarchical system analyzed so far, we can conclude that the evolution of matter on a star is also influenced by two main factors (remember the dualism that determines dynamics and evolution).

Table 4.4 compares a few elements found in planetary nebulae, the Orion Nebula and the Pegasi Nebula.

Table 4.4 Comparison of abundance of some elements in certain cosmic locations

Element	Planetary Nebulae	Orion Nebula	Pegasi
Ne	1500	12,000	12,600
S	900	2500	1500
C1	34	20	42
Ar	130	100	190

The data collected from the Universe shows a significant abundance of iron. Numerous theories attempt to explain this prevalence.

Even if hydrogen, carbon, nitrogen, and oxygen are abundant, their neighboring elements (or isotopes), such as lithium, beryllium, and boron, are rare. Among the nuclides, the most abundant are those whose atomic weights are multiples of 4, such as oxygen ($Z = 16$), neon ($Z = 20$), sodium isotope ($Z = 24$), magnesium ($Z = 24$), and silicon ($Z = 28$). It is observed by dividing the elements between those of even and those of odd atomic weight, but there needs to be a definitive answer. The most immediate explanation relates to a survival strategy. Regular iron is prone to oxidation, which can penetrate the material deeply. This observation underscores the importance of our research in understanding the composition and evolution of cosmic bodies.

Iron unites with oxygen to survive. If iron cannot defend itself from corrosion, such as aluminum, its survival strategy must be based on quantity (i.e., abundance). Of course, this assumption correlates with atomic bonds and configurations and must meet the stability criteria required for all elements.

Note that those with even-numbered weights are more abundant; these statistics result from stability factors and geometric configuration. (This topic will be discussed in the next chapter.)

As mentioned earlier in this chapter, the most credible theory of element formation is that elements were produced within the "star ovens." This theory assumes that stars were initially formed out of hydrogen. As hydrogen was burned, it produced helium. The burning of helium led to the formation of carbon, oxygen, neon, and probably magnesium. These led to further reactions determined by the specific conditions of each star. For example, here are some reactions that describe the formation of primary elements:

$$H^1 + H^1 \rightarrow H^2 + \beta + v$$
$$H^2 + H \rightarrow He^3 + \mathit{'Y}$$
$$He^3 + He^3 \rightarrow He^4 + 2H^1$$
$$He^3 + He^4 \rightarrow Be^7 + y$$
$$Be^7 + \beta \rightarrow Li^7$$
$$Li^7 + p \rightarrow 2He^4$$

We must note that these reactions occur at very high temperatures, and many are unstable. We will not detail the composition, diversity, and formation of stars, as this is not in the book's scope. However, we would like to point out that the Universe's hierarchical structure can be found at all material, energetic, and informational levels. Furthermore, these hierarchies prove to be interdependent, which implies an interdependent evolution of matter and intelligence. The material and energetic levels are assimilated as one interchangeable entity conventionally termed "matter."

Intelligence is strongly linked to material and energetic levels as a product of information. However, because of another factor not discussed thus far, geometry will be considered a separate but matter-dependent entity.

4.19 Role of Geometry in the Evolution of Matter, Intelligence, Life, and Consciousness

4.19.1 Basic Shapes

One needs to return to meteorites to establish a link between geometry, matter, intelligence, and consciousness since they are exposed to a dangerous, manic environment. Most meteorites that have collided with the Earth are chondrites. This type of meteoritic material contains chondrules: spherical bodies that appear to have developed during the cosmic journey of the meteorite. This supposition is based on the fact that the spherical material covering the core is mainly the same as the core, which melted and solidified. Therefore, chondrules are partially crystallized bodies. Of interest here, however, is the basic shape of chondrules. The sphere is a perfect geometric body that exhibits an unstable equilibrium. One might call this a dynamic equilibrium, as a sphere is always and never in equilibrium. How can this be explained? Well, with the friction in the Earth's atmosphere, the meteoritic material partially eroded. The rest became heated to the melting point. Since friction is a surface phenomenon, heating and melting occur only at the surface of the chondrites. The chondrites adapted to these dynamic conditions through geometric adaptation to minimize the influence. This geometrical solution proved to be the sphere. We know that most metallic crystals exhibit a cubic configuration and that this configuration is very stable. So, if we put together the resulting configuration, a chondrite, and a metallic crystal with cubic configuration, each of them has the best geometric configuration for its environmental conditions. The sphere could be considered the standard of stability and adaptation in a dynamic environment. In contrast, the cube could be considered the standard of stability and adaptation in a static (or quasistatic) environment.

One can see how geometry is important in matter, intelligence, and consciousness evolution. Why could mathematics be such a great tool in modeling reality? It is a product of human thought and is chiefly independent of experience. Even Albert Einstein stated that "as far as the laws of mathematics refer to reality, they are not certain; and as far as they are certain, they do not refer to reality." Since mathematics appeared and developed around reality, with more or less approximations, the following can be considered. Mathematics created different models of reality, each with certain degrees of error. These degrees of error are a consequence of reality in that the human mind cannot completely cover and understand its totality. Therefore, humans mimicked what they perceive and understand. When a model is to be compared to reality, another error level is added to the system for these reasons. Geometry plays a crucial role in modeling reality since nature is based on geometry and perfect geometric shapes are readily found in nature. Among the mathematical sciences, geometry seems to be the closest to nature. Even the name "geometry" comes from the Greek words for "Earth measuring." The Earth is obviously a part of the Universe, a part of reality. On the other hand, measuring involves a conventionally created scale of units that assign human values to real objects. According to Einstein, geometry can be divided into practical geometry, which refers directly to reality (based on experience), and axiomatic geometry, which is based on rules derived from reality (with a certain degree of abstractization). Practical geometry relies on physical observations and experiments and can be considered a physical science. On the other hand, one knows that geometry can be either Euclidean (which refers to static or quasistatic, two- or three-dimensional systems) or non-Euclidean (which refers to dynamic, multidimensional systems). The sphere and the tetrahedron represent the simplest, most perfect geometric form. We have already noted that chondrules adopt a survival strategy by self-modeling their shape into a sphere. Therefore, we can talk about an intelligent geometric design. Matter, intelligence, and geometry together form a powerful, dynamic system. Has there been an evolution of geometry? The answer is definitely positive, and an explanation will be developed within this chapter.

We can consider the evolution of geometry in two ways. First, we can talk about the evolution of geometrical science as a result of the evolution of human intelligence. One can also talk about the true geometry of the Universe, which is the result of the evolution of both matter and intelligence. However, as the goal of this book is to develop a theory about the interdependence between matter, intelligence, and geometry, only issues regarding the real geometry of the Universe will be addressed in this chapter. Humans have always been interested in understanding and modeling their environment and, eventually, the Universe. Different theories have been proposed and developed.

These theories are more or less sophisticated. From a geometrical point of view, however, they suggest a few recurring elements that form the basis of the geometry of the Universe. As the Universe is a dynamic system, its reference geometric form is the sphere, which is reducible to almost a point. Two points form a line. A line and an outer point form a surface.

A surface and an outer point form the basic solid, a tetrahedron. Based on this development, one can reach the cube, which is considered the reference solid for static geometry, earlier in this chapter. What does this mean? Well, it could explain why matter (as well as energy and information) has experienced a dynamic evolution before reaching the level of stability conferred upon the cubic shape. One should note that the cube represents a perfect reference geometric shape for Euclidean geometry. However, transposing this to non-Euclidean geometry, one encounters a hypercube, a representation of a cube in n-dimensions. Thus, a 1-hypercube is a line segment, a 2-hypercube is a square, a 3-hypercube is a regular cube, and a 4-hypercube is a "tesseract." This is visualized in Fig. 4.3.

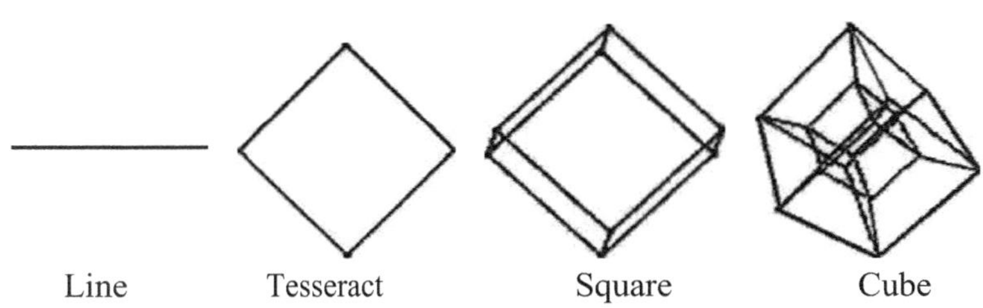

Figure 4.3 Hypercubes in 2-D, 3-D, and 4-D.

While Fig. 4.3 shows a projection of the tesseract in 3D space, Fig. 4.4 shows a symmetric projection into a plane. These geometrical forms can easily be considered an evolutionary structure within a hierarchic system.

It is crucial to acknowledge the pivotal role of the sphere in the evolution of geometry.

The sphere's dynamic nature is a recurring element in the Universe, from the microstructure of elements to the grand universal hierarchy. When viewed from the perspective of n-dimensional space, the sphere takes on different forms: In 2D, it is a circle; in 3D, it is a regular sphere; and in 4D, it is the "full sphere."

Even if theoretical models in n-dimensional spaces (the so-called Minkowski spaces) can be developed, they still need to be revised to be imagined and understood. One hopes that mathematics and physics will join hands to break the barrier of imagination that prohibits us from watching our system from an advanced dimension. As mentioned at the beginning of this book, a system cannot be accurately analyzed from inside the system. One must find a way to analyze it from the outside.

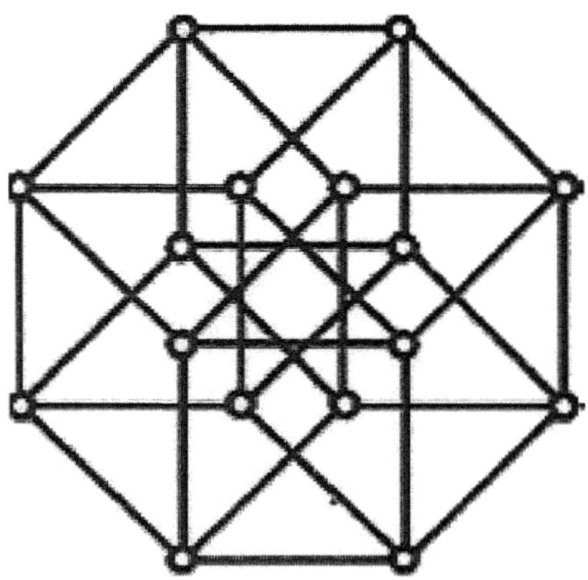

Figure 4.4 4D hypercube symmetrically projected into a plan.

4.19.2 The Pi Number

Circular shapes have always fascinated people. A circle can be considered a symbol of perfection of interest to scientists and artists. Is this just intuition or an intelligent inspiration? We will never know. The common element of a sphere in any dimensional space is the Pi number (π). The Pi number has been a constant known since ancient times and represents the ratio of the circumference of a circle to its diameter. It is an approximate value and is

$$\pi = 3.14159265358979323846264338327950288419716939937511$$

It cannot be expressed in terms of the ratio of two integers. This interesting property leads to a philosophical interpretation: The approximation of the Pi number leads to perfection. On the other hand, perfection is directly related to intelligence, and the sphere is related to dynamics and, therefore, evolution. Historically, the first theoretical calculation of the Pi number seems to have been carried out by Archimedes of Syracuse (287–212 BC), who obtained the approximation: $223/71 < \pi > 22/7$.

We should note that Archimedes knew the Pi number did not equal 22/7 and made no claim to have discovered the exact value. However, if we estimate the average of his two bounds, we obtain 3.1418, an error of about 0.0002 (Fig. 4.5).

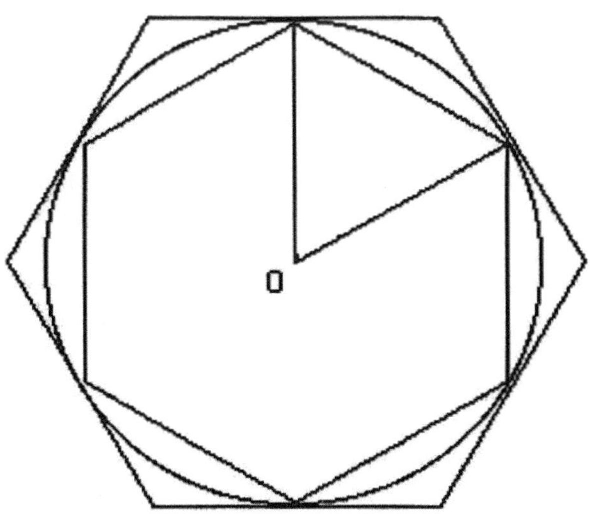

Figure 4.5 The bilateral convergence toward the value of π.

This bilateral convergence, which defines the value of the Pi number, can be compared with the macrocosmos–microcosmos dualism or the Universe–matter dualism. In both examples, however, we refer only to the converging elements. What represents the limits they are converging to? It might be related to Universal Intelligence because it is a universal number everywhere. If this is the case, we can also look at this inversely as a divergent process represented by the Universal Intelligence developing and evolving the Universe in the form of geometry and numbers. If this process is reversible, could it be pulsatory? Unfortunately, this question remains unanswered since the physical phenomena involved here are not completely understood. We know about matter transforming into energy and energy forming into matter, but matter transforming completely into intelligence is hard to understand, especially because intelligence still has no precise definition. If, at the dawn of Creation, there was light everywhere, and this energy created everything else, then it also had definite ubiquitous numerical and geometric intelligence.

This task is complicated by the lack of devices to perform these measurements. Thus, we cannot obtain data about the planetary magnetism or seismic waves of other planets. However, one can analyze their gross composition, which could be relevant. The analysis of meteorites is a good alternative until we can completely analyze the composition of other planets.

The Pi number can be found in a wide range of fields. It occurs in hundreds of equations, including those that describe the DNA double helix, rainbows, the ripples that radiate from a pool where a raindrop has fallen, superstrings, the gravitational field equations of Einstein, the equations of normal distribution of primes, in waves, navigation, and many, many more. It is present everywhere in the Universe. Even if Archimedes gave the most famous approximation of the Pi number, it is not the most accurate one. It will suffice, however, for regular applications. Other approximations include 355/113, which has an error of 0.00000849%, while the best approximation seems to be 104348/33215, which has an error of only 0.00000001056%.

Further theories and interpretations could be developed based on these approximations, but this is not our goal in this book. We are interested only in the role that the Pi number plays in the evolution of matter, geometry, intelligence, and consciousness, as well as their integration within the Universe.

We could deduce (or at least suppose) that the Pi number might directly relate to every system's internal impulse of evolution. However, we must also note that any system evolves according to certain laws, i.e., natural selection. The relationship between the laws of evolution and another constant called the Phi number will be discussed in the next section.

4.19.3 The Phi Number φ

The Phi number φ, also called "the Golden Number," has been known since ancient times. Fibonacci, who developed a theory about it, initially developed a model of species multiplication from generation to generation based on the reproduction of rabbits. Thus, he developed the so-called Fibonacci series, which is founded on the following numbers:

1, 1, 2, 3, 5, 8, 13, 21, 34, 55, 89, 144, 233, 377, 610, ...

The algorithm for this series considers the first two initial values, 1 and 1, as a starter. The next element of the series is the sum of the previous two. Thus, $a_n = a_{n-1} + a_{n-2}$ (n = 1, 2, 3, ..., N).

The interesting part of this series is that it can be used to compute the ratio of each of two consecutive elements from the Fibonacci series. From this, we get another series that converges toward a value equal to 1.618034, the Phi φ number (Fig. 4.6).

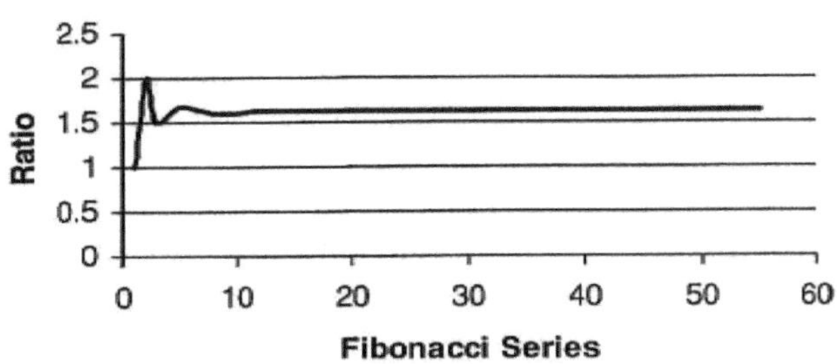

Figure 4.6 Convergence toward the Phi number

Table 4.5 shows the convergence of the ratio of the consecutive elements of the Fibonacci series and the table of values.

Table 4.5 Fibonacci series versus ratio of its consecutive elements

1	1	2	3	5	8	13	21	34	55	89	144
	1	2	1.5	1.666	1.6	1.625	1.615	1.619	1.617	1.618	1.618

You might ask why this Phi number is so important. First of all, it has been proved that it can be found at any level in the Universe, which makes it a good candidate for a universal number and universal consciousness. Furthermore, as will be seen immediately, the Phi number is the connection between geometry, the Universe (matter, geometry, intelligence, and consciousness), and consciousness evolution.

One must first assume some criteria for developing a series to prove this theory. Starting with the main derivatives of the Phi numbers that have been tabulated, we can establish a technique for identifying the Phi number in the Universe.

The best way to discover relationships between certain groups and the Phi number is to develop progressions based on the Phi number, starting from different reference elements. Thus, the main derivatives of the Phi number are shown in Table 4.6.

Table 4.6 Derivatives of the Phi number

φ	$\Phi^{(1/2)}$	$(\varphi+1)/2$
1.618	1.272	1.309
$1/\varphi$	$\varphi/2$	—
1.618	1.809	—

Take, for example, the planets of our galaxy. We can analyze the ratios between the distances to the sun of each of our neighboring planets, which leads to Table 4.7.

It is interesting to notice in this table that the mean value of the above ratios equals 1.688, which is very close to the Phi number. We could analyze the equatorial radius of Jupiter's satellites further. The results are presented in Table 4.8. However, we should remember that the distances used for computing the above ratios have a certain degree of error. This means that the ratios of the real distances might lead to a mean value even closer to the Phi number.

Table 4.7 Ratios of the distances to the sun of each of the two neighboring planets

Planet	Distance to Sun (Astronomic Units)	Ratio
Mercury	0.387	—
Venus	0.723	1.868
Earth	1.0	1.383
Mars	1.523	1.523
Asteroids	2.7	1.772
Jupiter	5.202	1.926
Saturn	9.536	1.833
Uranus	19.210	2.014
Neptune	30.138	1.568
Pluto	39.390	1.306

Table 4.8 Comparison between the relative radii of Jupiter's satellites and the deducted values based on the Phi number

Jupiter's Satellites	Equatorial Radius (Relative to the One of Jupiter = 1)	Value of the progression: V < p < R..,.,,..,
Io	5.91	5.91
Ganimede	9.40	9.56
Europe	15.0	15.47
Callisto	26.33	25.03

Again, one can observe that the deduced values are quite close to the real ones. Similar correlations with the Phi number were found in many other places in the Universe. We should mention that these correlate with the value of the galactic curve, and even the movement of the Universe tends toward the "red." All these facts strengthen the initial supposition that the Phi number is present almost anywhere in the Universe.

If the Phi number can be found almost anywhere in the macrocosmos, one could investigate whether the same happens at a microcosmos level. One could start by analyzing the composition of the dry air in the Earth's atmosphere and will use a progression of $\varphi^{1/2}$ for our correlation purpose.

As you can see, the correlation is almost perfect. Our correlation shows that the volumetric percentage of oxygen in the air is 20.94%, while its mass percentage is 23.14%. We also know that 100 g of water contains 89 g of oxygen.

To establish a correlation between the two values, one must develop a progression based on the Phi number starting from 20.94%. One will see that it intersects the 89% curve at 88.69%. The importance of this value will be discussed a little later when the presence of the Phi number at the human and animal levels is considered. The most important correlation in the atomic world might be dealing with the atomic number Z. In the previous table, the elements corresponding to hydrogen (H), sodium (Na), copper (Cu), rubidium (RB), and silver (Ag) are identified directly.

The values for lithium (Li) and francium (Fr) are calculated by using the geometric mean for the 4th and 5th elements and the 18th and 19th elements, respectively.

From the above tables, one can draw the following conclusions: Generally, the atomic numbers of the elements are related to the Phi number. However, it seems that this correlation is also based on the properties of the elements. Thus, one can observe that the correlation could hardly be established for group III. This might be related to the stability of these elements, which diminishes their dynamic behavior. Therefore, these elements might be related to other constants related to the static or quasistatic environment. However, one can continue to study the correlation between the Phi number and the periodic structure of the elements. In this analysis, one would study the correlation based on the progressions of both $\varphi^{1/2}$ and φ^2. Also, only the group's first and last elements would be analyzed. Indeed, one must admit that some elements do not fit perfectly, while others fit only if a certain type of progression is used.

From the previous table, the values corresponding to H, Li, Na, and Au are identified directly, while the remaining elements in the table use the geometric mean. This phenomenon indicates that each element has a space limitation imposed by the Phi number. Why does this occur? This question still awaits an answer. However, this is supposed to represent a mechanism of evolution for the material structures. Many other correlations exist between the material structures and the Phi number. Thus, an element's melting temperature, boiling temperature, ionic radius, van der Waals radius, ionization energy, and dissociation energy can be correlated with the Phi number within the same progression.

It has been proved that many of humankind's physiological, anatomical, or social features can be expressed by a progression of the Phi number. For example, in Table 4.9, you will find the normal values of some biochemical constants compared to the corresponding progression derived from the Phi number. Again, the procedure is to multiply the value of the first element in the table with $\varphi^{1/2}$ consecutively and then select the appropriate values.

Thus, considering this table, we obtain the following progression by multiplying 5 with $\varphi^{1/2}$: 5, 6.36, 8.08, 10.29, 13.08, 16.64, 21.17, and 26.93. From these values, the ones closest to the real values are picked, i.e., 5, 8, 16.6, and 26.9.

Table 4.9 Electrophoresis values of power

Electrophoresis Product	Normal Value (%)	.fij Progression
u1-globulin	5 (+/- 2%)	5
az-l(lobulio)	7.5	8.08
6-globulin	16	16.64
y-globulin	27.5	26.93

We can already develop different interpretations of these correlations. One could establish hierarchical and dependent relations between elements in the same progression.

If different factors are analyzed, even more interesting relations could be developed. It has been seen thus far that the Phi number could be easily found in almost everything in the Universe. However, it might be interesting to find out the relationship between the Phi number and geometry.

First, we must describe more properties of the Phi number. The Phi number satisfies the following equations:

$$\varphi = \varphi^2 - 1$$

$$1 + \varphi = \varphi^2;\ \varphi + = \varphi^3;\ \varphi^2 + \varphi^3 = \varphi^4;$$

$$\varphi = 1 + 1/(1 + 1/(1 + 1/(1 + 1/(1 + 1/ \ldots))))$$

$$\varphi = (\sec 72)/2 = (\csc 18)/2 = 1/(2\cos 72)\ 1/(2\sin 18)$$

$$= 2\sin 54 = 2\cos 36 = 2/(\csc 54) = 2/(\sec 36)$$

$$= 2\sin 54 = 2\cos 36 = 2/(\csc 54) = 2/(\sec 36)$$

The Phi number φ is also called the "Golden Ratio." This unique ratio is such that, given a line segment, the ratio of the whole segment to the larger portion of the segment is the same as the ratio of the segment's larger portion to the smaller one and equals the Phi number.

This ratio can be found, for example, in the famous pentagram (Fig. 4.7), which was considered sacred in antiquity.

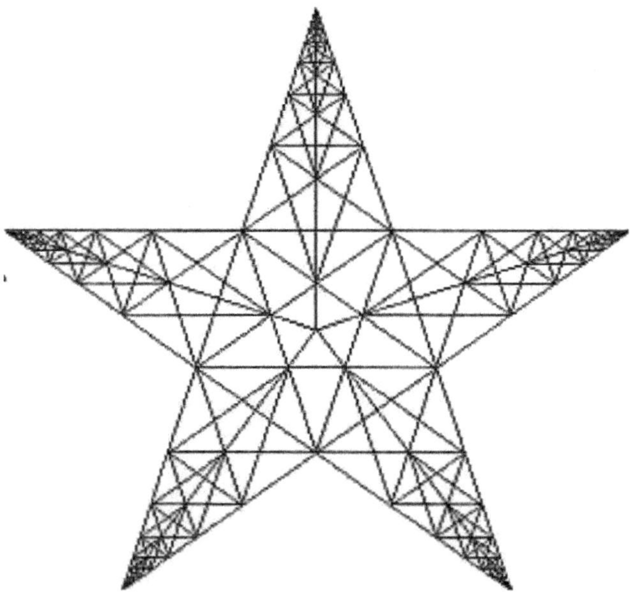

Figure 4.7 The Phi number in the pentagram.

In Fig. 4.7, each of the two adjacent points with the opposite point forms the so-called "Golden Triangle," an isosceles triangle with an angle of 36° and two angles of 72°. The pentagram was constructed after the Phi number since anything measurable in the Universe can be uniquely divided to follow the above criteria using the Phi number.

Now that the properties of the Phi number are known, let us reconsider the properties of the dynamic and static geometry mentioned earlier. The cube represents the reference element for the static geometry, while the sphere represents the reference for the dynamic geometry. By analyzing these two forms, one realizes that the volume of the cube is expressed only as a function of its dimensions and implies none of the Phi or Pi numbers, while the volume of the sphere is a function of these numbers. A cube can be further decomposed into six pyramids. Based on this, one could consider the pyramid a static form.

On the other hand, if one analyzes the dimensions of a specific pyramid, say the Great Pyramid of Giza, one will observe that its dimensions are also a function of the Pi and Phi numbers.

We could also consider it a tool to further investigate the link between static and dynamic geometry and between matter, geometry, intelligence, and consciousness.

The ancient Egyptians also had an interesting way of handling fractions and ratios. Whenever a non-integer number was needed, it was expressed as a sum of fractions, all with a numerator of one. Similarly, a fraction with numerator 1, closest to but smaller than the difference between the value of the initial fraction and the value of the fraction of numerator 1, was determined.

Such examples can be found in Egyptian documents dated about 1700 B.C., as the following:

$$2/7 = 1/4 + 1/28$$
$$2/97 = 1/56 + 1/679 + 1/776$$
$$2/99 = 1/66 + 1/198$$

Based on this procedure, one can deduce that the circle and the Pi number, possibly associated with the Phi number in advanced cases, exist in the background of this conversion.

Also, the Great Pyramid is supposed to have been built using the same procedure, which might be very useful in solving the controversy over its dimensions.

Thus, if one considers the Great Pyramid, as sketched in Fig. 4.8, one finds the following interesting correlation:

A circle, having a diameter formed by the apex of the pyramid and the center of the base of the pyramid, has a circumference twice the base length of the pyramid and an area equal to the pyramid's vertical sectional area through the apex.

1. Thus, the ratio f of the perimeter of the pyramid's base to its height is 2π. It is interesting to note here that for the Pyramid of the Sun in Mexico, the ratio equals 2π.
2. The ratio of the apothem of a face of the pyramid to the base length equals $\pi/2$. Or, in other words, the ratio of the apothem to the base length is less than $\pi/2$ (which is also an important number used in various Phi number progressions).
3. The ratio of the pyramid's perimeter to the pyramid's altitude equals 2π.

Many other interesting correlations could be developed from the geometry of the Great Pyramid, but for now, we can use the ones above for a deeper analysis. Consider the ratios between the pyramid's perimeter to the pyramid's altitude and between the pyramid's apothem and half of the pyramid's base. From these ratios, we can further write the following simple geometric deductions:

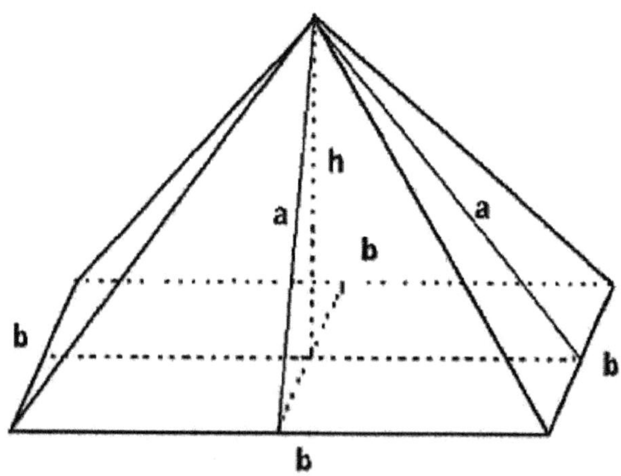

Figure 4.8 Sketch of the Great Pyramid.

The aforementioned discussion gives the relation between the Phi number and the number 4. Since both Pi and Phi are universal numbers, 4 is also universal. However, if we multiply the Pi number by the square root of Phi, the result is not exactly 4, but 3.996..., which is close to 4. This might mean that either the pyramid did not accurately reflect the relation between Pi and Phi or the builders tried to focus on the importance of the number 4. Another argument in the above equation might be the errors perpetuated by conversions from one measuring system to another and the initial errors arising from approximating various fractions. However, these last errors cannot be considerable since it is quite probable that the ancient Egyptians developed their fraction conversion procedure from practical geometrical elements. Therefore, building a structure that involves fractions would require reversing the conversion procedure. In other words, the Egyptians did not have to measure the dimensions of a structure since they knew them from geometrical applications.

These facts could lead to different interpretations. First, one observes that the Great Pyramid plays a very important role in geometry since it makes the link between static and dynamic geometry and has further implications for evolution and the structure of matter and intelligence. Also, the Great Pyramid can be considered a tool for projecting sphere segments on plane surfaces. This, again, proves the transition role of the Great Pyramid between static and dynamic geometry. In other words, the Great Pyramid represents a calculator that can transform the static geometry of angles into the dynamic geometry of curves. In addition to the Great Pyramid, we should also mention the so-called D&M pyramid on Mars. This pyramid is situated at 40.868 degrees north, which is exactly arctan, where *e* is the base of the Eulerian logarithm. In addition, many other geometric features of the D&M pyramid can be expressed as functions of *e* and *i*. Like the relation between π and ϕ or φ, one should also note the relation between *e* and *i*, discovered by Euler. Thus, Euler's formula is

$$e^{ix} = \cos x + i \sin x,$$

where i is the square root of −1, a complex number. When $x = \pi$, Euler's formula may be rewritten as $e^{i\pi} + 1 = 0$ or $e^{i\pi} = -1$, which is known as Euler's identity.

The relationship between π, the Phi number, and *e* can also be demonstrated geometrically. One can reproduce the shape of the Nautilus shell by using a spiral generated by a recursive series of Golden Triangles.

The complex result is a logarithmic spiral sum, demonstrating our initial assumption. The same spiral could be built from a recursive series of rectangles generated by the Golden Mean.

In Fig. 4.9, you can find the procedure for building the logarithmic spiral based on both Golden Triangles and Golden Rectangles.

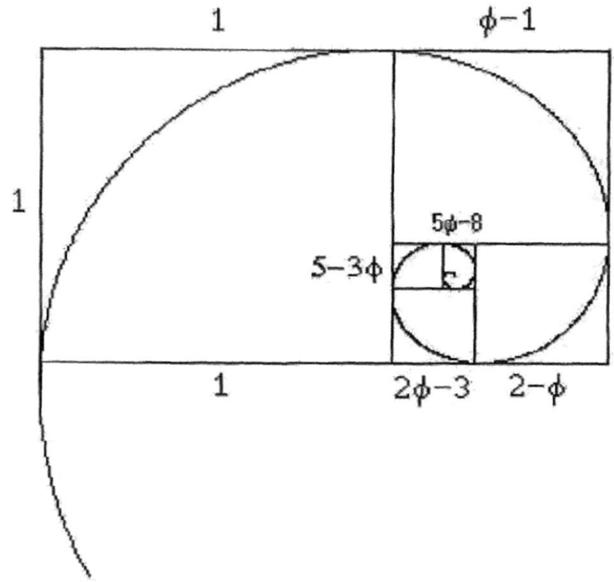

Figure 4.9 The logarithmic spiral built by triangles.

Returning to the universal number 4, we would like to add some very important aspects. It is known that three points can form a surface, which is a two-dimensional geometric element (in Euclidean geometry). However, a fourth point outside the surface creates the third dimension, since any point above or under the surface determined by three points forms, with the three points of a spatial shape, a tetrahedron. One should also remember the importance of the tetrahedron in static geometry, where it is a reference shape. The spatial–temporal universe is determined by four variables: the three spatial variables (length, width, and height) and the temporal variable, time. Therefore, any particle in the Universe can be localized with these four variables only.

4.20 Variable Minds Variable

The Golden Ratio examines the presence of this divine number in art and architecture throughout history, as well as its ubiquity among plants, animals, and even the cosmos. This gorgeous book—with lay-flat dimensions that closely approximate the Golden Ratio—features clear, enlightening, and entertaining commentary alongside stunning full-color illustrations by Venezuelan artist and architect Rafael Araujo. From the pyramids of Giza to quasicrystals to the proportions of the human face, the Golden Ratio can generate shapes with exquisite properties. This book invites you to take a new look at this timeless topic, with a compilation of research and information worthy of a textbook, accompanied by over 200 beautiful illustrations that transform this into the ultimate coffee table book. Author Gary Meisner shares the results of his 20-year investigation and collaboration with thousands of people across the globe in dozens of professions and walks of life. The evidence will close the gaps of understanding related to many claims of the Golden Ratio's appearances and applications and present new findings to further our knowledge. Whoever you are, and whatever you may know about this topic, you will find something new, interesting, and informative in this book and may find yourself challenged to see, apply, and share this unique number of mathematics and science in new ways.

If everybody else can understand dimensions and time and the subatomic potentiality more, we can experience a time where channeling and the internet become obsolete; we fully unclothe our inner technology (telepathy, bilocation, individual teleportation, etc.), have light beings teaching us in our living rooms, and will be able to walk off a cliff and not fall. First, one has to deconstruct our limiting belief systems and engage the right hemisphere into harmony with our ego male hemisphere, which has been dominating. I am currently teaching in depth our potential, the physics of it, and our dimensions.

The Fibonacci sequence is a series of numbers in which a given number is the addition of the two numbers before it. So, if you start with zero, the next number will be 1, followed by 1, followed by 2, followed by 3, and so on. As you can see, every number in this series or sequence is obtained by adding the two preceding numbers. This simple series of numbers is referred to as the Fibonacci sequence for the Fibonacci series. Individual numbers in this sequence are often called Fibonacci numbers. To the uninitiated, it may just seem like a series of numbers. Still, the Fibonacci sequence has been discovered and rediscovered in various forms, not only in mathematics but also in nature and our everyday lives. There is another exciting offshoot of the Fibonacci sequence—the Golden Ratio. Seashells are one of the most common examples of the Golden Spiral in nature. Ocean waves, hurricanes, flower buds, snail shells, and spider webs are some of the many naturally occurring examples.

References and Further Readings

Benveniste, J. (1998). From water memory effects to digital biology. *DigiBio.*

Bernardo, K. (1996). *Your Consciousness is Not in Your Head.* North American Conference on Smart Structures and Materials.

Biocybernaut Institute (1998). Alpha Neurofeedback Training, using alpha brain waves, a specific frequency range (8–13 Hz) of brain wave activity associated with states of relaxation, alertness, and heightened creativity.

Chalmers, D. (2010). *The Character of Consciousness, Philosophy of Mind.* Oxford University Press.

Ciofu, I. (1994). Numarul de Aur. Matrice a Evolutiei? (Golden Number: Matrix of Evolution?), Ed. Coresi, Bucharest, Romania.

Dunai, T. J., and Finlay, S. M. (2009). Reporting of cosmogenic nuclide data for exposure age and erosion rate determinations. *Quat. Geochronol.*, **4**(6), 437–440.

Einstein, A. (1920). *Ether and the Theory of Relativity.* University of Leyden.

Einstein, A. (1921). *Geometry and Experience.* Prussian Academy of Sciences.

Einstein, A. (1996). *Cum Vad Eu Lumea. Teoria Relativitatii pe Intelesul Tuturor* (How Do I See the World. Theory of Relativity on Everybody's Understanding), Ed. Humanitas, Bucharest, Romania.

Erhard, M., Krenn, M., and Zeilinger, A. (2020). Advances in high-dimensional quantum entanglement. *Nat. Rev. Phys.* **2**, 365–381.

Freeman, W. J. (1991). The physiology of perception. *Sci. American*, **264**(2), 78–85.

Frolov, A. V. (1995). *Matter as Process.* St. Petersburg, Russia.

Gamow, G. (1946). Expanding universe and the origin of elements. *Phys. Rev.* **70**, 572.

Greco, D. (1998). *Ether and Field Theories*. MIT.

Guth, A. (2004). Inflation. In: *Measuring and Modeling the Universe*, W. L. Freedman (Ed.). Carnegie Observatories Astrophysics Series, Vol. 2. Cambridge: Cambridge University Press.

Guth, A. H. (1981). Cosmic inflation. *Phys. Rev. D*, **23**, 347

Haldane, J. B. S. (1929). The origin of life. *Rationalist Annual*, **148**, 3–10.

Hardcastle, V. G. and Raja, V. and (Ref: Koch, C.) The Neural Correlates of Consciousness, Available from: https://www.researchgate.net/publication/344577349_www.routledge.com/The-Routledge-Handbook-of Consciousness/Gennaro/p/book/9780367571900

Hubble, E. (1929). Extra-galactic nebulae. *Proc. Natl. Acad. Sci.*, **15**(3), 168–173.

Lindemann, P. A. (2011). *Thermodynamics & Free Energy*. Borderlands.

Lusted, H. S., and Knapp, R. B. (1996). Controlling computers with neural signals. *Scientific American*, **275**(4), 82–87.

Merleau-Ponty, M. (1945). *Phénoménologie de la perception, 1945 (French), 1962 (English)*, English translation from French by Colin Smith (1st English translation), Donald Landes (2nd English translation), Éditions Gallimard, Routledge & Kegan Paul, 1945, English translation (1962), 466 (1965 Routledge edition), ISBN, 978-0415834339 (2012 Routledge edition).

Penrose, R. (2022). Roger Penrose: Consciousness must be beyond computable physics. *New Scientist*, 14 November 2022.

Popa, S. G., and Nicu, M. D. (1989). Unele consideratii asupra efectului de piramida (Some considerations regarding the effect of the pyramid), *Session of Scientific Communications*, Politehnica University of Bucharest.

Popa, S. G., Pop, V., and Serban, I. (1994). Probleme privind abordarea sistemica a related SNC-psychism (Problems regarding the systemic approach of the relationship Central Nervous System—Psychism). *Studies and Research on Biotechnology*, **26**.

Roland-Mieszkowski, M. (1998). *Life on Earth: Flow of Energy and Entropy*, Digital Recordings.

Shahinpoor, M. (1996). Intelligent materials and structures revisited. *Proc. SPIE 1996 North American Conference on. Smart Structures and Materials.* February, 25–29, 1996.

Shahinpoor, M. (1997). *Intelligent Civil Engineering Materials and Structures Revisited*. Engineering Mechanics Division/ASCE.

Shahinpoor, M. (2024). Immortal biomimetic humanoid robots with a human consciousness. *Int. J. Robotics and Automation*, **10**(3), 70–71.

Shahinpoor, M., and Gheshmi, S. (2015). *Robotic Surgery*. Singapore: Jenny Stanford Publishing.

Shahinpoor, M., and Thompson, M. S. (1995). The Venus flytrap as a model for biomimetic material with built-in sensors and actuators. *J. Mater. Sci. Eng.*, **C2**, 229–233.

Shahinpoor, M., and Wang, G. (1995). Design, modeling and performance evaluation of a novel large motion shape memory alloy actuator. In *Proceedings of SPIE (1995) North American Conference on Smart Structures and Materials*, February 28–March 2, San Diego, CA, paper no. 31, 2447.

Shahinpoor, M., and Wang, G. (1995). Electro-thermo-mechanics of SMA fiber bundles embedded in an elastic medium, in *Proc. SPIE 2427, Active Materials and Smart Structures*, vol. 2427, pp. 272–382.

Shahinpoor, M., Bar-Cohen, Y., Simpson, J., and Smith, J. (1998). Ionic polymer–metal composites (IPMC's) as biomimetic sensors, actuators and artificial muscles: A review. *Smart Mater. Struct. J.*, **7**, R15–R30.

Shannon, C. E. (1949). A mathematical theory of communication. *Bell System Tech. J.*, **27**(3): 379–423.

Tononi, G., and Koch, C. (2015). Consciousness: Here, there and everywhere? *Phil. Trans. Royal Soc.*, **370**(1668). doi:10.1098/rstb.2014.0167.

Wang, G., and Shahinpoor, M. (1997). A new design for a rotatory joint actuator made with shape memory alloy contractile wire. *J. Intell. Mater. Syst. Struct.*, **8**(3), 191–279.

Wang, G., and Shahinpoor, M. (1997). Design for shape memory alloy rotatory joint actuators using shape memory effect and pseudoelastic effect. *Smart Mater. Technol.*, **3040**, 23–30.

Wang, G., and Shahinpoor, M. (1997). Design, prototyping and computer simulation of a novel large bending actuator made with a shape memory alloy contractile wire. *Smart Mater. Struct. J.*, **6**(2), 214–221.

Zadeh, L. A. (1973). Outline of a new approach to the analysis of complex systems and decision processes. *IEEE Transactions on Systems, Man, & Cybernetics*, **3**(1), 28–44.

Chapter 5

Design, Development, and Construction of Biomimetic Humanoid Robots

5.1 Introduction

This chapter will introduce stimuli-responsive, smart, intelligent materials and artificial muscles to design, develop, fabricate, and construct biomimetic humanoid robots with a consciousness similar to human consciousness. It is important to assign an identity to the individual who will have consciousness. This will be called identity-vita-assigned consciousness (IVA-consciousness). It is important not to have just an AI intelligent computer or robot to have consciousness with no identity. Under these circumstances, the robot with consciousness may become out of control because of a lack of identity and develop undesirable scenarios.

This is the beginning of imparting some consciousness to a humanoid robot. It informs and alerts the humanoid robot that it will be assigned the identity of the human master as well as the human master's complete vita and resume and the story of his or her life so far. The humanoid robot knows from its memory bank that it has the same identity (male or female) as the human master. This is a kind of beginning of self-awareness for the humanoid to always know that it has an identity and corresponds to the human master, say Captain Kirk's humanoid.

Biomimetic Humanoid Robots with Human Consciousness
Mohsen Shahinpoor

ISBN 978-981-5129-87-8 (Hardcover), 978-1-003-71373-9 (eBook)
www.jennystanford.com

DOI: 10.1201/9781003713739-5

The humanoid robot also needs some kind of smart wearable clothing and outfit. The clothing should look the same, which may be exactly similar to the clothing worn by its human master.

The smart, intelligent, stimuli-responsive electroactive polymers are the smart clothing fabrics to be tailored and worn by humanoid robots. Of course, the robot should look very much like the master human and possibly in regular clothing.

Figures 5.1(a,b,c) show the human masters and the look-alike humanoid robots with their masters' consciousness.

Figure 5.1 (a, b, c) Humans and their humanoid robots.

If desired, humanoid robots can be fabricated much larger than the master human, especially for larger and heavier loads and activities, space travel, as well as for representing the humanoids as aliens from Earth! In this case, the gigantic humanoid robots are designated as humanoid robot number 2, such as Captain Kirk's humanoid-2 (see Fig. 5.1c).

Many scientists and researchers have focused on achieving efficiencies as high as 50% in the direct conversion of chemical to mechanical energy, as occurs in biological muscles. In comparison, most internal combustion engines and steam turbines have lower efficiency.

First, it would be useful to review electroactive polymers (EAPs) in general and other stimuli-responsive and multifunctional smart materials and artificial muscles. This chapter presents the materials for creating immortal biomimetic humanoids with consciousness.

This chapter will introduce the design, development, and construction of biomimetic humanoid robots with human consciousness using stimuli-responsive, smart, wearable intelligent materials and artificial muscles. It will also introduce stimuli-responsive, smart, intelligent materials and artificial muscles.

As described before, humanoid robots can help humans master any profession and even sports activity. They can learn all that through training and instructions. Please note that the current technology can make humanoid robots much more capable and flexible in moving their joints. They can be designed and fabricated to easily bend their fingers, elbows, and knees forward and backward or turn their necks backward if necessary.

5.2 A Brief History of Electroactive Polymers and Artificial/Synthetic Muscles

Röntgen (1880) appears to have been the first to make an EAP. He used a rubber band that could change shape on being charged or discharged. Later, Sacerdote (1899) formulated the strain response to electric field activation in polymers. In 1925, Eguchi (1925) reported the discovery of a piezoelectric polymer that he called an electret. He found that the resulting material was piezoelectric when molten carnauba wax, rosin, and beeswax were solidified by cooling in a direct current (DC) electric field. Generally, electrical excitation is only one type of stimulator that can induce elastic deformation in polymers. The polyvinylidene fluoride (PVDF) crystalline solids possess microscopic regions with dipole charges. Under mechanical stress, the internal arrangements of embedded electrical dipoles generate a voltage across the material boundaries. Conversely, an applied voltage to the material changes the embedded internal dipole charges' orientation and generates a deformation or strain in the solid. Zhang et al. (1998) observed substantial piezoelectric activity in PVF2-TrFE (polyvynilidene fluoride or difluoride-tri fluoroethylene or VF3) as early as 1998.

Other activation mechanisms include chemical (Katchalsky, 1949; Kuhn et al., 1950; Steinberg et al., 1966; Shahinpoor, 1992; Otero et al., 1995; Shahinpoor et al., 1997a, 1997b), thermal (Tobushi et al., 1992; Kishi et al., 1993; Li et al., 1999), pneumatic (Shahinpoor et al., 2001), optical (van der Veen and Prins, 1971), and magnetic (Zrinyi et al., 1997) mechanisms.

Chemically stimulated polymers were discovered more than half a century ago when it was shown that collagen filaments could reversibly contract or expand when dipped in acidic or alkaline solutions, respectively (Katchalsky, 1949). This early work pioneered synthetic polymers that mimic biological muscles (Steinberg et al., 1966; Shahinpoor et al., 1998a, 1998b).

However, electrical stimulation has remained the best means of EAP material actuation and sensing. Shahinpoor and Mojarrad (1994, 1996, 1997a, 1997b, 1997c, 1997d, 2000) were among the pioneers in making electrically active—in sensing and actuation—ionic polymer conductor nanocomposites (IPCNCs) and ionic polymer–metal nanocomposites (IPMNCs).

The most significant progress in developing EAP materials has occurred in the last 10 years when useful materials that can induce strains exceeding 100% have emerged (Perline et al., 1998). Generally, EAPs can be divided into two major categories of electronic and ionic polymers based on their activation mechanism. The electronic polymers (electrostrictive, electrostatic, piezoelectric, and ferroelectric) require high activation fields (~200 MV/m) close to the dielectric breakdown field levels in polymers.

The electronic EAP materials have a higher mechanical energy density and can operate in the air without significant constraints. Ionic EAP materials (gels, polymer–metal composites, conductive polymers (CPs), and carbon nanotubes and graphene), on the other hand, require drive voltages as low as a few volts and small fields of about a few thousand volts per meter (~2–4 kV/m).

The induced displacement of the electronic and ionic EAPs can be designed geometrically to bend, stretch, roll, twirl, twist, or contract. Next, we will describe some specific EAPs.

5.2.1 Electrically Conductive and Photonic Polymers

McGehee et al. (1999) described it as taking almost 20 years to develop synthetic metals or CPs such as polyaniline. The success of these studies has led to the emergence of CPs that exhibit electronic properties approaching the levels in metals and semiconductors (Cao et al., 1991) and offer the processing advantages and mechanical properties of polymers. High-performance devices, including light-emitting diodes, light-emitting electrochemical cells, photodiodes, and lasers, have been fabricated. The brightness of some light-emitting diodes based on photonic polymers is as high as that of a fluorescent lamp. The performance of some photonic polymers has been improved such that their performance is comparable to or better than that of their inorganic counterparts. Compared to some conventional charge-coupled devices (CCDs), EAP-based systems are expected to respond about 10 times faster, provide larger pixel arrays at low power, and effectively operate at low light levels.

A large number of conducting polymers are currently used industrially and medically. Well-known conducting polymers are polypyrrole (PPy), polyaniline, polythiophene, polyphenylene vinylene, and oxyacetylene, which can be manufactured by chemical or electrochemical oxidation and reduction (REDOX) procedures.

Early work on CPs reported that polyacetylene's conductivity increased millions of times when it was oxidized by "doping" with iodine vapor. CP's molecular structures possess single and double chemical bonds to enhance charge transfer. The pioneering work of Professors Heeger (2001), MacDiarmid (2001), and Shirakawa (2001) in these areas of CPs earned them the Nobel Prize in Chemistry in 2000.

5.2.2 Magnetically Activated Polymer Gels and Polymers

Magnetically activated gels, so-called ferrogels, are chemically cross-linked polymer networks that are swollen by the presence of a magnetic field (Zrinyi et al., 1999). Zrinyi et al. (1999) have been pioneers of this technology. Such a gel is a colloidal dispersion of monodomain magnetic nanoparticles. Such magnetic ferrogel materials deform in a spatially nonuniform magnetic field because their embedded nanoparticles move in reaction to the field.

The ferrogel material can be activated to bend, elongate, deform, curve, or contract repeatedly. It has a response time of less than 100 ms, independent of the particle size. Note that magnetic gels are softer, more stretchable, and maneuverable in the magnetic field. "An Intro to the Development of Ferrogels" was a classic paper by Rosenzweig in 1985 on Ferro hydrodynamics. A colloidal ferrofluid, or a magnetic fluid, is a colloidal dispersion of monodomain magnetic particles.

The monodomain magnetic particles are about 10–15 nm in size and are superparamagnetic, in which magnetization can randomly flip direction under the influence of temperature. Magnetic gels or ferrogels belong to the general family of magnetostrictive materials producing strain when exposed to a magnetic field. Magnetic gels belong to the family of hydrogels, polymeric gels, and polyelectrolyte gels. They are highly swollen molecular networks that are cross-linked, creating a hydrophilic solid.

5.2.3 Electronic EAPs/Ferroelectric Polymers

The conducting crystal or dielectric material exhibits spontaneous electric polarization. These are based on the phenomenon of piezoelectricity, which is found only in noncentrosymmetric materials such as PVDF. These polymers are partly crystalline, with an inactive amorphous phase, and have Young's modulus of elasticity of about 1–10 GPa. This relatively high elastic modulus offers high mechanical energy density. A large applied AC field (–200 MV/m) can induce electrostrictive (nonlinear) strains greater than 1%. Sen et al. (1984) investigated the effect of mixing heavy plasticizers (–65 wt%) of ferroelectric polymers, hoping to achieve large strains in reasonably applied fields. However, the plasticizer is also amorphous and inactive, decreasing Young's modulus, permittivity, and electrostrictive strains.

Recently, Zhang et al. (1998) introduced defects into the crystalline structure using electron irradiation to dramatically reduce the dielectric loss in a PVDF trifluoroethylene (PVDF-TrFE) copolymer. This copolymerization permits AC switching with much less generated heat. The electric field–induced change between nonpolar and polar regions is responsible for the large electrostriction observed in this polymer. As large as 4% of electrostrictive strains can be achieved with low-frequency driving fields having amplitudes of about 150 V/μm. As with ceramic ferroelectrics, electrostriction can be considered the origin of piezoelectricity in ferroelectric polymers (Furukawa and Seo, 1990). Unlike electrostriction, piezoelectricity is a linear effect, where the material will be strained when voltage is applied, and a voltage signal will be induced when stress is applied.

5.2.4 Electrets and Piezoelectric Polymers

Electrets, discovered in 1925, retain their electric polarization after being subjected to a strong electric field (Eguchi, 1925). Piezoelectric behavior in polymers also appears in electrets, which are essential materials with a geometrical combination of hard and soft phases (Sessler and Hillenbrand, 1999). The positive and negative charges within the material are permanently displaced along and against the field's direction, respectively, making a polarized material with a net zero charge. Piezoelectric materials are piezoceramics, such as lead-zirconate-titanate (PZT) and piezopolymers, such as PVDF.

The piezoelectric effect describes a reversible electrodynamic relation in some solid crystalline structures with embedded dipoles. These crystalline solids possess microscopic regions containing dipole charges. Under applied mechanical stress, they change the internal arrangements of embedded electrical dipoles, subsequently generating a voltage across the material boundaries. Conversely, an applied voltage to the solid crystalline changes the orientation of the embedded internal dipole charges and generates a deformation or strain in the solid.

5.2.5 Dielectric Elastomer EAPs

Polymers with a low elastic stiffness modulus and a high dielectric constant can be packaged with interdigitated electrodes to generate large actuation strains by subjecting them to an electric field. A parallel plate capacitor can represent this dielectric elastomer EAP (Perline et al., 1998).

The induced strain is proportional to the square of the electric field, multiplied by the dielectric constant, and is inversely proportional to the elastic modulus. Dielectric elastomer EAP actuators require large electric fields (100 V/μm) and can induce significant strain levels (10–200%).

Recently, Perline et al. (2000) introduced a new polymer class exhibiting an extremely high strain response. These acrylic-based elastomers have produced large strains of more than 200% but suffer because they require large electric fields in the range of hundreds of megavolts per meter.

If rubbery elastomers, such as a silicone rubber sheet, are sandwiched between two compliant electrodes, any imposed electric field induces electrostatic forces (attraction) between the electrodes. Thus, the rubber sheet between them can be compressed by the electrostatic forces, which then cause the rubbery sheet to expand sideways due to Poisson's ratio effect and, thus, actuation results.

Röntgen in 1880 demonstrated this actuation by using two glasses as dielectrics, and once the opposing surfaces of these glasses were charged, small thickness changes were observed by Röntgen. Later, electrostatically induced pressures acting to compress dielectrics became known as the "Maxwell stress." It was, however, Perline, Kornbluh, and Joseph in 1998 who introduced dielectric elastomer technology with compliant electrodes. They concluded that by deliberately choosing polymers with relatively low moduli of elasticity, the field-induced strain response due to Maxwell stress could be large. Polymer actuators designed to exploit Maxwell stress in this manner became known as "dielectric elastomers or DEs."

5.2.6 Liquid Crystal Elastomer Materials

Liquid crystal elastomers (LCEs) were pioneered at the Albert-Ludwig Universitat in Freiburg, Germany (Finkelmann et al., 1981). These materials can form an EAP actuator by inducing isotropic-nematic phase transition due to temperature increase via Joule heating. LCEs are composite materials consisting of monodomain nematic LCEs and CPs distributed within their network structure (Shahinpoor, 2000d; Finkelmann and Shahinpoor, 2002; Ratna et al., 2002).

LCEs have been made electroactive by creating a composite material consisting of monodomain nematic LCEs and a conductive phase such as graphite or conducting polymers distributed within their network structure. The actuation mechanism of these materials involves phase transition between nematic and isotropic phases for less than a second. The reverse process is slower, taking about 10 s, and it requires cooling to cause the expansion of the elastomer to its original length. The mechanical properties of LCE materials can be controlled and optimized by effectively selecting the liquid crystalline phase, density of cross-linking, flexibility of the polymer backbone, coupling between the backbone and liquid crystal group, and coupling between the liquid crystal group and the external stimuli. These materials can be robotic actuators that increase temperature by inducing a nematic–isotropic phase transition.

This thermal actuation causes them to shrink, as described in a thorough review of these intelligent multifunctional materials by Brand and Finkelmann (1998). The reverse process is slower, taking about 10 s, and requires cooling the LCE back to its initial temperature as it expands to its original size.

5.2.7 Ionic EAPs/Ionic Polymer Gels (IPGs)

Polymer gels can be synthesized to produce strong actuators with the potential to match the force and energy density of biological muscles. These materials, such as polyacrylonitrile (PAN), are generally activated by a chemical reaction, changing from an acid to an alkaline environment and causing the gel to become dense or swollen, respectively. This reaction can be stimulated electrically, as was shown by Shahinpoor and Mojarrad (1994, 1996, 1997a, 1997b, 1997c, 1997d, 2000).

Current efforts are directed toward developing thin layers and more robust electrode techniques. Researchers recently reported progress using a mix of conductive and PAN fibers at the University of New Mexico (Schreyer et al., 2000). Osada and Ross-Murphy (1993) describe the mechanism responsible for the chemomechanical behavior of ionic gels under electrical excitation.

Gong et al. (1994a, 1994b) describe the model for hydrogel behavior as a contractile EAP. Much research and development have been conducted in Hokkaido University, Japan, and applications using ionic gel polymers have been explored. These include the electrically induced bending of gels (Osada and Hasebe, 1985; Osada et al., 1992) and electrically induced reversible volume change of gel particles (Osada and Kishi, 1989).

5.2.8 Nonionic Polymer Gels/EAPs

Nonionic polymer gels containing a dielectric solvent can swell under a DC electric field with a significant strain. Hirai et al. (1995, 1999) at Shinshu University in Japan have created bending and crawling nonionic EAPs using a poly(vinyl alcohol) gel with dimethyl sulfoxide. A 10 × 3 × 2 mm actuator gel was subjected to an electrical field and exhibited bending at angles greater than 90° within 60 ms.

This phenomenon is attributed to charge injection into the gel and the flow of solvated charges that induce an asymmetric pressure distribution. Another nonionic gel is poly(vinyl chloride) (PVC), which is generally inactive when subjected to electric fields. However, if PVC is plasticized with dioctyl phthalate (DOP), a typical plasticizer, it can maintain its shape and behave as a nonionic elastic gel.

5.2.9 Ionic Polymer–Metal Composites

The ionic polymer–metal composite (IPMC) is an EAP that bends, rolls, and twists in response to a small electrical field (5–10 V/mm) due to the mobility of cations in the polymer network. In 1992, the IPMC was realized based on a chemical plating technique developed by Merlet, Pinneri, and coworkers in France and Kawami and Takanake in Japan in the 1980s. The first working actuators were built by Oguro et al. (1992) in Japan, and Shahinpoor (1992) and Mojarrad (2001) in the United States. The first working sensors of this kind were fabricated in the United States by Shahinpoor (1992) and Sadeghipour et al. (1992).

The operation as actuators is the reverse process of the charge storage mechanism associated with fuel cells (Heitner-Wirguin, 1996; Kim et al., 1998, 2000). A relatively low electric field is required (five orders of magnitude smaller than the fields required for PVDF-TrFE and dielectric elastomers to stimulate bending in IPMCs), where the base polymer provides channels for the mobility of positive ions in a fixed network of negative ions on interconnected clusters. To electrode the polymer films chemically, metal ions (platinum, gold, palladium, or others) are dispersed throughout the hydrophilic regions of the polymer surface and are subsequently reduced to the corresponding zero-valence metal atoms.

This chapter fully explains these methodologies and characteristics. Ionic polymeric networks contain conjugated ions that an imposed electric field can redistribute, consequently acting as distributed nanoactuators, nanosensors, and energy harvesters. The chapter briefly presents the manufacturing methodologies.

A linear irreversible thermodynamic model of the underlying actuation and sensing mechanisms is presented. These mechanisms are based on two driving forces: an electric field E, and a solvent pressure gradient Δp and two fluxes, electric current density J, and the ionic+plasticizer flux Q. Gel- and chitosan-based conductor composites have also been considered electrically active composite smart materials.

5.2.10 Conductive Polymers or Synthetic Metals

CPs operate under an electric field by reversible counter-ion insertion and expulsion during REDOX cycling (Gandhi et al., 1995; Otero et al., 1995). Oxidation and reduction occur at the electrodes, inducing a considerable volume change due mainly to the exchange of ions with an electrolyte. When a voltage is applied between the electrodes, oxidation occurs at the anode and reduction at the cathode. A liquid electrolyte containing conjugated ions or a solid polyelectrolyte medium near CPs, such as PPy, is often necessary to cause charge migration into and out of the CP.

Ions (H^+) migrate between the electrolyte and the electrodes to balance the electric charge. Adding the ions causes the polymer to swell; conversely, their removal results in shrinkage. As a result, the sandwich assembly bends. CP actuators generally require small electric fields in the range of 1–5 V/μm; the speed increases, with the voltage having relatively high mechanical energy densities of over 20 J/cm^3 but with low efficiencies at 1% or less. Several CPs have been reported in recent years, for example, PPy, polyethylene dioxythiophene, poly(*p*-phenylene vinylene)s, polyanilines, and polythiophenes. The operation of CPs as actuators at the single-molecule level is currently being studied, taking advantage of the intrinsic electroactive properties of individual polymer chains.

The initial attempts to create artificial muscles date back to the pioneering work of Kuhn et al. (1950) and Katchalsky et al. (1949) in connection with pH-activated muscles (or simply pH muscles)

(Steinberg et al., 1966; Shahinpoor, 1992, 1993; Otero et al., 1995). Note also the other means of activating artificial muscles, such as thermal (Tobushi et al., 1992; Kishi et al., 1993; Li et al., 1999), pneumatic (Shahinpoor et al., 2001), optical (van der Veen and Prins, 1971), and magnetic (Zrinyi et al., 1997) means.

Chemically stimulated polymers were discovered more than half a century ago when it was shown that collagen filaments could reversibly contract or expand when dipped in acidic or alkaline solutions, respectively (Katchalsky, 1949). This early work pioneered synthetic polymers that mimic biological muscles (Steinberg et al., 1966; Shahinpoor et al., 1998).

However, actuation and sensing have remained the best means to describe artificial muscle materials. Shahinpoor and Mojarrad (1994, 1996, 1997a, 1997b, 1997c, 1997d, 2000) were among the pioneers of making electrically active—in sensing and actuation—IPCNCs and IPMNCs (see also Mehran Mojarrad's PhD dissertation, 2001). Zhang et al. (1998) observed substantial piezoelectric activity in PVF2-TrFE as early as 1998.

The most progress in the development of artificial muscle materials has occurred in the last 10 years, where active materials that can induce strains exceeding 100% have emerged (Perline et al., 1998). All the preceding categories of EAPs also fall under the category of artificial muscles.

5.2.11 Shape-Memory Alloys and Shape-Memory Polymers

The history of shape-memory alloy (SMA) and shape-memory polymer (SMP) artificial muscles is extensive and will not be reported here. SMPs belong to the family of shape-memory materials (SMMs), which can deform into a predetermined shape under some imposed specific fields and stimuli such as temperature, electricity or magnetism, and strain and stress.

The pioneering works of Liang and Rogers (1990, 1992) and Liang et al. (1991) in developing SMA and SMP actuators are noteworthy. In their work, a load of a spring-biased SMA actuator was modeled as a dead weight. However, many practical applications involve varying loads, such as the cases of SMA rotatory joint actuators (Shahinpoor, 1995d; Wang and Shahinpoor, 1997a, 1997b, 1997c). A general design methodology of various types of bias-force SMA actuators has been investigated by Shahinpoor and Wang (1995) (see also Guoping Wang's PhD dissertation, 1998).

These transformations are due to the elastic energy stored in SMMs during the initial deformation. As a member of SMMs, SMPs are stimuli-responsive polymers. SMPs frequently use either heat or laser light energy as a stimulant to change shape. The thermally induced shape-memory effect can be observed by irradiation with infrared light, exposure to alternating magnetic fields, imposing an electric field, or immersion in water.

5.2.12 Metal Hydride Artificial Muscle Systems

The binary combination of hydrogen and a metal or metal alloy can absorb large amounts of hydrogen via surface chemisorption and subsequent hydriding reactions. This phenomenon can be used to fabricate artificial muscle systems as described in US Patent 6,405,532 (Kim et al., 2002; Lloyd et al., 2002; Shahinpoor, 2002c; Shahinpoor and Kim, 2002f). Useful characteristics of metal hydrides as artificial muscles are their large uptake/discharge capacity of hydrogen, safe operation (hydrogen desorption is a highly endothermic process), rapid kinetics, and environmentally benign characteristics. Metal hydrides are traditionally used for hydrogen storage and thermal devices.

5.2.13 Electrorheological Fluids Smart Materials

Electrorheological fluids (ERFs) are suspensions consisting of 0.1–100 m dielectric particles and a dielectric base fluid. ERFs are a class of smart materials capable of changing from a liquid phase to a much more viscous liquid to an almost solid phase in an electric field. Since the dielectric constant of suspension particles differs from the dielectric constant of the base fluid, the external electric field polarizes particles. These polarized particles interact and form chain-like or even lattice-like organized structures. Simultaneously, the rheological properties of the suspension change effectively; for example, the effective viscosity increases dramatically. ER suspensions also have a magnetic analog consisting of ferromagnetic particles and the base liquid. Because the viscosity of the ER liquid can be controlled with the electric field strength, the viscosity of the magnetorheological fluid (MRF) is sensitive to the magnetic field.

The response time of ERFs is of the order of 1–10 ms. In principle, this enables the use of these liquids in such applications as electrically controlled clutches, valves, and active damping devices. The use of ERFs as artificial muscles has not been reported anywhere. However, several publications in the pertinent literature (Gandhi et al., 1989a, 1989b; Furusha and Sakaguchi, 1999) concern the applications of ERF to robotics and as intelligent materials and composites. Some other relevant references are Huang et al. (2003) and Dwyer-Joyce et al. (1996).

The solid phase of an ERF has mechanical properties similar to a solid, like a gel. ERFs can perform phase change from liquid to a thicker liquid, such as honey, and then almost solid, or reversely from almost solid, they can transform into a thick liquid and then into a thin liquid in a few milliseconds. This effect is called the "Winslow effect" after its discoverer, Willis M. Winslow, who was awarded a US patent in 1947 and published an article on the effect in 1949.

Note that the change is in fluid viscosity and the emerging solid-like properties. The effect is an electric field–dependent yield shear stress, such as in Bingham plastic (a type of viscoelastic material like thick honey or wax), with a shear stress yield point dependent on the electric field strength. Once in a yielding shearing mode, the ERF behaves like a Newtonian fluid when there is no yield shear stress and stress is directly proportional to the shear rate γ.

5.2.14 Magnetorheological Fluids Smart Materials

MRFs are mostly suspensions of micron-sized, magnetizable particles in the oil. They are similar to ERFs but 20–50 times more reliable. They can also be operated directly from low-voltage power supplies and are far less sensitive to contaminants and temperature extremes.

Under normal conditions, an MRF is a free-flowing liquid with a consistency similar to that of motor oil. However, exposure to a magnetic field can transform the fluid into a near-solid in milliseconds. Just as quickly, the fluid can be returned to its liquid state by removing the field.

The degree of change in an MRF is proportional to the magnitude of the applied magnetic field. MRFs develop yield strength when subjected to the field and behave as Bingham solids. The change can appear as a substantial change in effective viscosity like that in ERFs.

Applications include automotive primary suspensions, truck seat systems, control-by-wire/tactile feedback, pneumatic control, seismic mitigation, and prosthetics. These applications are more than just a demonstration of MRF functionality. Each represents a commercially field-proven MR system that embodies all the necessary refinements to make it fully functional, reliable, cost-effective, and long-lived. Some relevant references are Jolly et al. (1996), Jolly and Carlson (2000), Carlson (1999a, 1999b), Carlson and Weiss (1994), and Weiss et al. (1994). MRFs are suspensions of micron-sized magnetic particles, such as carbonyl iron powder, in a liquid host. The host medium is oil with some additives to minimize particle sedimentation and wear and tear. When the MRF suspension is placed in a magnetic field, the suspended colloidal particles reconfigure to form chains in the direction of the magnetic flux and make the solution more solid-like than liquid.

5.2.15 Magnetic Shape-Memory Smart Materials

The magnetically controlled SMM is a new way to produce motion and force. The magnetic shape-memory (MSM) mechanism was suggested by Ullakko (1996) and O'Handley (1998) and was demonstrated for an Ni–Mn–Ga alloy as early as 1996. Magnetic SMAs (MSMAs), also called ferromagnetic SMAs (FSMAs), are an exciting extension of the class of SMMs. The MSM effect has demonstrated that certain SMMs that are also ferromagnetic can show substantial dimensional changes (6%) under the application of a magnetic field. These strains occur within the low-temperature (martensitic) phase.

Ferromagnetic shape-memory (FSM) materials are a new class of active materials that combine the properties of ferromagnetism with those of a diffusionless, reversible, martensitic transformation. Materials such as SMA Ni_2MnGa, which has a cubic Heusler structure in the high-temperature austenitic phase and undergoes a cubic-to-tetragonal martensitic transformation, clearly exhibit MSM effects.

The FSM effect refers to the reversible field-induced austenite-to-martensite transformation or the rearrangement of martensitic variants by an applied magnetic field, leading to an overall shape change.

Typically, contractile/expansive deformation of the order of 6% is routinely observed in these materials. See also Lavrov et al. (2002). The magnetic control of the shape-memory effect would lead to a more rapid response of the actuator than the thermal control. The magnetic field controls the reorientation of the twin variants as the stress controls the twin variants in standard SMAs.

The MSM effect has demonstrated that certain SMMs that are also ferromagnetic can show substantial dimensional changes (6–10%) under the application of a magnetic field. These strains occur within the low-temperature (martensitic) phase.

5.2.16 Giant Magnetostrictive Materials

Magnetostrictive materials allow the interchange of mechanical and magnetic energies that, for example, produce strains in the magnetic field. These strains are called magnetostriction λ. Magnetostriction in ferromagnetic materials causes them to change shape when subjected to a dynamic magnetic field. The effect was first identified in 1842 by James Joule when observing a nickel sample. This effect is known as the Joule effect. At a fundamental level, the dimension change results from the interactive coupling between an applied magnetic field and the magnetization and magnetic moments of the material's domains or magnetic dipoles.

The most advanced magnetostrictive materials, called giant magnetostrictive materials (GMMs), such as the commercially available TERFENOL-D, among other materials, exhibit $\lambda = 1000$ ppm (or about 0.1% strain) in $H = 80$ kA/m. They are alloys composed of iron (Fe), dysprosium (Dy), and terbium (Tb): Tb*x*Dy1−*x*Fey. In the applied magnetic field (*H*), the domains move or rotate so that the magnetic poles align, causing a dimensional change (*d*). Note that magnetostriction produces mechanical deformation in nearly all ferromagnetic materials.

5.2.17 Fibrous Ionic Polyacrylonitrile Gel (PAN, PANG) as Artificial Muscles

PAN fibers in an active form (PAN or PAN gel modified by annealing/cross-linking and partial hydrolysis) elongate and contract when immersed in pH solutions (caustic and acidic solutions, respectively). Active PAN fibers can also contract and expand in polyelectrolyte solutions when electrically and ionically activated with cations and anions. The change in length for these pH-activated fibers is typically greater than 100%. However, more than 900% contraction/expansion of PAN nanofibers (less than 1 μm in diameter) has been observed in the laboratories. PAN muscles present great potential as artificial muscles for linear actuation. The basic unit of commercially available PAN fiber (Mitsubishi Rayon Co., Japan, Orlon, or artificial silk) is a "single strand." One PAN strand consists of approximately 2000 filaments. The typical diameter of each filament is approximately 10 μm in the raw state and 30 μm in a fully elongated state (gel). The advantages of PAN fibers, among other electrolyte gels, are that the PAN fiber gel has excellent mechanical properties, which can be compared to mammalian biological muscles.

The substantial volume change of PAN fiber gel also reduces the gel's size, an essential factor in determining response time. PAN fibers can convert chemical energy directly into mechanical motion. Based on the ion diffusion theory, the response time of swelling will be proportional to the square of the gel fiber diameter. The surface/volume ratio also affects the response time. Note that such pH-induced contraction–expansion of modified PAN fibers can also be induced electrically in a chemical cell by electrolysis and producing H^+ and OH^- ions.

5.2.18 Piezoresistivity

Piezoresistivity is a property of specific materials such as metals and semiconductors for which the materials' electrical resistance changes due to mechanical pressure, force, acceleration, strain, and stress. Note that metals do not exhibit piezoresistivity as they do not have a bandgap. The resistance of strained metal samples changes due to dimensional changes—this may not be considered piezoresistivity.

The unit of piezoresistivity is ohm-meter or symbolically Ω-m. Metals and semiconducting materials exhibit such a property. The piezoresistive effect in semiconductors is generally several orders of magnitudes more significant than the geometrical effect. This effect is present in semiconductors such as germanium, amorphous silicon, polycrystalline silicon, and silicon carbide.

Semiconductor strain gauges can be designed, built, and operated in various smart sensor applications and as microelectromechanical (MEM) or nanoelectromechanical (NEM) devices and systems.

5.2.19 Electrostrictive Materials as Smart Actuators and Sensors

Electrostriction is the electromechanical coupling in all electrical nonconductors (dielectric materials). Under the application of an electric field, these materials show deformation, strain, and stress. All electrostrictive materials exhibit second-order nonlinear coupling between the elastic strains or stresses. The dielectric terms that couple the strain tensor with the applied electric field are a nonlinear product of the vectors of the electric fields. For a single uniaxial strain (deformation), the induced strain (deformation) is directly proportional to the square of the applied electric field (voltage). The domains of the material get polarized, and opposite sides of these domains become differently charged and attract each other, reducing material thickness in the direction of the applied field and increasing thickness in the orthogonal directions due to Poisson's ratio.

The resulting strain tensor S_{ij} $(i, j = 1, 2, 3)$ is proportional to the product of the polarization vectors P_k. For simple one-dimensional domains, the strain is proportional to the square of the applied electric field.

5.2.20 Hydrogels and Nanogels as Smart Actuators and Sensors

Hydrogels and nanogels can be used for many applications and are increasingly developed also because of their possible biocompatibility. Such smart materials can bind or release drugs, pollutants, and catalysts upon interacting with external effectors and swell or shrink under different pH, chemical compounds, temperatures, or light. Hydrogels typically have a water content between 80% and 99%, which can change by external stimuli; this is the basis of many applications. Natural sources of hydrogels are agarose, chitosan, methylcellulose, or hyaluronic acid. Smart nanogels are the most exciting innovations emerging in nanomedicine and biomedical applications.

With the recent advancements in the applications of biomaterials, nanogels have emerged as novel candidates for drug delivery, biosensing, imaging, and tissue engineering. Nanogels owe the synergistic properties of interpenetrating networks and the nanoscale properties such as small size and high surface-to-volume ratio. In brief, this chapter discusses the natural and synthetic polymers deployed for the synthesis of nanogels.

5.2.21 New Stimuli-Responsive Smart Materials Actuators and Sensors

5.2.21.1 Giant Magnetoresistive Materials

Magnetoresistance is defined as the property of a material to change its electrical conductivity or inverse electrical resistance when an external magnetic field is applied to it. William Thomson (Lord Kelvin), in 1851, discovered that when pieces of iron or nickel are placed within an external magnetic field, the electrical resistance increases when the current is in the same direction as the magnetic force, which is aligned with the magnetic N–S vector, and decreases when the current is perpendicular to the direction of the magnetic force. He noted that the magnitude of changes in conductivity or resistivity was greater with nickel than with iron.

This magnetoresistance effect is referred to as anisotropic magnetoresistance (AMR). Lord Kelvin could not reduce the electrical resistance of any metal by more than 5%. This effect is commonly called the ordinary magnetoresistance (OMR) effect to differentiate it from the more recent discoveries of giant magnetoresistance (GMR), colossal magnetoresistance (CMR), tunnel magnetoresistance (TMR), and extraordinary magnetoresistance (EMR). Giant magnetoresistive materials generally possess alternating ferromagnetic and nonmagnetic but conductive layers, such as iron–chromium and cobalt–copper.

5.2.21.2 Mechanochromic Smart Materials and Mechanical Metamaterials

This chapter reviews two recent families of smart materials: mechanochromic materials and mechanical metamaterials. Mechanochromic materials change their optical properties, particularly photoluminescence characteristics if subjected to mechanical loading or environmental interactions. Chemical and physical molecular changes across various length scales and the rearrangement of molecular chemical bonds to modifications in molecular arrangements in the nanometer regime generally trigger mechanochromic characteristics. Metamaterials define materials that are not ordinarily produced in nature. Note that "meta" means "beyond", and metamaterials have properties beyond conventional materials. Metamaterials are nanocomposite materials made of periodically repeated micro or nano units of metals, alloys, and plastics that exhibit properties different from the natural properties of the participating materials. In the following sections, these families of mechanochromic and metamaterials are further described.

5.2.21.3 Smart Nanogels for Biomedical Applications

Smart nanogels are among the most important innovations in nanomedicine and biomedical applications. With recent advancements in biomaterial applications, nanogels have emerged as novel candidates for drug delivery, biosensing, imaging, tissue engineering, and targeted delivery of bioactives. The nanoparticle form of hydrogel is known as "nanogels." Nanogels owe the synergistic properties of interpenetrating networks and the nanoscale properties such as small size and high surface-to-volume ratio. These hybrid materials owe high drug loading, can cross strong barriers, and are highly biocompatible.

5.3 A Brief History of Electromotive Polymers

Kuhn and Kunzle (Kuhn et al., 1948) of Basle University in Switzerland and Katchalsky (1949) of the Weizmann Institute of Science in Israel were among the first scientists to discover the shape change of ionized polymers such as a polyacid or polybase when stimulated by various pH solutions. We call this class of ionic polymers pH-activated ionic polymer gels (or merely pH muscles).

A mechanically stressed polyacrylic acid (PAA) foil containing glycerol and H_2SO_4 was heated to make a contractile filament. The ionization of the resulting polymeric acid caused a molecular shape change in an aqueous solution. The stretch of the polymer molecules was attributed to electrostatic repulsive forces between carboxylic ions present in the solution. The contraction of the poly-molecule was attributed to the Brownian motion resulting from the neutralization of charged groups. Kuhn Kunzle and Katchalsky used a methacrylic acid copolymer with divinylbenzene in their experiment. They used an intermittent wash cycle with distilled water to remove the salt formed between the application of acid and alkali. They proposed that equilibrium swelling of the polymeric acid gels was caused by the following:

- Solution tendency of polymeric molecules and osmotic pressure of the cations of the alkali bond by the gel
- Rubber-like contraction tendency of the stretched polymer molecules

They observed that the swelling capacity of the gel decreased with increasing degrees of cross-linking of the polymer. The degree of ionization depended on the charge distribution of the polymer chain. Maximum swelling could be achieved for about 50% neutralization of these charge groups.

Later, Hamlen et al. (1965), three research scientists at General Electric Company, were able to stimulate the copolymer of polyvinyl alcohol (PVA)-PAA electrically by making the polymer conductive with chemical treatment by the solution of platinic chloride and sodium borohydride. Thus, they could actuate it by electricity instead of the pH variation of the surrounding liquid environment. Although the resulting ionic polymer was slow in response relative to its pH-activated counterpart, it nevertheless proved the possibility of electrical stimulation of these polymers, making it attractive for robotics controls and manipulation. Because the PVA-PAA copolymer is a negatively charged gel (due to the $COOH^-$ side group in PAA), it swells or shrinks osmotically depending on total ionic concentration inside the polymer; this is determined by the degree of ionization of the weak carboxylic acid group ($COOH^-$).

When the external environment (electrolyte solution) is acidic, the dissociation degree is low, and the polymer shrinks in an alkaline solution. It expands similarly to the lengths of the pH muscles mentioned earlier. A conductor such as platinum can be included in the polymer and made to have lower voltage for hydrogen and oxygen evolution. This class of ionic polymers is called electrically activated ionic polymer gels (or merely electroactive muscles).

In these researchers' experiments, PVA-PAA fibers were treated eight times in platinum solution and submerged in a 0.01 N solution of NaCl (1% concentration). A counter-electrode of platinum wire was used and placed in a container holding the muscle and salt solution. A square wave of ±5 V amplitude at 40 mA and a 20 min period ($f = 0.0008$ Hz) were then applied. When the fiber is negative, hydrogen evolves, causing the solution to become alkaline, and the fiber expands. When the fiber is positive, the solution surrounding and within the fibers becomes acidic, causing its contraction.

Fragala et al. (1972) of the GE-Direct Energy Conversion Program experimented with weak acidic contractile polymeric membranes in a setup that forced a change in the pH of the solution surrounding the membrane by the electrodialysis process.

They developed mathematical formulations that adequately described the response of the artificial muscle to the applied field current. They concluded that a dissociation constant of more than 10^{-3} g-eq/L for weak acidic groups within the material was needed to obtain large deformation in the muscle membrane. Their apparatus consisted of a three-compartment container with a weak acidic polymeric muscle membrane immersed in a mixture of weak salt and acid solution in the middle compartment. This arrangement was separated by two weak cationic and anionic ion-exchange membranes to fill the other compartments with the same weak salt and acid concentration as the muscle membrane.

Next, they inserted two electrodes (Ag/AgCl) in the ion-exchange compartments. They applied a voltage gradient to change the pH of the solution surrounding the muscle membrane through an electrodialysis process. In effect, they were activating a pH-sensitive muscle by electrically varying the pH of the surrounding solution. They studied muscle membrane response as a function of pH value, solution concentration, compartment size, certain cations, and membrane fabrication.

The next section details a formulation Fragala et al. (1972) used to develop analytical relations among the applied field, hydrogen ion, and salt concentration that affect the pH and, ultimately, the muscle contraction and expansion. The bar over the variable here and in what follows indicates values within the membrane.

MIT's Yannas and Grodzinsky (1973) were among the first to study the deformation of collagen fiber from a rat-tail tendon in an electric field when constrained at two ends and submerged in an aqueous solution. They viewed their results as an electrophoresis or electro-osmosis phenomenon. They reported that, except at the isoelectric point, individual collagen molecules and macroscopic specimens such as fibers and membranes constituted from such molecules carry a net electrostatic charge. This charge can give rise to a very intense electric field of the order 10^8 V/cm at the molecular level, which means a very large potential drop over a distance defined by the Debye length of roughly 10–1000 Å. The charged polyelectrolyte is, therefore, surrounded by the mobile counter-ions. Their experimental observation supported evidence of the model of an electric double layer formed by the primary charge fixed on the polyelectrolyte and the diffuse layer of mobile counter-ions in the solution. Yannas and Grodzinsky estimated the Debye length or effective thickness of $1/k$ of the ionic layer surrounding individual fibrils' charged sites.

According to them, an increase in ionic strength results in a decrease in Debye length. On the other hand, the observed drop in isometric force with ionic strength should, in terms of the preceding model, result from a weakening of inter-fibrillar repulsion and a corresponding decrease in lateral swelling.

Grodzinsky and Melcher (1974) modeled the electromechanical transduction of collagen and other aqueous polyelectrolytes in the membrane form. In their study, they coupled membrane to mechanical load and observed the conversion of electrical to mechanical response and vice versa. Their model represented a membrane at the interfibrillar level with cylindrical pores relative to externally measured potentials, membrane deformations, current flow, mass fluxes to pore radius, fibril diameter, and the polyelectrolyte charge. Molecules of collagen, like other protein polyelectrolytes, possess many ionizable groups capable of dissociating and attaining net charge in various solvent media. On the electrical side, this primary charge can give rise to intense local electric fields as high as 10^8 V/cm. Therefore, collagen and other polyelectrolytes are susceptible to interactions with externally applied fields, whether isolated molecules, fibers, or membranes.

Besides, polyelectrolyte structures may interact with each other through their internal fields. On the mechanical side, the fibril–electrolyte matrix composing macroscopic polyelectrolyte fibers and membranes is often flexible and elastic in the hydrated state. Therefore, forces due to electric fields can result in motion and deformation of the polyelectrolyte.

Collagen is the body's primary structural protein in the extracellular space (usually in fibril form) and is a major constituent of vertebrate connective tissue. It is also found in blood vessels and organ walls, the cornea and vitreous humor, basement membranes, and other epithelial and endothelial linings. The physiochemical origin and location of charge sites on the molecules are fundamental to all electrochemical interactions with collagen and to our continuum models. In rat-tail tendon collagen, there are about 350 acidic and 265 basic groups among the ~3000 amino acid residues per tropocollagen molecule (predominantly carboxyl [–COOH] and amino [$-NH_2$] groups, respectively).

These groups can ionize as a function of electrolyte pH and ionic strength, leaving a net positive or negative charge fixed to the molecule. Titration methods could determine the number of these fixed charges in the specimen.

Tanaka et al. (1980) of MIT used the Flory and Huggins (1941) theory of shrinking–swelling to formulate further the mean free energy needed for the phase transition of electrolytic gels. They used partially hydrolyzed acrylamide gel for their experimental work. The solvent used was a mixture of acetone and water. The polymer was highly sensitive to temperature, solvent composition, pH, added salt concentration, and applied electricity. The degree of volume change of the gel was found to be 500%. This change results from the phase transition of the system of the charged polymer network, counter-ions, and fluid composition.

Three major competing forces on the gel, in turn, cause the phase transition:

1. Positive osmotic pressure of counter-ions
2. Negative pressure due to polymer–polymer affinity

3. Rubber elasticity of the polymer network

Electric forces on the network's charged sites produce a stress gradient along the gel's electric field lines. The gel shrinks or swells at the critical stress, depending on whether the stress developed is above or below the critical stress.

In their experiment, they prepared polyacrylamide (PAM) gels by free-radical polymerization of acrylamide (monomer), using *N, N′*-methylene bisacrylamide (as cross-linker), ammonium persulfate and N,N,N′,N′-tetramethylene diamine (TEMED) (as initiator)—all of which were dissolved in water. Gel formation was initiated after 5 min, and to remove excess monomer, the gel was immersed in water after 1 h. The gel was then hydrolyzed in a solution of TEMED (1.2% solution, pH 12) for one month. Approximately 20% of acrylamide groups were converted to acrylic acid groups, which in turn were ionized in water.

After complete hydrolysis, the gel was immersed in a 50% solution of acetone water to reach equilibrium before cutting into desired dimensions. To energize the resulting gel, platinum electrodes were used with a DC voltage of 0–5 V; the gel was placed between electrodes. It is noted that PAM is an anionic type of polymer gel, which means it is negatively charged.

Therefore, the anisotropy of deformation of the disk is uniquely determined by B. Namely, for positive B, the disk is compressed more in its length than in diameter ($\alpha > \beta$), and for negative B, the compression in the radial direction is more than axial ($\alpha < \beta$). By plotting α (radial expansion) versus β (axial expansion) of a rod-shaped gel, various values for B and τ can be obtained.

De Rossi et al. (1985) of the University of Pisa in Italy explained the dynamic behavior of these gels from a thermodynamic point of view according to the general expression:

$$dU = TdS - PdV + Fdl + \mu_i\, dn_i + \varepsilon\, dq \tag{5.1}$$

The isothermal conversion of chemical energy into mechanical work underlies the motility of all living organisms and can easily be seen, for instance, in muscle, flagella, and ciliary movement. All these biological systems are characterized by extremely high energy conversion efficiency. The high conversion efficiency of biological systems is largely due to the direct conversion of chemical energy without unnecessary intermediate heat-producing components.

Chemomechanical systems are the only artificial systems currently that can achieve this. The chemomechanical reaction may generate mechanical energy on a macroscopic level and transform information as a signal or receptor, whereby microscopic deformation plays an essential role in switches and sensors.

Osada further classified synthetic polymer gels according to the principle and type of reaction involved:

- Hydrogen ion transfer (pH muscle)
- Ion-exchange or chelation
- REDOX reaction (REDOX muscle)
- Steric isomerization
- Phase transition or order–disorder transition
- Polymer–polymer association or aggregation
- Electrokinetic processes

Several chemomechanical systems, such as polyelectrolyte fibers and membranes, have been investigated in the past. These materials expand and contract upon changing their solubility or degree of ionization. There are also thermosensitive and optically sensitive polymers. However, from the standpoint of robotic controls, most researchers have focused on electroactive polyelectrolytes. An explanation of the materials' behavior and their application as artificial muscles follows.

5.3.1 Contraction

For a polyelectrolyte undergoing shape changes by applying DC current, the velocity of shape change is proportional to the charge density in the gel. This shape change may be the first model of an electroactive artificial muscle working in an aerobic and aqueous medium system. The gel contracts and dilates reversibly when stimulated electrically under isothermal conditions.

The electrical control makes use of cross-linked polyelectrolyte gels. The system is quite simple. For instance, a water-swollen polymer gel is inserted between electrodes connected to a DC source. When the electricity is turned on, the polymer gel starts to shrink. This procedure has been verified and quantified experimentally in the case of several ionic gels, such as poly(2-acrylamido-2-methyl-1-propane sulfonic) acid (PAMPS). The degree of swelling changes as other media, such as a mixture of water and ethanol or glycerin or other solvents, are used compared with pure water only.

5.3.2 Mechanisms

A quantitative interpretation of the phenomena observed is that the application of an electric field causes the pumping of largely mobile ions, partly macro-network ions, and surrounding hydrated water in opposite directions until they reach the electrode. In general, the velocity of migration and the velocity of the gel contraction are governed by the number of mobile ions, q_n, and the gradient of the electric field, ΔE, which drives these ions.

The force produced in the gel is proportional to the product of q_n and ΔE:

$$F = \Delta E \times q_n \tag{5.2}$$

5.4 Role of Microparticles in Contraction of Gels

Microparticles of the sodium salt of PAA gel were synthesized to establish the system with minimized response time. The size change of the particle with time under various electric fields was measured. Experiments showed that there is a threshold voltage below which no contraction occurs. As the electric voltage increased, the contraction increased as well. This also affected the volumetric reduction in the size of the sample. Volume reduction by 30 or 3000% was easily achieved within less than 1 min under 6 V DC current. After removal of the electrical current, the gel returned to its original size within 5 min.

The rate of volume change is a function of the particle's size. The relative volume change decreased with the increasing size of the particle. The experimental results verified that this rate is inversely proportional to the square of particle size. This finding aligns with Tanaka's proportionality with the square of the characteristic length of the sample. Shahinpoor and Osada (1995a) formulated a theoretical model for a cylindrical gel sample describing the dynamics of contraction of ionic polymeric gels in the presence of an electric field. Their model considered the dynamic balance between the internal forces during the contraction.

These forces are assumed to be due to the viscous effects caused by the motion of the liquid solvent medium within the polymer network, the internal forces due to the motion of the liquid in and out of the network, and the electrophoretic forces due to the motion of the charged ions in the solvent as it exudes from the ionic polymeric gel network. The effects of the rubber elasticity of the network and ion–ion interactions were assumed to be negligible compared to inertial, viscous, and electrophoretic effects. The governing equations were then solved for the velocity of the liquid exudation (water, ethanol, acetone, or mixture of other solvents) from the network as a function of the time and radial distance in the cylindrical sample.

The relative weight of the gel was then related to the velocity by an integral equation. This problem can be solved numerically to obtain a relationship between the amount of contraction as a function of time, electric field, strength, and other pertinent materials and geometrical parameters. The results of the numerical simulation in the case of PAMPS polymer indicated close agreement with experimental data, as described later in the book. Caldwell and Taylor (1989) of the University of Hull in the United Kingdom attempted to describe the force–velocity relationship of the contraction–expansion mechanism of the PVA-PAA copolymer gel. They simulated flexor and extensor muscle pairs of humans to power a robot gripper. They used water and acetone for the expansion–contraction of the copolymer gel.

References and Further Readings

Abe, Y., Mochizuki, A., Kawashima, T., Tamashita, S., Asaka, K., and Oguro, K. (1998). Effect on bending behavior of counter cation species in perfluorinated sulfonate membrane-platinum composite. *Polym. Adv. Technol.* **9**:520–526.

Adolf, D., Shahinpoor, M., Segalman, D., and Witkowski, W. (1993). Electrically controlled polymeric gel actuators. U.S. Patent no. 5,250,167.

Akazawa, K. (1991). Neuromuscular control system and hardware models. *Adv. Robot.* **5**(1):75–85.

Akazawa, K., and Fuji, K. (1986). Theory of muscle contraction and motor control. *Adv. Robot.* **1**(4):379–390.

Asahi Chemical Industry Co., Ltd. (1995). Aciphex formula. Public release.

Asaka, K., and Oguro, K. (2000). Bending of polyelectrolyte membrane platinum composites by electric stimuli. Part II. Response kinetics. *J. Electroanal. Chem.* **480**:186–198.

Asaka, K., Oguro, K., and Takenaka, H. (1994). Bending response of polyelectrolyte membrane-Pt composite. In *Preprints Sapporo Symposium on Intelligent Polymer Gels*, October 6–8, Sapporo, Japan, 87–88.

Asaka, K., Oguro, K., Nishimura, Y., Misuhata, M., and Takenaka, H. (1995). Bending of polyelectrolyte membrane-platinum composites by electric stimuli. I. Response characteristics to various waveforms. *Polym. J.* **27**:436–440.

Ashton-Miller, J. A., and Pandy, M. G. (1990). Issues in modeling and control of biomechanical systems. In *Proceedings of the Winter Annual Meeting of the American Society of Mechanical Engineers*, November 25–30, Dallas, TX. ASME Publications, DSC-Vol. 25.

Atkins, P. W. (1982). *Physical Chemistry*, 2nd ed. London: Oxford University Press.

Aviram, A. (1978). Mechanophotochemistry. *Macromolecules* **11**:1275.

Bar-Cohen, Y., Leary, S. P., Shahinpoor, M., Simpson, J. O., and Smith, J. (1999a). Flexible low-mass devices and mechanisms actuated by electro-active polymers. In *Electroactive Polymers*, SPIE publication no. 3669-38, 51–56.

Bar-Cohen, Y., Xue, T., Joffe, B., S.-S. Lih, Shahinpoor, M., Simpson, J., Smith, J., and Willis, P. (1997a). Electroactive polymers (IPMC) low-mass muscle actuators. In *Proceedings of (1997) SPIE Conference on Smart Materials and Structures*, March 5, San Diego, CA.

Bar-Cohen, Y., Xue, T., Joffe, B., S.-S. Lih, Willis, P., Simpson, J., Smith, J., and Shahinpoor, M. (1997b). Electroactive polymers (EAP) low-mass muscle actuators. In *Proceedings of SPIE 3041, Smart Structures and Materials (1997) Symposium, Enabling Technologies: Smart Structures and Integrated Systems*, ed. M. E. Regelbrugge. Bellingham, WA: SPIE, 697–701. ISBN 0-8194-2454-4.

Bar-Cohen, Y., Xue, T., Shahinpoor, M., Salehpoor, K., Simpson, J., Smith, J., and Willis, P. (1998a). Low-mass muscle actuators using electroactive polymers (EAP). In *Proceedings of SPIE Smart Materials and Structures Conference*, March 3–5, San Diego, CA, SPIE publication no. 3324-32.

Bar-Cohen, Y., Xue, T., Shahinpoor, M., Simpson, J., and Smith, J. (1998b). Flexible low-mass robotic arm actuated by electroactive polymers

(EAP). In *Proceedings of SPIE Smart Materials and Structures Conference*, March 3–5, San Diego, CA, SPIE publication no. SPIE 3329-07. (1998c). Flexible, low-mass robotic arm actuated by electroactive polymers and operated equivalently to a human arm and hand. In *Proceedings of the Space '98-Robotics '98 Conference, Third International Conference Exposition on Robotics for Challenging Environment*, eds. L. A. Demsetz, R. H. Byrne, and J. P. Weyzel. April 26–30, Albuquerque, NM: American Society of Civil Engineers.

Baughman, R. H. (1996). Conducting polymer artificial muscles. *Synth. Met.* **78**:339–353.

Baughman, R. H., Cui, C., Zakhidov, A. A., Iqbal, Z., Basrisci, J. N., Spinks, G. M., Wallace, G. G., Mazzoldi, A., D. de Rossi, Rinzier, A. G., Jaschinski, O., Roth, S., and Kertesz, M. (1999). Carbon nanotube actuators. *Science* **284**:1340–1344.

Baughman, R. H., Shacklette, L. W., Elsenbaumer, R. L., Plichta, E. J., and Becht, C. (1991). Microelectromechanical actuators based on conducting polymers. In *Molecular Electronics*, ed. P. I. Lazarev. Dordrecht: Kluwer Academic Publishers.

Beatty, M. F. (1987). Topics in finite elasticity: Hyperelasticity of rubber, elastomers, and biological tissues—With examples. *Appl. Mech. Rev.* **40**:1699–1733. (Reprinted with minor modifications as "Introduction to Nonlinear Elasticity." In *Nonlinear Effects in Fluids and Solids*, eds. M. M. Carroll and M. A. Hayes. New York, NY: Plenum Press, 16–112, 1996.)

Bejczy, A. K., and Salisbury, J. K. (1983). Controlling remote manipulators through kinesthetic coupling. *Comput. Mech. Eng.* **2**(1).

Bennet, M., and Leo, D. J. (2003). Manufacture and characterization of ionic polymer transducers with non-precious metal electrodes. *J. Smart Mater. Struct.* **12**(3):424–436.

Bernardi, D. M., and Verbugge, M. W. (1992). A mathematical model of a solid polymer electrolyte fuel cell. *J. Electrochem. Soc.* **139**(9):2477–2491.

Bernardi, P., D'Inzeo, G., and Pisa, S. (1994). A generalized ionic model of the neuronal membrane electrical activity. *IEEE Trans. Biomed. Eng.* **41**(2):125–133.

Bone, Q., and Marshall, N. B. (1982). *Biology of Fishes*. London: Blackie & Son.

Brand, H. R., and Finkelmann, H. (1998). Physical properties of liquid crystalline elastomers. In *Handbook of Liquid Crystals. Vol. 3: High Molecular Weight Liquid Crystals*, eds. D. Demus, J. Goodby, G. W. Gray, H.-W. Spiess, and V. Vill. Weinheim: Wiley–VCH, pp. 277–289.

Brand, P. W., and Hollister, A. (1993). *Clinical Mechanics of the Hand*, 2nd ed. Mosby Year Book.

Brandt, H. R., and Pleiner, H. (1994). Electrohydrodynamics of nematic liquid crystalline elastomers. *Phys. A* **208**:359.

Brock, D. (1991a). *Artificial Muscle Research Review*. Cambridge, MA: MIT Artificial Intelligence Lab. (1991b). *Design and Control of an Artificial Muscle*. Cambridge, MA: MIT Artificial Intelligence Lab. (1991c). *Review of Artificial Muscle Based on Contractile Polymers*. MIT Artificial Intelligence Lab. AI Memo No. 1330.

Brock, D., Lee, W., Segalman, D., and Witkowski, W. (1994a). A dynamic model of a linear actuator based on polymer hydrogel. In *Proceedings of the International Conference on Intelligent Materials*, 210–222. (1994b). A dynamic model of a linear actuator based on polymer hydrogel. *J. Intell. Mater. Syst. Struct.* **5**(6):764–771.

Burgmayer, P., and Murray, R. W. (1982). An ion gate membrane: Electrochemical control of ion permeability through a membrane with an embedded electrode. *J. Am. Chem. Soc.* **104**:6139.

Caldwell, D. 1993. Natural and artificial muscle elements as robot actuators. *Mechatronics* **3**(3):269–283.

Caldwell, D. G., and Taylor, P. M. (1989). An artificial muscle actuator for robots. In Proceedings of the fourth

Caldwell, D., and Taylor, P. (1990). Chemically stimulated pseudo-muscular actuation. *Int. J. Eng. Sci.* **28**(8):797–808.

Cao, Y., Smith, P., and Heeger, A. J. (1991). Mechanical and electrical properties of polyacetylene films oriented by tensile drawing. *Polymer* **32**:1210.

Carlson, J. D. (1999a). Low-cost MR fluid sponge devices. *J. Intell. Syst. Struct.* **10**:589–594. (1999b). Magnetorheological fluid actuators. In *Adaptronics and Smart Materials*, ed. H. Janocha. Berlin: Springer-Verlag, pp. 180–195.

Carlson, J. D., and Weiss, K. D. (1994). A growing attraction to magnetic fluids. *Mach. Design* **8**:61–66.

Chen, Z., Tan, X., and Shahinpoor, M. (2005). Quasistatic positioning of ionic polymer–metal composite (IPMC) actuators. In *Proceedings of the IEEE/ASME Conference on Advanced Intelligent Mechatronics* (AIM 2005), July 24–28, Monterey, CA, 60–65.

Chiang, C. K., Druy, A. A., Gau, S. C., Heeger, A. J., Shirakawa, H., Louis, E. J., Gau, S. C., Mac Diarmid, A. G., and Park, W. (1978). Synthesis of highly conducting films of derivatives of polyacetylene, (CH)x. *J. Am. Chem. Soc.* **100**:1013.

Chiang, C. K., Fischer, C. R., Park, Y. W., Heeger, A. J., Shirakawa, H., Louis, E. J., Gau, S. C., and Mac Diarmid, A. G. (1977). Electrical conductivity in doped polyacetylene. *Phys. Rev. Lett.* **39**:1098.

Chiarelli, P., and De Rossi, D. (1988). Determination of mechanical parameters related to swelling kinetics in an electrically activated contractile gel. *Prog. Colloid Polym. Sci.* **78**:4–8.

Chiarelli, P., De Rossi, D., and Umezawa, K. (1989). Progress in the design of an artificial urethral sphincter. In *Proceedings of the Third Vienna International Workshop on Functional Electrostimulation*, September, Vienna, Austria.

Chiarelli, P., Della Santa, A., De Rossi, D., and Mazzoldi, A. (1994). Actuation properties of electrochemically driven polypyrrole free-standing films. In *Proceedings of the International Conference on Intelligent Materials*, Vol. ICIM-3, June 1996, Lyon, France, 352–360.

Chiarelli, P., Umezawa, K., and Rossi, D. D. (1991). A polymer composite showing electrocontractile response. *Polym. Gels*: 195–201.

Choi, K., Kim, K. J., Kim, D., Manford, C., Heo, S., and Shahinpoor, M. (2006). Performance characteristics of electrochemically driven polyacrylonitrile fiber bundle actuators. *J. Intell. Mater. Syst. Struct.* **17**(7):563–576.

Crowson, A. (1996). Smart materials technologies and biomimetics. In *Proceedings of the SPIE Smart Structures and Materials Conference*, February, San Diego, CA.

Crowson, A., and Bailey, J. A. (1993a). *U.S. Army Research Office Publications*, 78–89. (1993b). Microelectro-mechanics of ionic polymeric gels as artificial muscles for robotic applications. In *Proceedings (1993) IEEE International Conference on Robotics & Automation*, May, Atlanta, GA, Vol. 2, 380–385. (1993c). Current-voltage curves of bipolar membranes. *J. Appl. Phys.* **72**(1):259–264.

Dautzenberg, H., Jaeger, W., Kotz, J., Philipp, B., Seidel, C., and Stscherbina, D. (1994). *Polyelectrolytes, Formulation, Characterization, and Application*. Munich: Hanser Publishers.

Davis, T. A., Genders, J. D., and Pletcher, D. (1997). *A First Course in Ion Permeable Membranes*. Romsey: Electrochemical Consultancy.

De Gennes, P. G., Hebert, M., and Kant, R. (1997). Artificial muscles based on nematic gels. *Macromol. Symp.* **113**:39.

De Gennes, P. G., Okumura, K., Shahinpoor, M., and Kim, K. J. 2000. Mechanoelectric effects in ionic gels. *Europhys. Lett.* **50**(4):513–518.

De Rossi, D., Charelli, P., Buzzigoli, G., Domenici, C., and Lazzeri, L. (1986). Contractile behavior of electrically activated mechanochemical polymer actuators. *Trans. Am. Soc. Artif. Intern. Organs* **XXXII**:157–162.

De Rossi, D., Domenici, C., and Charelli, P. (1988). Analogs of biological tissues for mechanotransduction: Tactile sensors and muscle-like actuators. In *Sensors and Sensory Systems for Advanced Robots (NATO ASI Serie)*, Vol. F43, 201–218.

De Rossi, D., Parrini, D., Chiarelli, P., and Buzzigoli, G. (1985). Electrically induced contractile phenomena in charged polymer networks: Preliminary study on the feasibility of muscle-like structures. *Trans. Am. Soc. Artif. Intern. Organs* **XXXI**:60–65.

De Rossi, D., Suzuki, M., Osada, Y., and Morasso, P. (1992). Pseudomuscular gel actuators for advanced robotics. *J. Intell. Mater. Syst. Struct.* **3**:75–95.

De Torresi, C. (1995). Ionic exchanges in dodecylbenzene sulfonate doped polypyrrole. I—Optical beam deflection study. *Synth. Met.* **72**:59.

De, S. K., Aluru, N. R., Johnson, B., Crone, W. C., Beebe, D. J., and Moore, J. (2002). Equilibrium swelling and kinetics of pH-responsive hydrogel: Models, experiments, and simulation. *J. Microelectromech. Syst.* **11**(5):544–555.

Della Santa, A., De Rossi, D., and Mazzoldi, A. (1997). Characterization and modeling of a conducting polymer muscle-like linear actuator. *Smart Mater. Struct.* **6**:23–24.

Deole, U., Lumia, R., and Shahinpoor, M. (2004). Characterization of impedance properties of ionic polymer metal composite actuators. In *Proceedings of the Second World Congress on Biomimetics and Artificial Muscle (Biomimetics and Nano-bio 2004)*, December 5–8, Albuquerque, NM.

Doi, M., Matsumoto, M., and Hirose, Y. (1992). Deformation of ionic polymer gels by electric fields. *Macromolecules* **25**:5504–5511.

Dorfner, K. (1972). *Ion Exchangers Properties and Applications*, 3rd ed. Ann Arbor, MI: Ann Arbor Science Publishers, Inc.

Dukhin, S. S., and Shilov, V. N. (1974). *Dielectric Phenomena and the Double Layer in Disperse Systems and Polyelectrolytes.* Jerusalem: Keter Publishing House Ltd.

Dunai, T. J., and Finlay, S. M. (2009). Reporting of cosmogenic nuclide data for exposure age and erosion rate determinations. *Quaternary Geochronology*, **4**(6):437–440.

Dusek, K., (ed.) (1993). *Advances in Polymer Science*, vols. 109 and 110, *Responsive Gels, Transitions I and II*. Berlin: Springer-Verlag.

Dwyer-Joyce, R. S., Bullough, W. A., and Lingard, S. (1996). Elastohydrodynamic performance of unexcited electro-rheological fluids. *Int. J. Mod. Phys. B* **10**(23–24):3181–3189.

Eckerle, J. S., Andeen, G. B., and Kornbluh, R. D. (1992). I am exploring artificial muscles as robot actuators. *Rob. Int. Soc. Manuf. Eng.* **5**(1):1–4.

Eguchi, M. (1925). Piezoelectric polymers. *Phil. Mag.* **49**.

Eisenberg, A., and Bailey, F. E. (eds.) (1986). *Coulombic Interactions in Macromolecular Systems*, Vol. 302. ACS Sym. Series.

Eisenberg, A., and King, M. (1977). *Ion-Containing Polymers*. New York, NY: Academic Press.

Eisenberg, A., and Yeager, H. L. (eds.) (1982). *Perfluorinated ionomer membranes*, Vol. 180. Washington, DC: American Chemical Society.

Ellington, C. P., and Pedley, T. J. (1995). Biological fluid dynamics. In *Proceedings of Symposia of the Society for Experimental Biology*, **XLIX**, Society for Experimental Biology.

Engdahl, G., and Mayergoyz, I. D. (2000). *Handbook of Giant Magnetostrictive Materials*, 1st ed. New York, NY: Academic Press.

Erhard, M., Krenn, M., and Zeilinger, A. (2020). Advances in high-dimensional quantum entanglement. *Nat. Rev. Phys.* **2**, 365–381.

Escoubes, M., and Pineri, M. (1982). *Perfluorinated Ionomer Membranes*, eds. A. Eisenberg and H. L. Yeager. Washington, DC: American Chemical Society.

Evans, R. B., and Thompson, D. E. (1993). The application of force to the healing tendon. *J. Hand Ther.* 266–284.

Ferrara, L., Shahinpoor, M., Kim, K. J., Schreyer, B., Keshavarzi, A., Benzel, E., and Lantz, J. (1999). Use of ionic polymer–metal composites (IPMCs) as a pressure transducer in the human spine. In *Electroactive Polymers*, SPIE publication no. 3669-45, 394–401.

Finkelmann, H., and Brand, H. R. (1994). Liquid crystalline elastomers: A class of materials with novel properties. *Trends. Polym. Sci.* **2**:222.

Finkelmann, H., and Shahinpoor, M. (2002). Electrically controllable liquid crystal elastomer–graphite composite artificial muscles. In *Proceedings of SPIE 9th Annual International Symposium on Smart Structures and Materials*, March, San Diego, CA, 4695–4653.

Finkelmann, H., Kock, H. J., and Rehage, G. (1981). Investigations on liquid crystalline siloxanes: 3. Liquid crystalline elastomer—A new type of liquid crystalline material. *Makromol. Chem. Rapid. Commun.* **2**:317–323.

Firoozbakhsh, K., and Shahinpoor, M. (1998). Mathematical modeling of ionic interactions and deformation in ionic polymeric metal composite artificial muscles. In *Proceedings of SPIE Smart Materials and Structures Conference*, March 3–5, San Diego, CA, publication no. SPIE 3323-66.

Flory, P. J. (1941). Thermodynamics of high polymer solutions. *J. Chem. Phys.* **9**(8):660.

Flory, P. J. (1953a). *Principles of Polymer Chemistry*. Ithaca, NY: Cornell University Press. (1953b). *Statistical Mechanics of Swelling Network Structures*. Ithaca, NY: Cornell University Press; 1969. *Statistical Mechanics of Polymer Chains*. New York, NY: Interscience Publishers.

Fragala, A., Enos, J., LaConti, A., and Boyack, J. (1972). Electrochemical activation of synthetic artificial muscle membrane. *Electrochem. Acta* **17**:1507–1522.

Full, R. J., and Meijer, K. (2001). Metrics of natural muscle. In *Electroactive Polymers (EAP), Such as Artificial Muscles, Reality Potential, and Challenges*, ed. Y. Bar-Cohen. SPIE & William Andrew/Noyes Publications, 67–83.

Full, R. J., Kubow, T., Schmitt, J., Holmes, P., and Koditschek, D. (2002). I am quantifying dynamic stability and maneuverability in legged locomotion. *Int. Comp. Biol.* **42**:149–157.

Furukawa, T., and Seo, N. (1990). Electrostriction is the origin of piezoelectricity in ferroelectric polymers. *Jpn. J. Appl. Phys.* **29**(4):675 –680.

Furusha, J., and Sakaguchi, M. S. (1999). New actuators using ER fluids and their applications to force display devices in virtual reality and medical treatment. *Int. J. Mod. Phys. B* **13**(14–16):2051–2059.

Gamow, G. (1946). Expanding universe and the origin of elements. *Phys. Rev.* **70**, 572.

Gandhi, M. R., Murray, P., Spinks, G. M., and Wallace, G. G. (1995). Mechanisms of electromechanical actuation in polypyrrole. *Synth. Met.* **75**:247–256.

Gandhi, M. V., Thompson, B. S., and Choi, S.-B. (1989a). A new generation of innovative ultra-intelligent composite materials featuring electro-rheological: An experimental investigation. *J. Compos. Mater.* **23**:1232–1255.

Gandhi, M. V., Thompson, B. S., Choi, S.-B., and Shakair, S. (1989b). Electro-rheological fluid-based articulating robotic systems. *J. Mech. Trans. Automation.* **111**:328–336.

Gebel, G., Aldebert, P., and Pineri, M. (1987). Structure and related properties of solution-case perfluorosulfonate ionomer films. *Macromolecules* **20**:1425–1428.

Genuini, G., Casalino, G., Chiarelli, P., and De Rossi, D. (1990). *Pseudomuscular Linear Actuators: Modeling and Simulation Experiences in the Motion of Articulated Chains.* Maratea, Italy: NATO ACI Science.

Gierke, T. D., and Hsu, W. Y. (1982). The cluster-network model of ion clustering in perfluoro sulfonate membranes. In *Perfluorinated Ionomer Membranes*, eds. A. Eisenberg and H. L. Yeager. Washington, DC: ACS, 283–307.

Gierke, T. D., Munn, G. E., and Wilson, F. C. (1982). Morphology of perfluorosulfonated membrane products—Wide-angle and small-angle x-ray studies. *ACS Symp. Ser.* **180**:195–216.

Gobin, P. F., and Tatibouet, J. (eds.) (1996). *Proceedings of the Third International Conference on Intelligent Materials*, Vol. 2779, The International Society for Optical Engineering.

Gong, J. P., and Osada, Y. (1994). Modeling and simulation of ionic polymer network. In *Preprints of the Sapporo Symposium on Intelligent Polymer Gels*, October 6–8, Sapporo, Japan, 21–22.

Gong, J. P., Nitta, T., and Osada, Y. (1994a). Electrokinetic modeling of the contractile phenomena of polymeric-truly gels—One-dimensional capillary model. *J. Phys. Chem.* **98**:9583–9587.

Grimshaw, P. E., Nussbaum, J. H., Grodzinsky, A. J., and Yarmush, M. L. (1990a). Kinetics of electrically and chemically induced swelling in polyelectrolyte gels. *J. Chem. Phys.* **93**(6):4462–4472.

Grimshaw, P. E., Nussbaum, J. H., Yarmush, M. L., and Eisenberg, S. R. (1989). Dynamic membranes for protein transport: Chemical electrical control. *Chem. Eng. Sci.* **44**(4):827–840.

Grodzinsky, A. J. (1974). *Electromechanics of Deformable Polyelectrolyte Membranes*. Sc.D. dissertation. MIT, Cambridge, MA.

Grodzinsky, A. J. (1975). Fields, forces, and flows in biological tissues and membranes. Lecture notes.

Grodzinsky, A. J., and Melcher, J. R. (1974). Electromechanics of deformable, charged polyelectrolyte membranes. In *Proceedings of the 27th Annual Conference on Engineering in Medicine and Biology*, 16, paper 53.2. (1976). Electromechanical transduction with charged polyelectrolyte membranes. *IEEE Trans. Biomed. Eng.* **23**(6):421–433.

Guo, S., Fukuda, T., Kosuge, K., Arai, F., Oguro, K., and Negoro, M. (1994). *Micro Catheter System with Active Guide Wire Structure, Experimental Results, and Characteristic Evaluation of Active Guide Wire Catheter Using ICPF Actuator*. Osaka: Osaka National Research Institute, 191–197. (1995). *Micro Catheter System with Active Guide Wire*. Preprint, Osaka, Japan.

Guth Alan, H. (2004). Inflation, In *Measuring and Modeling the Universe, Carnegie Observatories Astrophysics Series*, Vol. 2, ed. W. L. Freedman. Cambridge: Cambridge University Press.

Guth, A. H. (1981). Cosmic inflation. *Phys. Rev. D*, **23**, 347.

Halpert, and Landgrebe, A. R. (eds.). (1995). *The Electrochemical Society Proceedings Series*. Pennington, NJ: PV 95–23, p. 193.

Hamlen, R. P., Kent, C. E., and Shafer, S. N. (1965). Electrolytically active polymers. *Nature* **206**:1149–1150.

Happel, J., and Brenner, H. (1973). *Low Reynolds Number Hydrodynamics*. Englewood Cliffs, NJ: Prentice Hall.

Hawkins, G. F., O'Brien, M. J., and Creasy, T. S. (2004). Nastic materials using internally generated pressure. In *International Conference on Adaptive Structures and Technologies*, CAST 2004, October, Bar Harbor, ME.

Hebert, M. R. K., and de Gennes, P. G. (1997). Dynamics and thermodynamics of artificial muscles based on nematic gels. *J. Phys. I France* **7**:909–918.

Heeger, A. J. (2001). Semiconducting and metallic polymers: The fourth generation of polymeric materials. The Noble Prize 2000 lecture. *Curr. Appl. Phys.* **1**:247–267.

Heitner-Wirguin, C. (1996). Recent advances in perfluorinated ionomer membranes: Structure, properties and applications. *J. Membr. Sci.* **120**(1):1–33.

Helfferich, F. (1995). *Ion Exchange*. New York, NY: Dover Publications, Inc.

Henderson, B., Lane, S., Shahinpoor, M., Kim, K., and Leo, D. 2001. Evaluation of ionic polymer-metal composites for use as near-DC mechanical sensors. In *AIAA Space 2001—Conference and Exposition*, Albuquerque, NM, AIAA paper 2001–4600.

Hess, C., and Li, L. (1989). Smart hands for EVA retriever. In *NASA Conference on Space Telerobotics*, January, Pasadena, CA.

Higa, M., and Kira, A. (1994). A new equation of ion flux in a membrane: Inclusion of frictional force generated by the electric field. *J. Phys. Chem.* **98**(25):6339–6342.

Hirai, M., Hirai, T., Sukumoda, A., Nemoto, H., Amemiya, Y., Kobayashi, K., and Ueki, T. (1995). Electrically induced reversible structural change of a highly swollen polymer gel network. *J. Chem. Soc. Faraday Trans.* **91**:473–477.

Hirai, T., Zheng, J., and Watanabe, M. (1999). Solvent-drag bending motion of polymer gel induced by an electric field. In *Proceedings of the SPIE 6th Annual International Symposium on Smart Structures and Materials*, Vol. 3669, ed. Y. Bar-Cohen, 209–217.

Hirokawa, Y., and Tanaka, T. (1984). Volume transition in nonionic gel. *J. Chem. Phys.* **81**:6379.

Hirotsu, S., Hirokawa, Y., and Tanaka, T. (1987). Volume-phase transitions of ionized n-isopropylacrylamide gels. *J. Chem. Phys.* **87**(2):1392–1395.

Hsu, W. Y., and Gierke, T. D. (1982). Ion clustering and transport in Nafion perfluorinated membranes. *J. Electrochem. Soc.* **129**(3):C121–C129.

Hu, X. (1996). Molecular structure of polyacrylonitrile fibers. *J. Appl. Polym. Sci.* **62**:1925–1932.

Huang, J. P., Karttunen, M., Yu, K. W., and Dong, L. (2003). Dielectrophoresis of charged colloidal suspensions. *Phys. Rev. E* **67**:021403.

Hubble, E. (1929). Extra-galactic nebulae. *Acad. Sci.* **15**(3):168–173.

Huggins, M. L. (1941). Solutions of long chain compounds. *J. Chem. Phys.* **9**(15):440.

Huxley, A. F. (1957). Muscle structure and theories of contraction. *Prog. Biophys. Chem.* **7**:255.

Ichijo, H., Hirasa, O., Kishi, R., Oowada, M., Sahara, K., Kokufuta, E., and Kohno, S. (1995). Thermo-responsive gels. *Radiat. Phys. Chem.* **46**(2):185–190.

Ito, S. (1989). Phase transition of an aqueous solution of poly (N-alkyl acrylamide) derivatives: Effects of side chain structure. *Kobunsha* **46**(7):437.

Itoh, Y., Okui, N., Matsumura, T., Umemoto, S., and Sakai, T. (1987). Contraction/elongation mechanism of acrylonitrile gel fibers. *Polym. Prepr.* **36**(9):2897–2899.

Jacobsen, S. C. (1989). The state of the art in dexterous robotics. In *Conference Dinner, Speaker, IEEE International Conference on Robotics and Automation*, May, Scottsdale, AZ.

Jacobsen, S. C., Iverson, E. K., Knutti, D. F., Johnson, R. T., and Biggers, K. B. (1986). Design of the UTAH/M.I.T. dexterous hand. In *IEEE International Conference on Robotics and Automation*, April, San Francisco.

Jang, B. Z., and Zhang, Z. J. (1994). Thermally and phase transformation-induced volume changes of polymers for actuator applications. *J. Intell. Mater. Syst. Struct.* **5**:758–763.

Jolly, M. E., Carlson, J. D., and Muñoz, B. C. (1996). A model of the behavior of magnetorheological materials. *Smart Mater. Struct.* **5**:607–614.

Jolly, M. R., and Carlson, J. D. (2000). Composites with field responsive rheology. In *Comprehensive Composite Materials*, Vol. 5. New York, NY: Elsevier Science Ltd., Chapter 27, 86.

Kaga, Y., Okuzaki, H., Yasunaga, H., and Osada, Y. (1994). Electrically controlled insulin release from polyelectrolyte gel. In *Proceedings of the International Conference on Intelligent Materials*, 711–718.

Kagami, Y., Matsuda, A., Yasunaga, H., and Osada, Y. (1994). Order–disorder transition of hydrogel with n-alkyl acrylate and shape memory function as a smart diaphragm. In *Preprints of the Sapporo Symposium on Intelligent Polymer Gels*, October 6–8, Sapporo, Japan, 129–130.

Kajiwara, K., and Ross-Murphy, S. B. (1992). Synthetic gels on the move. *Nature* **355**(6357):208–209.

Kajiyama, T., Oishi, Y., Takahara, A., and He, X. (1994). Higher order structures and thermoresponsive properties of polymeric gel with stearyl acrylate. In *Preprints of the Sapporo Symposium on Intelligent Poly-Gels*, October 6–8, Sapporo, Japan, 27–30.

Kaneto, K., Kaneko, M., Min, Y., and MacDiarmid, A. G. (1995). Artificial muscle: Electromechanical actuators using polyaniline films. *Synth. Met.* **71**:2211.

Kanno, R., Hattori, M., Tadokoro, S., Takamori, T., and Oguro, K. (1994). *Modeling of Electric Characteristics of ICPF Actuator*. Kobe: Kobe University Preprint.

Kanno, R., Kurata, A., Hattori, M., Tadokoro, S., Takamori, T., and Oguro, K. (1994a). Characteristics and modeling of ICPF actuators. In *Proceedings of Japan–USA Symposium on Flexible Automation*, Vol. 2, 692–698.

Kanno, R., Tadokoro, S., Takamori, T., and Hattori, M. (1996). Linear approximate dynamic model of ICPF actuator. In *Proceedings of the IEEE International Conference on Robotics and Automation*, 219–225.

Katchalsky, A. 1949. Rapid swelling and deswelling of reversible gels of polymeric acids by ionization. *Experientia* **V**:319–320.

Keshavarzi, A., Shahinpoor, M., Kim, K. J., and Lantz, J. (1999). Using ionic polymer-metal composite sensors, blood pressure, pulse rate, and rhythm measurement. In *Electroactive Polymers*, SPIE publication no. 3669-36, 369–376.

Kim, D., and Kim, K. J. (2005). Self-oscillatory behavior of ionic polymer–metal composite (IPMC): A new finding. In *SPIE Smart Materials and Structures Conference*, March, #5759-7.

Kim, J., Kim, J.-Y., and Choe, S.-J. (2000). Electro-active paper: Its possibility as actuators. In *Proceedings of the SPIE EAPAD Conference, Part of the*

7th Annual International Symposium on Smart Structures and Materials, SPIE Proceedings, Vol. 3987, ed. Y. Bar-Cohen, 203–209.

Kim, K. J., and Shahinpoor, M. (1999). Effect of the surface-electrode resistance on the actuation of the ionic polymer–metal composite (IPMC) artificial muscles. In *Electroactive Polymers*, SPIE publication no. 3669-43, 308–319.

Kim, K. J., and Shahinpoor, M. (2001a). Development of three-dimensional polymeric artificial muscles. In *Proceedings of SPIE 8th annual international symposium on smart structures and materials*, March, Newport Beach, CA, 4329–(58). (2001b-2003a). Ionic polymer–metal composites—II. Manufacturing techniques, smart materials, and structures (SMS). *Inst. Phys. Publ.* **12**(1):65–79. (2003b). Effective diffusivity of nanoscale ion–water clusters within ion-exchange membranes determined by a novel mechano-electrical technique. *Int. J. Hydr. Energy* **28**(1):99–104.

Kim, K. J., Caligiuri, J., and Shahinpoor, M. (2003). Contraction/elongation behavior of cation-modified poly-acrylonitrile fibers. In *Proceedings of SPIE 10th Annual International Symposium on Smart Structures and Materials*, March 2–6, San Diego, CA, SPIE publication no. 5051-23, 207–213.

Kim, K. J., Caligiuri, J., Choi, K., Shahinpoor, M., Norris, I. D., and Mattes, B. R. (2002). Polyacrylonitrile nanofibers as artificial nano-muscles. In *Proceedings of the First World Congress on Biomimetics and Artificial Muscle (Biomimetics 2002)*, December 9–11, Albuquerque, NM.

Kim, K. J., Shahinpoor, M., and Razani, R. (1998). Solid polymer fuel cells for the next century. *Int. J. Environ. Conscious Des. Manuf.* **7**(3):17–46. (1999). Electro-active polymer materials for solid polymer fuel cells. In *Electroactive Polymers*, SPIE publication no. 3669-42, 385 –393. (2000a). Preparation of IPMCs for fuel cells, electrolysis, and hydrogen sensors. In *SPIE Smart Materials and Structures*, SPIE publication no. 3987-41, 311–320. (2000b). Preparation of IPMCs for fuel cells, electrolysis, and hydrogen sensors. In *Proceedings of SPIE 7th International Symposium on Smart Structures and Materials*, Vol. 3687, 110–120.

Kim, K., Detweiler, J., Lloyd, G., Shahinpoor, M., and Razani, A. (2002). Experimental and theoretical investigation of a metal hydride artificial muscle. In *Proceedings of the First World Congress on Biomimetics and Artificial Muscle (Biomimetics 2002)*, December 9–11, Albuquerque, NM.

Kishi, R., Hasebe, M., Hara, M., and Osada, Y. (1990). Mechanism and process of chemomechanical contraction of polyelectrolyte gels under electric field. *Polym. Adv. Technol.* **1**:19–25.

Kishi, R., Ichijo, H., and Hirasa, O. (1993). Thermo-responsive devices using poly(vinyl methyl ether) hydrogels. *J. Intell. Mater. Syst. Struct.* **4**: 533–537.

Koch, C. *Consciousness and Its Physical Substrate*, NCC Neuronal Correlates of Consciousness (NCC).

Kohno. (1995). Thermo-responsive gels. *Radiat. Phys. Chem.* **46**:185–190.

Kolde, J. A., Bahar, B., Wilson, M. S., and Zawodzinski, T. A. (1995). In *Proton Conducting Membrane Fuel Cells I*, eds. S. Gottesfeld, G. Halpert, and A. Landgrebe. Pennington, NJ: The Electrochemical Society, PV 95–23, p.193.

Kolosov, O., Suzuki, M., and Yamanaka, K. (1993). Microscale evaluation of the viscoelastic properties of polymer gel for artificial muscles using transmission acoustic microscopy. *J. Appl. Phys.* **74**(10):6407–6412.

Komoroski, R. A., and Mauritz, K. A. (1982). Nuclear magnetic resonance studies and the theory of ion pairing in perfluorinated ionomers. In *ACS symposium series*, Vol. 180. Washington, DC: The American Chemical Society.

Kottke, E. A., Partridge, L. D., and Shahinpoor, M. (2004). Bio-potential neural activation of artificial muscles. In *Proceedings of the Second World Congress on Biomimetics and Artificial Muscle (Biomimetics and Nano-Bio 2004)*, December 5–8, Albuquerque, NM. (2007). Bio-potential activation of artificial muscles. *J. Intell. Mater. Syst. Struct.* **18**(2).

Kuhn, W. (1949). Reversible Dehnung und Kontraktion bei Anderung der Ionisation eines Netzwerks Polyvalenter Fadenmolekulionen. *Experientia* **V**:318–319.

Kuhn, W., and Hargitay, B. (1951). Muskelahnliche Kontraktion und Dehnung von Netzwerken Polyvalenter Fadenmolekulionen. *Experientia* **VII**:1–11.

Kuhn, W., Hargitay, B., Katchalsky, A., and Eisenberg, H. (1950). Reversible dilation and contraction by changing the ionization state of high-polymer acid networks. *Nature* **165**:514–516.

Kuhn, W., Kunzle, O., and Katchalsky, A. (1948). Verhalten polyvalenter fademolekelionen in losung. *Helvetica Chem. Acta* **31**:1994–2037.

Kuntz, W. H., Larter, R., and Uhegbu, C. E. (1987). Enhancement of membrane transport of ions by spatially nonuniform electric fields. *J. Am. Chem. Soc.* **109**(9):2582–2585.

Laverack, M. S. (1985). Physiological adaptations of marine animals. In *Symposia of the Society for Experimental Biology. No. XIX*, Society for Experimental Biology.

Lavrov, A. N., Komiya, S., and Ando, Y. (2002). Antiferromagnets: Magnetic shape-memory effects in a crystal. *Nature* **418**:385–386.

Leo, D. J., and Cuppoletti, J. (2004). High-energy density actuation based on biological transport mechanisms. In *International Conference on Adaptive Structures and Technologies (CAST 2004)*, October, Bar Harbor, ME.

Li, F. K., Zhu, W., Zhang, X., Zhao, C. T., and Xu, M. (1999). Shape memory effect of ethylene-vinyl acetate copolymers. *J. Appl. Polym. Sci.* **71**(7):1063–1070.

Li, J. Y., and Nemat-Nasser, S. (2000). Micromechanical analysis of ionic clustering in Nafion perfluorinated membrane. *Mech. Mater.* **32**(5):303–314.

Li, Y., and Tanaka, T. (1989). Study of the universality class of the gel network system. *J. Chem. Phys.* **90**(9):5161–5166.

Liang, C., and Rogers, C. A. (1990). One-dimensional thermomechanical constitutive relations for shape-memory materials. *J. Intell. Mater. Syst. Struct.* **1**(2):54–59. (1992). Design of shape memory alloy actuators. *ASME J. Mech. Des.* **114**:223–230.

Liang, C., Rogers, C. A., and Malafeew, E. (1991). Preliminary investigation of shape memory polymers and their hybrid composites. In *ASME Conference on Smart Structures and Materials*, Vol. 123, 97–105.

Lifson, S., and Katchalsky, A. (1954). The electrostatic free energy of polyelectrolyte solutions—II. Fully stretched macromolecules. *J. Polym. Sci.* **13**:43 –55.

Liu, Z., and Calvert, P. (2000). Multilayer hydrogens and muscle-like actuators. *Adv. Mater.* **12**(4):288–291.

Lloyd, L. G., Kim, K. J., Razani, A., and Shahinpoor, M. (2002). Investigation of a solar-thermal biomimetic metal hydride actuator. In *Proc. Solar 2002 Conf. (Reno, NV); Proc. Solar Eng.* 2002, SED 2002-1066, 301–308. (2003). Investigation of a solar-thermal bio-mimetic metal hydride actuator. *ASME J. Sol. Energy Eng.* **125**:95–100.

Lumia, R., and Shahinpoor, M. (1999). Microgripper design using electro-active polymers. In *Electroactive Polymer*, SPIE publication no. 3669-30, 322–329. (2002). Artificial muscle micro-gripper. In *Proceedings of the First World Congress on Biomimetics and Artificial Muscle (Biomimetics 2002)*, December 9–11, Albuquerque, NM.

MacDiarmid, A. G. (2001). Synthetic metals: A novel role for organic polymers. The Noble Prize 2000 lecture. *Curr. Appl. Phys.* **1**:269–279.

Maddock, L., Bone, Q., and Rayner, J. M. V. (1994). *Mechanics and Physiology of Animal Swimming*. Cambridge: Cambridge University Press.

Mallavarapu, K., and Leo, D. J. (2001). Feedback control of the bending response of ionic polymer actuators. *J. Intell. Mater. Syst. Struct.* **12**:143–155.

Margolis, J. M. (1989). *Conductive Polymers and Plastics*. London: Chapman & Hall.

Marieb, E. N. (1992). *Human Anatomy and Physiology*, 2nd ed. Redwood City, CA: Benjamin/Cummings Publishing.

Matsui, H., and Kobayashi, K. (1983a). Biomechanics VIII-A. International series on biomechanics. In *Proceedings of the 8th International Congress of Biomechanics*, Vol. 4A. Nagoya: Human Kinetics Publishers, Inc. (1983b). Biomechanics VIII-B. International series on biomechanics. In *Proceedings of the 8th International Congress of Biomechanics*, Vol. 4B. Nagoya: Human Kinetics Publishers, Inc.

Matsukata, M., Aoki, T., Sanui, K., Ogata, N., Kikuchi, A., Sakurai, Y., and Okano, M. (1994). New temperature-responsive biosystems by IPAA-modified enzymes. In *Preprints of the Sapporo Symposium on Intelligent Polymer Gels*, October 6–8, Sapporo, Japan, 37–38.

Matsuo, E. S., and Tanaka, T. (1988). Kinetics of discontinuous volume-phase transition of gels. *J. Chem. Phys.* **89**(3):1695–1703.

McGehee, M. D., Miller, E. K., Moses, D., and Heeger, A. J. (1999). Twenty years of conductive polymers: From fundamental science to applications. In *Advances in Synthetic Metals: Twenty Years of Progress in Science and Technology*, eds. P. Bamier, S. Lefrant, and Bidan, G. New York, NY: Elsevier, 98–203.

Meghdari, A., Jafarian, M., Mojarrad, M., and Shahinpoor, M. (1993). Exploring artificial muscles as actuators for artificial hands. In *Intelligent Structures, Materials, and Vibrations*, ASME publication DE-Vol. 58, eds. M. Shahinpoor and Tzou, H. S., 21–26.

Merleau-Ponty, M. *Phénoménologie de la perception, 1945 (French), 1962 (English)*, English translation from French by Colin Smith (1st English translation), Donald Landes (2nd English translation), Éditions Gallimard, Routledge & Kegan Paul, 1945, English translation (1962), 466 (1965 Routledge edition), ISBN, 978-0415834339 (2012 Routledge edition).

Michopolous, J. G., and Shahinpoor, M. (2002a). Continuous electrodynamic estimation of impedance associated with multi-dimensional ionic polymeric artificial muscles. In *Proceedings of the First World Congress on Biomimetics and Artificial Muscles (Biomimetics 2002)*, December 9–11, Albuquerque, NM. (2002b). Towards a multiphysics formulation of electroactive large deflection plates made from ionic polymeric artificial muscles. In *Proceedings of the First World Congress on Biomimetics and Artificial Muscle (Biomimetics 2002)*, December 9–11, Albuquerque, NM. (2004). Experimental calibration of non-linear continuum multi-field ionic polymer plate modeling. In *Proceedings of the Second World Congress on Biomimetics and Artificial Muscle (Biomimetics and Nano-Bio 2004)*, December 5–8, Albuquerque, NM.

Millet, P., Pinneri, M., and Durand, R. (1989). New solid polymer electrolyte composites for water electrolysis. *J. Appl. Electrochem.* **19**:162–166.

Mojarrad, M. (1997). Autonomous robotic swimming vehicle employing artificial muscle fin mimicking fish propulsion. In *AUSI Conference on Unmanned Untethered Submersible Technology*, September 7–10, Durham, NH. (1999). Design of composite artificial muscle (CAM) fin for aquatic vehicle propulsion. In *AUSI Conference on Unmanned Untethered Submersible Technology*, August 23–25, Durham, NH.

Mojarrad, M. (2001). Study of ionic polymeric gels as smart materials and artificial muscles for biomimetic swimming robotic applications. Ph.D. thesis. Department of Mechanical Engineering, University of New Mexico, Albuquerque, NM.

Mojarrad, M., and Shahinpoor, M. (1996a). Noiseless propulsion for swimming robotic structures using polyelectrolyte ion-exchange membranes. In *Proceedings of SPIE 1996 North American Conference on Smart Structures and Materials*, February 26–29, San Diego, CA, 2716, paper no. 27, 183–192. (1996b). Ion exchange membrane-platinum composites as electrically controllable artificial muscles. In *Proceedings of the Third International Conference on Intelligent Materials*, June 3–5, Lyon, France, 1012–1016. (1997a). Ion-exchange-metal composite sensor films. In *Proceedings of SPIE Conference on Intelligent Structures and Materials*, March 3–6, San Diego, CA. (1997b). Ion-exchange-metal composite artificial muscle actuator load characterization and modeling. In *Proceedings of SPIE Conference on Intelligent Structures and Materials*, March 3–6, San Diego, CA. (1997c). Biomimetic robotic propulsion using polymeric artificial muscles. In *Proceedings of (1997) IEEE Robotics and Automation Conference*, April 20–25, Albuquerque, NM.

Mojarrad, M., and Shahinpoor, M. (1997a). Biomimetic robotic propulsion using ion-exchange membrane metal composite artificial muscles. In *Proceedings (1997) of IEEE Robotic Automation Conference*, April, Albuquerque, NM. (1997b). Ion-exchange-metal composite sensor films. In *Proceedings (1997) of SPIE Smart Materials and Structures Conference*, March, San Diego, CA, publication no. 3042-10. (1997c). Ion-exchange-metal composite artificial muscle actuator load characterization and modeling. *Smart Mater. Technol.* **3040**:294–301. (1997d). Electrically induced large amplitude vibration and resonance characteristics of ionic poly-metric membrane-metal composites. In *Proceedings of SPIE conference on intelligent structures and materials*, March 3–6, San Diego, CA. (2000). Soft actuators and artificial muscles. U.S. Patent no. 6,109,852.

Mojarrad, M., and Wilson, D. (2000). Electroactive polymeric composite fin design for propulsion of autonomous aquatic vehicles. In *Proceedings of the Fourth International Conference and Exposition/Demonstration on Robotics for Challenging Situations and Environments*, February 27–March 2.

Moneim, M. S., Keikhosrow, F., Mustapha, A.-A., Larsen, K., and Shahinpoor, M. (2002). Flexor tendon repair using shape memory alloy suture: A biomechanical evaluation. *Clin. Orthop. Relat. Res.* (402):251–259.

Moor, R. B., Cable, K. M., and Croley, T. L. (1992). Barriers to flow in semicrystalline ionomer a procedure for preparing melt-processes perfluorosulfonate ionomer films and membranes. *J. Membr. Sci.* **75**:7–14.

Moor, W. (1972). *Physical Chemistry*, 4th ed. Englewood Cliffs, NJ: Prentice-Hall.

Motamedi, A. R., Blevins, F. T., Willis, M. C., McNally, T. P., and Shahinpoor, M. (2000). Biomechanics of the coracoclavicular ligament complex and augmentations used in its repair and reconstruction. *Am. J. Sports Med.* **28**(3):380–384.

Nagasawa, M. (1988). Molecular conformation and dynamics of macromolecules in condensed systems. In *Studies in Polymer Science*. New York, NY: Elsevier.

Nagatake, and Tsuchiya, K. (1992). Theoretical analysis of an electrostatic linear actuator developed as a biomimicking skeletal muscle. *JSME Int. J., Ser. III*, **35**(3):400–405.

Narita, T. M., Gong, J. P., and Osada, Y. (1998). Kinetic study of surfactant binding into polymer gel—Experimental and theoretical analyses. *J. Phys. Chem. B* **102**:4566–4572.

Naumann, H. (1987). Conjugated polymers. In *Electronic Properties of Conjugated Polymers*, eds. H. Kuzmany, M. Mehring, and S. Roth. New York, NY: Springer-Verlag.

Nemat-Nasser, S. (2002). Micro-mechanics of actuation of ionic polymer–metal composites (IPMCs). *J. Appl. Phys.* **92**(5):2899–2915.

Nemat-Nasser, S., and Li, J. Y. (2000). Electromechanical response of ionic polymer–metal composites. *J. Appl. Phys.* **87**(7):3321–3331.

Nemat-Nasser, S., and Wu, Y. (2003). Comparative experimental study of ionic polymer–metal composites with different backbone ionomers and in various cation forms. *J. Appl. Phys.* **93**:5255–5267.

Newbury, K. M. (2002). Characterization, modeling, and control of ionic polymer transducers. Ph.D. dissertation. Virginia Tech.

Newbury, K. M., and Leo, D. J. (2002). Electrically induced permanent strain in ionic polymer–metal composite actuators. In *Proceedings of SPIE (2002) North American Conference on Smart Structures and Materials*, March, San Diego, CA, Vol. 4695, 67–77.

Nicoli, D., Young, C., Tanaka, T., Pollak, A., and Whitesides, G. (1983). Chemical modification of acrylamide gels: Verification of the role of ionization in phase transitions. *Macromolecules* **16**:887–891.

Nitta, T., Akama, K., Gong, J. P., and Osada, Y. (1994). Ionic conduction and water transport in the charged polymer networks. In *Preprints of the Sapporo Symposium on Intelligent Polymer Gels*, October 6–8, Sapporo, Japan, 119–120.

O'Handley, R. C. (1998). Model for strain and magnetostriction in magnetic shape memory alloys. *J. Appl. Phys.* **83**:3263–3271.

O'Handley, R. C., Ullakko, K., Huang, J. K., and Kantner, C. (1996). Large magnetic-field-induced strains in Ni_2MnGa single crystals. *Appl. Phys. Lett.* **69**:1966–1971.

Ogston, A. G., Preston, B. N., and Wells, J. D. (1973). On the transport of compact particles through solutions of chain-polymers. *Proc. R. Soc. Lond.* **333**:297.

Oguro, K., Asaka, K., and Takenaka, H. (1993). Polymer film actuator is driven by low voltage. In *Proceedings of the 4th International Symposium of Machines and Human Science*, Nagoya, Japan, 39–40.

Oguro, K., Fujiwara, N., Asaka, K., Onishi, K., and Sewa, S. (1999). Polymer electrolyte actuator with gold electrodes. In *Proceedings of the SPIE 6th Annual International Symposium on Smart Structures and Materials*, SPIE Proceedings 3, Vol. 669, 64–71.

Oguro, K., Kawami, Y., and Takenaka, H. (1992). Bending of an ion-conducting polymer film-electrode composite by an electric stimulus at low voltage. Trans. *J. Micromach. Soc.* **5**:27–30.

Oguztoreli, M. N., and Stein, R. B. (1983). Optimal control of antagonistic muscles. *Biol. Cybern.* **48**:1–99.

Ohmine, I., and Tanaka, T. (1982). Salt effects on the phase transitions of polymer gels. *J. Chem. Phys.* **77**:5725.

Okuzaki, H., and Osada, Y. (1994a). Chemomechanical polymer gel with electrically driven motility. In *Proceedings of the International Conference on Intelligent Materials*, 960–970. (1994b). Effects of hydrophobic interaction on the cooperative binding of surfactant to a polymer network. *Macromolecules* **27**:502–506. (1994c). Electro-driven chemomechanical polymer gel as an intelligent soft material. *J. Biomater. Sci. Polym. Ed.* **5**(5):485–496.

Okuzaki, H., Katsuyama, Y., and Osada, Y. (1994). Electrically driven chemomechanical polymer gel based on molecular assembly reaction. In *Preprints of the Sapporo Symposium on Intelligent Polymer Gels*, October 6–8, Sapporo, Japan, 115–116.

Onishi, K., Sewa, S., Asaka, K., Fujiwara, N., and Oguro, K. (2000). Bending response of polymer electrolyte actuator. In *Proc. Smart Structures and Materials 2001: Electroactive Polymer Actuators and Devices.*

Osada, Y. (1991). Chemical valves and gel actuators. *Adv. Mater.* **3**(2):107–108. (1992a). A chemomechanical polymer gel with electrically driven motility. In *Proceedings of the Conference on Recent Advances in Adaptive and Sensory Materials and Their Applications*, 783–790. (1992b). Electro-stimulated chemomechanical system using polymer gels (an approach to an intelligent artificial muscle system). In *Proceedings of the International Conference on Intelligent Materials*, 155–161.

Osada, Y., and Hasebe, M. (1985). Electrically activated mechanochemical devices using polyelectrolyte gels. *Chem. Lett.* **4**:1285–1288.

Osada, Y., and Kishi, R. (1989). Reversible volume change of microparticles in an electric field. *J. Chem. Soc.* **85**:655–662.

Osada, Y., and Matsuda, A. (1995). Shape memory in hydrogels. *Nature* **376**:219.

Osada, Y., and Ross-Murphy, S. B. (1993). Intelligent gels. *Sci. Am.* **268**:82–87.

Osada, Y., Okuzaki, H., and Hori, H. (1992). A polymer gel with electrically driven motility. *Nature* **355**:242–244.

Osada, Y., Okuzaki, H., Gong, J. P., and Nitta, T. (1994). Electro-driven gel motility on the base of cooperative molecular assembly reaction. *Polym. Sci.* **36**:340–351.

Oster, G., and Auslander, D. (1971). Topological representations of thermodynamic systems—II. Some elements are subunits for irreversible thermodynamics. *J. Franklin Inst.* **292**:77–92.

Otake, M., Inaba, M., and Inoue, H. (1999). Development of gel robots made of electro-active polymer PAMPS gel. In *Proceedings of IEEE International Conference on Systems, Man and Cybernetics*, WA20-2, CDROM (1999).

Otake, M., Kagami, Y., Inaba, M., and Inoue, H. (2000b). The behavior of a mollusk-type robot made of electro-active polymer gel under spatially varying electric fields. In *Intelligent Autonomous Systems*, Vol. 6, eds., E. Pagello et al. IOS Press, 686–691.

Otake, M., Kagami, Y., Inaba, M., and Inoue, H. (2002b). Motion design of a starfish-shaped gel robot made of electro-active polymer gel. *Rob. Auton. Syst.* **40**:185–191. (2002c). Starfish-shaped gel robots made of EAP. *WW-EAP Newsletter* **4**(2):7–8.

Otero, T. F. (1997). Artificial muscles, electrode solution, and REDOX processes in conducting polymers. In *Handbook of Organic Conductive Molecules and Polymers*, ed. H. S. Nalwa. New York, NY: John Wiley & Sons Ltd.

Otero, T. F., and Rodríguez, J. (1992). Electrochemomechanical and electro-chemopositioning devices: Artificial muscles. In *Intrinsically Conducting Polymers: An Emerging Technology*, ed. M. Aldissi. The Netherlands: Kluwer Academic Publishers, 40.

Otero, T. F., and Sansifiena, J. M. (1998). Soft and wet conducting polymers for artificial muscles. *Adv. Mater.* **10**(6):491– 494.

Otero, T. F., and Sansinena, J. M. (1995). Artificial muscles based on conducting polymers. *Bioelectrochem. Bioenerg.* **38**:411–414.

Otero, T. F., Angulo, E., Rodríguez, J., and Santamaría, C. (1992). Electrochemomechanical properties from a bilayer: Polypyrrole/non-conducting and flexible material—artificial muscle. *J. Electroanal. Chem.* **341**:369–375.

Otero, T. F., Grande, H., and Rodriguez, J. (1995). A new model for electrochemical oxidation of polypyrrole under conformational relaxation control. *J. Electrical. Chem.* **394**:211–216. (1996a). Reversible electrochemical reactions in conducting polymers: A molecular approach to artificial muscles. *J. Phys. Org. Chem.* **9**:381. (1996b). Influence of the counterion size on the rate of electrochemical relaxation in polypyrrole. *Synth. Met.* **9**:285.

Otero, T. F., Rodríguez, J., and Santamaría, C. (1994). Conductive polymers. *Mater. Res. Soc. Symp. Proc.* **330**:333.

Otero, T. F., Rodriguez, J., Angulo, E., and Santamaria, C. (1993). Artificial muscles from bilayer structures. *Synth. Met.* **55–57**:3713–3717.

Paquette, J., and Kim, K. J. (2002). An electric circuit model for ionic polymer-metal composites. In *Proceedings of the First World Congress on Biomimetics and Artificial Muscles*, December 9–11, Albuquerque, NM.

Park, I.-S., Kim, K. J., and Kim, D. (2006). Multi-fields responsive ionic polymer–metal composites. In *Proceedings of SPIE Smart Materials and Structures Conference*, March, 6168–6136.

Park, Y. H., and Han, M. H. (1992). Preparation of conducting polyacrylonitrile/polypyrrole composite films by electrochemical synthesis and their electrical properties. *J. Appl. Polym. Sci.* **45**:1973–1982.

Peace, G. S. (1993). *Taguchi Methods: Hands-on Approach*. New York, NY: Addison–Wesley Publishing Company, Inc.

Pei, Q., and Inganäs, O. (1993a). Electrochemical muscles: Bending strips built from conjugated polymers. *Synth. Met.* **55–57**:3718–3723. (1993b). Electrochemical applications of the bending beam method. 2. Electroshrinking and slow relaxation in polypyrrole. *J. Phys. Chem.* **97**:6034.

Pei, Q., Inganas, O., and Lundstrom, I. (1993). Bending bilayer strips built from polyaniline for artificial electrochemical muscles. *Smart Mater. Struct.* **2**(1):1–5.

Perline, R., Kornbluh, R., and Joseph, J. P. (1998). Electrostriction of polymer dielectrics with compliant electrodes as a means of actuation. *Sens. Actuators* **64**:77–85.

Perline, R., Kornbluh, R., Pei, Q., and Joseph, J. (2000). High-speed electrically actuated elastomers with strain greater than 100%. *Science* **287**: 836–839.

Phadke, M. S. (1989). *Quality Engineering Using Robust Design*. Englewood Cliffs, NJ: Prentice Hall.

Price, W. E., and Wallace, G. G. (1994). Conducting polymer membranes as intelligent separation systems. In *Proceedings of the International Conference on Intelligent Materials*, 994–1002.

Ramirez, P., Rapp, H. J., Reichle, S., Strathmann, H., and Mafe, S. (1992). *Life*. Seattle, WA: Ebner and Sons.

Rashid, T., and Shahinpoor, M. (1999). Force optimization of ionic polymeric platinum composite artificial muscles using an orthogonal array manufacturing method. In *Electroactive Polymers*, SPIE publication no. 3669-28, 289–298.

Ratna, B. R., Selinger, J. V., and Jeon, H. G. (2002). Isotropic-nematic transition in liquid-crystalline elastomers. *Phys. Rev. Lett.* **89**:225701.

Recent advances in ionic polymer conductor composite materials such as distributed nanosensors, nanoactuators, and artificial muscles. In *Proceedings of SPIE 12th Annual International Symposium on Smart Structures and Materials*, March 7–10, San Diego, CA, publication no. 5759, 49–63.

Rieder, W. G., and Busby, H. R. (1990). *Introductory Engineering Modeling Emphasizing Differential Models and Computer Simulations.* Malabar, FL: Robert E. Krieger Publishing Company.

Rohen, I. W., Yokochi, C., Lutjen-Drecoll, E. (2006). *Color Atlas of Anatomy: A Photographic Study of the Human Body*, 5th ed. Philadelphia, PA: Lippincott Williams & Wilkins, 208–209.

Röntgen, W. C. (1880). About the changes in shape and volume of dielectrics caused by electricity. *Ann. Phys. Chem.* **I**(1):771–786.

Rosen, M. W. (1959). Water flows about a swimming fish. Master's thesis. U.S. Naval Ordinance Test Station.

Sacerdote, M. P. (1899). Strains in polymers due to electricity. *J. Phys.* **3**:31.

Sadeghipour, K., Salomon, R., and Neogi, S. (1992). Development of a novel electrochemically active membrane and "smart" material-based vibration sensor/damper. *Smart Mater. Struct.* **1**:172–179.

Sakurada, I., Nakajima, A., and Fujiwara, H. (1959). Vapor pressures of polymer solutions. II. Vapor pressure of the poly(vinyl alcohol)-water system. *J. Polym. Sci.* **35**:497–505.

Salisbury, J. K. (1984). Design and control of an articulated hand. In *International Symposium of Design Synthesis*, July, Tokyo.

Samec, Z., Trojanek, A., and Samcova, E. (1994). Evaluation of ion transport parameters in a Nafion membrane from ion-exchange measurements. *J. Phys. Chem.* **98**(25):6352–6358.

Schmitz, K. S. (1994). Macro-ion characterization from dilute solutions to complex fluids. In *ACS Symposium Series 548*. New York, NY: American Chemical Society.

Schreyer, H. B., Gebhart, N., Kim, K. J., and Shahinpoor, M. (2000). Electric activation of artificial muscles containing polyacrylonitrile gel fibers. *Biomacromol. J.* **1**:42–647.

Schreyer, H. B., Shahinpoor, M., and Kim, K. J. (1999). Electrical activation of PAN-Pt artificial muscles. In *Proceedings of SPIE/Smart Structures and Materials/Electroactive Polymer Actuators and Devices*, March, Newport.

Segalman, D. J., and Witkowski, W. R. (1994). Two-dimensional finite element analysis of a polymer gel drug delivery system. In *Proceedings of the International Conference on Intelligent Materials*, 1055–1066.

Segalman, D., Witkowski, W., Adolf, D., and Shahinpoor, M. (1991). Electrically controlled polymeric gels as active materials in adaptive structures. In *Proceedings of the ADPA/AIAA/ASME/SPIE Conference on Active Materials and Adaptive Structures*, 335–345. (1992a). Theory of electrically controlled polymeric muscles as active materials in adaptive structures. *Int. J. Smart Mater. Struct.* **1**(1):44–54. (1992b). Numerical simulation of dynamic behavior of polymeric gels. In *Proceedings of the 1st International Conference on Intelligent Materials, ICIM'92*, July, Tsukube, Japan, Technomic Publishing Co., 310–313. (1992c). Theory and application of electrically controlled polymeric gels. *Smart Mater. Struct.* **1**:95–100.

Segalman, D., Witkowski, W., Rao, R., Adolf, D., and Shahinpoor, M. (1993). Finite element simulation of the 2D collapse of a polyelectrolyte gel disk. In *Proceedings (1993) of SPIE North American Conference on Smart Structures And Materials*, February, Albuquerque, NM, Vol. 1916, 14–22.

Sen, A., Scheinbeim, J. I., and Newman, B. A. (1984). The effect of plasticizer on the polarization of poly(vinylidene fluoride) films. *J. Appl. Phys.* **56**(9):2433–2439.

Senador, A. E., Shaw, M. T., and Mather, P. T. (2001). *MRS Symposium Proceedings*. Warrendale, PA: Materials Research Society, 661, KK5.9.1.

Sessler, G. M., and Hillenbrand, J. (1999). Novel polymer electrets. *MRS Symp. Proc. Electroact. Polym. (EAP)* 600:143–158.

Shahinpoor, M. (1991). Conceptual design, kinematics and dynamics of swimming robotic structures using active polymer gels. In *Proceedings of ADPA/AIAA/ASME/SPIE Conference on Active Materials & Adaptive Structures*, November, Alexandria, VA.

Shahinpoor, M. (1991a). Design and development of micro-actuators using ionic polymeric micromuscles. In *Proceedings of the ASME design engineering technical conference*, September, Boston. (1991b). Intelligent materials and structures revisited. In *Proceedings of SPIE Conference on Intelligent Structures and Materials*, February 26–29, San Diego, CA, 238–250. (1996). Ionic polymeric gels as artificial muscles for robotic and medical applications. *Int. J. Sci. Technol.* **20**(1):89–136.

Shahinpoor, M. (1992). Conceptual design, kinematics and dynamics of swimming robotic structures using ionic poly- meric gel muscles. *Smart Mater. Struct.* **1**(1):91–94. (1993). Novel applications of ionic polymeric gels as smart materials and artificial muscles. In Interdisciplinary research in smart materials.

Shahinpoor, M. (1995). Spring-loaded ionic polymeric gel linear actuator. U.S. patent no. 5,389,222. U.S. Patent Office.

Shahinpoor, M. (1995). The Venus flytrap as a model for biomimetic material with built-in sensors and actuators. *J. Mater. Sci. Eng.* **2**(4):229–233.

Shahinpoor, M. (1995f). Micro-electro-mechanics of ionic polymeric gels as electrically controllable artificial muscles. *Int. J. Intell. Mater. Syst.* **6**(3):307–314.

Shahinpoor, M. (1997b). Linear and platform-type robotic actuators made from ion-exchange-membrane-metal composites. In *Proceedings of SPIE Conference on Intelligent Structures and Materials*, March 3–6, San Diego, CA.

Shahinpoor, M. (1999). Electro-mechanics of iono-elastic beams as electrically controllable artificial muscles. In *Proceedings of the SPIE*, Vol. 3669, 109–121.

Shahinpoor, M. (2000d). Potential applications of electroactive polymer sensors and actuators in MEMS technologies. In *SPIE Smart Materials & MEMS*, publication no. 4234-40, 450–459.

Shahinpoor, M. (2002a). Electrically activated artificial muscles are made with liquid crystal elastomers. In *Proceedings of the SPIE 7th Annual International Symposium on Smart Structures and Materials*, ed. Y. Bar-Cohen. EAPAD conference, **3987**, 187–192.

Shahinpoor, M. (2003a). Linear electromechanical model of ionic polymer transducers, Part I: Model development. *J. Intell. Mater. Syst. Struct.* **14**(6):333–342. (2003b). Linear electromechanical model of ionic polymer transducers, Part II: Experimental validation. *J. Intell. Mater. Syst. Struct.* **14**(6):343–358.

Shahinpoor, M. (2002). Development of electric environment to control mollusk-shaped gel robots made of electro-active polymer PAMPS gel. In *Proceedings of the SPIE Electroactive Polymer Actuators and Devices (EAPAD)*, Vol. 3987, 321–330. (2002a). Kinematics of gel robots made of electro-active polymer PAMPS gel. In *Proceedings of the IEEE International Conference on Robotics and Automation*, San Francisco, 488–493.

Shahinpoor, M. (1994). In *Proceedings of the International Conference on Intelligent Materials*, 1095–1104. (1994b). Electro-mechanics of resilient contractile fiber bundles with applications to ionic polymeric gel and SMA robotic actuators. In *Proceedings (1994) IEEE*

International Conference on Robotics & Automation, May, San Diego, CA, Vol. 2, 1502–1508. (1994c). Design and modeling of a novel spring-loaded ionic polymeric gel actuator. In *Proceedings of SPIE 2189, Smart Structures and Materials 1994: Smart Materials*. https://doi.org/10.1117/12.174062.

Shahinpoor, M. (1994). In *Proceedings SPIE (1994) North American Conference on Smart Structures and Materials*, February, Orlando, FL, Vol. 2189, paper no. 26, 255–264. (1994d). Microelectro-mechanics of ionic polymeric gel as synthetic robotic muscles. In *Proceedings SPIE (1994) North American Conference on Smart Structures and Materials*, February, Orlando, FL, Vol. 2189, paper no. 27, 265–274. (1994e). Continuum electromechanics of ionic polymeric gels as artificial muscles for robotic applications. *Smart Mater. Struct. Int. J.* **3**:367–372. (1994f). Micro-electro-mechanics of ionic polymeric gels as electrically controlled synthetic muscles. In *Biomedical Engineering Recent advances*, Vol. 1, ed. Vossoughi, J. Washington, DC: University of District of Columbia Press, 756–759. (1995a). A new effect in ionic polymeric gels: The ionic flexogelectric effect. In *Proceedings SPIE (1995) North American Conference on Smart Structures Materials*, February 28–March 2, San Diego, CA, paper no. 05, 2441.

Shahinpoor, M., Ahghar, M., Kim, K. J., and Sillerud, L. O. 2002. Industrial and medical applications of ionic polymer–metal composites as biomimetic sensors, actuators, and artificial muscles. In *Proceedings of SPIE 9th Annual International Symposium on Smart Structures and Materials*, March, San Diego, CA, publication no. 4695-43.

Shahinpoor, M., and Ahghar, M. (2002). Modeling of electrochemical deformation in polyacrylonitrile (PAN) artificial muscles. In *Proceedings of the First World Congress on Biomimetics and Artificial Muscle (Biomimetics 2002)*, December 9–11, Albuquerque, NM.

Shahinpoor, M., and Alvarez, R. (2002). Simulation and control of iono-elastic beam dynamic deformation model. In *Proceedings of SPIE 9th Annual International Symposium on Smart Structures and Materials*, March, San Diego, CA, publication no. 4695-40.

Shahinpoor, M., and Gheshmi, S. (2015). *Robotic Surgery*. Singapore: Jenny Stanford Publishing.

Shahinpoor, M., and Guran, A. (2003). Ionic polymer-conductor composites (IPCCs) as biomimetic sensors, actuators, and artificial muscles. In *Selected Topics in Structronics and Mechatronic Systems*, eds. A. Belyaev and A. Guran. London: World Scientific Publishers, 417–436.

Shahinpoor, M., and Kim, K. (2001). Fully dry solid-state artificial muscles exhibiting giant electromechanical effect. In *Proceedings of SPIE 8th Annual International Symposium on Smart Structures and Materials*, March, Newport Beach, CA, publication no. 4329-58.

Shahinpoor, M., and Kim, K. J. (2000a). The effect of surface-electrode resistance on the performance of ionic polymer–metal composite (IPMC) artificial muscles. *Smart Mater. Struct.* **9**:543–551.

Shahinpoor, M., and Kim, K. (2002). Metal hydride artificial muscle systems. In *Proceedings of the First World Congress on Biomolecular-Metrics and Artificial Muscle* (Biomimetics 2002), December 9–11, Albuquerque, NM.

Shahinpoor, M., and Lumi R. (1995d). Design, model, and fabricate micro-robotic actuators with ionic polymeric gel and SMA micro-muscles. In *Proceedings (1995) ASME Design Engineering Technical Conference*, September, Boston.

Shahinpoor, M., and Mojarrad, M. (1994). Active musculoskeletal structures equipped with a circulatory system and a network of ionic polymeric gel muscles. In *Proceedings of the International Conference On Intelligent Materials*, 1079–1085. Also, preprints of the Sapporo symposium on intelligent polymer gels, October 6–8, Sapporo, Japan, 127–128.

Shahinpoor, M., and Mojarrad, M. (1996). Ion-exchange membrane-platinum composites as electrically controllable artificial muscles. In *Proceedings (1996) of Third International Conference on Intelligent Materials, ICIM '96, and Third European Conference on Smart Structures and Materials*, June, Lyon, France, 1012–1017.

Shahinpoor, M., and Mojarrad, M. (1997a). Biomimetic robotic propulsion using ion-exchange membrane metal composite artificial muscles, In *Proceedings of IEEE Robotic Automation Conference*, April 1997, Albuquerque, NM, USA.

Shahinpoor, M., and Mojarrad, M. (1997b). Ion-exchange-metal composite sensor films, In *Proceedings of SPIE Smart Materials and Structures Conference*, March 1997, San Diego, CA, publication no. 3042-10.

Shahinpoor, M., and Mojarrad, M. (1997c). Ion-exchange-metal composite artificial muscle actuator load characterization and modeling, *Smart Mater. Technol.* **3040**:294–301.

Shahinpoor, M., and Mojarrad, M. (1997d). Electrically induced large amplitude vibration and resonance characteristics of ionic polymeric membrane-metal composites. In *Proceedings of SPIE Conference on Intelligent Structures and Materials*, March 3–6, San Diego, CA.

Shahinpoor, M., and Osada, Y. (1995a). Electrically induced dynamic contraction of ionic polymeric gels. In *Preprints of the Sapporo Symposium on Intelligent Polymer Gels*, October 6–8, 1994, Sapporo, Japan. Also in *Proceedings of SPIE Conference on Smart Materials and Structures*, February 28–March 2, San Diego, CA. (1995b). Heart tissue replacement with ionic polymeric gels. In *Proceedings (1996) of ASME Winter Annual Meeting*, November 12–18, San Francisco.

Shahinpoor, M., and Popa, S. G. (2002). Recent technology development in contactless monitoring of the electromagnetic activities of the human heart and brain. In *Proceedings of SPIE 9th Annual International Symposium on Smart Structures and Materials*, March, San Diego, CA, publication no. 4694-44.

Shahinpoor, M., and Thompson, M. S. (1994). The Venus fly trap and the waterwheel plant as smart carnivorous botanical structures with built-in sensors and actuators. In *Proceedings (1994) of the International Conference on Intelligent Materials*, ICIM '94, June, Williamsburg, VA, 1086–1094.

Shahinpoor, M., and Tzou, H. S. (1993). Intelligent structures, materials, and vibrations. In *Proceedings of the 14th Biennial Conference on Mechanical Vibration and Noise*, September 19–22. Albuquerque, NM: ASME Publications.

Shahinpoor, M., and Wang, G. (1995). Design, modeling and performance evaluation of a novel large motion shape memory alloy actuator. In *Proceedings of SPIE (1995) North American Conference on Smart Structures and Materials*, February 28–March 2, San Diego, CA, paper no. 31, 2447.

Shahinpoor, M., and Wang, G. (1995). Electro-thermo-mechanics of SMA fiber bundles embedded in an elastic medium, In *Active Materials and Smart Structures*, G.L. Anderson and Dimitris C. Lagoudas (eds.), SPIE Publication, vol. 2427, pp. 272–382.

Shahinpoor, M., Bar-Cohen, Y., Simpson, J., and Smith, J. (1998a). Ionic polymer–metal composites (IPMCs) as biomimetic sensors, actuators and artificial muscles—A review. *Smart Mater. Struct. J.* **7**:R15–R30. (1999). Ionic polymer–metal composites (IPMCs) as biomimetic sensors and actuators. In *Field-Responsive Polymers*, eds. I. M. Khan and J. S. Harrison. American Chemical Society Publication, ACS-FRP, ACS Symposium Series 726. Oxford: Oxford University Press, 25–50.

Shahinpoor, M., Bar-Cohen, Y., Xue, T., Simpson, J., and Smith, J. (1998b). Some experimental results on ion-exchange polymer–metal composites as biomimetic sensors and actuators. In *Proceedings of*

SPIE Smart Materials and Structures Conference, March 3–5, San Diego, CA, publication no. 3324-37.

Shahinpoor, M., Kim, K. J., and Leo, D. (2003). Ionic polymer–metal composites as multifunctional materials. *Polym. Compos.* **24**(1):24–33.

Shahinpoor, M., Kim, K. J., and Mojarrad, M. (2005). *Ionic Polymeric Conductor Composite Artificial Muscles*, 2nd ed. Albuquerque, NM: ERI/AMRI Press.

Shahinpoor, M., Kim, K. J., and Schreyer, H. B. (2000a). Artificial sarcomere and muscle made with conductive polyacrylonitrile (C-PAN) fiber bundles. In *Proceedings of SPIE 3987, Smart Structures and Materials 2000: Electroactive Polymer Actuators and Devices* (EAPAD), 243–251. (2000b). Effects of counter-ions on the performance of IPMCs. In *SPIE Smart Materials and Structures*, publication no. 3987-18, 110–120.

Shahinpoor, M., Kim, K. J., Griffin, S., and Leo, D. (2001). Sensing capabilities of ionic polymer–metal composites. In *Proceedings of SPIE 8th Annual International Symposium on Smart Structures and Materials*, March, Newport Beach, CA, publication no. 4329-28.

Shahinpoor, M., Kim, K. J., Sillerud, L. O., Norris, I. D., and Mattes, B. R. (2002). Electroactive polyacrylonitrile nanofibers as artificial nano muscles. In *Proceedings of SPIE 8th Annual International Symposium on Smart Structures and Materials*, March, San Diego, CA, publication no. 4695-42.

Shahinpoor, M. (2002a). Metal hydride artificial muscle systems. In *Proceedings of the First World Congress on Biomolecular-Metrics and Artificial Muscle (Biomimetics 2002)*, December 9–11, Albuquerque, NM. (2002b). Applications of ionic polymer conductor composites (IPCCs) to nanotechnology and nanorobots. In *Proceedings of the First World Congress on Biomimetics and Artificial Muscle (Biomimetics 2002)*, December 9–11, Albuquerque, NM. 2002c. Metal hydride artificial muscle systems. In *Proceedings of the First World Congress on Biomolecular-Metrics and Artificial Muscle (Biomimetics 2002)*, December 9–11, Albuquerque, NM.

Shahinpoor, M., Norris, I. D., Mattes, B. R., Kim, K. J., and Sillerud, L. O. (2002). Electroactive polyacrylonitrile nanofibers as artificial nano-muscles. In *Proceedings of the 2002 SPIE Conference on Smart Materials and Structures*, March, San Diego, CA, publication no. 4695-42, 169–173.

Shahinpoor, M., Salehpoor, K., and Razani, A. (1998). Role of ion transport in dynamic sensing and actuation of ionic polymeric platinum composite artificial muscles. In *Proceedings of SPIE Smart Materials and Structures Conference*, March 3–5, San Diego, CA, publication no. 3330-09.

Shahinpoor, M., Sillerud, L. O., and Popa, S. G. (2002). Smart fiber optic magnetometer. In *Proceedings of the First World Congress on Biomimetics and Artificial Muscle (Biomimetics 2002)*, December 9–11, Albuquerque, NM.

Shahinpoor, M., Wang, G., and Mojarrad, M. (1994). Electro-thermo-mechanics of spring-loaded contractile fiber bundles with applications to ionic polymeric gel and SMA actuators. In *Proceedings of the International Conference on Intelligent Materials*, 1105–1116.

Shainpoor, M., et. al. (1993). Patent, USPTO.gov., 1993. Actuator element. US patent no. composite 5,268,082.

Shiga, T. 1997. Deformation and viscoelastic behavior of polymer gels in electric fields. *Adv. Polym. Sci.* **134**:131–163.

Shiga, T., and Karachi, T. (1990). Deformation of polyelectrolyte gels under the influence of electric field. *J. Appl. Polym. Sci.* **39**:2305–2320.

Shiga, T., Hirose, Y., Okada, A., and Kurauchi, T. (1993). Bending of ionic polymer gel caused by swelling under sinusoidally varying electric fields. *J. Appl. Polym. Sci.* **47**:113–119.

Shinohara, S., Tajima, N., and Yanagisawa, K. (1994). Photo fabrication for small polymer gels and their properties. In *Preprints of the Sapporo Symposium on Intelligent Polymer Gels*, October 6–8, Sapporo, Japan, 91–92.

Shirakawa, H. (2001). The discovery of polyacetylene films—The dawning of an era of conductive polymers. The Noble Prize 2000 lecture. *Curr. Appl. Phys.* **1**:281–286.

Shirakawa, H., Louis, E. J., MacDiarmid, A., Chiang, C. K., and Heeger, A. J. (1977). Synthesis of electrically conducting organic polymers: Halogen derivatives of polyacetylene, (CH)x. *J. C. S. Chem. Commun.* **285**:578.

Singh, D., Lu, D. M., and Djilali, N. (1999). A two-dimensional analysis of mass transport in proton exchange membrane fuel cells. *Int. J. Eng. Sci.* **37**:431–452 .

Skalak, R., and Chien, S. (1987). *Handbook of Bioengineering*. New York, NY: McGraw-Hill.

Smela, E., and Gadegaard, N. (2001). Volume change in polypyrrole studied by atomic force microscopy. *J. Phys. Chem. B* **105**:9395.

Smela, E., Inganäs, O., and Lundström, I. (1995). Controlled folding of micrometer-size structures. *Science* **268**:1735–1738.

Smela, E., Inganäs, O., Pei, Q., and Lundström, I. (1993). Electrochemical muscles: Micromachining fingers and corkscrews. *Adv. Mater.* **5**(9):630–632.

Soltanpour, D., and Shahinpoor, M. (2002). Development of a synthetic-muscle-based miniature diaphragm pump for medical applications. In *Proceedings of the First World Congress on Biomimetics and Artificial Muscle (Biomimetics 2002)*, December 9–11, Albuquerque, NM.

Soltanpour, D., Shahinpoor, P., and Shahinpoor, M. (2002). Development of an artificial muscle-based smart band to correct refractive errors of the human eye. In *Proceedings of the First World Congress on Biomolecular-Metics and Artificial Muscle (Biomimetics 2002)*, December 9–11, Albuquerque, NM.

Springer, T. E., Wilson, M. S., and Gottesfeld, S. (1993). Modeling and experimental diagnostics in polymer electrolyte fuel cells. *J. Electrochem. Soc.* **140**(12).

Springer, T. E., Zawodzinski, T. A., and Gottesfeld, S. (1991). Polymer electrolyte fuel cell model. *J. Electrochem. Soc.* **138**(8).

Stein, J. L., Ashton-Miller, J. A., and Pandy, M. G. (1989). Issues in modeling and control of biomechanical systems. In *Proceedings of the Winter Annual Meeting of the American Society of Mechanical Engineers*, December 10–15. San Francisco, CA: ASME Publications, DSC-Vol. 17.

Steinberg, I. Z., Oplatka, A., and Katchalsky, A. (1966). Mechanochemical engines. *Nature* **210**:568–571.

Steinmetz, C. G., and Larter, R. (1988). Electrostatic model for enhancement of membrane transport by a nonuniform electric field. *J. Phys. Chem.* **92**(21):6113–6120.

Stone, R. J., and Stone, J. A. (1990). *Atlas of the Skeletal Muscles*. Dubuque, IA: Wm. C. Brown Publishers.

Strobel, M., Lyons, C. S., and Mittal, K. L. (1994). *Plasma Surface Modification of Polymers: Relevance to Adhesion*. Utrecht: VSP Publication.

Tadokoro, S. (2000). An actuator model of ICPF for robotic applications on the basis of physicochemical hypotheses. In *Proceedings of the IEEE*, ICRA, 1340–1346.

Tadokoro, S., Takamori, T., and Oguro, K. (2001). Application of the Nafion–platinum composite actuator. In *Proceedings of the SPIE*, Vol. 4329, 28–42.

Tadokoro, S., Yamagami, S., Takamori, T., and Oguro, K. (2000). Modeling of Nafion-Pt composite actuators (ICPF) by ionic motion. In *Proceedings of the SPIE*, Vol. 3987, 92–102.

Takenaka, H., Torikai, E., Kawami, Y., and Wakabayshi, N. (1982). Solid polymer electrolyte water electrolysis. *Int. J. Hydrogen Energy* **7**:397–403.

Tal, J. (1994). *Step-by-Step Design of Motion Control Systems.* Ontario: Electromate Industries Publication.

Tanaka, T., Sun, S., Hirokawa, Y., Katayama, S., Kucera, J.P., Hirose, Y., and Amiya, T. (1987). Mechanical instability of gels at the phase transition. *Nature* **325**(6107):796–798. *Nature*, **325**:796–798.

Tobushi, H., Hayashi, S., and Kojima, S. (1992). Mechanical properties of shape memory polymer of polyurethane.

Tononi, G., and Koch, C. (2015). Consciousness: Here, there and everywhere? *Phil. Trans. Biol. Sci.*, **370**(1668):1–18.

Tortora, G., and Grabowski, S. R. (1993). *Principles of Anatomy and Physiology*, 7th ed. New York, NY: Harper-Collins College Publishers.

Tourillon, G., and Garnier, F. (1984). Structural effect on the electrochemical properties of polythiophene and derivatives. *J. Electroanal. Chem.* **161**:51. (1994). Effect of dopant on conjugated polymers. *J. Polym. Sci., Polym. Phys. Ed.* **22**:33.

Tozzi, P., Shahinpoor, M., Hayoz, D., and L. von Segesser. (2004). Electroactive polymers to assist failing heart: The future is now. In *Proceedings of the Second World Congress on Biomimetics and Artificial Muscle (Biomimetics and Nano-Bio 2004)*, December 5–8, Albuquerque, NM.

Triantafyllou, M. S., and Triantafyllou, G. S. (1995). An efficient swimming machine. *Sci. Am.* 64–70.

Truesdell, C. A., and Noll, W. (1965). *The Non-Linear Field Theories of Mechanics*, ed. S. S. Antman. Berlin, Heidelberg: Springer.

Tyldesley, B., and Grieve, J. I. (1989). *Muscles, Nerves, and Movement.* Glasgow: Blackwell Scientific Publications.

Tyson, J., Schmidt, T., Galanulis, K., and Shahinpoor, M. (2002). Full-field deformation and strain measurement in biomechanics and biomimetics. In *Proceedings of the First World Congress on Biomimetics and Artificial Muscle (Biomimetics 2002)*, December 9–11, Albuquerque, NM.

Tyson, J., Schmidt, T., Shahinpoor, M., and Galanulis, K. (2003). Biomechanics deformation and strain measurements with 3D image correlation photogrammetry. *J. Exp. Tech. Soc. Exp. Mech.* **27**(4):32–46.

Tzou, H. S., and Fukuda, T. (1992). *Precision Sensors, Actuators and Systems.* Dordrecht: Kluwer Academic Publishers.

Tzou, H. S., Anderson, G. L., and Natori, M. C. (1995c). Active polyelectrolyte gels are electrically controllable artificial muscles and intelligent network structures. In *Active Structures, Devices, and Systems.* Lexington, KY: World Science Publishing.

Ueoka, Y., Isogai, N., and Nitta, T. (1994). Eel-like gel actuator with biomimetic movement. In *Preprints of the Sapporo Symposium on Intelligent Polymer Gels*, October 6–8, Sapporo, Japan, 117–118.

Ugural, A. C., and Fenster, S. K. (1987). *Advanced Strength and Applied Elasticity*. New York, NY: Elsevier.

Ullakko, K. (1996). Magnetically controlled shape memory alloys: A new class of actuator materials. *J. Mater. Eng. Perform.* **5**:405–409.

Umemoto, S., Okui, N., and Sakai, T. (1991). Contraction behavior of poly(acrylonitrile) gel fibers. In *Polymer Gels*, eds. D. DeRossi, K. Kajiwara, Y. Osada, and A. Yamauchi. New York, NY: Plenum Press, 257–270.

Urayama, K., Takaigawa, T., Masuda, T., and Kohjiya, S. (1994). Stress relaxation and creep of polymer gels in a solvent under various deformation modes. In *Preprints of the Sapporo Symposium on Intelligent Poly-Gels*, October 6–8, Sapporo, Japan, 89–90.

Van der Veen, G., and Prins, W. (1971). Photomechanics directs the bending of a polymer film by light. *Phys. Sci.* **230**:70.

Van der, A. J., Sherman, J. H., and Luciano, D. S. (1985). *Human Physiology: The Mechanism of Body Function*, 4th ed. New York, NY: McGraw-Hill, 255–298.

Veltink, P. H., Chizeck, H. J., Crago, P. E., and El-Bialy, A. (1992). Nonlinear joint angle control for artificially stimulated muscle. *IEEE Trans. Biomed. Eng.* **39**(4):368–380.

Verbrugge, M. W., and Hill, R. F. (1993). Ion and solvent transport in ion-exchange membranes. *J. Electrochem. Soc.* **140**(5):1218–1225.

Wang, G. (1998). A general design of bias force shape memory alloy (BFSMA) actuators and an electrically controlled SMA knee and leg muscle exerciser for paraplegics and quadriplegics. Ph.D. dissertation. Department of Mechanical Engineering, University of New Mexico, Albuquerque.

Wang, G., and Shahinpoor, M. (1997a). Design for shape memory alloy rotatory joint actuators using shape memory effect and pseudoelastic effect. *Smart Mater. Technol.* **3040**:23–30. (1997b). Design, prototyping and computer simulation of a novel large bending actuator made with a shape memory alloy contractile wire. *Smart Mater. Struct. Int. J.* **6**(2):214–221. (1997c). A new design for a rotatory joint actuator made with shape memory alloy contractile wire. *Int. J. Intell. Mater. Syst. Struct.* **8**(3):191–279. (1998). Design of a knee and leg muscle exerciser using a shape memory alloy rotary actuator. In *Proceedings of SPIE Smart Materials and Structures Conference*, March 3–5, San Diego, CA, publication no. 3324-29.

Wang, Q., Du, X., Xu, B., and Cross, L. E. (1999). Electromechanical coupling and output efficiency of piezoelectric bending actuators. *IEEE Trans. Ultrason. Ferroelectric. Freq. Control* **46**(3):638–646.

Wang, T. T., Herbert, J. M., and Glass, A. M. (eds.) 1988. *The Applications of Ferroelectric Polymers*. New York, NY: Chapman & Hall.

Webb, P. W., and Weihs, D. (1983). *Fish Biomechanics*. New York, NY: Praeger.

Weiss, K. D., Carlson, J. D., and Nixon, D. A. (1994). Viscoelastic properties of magneto- and electro-rheological fluids. *J. Intell. Mater. Syst. Struct.* **5**:772–775.

Whiting, C. J., Voice, A. M., Olmsted, P. D., and McLeish, T. C. B. (2001). Shear modulus of polyelectrolyte gels under electric field. *J. Phys.: Condens. Matter.* **13**:1381–1393.

Williams, W., and Bannister, D. *Gray's Anatomy*, 37th ed. Edinburgh: Churchill Livingstone, 614–616.

Winter, D. A. (1990). *Biomechanics and Motor Control of Human Movement*. New York, NY: Wiley-Interscience.

Winter, D., Norman, R. W., Wells, R. P., Hayes, K. C., and Patla, A. E. (1985a). Biomechanics IX—A, international series on biomechanics. In *Proceedings of the Ninth International Congress of Biomechanics*, Vol. 5A. Waterloo: Human Kinetics Publishers, Inc. (1985b). Biomechanics IX—B, international series on biomechanics. In *Proceedings of Ninth International Congress of Biomechanics*, Vol. 5B. Waterloo: Human Kinetics Publishers, Inc.

Wood, J. E., Meek, S. G., and Jacobsen, S. C. (1989a). Quantitation of human shoulder anatomy for prosthetic arm control I. Surface modeling. *J. Biomech.* **22**(3):273–292. (1989b). Quantitation of human shoulder anatomy for prosthetic arm control II. Anatomy matrices. *J. Biomech.* **22**(4):309–325.

Woojin, L. (1996). Polymer gel-based actuator: Dynamic model of gel for real-time control. Ph.D. thesis. Massachusetts Institute of Technology.

Wu, Y. T., Brokaw, C. J., and Brennen, C. (1975). *Swimming and Flying in Nature*, Vols. I and II. New York, NY: Plenum Press.

Yamada, H. (1970). *Strength of Biological Materials*. Baltimore, MD: The Williams & Wilkins Company.

Yannas, I. V., and Grodzinsky, A. J. (1973). Electromechanical energy conversion with collagen fibers in an aqueous medium. *J. Mechanochem. Cell Motil.* **2**:113–125.

Yasuda, K., Gong, P., Katsuwama, Y., Nakavama, A., Tanabe, Y., Kondo, E., Ueno, M., and Osada, Y. (2005). Biomechanical properties of high-toughness double network hydrogels. *Biomater. J.* **26**(21):4468–4475.

Yeager, H. L. (1982). Perfluorinated ionomer membranes. In *Perfluorinated Ionomer Membranes*, eds., A. Eisenberg and H. L. Yeager. American Chemical Society Symposium Series, 180.

Yen, C. C., and Chang, T. C. (1989). Preparation of electric-conducting film from polyacrylonitrile-silver nitrate complex. *J. Appl. Polym. Sci.* **40**:267–277.

Yoshida, H., and Miura, Y. (1992). The behavior of water in perfluorinated ionomer membranes having various monovalent cations. *J. Membr. Sci.* **68**:1–10.

Yoshida, R., Yamaguchi, T., and Ichijo, H. (1996). Novel oscillation, swelling-deswelling dynamic behavior for pH-polymer gels. *Mater. Sci. Eng. C* **4**:107–113.

Yoshida, T. (1987). Electrochemical studies of polyaniline and its applications. *Synth. Met.* **18**:365.

Young, R. J., and Lovell, P. A. 1991. *Introduction to Polymers*, 2nd ed. London: Chapman & Hall, 353.

Yuh, J. 1994. Underwater robotic vehicle: Design and control. In *NSF Workshop on Future Research Directions in Underwater Robotics*, Maui, HI.

Zhang, Q. M., Bharti, V., and Zhao, X. (1998). Giant electrostriction and relaxor ferroelectric behavior in electron-irradiated poly(vinylidene fluoride-tetrafluoroethylene) copolymer. *Science* **280**:2101–2104.

Zhang, Q. M., Furukawa, T., Bar-Cohen, Y., and Scheinbeim, J. (eds.) (1999). *Proceedings of the Fall MRS Symposium on Electroactive Polymers (EAP)*, Vol. 600. Warrendale, PA: Materials Research Society, 1–336.

Zrinyi, M., Barsi, L., Szabo, D., and Kilian, H. G. (1997). Direct observation of abrupt shape transition in ferrogels induced by a nonuniform magnetic field. *J. Chem. Phys.* **106**(13):5685–5692.

Zrinyi, M., Szabo, D., and Feher, J. (1999). Comparative studies of electro- and magnetic field-sensitive polymer gels. In *Proceedings of SPIE 6th Annual International Symposium of Smart Structures and Materials*, EAPAD, Vol. 3669, ed. Y. Bar-Cohen. 406–413.

Chapter 6

Fundamentals of Robotics Toward Design and Development of the Robotic Part of the Humanoid Robot

6.1 Introduction

In this chapter, the fundamentals of robotics have been discussed, along with the design and development of the linkages and linkage dynamics of the robotic part of humanoid robots. This chapter presents some fundamental aspects of robotic transformations, inverse kinematics, and inverse dynamics. Of course, the present position is that this technology is now well-developed regarding humanoid robots and that the associated consciousness is not yet fully implemented.

The humanoid robot will be designed and constructed to resemble the human master. It will have an embedded smart computer and microprocessor that will record all events in its life and can transfer all that knowledge and know-how to the memory of its human master. The humanoid robot will live with its owner (man or woman), be his or her life companion, gradually learn or become aware and knowledgeable of its owner's consciousness, and transform into the consciousness of its owner, a human.

Biomimetic Humanoid Robots with Human Consciousness
Mohsen Shahinpoor

ISBN 978-981-5129-87-8 (Hardcover), 978-1-003-71373-9 (eBook)
www.jennystanford.com

DOI: 10.1201/9781003713739-6

This book presents some fundamental aspects of robotic transformations, inverse kinematics, and inverse dynamics. Some of the materials in this chapter are also covered in *Robotic Surgery* by M. Shahinppor and S. Gheshmi (2015). The future humanoid robots will also be able to help humans in various endeavors such as biomedical engineering and performing robotic surgery like surgeons.

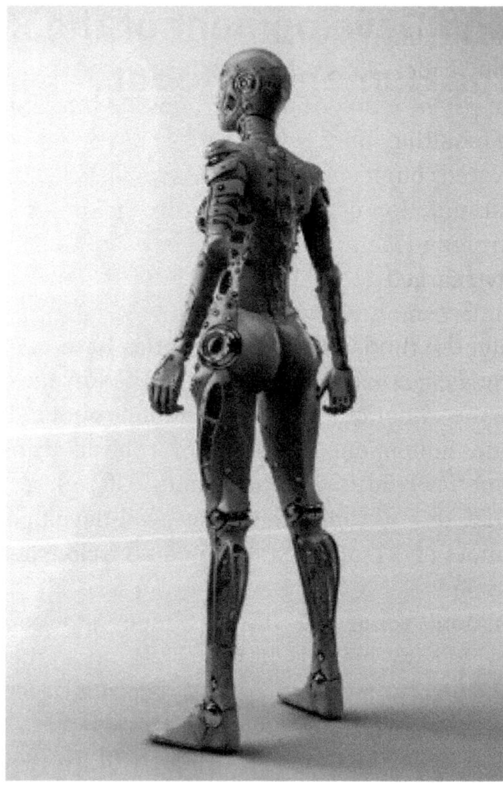

Figure 6.1 A humanoid robot (iStock through Shutterstock).

The current advanced robotic applications, such as surgical systems, evolved from the laparoscopic advanced robotic applications, such as surgical procedures, and made it possible for surgeons to perform surgery away from the patient with much more concentration and ease. However, what the surgeons lost in this transition was the sensation of tissues and organs and kinesthetic force feedback during surgery. Interestingly, even during laparoscopic surgery, surgeons can still feel and sense the tissues and organs they are handling and operating on with laparoscopic/endoscopic tools and feel the kinesthetic forces at work. However, the kinesthetic force feedback was replaced with visual feedback during robotic surgery. It will be great to create such soft skin, tissue, and organ sensing by the proposed biomimetic humanoid robots (Fig. 6.1). It is to be noted that some of this kinesthetic force feedback was lost in the transition from open to laparoscopic surgery due to trocar friction and varying lever arms, anyway.

However, with smart materials such as ionic polymer–metal composites (IPMCs) and appropriate calibration and tuning, one may recover the kinesthetic force feedback during surgery using IPMCs. IPMCs are great for robotic force feedback applications because they work perfectly well in the wet human body environment and generate millivolt-level sensing signals for kinesthetic force feedback. One can also produce highly maneuverable surface tissues and face tissue membranes with IPMCs. These issues on face tissues enable humanoid robots to display facial gestures and to enable them to look very much like real human beings.

Some additional robotic developments are as follows: Figures 6.2 and 6.3 show Atlas 1 and Atlas 2 from Boston Dynamics. Figure 6.4 shows another humanoid robot.

Figure 6.2 Atlas 1 from Boston Dynamics.

Figure 6.3 Atlas 2 from Boston Dynamics.

Figure 6.4 Some humanoid robots. *Source*: FastCompany.

Jia Jia is China's first humanoid robot (Fig. 6.5). This Chinese humanoid robot puts on a charm in Shanghai. People worldwide admire Jia Jia for her realistic and alluring appearance. Jia Jia was created by the University of Science and Technology research team in China. This astounding beauty can hold a normal conversation with a person with a microbial facial expression; she does that with the help of speech-generation algorithms and facial recognition technologies.

Figure 6.5 Jia Jia. *Source*: Digital Trends.

Sophia is considered the most advanced humanoid robot (Fig. 6.6). She debuted in 2016. She was one of a kind, and her interaction with people was the most unlikely thing you can ever see in a machine. She was designed by a Hong Kong–based company called Hanson Robotics and was created to look like Audrey Hepburn, a famous Hollywood actress. The creator's goal was to fit her as an elderly companion in nursing homes or a crowd manager at events.

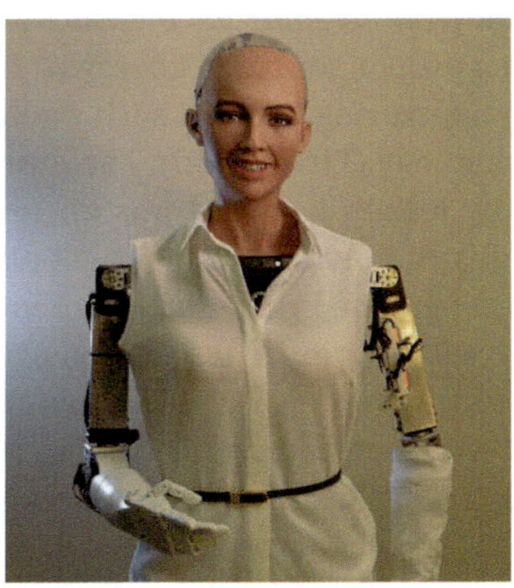

Figure 6.6 Sophia. *Source*: Research Gate.

Sophia is the world's first robot citizen and the first robot innovation ambassador for the United Nations Development Program. The purpose of creating Sophia was to make a robot capable of gaining social skills. Sophia has been embedded with neural networks and artificial intelligence to recognize human faces and understand their gestures and emotions. She can also interact with different people and also respond appropriately.

6.2 Introduction to Humanoid Robots: General Configurations

6.2.1 History of Robotics

Malone (1978) mentions that Aristotle was the first to discuss the concept of automation as a means to avoid the need for servants. The first versions of robots mostly consisted of clocks, such as Clepsydra (the water clock, which measures time through a graduated flow of liquid passing through a small opening (Bedini, 1962)), pioneered by Ctesibius of Alexandria (c. 270 BC) (Rosheim, 1994), subsequently followed by self-moving machines or automatons. The use of automatons was also related to clocks, such as the case of 1497, where two bell-striking giants decorated the clock tower in Piazza San Marco, Venice. Later in history, cuckoo clocks emerged and gained popularity, especially in Germany. Leonardo da Vinci did considerable and notable work on robotics, mostly found in his renowned book *Codex Atlanticus*. Da Vinci planned to build an *anthrobot*, though a proper source of energy or the necessary high-precision part manufacturing to build such a robot did not exist in contemporary technology (Pires, 2000). The invention of the textile machine in 1801 by Joseph Jacquard was one of the catalysts and symbols of the industrial revolution that took place in 1750–1850. Seward Babbitt designed the first industrial robot in 1892. This was a motorized crane with a gripper for the removal of ingots from a furnace. Tesla (1898) made his precious contribution to robotics through his patented remotely controlled device, the first of its kind, among many other inventions that are products of his work.

The word *robot* seems to have first become popular when the Czech playwright Karel Capek's play, titled R.U.R. (or Rossum's

Universal Robots), was first performed in Paris, France, in the 1920s. In that play, small, artificial, and anthropomorphic creatures strictly obeyed their master's orders. In Czech and Russian, these creatures were called robotic, from robotna, which are the Czech and Russian words for "drudgery" and "hard work." *Robotics* as a term, on the other hand, was introduced later, in 1942, by Isaac Asimov in the story "Runaround," in which the author also submitted the Laws of Robotics. These laws can be summarized as follows:

1. **Law one:** A robot may not harm a human being or, through inaction, allow a human being to come to harm.
2. **Law two:** Robots must obey orders given by humans, except those that would conflict with the higher-order laws.
3. **Law three:** Robots must protect their existence as long as such protection does not conflict with the higher-order laws.

Asimov's laws have found real-world applications, particularly in modern advanced robotic applications such as surgical robots. According to Shahinpoor's book *Intelligent Robotic Systems*, a robot is a reprogrammable multifunctional manipulator designed to move materials, parts, tools, or specialized devices through variable programmed motions for various tasks. This definition covers a broad spectrum of robot manipulators, and within this definition, there are different classes of robots, which include the following:

1. **Automated or flexible manufacturing:** These "industrial" robots are employed in a wide range of manufacturing processes, including parts assembly and inspection, materials handling, welding, and materials painting.
2. **Remote exploration:** This class of robotic manipulators is designed to survive in environments that humans cannot tolerate. They can be used to explore the unknown, from the edge of our solar system to the depths of Earth's oceans.
3. **Prosthetic and biomedical:** Robotic technology and its accompanying sensor technology can be teamed up with one another to provide prosthetic limbs with touch sensation. Humanoid robots also fall into this category. Miniature robots under a surgeon's control can probe the human body to operate on patients from within their bodies.
4. **Hazardous material handling:** Robots in this class have been employed to remove bombs and handle hazardous materials.

5. **Service:** Some present uses for service robots include security, janitorial, mail delivery, fire sentry, firefighter, and voice-commanded errand robots. Service robots will increase as technology progresses and manufacturing costs fall.

Westinghouse conceived two robots in 1940 that utilized electric motors for comprehensive body motion, and, among other activities, they imitated human and animal behavior. One exhibited human behavior by dancing and counting to 10. The other exhibited animal behavior by walking, standing on hind legs, and barking. The year 1946 marks the beginning of the computer age with the introduction of several inventions that will be expounded on herein. George Devol invented a playback device for controlling machines by introducing a magnetic process recorder. J. Presper Eckert and John Mauchly are credited for building the first computer that used electronic components, ENIAC. In contrast, the first digital computer was conceived at the Massachusetts Institute of Technology (MIT) and was called Whirlwind. Norbert Wiener published a book on *Cybernetics* that described the concept of communications and control in mechanical, biological, and electronic systems (Diodato et al., 2004).

The invention of the transistor in 1948 marks the start of a new era of inventions and advent in computing, which expedited the development of robots that functioned in conjunction with this new generation of computers. Raymond Goetz invented an articulated arm equipped with a teleoperator for the Atomic Energy Commission (AEC) in 1951. Devol and Engelberger were the first to develop a programmable robot in 1954, called Unimate, and linked it to the term "universal automaton" (please refer to the previous reference for the term automaton). Engelberger went on to establish Unimation, the world's first robot company.

Planet Corporation made the first commercial robot available in the market in 1959. In 1960, Condec Corporation purchased Unimation and began the development of the Ultimate Robot System. In 1962, General Motors started equipping production lines in Trenton, New Jersey, with robots. By 1964, MIT, Stanford University, and the University of Edinburgh had laboratories devoted to research on artificial intelligence. Hughes Aircraft developed the remotely controlled Mobots, specifically designed for use in "environments beyond [human] capacity and for tasks beyond [human] capability"

(Asimov et al., 1985), including construction, chemical testing, and interaction in nuclear reactor environments. In 1968, researchers at the Stanford Research Institute developed Shakey, a robot equipped with visual capabilities. In 1970, Stanford University introduced an electrically powered robotic arm. In 1973, Richard Hohn designed the first commercial minicomputer-controlled robot, T3, or the Tomorrow Tool. In 1974, Scheinman incorporated the company Vicarm to market an industrial version of the computer-controlled robotic arm developed by the Stanford research group. NASA would use this robotic arm on the Viking space probes. In 1978, Unimation, under continuous support from General Motors, developed the PUMA (Programmable Universal Machine for Assembly).

The computer industry experienced the beginning of sustained success during the 1980s, the profits of which were also conveyed to the robotic industry. Fujitsu Fanuc Co. started the first completely automated factory in 1980, while many new robotics companies were entering the market. By 1990, just 40 Japanese and 12 American companies were controlling a $170 billion industry due to numerous purchases of small companies that these companies made. These robotic companies improved the human–robot interface, which resulted in the development of the first visual-servo-controlled systems. On the other hand, feedback systems were continuously being improved, which sparked interest in a novel market for robotics: medicine. The first tests of robotics in medicine were successful, which encouraged a wave of innovations and enthusiasm stemming from the belief that the convergence of robotics with medicine would yield extraordinary results in the future (Patel, 2008).

Computer Motion and Intuitive Advanced were the two major companies in developing and marketing advanced robotic applications, such as surgical robotic systems, until Intuitive Advanced purchased Computer Motion in 2003. Computer Motion, Inc. (Goleta, CA), founded in 1989 by Yulun Wang, PhD, introduced a voice-controlled robotic arm, AESOP®, in 1993 for use in laparoscopy. In 1994, AESOP® was the first advanced robotic application to be cleared by the Food and Drug Administration (FDA), while a further generation of AESOP®, AESOP® 2000, became the first voice-controlled robot to be cleared by the FDA in 1996. Another product by Computer Motion, ZEUS® Robotic Microadvanced, was introduced in 1998 and consisted of a slave robot with three robotic arms and a master surgeon's console, from which the surgeon telemanipulates the robotic arms to conduct surgery. Intuitive Advanced (Sunnyvale, CA) was founded in 1995 by Frederic Moll, MD, Robert Younger, and John Freund, MD, and was based on the technology developed at the Stanford Research Institute.

The most important product of Intuitive Advanced is the da Vinci® Advanced System, consisting of a slave robotic system that performs surgery through four manipulator arms and a surgeon console that houses a surgeon as master of the surgery. The da Vinci® system is currently the most widely used system in general surgery and is also the first robotic system to be used in cardiac interventions: in a mitral valve procedure in 1998 in Paris (Carpentier et al., 1998) by Alain F. Carpentier, MD, and in a coronary artery bypass graft procedure (CABG) performed by Friedrich Mohr, MD, in Leipzig in the same year (Mohr et al., 1999), etc.

6.3 Fundamentals of Robotics

6.3.1 Kinematics of Robotic Manipulators

6.3.1.1 Introduction to kinematics of robotic manipulators

Kinematics is the study of the motion of objects without consideration of forces that generate the motion. The kinematics of robotic manipulators is the analysis of the movements, geometrical configurations, and constraints of robotic structures during manipulation. It deals with geometrical configurations and constraints of robotic structures during manipulation. It deals with the geometrical properties of the robotic system and time derivatives of position variables such as velocity and acceleration.

In this chapter, we start with a general description of robotic manipulators and continue with an introduction to mathematical notation, which is mostly used in the kinematic analysis of robots. Then, some mathematical tools are further described as prerequisites to this knowledge, which assist us in finding out the kinematic attitude of one link concerning an adjoining link in a robotic system. In other words, one can find out how two adjacent links move concerning each other when position variables change. This eventually leads to the derivation of the Denavit–Hartenberg homogeneous transformation. Direct and inverse kinematics analyses of robotic manipulators are covered in this chapter, and some interesting robotic engineering problems are discussed.

6.3.1.2 General description of robotic manipulators

A robotic manipulator is an open-loop chain of links connected in series by prismatic or revolute joints. One end is stationary and attached to a supporting base, while the other is relatively free and commonly attached to a specialized tool such as an endoscopic camera.

The free end can reach different points of its workspace to perform a specific task. For instance, it can carry an electrode to weld two objects together; it can have a gripper to pick objects from one location and place them in another; it can be facilitated with medical instruments such as trocars, grippers, and suturing needles to perform advanced tasks robotically.

The location and orientation of the free end result from the collective effect of translation and rotation of each joint of a robotic manipulator chain of links. Such motions are controlled by electrical, magnetic, hydraulic, or pneumatic actuators.

The central issue in industrial robotic manipulation is the ability to position the robotic free end at a specified location with a specified orientation at a given time, which is the core of flexible and automated manufacturing. Figures 6.7 and 6.8 show a standard six-axis robotic manipulator possessing a base (waist), shoulder, elbow, and wrist capable of pitch, roll, and yaw motions as well as gripping motion.

The combination of the end-effector's spatial location and orientation (kinematic attitude) can be described mathematically by 4 × 4 homogeneous transformations. These homogeneous transformations are used to solve both the direct and inverse kinematic problems of robotic manipulation.

Referring to Figs. 6.7 and 6.8, the direct kinematics problem in robotics is to find the kinematic attitude given the vector of the joint displacements, $\theta_i = [\theta_1\theta_2\theta_3 ... \theta_n]^T$, for an n-axis robotic manipulator.

On the other hand, the inverse kinematics problem for robotic manipulators involves finding the vector of the joint displacements

θ_i, i = 1, 2,..., N, for *n*-axis robotic manipulators given the kinematic attitude of the gripper with respect to the base coordinates.

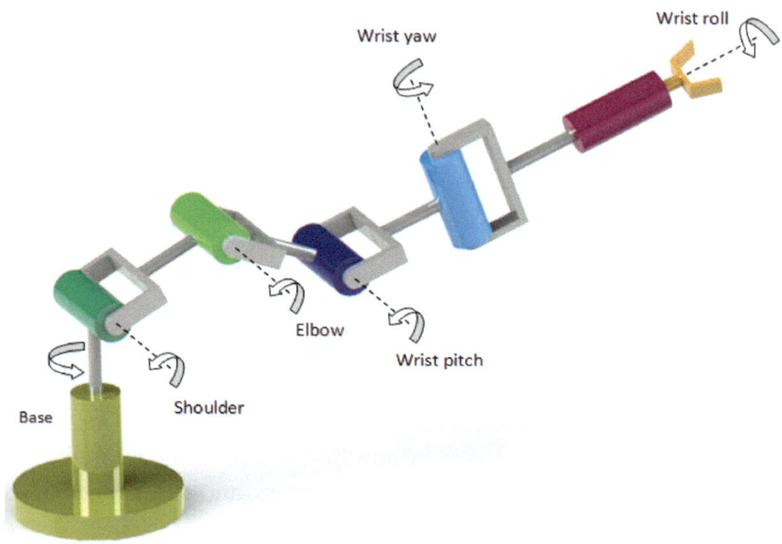

Figure 6.7 A typical six-axis revolute robotic manipulator.

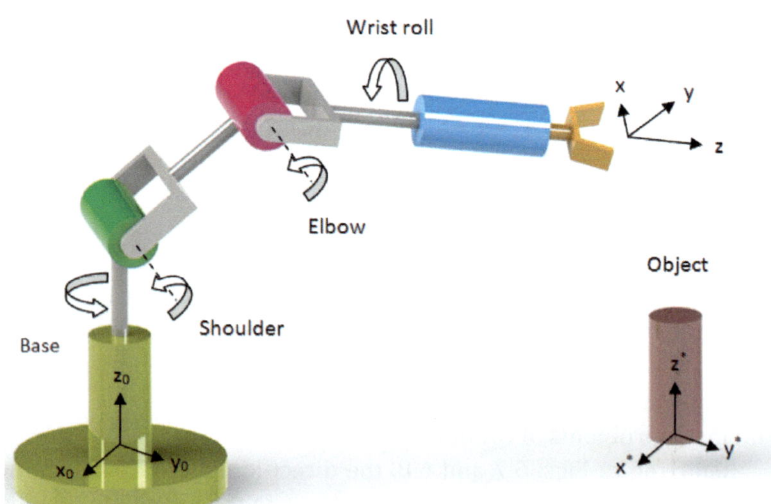

Figure 6.8 Relative configuration of the gripper and base coordinate in a robotic manipulator.

Normally, the latter is the most desirable problem to solve because it is at the heart of flexible automated manufacturing operations and assembly processes. Note Fig. 6.9 for the definitions of direct and inverse kinematics.

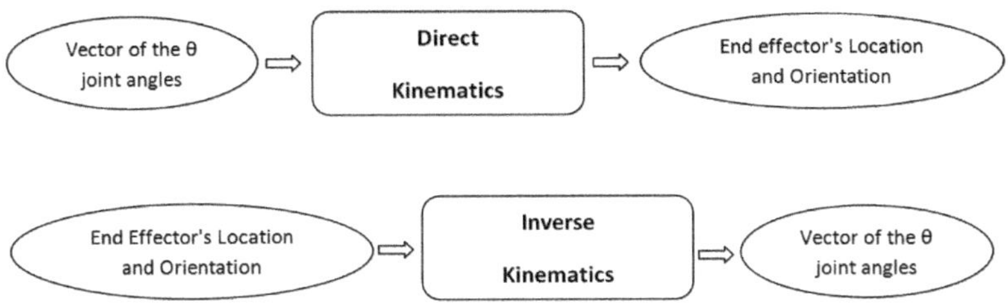

Figure 6.9 Definitions of direct and inverse kinematics.

On the other hand, direct kinematics solutions are used for special applications such as direct trajectory planning or obstacle collision prevention algorithms. In the following, a brief description of the mathematical notations used throughout this text is provided.

6.3.1.3 Brief description of mathematical notations

Conventional notations for the representation of vectors, scalars, and matrices are used throughout the text. Pre-superscripts denote descriptive information regarding coordinate frames. For instance, ${}^{A}r$ is a position vector described with respect to frame A. Frame A itself is represented by a 4 × 4 homogenous transformation that describes the location of its origin and relative rotation concerning a universal inertial reference frame.

- An ith frame is sometimes denoted by A_i.
- A_j^i sometimes denotes a frame i described concerning frame j.
- The following compact notation is used for trigonometric functions:

$$S_{ijk} = \sin(\theta_i + \theta_j + \theta_k)$$

$$C_{ijk} = \cos(\theta_i + \theta_j + \theta_k)$$

- T is generally used to denote transformations, while H is used for homogenous transformations.

6.3.1.4 Mathematical preliminaries on vectors and matrices

A vector is defined concerning a coordinate frame. Hence, a point can be described by different vectors defined in different coordinate frames. For instance, in Fig. 6.10, vectors A and B show the same point but are different since A is described with respect to the $X_1Y_1Z_1$ coordinate frame, and B is described concerning the $X_2Y_2Z_2$ coordinate frame.

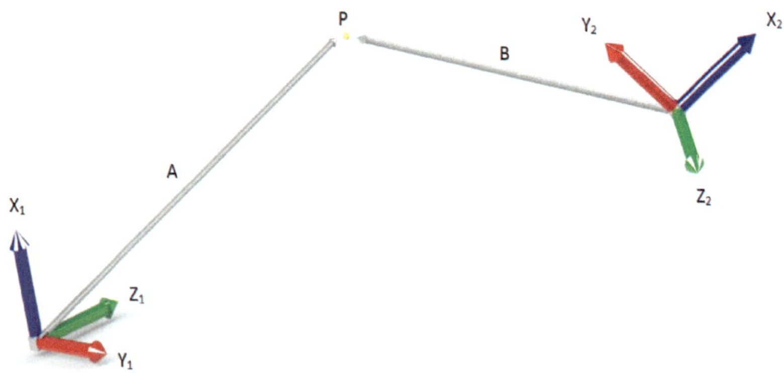

Figure 6.10 Description of the same point in two different coordinate frames.

Generally, the inverse of a matrix can be calculated as

$$A_{ij}^{-1} = \frac{\text{Transpose}\,(\text{Cofactor } A_{ij})}{\det A_{ij}} \tag{6.1}$$

Therefore, to calculate the inverse of matrix A, we need to calculate the transpose of the cofactor of matrix A and its determinant. You can refer to linear algebra textbooks to learn how the cofactor of matrices and their determinants are calculated.

The multiplication of A and the calculated A^{-1} results in a 3×3 unitary matrix.

6.3.1.5 Homogenous representation of points and objects

Before describing the homogenous representation of objects, the concept of a homogenous vector should be introduced. Homogenous vectors have the same direction but different magnitudes and components. Figure 6.11 shows several homogenous vectors.

A vector has three components in space, namely, X = a. w, Y = b. w, and Z = c. w, and can be shown as $[XYZw]^T$, in which w is the scaling factor. A similar definition for homogenous planes can be stated since planes can be represented by their outward normal vector.

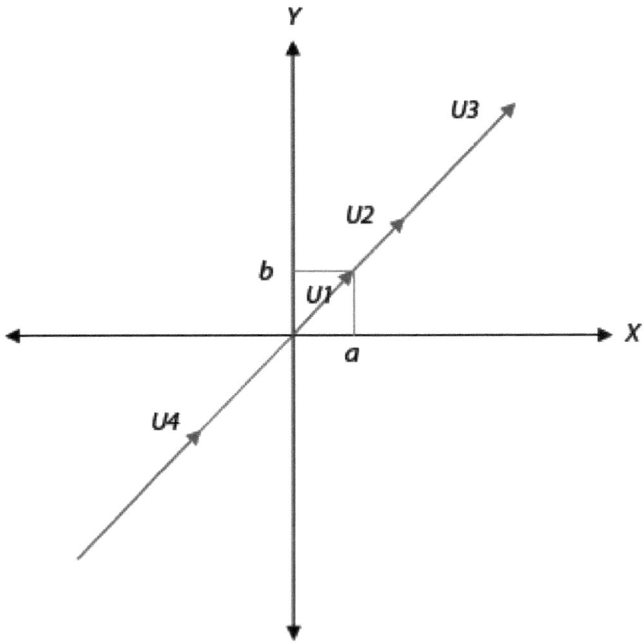

Figure 6.11 Representation of homogenous vectors.

Points can be represented as homogenous position vectors such that a point *p* having coordinates a, b, and c can be represented as a vector u = ai + bj + ck and generally can be represented by u = $[XYZw]^T$, where X = a. w, Y = b. w, and Z = c. w and w is the scaling factor. Similarly, objects can be expressed as a set of points, that is, homogenous column vectors that normally are packed into a 4 × *n* homogenous matrix with *n* representing the number of characteristic points peculiar to the object in a geometrical sense.

For example, an inverted pyramid (Fig. 6.12) can be described easily by a 4 × 5 homogenous transformation.

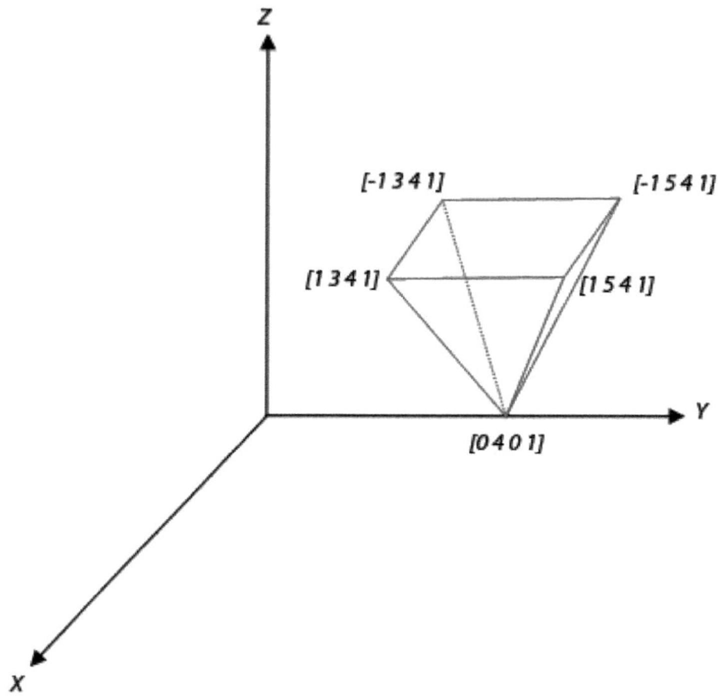

Figure 6.12 Object representation utilizing homogenous transformation made up of the object's characteristic homogenous.

Then the inverted pyramid can be represented by a homogenous transformation A such that

$$A = \begin{bmatrix} 0 & 1 & -1 & -1 & 1 \\ 4 & 5 & 5 & 3 & 3 \\ 0 & 4 & 4 & 4 & 4 \\ 1 & 1 & 1 & 1 & 1 \end{bmatrix} \quad (6.2)$$

The order of appearance of columns in A is arbitrary. However, once set, it must remain the same. For example, the first column is the top vertex of the pyramid and no matter what transformation the pyramid has undergone, the first column will remain as the top vertex. Therefore, under a translation of a units along the x direction, the proper transformation is

$$T(x,a)=\begin{bmatrix}1 & 0 & 0 & a\\ 0 & 1 & 0 & 0\\ 0 & 0 & 1 & 0\\ 0 & 0 & 0 & 1\end{bmatrix} \tag{6.3}$$

Once the transformation is applied to the inverted pyramid, it translates the pyramid along the direction by a units, and the new object is given by A_{new} such that

$A_{new} = T.\, A =$

$$\begin{bmatrix}1 & 0 & 0 & a\\ 0 & 1 & 0 & 0\\ 0 & 0 & 1 & 0\\ 0 & 0 & 0 & 1\end{bmatrix}\begin{bmatrix}0 & 1 & -1 & -1 & 1\\ 4 & 5 & 5 & 3 & 3\\ 0 & 4 & 4 & 4 & 4\\ 1 & 1 & 1 & 1 & 1\end{bmatrix}\begin{bmatrix}a & 1+a & -1+a & -1+a & 1+a\\ 4 & 5 & 5 & 3 & 3\\ 0 & 4 & 4 & 4 & 4\\ 1 & 1 & 1 & 1 & 1\end{bmatrix} \tag{6.4}$$

Now the pyramid's top vertex or the first column is the point $[a\ 4\ 0\ 1]$. Similar transformations may be applied to the object to rotate it around and translate it. However, all columns preserve their original identity as if we had labeled them with certain names such as *A*, *B*, *C*, *D*, and *E*.

6.3.1.6 Homogenous transformations

A homogenous transformation is defined as a 4 × 4 matrix that generally represents translation, rotation, scaling, and perspective projection of points, vectors, and objects. It generally consists of a 3 × 3 rotation matrix, a 3 × 1 translation vector, a 1 × 3 perspective projection vector, and a 1 × 1 scaling matrix. Thus,

$$T=\begin{bmatrix}\text{Rotation }(3\times3) & \text{Traslation }(3\times1)\\ \text{Perspective projection }(1\times3) & \text{Scaling }(1\times1)\end{bmatrix} \tag{6.5}$$

Some important homogenous transformation matrices are given in Table 6.1.

Table 6.1 Common homogenous transformations

Rotation around the *X* coordinate by an angle α:

$$\text{Rotation}(X,\alpha)=\begin{bmatrix}1 & 0 & 0 & 0\\ 0 & \cos\alpha & -\sin\alpha & 0\\ 0 & \sin\alpha & \cos\alpha & 0\\ 0 & 0 & 0 & 1\end{bmatrix}$$

Rotation around the *Y* coordinate by an angle θ:

$$\text{Rotation}(Y,\theta)=\begin{bmatrix}\cos\theta & 0 & \sin\theta & 0\\ 0 & 1 & 0 & 0\\ -\sin\theta & 0 & \cos\theta & 0\\ 0 & 0 & 0 & 1\end{bmatrix}$$

Rotation around the *Z* coordinate by an angle β:

$$\text{Rotation}(Z,\beta)=\begin{bmatrix}\cos\beta & -\sin\beta & 0 & 0\\ \sin\beta & \cos\beta & 0 & 0\\ 0 & 0 & 1 & 0\\ 0 & 0 & 0 & 1\end{bmatrix}$$

Transformation for "*a*" along the *X* axis, "*b*" along the *Y* axis, and "*c*" along the *Z* axis:

$$\text{Translation}(a,b,c)=\begin{bmatrix}1 & 0 & 0 & a\\ 0 & 1 & 0 & b\\ 0 & 0 & 1 & c\\ 0 & 0 & 0 & 1\end{bmatrix}$$

Rotation around an arbitrary direction *K* by an angle θ ($K = k_1 i + k_2 j + k_3 k$):

$$\text{Rotation}(\mathrm{K},\theta)=\begin{bmatrix}k_1\cdot k_1\cdot(1-\cos\theta)+\cos\theta & k_2\cdot k_1\cdot(1-\cos\theta)-k_3\cdot\sin\theta & k_3\cdot k_1\cdot(1-\cos\theta)+k_2\cdot\sin\theta & 0\\ k_1\cdot k_2\cdot(1-\cos\theta)+k_3\cdot\sin\theta & k_2\cdot k_2\cdot(1-\cos\theta)+\cos\theta & k_3\cdot k_2\cdot(1-\cos\theta)-k_1\cdot\sin\theta & 0\\ k_1\cdot k_3\cdot(1-\cos\theta)-k_2\cdot\sin\theta & k_2\cdot k_3\cdot(1-\cos\theta)+k_1\cdot\sin\theta & k_3\cdot k_3\cdot(1-\cos\theta)+\cos\theta & 0\\ 0 & 0 & 0 & 1\end{bmatrix} \tag{6.6}$$

Example 1

Find the homogenous transformation that moves the pyramid in Fig. 6.12 to the position illustrated in Fig. 6.13.

Solution. As you can see in the figures, the object undergoes a translation for 1 unit along the X axis, a rotation around the X axis by 180°, a rotation around the Z axis by −90°, and a translation along the Z axis for −4 units, respectively. Negative signs are movements in negative directions. Thus,

H = Translation (X, 1). Rotation (X, 180 degrees)

Rotation (Z, −90 degrees). Translation (Z, −4)

Each of the terms in the above equation can be easily obtained as they were mentioned previously; therefore,

$$\mathrm{H}=\begin{bmatrix}1&0&0&1\\0&1&0&0\\0&0&1&0\\0&0&0&1\end{bmatrix}.\begin{bmatrix}1&0&0&0\\0&-1&0&0\\0&0&-1&0\\0&0&0&1\end{bmatrix}.\begin{bmatrix}0&1&0&0\\-1&0&0&0\\0&0&1&0\\0&0&0&1\end{bmatrix}.\begin{bmatrix}1&0&0&0\\0&1&0&0\\0&0&1&-4\\0&0&0&1\end{bmatrix}$$

Then,

$$\mathrm{H}=\begin{bmatrix}0&1&0&1\\1&0&0&0\\0&0&-1&4\\0&0&0&1\end{bmatrix}, \tag{6.7}$$

and the new positions of the vectors are

$$\mathrm{A_{new}}=\mathrm{HA}=\begin{bmatrix}0&1&0&1\\1&0&0&0\\0&0&-1&4\\0&0&0&1\end{bmatrix}.\begin{bmatrix}0&1&-1&-1&1\\4&5&5&3&3\\0&4&4&4&4\\1&1&1&1&1\end{bmatrix}$$

$$\mathrm{A_{new}}=\begin{bmatrix}5&6&6&4&4\\0&1&-1&-1&1\\4&0&0&0&0\\1&1&1&1&1\end{bmatrix} \tag{6.8}$$

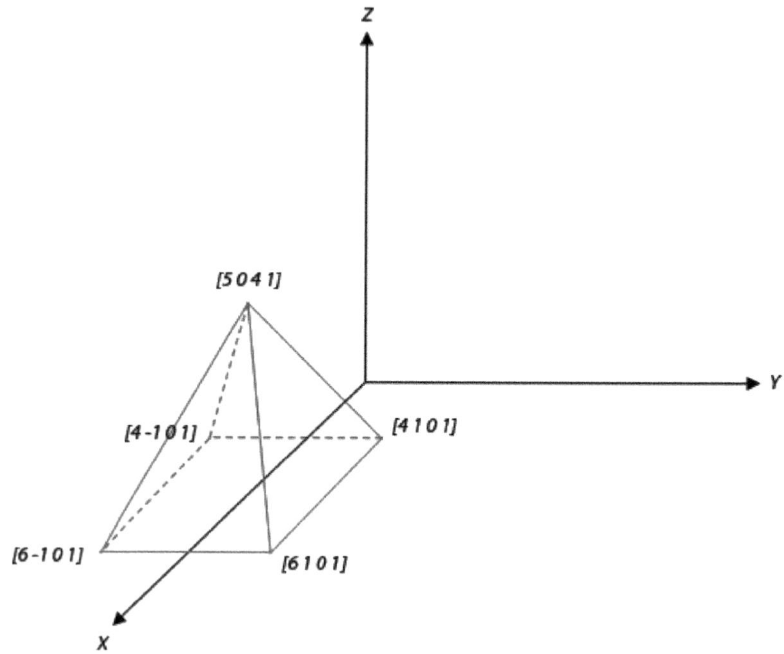

Figure 6.13 Object manipulation.

6.3.1.7 Robotic manipulator joint coordinate systems

A manipulator consists of links connected by a series of joints. Homogenous transformations concerning local joint coordinates are called A matrices (i.e., Denavit–Hartenberg transformations). Let A_1 describe the position and orientation of the first link with respect to the base, A_2 that of the second link with respect to the first link, A_3 that of the third link with respect to the second link, and so on. Then, the position and orientation of the nth link with respect to the base coordinate will be

$$T_{\text{n}} = A_1A_2A_3...A_{\text{n}-1}A_{\text{n}} \tag{6.9}$$

The products of the A matrices are called T matrices. T_{n} is designated as the end-effector transformation, so the end-effector origin has a position vector p. Attached to the origin is a rectangular Cartesian coordinate system whose orientation designates the orientation of the end-effector.

For any link joint coordinate i, the link direction at the joint is in the approach vector direction (a_i), the direction of the link-to-link rotation is in the o_i direction (the orientation vector), and the normal unit vector n_i forms a right-handed system with o_i and a_i.

The position vector of this i^{th} joint with respect to the base coordinate is p_i; thus, the transformation T_i of this joint coordinate is

$$T_i = \begin{bmatrix} n_{ix} & o_{ix} & a_{ix} & p_{ix} \\ n_{iy} & o_{iy} & a_{iy} & p_{iy} \\ n_{iz} & o_{iz} & a_{iz} & p_{iz} \\ 0 & 0 & 0 & 1 \end{bmatrix} \qquad (6.10)$$

6.3.1.8 Denavit–Hartenberg (D–H) representations

As defined previously, a generalized robotic arm may be considered a kinematic chain interconnected at joints whose motions can be servo-controlled by proper actuators. The interconnections are either revolute (rotary), prismatic (telescopic), or a combination.

1. In 1955, Denavit and Hartenberg defined the concept of a "lower pair" joint as one created by contacting surfaces. In this sense, "upper pair" joints were the ones created by either point or line contacts between two bodies. Thus, in Fig. 6.14, the joints i's are the lower pairs, while the joints (i+1)'s and (i-1)'s are the upper pairs.
2. Now consider a pair of adjacent robotic links interconnected by lower pairs capable of rotation and telescopic motion (Fig. 6.14). The coordinates are chosen as follows: The distance between the two common normal a_i and a_{i-1} is called the link distance d_i.
3. Z_i is along the axis of motion or rotation of the i + 1th joint.
4. The X_i axis is in the direction normal to both the Z_i and Z_{i-1} axes, pointing away from the Z_{i-1} axis (such as to make a right-handed coordinate with either Z_i and Z_{i-1} or Z_{i-1} and Z_i).

The Y_i coordinate is chosen to make the $X_iY_iZ_i$ coordinate system a right-handed coordinate system. The length of the normal a_i is the minimum distance between the Z_i and Z_{i-1} axes. If this is zero, the direction of a_i becomes arbitrary. Note that a_i is also called the length of the ith link. The relative orientation of the X_i axis concerning the X_{i-1} axis is called θ_i or the vector of the joint angles.

The relative orientation of the Z_i axis concerning the Z_{i-1} axis is called α_i or the vector of twist angles. Denavit–Hartenberg transformations will be applied to these frame transformations.

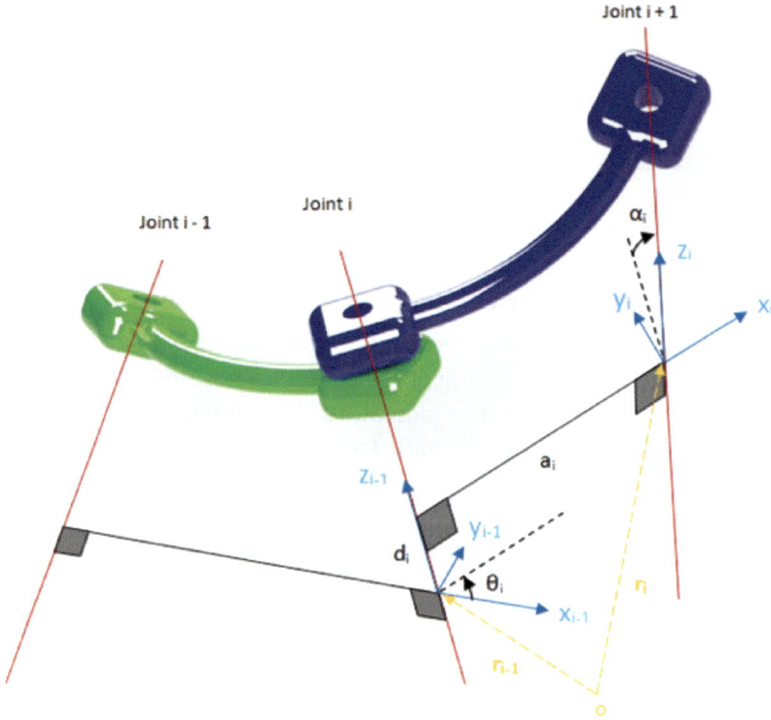

Figure 6.14 Generalized robotic link coordinate systems.

The four parameters d_i, θ_i, a_i, and α_i constitute a minimally sufficient set to determine the kinematic configuration of each link of the robotic arm. Note that d_i is the joint distance, θ_i is the joint angle, a_i is the link length, and α_i is the link twist angle.

For a plane revolute joint, generally d_i, a_i, and α_i are all constant, while θ_i varies as the link i rotates about the axis of joint i. On the other hand, for a prismatic joint, θ_i, a_i, and α_i are constant, while d_i varies as the link i slides along the axis of joint i.

Thus, for both cases, a_i and α_i are generally constant and depend on the design of the robot. For example, when the joint axes of adjacent joints intersect, the link length a is also zero (such is the case with prismatic joints).

Once the D–H coordinate system for each link is established, a homogenous transformation matrix can be developed easily relating the ith coordinate frame. Referring to Fig. 6.7, we can see that a point expressed in the ith coordinate system may be expressed in the $(i - 1)^{th}$ coordinate system by performing the following successive transformations:

1. A rotation around the Z_{i-1} axis by an angle θ_i to align the X_{i-1} and X_i axes
2. A translation along the Z_{i-1} axis for a distance d_i to bring the X_{i-1} and X_i axes
3. A translation along the X_i axis for a distance a_i to bring the two origins into coincidence
4. A rotation around the X_i axis by an angle α_i to make the two coordinate systems coincide completely

Thus, the complete transformation of the link i concerning the link $i - 1$ or the joint i concerning the joint $i - 1$ is

$$H_{i-1}^{i} = T_{i-1}^{i} = A_{i-1}^{i}$$
$$= \text{Rotation }(Z_{i-1}, \theta_i).\ \text{Translation }(Z_{i-1}, d_i).\ \text{Translation }(X_i, a_i)$$

Rotation (X_i, α_i) or

$$A_{i-1}^{i} = \begin{bmatrix} \cos\theta_i & -\sin\theta_i & 0 & 0 \\ \sin\theta_i & \cos\theta_i & 0 & 0 \\ 0 & 0 & 1 & 0 \\ 0 & 0 & 0 & 1 \end{bmatrix} \cdot \begin{bmatrix} 1 & 0 & 0 & 0 \\ 0 & 1 & 0 & 0 \\ 0 & 0 & 1 & d_i \\ 0 & 0 & 0 & 1 \end{bmatrix} x$$

$$x \begin{bmatrix} 1 & 0 & 0 & a_i \\ 0 & 1 & 0 & 0 \\ 0 & 0 & 1 & 0 \\ 0 & 0 & 0 & 1 \end{bmatrix} \begin{bmatrix} 1 & 0 & 0 & 0 \\ 0 & \cos\alpha_i & -\sin\alpha_i & 0 \\ 0 & \sin\alpha_i & \cos\alpha_i & 0 \\ 0 & 0 & 0 & 1 \end{bmatrix} \tag{6.11}$$

$$A_{i-1}^{i} = A_i = \begin{bmatrix} \cos\theta_i & -\cos\alpha_i \cdot \sin\theta_i & \sin\alpha_i.\sin\theta_i & a_i \cdot \cos\theta_i \\ \sin\theta_i & \cos\alpha_i \cdot \cos\theta_i & -\sin\alpha_i \cdot \cos\theta_i & a_i \cdot \sin\theta_i \\ 0 & \sin\alpha_i & \cos\alpha_i & d_i \\ 0 & 0 & 0 & 1 \end{bmatrix}$$

A_i shows the transformation pertaining to the ith link. Furthermore, if r_i is the homogenous coordinate of the ith joint and r_{i-1} is the homogenous coordinate of the $(i-1)^{th}$ joint, it is clear that

$$r_{i-1} = A_{i-1}^{i}.r_i \tag{6.12}$$

The following algorithm completely assigns and establishes link coordinate systems compatible with D–H transformations for a given robotic arm with n degrees of freedom. Adjacent links can be related to each other kinematically through a set of 4 × 4 homogenous transformation matrices. The first coordinate system pertaining to the base is denoted by a homogenous system $[X_0 Y_0 Z_0\ 1]^T$ at the supporting base. The origin of this system is denoted as the 0th joint.

- Establish the base coordinate $[X_0Y_0Z_0]$ such that the Z_0 axis lies along the axis of motion of joint 1.
- Initialize and loop for each $i = 1,2,\ldots,n$.
- Align all Z_i with the axis of motion or rotation of the joint $i + 1$.
- Establish the origin of the ith coordinate system, either at the intersection of the Z_i and Z_{i-1} axes or at the intersection of the common normal between the Z_i and Z_{i-1} axes.

Establish the X_i axis at each ith joint, either by $\pm(Z_{i-1} \times Z_i)$ or along the common normal between Z_{i-1} and Z_i when they are parallel.

- Establish the Y_i axis by $Y_i = +(Z_i \times X_i)$ to complete the right-handed coordinate system.
- Find d_i as the distance from the origin of the $(i-1)^{th}$ coordinate system to the intersection of then Z_{i-1} and X_i axes.
- Find a_i as the distance from the intersection of the Z_{i-1} and X_i axes to the origin of the ith coordinate system.
- Find θ_i as the angle of rotation from the X_{i-1} axis to the X_i axis.
- Find α_i as the angle of rotation from the Z_{i-1} axis to the Z_i axis about the Z_i axis.

In prismatic joints, the Z axes can also be established parallel to the actuation direction for ease of calculations.

Example 2

Carry out the direct and inverse kinematics of the robotic arm depicted in Fig. 6.15.

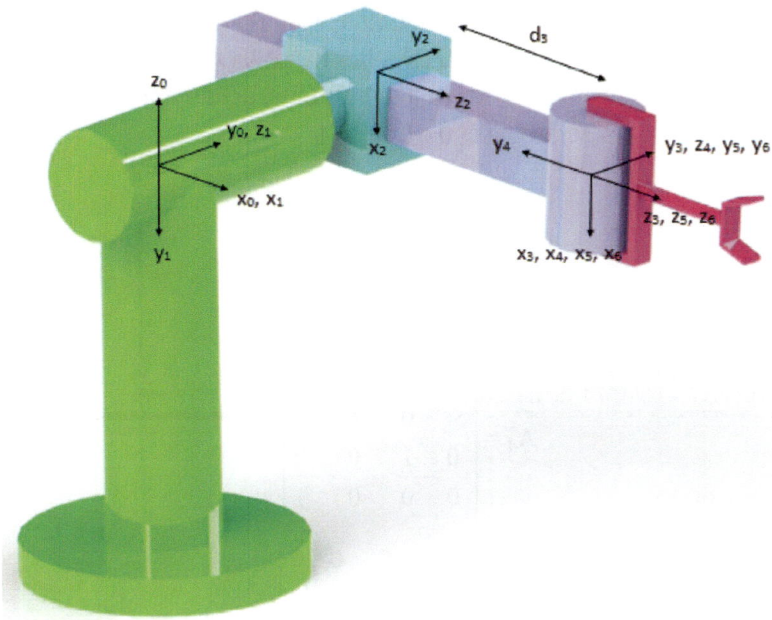

Figure 6.15 A cylindrical robotic manipulator.

Solution. This robotic arm consists of one telescopic motion and five rotary motions. Moreover, there are two rolling motions involved before and after the pitch motion to assist the robotic arm simulate the yaw motion. Joint coordinate systems are shown in the figure. Note that in the following, $S_i = \sin\theta_i$ and $C_i = \cos\theta_i$.

$$A_0^1 = \begin{bmatrix} C_1 & 0 & -S_1 & 0 \\ S_1 & 0 & C_1 & 0 \\ 0 & -1 & 0 & 0 \\ 0 & 0 & 0 & 1 \end{bmatrix};$$

$$A_1^2 = \begin{bmatrix} C_2 & 0 & S_2 & 0 \\ S_2 & 0 & -C_2 & 0 \\ 0 & 1 & 0 & d_2 \\ 0 & 0 & 0 & 1 \end{bmatrix};$$

$$A_2^3 = \begin{bmatrix} 1 & 0 & 0 & 0 \\ 0 & 1 & 0 & 0 \\ 0 & 0 & 1 & d_3 \\ 0 & 0 & 0 & 1 \end{bmatrix};$$

$$A_3^4 = \begin{bmatrix} C_4 & 0 & -S_4 & 0 \\ S_4 & 0 & C_4 & 0 \\ 0 & -1 & 0 & 0 \\ 0 & 0 & 0 & 1 \end{bmatrix};$$

$$A_4^5 = \begin{bmatrix} C_5 & 0 & S_5 & 0 \\ S_5 & 0 & -C_5 & 0 \\ 0 & 1 & 0 & 0 \\ 0 & 0 & 0 & 1 \end{bmatrix};$$

$$A_5^6 = \begin{bmatrix} C_6 & -S_6 & 0 & 0 \\ S_6 & C_6 & 0 & 0 \\ 0 & 0 & 1 & 0 \\ 0 & 0 & 0 & 1 \end{bmatrix}$$

To find T_0^6, multiply the above matrices:

$$T_0^6 = A_0^1 \cdot A_1^2 \cdot A_2^3 \cdot A_3^4 \cdot A_4^5 \cdot A_5^6 = \begin{bmatrix} n_x & o_x & a_x & p_x \\ n_y & o_y & a_y & p_y \\ n_z & o_z & a_z & p_z \\ 0 & 0 & 0 & 1 \end{bmatrix}$$

The T_0^6 matrix elements can easily be calculated:

$$n_x = C_1\left[C_2\left(C_4\,C_5\,C_6 - S_4\,S_6\right) - S_2\,S_5\,S_6\right] - S_1\left(S_4\,C_5\,C_6 + C_4\,C_6\right),$$

$$n_y = S_1\left[C_2\left(C_4\,C_5\,C_6 - S_4\,S_6\right) - S_2\,S_5\,S_6\right] + C_1\left(S_4\,C_5\,C_6 + C_4\,C_6\right),$$

$$n_z = -S_2\left(C_4\,C_5\,C_6 - S_4\,S_6\right) - C_2\,S_5\,C_6,$$

$$o_x = C_1\left[-C_2\left(C_4\,C_5\,S_6 - S_4\,C_6\right) - S_2\,S_5\,S_6\right] - S_1\left(-S_4\,C_5\,S_6 + C_4\,C_6\right),$$

$$o_y = S_1\left[-C_2\left(C_4\,C_5\,S_6 - S_4\,C_6\right) - S_2\,S_5\,S_6\right] + C_1\left(-S_4\,C_5\,S_6 + C_4\,C_6\right),$$

$$o_z = S_2\left(C_4\,C_5\,S_6 + S_4\,C_6\right) + C_2\,S_5\,S_6,$$

$$a_x = C_1 (C_2 C_4 S_5 + S_2 C_5) - S_1 S_4 S_5,$$

$$a_y = S_1 (C_2 C_4 S_5 + S_2 C_5) + C_1 S_4 S_5,$$

$$a_z = -S_2 C_4 S_5 + C_2 C_5,$$

$$p_x = C_1 S_2 d_3 - S_1 d_2,$$

$$p_y = S_1 S_2 d_3 + C_1 d_2,$$

$$p_z = C_2 d_3.$$

Twelve equations relate joint parameters to the position and orientation of the end-effector and vice versa. If the joint parameters are known, the position and orientation of the end-effector can be easily obtained using the 12 equations above. However, if we know the position and orientation of the end-effector and want to calculate the joint parameters, we have to solve the above-mentioned equations for θ_1, $\theta_2,\ldots,\theta_6$. This process is called inverse kinematics analysis. To solve these equations, some mathematical prerequisites are essential, which are beyond the scope of this book. In the following, the inverse kinematic analysis is illustrated through simpler problems.

6.3.1.9 Direct and inverse kinematics in robotics

In a robotic arm with n degrees of freedom, A's can be calculated and multiplied to obtain the T_n matrix. T_n shows the relative position and orientation of the end-effector coordinate frame with respect to the base coordinate, which is a function of the joint parameters $\theta_i = [\theta_1 \theta_2 \theta_3 \ldots, \theta_n]^T$.

If the joint parameters are known in a robotic arm, T_n can be calculated with the help of D–H transformation.

In other words, the relative position and orientation of the robotic arm end-effector with respect to the base coordinate frame can be shown as a function of the joint parameters. This procedure is called direct kinematic analysis of robotic manipulators.

If the relative position and orientation of the robotic arm end-effector with respect to the base are known, the joint parameters to lead to that position and orientation can be calculated by solving a set of trigonometric equations obtained from D–H transformation analysis. This process is called inverse kinematic analysis of robotic manipulators.

Inverse kinematic analysis of robotic arms is more applicable to engineering problems. For instance, to perform intraocular robotic surgery, a special point in the eye has to be reached at a specific orientation; therefore, knowing what combination of joint parameters leads the robotic arm to that position and orientation seems necessary.

In addition to the D–H method for analyzing the kinematic attitude of robotic arms, geometrical relationships between the robotic links can be employed to perform direct and inverse kinematic analyses. The following examples show this.

Example 3

Carry out the direct and inverse kinematics of the robotic arm depicted in Fig. 6.16.

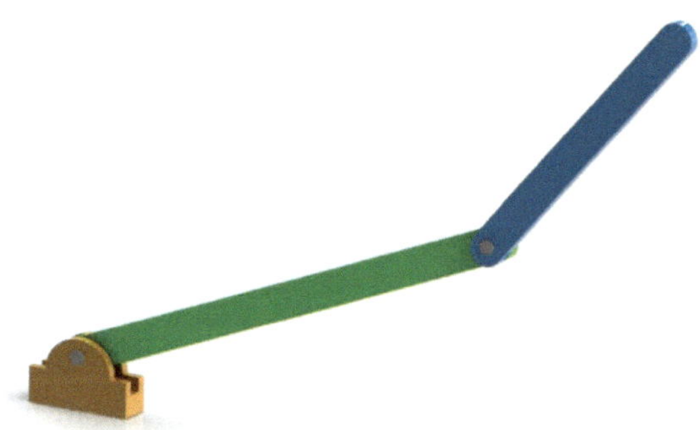

Figure 6.16 A two-link robotic manipulator.

Solution. The following trigonometric equations can be easily obtained from Fig. 6.18. All the constants are illustrated in Fig. 6.17. We have

$$X = l_1 C_1 + l_2 C_{12}$$

$$Y = l_1 S_1 + l_2 S_{12}$$

This is the direct kinematic analysis of a two-link robotic arm. Now we solve these two equations for θ_2. First, we take the square of both sides of each of the previous equations:

$$X^2 = l_1^2 \cdot C_1^2 + l_2^2 \cdot C_{12}^2 + 2l_1 \cdot l_2 \cdot C_1 \cdot C_{12}$$

$$Y^2 = l_1^2 \cdot S_1^2 + l_2^2 \cdot S_{12}^2 + 2l_1 \cdot l_2 \cdot S_1 \cdot S_{12}$$

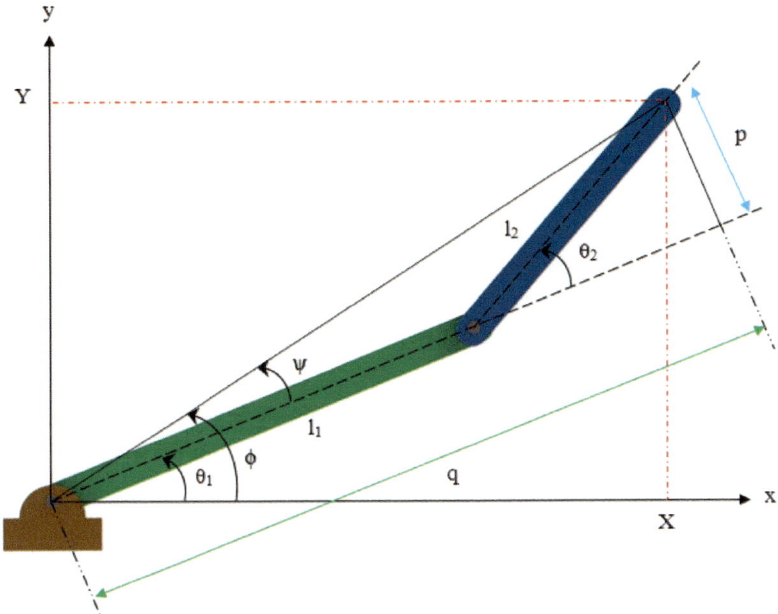

Figure 6.17 A two-link robotic manipulator's geometrical properties.

Adding these equations, we have

$$X^2+Y^2=l_1^2\cdot\left(S_1^2+C_1^2\right)+l_2^2\cdot\left(S_{12}^2+C_{12}^2\right)+2l_1\cdot l_2\cdot\left(C_1\cdot C_{12}+S_1\cdot S_{12}\right)$$

$$X^2+Y^2=l_1^2+l_2^2+2l_1\cdot l_2\cdot C_2$$

$$\mathrm{C}_2=\frac{X^2+Y^2-l_1{}^2-l_2{}^2}{2\cdot l_1\cdot l_2}=\mathrm{a}^*$$

$$\mathrm{S}_2=\sqrt{1-a^{*2}}$$

$$\tan\theta_2=\frac{\sqrt{1-a^{*2}}}{a^*}\theta_2=\tan^{-1}(\frac{\sqrt{1-a^{*2}}}{a^*})$$

$$\theta_2=\tan^{-1}\left(\frac{\sqrt{4\cdot l_1^2\cdot l_2^2-\left(X^2+Y^2-l_1{}^2-l_2{}^2\right)^2}}{X^2+Y^2-l_1{}^2-l_2{}^2}\right)$$

We also know from the geometry of the two-link robot (Fig. 6.18) that

$$\theta_1 = \phi - \psi = \tan^{-1}\left(\frac{Y}{X}\right) - \tan^{-1}\left(\frac{p}{q}\right)$$

Thus, $\theta_1 = \tan^{-1}\left(\frac{Y}{X}\right) - \tan^{-1}\left(\frac{l_2 \cdot S_2}{l_1 + l_2 \cdot C_2}\right)$

Using the inverse kinematic solution of the two-link robotic manipulator, we can calculate the joint parameters (θ_1, θ_2) if we know the geometrical constants and the position of the end-effector (l_1, l_2, X, Y). Therefore, we know how much to actuate the joint actuators to reach a specific position.

Example 4

Determine the joint parameters in both two-link robotic arms shown in Fig. 6.18 so that they keep the rectangular object in a specific position (a, b) at an angle Ψ.

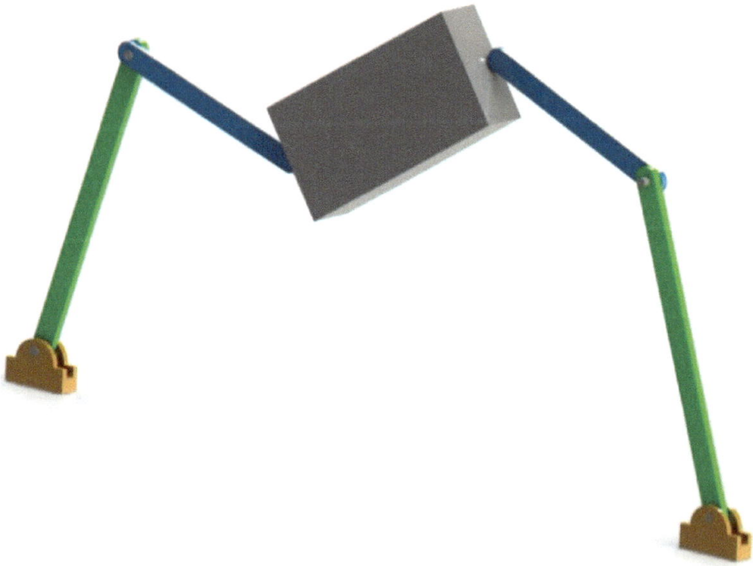

Figure 6.18 Two two-link robotic arms manipulating an object.

Solution. We assume that the object is a homogenous rectangle $w \times s$ and the center of mass is in the middle (Fig. 6.19).

The origin of the X_1Y_1 coordinate system is at (X_1, 0), and the origin of the X_2Y_2 coordinate system is at ($X_1 + d$, 0).

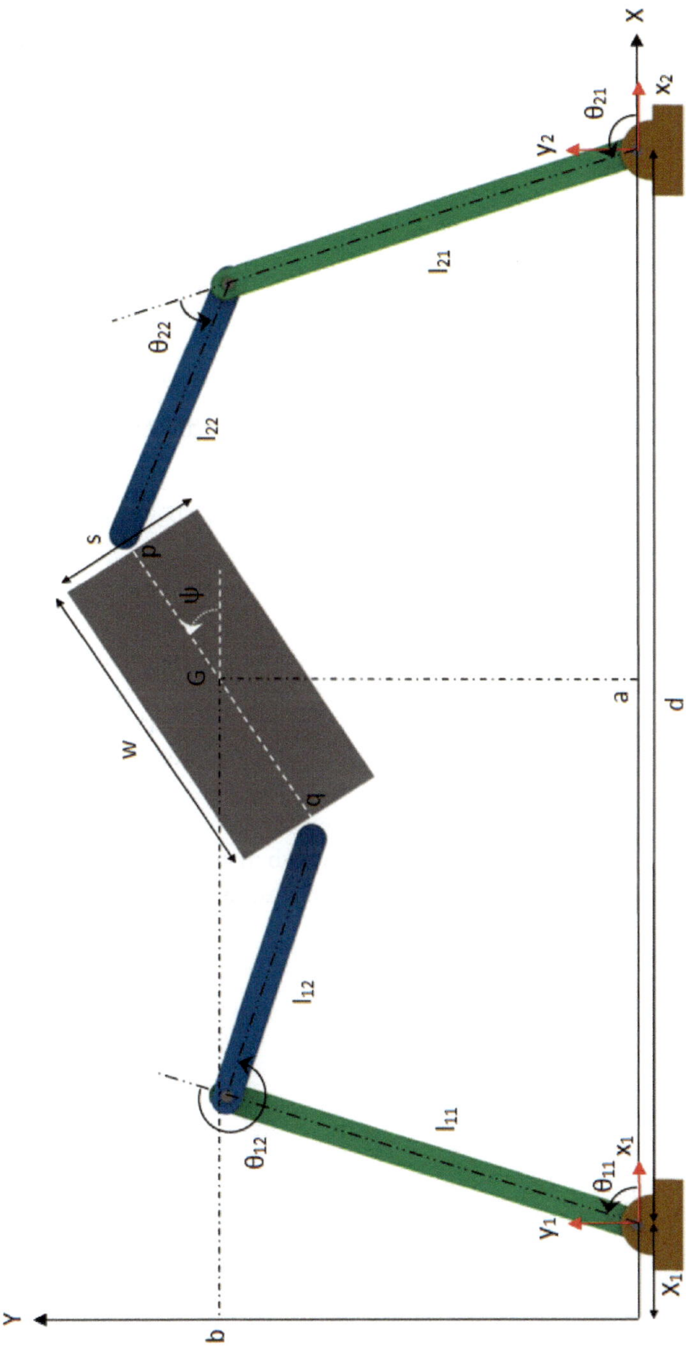

Figure 6.19 Geometrical properties of two two-link robotic arms.

From Fig. 6.19 it is clear that the tip positions p and q are given by

$$p=\left(a+\frac{w}{2}\cdot\cos\psi\right)i+\left(b+\frac{w}{2}\cdot\sin\psi\right)j$$

$$q=\left(a-\frac{w}{2}\cdot\cos\psi\right)i+\left(b-\frac{w}{2}\cdot\sin\psi\right)j$$

In the XY coordinate system, p is at $(a+\frac{w}{2}\cdot\cos\psi, b+\frac{w}{2}\cdot\sin\psi)$, and therefore, the location of p in the X_2Y_2 coordinate system is $(a+\frac{w}{2}\cdot\cos\psi - X_1 - d, b+\frac{w}{2}\cdot\sin\psi)$.

In the XY coordinate system, q is at $(a-\frac{w}{2}\cdot\cos\psi, b-\frac{w}{2}\cdot\sin\psi)$, and therefore, the location of q in the X_1Y_1 coordinate system is $(a-\frac{w}{2}\cdot\cos\psi - X_1, b-\frac{w}{2}\cdot\sin\psi)$.

Now we solve the two inverse kinematics problems separately. For the left two-link robotic arm, we know the position of q in the X_1Y_1 coordinate system; thus, we can easily determine the θ's. This also holds for the right arm.

We already solved the inverse kinematics problem of a two-link robotic arm. Now we need to use the solution to the previous example and substitute new constants into it. We have the following:

For the left two-link robotic arm:

$$l_1 = l_{11}, l_2 = l_{12}$$

$$X = a-\frac{w}{2}\cdot\cos\psi - X_1 \Rightarrow$$ We now substitute these into the equations obtained in the previous example.

$$Y = b-\frac{w}{2}\cdot\sin\psi$$

$$\theta_1 = \theta_{11}$$

$\theta_2 = \theta_{12}\ \theta_{12}$

$$=\tan^{-1}\left(\frac{\sqrt{4\cdot l_{21}^2\cdot l_{22}^2-\left(\left(a+\frac{w}{2}\cdot\cos\psi-X_1-d\right)^2+\left(b+\frac{w}{2}\cdot\sin\psi\right)^2-l_{21}{}^2-l_{22}{}^2\right)^2}}{\left(a+\frac{w}{2}\cdot\cos\psi-X_1-d\right)^2+\left(b+\frac{w}{2}\cdot\sin\psi\right)^2-l_{21}{}^2-l_{22}{}^2}\right)$$

$$\theta_{11} = \tan^{-1}\left(\frac{b - \frac{w}{2}\cdot\sin\psi}{a - \frac{w}{2}\cdot\cos\psi - X_1}\right) - \tan^{-1}\left(\frac{l_{12}\cdot\sin\theta_{12}}{l_{11} + l_{12}\cdot\cos\theta_{12}}\right)$$

For the right two-link robotic arm:

$$l_1 = l_{21}, l_2 = l_{22}$$

$$X = a + \frac{w}{2}\cdot\cos\psi - X_1 - d \Rightarrow$$ We now substitute these into the equations obtained in the previous example.

$$Y = b + \frac{w}{2}\cdot\sin\psi$$

$$\theta_1 = \theta_{21}$$

$\theta_2 = \theta_{22}$ θ_{22}

$$= \tan^{-1}\left(\frac{\sqrt{4\cdot l_{21}^2\cdot l_{22}^2 - \left(\left(a + \frac{w}{2}\cdot\cos\psi - X_1 - d\right)^2 + \left(b + \frac{w}{2}\cdot\sin\psi\right)^2 - l_{21}{}^2 - l_{22}{}^2\right)^2}}{\left(a + \frac{w}{2}\cdot\cos\psi - X_1 - d\right)^2 + \left(b + \frac{w}{2}\cdot\sin\psi\right)^2 - l_{21}{}^2 - l_{22}{}^2}\right)$$

$$\theta_{21} = \tan^{-1}\left(\frac{b + \frac{w}{2}\cdot\sin\psi}{a + \frac{w}{2}\cdot\cos\psi - X_1 - d}\right) - \tan^{-1}\left(\frac{l_{22}\cdot\sin\theta_{22}}{l_{21} + l_{22}\cdot\cos\theta_{12}}\right)$$

If we want to keep a rectangular object in a specific position with a specific orientation using two two-link robotic arms, we can easily calculate the joint parameters $(\theta_{11},\theta_{12},\theta_{21},\theta_{22})$ from the previous equations and consequently actuate the actuators properly to reach that position and orientation.

6.3.1.10 Robotic workspace

The workspace of a robotic manipulator is defined as the set of all three-dimensional points that can be reached by a reference point located on the robotic hand. A restricted version of a robotic workspace is also defined as the set of all points that can be reached by a fixed orientation of the robotic hand. The knowledge of robotic workspaces is important in arranging the associated advanced tools, personnel, objects, and devices around advanced robotic applications such as surgical robots and assessing the efficiency of the operating room in which the advanced robot is located.

In general, the boundary of a robotic workspace, which is called the robotic work envelope, is a complex surface difficult to represent explicitly by geometrical equations.

To derive mathematical expressions for robotic work surfaces, we customarily employ the D–H homogeneous transformations to describe the locus of the trajectories produced by the robotic hand. Seeking analytical solutions for the workspace of a robotic manipulator is a tedious task. However, using numerical methods, we can easily get an understanding of the workspace of a robotic arm. For example, consider a two-dimensional two-link robotic arm shown in Fig. 6.20.

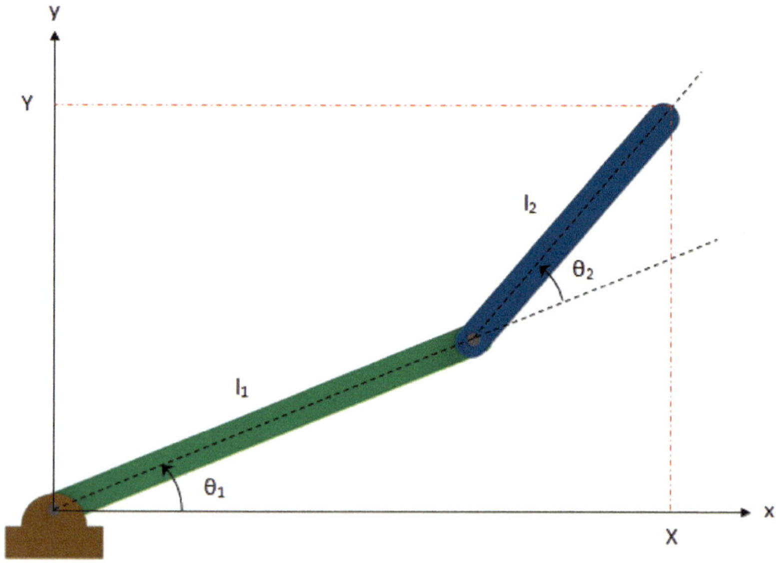

Figure 6.20 A two-dimensional two-link robotic manipulator.

The position of the tip of the robot can be expressed by the following equations:

$$X = l_1.\cos\theta_1 + l_2.\cos(\theta_1 + \theta_2)$$

$$Y = l_1.\sin\theta_1 + l_2.\sin(\theta_1 + \theta_2)$$

The lengths of these two links are constant, while θ_1 and θ_2 are the only variables. We can easily employ numerical analysis software, such as MATLAB, to draw the cloud of the tip positions with all possible sets of incremental variables.

We must concern ourselves with the techniques of motion trajectory design for humanoid robots. Either we need to describe the desired motion of robotic manipulators in the joint space, the three-dimensional workspace, or the hand coordinates, since the time histories of position, orientation, linear velocity, angular velocity, linear acceleration, and angular acceleration are concerned. For instance, in a pick-and-place robotic system, the mission is to pick an object from one location and place it in another. However, we might need to program the robotic system in more detail. There may be some obstacles in the way of the robotic hand, which we must avoid to prevent collision. Thus, the robotic manipulator hand's path to perform its eventual mission is important.

To design the trajectory of a robotic hand, we need to define the functionality of joint parameters concerning each other. We will not dwell too much on this topic.

References and Further Readings

Alexander, E. III, and Maciunas, R. J. (1999). *Advanced Neuroadvanced Navigation*. Thieme Medical Publishers, Inc., New York, pp. 333–338.

Allen, B. F., Jordan, B., Pannell, W., Lewis, C., Dutson, E., and Faloutsos, P. (2010). Laparoscopic advanced robot for remote in vivo training. *Advanced Robotics*, **24**:1679–1694.

Al-Niaimi, A. N., Einstein, M. H., Perry, L. T., Hartenbach, E. M., and Kushner, D. M. (2011). Uterine artery sparing robotic radical trachelectomy (AS-RRT) for early cancer of the cervix. *International Journal of Gynecology and Obstetrics*, **112**(2011):76–80.

Argenziano, M., Oz, M. C., DeRose, J. J. Jr., Ashton, R. C. Jr, Beck, J., Wang, F., Chitwood, W. R., Nifong, L. W., Dimitui, J., Rose, E. A., and Smith, C. R. (2002). Totally endoscopic atrial septal defect repair with robotic assistance. *The Heart Surgery Forum*, **5**:194–297.

Asimov, I. Retrieved from http://www.used-robots.com/robot-education.php?page=asimov, November 07, 2012, 2:20 pm EST.

Asimov, I., and Frenkel, K. (1985). Robots: Machines in man's image. New York: Harmony Books, p. 19.

Bann, S., Khan, M., Hernandez, J., Munz, Y., Moorthy, K., Datta, V., Rockall, T., and Darzi, A. (2003). Robotics in surgery. *Journal of the American College of Surgeons*, **196**(5): 784–795.

Bann, S., Khan, M., Hernandez, J., Munz, Y., Moorthy, K., Datta, V., Rockall, T., and Darzi, A. Robotics in surgery. *Journal of the American College of Surgeons*, **196**(5): 784–795.

Bedini, S. A. (1962). The compartmented cylindrical clepsydra. *Technology and Culture*, **3**(2):115–141.

Bochkarev, V., Ringley, C. D., and Oleynikov, D. (2005). Robotic-assisted operative techniques in general surgery. *Operative Techniques in General Surgery*, **7**(4):188–200.

Bochkarev, V., Ringley, C. D., and Oleynikov, D. (2005). Robotic-assisted operative techniques in general surgery. *Operative Techniques in General Surgery*, **7**(4):153–210.

Bourla, D. H., Hubschman, J. P., Culjat, M., Tsirbas, A., Gupta, A., and Schwartz, S. D. (2008). Feasibility study of intraocular robotic surgery with the da Vinci advanced system. *Retina*, **28**(1):154–158.

Brandt, G, Radermacher, K., Zimolong, A., Rau, G., Merloz, P., Klos, T. V., Robb, J., and Staudte, H. W. (2000). CRIGOS: Development of a compact robot for image-guided orthopedic surgery. *Orthopedic*, **29**(7):645–649.

Butner, S. E., and Ghodoussi, M. Transforming advanced robot for human telesurgery. *Transactions on Robotics and Automation*, **19**(5).

Cadeddu, J. A., Bzostek, A., Schreiner, S., Barnes, A. C., Roberts, W. W., Anderson, J. H., Taylor, R. H., and Kavoussi, L. R. (1997). A robotic system for percutaneous renal access. *Journal of Urology*, **158**:1589.

Cadiere, G., Himpens, J., Vertruyen, M., and Favretti, F. (1999). The world's first obesity surgery performed by a surgeon at a distance. *Obesity Surgery*, **9**:206–209.

Carpentier, A., Loulmet, D., Aupecle, B., Kieffer, J. P., Tournay, D., Guibourt, P., Fiemeyer, A., Méléard, D., Richomme, P., and Cardon, C. (1998). Computer-assisted open heart surgery: First case operated on with success. *Comptes rendus de l'Académie des Sciences*, **321**:437–442.

Casale, P., and Kojima, Y. (2009). Robotic-assisted laparoscopic surgery in pediatric urology: An update. *Scandinavian Journal of Surgery*, **98**:110–119.

Cassilly, R., Diodato, M. D., Bottros, M., and Damiano, R. J. Jr. (2004). Optimizing motion scaling and magnification in robotic surgery. *Surgery*, **136**(2):291–294.

Castle, S. L., and Kernstine, K. H. (2008). Robotic-assisted surgery. In *Seminars in Thoracic and Cardiovascular Surgery*, **20**(4):326–331.

Chan, F., Kassim, I., Lo, C., Ho, C.L., Low, D., Ang, B.T., and Ng I. (2009). Image-guided robotic neurosurgery: An in vitro and in vivo point accuracy evaluation experimental study. *Advanced Neurology*, **71**: 640–648.

Chen, W., Fu, G., Gong, J., He, Y., and Dong, S. (2002). A new design conception for large-span deployable flat grid structures. *International Journal of Space Structures*, **17**(4):293–299.

Davies, B. L., Hibberd, R. D., Coptcoat, M. J., and Wickham, J. E. (1989). A surgeon robot prostatectomy: A laboratory evaluation. *Journal of Medical Engineering and Technology*, **13**:273–277.

De Gennes, P. G., Okumura, K., Shahinpoor, M., and Kim, K. J. (2000). Mechanoelectric effects in ionic gels. *Europhysics Letters*, **50**(4): 513–518.

Degueldre, M., Vandromme, J., Huong, P. T., and Cadiere, G. B. (2000). Robotically assisted laparoscopic micro advanced tubal anastomosis: A feasibility study. *Fertility and Sterility*, **74**:1020–1023.

Del Grosso, A. E., and Basso, P. (2010). Adaptive building skin structures. *Smart Materials and Structures*, **19**(12):124011.

Deole, U., Lumia, R., Shahinpoor, M., and Bermudez, M. (2008). Design and test of IPMC artificial muscle microgripper. *Journal of Micro-Nano Mechatronics*, **4**: 95–102.

Diaz-Arrastia, C., Jurnalov, C., Gomez, G., and Townsend, C. Jr. (2002). Laparoscopic hysterectomy using a computer-enhanced advanced robot. *Surgical Endoscopy*, **16**:1271–1273.

Diodato, M., Prasad, S., Klingensmith, M., et al. (2004). Robotics in surgery. *Current Problems in Surgery*, **41**:752–810.

Diolaiti, N. (2010). Minimally invasive advanced systems. U.S. Patent No. 7,725,214.

Drasin, T., Dutson, E., and Gracia, C. (2004). Use of a robotic system as advanced first assistant in advanced laparoscopic surgery. *Journal of the American College of Surgeons*, **199**(3):368–373.

Fankhauser, H., Glauser, D., Flury, P., Piguet, Y., Epitaux, M., Favre, J., and Meuli, R. A. (1994). Robot for CT-guided stereotactic neurosurgery. *Stereotactic and Functional Neurosurgery*, **63**(1–4):93–98.

Fest, E., Shea, K., Domer, B., and Smith, I. F. C. (2003). Adjustable tensegrity structures. *Journal of Structural Engineering*, **129**(4):515–526.

Gantes, C. J., and Konitopoulou, E. (2004). Geometric design of arbitrarily curved bistable deployable arches with discrete joint size. International Journal of Solids and Structures, **41**(20):5517–5540.

Giorgi, C., Sala, R., Riva, D., Cossu, A., and Eisenberg, H. (2000). Robotics in child neurosurgery. *Child's Nervous System*, **16**(10–11): 832–834.

Gomes, P. (2011). Advanced robotics: Reviewing the past, analyzing the present, imagining the future. *Robotics and Computer-Integrated Manufacturing*. **27**(2):261–266.

Guillonneau, B., Jayet, C., Tewari, A., and Vallancien, G. (2001). Robot-assisted laparoscopic nephrectomy. *Journal of Urology*, **166**:200–201.

Haber, G. P., Crouzet, S., and Gill, I. S. (2008). Laparoscopic and robotic assisted radical cystectomy for bladder cancer: A critical analysis. *European Urology*, **54**(2008): 54–64.

Haidegger, T., and Benyo, Z. (2008). Advanced robotic support for long duration space missions. *Acta Astronautica*, **63**(2008): 996–1005.

Hemal, A. K., and Menon, M. (2004). Robotics in urology. *Current Opinion in Urology*, **14**(2):89–93.

Himpens, J., Leman, G., and Cadiere, G. B. (1998). Teleadvanced laparoscopic cholecystectomy. *Surgical Endoscopy*, **12**:091.

Hoberman, C. (1990). Reversibly expandable doubly-curved truss structure. U.S. Patent 4,942,700.

Hoberman, C. (1991). Radial expansion/retraction truss structures. U.S. Patent 5,024,031.

Hoberman, C. (2007). Unfolding Structures. (http://www.hoberman.com).

Horgan, S., and Vanuno, D. (2001). Robots in laparoscopic surgery. *Journal of Laparoendoscopic & Advanced Techniques*, **11**(6).

Hoznek, A., Zaki, S. K., Samadi, D. B., Salomon, L., Lobontiu, A., Lang, P., and Abbou, C. C. (2002). Robotic-assisted kidney transplantation: An initial experience. *Journal of Urology*, **167**:1604–1606.

Iordachita, I., Kapoor, A., Mitchell, B., Kazanzides, P., Hager, G., Handa, J., and Taylor, R. (2006). *Steady-Hand Manipulator for Retinal Surgery*. The Johns Hopkins University.

Jakopec, M., Harris, S. J., Rodriguez y Baena, F., Gomes, P., Cobb, J., and Davies, B. L. The first clinical application of a "hands-on" robotic knee surgery system. *Computer Aided Surgery*, **6**:329–339.

Kaiser, W. A., Fischer, H., Vagner, J., and Selig, M. (2000). Robotic system for biopsy and therapy of breast lesions in a high-field whole-body magnetic resonance tomography unit. *Investive Radiology*, **35**: 513–519.

Kassabian, P., You, Z., and Pellegrino, S. (1999). Retractable roof structures. *Proceedings Institution of Civil Engineers Structures and Buildings* **134**:45–56.

Kim, K. J., and Shahinpoor, M. (2002). A novel method of manufacturing three-dimensional ionic polymer-metal composites (IPMC's) biomimetic sensors, actuators and artificial muscle. *Polymer*, **43**(3):797–802.

Koren, Y. (1985). *Robotics for Engineers*. McGraw & Hill.

Kwoh, Y. S., Hou, J., Jonckheere, E. A., and Hayati, S. (1988). A robot with improved absolute positioning accuracy for CT-guided stereotactic brain surgery. *IEEE Transactions on Biomedical Engineering*, **35**:153–160

Kypson, A. P., Nifong, L. W., and Chitwood, W. R. Jr. (2003). Robotic cardiac surgery. *Journal of Long-Term Effects of Medical Implants*, **13**(6):451–464.

Larkin, D. Q., and Shafer, D. C. (2011). Robotic surgery system including position sensors using fiber Bragg gratings. U.S. Patent No. 7,930,065.

Le Roux, P. D., Das, H., Esquenazi, S., and Kelly, P. J. (2001). Robot-assisted microsurgery: A feasibility study in the rat. *Neurosurgery*, **48**:584–589.

Lum, M. J. H., Rosen, J., Lendvay, T. S., Wright, A. S., Sinanan, M. N., and Hannaford, B. (2008). TeleRobotic fundamentals of laparoscopic surgery (FLS): Effects of time delay—Pilot study. *30th Annual International IEEE EMBS Conference 2008.*

Ma, J., and Berkelman, P. (2007). Task evaluations of a compact laparoscopic advanced robot system. *IEEE/RSJ International Conference on Intelligent Robots and Systems*, IROS 2007, October 29-November 2, 2007.

Maden, F., Korkmaza, K., and Akgünb, Y. (2011). A review of planar scissor structural mechanisms: Geometric principles and design methods. *Architectural Science Review*, **54**(3):246–257.

Malone, R. (1978). *The Robot Book*. New York: Push Pin Press, p. 26.

Mao, S. P., Lai, H. C., Chang, F. W., Yu, M. H., and Chang, C. C. (2007). Laparoscopy-assisted robotic myomectomy using the da Vinci system. *Taiwanese Journal of Obstetrics and Gynecology*, **46**(2):174–176.

Marescaux, J., Smith, M., Fölscher, D., Jamali, F., Malassagne, B., and Leroy, J. (2001). Telerobotic laparoscopic cholecystectomy: Initial experience with 25 patients. *Annals of Surgery*, **234**:1–7.

Margossian, H., Garcia-Ruiz, A., Falcone, T., Goldberg, J. M., Attaran, M., and Gagner, M. (1998). Robotically assisted laparoscopic micro advanced uterine horn anastomosis. *Fertility and Sterility*, **70**:530–534.

Martinez, B. D., and Wiegand, C. S. (2004). Robotics in vascular surgery. *The American Journal of Surgery*, **188**:57S–62S.

Meaning, H. C. M., Hendrix, R., Rosielle, P. C. J. N., Steinbuch, M., Nijmeijer, H., and de Smet, M. C. A master-μslave robot for vitreoretinal eye surgery. *Proceedings of the Euspen International Conference – Delft*, June 2010.

Micali, S., Virgili, G., Vannozzi, E., Grassi, N., Jarrett, T. W., Bauer, J. J., Vespasiani, G., and Kavoussi, L. R. (2000). Feasibility of telementoring between Baltimore (USA) and Rome (Italy): The first five cases. *Journal of Endourology*, **14**:493–496.

Mirbagheri, A., Farahmand, F., Meghdari, A., and Karimian, F. (2011). Design and development of an effective low-cost robotic cameraman for laparoscopic surgery: RoboLens. *Scientia Iranica*, **18**(1): 105–114.

Mitchell, B., Koo, J., Iordachita, I., Kazanzides, P., Kapoor, A., Handa, J., Hager, G., and Taylor, R. (2007). Development and application of a new steady-hand manipulator for retinal surgery. *IEEE International Conference on Robotics and Automation*, Roma, Italy, 10–14 April 2007.

Mohr, F. W., Falk, V., Ziegler, A., and Autschback, R. (1999). Computer-enhanced coronary artery bypass surgery. *The Journal of Thoracic and Cardiovascular Surgery*, **117**:1212–1214.

Moradi Dalvand, M., and Shirinzadeh, B. (2013). Motion control analysis of a parallel robot-assisted minimally invasive surgery/microsurgery system (PRAMiSS). *Robotics and Computer-Integrated Manufacturing*, **29**(2):318–327.

Munz, Y., Moorthy, K., Kudchadkar, R., Hernandez, J. D., Martin, S., Darzi, A., and Rockall, T. (2004). Robotic-assisted rectopexy. *The American Journal of Surgery*, **187**:88–92.

Ng, W. S., Davies, B. L., Hibberd, R. D., and Timoney, A. G. (1993). A first-hand experience in transurethral resection of the prostate. *IEEE EMBS Journal*:123–125.

Nowlin, W. C., Mohr, P. W., Schena, B. M., Larkin, D. Q., and Guthart, G. (2011). Software center and highly configurable robotic systems for surgery and other uses. U.S. Patent No. 8,004,229.

Olsen, L. H. (2006). Robotics in pediatric urology. *Journal of Pediatric Urology*, **2**:40e45.

Onnasch, J. F., Schneider, F., Falk, V., Mierzwa, M., Bucerius, J., Mohr, F. W. (2002). Five years of less invasive minimal surgery: From experimental to routine. *Heart Surgery Forum*, **5**:132–135.

Onoda, J., Fu, D.-Y., and Minesugi, K. (1996). Two-dimensional deployable hexapod truss. *Journal of Spacecraft and Rockets*, **33**:416-421.

Patel, K. (2008). Robotics the future of surgery. *International Journal of Surgery*, **6**:441–442.

Patel, M. N., Menon, M., and Rogers, C. G. (2010). Robotic partial nephrectomy: A comparison to current techniques. *Urologic Oncology: Seminars and Original Investigations*, **28**:74–76.

Pellegrino, S., and Calladine, C. R. (1986). Matrix analysis of statically and kinematically indeterminate frameworks. *International Journal of Solids and Structures*, **22**:409–2

Pinero, E. P. (1961). Project for a mobile theatre. *Architectural Design*, **12**, 570.

Pires, N. J. (2000). Using actual industrial robot manipulators with construction tasks. *Proceedings of the 17th ISARC (2000)*, Taipei, Taiwan, pp. 1–5.

Prasad, S. M., Maniar, H. S., Soper, N. J., Damiano, R. J. Jr., and Klingensmith, M. E. (2002). The effect of robotic assistance on learning curves for basic laparoscopic skills. *The American Journal of Surgery*, **183**:702–707.

Prasad, S. M., Prasad, S. M., Maniar, H. S., Chu, C., Schuessler, R. B., and Damiano, R. J. Jr. (2004). Advanced robotics: Impact of motion scaling on task performance. *Journal of the American College of Surgeons*, **199**(6):863–868.

Prasad, S. M., Prasad, S. M., Maniar, H. S., Chu, C., Schuessler, R. B., and Damiano, R. J. (2004). Advanced robotic applications such as surgical robotics: Impact of motion scaling on task performance. *Journal of the American College of Surgeons*, **199**(6):863–868.

Rosheim, M. E. (1994). *Robot Evolution: The Development of Anthrobotics*. John Wiley and Sons, Inc., p. 2.

Sabharwal, A., Pradhan, S., and Kumar, A. (2006). Current role of robotics in urology. *Apollo Medicine*, **3**(4):365–370.

Shahinpoor, M. (1996). Multifingered grabbers as smart structures for robotic applications. *Proceedings of SPIE 2779*, April 1996.

Shahinpoor, M. (2000). Ion-exchange membrane-metal composite as biomimetic sensors and actuators. In *Polymer Sensors and Actuators*, Y. Osada and D. De Rossi (Eds.). Springer-Verlag-Heidelberg, pp. 325–359.

Shahinpoor, M. (2002). Artificial muscles. In *Encyclopedia of Biomaterials and Biomedical Engineering*, G. Wnek and G. Bowlin (Eds.). New York: Marcel Dekker Publishers, pp. 43–52.

Shahinpoor, M. (2003). Ionic polymer-conductor composites as biomimetic sensors, robotic actuators and artificial muscles: A review. *Electrochimica Acta*, **48**(14–16):2343–2353.

Shahinpoor, M. (2005). Soft plastic robots and artificial muscles. *International Journal of Advanced Robotic Systems*, **2**(2):161–174.

Shahinpoor, M. (2007). *Advanced Polymeric Nano-Composites*. Taylor and Francis Publishers.

Shahinpoor, M. (2008). Ionic polymeric conductor nano composites (IPCMCs) as distributed nanosensors and nanoactuators. *Advances in Science and Technology*, **54**:70–81.

Shahinpoor, M. (2009). Biomimetics nananosensors and nanoactuators. In *Biomimetics and Bioinspired Nanomaterials*, S. S. Challa and R. Kumar (Eds.). Weinheim: John Wiley and Sons, pp. 1–26.

Shahinpoor, M. (2009). Recent advances in ionic polymer metal nanocomposites as distributed biomimetic nanosensors, nanoactuators and artificial muscles. *Journal of Physics: Conference Series*, **127**.

Shahinpoor, M. (2011). *Intelligent Robotic Systems: Modeling & Simulation*, 2nd edition. Albuquerque, New Mexico: ERI Press.

Shahinpoor, M., and Gheshmi, S. (2012). Space-saving laparoscopic advanced slave robot. U.S. Provisional Patent Application No. 61718822, November 2012.

Shahinpoor, M., and Gheshmi, S. (2015). *Robotic Surgery*, Jenny Stanford Publishing, Singapore.

Shahinpoor, M., and Kim, K. J. (2002). A solid-state soft actuator exhibiting large electromechanical effect. *Applied Physics Letters (APL)*, **80**(18):3445–3447.

Shahinpoor, M., and Kim, K. J. (2005). Ionic polymer-metal composites–IV. Industrial and medical applications (Review Paper). *Smart Materials and Structures*, **14**(1): 197–214.

Shahinpoor, M., and Schneider, H. J. (2008). *Intelligent Materials*, 1st. edition. Royal Society of Chemistry (RSC) Publishers.

Shahinpoor, M., Gheshmi, S., and Soltanpour, D. (2012). Intraocular robotic surgical system, US Provisional Patent Application No. 61716718, 205 pages, November, 2012.

Shahinpoor, M., Kim, K. J., and Mojarrad, M. (2007). *Artificial Muscles: Applications of Advanced Polymeric Nano-Composites*. London and New York: CRC Press, Taylor and Francis Publishers.

Shew, S. B., Ostlie, D. J., and Holcomb III, G. W. (2003). Robotic telescopic assistance in pediatric laparoscopic surgery. *Pediatric Endosurgery & Innovative Techniques*, **7**(4).

Siwek, L. G., and Reynolds, B. (2007). Totally robotic mitral valve repair. *Operative Techniques in Thoracic and Cardiovascular Surgery: A Comparative Atlas*, **12**(4):235–249.

Sofla, A., Elzey, D., and Wadley, H. (2009). Shape morphing hinged truss structures. *Smart Materials and Structures*, **18**, 065012.

Strong, M. (2004). Protein nanomachines. *PLoS Biology*, **2**:0305.

Sutherland, G. R., Louw, D. F., McBeth, P. B., Fielding, T., and Gregoris, D. J. (2012). U.S. Patent No. 8170717, May 1, 2012.

Sutherland, G. R., Louw, D. F., McBeth, P. B., Fielding, T., and Gregoris, D. J. (2006). Microadvanced robot system. U.S. Patent No. 7155316, December 26, 2006.

Sweeney, T., and Rattner, D. W. (2002). Robotically assisted minimally invasive biliary surgery in a porcine model. *Surgical Endoscopy*, **16**:138–141.

Taylor, R. H. (2003). *Medical Robotics in Computer-Integrated Surgery. IEEE Transactions on Robotics and Automation*, **19**(5).

Tchartchian, G., Dietzel, J., Bojahr, B., Hackethal, A., and De Wilde, R. (2011). Decreasing strain on the surgeon in gynecologic minimally invasive surgery by using semi-active robotics. *International Journal of Gynecology and Obstetrics*, **112**:72–75.

Terris, D. J., and Amin, S. H. (2008). Robotic and endoscopic surgery in the neck. *Operative Techniques in Otolaryngology-Head and Neck Surgery*, **19**(1):36–41.

Tesla, N. (1898). Method of and apparatus for controlling mechanism of moving vessels of vehicles. U.S. Patent No. 613809, November 8, 1898.

Tewari, A., Peabody, J., Sarle, R., Balakrishnan, G., Hemal, A., Shrivastava, A., and Menon, M. (2002). The technique of da Vinci robot-assisted anatomic radical prostatectomy. *Urology*, **60**:569–572.

Torraca, L., Ismeno, G., Quarti, A., and Alfieri, O. (2002). Totally endoscopic atrial septal defect closure with a robotic system: Experience with seven cases. *Heart Surge Forum*, **5**:125–127.

Tsirbas, A., Mango, C., and Dutson, E. (2007). Use of robotics for intraocular surgery. *British Journal of Ophthalmol*, **91**(1):18–21.

Tsui, I., Tsirbas, A., Mango, C. W., Schwartz, S. D., and Hubschman, J. P. (2010). *Robotic Surgery in Ophthalmology*, S. H. Baik (Ed.). InTech.

Tsutomu, K., and Tokai, H. (1997). Cable scissors arch-marionettes structure. Structural morphology, towards the new millennium. *Proceedings of International Conference of IASS*, University of Nottingham, 107–116.

Turchetti, G., Palla, I., Pierotti, F., and Cuschieri, A. (2012). Economic evaluation of da Vinci–assisted robotic surgery: A systematic review. *Surgical Endoscopy Volume*, **26**:598–606.w

Ueta, T., Yamaguchi, Y., Shirakawa, Y., Nakano, T., Ideta, R., Noda, Y., Morita, A., Mochizuki, R., Sugita, N., Mitsuishi, M., and Tamaki, Y. (2009). Robot-assisted vitreoretinal surgery: Development of a prototype and feasibility studies in an animal model. *Ophthalmology*, **116**(8):1538–1543.

Van Der Brug, W. P., De Bliek, H. L. T., and Gerritsen, F. A. (1999). Image-guided surgery system. U.S. Patent No. 6,006,127.

White, M. A., Haber, G. P., Autorino, R., Khanna, R., Forest, S., Yang, B., Altunrende, F., Stein, R. J., and Kaouk, J. H. (2010). Robotic laparoendoscopic single-site radical prostatectomy: Technique and early outcomes. *European Urology*, **58**:544–550.

Wisselink, W., Cuesta, M. A., Gracia, C., and Rauwerda, J. A. (2002). Robot-assisted laparoscopic aortabifemoral bypass for aortoiliac occlusive disease: A report of two cases. *Journal of Vascular Surgery*, **36**:1079–1082.

Yildrim, Y. (2010). *Cytoreductive Surgery in Gynecologic Oncology: A Multidisciplinary Approach*. Kerala: Transworld Research Network, pp. 213–232.

Chapter 7

Development of a Portable Small Nuclear Battery for Biomimetic Humanoid

7.1 Introduction

The development of a portable small nuclear battery to provide energy for the activities of a biomimetic humanoid robot (humanoid or animaloid) has been needed for a long time. Nuclear batteries are the portable power of the future. These portable power supplies will be replaceable if needed. Note that the humanoid robot will have no internal bio-organs like normal human beings. All movements are electromechanical and sensory, and the adjoining smart (intelligent) stimuli-responsive materials worn by the biomimetic humanoid robot replace motor neurons here. The humanoid robot with human consciousness will be entirely electromechanical and capable of surviving immortally in time. Please see Chapters 5 and 6 for a description of wearable stimuli-responsive smart materials, robotic manipulators, and humanoid robots. As described in these chapters, the humanoid robots will need energy to operate their various electromechanical actuators, sensors, related instrumentation, and the resident identity-vita-assigned consciousness (IVA-

Biomimetic Humanoid Robots with Human Consciousness
Mohsen Shahinpoor

ISBN 978-981-5129-87-8 (Hardcover), 978-1-003-71373-9 (eBook)
www.jennystanford.com

DOI: 10.1201/9781003713739-7

consciousness) computer in the humanoid robot. The solution appears to be nuclear batteries,[1] which will be discussed here in this chapter. Note that some nuclear batteries can last for up to 28,000 years.[2]

In 2024, the Chinese company Betavolt announced a coin-sized nuclear battery using radioactive nickel sandwiched between thin layers of diamond, which acts as a semiconductor that could power devices such as mobile phones, laptops, and drones for half a century, with an energy density 10 times higher than our current, most powerful lithium-ion batteries. A small nuclear battery could last for more than 50 years (Fig. 7.1).

Figure 7.1 Nuclear Betavolt battery by Betavolt Company. *Credit*: Betavolt Technology.

In a nuclear battery, the power source is a piece of radioactive material. These ideas are not new. The Voyager 1 space probe,

[1]Nuclear Batteries, the Portable Powerofthe Future? https://www.bbvaopenmind.com/en/technology/innovation/nuclear-batteries-portable-power-of-the future/#:~:text=In%202024%2C%20the%20Chinese%20company%20Betavolt%20announced%20a%20coin%2Dsized,times%20higher%20than%20our%20current| OpenMind (bbvaopenmind.com))

[2]Diamond Batteries Explained (Technology Innovation: https: //www.bbvaopenmind.com/en/technology/)

launched in 1977, has a nuclear battery. It is now over 15 billion miles away, and it still has a little juice. The specific type on Voyager is called a radioisotope thermoelectric generator, which is a big name for what is a hunk of plutonium in a box. As the plutonium decays, it converts mass to energy, producing heat. The difference in temperature between the hot and cold metals produces voltage and causes an electric current to flow.

This new battery announced by Betavolt uses a different technology called betavoltaic generation. Instead of tapping thermal energy, it captures the ejected electrons, known as beta particles, from a radioactive isotope of nickel to form an electric circuit. It is made up of several layers of nickel sandwiched between plates of diamond, which serve as a semiconductor.

7.2 What Happens in Radioactive Decay?

Nickel-63 is an isotope of the stable version of the element nickel-58. That number is the atomic weight—the total number of protons and neutrons in the atom's nucleus. Nickel-63 has five extra neutrons, which make it unstable. Over time, one of those extra neutrons will decay into a proton and produce a new electron. With an extra proton, the atom will now be copper-63, the next element in the periodic table. This nuclear reaction produces energy, shooting the electron out of the atom at high speed. It is important to know that the rate of radioactive decay is not constant; it depends on the number of atoms of the material present, so the production of electrons declines exponentially over time.

Let us face it: EVs are not catching on as much as everybody wanted. Their high price tag, slow charging times, and somewhat compromising range have been among the biggest setbacks for EVs, all of which stem from one issue: Tesla has just announced the diamond nuclear battery.

The concept of a nuclear battery is different because of the physical scale and power output of this machine—about 10 MW. It is so small that a whole power plant is built in a factory and fits within a standard container. This provides several benefits from an economic point of view.

1. news.mit.edu › 2021 › 3Q: Why "nuclear batteries" offer a new approach to carbon-free energy

Jun 25, 2021, · A new generation of relatively small and inexpensive factory-built nuclear reactors designed for autonomous plug-and-play operation is on the horizon, says a group of nuclear experts at MIT and elsewhere. These proposed "nuclear batteries" could help reduce greenhouse gas emissions if adopted widely.

2. scitechdaily.com ›"Nuclear Batteries" Offer a New Approach to Carbon-Free Energy

Jun 25, 2021, · Jacopo Buongiorno and others say factory-built microreactors trucked to usage sites could be a safe, efficient option for decarbonizing electricity systems. We may be on the brink of a new paradigm for nuclear power, a group of nuclear specialists suggested recently in The Bridge, the journal of the National Academy of Engineering.

3. www.bbvaopenmind.com › en › Nuclear Batteries, the Portable Power of the Future? | OpenMind

Mar 13, 2024, · In 1913, decades before the discovery of nuclear fission, the British physicist Henry Moseley demonstrated that beta particles—high-energy electrons or positrons released by the decay of a radioactive nucleus—emitted by radium produce an electric current, thus inventing the atomic battery.

4. link.springer.com › article › Recent progress and perspective on batteries made from nuclear waste

Mar 15, 2023 · The reported specific energy of a nuclear β cell battery (Schottky barrier-based diamond diode) using 63 Ni (25% enriched) source is about 3300 mWh/g, which is ten times higher than the commercially available chemical batteries such as the Li-ion battery which has a specific energy of about 100–265 mWh/g .

5. onlinelibrary.wiley.com › doi › Nuclear batteries: Current context and near-term expectations

Sep 7, 2022 · Summary. The batteries fueled by radioisotopes have represented a significant technological solution for planetary science and exploration missions since the beginning of the space era. Now emerging researches and new concepts are making the nuclear batteries attractive also for relevant terrestrial applications.

6. www.nei.org › news › How Nuclear, Batteries and Energy Storage Can Build a Carbon ...

Dec 6, 2018 · December 6, 2018. Energy storage technologies—and batteries in particular—are often seen as the "holy grail" to fully decarbonizing our future electricity grid, along with renewables and nuclear energy—which provides more than 56 percent of America's carbon-free electricity.

7. link.springer.com › content › Recent progress and perspective on batteries made from nuclear

Various types of nuclear waste can be categorized as uranium tailings (a by-product of uranium extraction from ore), transuranic (TRU) waste (a by-product during nuclear research and nuclear weapon development), low-level waste (materials containing radioactive contamination or exposure in nuclear fission), and intermediate-level waste (nuclear reactor).

7.3 Beginnings of Atomic Batteries

In 1913, decades before the discovery of nuclear fission, the British physicist Henry Moseley (1913) demonstrated that beta particles—high-energy electrons or positrons released by the decay of a radioactive nucleus—emitted by radium produce an electric current, thus inventing the atomic battery.

Figure 7.2 Diamond batteries from NDP.

Companies such as NDB Home introduced diamond batteries. Nano Diamond Battery (NDB) (Fig. 7.2) is an innovative energy generator and storage that redefines and revolutionizes the battery, as we know it.

7.4 Nanotechnology for the General-Purpose Atomic Battery

Advances in non-thermal nuclear batteries have been made over the past few decades, but recent developments in nanotechnology have provided new tools. For example, companies such as NDB and others are developing nanodiamond batteries based on radioisotopes encapsulated in synthetic diamonds. This company uses radioactive waste from nuclear power plants, something Asimov foresaw in his 1964 prediction. NDB says its batteries could last up to 28,000 years, powering everything from smartphones and medical devices to cars and planes.

Several companies are already producing some form of a nuclear battery, but so far, only for specialized applications. But the general-purpose atomic battery is getting closer. In 2024, the Chinese company Betavolt announced a coin-sized nuclear battery using radioactive nickel sandwiched between thin layers of diamond, which acts as a semiconductor that could power devices such as mobile phones, laptops, and drones for a half a century, with an energy density 10 times higher than our current lithium-ion batteries. Betavolt hopes to begin industrial production in 2025. A common objection to any nuclear-powered device is the presence of a hazardous material, which poses no risk as long as it remains inside the battery but does pose a risk if the battery ruptures.

All batteries do the same thing: They produce an electric current to do some work. However, energy is not free. If that work is blasting music on your Bluetooth speakers, there must be something that decreases energy. In a good old AA, there is a chemical reaction to produce the current. That chemical reaction does not last forever, so the battery will eventually die.

It is crazy that a temperature difference alone can generate electricity, but you can test this at home using some copper wire and a paper clip (without the plutonium) by sticking one end in ice water and the other in hot water. This type of power source is great for space probes because it has no moving parts, so it will not break down, and it lasts for decades.

It is made up of several layers of nickel sandwiched between plates of diamond, which serves as a semiconductor. It is important to know that the rate of radioactive decay is not constant; it depends on the number of atoms of the material present, so the production of electrons declines exponentially over time. In the case of nickel-63, half of the atoms will decay in about 96 years—we say it has a "half-life" of 96 years (Fig. 7.3).

Note that an electrical current is just a flow of electrons in a circuit. The flow rate is measured in amperes: 1 amp = 6.24×10^{18} electrons flowing through a certain point per second.

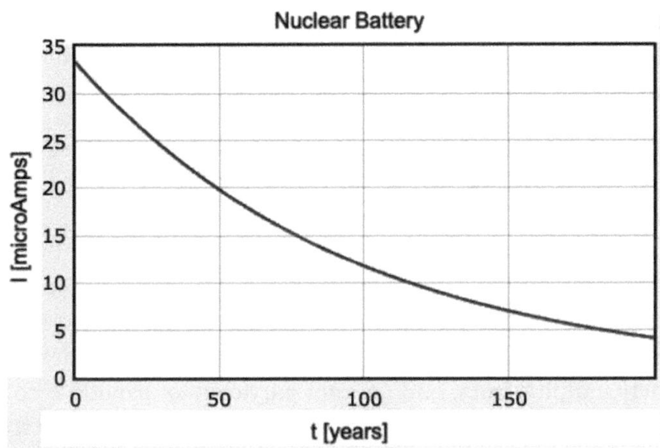

Figure 7.3 Decay of nuclear batteries in time.

The power supplied (P), measured in watts, can be calculated by multiplying the electrical current (I) by the voltage (V). One watt equals 1 joule of energy per second. Multiplying power by a period (Δt) gives you the total energy used (ΔE), usually measured in kilowatt-hours.

$$P = IV$$

$$\Delta E = P\Delta t$$

Scientists have been studying nuclear power's potential capabilities for decades; figuring out how to store that energy in a contained space has been challenging. Certain radioactive isotopes are volatile, toxic, difficult to shield, and unsuitable for use as part of a direct conversion power source.

However, other isotopes are stable, relatively benign, and have the potential to power remote electronics for extensive periods. Using radioisotopes such as tritium, scientists and engineers have begun creating practical nuclear batteries for powering low-energy devices.

7.5 What Is a Nuclear Battery?

A nuclear battery is any device that harnesses energy from radioactive element isotope decay to generate electricity. The terms nuclear battery, atomic battery, and radioisotope generator are interchangeable and indicate how the power source creates a current.

7.6 How Are Nuclear Batteries Different?

Nuclear batteries differ from traditional batteries in their cost, lifespan, applications, and function.

Traditional batteries use electrochemical reactions as their power supply. Radioisotope generators capitalize on the decay of radioactive alpha, beta, and gamma particles to provide a constant energy source. As these particles are emitted, they stir electrons in the battery system to create a current.

Due to their increased capabilities, nuclear batteries are much more expensive than traditional batteries of the same size. This is one of the limitations currently existing with nuclear battery research and use.

7.7 How Do Atomic Batteries Work?

Atomic and nuclear batteries generate electricity through the decay of radioactive particles. Some batteries use this decay to generate heat and then harvest with thermocouples; others harness diode junctions to facilitate non-thermal conversion. Regardless of the method, all nuclear batteries draw energy from a radioactive source.

7.8 Types of Nuclear Batteries

Different nuclear batteries use different systems to generate power for their devices. Each type has its benefits, limitations, and use cases.

Non-thermal conversion batteries, including betavoltaic power sources, use the incident energy released during the radioactive decay to cycle electrons into a current. By converting a fraction of the nuclear energy created during the decay process, these batteries can create a stream of electricity without relying on temperature differences.

Direct conversion betavoltaics are some of the most efficient nuclear batteries on the market because the beta particle decay is more effectively converted into usable electrical power than it is with other particles. Indirect conversion betavoltaics uses light emission and a photovoltaic cell (instead of a betavoltaic cell) to produce electrical current. These devices are less efficient than direct conversion devices and do not last as long due to degradation of the light-emitting phosphors, but can reach high powers for short periods.

7.9 Nuclear Diamond Batteries

One of the most exciting areas of atomic battery technology is the ongoing research to improve the field. Scientists are currently developing a nuclear diamond battery that produces power from the radioactive decay of diamonds (carbon-14). Like all nuclear batteries, this diamond battery produces power proportionally to the half-life of the radioactive source. The difference is that carbon-14 has a half-life of 5700 years!

These diamond batteries are still in their infancy, but tritium betavoltaics—which offer similar benefits—are already in use. They demonstrate a tremendous opportunity for repurposing existing nuclear waste while offering a long-term, steady flow of electricity.

7.10 Breakdown of Radioactive Elements for Battery Usage

The type of nuclear battery used often depends on which radioactive isotope acts as a power supply. How energy from alpha particles, beta particles, and gamma rays is captured differs. Here are some of the more commonly used and tested radioactive isotopes.

7.10.1 Uranium Power

Uranium is a popular radioactive nuclear element for power supply because it has been used as the primary energy source in nuclear power plants for over 60 years. Most plants use the uranium-235 isotope because its atoms are easier to break apart. Uranium can be mined as a solid and is considered weakly radioactive.

Uranium outputs weak alpha particles that cannot penetrate a piece of paper, and its half-life is around 700 million years. Unfortunately, uranium-235 is not suitable for use in batteries, and this isotope is out of the question for small remote devices.

7.10.2 Plutonium Batteries

One of the other more recognizable radioactive elements—plutonium—has already been used in nuclear batteries in the past. Isotope plutonium-238 has a half-life of 87.7 years and acted as a cardiac pacemaker power supply for a short time in the 1970s. There were two main issues with plutonium-238 batteries.

First, they were bigger than other batteries. The barriers needed to slow down plutonium radiation made the pacemakers inconvenient and unpleasant for those who had them. Second, in what would have been a worst-case scenario, they were still very toxic to humans.

7.11 Nuclear Battery Applications

Atomic batteries are already being used in devices such as moon landers and satellites; RTGs are even helping to power the Perseverance Mars rover! As research develops effective ways to harness and contain radioactive decay, the number of potential uses for radioisotope power sources will increase dramatically, including wireless sensors, low-power electronics, oil well monitoring, and other exciting applications. In this book, it is proposed that nuclear batteries for humanoid robots be used to make them last for a long time before replacement.

7.12 Nuclear Battery Lifespan

A reason nuclear batteries are so promising is their predictability. As we continue discovering more about optimizing the non-radioactive components of a power source, we are learning how to take advantage of its full lifespan.

Because electricity comes from a steady decay of particles, the battery does not deplete faster because of increased usage. Studies of radioisotope half-life tendencies allow researchers to predict how much energy a nuclear battery can output at any given time throughout its use.

7.13 Disadvantages of Nuclear Batteries: Do Batteries Give Off Radiation?

In the past, humans did not have a good understanding of radiation—or strategies for handling it safely. One of the largest hurdles for nuclear battery manufacturers is the public's negative perspective on nuclear energy. City Labs continues to address this issue by educating people on how nuclear energy using tritium can be eco-friendly, efficient, and safe.

7.14 Nuclear Battery Cost

The cost of producing nuclear batteries is impractical for certain applications. Radioisotopes can be rare, and the technology necessary to utilize them effectively can be expensive. Historically, nuclear battery prices have been too high to justify mass production and use.

With less demanding isotopes such as tritium, the commercialization of these products has become more realistic. With wider adoption, products with tritium batteries will be more accessible and less costly.

7.15 Ongoing Research and Development of City Labs' Batteries (NanoTritium™ Technology)

Certain radioactive isotopes are volatile, toxic, difficult to shield, and unsuitable for direct conversion power source use. However, humanoid robots can easily use nuclear batteries. Other isotopes are stable, relatively benign, and have the potential to power remote electronics for extensive periods.

City Labs' NanoTritium™ batteries power a wide range of low-energy electronic devices. NanoTritium™ batteries are used in things such as SRAMs to power encryption keys when the processors are powered down. The P200 betavoltaic micro-batteries improve upon the last series and aim to expand the applications to wireless sensors, security devices, and cardiac pacemakers. These new batteries (Fig. 7.4)—in addition to supplying power between 5 and 10 microwatts—can output milliwatt power bursts with the help of additional electronics.

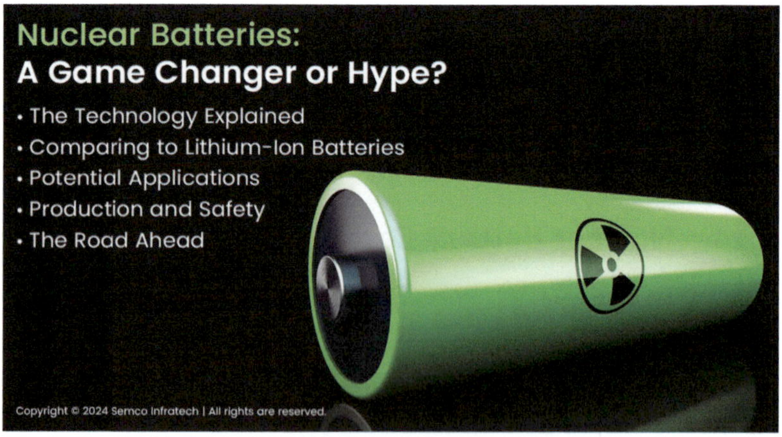

Figure 7.4 Nuclear batteries: A game changer or hype?

7.16 The Road Ahead

Nuclear batteries hold significant potential in the realm of nanotechnology and long-lasting energy sources. However, extensive research and development are still needed to overcome production complexities and ensure safety.

References and Further Readings

Garrett, A. B. (1956). Nuclear batteries. *Journal of Chemical Education*, **33**(9):446.

He, M., Wang, M., and Wang, Z. (2022). The new-type batteries with ultimate energy density. *Journal of Physics: Conference Series*, **2247**: 012013. Hughes, K. (2024). Nuclear power in your pocket? 50-year battery innovation. CAS. Retrieved from: https://www.cas.org/resources/cas-insights/nuclear-power-your-pocket-50-year-battery-innovation.

Katiyar, N. K., and Goel, S. (2023). Recent progress and perspective on batteries made from nuclear waste. *Nuclear Science and Techniques*, **34**(33). DOI: https://doi.org/10.1007/s41365-023-01189-0.

Naseem, M. B., Kim, H. S., Lee, J., Kim, C. H., and In, S.-I. (2023). Betavoltaic nuclear battery: A review of recent progress and challenges as an alternative energy source. *The Journal of Physical Chemistry C*, **127**(16):7565–7579.

Nikolic, R. (2022). *Nuclear Batteries with Potential*. Lawrence Livermore National Laboratory.

Prelas, M., Weaver, C. L., Watterman, M. L., Lukosi, E., Schott, R. J., and Wisniewski1, D. (2014). A review of nuclear batteries. *Progress in Nuclear Energy*, **75**:117–148.

Santiago, A. A., and Parsons, J. E. (n.d.). Developing a suitable business model for nuclear batteries, one MIT Leader for Global Operations, School of Engineering and Sloan School of Management.

Chapter 8

Design and Development of Advanced Intelligent AI Computers

8.1 Introduction

This chapter describes the methods to design and develop advanced intelligent AI computers and software to learn how to think like humans at any age and take possible related actions like humans. It also discusses the brain anatomy, major parts such as the cerebellum and cerebral cortex, and the adjoining neurons and associated axons, neurons, dendrites, synapses, and their collaborative interactions.

This chapter also discusses the connection between the brain and consciousness and the role of microtubules in storing conscious understanding and awareness. The chapter also briefly discusses the microtubules and how they control and interact with identity-vita-assigned consciousness (IVA-consciousness). According to a highly disputed theory proposed by Stuart Hameroff and Roger Penrose and their colleagues (1990, 1995, 1996) in the mid-1990s, consciousness is based on quantum vibrations in tubulin/microtubules inside brain neurons and the collapse of the quantum wave function.

Another theory, "orchestrated objective reduction" (Orch OR), was first proposed in the mid-1990s by eminent mathematical

Biomimetic Humanoid Robots with Human Consciousness
Mohsen Shahinpoor

ISBN 978-981-5129-87-8 (Hardcover), 978-1-003-71373-9 (eBook)
www.jennystanford.com

DOI: 10.1201/9781003713739-8

physicist Roger Penrose and prominent anesthesiologist Stuart Hameroff. They suggested that quantum vibrational computations in microtubules were "orchestrated" ("Orch") by synaptic inputs and memory stored in microtubules and were termed by Penrose "objective reduction" (OR), hence "Orch OR." Microtubules are major components of the cell's structural skeleton.

Orch OR was harshly criticized, as the brain was considered too "warm, wet, and noisy" for seemingly delicate quantum processes. However, evidence has shown warm quantum coherence in plant photosynthesis, bird brain navigation, sense of smell, and brain microtubules.

According to Hameroff (2022) and as shown in Fig. 8.1, they show that the evidence clarifies Orch OR quantum bits, or "Qubits," as helical pathways in microtubule lattices.

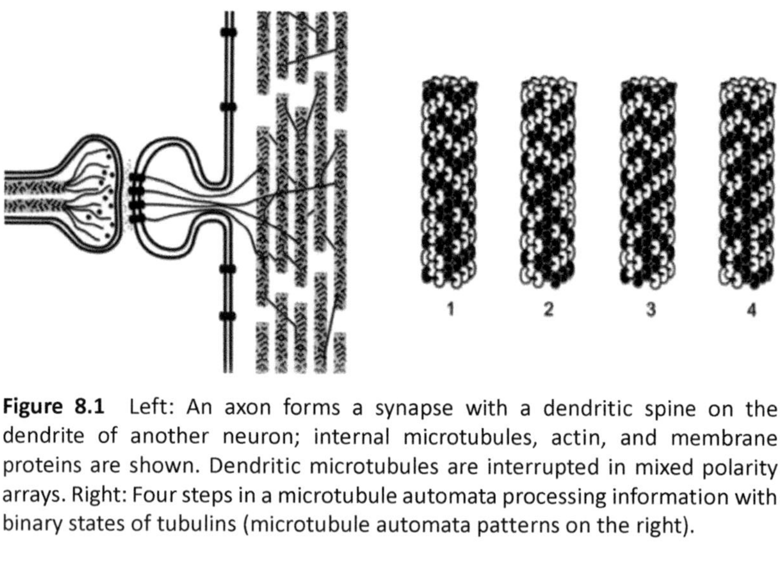

Figure 8.1 Left: An axon forms a synapse with a dendritic spine on the dendrite of another neuron; internal microtubules, actin, and membrane proteins are shown. Dendritic microtubules are interrupted in mixed polarity arrays. Right: Four steps in a microtubule automata processing information with binary states of tubulins (microtubule automata patterns on the right).

Computer scientists are trying to model human behavior using neural networks that treat individual neurons as the base unit. However, according to Justin Riddle, unicellular organisms can do many things that we consider to be similar to human behavior. Many think that DNA holds some secret code or algorithm that executes the decision-making process of the cell. However, the microscope reveals a different story where the microtubules are performing a vast array of complex behaviors: swimming toward food, away from predators, and coordinating protein delivery and creation within the cell.

This begs the question: how do microtubules work? Well, they are single proteins organized into helical cylinders. Typically, one thinks of a protein's function as being determined by its structure, but the function of a single protein repeated into tubes is tough to unravel. Hameroff proposed that perhaps these tubulin proteins act as bits of information (Qubits), and the whole tube works as a universal computer that can be programmed to fit any situation. Given the limitations of digital computation, Penrose (1996) looked for a quantum computer in biology, and Hameroff looked for more than a digital computation explanation. Hence, the Hameroff–Penrose (1995, 1996) model of microtubules as quantum computers was born. If microtubules are quantum computers, each cell would possess a central executive hub for *rapidly integrating information* from across the cell and turning that information into a single action plan that could be quickly disseminated. Furthermore, the computation would get a "quantum" speed-up in that exponentially large search spaces could be tackled reasonably. If microtubules are indeed quantum computers, then modern science has greatly underestimated the processing power of a single cell, let alone the entire human brain.

8.2 Anesthesiology and Consciousness

Hameroff believes that "anesthetic action links consciousness to quantum vibrations in brain microtubules." Hameroff is a professor of anesthesiology and psychology and the director of the Center for Consciousness Studies Banner-University Medical Center at the University of Arizona, Tucson, Arizona.

Hypothesis: Somewhere in the brain, collective pi resonance quantum oscillations critical to consciousness are dampened and dispersed by anesthetic van der Waals couplings.

Van der Waals forces are forces of attraction between molecules that are very close together. These forces between molecules are much weaker than the chemical bonds between the atoms holding a molecule together. Anesthetics appear to act in non-polar pi resonance regions in tubulin, components of microtubules.

According to Arsha Bodha, neuroscience has made giant strides in explaining how intricate networks of neurons in our brain endow us with sight, speech, memory, and even emotions. Some researchers believe that the origin of consciousness itself will eventually be traced to neurons. However, according to Advaita Vedanta, the brain cannot produce consciousness, nor can consciousness be studied by conventional science. The *Quest of Neuroscience* suggests that the source of consciousness is in experience. Neuroscience has made huge strides in understanding the brain and its 100 billion neurons. Particular brain regions involved in sight, speech, memory, balance, and so on are being methodically explored and mapped out in detail. Brain tissue is microscopically studied to see how neurons are interconnected. Directly probing the brain or indirectly using EEG instruments and magnetic stimulation measures the electrical signals that neurons use to communicate. More recently, functional MRI and PET scans have created highly defined images of neural activity throughout the brain. In the future, new technologies might make it possible to accurately measure the neural activity in your brain so that your innermost thoughts and feelings can be decoded.

Will scientific research ever locate a particular network of brain neurons responsible for consciousness itself? Some researchers considered these ideas decades ago, but ongoing studies have completely ruled out the notion that consciousness arises from a single, localized source in the brain. All current theories suggest that the source of consciousness is decentralized or distributed. Bernard Bars describes the origin of consciousness in the brain through his Global Workspace Theory. By a global workspace, he means a decentralized network of neurons that functions like a screen, a screen onto which various images and ideas are projected. According to Bars, consciousness emerges from the interaction of neurons in that global workspace.

Francis Crick received the Nobel Prize for discovering the structure of DNA. Later in his career, he collaborated with a researcher who considered consciousness a fundamental property of complex neural networks. Together, they theorized that neurons become synchronized with each other in a part of the brain known as the claustrum, and their synchronous activity gives rise to consciousness.

Giulio Tononi developed a mathematical model of consciousness called Integrated Information Theory. He claims that consciousness is nothing but highly integrated information. According to Tononi, the enormous integration of information in the brain's powerful cerebral cortex gives rise to consciousness.

According to the Attention Schema Theory of Michael Gaziano, when the faculty of attention filters the interactions of neurons throughout the brain, a simplified model or representation is created. For Gaziano, that representation or schema is responsible for consciousness.

Finally, Roger Penrose is the Nobel Laureate in physics who believes that consciousness cannot be explained through ordinary physical and mathematical laws. Therefore, he postulates the existence of quantum gravity and concludes that consciousness results from quantum effects, which are thought to occur in the microtubules inside cells. Those theories are highly speculative and extremely difficult to verify. Such theories are called materialist or physicalist. They are physicalists because they accept the existence of matter and energy alone, but they reject the existence of any non-material, non-physical reality. But in Advaita Vedanta, consciousness is a non-material, non-physical fundamental reality. "The hard problem of consciousness" is an expression coined by a philosopher named David Chalmers. He uses it to describe the apparently insurmountable obstacles that prevent neuroscientists from directly observing or studying consciousness. Much like in Advaita Vedanta, Chalmers differentiates the objective existence of thoughts and emotions from your subjective, conscious experience of them. He proposes an alternative to the physicalist worldview, the view that accepts only matter and energy as being fundamental. Chalmers says that consciousness is another fundamental reality besides matter and energy. Other philosophers propose idealism and neutral monism. However, none of these theories is widely accepted nor offers a completely satisfactory solution to the hard problem of consciousness.

8.3 Roger Penrose's Mind-Bending Theory of Reality

Nobel Laureate Roger Penrose's Orch OR theory of consciousness could change what we know about time, the universe, and reality by incorporating the physics of consciousness. Recent advancements in AI and robotics have led to significant breakthroughs, including a robot with a brain-on-a-chip in China and Skild AI's development of a universal robot brain for complex tasks. Meanwhile, Zen Technologies in India has introduced Prahasta, a four-legged robot with advanced AI for defense purposes. It is capable of navigating difficult terrains and carrying heavy loads.

References and Further Readings

Froes, M. M., Correia, A. H. P., Garcia-Abreu, J., Spray, D. C., Campos De Carvalho, A. C., and Neto, V. M. (1999). Gap-junctional coupling between neurons and astrocytes in primary central nervous system cultures. *Proceedings of the National Academy of Sciences*, **96**(13):7541–7546.

Hameroff, S. R. (1994). Quantum coherence in microtubules: A neural basis for emergent consciousness. *Journal of Consciousness Studies*, **1**:91–118.

Hameroff, S. R. (2006). The entwined mysteries of anesthesia and consciousness: Is there a common underlying mechanism? *Anesthesiology*, **105**:400–412.

Hameroff, S. R. (2021). 'Orch OR' is the most complete, and most easily falsifiable theory of consciousness. *Cognitive Neuroscience*, **12**(2):74–76.

Hameroff, S. R. (2022). Consciousness, cognition and the neural cytoskeleton: A new paradigm needed in neuroscience. *Frontiers in Molecular Neuroscience*, **15**:869935.

Hameroff, S., and Penrose, R. (1996). Orchestrated reduction of quantum coherence in brain microtubules: A model for consciousness. *Mathematics and Computers in Simulation*, **40**(3-4):453–480.

Hameroff, S. and Penrose, R. (2014). Consciousness in the universe: A review of the 'Orch OR, *Physics of Life Reviews*, **11**(1):39–78.

Penrose, R. (1989). *The Emperor's New Mind: Concerning Computers, Minds, and the Laws of Physics*. Oxford: Oxford University Press.

Penrose, R. (1996). On gravity's role in quantum state reduction. *General Relativity and Gravitation*, **28**:581–600.

Penrose, R. (2022). New physics for the Orch OR consciousness proposal. In *Consciousness and Quantum Mechanics*, S. Gao (Ed.). Oxford: Oxford University Press.

Penrose, R., and Hameroff, S. (1995). What gaps? Reply to Grush and Churchland. *Journal of Consciousness Studies*, **2**:98–112.

Rasmussen, S., Karampurwala, H., Vaidyanath, R., Jensen, K. S., and Hameroff, S. (1990). Computational connectionism within neurons: A model of cytoskeletal automata subserving neural networks. *Physica D: Nonlinear Phenomena*, **42**:428–449.

Chapter 9

Steps Toward Designing and Developing Biomimetic Humanoid Robots

9.1 Introduction

This chapter addresses how to design, fabricate, and operate biomimetic humanoid robots that look and behave similar to humans. Thus, it presents the steps toward designing and developing such robots, making them behave and look like normal humans.

This means soft movement of arms, legs, fingers, neck, waist, muscles, and other body parts. One must also design and develop clothing and soft wearable braces and suits for the humanoid robot. The design and development of biomimetic soft wearable robotic structures equipped with artificial muscles, such as ionic polymeric nanocomposites (IPNCs), shape-memory alloys (SMAs) artificial muscles, piezoelectric muscles, and possibly dielectric elastomer muscles, metal hydride muscles, electrostrictive and magnetostrictive muscles, and many more, have been considered in this chapter. These wearables and muscles will also have deformation sensing and activation capabilities.

This chapter also covers the possible design of the facial expressions of biomimetic humanoid robots using ionic polymer–metal composites (IPMCs) as artificial robotic bodies, skin faces, and muscles.

Biomimetic Humanoid Robots with Human Consciousness
Mohsen Shahinpoor

ISBN 978-981-5129-87-8 (Hardcover), 978-1-003-71373-9 (eBook)
www.jennystanford.com

DOI: 10.1201/9781003713739-9

One of the important areas of biomimetic robotics is creating facial expressions by moving various parts of the robot's facial muscles. This process is quite complicated but creates more human-like facial expressions. This chapter proposes a novel design for facial masks using IPMCs, as well as their fabrication.

A new family of IPMC sensors and actuators is proposed for flexible surface masks. The surface masks made with IPMCs will be experimentally capable of bending, rolling, turning, twisting, and simultaneous sensing. However, their sensing characteristics as a soft biomimetic surface actuator and sensor are shown to have great potential for ubiquitous robot–human interactions.

Upon various types of deformation, they are shown to generate unique output voltage signals and transient currents to be correlated to the surface mask feedback force. Furthermore, a flexible sheet of IPMC can be actuated simultaneously on the fly by a small power supply embedded in the humanoid robot. The active surface mask version of IPMC can be applied as smart skin for all body parts of the humanoid robot to develop human-like dexterous and soft manipulation. This chapter introduces a possible design for an IPMC robotic surface mask or muscles with soft actuation and sensing in a flexible surface configuration.

The human face possesses approximately 43 muscles and over 24 individual muscles on each side, possibly 30, depending on how they are counted. It takes 12 muscles to smile and 43 muscles to frown.

Shahinpoor et al. (1998) published an early version and review of IPMCs in 1998. See the research papers of Osada (1985, 1989, 1991, 1992, 1994, 1995), Oguro, Kawami, and Takenaka (1993), Oguro, Asaka, and Takenaka. (1993), and Shahinpoor and Kim (2000a, 2002) for their pioneering works (Shahinpoor, et al. 1998) the 1992–2000 period. The electrodynamics of cation generation and transportation in IPMCs is governed by the Poisson–Nernst–Planck field equations (Sparks, 1988). Biomimetic soft robotic actuation and sensing of these materials display artificial muscle behavior.

One of the important areas of biomimetic robotics is to create facial expressions by moving various parts of the robot's facial muscles. It is not very easy, but it does create more human-like facial expressions. A novel design for facial masks using IPMCs has been proposed. The surface masks made with IPMCs will be experimentally capable of bending, rolling, turning, twisting, and simultaneous sensing. However, their sensing characteristics as soft biomimetic surface actuators and sensors conclude that consciousness results from quantum effects on various types of deformation. They are shown to generate unique output voltage signals and transient currents to be correlated to the surface mask feedback force.

Furthermore, a small power supply embedded in the humanoid robot can simultaneously actuate a flexible sheet of IPMC on the fly. The active surface mask version of IPMC can be applied as smart skin to develop human-like dexterity and soft manipulation. This chapter introduces a possible design for an IPMC robotic surface mask or muscles with soft actuation and sensing in a flexible surface configuration (von Arx, 2018). The facial muscles are striated muscles that link the face's skin to the skull's bone to perform important functions for daily life (Fig. 9.1).

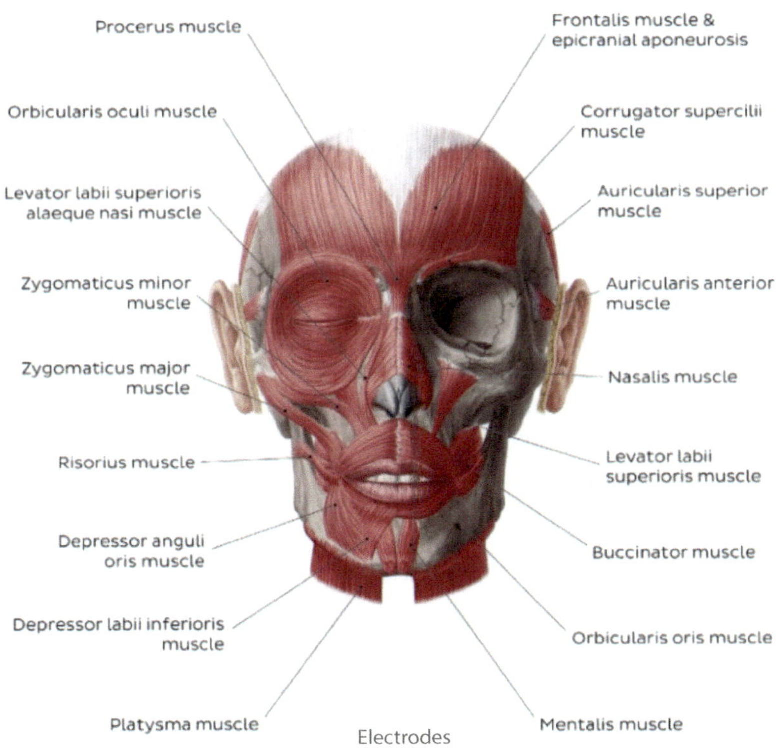

Figure 9.1 Facial muscles. Reprinted from Kenhub.com with permission.

A soft biomimetic surface mask made with IPMCs may be limited. IPMCs are relatively lightweight and have limited load-bearing capabilities. This limitation can restrict the transportation of significant payloads or equipment, which may be essential for certain applications. Several water molecules tend to attach or bond with cations. This is called the hydration number: 4 for Na^+ and 6 for Li^+. IPMCs typically require a voltage to induce deformation, which may demand substantial power sources or energy storage systems.

The chapter shows only the simulation results and does not provide a detailed theoretical analysis. One can use IPMCs with special ionic liquids that are not temperature sensitive. Temperature-insensitive actuators and sensors, such as piezoceramics (PZT), dielectric elastomers, or electromagnetic interactive actuator systems, may also be used with temperature limitations. SMAs may also be used for actuation and sensing.

9.2 Actuation and Sensing Configurations

IPMCs, as shown in Fig. 9.2, undergo cation migrations and rearrangements when subjected to either an electric field or a deformation field. Small samples of IPMC cantilevered strips (0.5 cm × 3 cm × 0.2 mm) can generate a tip-blocking force density equal to 40. Several water molecules tend to attach or bond with cations. This is called the hydration number: 4 for Na^+ and 6 for Li^+. This capability means they can lift an object 40 times their weight (Shahinpoor, 2020). For example, if the weight of an IPMC strip with a density of 2 g/cm^3 is 0.1 gmf, it can produce a tip-blocking force of about 4 gmf.

The Poisson–Nernst–Planck phenomena (Zheng and Wei, 2011; Song and Cao, 2018) govern such ion dynamics, which we will not consider theoretically in this chapter. Designing and operating a highly maneuverable robotic mask is desirable for many soft biomimetic humanoid robotic applications.

They have a force density of about 40 in a cantilever configuration with typical sizes of 10 mm × 30 mm × 0.2 mm, meaning they can generate a tip force of almost 40 times their weight in a cantilever mode. In this case, the weight of the cantilever is about 0.06 gmf based on a density of 2 gm/cm^3 for IPMCs, which means it can produce a tip-blocking force of 2.4 gmf.

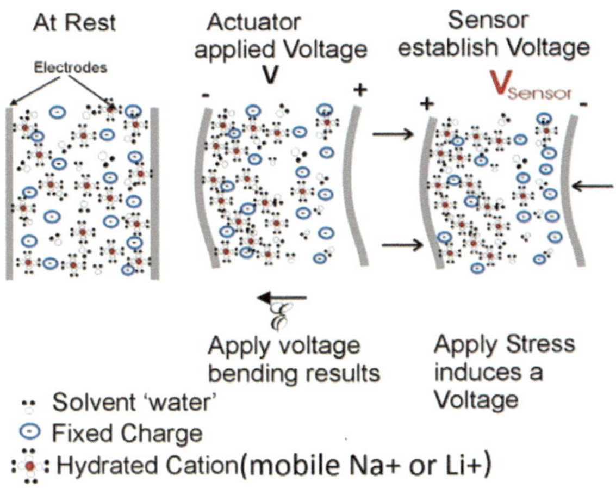

Figure 9.2 Essential mechanisms of actuation and sensing in IPMCs.

Thus, such a typical sample of IPMCs in actuation, sensing, and energy-harvesting modes has a very broad bandwidth to kilo HZ and higher. IPMCs were introduced in 1998 by Shahinpoor, Bar-Cohen, Xue, Simpson, and Smith (1997, 1998). However, the original idea of ionic polymer actuators and sensors goes back to the 1992–93 results by Osada et al. (1992), Oguro et al. (1992, 1993, 1995), Adolf et al. (1993), and Shahinpoor (2005).

The essential mechanism for IPMCs' actuation and sensing/energy-harvesting capabilities is the migration of cations (Na^+, Li^+), which are loosely adjoined to the underlying molecular network with anions, toward the cathode electrode and away from the anode electrode due to either an imposed electric field (actuation) or an imposed deformation field (sensing/energy harvesting).

Figure 9.2 graphically displays the actuation and sensing mechanisms in IPMC cantilever strips. Thus, this scenario forces the strip to bend accordingly.

Note that if the electrodes are not placed symmetrically on the IPMC strip, they can bend and twist. Figures 9.3a and 9.3b depict the deformation of small strips of IPMCs (4 cm × 1 cm × 0.2 mm) in a small electric field (of voltage 4 V) or 20 kV/m.

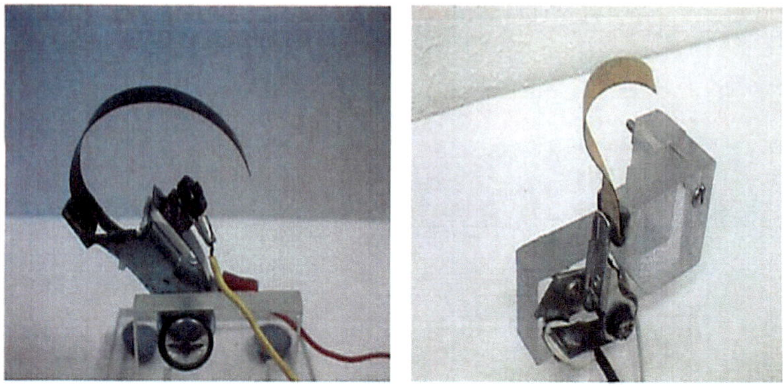

(a) (b)

Figure 9.3 Deformation [bending (a), bending and twisting (b)] of small strips of IPMCs (4 cm × 1 cm × 0.2 mm) in a small electric field of 20 kV/m.

Figures 9.4 and 9.5 depict typical graphical displays of the deformation of IPMC strips in a cantilever configuration versus voltage and current, both in actuation and sensing modes.

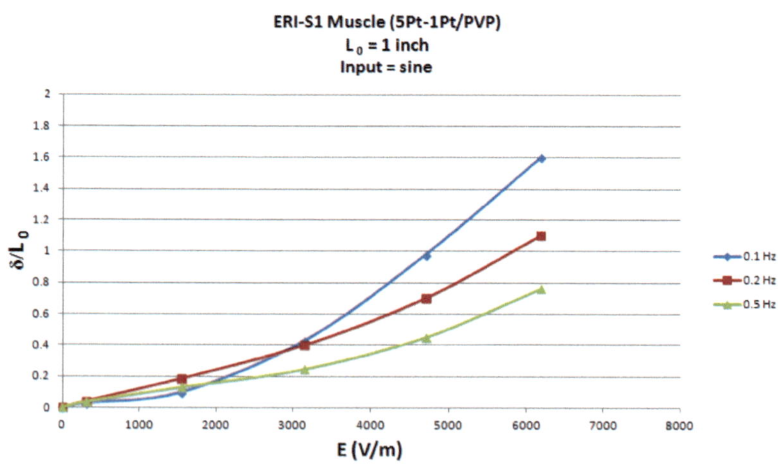

Figure 9.4 One-dimensional IPMC cantilever (1 cm × 4 cm × 0.2 mm) tip deflection versus the imposed sinusoidal electric field for three different frequencies (0.1–0.5 Hz).

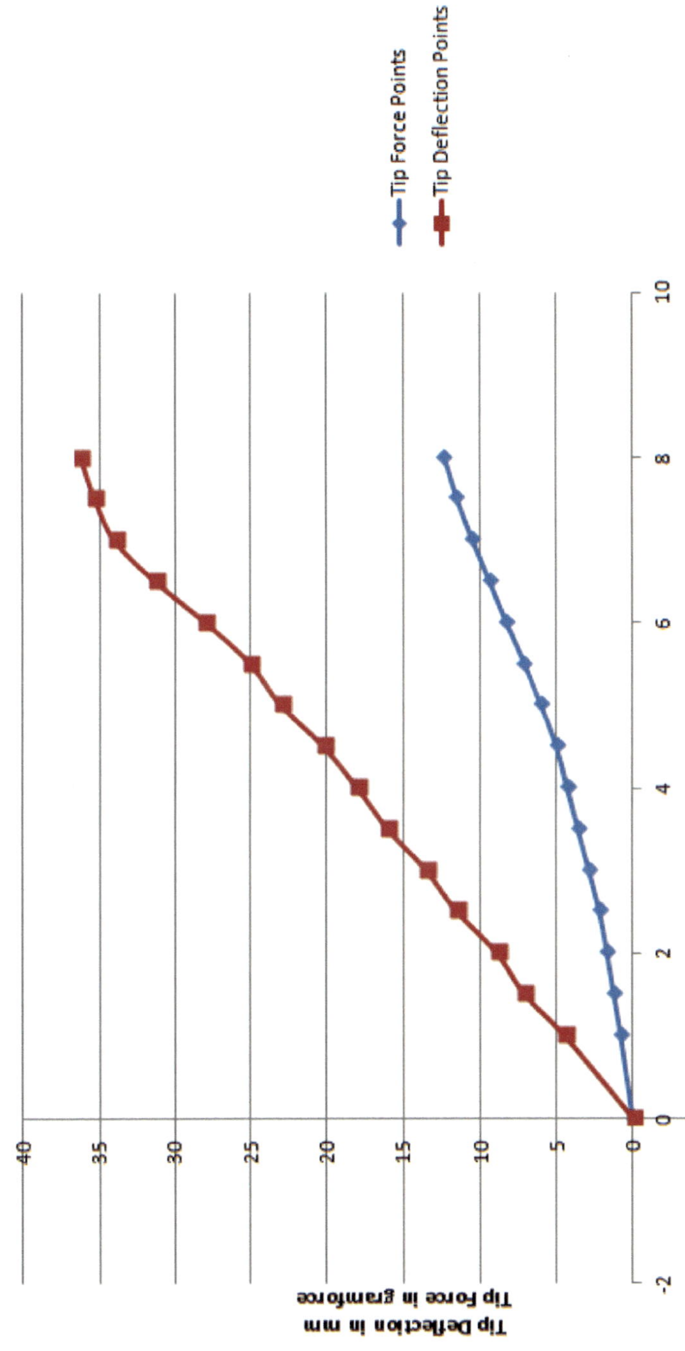

Figure 9.5 IPMC cantilever (1 cm × 4 cm × 0.2 mm) tip deflection and tip-blocking force versus the imposed step voltage.

Figure 9.6 displays an IPMC cantilever (1 cm × 4 cm × 0.2 mm) in a sensing/energy-harvesting mode showing tip deflection versus output oscillatory voltage signal.

IPMCs are two-phase systems comprising a polar medium such as water. They contain ion cluster networks surrounded by an ion-containing hydrophobic polytetrafluoroethylene (PTFE or Teflon).

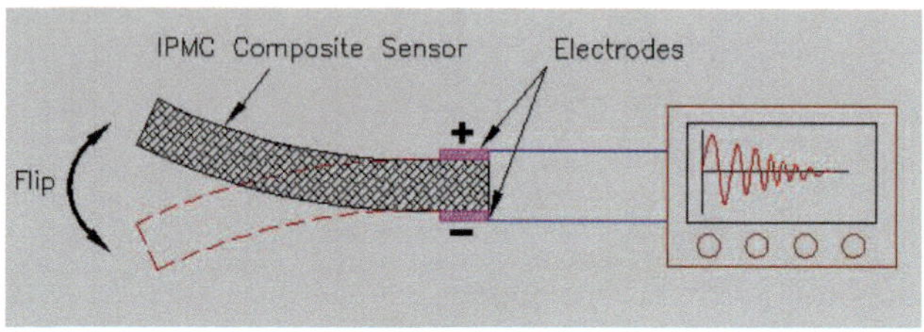

(a)

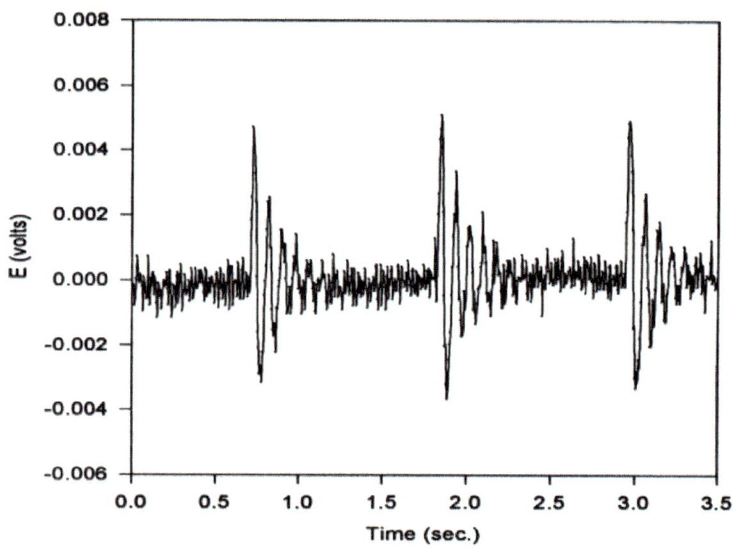

Dynamic sensing characteristics of an IPMC

(b)

Figure 9.6 IPMC cantilever (1 cm × 4 cm × 0.2 mm) in a sensing/energy-harvesting mode (a) showing tip deflection versus output oscillatory voltage signal (b).

The structural stability of the ion-containing polymer is provided by the PTFE backbones and the hydrophilic clusters, which facilitate the transport of ions and hydrated water molecules attached to them in the ionic polymer. These nanoclusters (3–5 nanometers) contain an interfacial region of hydrated, sulfonate-terminated perfluoro ether side chains surrounding a central region of polar fluids with cations such as Na^+ or Li^+.

As reported by Shahinpoor and (2005), Shahinpoor, Kim, and Mojarrad (2007), and Kim and Shahinpoor (2003), ion-containing polymers in a nanocomposite with a conductor phase can be manufactured three-dimensionally to any complex shape.

9.3 Novel Family of IPMCs as Active Robotic Surface Mask

Active robotic surface masks can be assembled, as shown in Fig. 9.7, to form an active stimuli-responsive surface mask with a feedback sensor. Figures 9.7a–d depict some configurations for the surface robotic mask operations.

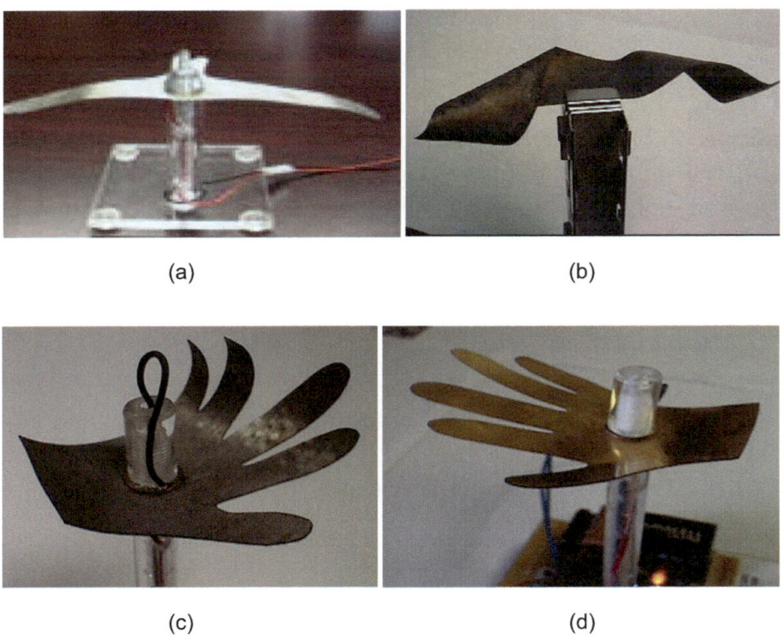

Figure 9.7 Configurations for surface mask operations.

9.4 IPMC Modeling and Simulation

Here we present a very brief review of the mathematical modeling of the dynamic deformation of the robotic mask. De Gennes et al. (2000) presented the first phenomenological theory for sensing and actuation in IPMCs. Asaka and Oguro (2000) discussed the bending of polyelectrolyte membrane–platinum composites by electric stimuli. They presented a theory on actuation mechanisms in IPMCs by considering the electro-osmotic drag term in transport equations. Let us now summarize the underlying principle of the IPNC actuation and sensing capabilities, which can be described by the standard Onsager formulation using linear irreversible thermodynamics.

When *static conditions* are imposed, a simple description of the *mechanoelectrical effect is possible based upon two forms of transport: ion transport (with a current density normal to the material) and solvent transport (with a flux; we can assume that this term is water flux*). The conjugate forces include the electric field and the pressure gradient. The resulting equation has the following concise form:

$$\underset{\sim}{J}(x, y, z, t) = \sigma \underset{\sim}{E}(x, y, z, t) - L_{12} \underset{\sim}{\nabla} p(x, y, z, t) \tag{9.1}$$

$$\underset{\sim}{Q}(x, y, z, t) = L_{21} \underset{\sim}{E}(x, y, z, t) - K \underset{\sim}{\nabla} p(x, y, z, t) \tag{9.2}$$

where σ and K are the material electric conductance and the Darcy permeability, respectively. A cross coefficient is usually $L = L_{12} = L_{21}$. The simplicity of Eqs. 9.1 and 9.2 provides a compact view of the underlying principles of actuation, transduction, and sensing of the IPNCs. When we measure the *direct* effect (actuation mode), we work (ideally) with electrodes impermeable to ion species flux, and thus we have $\underset{\sim}{Q}$ = zero. This gives

$$\underset{\sim}{\nabla} p(x, y, z, t) = \frac{L}{K} \underset{\sim}{E}(x, y, z, t) \tag{9.3}$$

This will, in turn, induce a curvature proportional to $\nabla p(x,y,z,t)$. De Gennes, Okumura, Shahinpoor, and Kim [17] fully derived and described the relationships between the curvature and pressure gradient. Let us mention that

$$(1/\rho_c) = M(E)/YI \tag{9.4}$$

where $M(E)$ is the local induced bending moment and is a function of the imposed electric field E; Y is Young's modulus (elastic stiffness) of the strip, which is a function of the hydration H of the ionic polymer–metal nanocomposite.

Note that I denotes the moment of inertia of the strip. Also note that locally $M(E)$ is related to the pressure gradient such that in a simplified scalar format:

$$\nabla p(x, y, z, t) = (2P/t^*) = (M/I) = Y/\rho_c = \mathrm{Y} \tag{9.5}$$

From Eq. (9.4) it is clear that the vectorial form of the curvature is related to the imposed electric field E by $\underset{\sim}{\kappa}_E = (L/KY)\,\underset{\sim}{E}$. Based on this simplified model, the tip bending deflection $a^{\cdot\cdot}{}_{\max}$ of an IPMC strip of length l_g should be almost linearly related to the imposed electric field because

$$\underset{\sim}{\kappa}_E \cong [2\underset{\sim}{\delta}_{\max} / (l_g^2 + \underset{\sim}{\delta}_{\max}^2)] \cong 2\underset{\sim}{\delta}_{\max} / l_g^2 \cong (\mathrm{L/KY})\underset{\sim}{E} \tag{9.6}$$

The experimental deformation characteristics of IPMCs (Shahinpoor, 2005; Shahinpoor, Kim, and Mojarrad, 2007) are consistent with the previous predictions obtained by the earlier linear irreversible thermodynamic formulation, which is also consistent with Eqs. 9.1 and 9.2 in the steady state conditions and has been used to estimate the value of the Onsager coefficient L to be of the order of 10^{-8} m^2/V-s.

Here we have used a low-frequency electric field to minimize the effect of loose water back diffusion under a step voltage or a DC electric field. Other parameters have been experimentally measured to be $K \sim 10^{-18}$ m^2/CP, $\sigma \sim 1$ A/mV or S/m.

Figure 9.8 depicts a more detailed dataset about the Onsager coefficient L.

On the other hand, one may consider charge transport modeling of actuation and sensing, which we refrain from performing and refer the reader to Bahramzadeh and Shahinpoor (2011a, 2011b) and Shahinpoor (2011).

Considering the angled or helical concept, the membranes are at angle α formation. As a result, tip displacement would be $\delta ver = \delta \sin\alpha$. In the case of a flat actuator, we have $\delta hor = \delta \cos\alpha$, and for the spiral, the rotation will be $\omega = 2\pi\delta \cos\alpha D$ in which D is the diameter of the actuator. Please note that a good amount of literature in this paper has already been published, as depicted in the list of references. However, the unique idea of the possibility of making an active robotic surface mask with IPMCs is the essential originality of the current paper. Eventually, an active surface mask version will be built from IPMCs, and its deformation and sensing capabilities will be demonstrated.

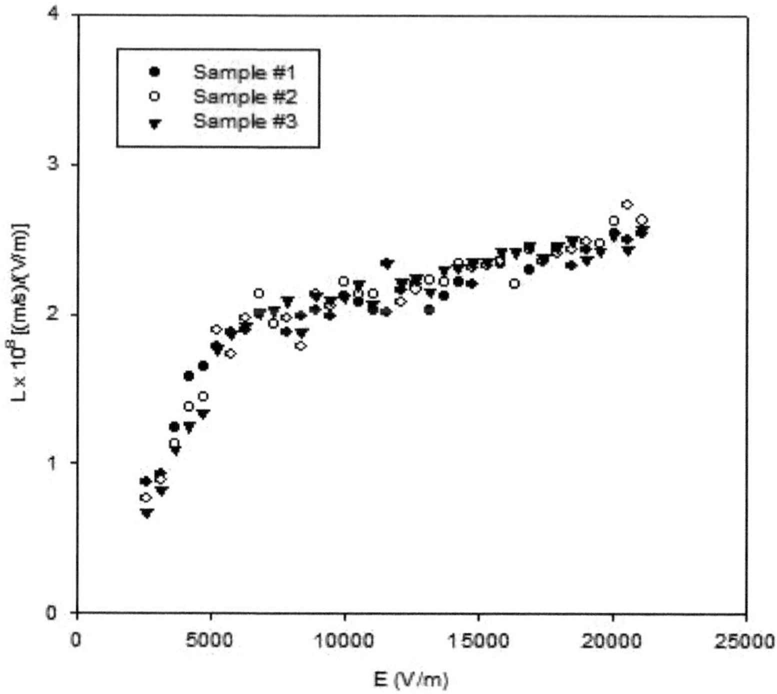

Figure 9.8 Experimental determination of the Onsager coefficient L_{ij}.

The chapter presents a potential novel design for an active robotic stimuli-responsive surface mask made with IPMC artificial muscles, a concept that is yet to be realized. When constructed with IPMCs, this surface mask is expected to demonstrate bending, rolling, turning, twisting, and simultaneous sensing capabilities. It is important to note that while some materials are referenced from previous works, the unique idea of an active robotic surface mask with IPMCs is the key originality of this chapter.

In this chapter, we have introduced many smart materials and artificial muscles that can be employed during the preparation of humanoid robots as well as help with robotic surgery to enhance the quality of advanced robotic applications such as surgical operations with robotic structures and to provide force, haptic and kinesthetic feedback to surgeons during robotic surgery. Smart materials are generally defined as multifunctional materials that can perform sensing, energy harvesting, and actuation in addition to providing additional signals of their environmental disturbances and changes. Due to the requirement of biocompatibility, not all smart materials can be easily used in robotic surgery.

For example, piezoceramic materials such as PZT (lead zirconate titanate) are not recommended for use in a biomedical environment due to the presence of lead-related materials.

However, piezo polymeric materials such as polyvinylidene fluoride or PVDFT may be used. Here we introduce biomimetic IPMCs as electroactive polymers (EAPs) and artificial muscles, conductive and conjugated polymers as electroactive polymers and artificial muscles, metal hydride artificial muscles, chemo electromechanical contractile artificial muscles such as polyacrylonitrile fibrous gels (PAN gels), biopolymeric artificial muscles such as chitosan gels, magnetic gels, SMAs, and shape-memory polymers (SMPs) to robotic surgery and discuss possible applications of other multifunctional smart materials and artificial muscles to robotic surgery.

9.5 Applications of IPMCs to Humanoid Robots

9.5.1 Brief Introduction to IPMCs as Multifunctional Materials

Ionic polymer metal composites (IPMCs) or ionic polymer conductor nanocomposites (IPCNCs) are chemically plated ionic polymers manufactured by an oxidation–reduction (REDOX) operation with a noble metal such as platinum or gold to keep them biocompatible. Refer to a seminal publication by Shahinpoor, Kim, and Mojarrad (2007) for a comprehensive coverage of various properties and applications of such materials.

The basic material is commonly ionic Teflon with relatively few fixed ionic groups. Once an electric field is imposed on such a network, the conjugated and hydrated cations rearrange to accommodate the local electric field. Thus, the network deforms; in the simplest of cases, such as in thin membrane sheets, spectacular bending is observed (Fig. 9.3) under small electric fields such as 10s of volts per millimeter. Typical experimental deflection curves are depicted in Figs. 9.9 and 9.10a,b.

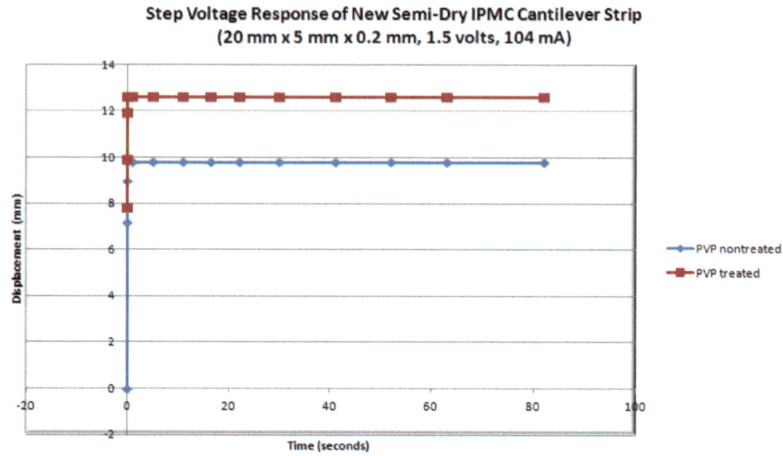

Figure 9.9 Step response displacement characteristics of IPMNC samples (£: arc length, L_o: effective beam length) and L_o = 1.5 inch (bottom).

Once an electric field is imposed on an IPMC cantilever, in the cantilever polymeric network, the hydrated cations migrate to accommodate the local electric field. This creates a pressure gradient across the thickness of the beam, and thus the beam undergoes bending deformation (Fig. 9.10) under small electric fields such as 10s of volts per millimeter.

Figure 9.11 depicts typical force and deflection characteristics of cantilever samples of IPMNC artificial muscles.

IPMCs can generate electrical power like an electromechanical battery if flexed, bent, twisted, torsioned, or squeezed. Keshavarzi, Shahinpoor, Kim, and Lantz (1999) applied the transduction capability of IPMC to the measurement of blood pressure, pulse rate, and rhythm measurement using thin sheets of IPMCs during surgery.

Motivated by the idea of measuring pressure in the human spine, Ferrara, Shahinpoor, Kim, Schreyer, Keshavarzi, Benzel, and Lantz (1999) applied pressure across the thickness of an IPMC strip while measuring the output voltage.

Typically, flexing such material in a cantilever form sets it into a damped vibration mode that can generate a similar damped signal in the form of electrical power (voltage or current), as shown in Fig. 9.11.

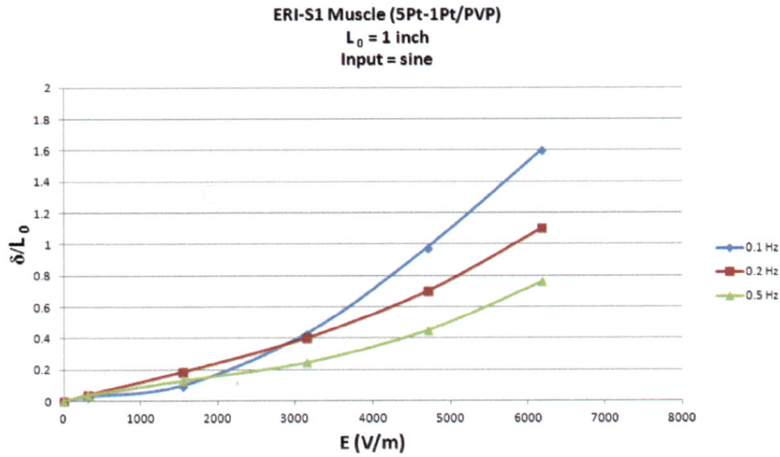

(a)

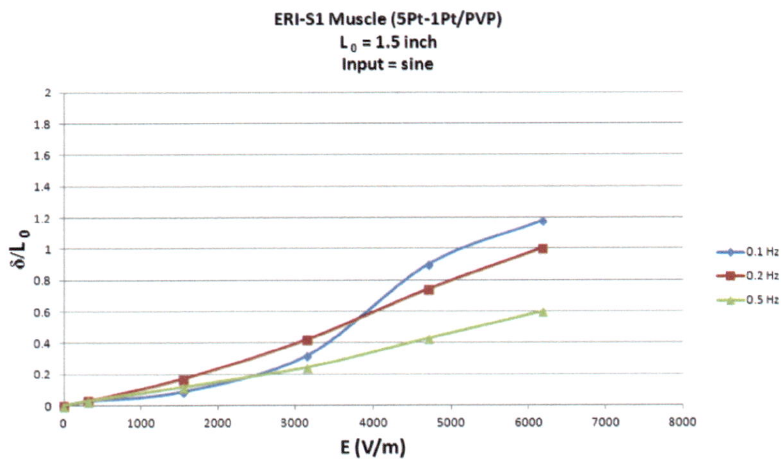

(b)

Figure 9.10 Displacement characteristics of an IPMC, ERI-S1: (a) L_o = 1.0 inch and (b) L_o = 1.5 inch (δ: arc length, L_o: effective cantilever).

The experimental results showed that almost a linear relationship exists between the voltage output and the imposed displacement of the tip of the IPMNC sensor. As far as force generation is concerned, IPMNCs generally have a very high force. Figure 9.12 displays the cantilever and load cell configuration for measuring the tip-blocking force of typical samples of IPMNCs.

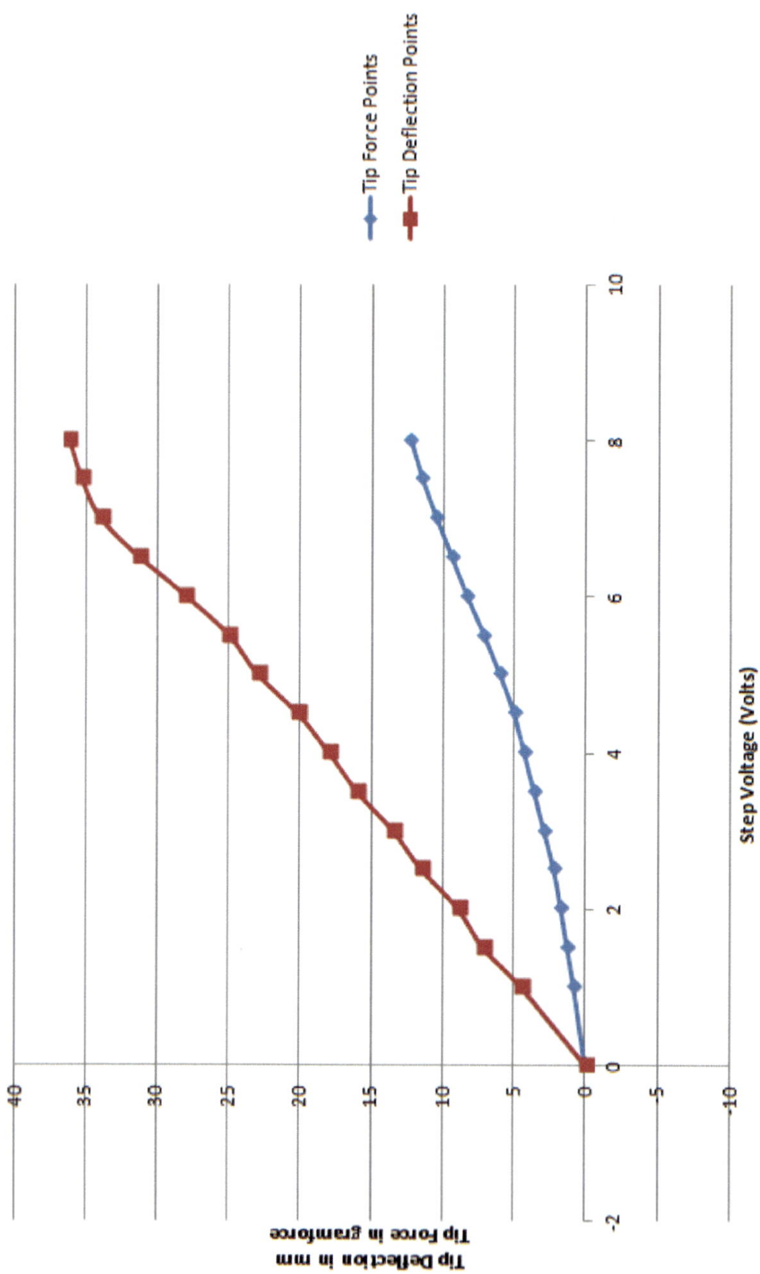

Figure 9.11 Variation of tip-blocking force and the associated deflection if allowed to move versus the applied step voltage for a 1 cm × 5 cm × 0.3 mm IPMNC Pt–Pd sample in a cantilever configuration.

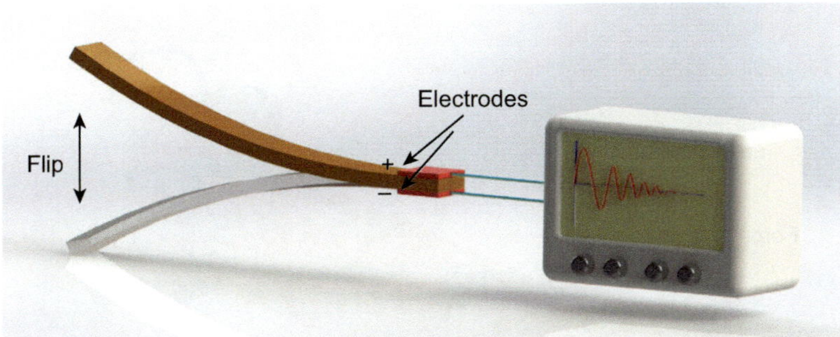

Figure 9.12 IPMC configuration in sensing and actuation.

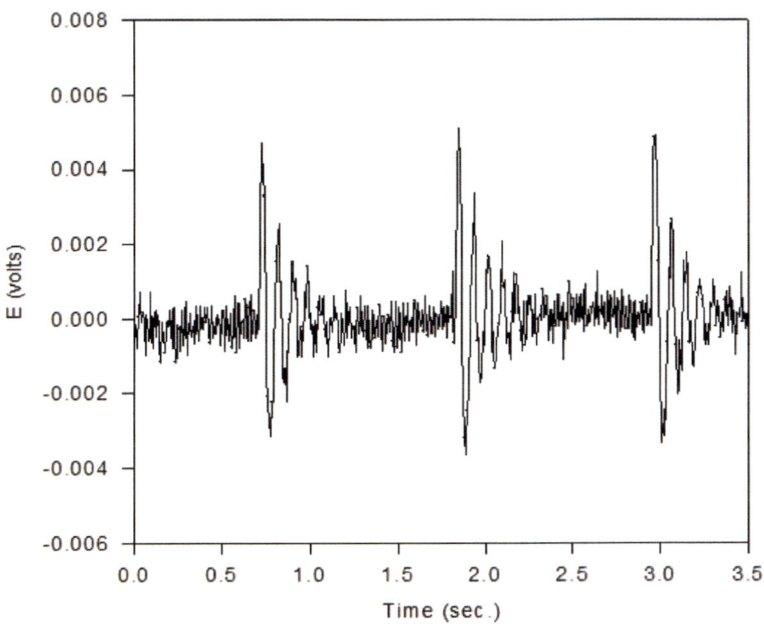

Figure 9.13 A typical voltage response of an IPMC strip (1 cm × 4 cm × 0.2 mm) under oscillatory mechanical excitations.

Figure 9.14 Cantilever and load cell configuration for measuring the tip-blocking force of IPMNC samples.

9.6 Feasibility of Providing Kinesthetic Force Feedback to Humanoid Robots by Electroactive Polymeric Sensors (IPMCs)

One can integrate IPMCs as electroactive polymeric nanosensors and nanoactuators with advanced robotic applications such as surgical end-effectors, like intuitive grasping forceps, to provide kinesthetic force/torque feedback to surgeons during robotic surgery. The application employs IPMCs as surgeons' feel/haptic sensors for the kinesthetics of internal organs in interaction with various advanced robotic applications such as surgical robotic end-effectors. The application integrates the kinesthetic force feedback signals with joysticks and foot pedals for surgeons to receive kinesthetic force feedback, on the fly, during robotic surgery.

In achieving these objectives, suitable IPMC strips and loops are attached to the end-effectors and wired through the end-effectors to the electronics providing kinesthetic force or torque feedback to surgeons. To provide that force or torque sensation to the surgeons, the specific IPMC sensor, say a tip bender, will be subjected to a bending force to create an output signal in millivolts. This signal will then be amplified electronically and fed into a linear actuator or servomotor to generate the same force or torque and affect the operational forces/torques in the joysticks or foot pedals used by surgeons.

If the tip of a 3 cm × 1 cm × 0.2 mm IPMC strip experiences a blocking force by contacting an organ/tissue during surgery, it will develop a blocking kinesthetic force of about 20 g. The same strip in a cantilever configuration, if moved by the kinesthetics of internal organs and end-effectors during surgery, will generate about 4 millivolts, which can be correlated to the kinesthetic forces of the internal organ movement during robotic surgery. Our experimentally obtained data indicate that IPMCs may provide dynamic feedback of kinesthetic forces to surgeons during surgery and gradually train surgeons to feel out the kinesthetics and kinesthetic forces and torques applied to internal organs and tissues during surgery. The fact that IPMCs can work well in the wet human body environment during robotic surgery will be an advantage for developing this technology.

The IPMCs are biocompatible because they are Teflon-based plastics in a nanocomposite form with a noble metal such as platinum or gold. They are electrically safe and self-powered and do not need any source of voltage or current to provide kinesthetic force feedback in millivolts, and they are autoclavable and hardly wear out. IPMCs also work well in an electrocautery environment because IPMCs are ionic Teflon with platinum electrodes that can withstand the high temperature of cauterization without melting or burning during surgery. The current advanced robotic applications such as surgical systems evolved from the laparoscopic advanced robotic applications such as surgical procedures and made it possible for surgeons to perform surgery away from the patient with much more concentration and ease. However, in this transition, the surgeons lost the sensation of tissues and organs and the kinesthetic force feedback during surgery.

It is interesting to note that even during laparoscopic surgery, surgeons can still feel and sense the tissues and organs they are handling and operating on with laparoscopic/endoscopic tools and feel the kinesthetic forces at work. However, the kinesthetic force feedback was replaced with visual feedback during robotic surgery.

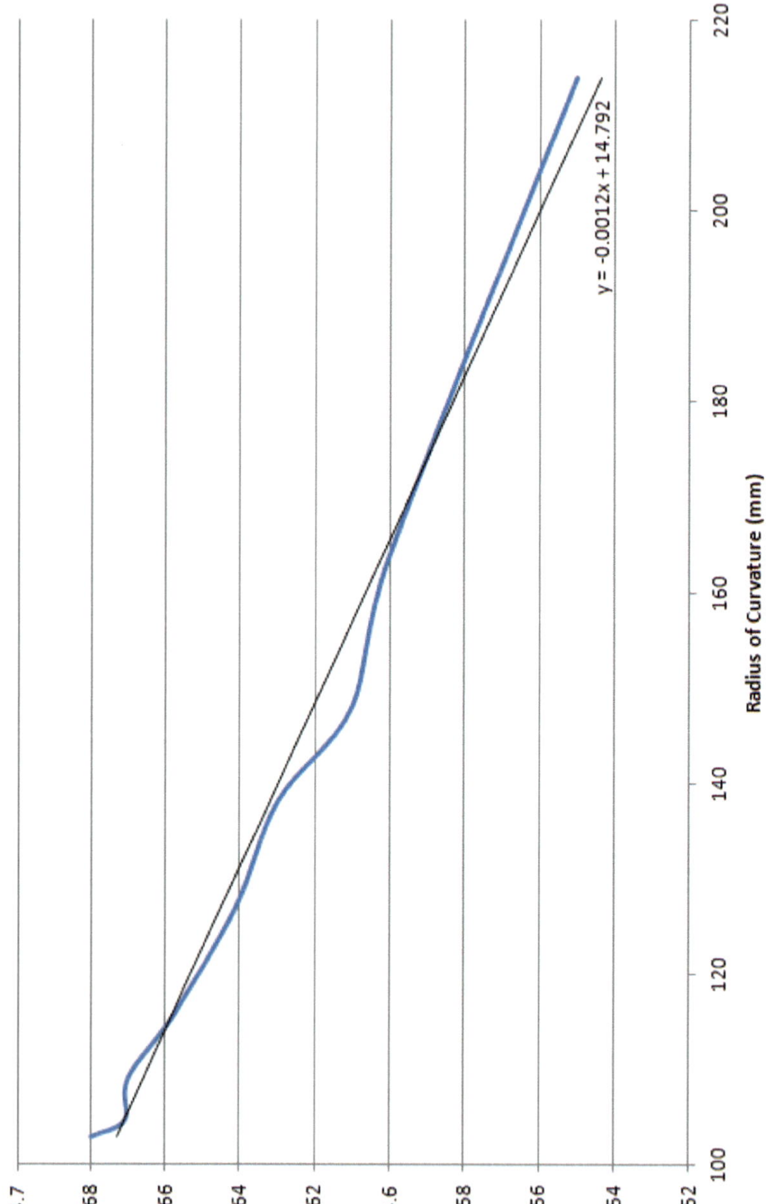

Figure 9.15 Typical sensing response of IPMC strips in bending. The sensing response is in millivolts, which can be correlated to tip the kinesthetic force.

It is to be noted that some of this kinesthetic force feedback was lost in the transition from open to laparoscopic surgery due to trocar friction and varying lever arms, anyway. However, with smart materials such as IPMCs and appropriate calibration and tuning, one may be able to recover the kinesthetic force feedback during surgery. IPMCs are great for such robotic force feedback applications because they work perfectly well in the wet human body environment and generate millivolt-level sensing signals for kinesthetic force feedback. Figure 9.15 depicts the typical sensing output of IPMC strips in bending and how the bending force is measured by a load cell.

Note that the output voltage of an IPMC strip is a function of the curvature and its rate of change. While an output voltage of 1–2 mV can be derived by dynamic sensing from a sample with dimensions of 10 mm × 30 mm × 0.2 mm, the achievable voltage is smaller in quasi-static sensing case using the same sample. Figure 9.16 depicts the experimental measurement of force by IPMC strips.

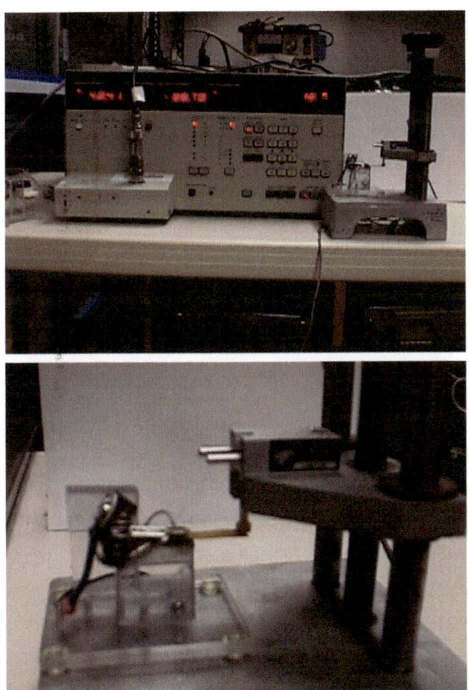

Figure 9.16 Experimental setup for the measurement of bending force and curvature of IPMC cantilever strips using a high-resolution load cell and impedance analyzer.

IPMCs generate signals in the range of a few millivolts in the presence of deformation. IPMC sensors have proven to be highly sensitive to the applied deformation over a large frequency range. Figure 9.17 shows the general response of an IPMC sensor to fast excitations followed by slow bending accompanied by high-frequency noise.

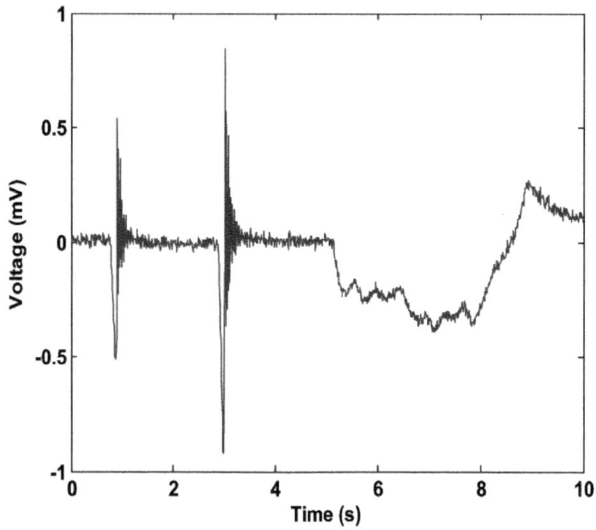

Figure 9.17 General response of IPMC sensors to fast excitations followed by slow bending.

To obtain kinesthetic force feedback information from IPMCs, two calibration procedures are required. To this end, the calibration of the deformation of the IPMC sensor for the generated signal and then the bending force of the IPMC actuator can be easily related to the observed deformation.

It should be emphasized that the results of using IPMCs as kinesthetic force feedback to surgeons during robotic surgery or contact between humanoid robots and humans are very promising in that kinesthetic force feedback may be possible using IPMCs in bending, twisting, looping, or compression loading.

In the next section, we will elaborate on some additional experimental data that may help achieve our objectives.

9.7 Integrating IPMCs with Robotic End-Effectors for Kinesthetic Force Feedback to Humanoid Robots in Touching and Contacting Human Flesh or Organs by Electroactive Polymeric Sensors

Ionic polymeric nanocomposites with distributed nanosensing and nanoactuation can be employed to provide kinesthetic force feedback to humanoid robots. Several apparatuses for modeling and testing the various IPMC artificial muscles are described to show the viability of the application of electroactive. IPMCs are used to provide users with kinesthetic force feedback.

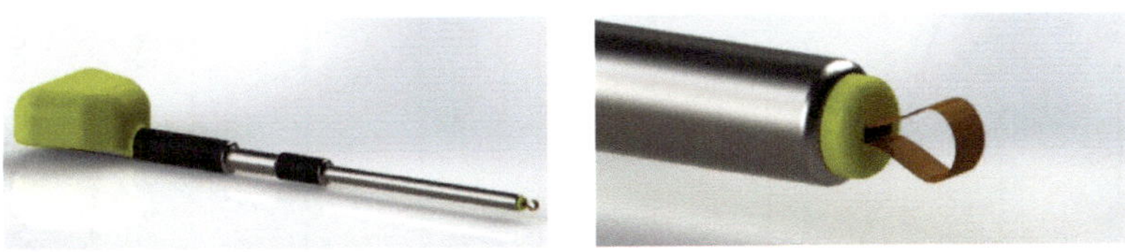

(a) (b)

Figure 9.18 Kinesthetic force feedback loop for haptic interaction with bodily organs and tissues.

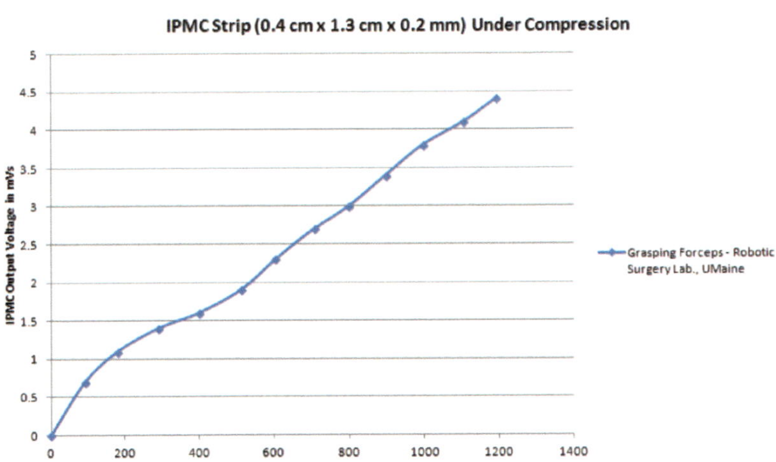

Figure 9.19 Typical strong sensing signal in millivolt (mV) out of the IPMC strip in compression mode (direct compression of IPMCs with a normal load).

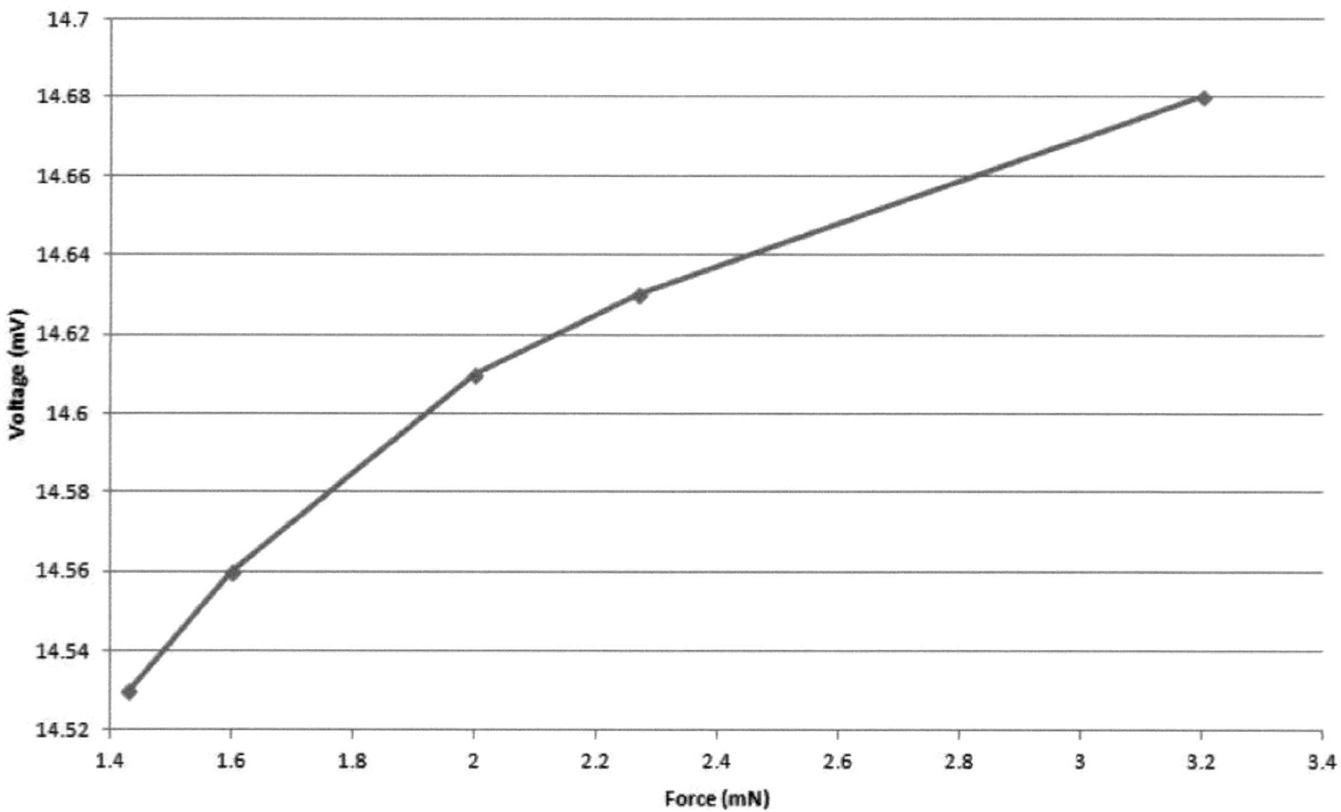

Figure 9.20 Typical strong sensing signal in millivolt (mV) out of the IPMC strip in compression mode (direct compression of IPMCs with a normal load).

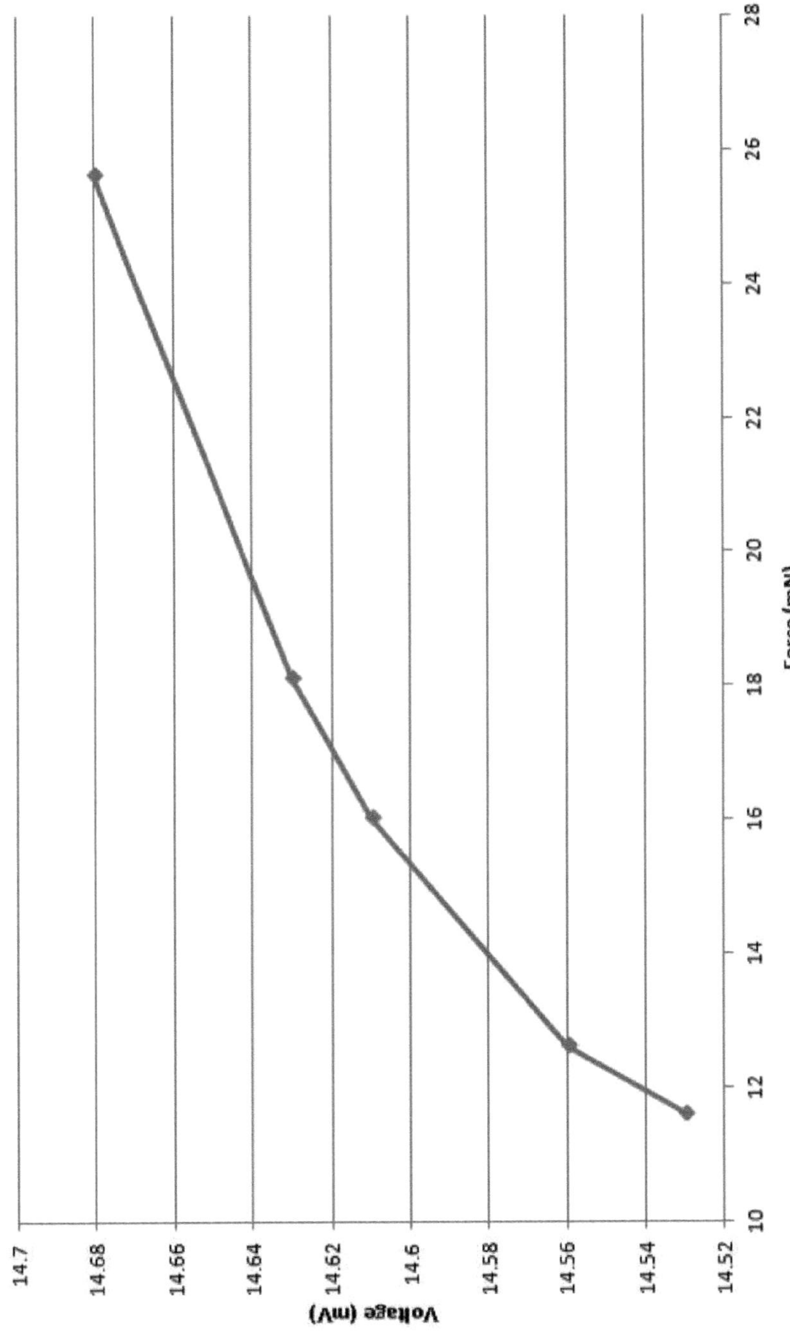

Figure 9.21 Typical force sensing signal in milli-Newton (mN) out of the IPMC strip (top: 10 mm × 30 mm × 0.2 mm; bottom: 10 mm × 30 mm × 0.4 mm).

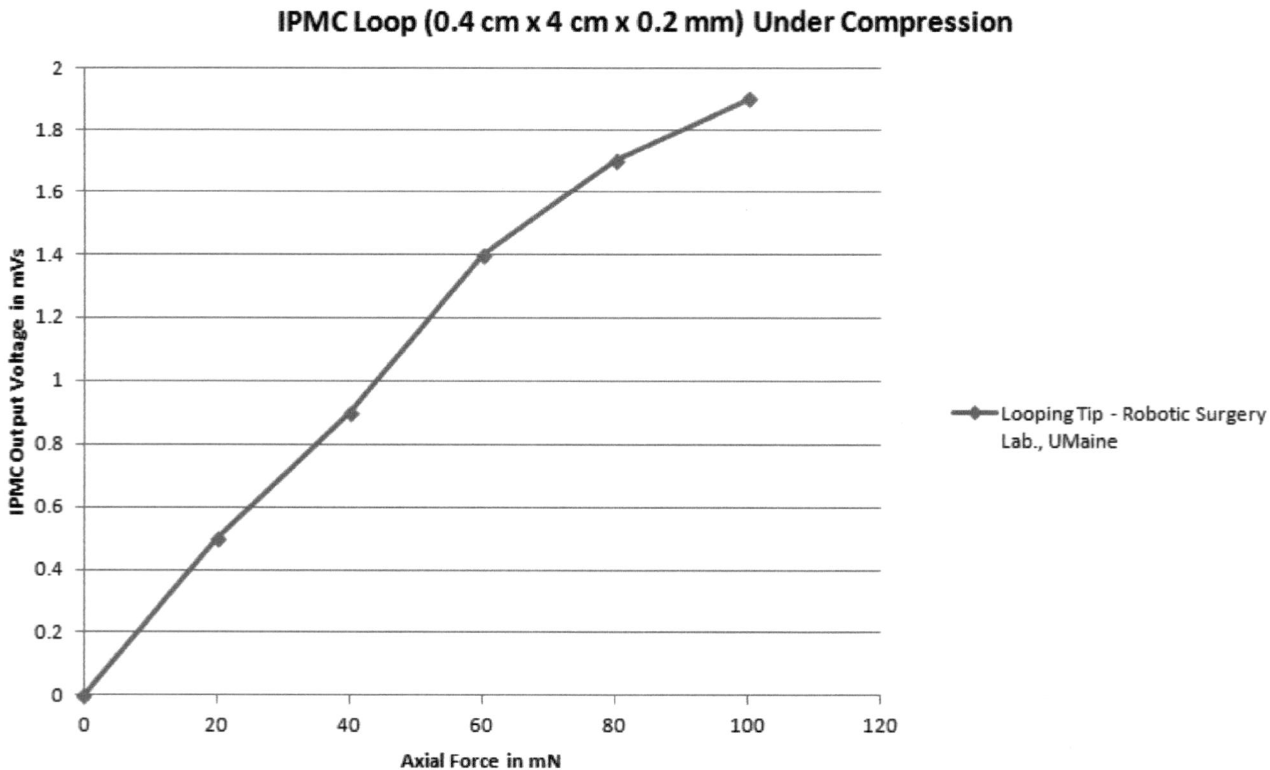

Figure 9.22 Typical sensing signal in millivolt (mV) out of the IPMC in a loop configuration (loop deformation of IPMCs due to kinesthetic interaction of da Vinci end-effectors and plastic body organs). The voltage output can be correlated with the kinesthetic normal force applied to the strip.

One can also explore the bending and loop configurations for IPMCs (Figs. 9.18a,b) to interact with bodily organs and tissues. The bending of IPMC strips or the deformation of the loop provides a kinesthetic force signal that can be correlated to the force exerted.

Kinesthetic force feedback signals in a few millivolt range can be generated by touching soft plastic organs and can be correlated with the grasping forces by users.

Figures 9.19, 9.20, and 9.21 show some typical sensing signals out of the IPMC strip attached to advanced humanoid robotic applications in compression, bending, and loop configurations.

By compression we mean direct compression of IPMCs with a normal load such as in grasping forceps. Note that the voltage output can be correlated with kinesthetic normal force applied to the strip, electronically, as described below.

The relation between the bending moment M and the radius of curvature ρ of the neutral axis of the beam is as follows:

$$M = \frac{EI}{\rho}$$

where ρ is the radius of curvature and $I = \frac{1}{12} b \cdot h^3$. Note that based on the dimensions given in Fig. 9.6 (10 mm × 30 mm × 0.2 mm), $I = \frac{1}{12} \times 0.01 \times 0.0002^3 = 6.67 \times 10^{-15} m^4$ and with E = 1200 MPa for IPMC, and considering pure bending, we can calculate the required force for bending as $F = \frac{M}{L} = \frac{M}{0.03} = 33.3M$. Thus, based on the curvatures measured in Fig. 9.22, one can calculate the corresponding M and calculate the equivalent force experienced by bending the IPMC during surgery. For example, for ρ = 100 mm, M = 81×10^{-6} Nm and $F = 2.74 \times 10^{-3}$ N = 2.74 mN.

Thus, in order to make robotic surgery more intelligent and haptics-based, one should utilize advanced robotic applications such as surgical robotic end-effectors with smart nanocomposites such as IPMCs capable of force, haptic, and impedance sensing, which can be fed back to the surgeon. Thus, one will be able to correlate the signal out of the IPMC mounted on an end-effector to the kinesthetic force experienced by the IPMC strip. In order to translate the kinesthetic force feedback voltage signal from the IPMC strips to the kinesthetic force feedback to surgeons' hands during surgery, the voltage signal will be amplified electronically and applied to a servo integrated with joysticks to simultaneously provide the surgeons with the kinesthetic force feedback during surgery. For other kinesthetic configurations of IPMCs such as bending kinesthetic or loop kinesthetic, similar operations are applied. Figure 9.23 depicts the general experimental setup to correlate the sensing voltage signal coming off the bending or loop configurations of IPMCs in kinesthetic interaction with end-effectors and organs with the actual kinesthetic forces at work in Newton.

The IPMC bending sensor is attached to a cantilever beam so that the IPMC strip follows the imposed curvature of the beam shape. One end of the sample is clamped to the fixed end of the beam. Both the curvature and the rate of change of curvature are controlled using a servomotor, which bends the tip of the beam. An AX-12 Dynamixel servomotor with a step size of 0.29° was used to control the tip bending of a cantilever beam. The servo is also controlled through LabVIEW software. For voltage measurement, an NI-9219 A/D data acquisition module was used, and the data was processed in LabVIEW. To reduce the signal noise, a bandpass filter was used to filter low (below 0.01 Hz) and high (higher than 5 Hz) frequencies. The output voltage was amplified by a factor of 10 for easier data processing. To calibrate the sensor, different curvature inputs were applied to the cantilever at different rates.

Incorporating haptic force feedback may also enable the expansion of robotic surgery to other advanced robotic applications, such as surgical procedures like intraocular surgery or microsurgery, that are difficult to perform without a sense of touch or force feedback integrated with advanced robotic applications such as surgical robotic end-effectors. These robotic end-effectors, such as needle holders, grasping forceps, dissecting forceps, scissors, biopsy spoons, and retractors, as well as electro-advanced robotic applications such as surgical tips and retractors and uterine manipulators, play a fundamental role in robotic surgery.

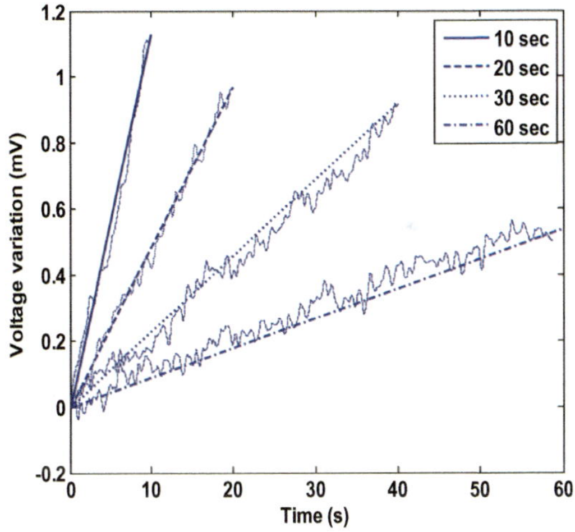

(a)

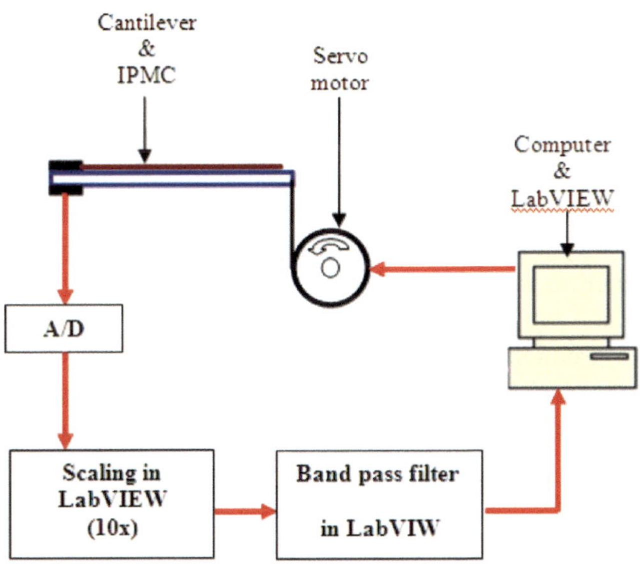

(b)

Figure 9.23 (a) Schematic of experimental setup to measure the dynamic kinesthetic output voltage of IPMC strips in bending and electronically correlate that to the forces generated via torque measurements of the servomotors. (b) Ramp response of IPMC sensor at four different curvature rates of 10 s, 20 s, 40 s, and 60 s. The IPMC strip was dynamically bent for an amount of 10 mm, which is equal to a 500 mm radius of curvature.

9.8 Help for the Robotic Surgery

Humanoid robots can be trained to directly perform robotic surgery and reduce or eliminate current robotic surgery procedures that lack the actual touch and tactile sensing of the organs by the surgeon while performing surgery and be content with visual feedback and commanding the robotic surgical tools to operate. Advanced robotic applications such as surgical slave robots perform the surgery on a patient's body. The instrument holder is in the workspace of the slave robot, and the robotic arms can easily pick up any of the advanced robotic applications such as surgical instruments. The robotic end-effectors are equipped with haptic feedback sensors, and force and optical sensors, which help detect forces or disturbances experienced by the robotic end-effectors by engagement with the human anatomy.

A robot's facial expression is very important in creating a lookalike humanoid robot. However, with IPMCs working as sensors and actuators, one can create realistic human-like facial expressions by integrating IPMCs into the facial expressions of humanoid robots. With smart materials such as IPMCs and appropriate calibration and tuning, one may recover the kinesthetic force feedback during surgery. IPMCs are great for robotic force feedback applications because they work perfectly well in the wet human body environment and generate millivolt-level sensing signals for kinesthetic force feedback.

In a groundbreaking advancement in robotics, researchers in Tokyo unveiled lab-grown human skin for robots! This living skin can repair itself and integrate sensory functions such as touch and temperature detection, pushing the boundaries of what is possible in the field of artificial intelligence. Some of the challenges these innovative scientists faced include maintaining a sterile environment and manipulating delicate biological tissues during development.

References and Further Readings

Adolf, D., Shahinpoor, M., Segalman, D., and Witkowski, W. (1993). US Patent Office, US Patent No. 5,250,167, Issued October 5, 1993.

Asaka, K., and Oguro, K. J. (2000). Bending of polyelectrolyte membrane platinum composites by electric stimuli: Part II. Response kinetics. *Journal* of *Electroanalytical Chemistry,* **480**:186–198

Asanuma, H., Asaka, K., Sato, S., and Poubel, L. P. (2014). Actuator vibration system. Japanese Patent No. 5594690, Issued August 15, 2014.

Bahramzadeh, Y., and Shahinpoor, M. (2011a). A review of ionic polymeric soft actuators and sensors. *Soft Robotics*, **1**(1): 38–52.

Bahramzadeh, Y., and Shahinpoor, M. (2011b). Dynamic curvature sensing employing ionic-polymer–metal composite sensors. *Smart Materials and Structures*, **20**(9). DOI: 10.1088/0964-1726/20/9/094011.

Bahramzadeh, Y., and Shahinpoor, M. (2012). Ionic polymer-metal composites (IPMCs) as dexterous manipulators and tactile sensors for minimally invasive robotic surgery, Proceedings Volume 8340, Electroactive Polymer Actuators and Devices (EAPAD) 2012; 834020. https://doi.org/10.1117/12.917432. Event: SPIE Smart Structures and Materials + Nondestructive Evaluation and Health Monitoring, 2012, San Diego, California, United States.

De Gennes, P. G., Okumura, K., Shahinpoor, M., and Kim, K. J. (2000). Mechanoelectric effects in ionic gels. *Europhysics Letters*, **50**(4): 513–518.

Doi, M., Matsumoto, M., and Hirose, Y. (1992). Deformation of ionic polymer gels by electric fields. *Macromolecules*, **25**:5504–5511.

Kim, K. J., and Shahinpoor, M. (2002). A novel method of manufacturing three-dimensional ionic polymer-metal composites (IPMC's) biomimetic sensors, actuators and artificial muscle. *Polymer*, **43**(3): 797–802.

Kim, K. J., and Shahinpoor, M. (2003). Ionic polymer–metal composites: II. Manufacturing techniques, Smart materials and structures. *Smart Materials and Structures*, **12**(1): 65–79.

Maksimkin, A. V., Dayyoub, T., Telyshev, D. V., and Gerasimenko, A. Y. (2022). Electroactive polymer-based composites for artificial muscle-like actuators: A review. *Nanomaterials*, **12**:2272.

Oguro, K., Asaka, K., and Takenaka, H. (1993). *Proceedings of the 4th International Symposium of Micro Machines and Human Science*, Nagoya, pp. 38–40.

Oguro, K., Kawami, Y., and Takenaka, H. (1992). *Journal of Micromachine Society*, **5**:27–30.

Oguro, K., Kawami, Y., and Takenaka, H. (1993). US Patent Office, US Patent No. 5,268,082, Issued December 7, 1993.

Osada, Y., Okuzaki, H., and Hori, H. (1992). *Nature*, **355**:242–244.

Poubel, L. P., Sato, S., Ishibashi, S., Asanuma, H., and Asaka, K. (2010). *Proceedings of the 18th Materials and Processing Conference of JSME (M&P2010)*, November 27–28, Tokyo.

Segalman, D. J., Witkowski, W. R., Adolf, D. B., and Shahinpoor, M. (1992). *International Journal of Smart Material and Structures*, **1**:95–100.

Shahinpoor, M. (1992). *International Journal of Smart Material and Structures*, **1**:91–94.

Shahinpoor, M. (2003). *Electrochimica Acta*, **48**(14–16):2343–2353. Shahinpoor, M., and Kim, K. J. (2001). *International Journal of Smart Materials and Structures*, **10**(4):819–833.

Shahinpoor, M. (2005). Soft plastic robots and artificial muscles. *International Journal of Advanced Robotic Systems*, **2**(2):161–174.

Shahinpoor, M. (2009). *Intelligent Robotic Systems: Modeling & Simulation*, 2nd edition. Albuquerque, New Mexico: ERI Press.

Shahinpoor, M. (2011). Biomimetic robotic venus flytrap (Dionaea Muscipula Ellis) made with ionic polymer metal composites (IPMCs), *Bioinspiration and Biomimetics*, **6**:046004, pp. 1–11, Institute of Physics (IOP) Publishing Ltd., London, UK.

Shahinpoor, M., and Kim, K. J. (2002). *Actuators and Sensors A, Physical*, **96**(2/3):125–132.

Shahinpoor, M., and Kim, K. J. (2002). *Applied Physics Letters*, **80**(18):3445–3447.

Shahinpoor, M., Bar-Cohen, Y., Simpson, J. O., and Smith, J. (1998). *International Journal of Smart Materials and Structures*, **7**(6):R15–R30.

Shahinpoor, M., Bar-Cohen, Y., Xue, T., Simpson, J. O., and Smith, J. (1998). *Proceedings of SPIE's 5th Annual International Symposium on Smart Structures and Materials*, March 1–5, 1998, San Diego, California.

Shahinpoor, M., Kim, K. J., and Mojarrad, M. (2007). *Artificial Muscles: Applications of Advanced Polymeric Nano Composites*, 1st edition. London: CRC Press, Taylor & Francis Publishers.

Song, Z., and Cao, X. (2018). Electroneutral models for dynamic Poisson-Nernst-Planck systems, *Phys. Rev. E*, **97**:012411.

Von Arx, T., Tamura, K., Yukiya, O., and Lozanoff, S. (2018). The face: A vascular perspective. A literature review. *Swiss Dental Journal*, **128**(5):382–392.

Westbrook, K. E., Nessel, T. A., Hohman, M. H., and Varacallo, M. (2024). *Anatomy, Head and Neck: Facial Muscles*. StatPearls Publishing LLC.

Zheng, Q., and Wei, G.-W. (2011). Poisson–Boltzmann–Nernst–Planck model, *J Chem Phys.*, 134.

Chapter 10

Quantum Fields and Quantum Entanglement

10.1 Introduction

Having completed the development of the humanoid robots and getting them ready to start their immortal lives in the universe, one needs to develop strategies for spatial travel in this huge universe. Here is when the quantum fields and effects could be of enormous value, and in particular, the notion and properties of *quantum entanglement* will be of great value. These issues will be discussed in this chapter. When humanoid robots with identity assigned (IA) consciousness travel through space, they must develop quick displacement and relocation systems using their IA consciousness toward the collapse of the wave function and producing the entanglement effect to transport the humanoid from one part of the universe to another part and possibly another time. This is quite an exciting notion for the future of humanity. The 2022 Nobel Prize in Physics was awarded to researchers Alain Aspect, John Clauser, and Anton Zeilinger for their research work on the foundation of quantum entanglement.

The Nobel Prize in Physics is typically awarded to scientists. However, in 2022, the Nobel Prize was awarded to three physicists

Biomimetic Humanoid Robots with Human Consciousness
Mohsen Shahinpoor

ISBN 978-981-5129-87-8 (Hardcover), 978-1-003-71373-9 (eBook)
www.jennystanford.com

DOI: 10.1201/9781003713739-10

who revealed that the universe is even stranger than we know due to quantum entanglement. The American Physical Society has announced that the Nobel Prize in Physics on quantum entanglement has been awarded, and the findings are truly amazing. In short, researchers Alain Aspect, John Clauser, and Anton Zeilinger (Fig. 10.1) have discovered that entangled particles behave like a single unit even when separated far away.

Figure 10.1 Alain Aspect, Anton Zeilinger, and John Clauser (2022 Nobel Prize in Physics, for quantum entanglement) (Erhard et al., 2020).

Their results have made an impact on quantum computing and quantum cryptography, which will also be of interest in this book.

Once described as "spooky action at a distance" by the world's most famous physicist, Albert Einstein, entanglement—the idea that two particles separated by vast distances could instantly influence each other—lies at the very heart of what makes *quantum physics* so strange and counterintuitive.

On its website, the Nobel Committee says it jointly awarded the 2022 Nobel Prize in Physics to the trio for their separate "experiments with entangled photons, establishing the violation of Bell inequalities, and pioneering quantum information science. One of the most fascinating predictions of quantum mechanics is entanglement, where widely separated particles can be prepared so that they behave as a single unit," Ulf Danielsson, secretary of the Nobel Committee for Physics, tells *Popular Mechanics.* "The groundbreaking experiments of Clauser, Aspect, and Zeilinger show that this mind-boggling phenomenon persists at macroscopic distances, demonstrating the deficiency of our classical intuition." Danielsson, a professor of theoretical physics at Uppsala University in Sweden, refers to the fact that this phenomenon of an instant quantum connection between particles across vast distances is not accounted for in classical physics of the everyday world.

The humanoid robots with IA consciousness developed in our laboratory chambers can travel across the universe using quantum entanglement.

In quantum teleportation, a pair of entangled particles transmit information about a third object instantaneously from one place to another. The original particle with information to be teleported is scanned. The scanning process disrupts the original particle and modifies both the entangled particles separated by a large distance instantaneously. The treatment process recreates the properties of the original particle.

Does consciousness collapse the quantum wave function? John von Neumann and Eugene Wigner took this idea seriously but have now widely dismissed it. We develop it by combining a mathematical theory of consciousness (integrated information theory, IIT, Guliu Tonini) with an account of quantum collapse dynamics (continuous spontaneous localization).

The nature of the relationship between human consciousness and the physical world has intrigued philosophers for many years. Virtually all of the founders of quantum theory—Planck, de Broglie, Heisenberg, Schrödinger, and Einstein—considered this subject in depth, and contemporary physicists continue this tradition.

We discuss these questions and build a quantum simulation of a two-qubit quantum computer. We explore concepts such as superposition and entanglement and how to create them. Quantum entanglement is possible between quantum systems. When a coin spins on a flat surface, it is in a state of superposition between its two faces—head and tails. Similarly, electrons in their natural state exist as a superposition of both up and down spin. Only when measured, do they give a definite value of up or down, which, in technical terms, is referred to as the "**collapse of the wavefunction Ψ**"? When a pair of electrons are generated, interact, or share spatial proximity, their spin states can get entangled, which is what scientists call the quantum entanglement of electrons. It would be relevant to recall Schrodiger's equations for the quantum wave function. In this book, quantum entanglement is described in simple terms so that it becomes accessible to people interested in knowing about quantum entanglement.

The time-independent Schrödinger equation is as follows:

$$\hat{H}^\wedge\psi = E\psi$$

The eigenvalues of the Hamiltonian ($\hat{H}$) are the energies (E) of the stationary states (ψ). The function responsible for evolving a quantum system in time ($\hat{H}$) has the states (ψ), which remain the same up to a constant scaling factor (E) under its action, and the scaling constant is the energy of the respective state.

The time-dependent Schrödinger equation (for a single particle moving in an electric potential) is as follows:

$$i\hbar\frac{\partial}{\partial t}\psi = \left(\frac{\hbar^2}{2m}\nabla^2 + V\right)\psi$$

Up to various constants ($i\hbar$), the wavefunction (ψ) satisfies the diffusion equation $\left(\frac{\partial\psi}{\partial t} = \frac{\hbar^2}{2m}\nabla^2\psi\right)$ with an extra term ($+V\psi$) consisting of the potential energy (V) multiplied by the wavefunction.

The rate of change ($\partial/\partial t$) of the wavefunction (ψ) at any point is proportional to a measure of its curvature ($\nabla^2\psi$) at that point multiplied by a constant ($\hbar^2/2m$), added to the potential (V) applied to the system multiplied by the wavefunction itself.

The time-dependent Schrödinger equation (general) is as follows:

$$i\hbar\frac{\partial}{\partial t}\psi = \widehat{H}\psi$$

Up to various constants ($i\hbar$), the time derivative of the wavefunction $\left(\frac{\partial}{\partial t}\psi\right)$ is given by the action of the Hamiltonian ($\hat{H}$) on the wavefunction.

The rate of change of the wavefunction at a point $\left(\frac{\partial}{\partial t}\psi\right)$ is proportional to the action of the function responsible for evolving a quantum system in time ($\hat{H}$) on the wavefunction.

10.2 Quantum Entanglement

Quantum entanglement is a physical resource, like energy, associated with the peculiar nonclassical correlations that are possible between separated quantum systems. Entanglement can be measured, transformed, and purified. A pair of quantum systems in an entangled state can be used as a quantum information channel to perform computational and cryptographic tasks that are impossible for classical systems. The general study of the information-processing capabilities of quantum systems is the subject of quantum information theory.

What Schrödinger showed was that if two particles are prepared in an **Einstein–Podolsky–Rosen (EPR)** quantum state, where there are matching correlations for two "canonically conjugate" dynamical quantities (quantities such as position and momentum whose values suffice to specify all the properties of a classical system), then there are infinitely many dynamical quantities of the two particles for which there exist similar matching correlations: Every function of the canonically conjugate pair of the first particle matches with the same function of the canonically conjugate pair of the second particle. So (Schrödinger, 1935; p. 559) system No. 1 "does not only know these two answers but a vast number of others, and that with no technical help whatsoever." Schrödinger coined the term "entanglement" to describe this peculiar connection between quantum systems (Schrödinger, 1935; p. 555):

When two systems, of which we know the states by their respective representatives, enter into temporary physical interaction due to known forces between them, and when, after a time of mutual influence, the systems separate again, then they can no longer be described in the same way as before. The interaction has entangled the two representatives (the quantum states).

He added (Schrödinger, 1935; p. 555): Another way of expressing the peculiar situation is the best possible knowledge of a *whole* does not necessarily include the best possible knowledge of all its *parts*, even though they may be entirely separate and therefore virtually capable of being 'best possibly known,' i.e., of possessing, each of them, a representative of its own. The lack of knowledge is by no means due to the interaction being insufficiently known—at least not in the way that it could be known more completely—it is due to the interaction itself.

Schrödinger, in the second part of the paper, showed that an experimenter, by a suitable choice of operations carried out on one member of an entangled pair, possibly using additional "ancilla" or helper particles, can "steer" the second system into a chosen mixture of quantum states, with a probability distribution that depends on the entangled state. The second system cannot be steered into a *particular* quantum state at the whim of the experimenter, but for many copies of the entangled pair, the experimenter can constrain the quantum state of the second system to lie in a chosen set of quantum states, where these states are correlated with the possible outcomes of measurements carried out on the entangled paired systems, or the paired systems plus ancillas. He found this conclusion sufficiently unsettling to suggest that the entanglement between two separating systems would persist only for distances small enough that the time light takes to travel from one system to the other could be neglected, compared with the characteristic periods associated with other changes in the composite system. He speculated that for longer distances, the two systems might, in fact, be in a correlated mixture of quantum states determined by the entangled state.

10.3 Exploiting Entanglement: Quantum Teleportation

To transfer the qubit for actual teleportation, an entangled quantum state must be created. Entanglement imposes statistical correlations between otherwise distinct physical systems by creating or placing two or more separate particles into a single, shared quantum state.

Quantum teleportation is the transfer of quantum states (in qubit) to another quantum state. It is not about transferring the information physically, but instead about transferring the state of the information. It sounds a little confusing, but a further explanation will help.

10.4 Quantum Information

Formally, the amount of classical information we gain, on average, when we learn the value of a random variable (or, equivalently, the amount of uncertainty in the value of a random variable before we learn its value) is represented by a quantity called the Shannon entropy, measured in bits (Shannon and Weaver, 1949). A random variable is defined by a probability distribution over a set of values. In the case of a binary random variable, with equal probability for each of the two possibilities, the Shannon entropy is one bit, representing maximal uncertainty. The Shannon entropy is less than one for all other probabilities—intuitively, representing some information about which alternative is more likely. For the case of maximal knowledge or zero uncertainty about the alternatives, where the probabilities are 0 and 1, the Shannon entropy is zero. (Note that the term "bit" refers to the basic unit of classical information in terms of Shannon entropy and to an elementary two-state classical system considered to represent the possible outputs of an elementary classical information source.)

Since information is always embodied in the state of a physical system, what happens if we use the quantum states of physical systems to store information rather than classical states? It turns out that quantum information is radically different from classical information. The unit of quantum information is the "qubit," representing the amount of quantum information that can be stored in the state of the simplest quantum system, for example, the polarization state of a photon. The term is due to Schumacher (1995), who proved a quantum analog of Shannon's noiseless coding theorem. (By analogy with the term "bit," the term "qubit" refers to the basic unit of quantum information in terms of the von Neumann entropy and to an elementary two-state quantum system considered as representing the possible outputs of an elementary quantum information source.) An arbitrarily large amount of classical information can be encoded in a qubit. This information can be processed and communicated, but because of the peculiarities of quantum measurement, at most one bit can be accessed. According to a theorem by Holevo, the accessible information in a probability distribution over a set of alternative qubit states is limited by the von Neumann entropy, which is equal to the Shannon entropy only when the states are orthogonal in the space of quantum states and is otherwise less than the Shannon entropy.

While classical information can be copied or cloned, the quantum "no cloning" theorem (Dieks, 1982; Wootters and Zurek, 1982) asserts the impossibility of cloning an unknown quantum state. To see why, consider how we might construct a classical copying device. A NOT gate is a device that takes a bit as input and produces as output either a 1 if the input is 0, or a 0 if the input is 1. In other words, a NOT gate is a 1-bit gate that flips the input bit. A controlled-NOT gate, or CNOT gate, takes two bits as inputs, a control bit and a target bit, and flips the target bit if and only if the control bit is 1 while reproducing the control bit. So there are two inputs, the control and target, and two outputs: the control, and either the target or the flipped target, depending on the value of the control. A CNOT gate functions as a copying device for the control bit if the target bit is set to 0 because the output of the target bit is then a copy of the control bit: the input 00 produces output 00, and the input 10 produces output 11 (here the first bit is the control and the second bit is the target). Insofar as we can think of a measurement as simply a copying operation, a CNOT gate is the paradigm of a classical measuring device. Imagine Alice equipped with such a device, with input and output control and target wires, measuring the properties of an unknown classical world. The input control wire is a probe for the presence or absence of a property represented by a one or a 0. The target wire is the pointer, initially set to 0. The output of the target is a one or a 0, depending on the presence or absence of the property.

10.5 Quantum Cryptography

Copying the key without revealing that it has been copied is also a problem for the shared key that Alice and Bob each store in some supposedly secure way. Alice and Bob notation is a simple notation for describing security protocols as sequences of message exchanges. However, the laws of physics in a classical world cannot guarantee that a storage procedure is completely secure, and they cannot guarantee that breaching the security and copying the key will always be detected. So, apart from the key distribution problem, there is a key storage problem.

Quantum entanglement solves these problems through the "monogamy" of entangled state correlations: no third party can share entanglement correlations between Alice and Bob. Moreover, any attempt by Eve to measure the quantum systems in the entangled state shared by Alice and Bob will destroy the entangled state. Alice and Bob can detect this by checking a Bell inequality.

While the difference between classical and quantum information can be exploited to achieve successful key distribution, other cryptographic protocols are thwarted by quantum entanglement. Bit commitment is a key cryptographic protocol that can be used as a subroutine in various important cryptographic tasks. In a bit commitment protocol, Alice supplies an encoded bit to Bob. The information available in the encoding should be insufficient for Bob to ascertain the value of the bit but sufficient, together with further information (supplied by Alice at a subsequent stage when she is supposed to reveal the value of the bit), for Bob to be convinced that the protocol does not allow Alice to cheat by encoding the bit in a way that leaves her free to reveal either 0 or 1 at will.

To illustrate the idea, suppose Alice claims the ability to predict advances or declines in the stock market daily. To substantiate her claim without revealing valuable information (perhaps to a potential employer, Bob), she suggests the following demonstration: She proposes to record her prediction before the market opens by writing a 0 (for "decline") or a 1 (for "advance") on a piece of paper, which she will lock in a safe. The safe will be handed to Bob, but Alice will keep the key. At the end of the day's trading, she will announce the bit she chose and prove that she committed earlier by handing Bob the key. Of course, the key-and-safe protocol is not probably secure from being cheated by Bob because no principle of classical physics prevents Bob from opening the safe and closing it again without leaving any trace.

The question is whether a quantum analog of this procedure exists that is unconditionally secure: probably secure by the laws of physics against cheating by either Alice or Bob. Bob can cheat if he can obtain *some* information about Alice's commitment before she reveals it (which would give him an advantage in repetitions of the protocol with Alice). Alice can cheat if she can delay committing the final stage when she is required to reveal her commitment, or if she can change her commitment at the final stage with a very low probability of detection.

It turns out that unconditionally secure two-party bit commitment, based solely on the principles of quantum or classical mechanics (without exploiting special relativistic signaling constraints or principles of general relativity or thermodynamics), is impossible. See Mayers (1997), Lo and Chau (1997), and Low's article "Quantum Cryptology" in Lo, Popescu, and Spiller (1998) for further discussion. Kent (1999) has shown that one can implement a secure classical bit commitment protocol by exploiting relativistic signaling constraints in a timed sequence of communications between verifiably separated sites for both Alice and Bob. Roughly, the impossibility arises because, at any step in the protocol where either Alice or Bob is required to make a determinate choice (perform a measurement on a particle in the quantum channel, choose randomly and perhaps conditionally between a set of alternative actions to be implemented on the particle in the quantum channel, etc.), the choice can be delayed by entangling one or more ancillary particles with the channel particle in an appropriate way. By suitable operations on the ancilla, the channel particle can be "steered," so this cheating strategy is undetectable. If Bob can obtain no information about the committed bit, then entanglement will allow Alice to "steer" the bit to either 0 or 1 at will.

In 2022, the US National Institute of Standards and Technology (NIST) announced a suite of encryption protocols designed to be secure against attacks by a quantum computer.

All our former experience with applying quantum theory seems to say that what is predicted by quantum formalism must occur in the laboratory. But the essence of quantum entanglement is one of the most subtle and intriguing phenomena in nature: quantum cryptography and quantum dense coding.

Quantum entanglement, a term coined by Erwin Schrödinger in 1935, is a mechanical phenomenon at the quantum level wherein the quantum states of two (or more) particles must be described concerning each other. However, these particles may be spatially separated. This phenomenon leads to paradox and has puzzled us for a long time. The behavior of entangled particles is inexplicable, incomprehensible, and like magic at work. Could two subatomic particles on opposite sides of the universe be really instantaneously connected? Is any theory that predicts such a connection essentially flawed or incomplete? Are the results of experiments that demonstrate such a connection being misinterpreted? These questions challenge our most basic concepts of spatial distance and time. Modern physics is in the process of dismantling the space all around us, and the universe will never be the same. Quantum entanglement involves utilizing cutting-edge technology and will bring great benefits to society. This chapter traces the development of quantum entanglement and presents some possible explanations for the strange behavior of entangled particles.

This chapter aims to provide strategies for detecting mesoscopic/macroscopic quantum superpositions and EPR paradoxes in mixed states that accurately represent the output of physical systems that generate squeezing and entanglement. The paradox of macroscopic entanglement occurs when we have a quantum superposition of two macroscopically distinguishable entities.

The wave–particle duality is a fundamental property of nature and one of the greatest mysteries of modern physics. This gave rise to a whole direction in quantum physics—the interpretation of quantum mechanics.

10.6 Introduction to Multiple Quantum Entanglement

The phenomenon of quantum entanglement involving two particles has puzzled scientists for a long time. People also ask, is there any proof of quantum entanglement? Quantum entanglement is experimentally demonstrated with photons, electrons, top quarks, molecules, and even small diamonds. The use of entanglement in communication, computation, and quantum radar is an active area of research and development.

Later, however, the counterintuitive predictions of quantum mechanics were verified in tests where polarization or spin of entangled particles was measured at separate locations. In earlier tests, it could not be ruled out that the result at one point could have been *subtly transmitted* to the remote point, affecting the outcome at the second location.

10.6.1 Entropy

In this section, the entropy of a mixed state is again discussed. It is also discussed how it can be viewed as a measure of quantum entanglement. Botzman introduced the entropy formula in terms of several microscopic states of a system. This equation reads:

$$S = k_B \ln W \tag{10.1}$$

where k_B is the *Boltzmann constant* (also written as simply k) and is equal to 1.380649×10^{-23} J/K, and ln is the *natural logarithm* function. W can be counted as the number N of possible i microscopic entities using the formula for *permutations*:

$$W = \frac{N!}{\Pi_i N_i!} \tag{10.2}$$

where i ranges over all possible molecular conditions and the dot (.) denotes *factorial*.

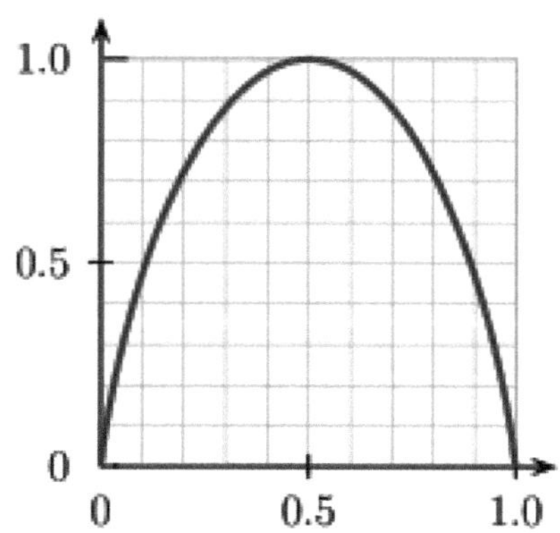

Figure 10.2 The plot of von Neumann entropy versus eigenvalue for a bipartite. When the eigenvalue has a value of 0.5, the von Neumann entropy is at a maximum, corresponding to maximum entanglement.

As in *statistical mechanics*, the more uncertainty (number of microstates) the system possesses, the larger the entropy. For example, the entropy of any pure state is zero, which is unsurprising since there is no uncertainty about a system in a pure state. The entropy of any of the two subsystems of the entangled state discussed earlier is log(2) (which can be shown to be the maximum entropy for 2 × 2 mixed states).

It is a classical result that the Shannon entropy achieves its maximum at, and only at, the uniform probability distribution $\{1/n, ..., 1/n\}$. Therefore, a bipartite pure state $\rho \in H_A \otimes H_B$ is said to be a maximally entangled state if the reduced state of each subsystem of ρ is the diagonal matrix.

Also, for $M > 2$ qubits, there are *spin-squeezed states*, a class of *squeezed coherent states* satisfying certain restrictions on the uncertainty of spin measurements, which are necessarily entangled.[1] Spin-squeezed states are good candidates for enhancing precision measurements using quantum entanglement.[2]

It is also possible to create entanglement between quantum systems that never directly interacted through the use of *entanglement swapping*. Two independently prepared, identical particles may also be entangled if their wave functions merely spatially overlap, at least partially.[3]

10.6.2 Testing a System for Entanglement

A density matrix ρ is called separable if it can be written as a convex sum of product states, namely with probabilities. By definition, a state is entangled if it is not separable.

For 2-qubit and qubit–qutrit systems (2×2 and 2×3, respectively), the simple *Peres–Horodecki criterion* provides both a necessary and a sufficient criterion for separability, and thus—inadvertently—for detecting entanglement. Yin et al. (2017) have reported setting a new quantum entanglement distance record of 1203 km, demonstrating the survival of a two-photon pair. The electron shells of multi-electron atoms always consist of entangled electrons. The correct ionization energy can be calculated only by consideration of electron entanglement.

10.6.3 Entanglement of Macroscopic Objects

Physicist John Bell depicted the Einstein camp in his article entitled "Bertlmann's socks and the nature of reality," p. 143, in *Speakable and Unspeakable in Quantum Mechanics*: "For EPR (The Einstein–Podolsky–Rosen (EPR) paradox is a thought experiment proposed by physicists Albert Einstein, Boris Podolsky, and Nathan Rosen which argues that the description of physical reality provided by quantum mechanics is incomplete, that would be an unthinkable 'spooky action at a distance'. To avoid such action at a distance, they have to attribute real properties in advance of observation to the space-time regions in question and correlated properties, which predetermine the outcomes of these particular observations. Since these real properties, fixed in advance of observation, are not contained in quantum formalism, that formalism for EPR is incomplete. It may be correct, as far as it goes, but the usual quantum formalism cannot be the whole story." And again, on p. 144, Bell says: "Einstein had no difficulty accepting that affairs in different places could be correlated. He could not accept that an intervention at one place could immediately influence affairs at the other."

10.7 Conclusions

As quantum entanglement may result from tachyons, i.e., faster than light particles, at work, it may thus utilize cutting-edge tachyons, which is another outstanding challenge in physics. In addition, according to the Copenhagen interpretation of quantum physics, waveforms collapsing to provide the second version of the particles give matching results when measured. Using this mini-wormhole, two particles that appear to be apart could be adjacent or perhaps even the same thing when seen from two different angles. Since what happens in one place depends on what happens elsewhere in the universe, quantum entanglement may also be a case of nonlocality at work.

Entanglement may also be likened to the case whereby a light switch controls two (or more) light bulbs, and when the light switch is turned on, the two (or more) light bulbs are lighted simultaneously.

The important question is whether one of those mentioned above truly explains the strange behavior of entangled particles, wherein experimental evidence would incontrovertibly validate the explanation.

References and Further Readings

Abhijith, J., Adedoyin, A., Ambrosiano, J., Anisimov, P., Casper, W., Chennupati, G., Coffrin, C., Djidjev, H., Gunter, D., Karra, S., Lemons, N., Lin, S., Malyzhenkov, A., Mascarenas, D., Mniszewski, S., Nadiga, B., O'Malley, D., Oyen, D., Pakin, S., Prasad, L., Roberts, R., Romero, P., Santhi, N., Sinitsyn, N., Swart, P. J., Wendelberger, J. G., Yoon, B., Zamora, R., Zhu, W., Eidenbenz, S., Bärtschi, A., Coles, P. J., Vuffray, M., and Lokhov, A. Y. (2022). Quantum algorithm implementations for beginners. *ACM Transactions on Quantum Computing*, **3**:1–92.

Akopian, N. (2006). Entangled photon pairs from semiconductor quantum dots. *Physical Review Letters*, **96**(2):130501.

Alcock, J., Brunner, N., Pawlowski, M., and Scarani, V. (2009). Recovering part of the quantum boundary from information causality. *Physical Review A*, **80**:040103.

Al-Safi, S. W., and Short, A. J. (2014). Reversible dynamics in strongly non-local boxworld systems. *Journal of Physics A: Mathematical and Theoretical*, **47**:325303.

Aspect, A., Dalibard, J., and Roger, G. (1982). Experimental test of Bell's inequalities using time-varying analyzers. *Physical Review Letters*, **49**:1804–1807.

Augusiak, R., Demianowicz, M., Tura, J., and Acín, A. (2015). Entanglement and nonlocality are inequivalent for any number of parties. *Physical Review Letters*, **115**(3):030404.

Barrett, J. (2007). Information processing in generalized probabilistic theories. *Physical Review A*, **75**:032304.

Barrett, J., Hardy, L., and Kent, A. (2005). No signaling and quantum key distribution. *Physical Review Letters*, **95**:010503.

Beiser, A. (1995). *Concepts of Modern Physics*, 5th edition. McGraw-Hill.

Bell, J. S. (1964). On the Einstein–Podolsky–Rosen paradox. *Physics*, **1**:195–200.

Bengtsson, I., and *Życzkowski*, K. (2006). *Geometry of Quantum States. An Introduction to Quantum Entanglement.* Cambridge: Cambridge University Press.

Bennett, C. H., and Di Vincenzo, B. D. (2000). Quantum information and computation. *Nature*, **404**: 247–255.

Bennett, C. H., Brassard, G., Crepeau, C., Jozsa, R., Peres, A., and Wotters, W. K. (1993). Teleporting an unkown quantum state via dual classical and Einstein–Podolsky–Rosen channels. *Physical Review Letters*, **70**:1895–1899.

Bernstein, J. (2013). *A Palette of Particles*. Harvard University Press.

Bhaskara, V. S., and Panigrahi, P. K. (2017). Generalized concurrence measure for faithful multiparticle pure state entanglement quantification using Lagrange's identity and wedge product. *Quantum Information Processing*, **16**(5):118.

Boette, A., Rossignoli, R., Gigena, N., and Cerezo, M. (2016). System-time entanglement in a discrete-time model. *Physical Review A*, **93**(6):062127.

Bohr, N. (1935). Can quantum-mechanical description of physical reality be considered complete? *Physical Review*, **38**:696–702.

Bokulich, A., and Jaeger, G. (2010). *Philosophy of Quantum Information and Entanglement*. Cambridge University Press, xv.

Born, M. (ed.) (1992). *The Born-Einstein Letters*. Dordrecht: Reidel.

Brassard, G. (2005). Is information the key? *Nature Physics*, **1**:2–4.

Bub, J. (2006). Quantum information and computation. In: J. Earman and J. Butterfield (Eds.), *Philosophy of Physics (Handbook of Philosophy of Science)*. Amsterdam: North Holland, pp. 555–660.

Bub, J. (2019). Quantum entanglement and information. In: *Stanford Encyclopedia of Philosophy*. Stanford, California: Stanford University.

Bub, T., and Bub, J. (2018). *Totally Random: Why Nobody Understands Quantum Mechanics (A Serious Comic on Entanglement)*. Princeton: Princeton University Press.

Chiribella, G., and Spekkens, R. (2016). *Quantum Theory: Informational Foundations and Foils*, New York, Springer.

Clauser, J. F., Horne, M. A., Shimony, A., and Holt, R. A. (1969). Proposed experiment to test local hidden-variable theories. *Physical Review Letters*, **23**:880.

Cramer, J. G. (2015). *The Quantum Handshake: Entanglement, Nonlocality and Transactions*. Springer Verlag.

Deutsch, D. (1985). Quantum theory, the Church–Turing principle and the universal quantum computer. *Proceedings of the Royal Society (London)*, **A400**:97–117.

Deutsch, D. (1997). *The Fabric of Reality*. London: Penguin.

Dickson, W. M. (2005). *Quantum Chance and Non-Locality: Probability and Non-locality in the Interpretations of Quantum Mechanics*. Cambridge, United Kingdom: Cambridge University Press.

Dieks, D. (1982). Communication by EPR Devices. *Physics Letters A*, **92**:271–272.

Dirac, P. A. M. (2019). *The Principles of Quantum Mechanics*. Clarendon Press. Duarte, F. J. (2019). *Fundamentals of Quantum Entanglement*. Bristol, UK: Institute of Physics.

Duncan, A. (2012). *The Conceptual Framework of Quantum Field*. Oxford University Press.

Einstein, A., Podolsky, B., and Rosen, N. (1935). Can quantum-mechanical description of physical reality be considered complete? *Physical Review*, **47**:777–780.

Ekert, A. (1991). Quantum cryptography based on Bell's theorem. *Physical Review Letters*, **67**:661–663.

Ekert, A., and Renner, R. (2014). The ultimate physical limits of privacy. *Nature*, **507**:443–447.

Erhard, M., Krenn, M., and Zeilinger, A. (2020). Advances in high-dimensional quantum entanglement. *Nature Reviews Physics*, **2**:365–381.

Everett, H. (1957). "Relative state" formulation of quantum mechanics. *Reviews of Modern Physics*, **29**:454–462.

Feynman, R. (1996). *Feynman Lectures on Computation*, J. G. Hey and R. W. Allen (Eds.). Reading, MA: Addison-Wesley Publishing Company.

Freedman, S. J., and Clauser, J. F. (1972). Experimental test of local hidden-variable theories. *Physical Review Letters*, **28**:938.

Friis, N., Vitagliano, G., Malik, M., and Huber, M. (2019). Entanglement certification from theory to experiment. *Nature Reviews Physics*, **1**:72–87.

Fuchs, C. A. (2014). An introduction to QBism with an application to the locality of quantum mechanics. *American Journal of Physics*, **82**:749–754.

Georgiev, D. D., and Gudder, S. P. (2022). Sensitivity of entanglement measures in bipartite pure quantum states. *Modern Physics Letters B*, **36**(22):22501012250255.

Gharibian, S. (2010). Strong NP-hardness of the quantum separability problem. *Quantum Information and Computation*, **10**(3&4):343–360.

Gour, G., and Wallach, N. R. (2013). Classification of multipartite entanglement of all finite dimensionality. *Physical Review Letters*, **111**(6):060502.

Grassl, M., *Rötteler, M.*, and Beth, T. (1998). Computing local invariants of quantum-bit systems. *Physical Review A*, **58**(3):1833–1839.

Gühne, O., and Tóth, G. (2009). Entanglement detection. *Physics Reports*, **474**(1–6):1–75.

Gurvits, L. (2003). Classical deterministic complexity of Edmonds' problem and quantum entanglement. In: *Proceedings of the Thirty-Fifth Annual ACM Symposium on Theory of Computing*. New York: ACM Press, p.10.

Hardy, L. (1992). Quantum mechanics, local realistic theories, and Lorentz-invariant realistic theories. *Physical Review Letters*, **68**(20):2981–2984.

Herbst, T., Scheidl, T., Fink, M., Handsteiner, J., Wittmann, B., Ursin, R., and Zeilinger, A. (2015). Teleportation of entanglement over 143 km. *Proceedings of the National Academy of Sciences of the United States of America*, **112**:14202–14205

Hesketh, G. (2016). *The Particle Zoo: The Search for the Fundamental Nature*. Quercus.

Hillery, M., and Zubairy, M. S. (2006). Entanglement conditions for two-mode states. *Physical Review Letters*, **96**(5):050503.

Holevo, A. S. (1973). Statistical problems in quantum physics. In: G. Murayama and J. V. Prokhorov (Eds.). *Proceedings of the Second Japan-USSR Symposium on Probability Theory*, Berlin: Springer, pp. 104–109.

Holland, M. J., and Burnett, K. (1993). Interferometric detection of optical phase shifts at the Heisenberg limit. *Physical Review Letters*, **71**(9):1355–1358.

Horodecki, M., Horodecki, P., and Horodecki, R. (1998). Mixed-state entanglement and distillation: Is there a bound entanglement in nature? *Physical Review Letters*, **80**(1998):5239–5242.

Horodecki, R., Horodecki, P., Horodecki, M., and Horodecki, K. (2009). Quantum entanglement. *Reviews of Modern Physics*, **81**(2):865–942.

Huang, Y. (2010). Entanglement criteria via concave-function uncertainty relations. *Physical Review A*, **82**(1):012335.

Huang, Y. (2013). Entanglement detection: Complexity and Shannon entropic criteria. *IEEE Transactions on Information Theory*, **59**(10): 6774.

Jaeger, G. (2009). *Entanglement, Information, and the Interpretation of Quantum Mechanics*. Heildelberg: Springer.

Jozsa, R., and Linden, N. (2002). On the role of entanglement in quantum computational speed-up. *Proceedings of the Royal Society A: Mathematical, Physical and Engineering Sciences*, **459**(2036):2011–2032.

Kent, A. (1999). Unconditionally secure bit commitment. *Physical Review Letters*, **83**:1447–1450.

Kitagawa, M., and Ueda, M. (1993). Squeezed Spin States. *Physical Review A*, **47**(6):5138–5143.

Kocher, C. A. (1971). Time correlations in the detection of successively emitted photons. *Annals of Physics*, **65**(1):1–18.

Kotler, S., Peterson, G. A., Shojaee, E., Lecocq, F., Cicak, K., Kwiatkowski, A., Geller, S., Glancy, S., Knill, E., Simmonds, R. W., Aumentado, J., and Teufel, J. D. (2021). Direct observation of deterministic macroscopic entanglement. *Science*, **372**(6542):622625.

Lami, L., and Regula, B. (2023). No second law of entanglement manipulation after all. *Nature Physics*, **19**(2):184–189.

Leinaas, J. M., Myrheim, J., and Ovrum, E. (2006). Geometrical aspects of entanglement. *Physical Review A*, **74**(1):012313.

Lo, H.-K., and Chau, H. F. (1997). Is quantum bit commitment possible? *Physical Review Letters*, **78**:3410–3413.

Lo, H.-K., Popescu, S., and Spiller, T. (1998). *Introduction to Quantum Computation and Information*. Singapore: World Scientific.

Ma, X.-S., Zotter, S., Kofler, J., Ursin, R., Jennewein, T., Brukner, Č., and Zeilinger, A. (2012). Experimental delayed-choice entanglement swapping. *Nature Physics*, **8**(6):480485.

Markoff, J. (2015). Sorry, Einstein. Quantum study suggests 'spooky action' is real. *The New York Times*. Retrieved October 21, 2015.

Marletto, C., Coles, D. M., Farrow, T., and Vedral, V. (2018). Entanglement between living bacteria and quantized light witnessed by Rabi splitting. *Journal of Physics Communications*, **2**(10):101001.

Mayers, D. (1997). Unconditionally secure quantum bit commitment is impossible. *Physical Review Letters*, **78**:3414–3417.

Merzbacher, E. (1970). *Quantum Mechanics*, 2nd edition. John Wiley & Sons.

Modinos, A. (1996). *Quantum Theory of Matter*. John Wiley & Sons.

Moreva, E. (2014). Time from quantum entanglement: An experimental illustration. *Physical Review A*, **89**(5):052122.

Navascues, M., and Wunderlich, H. (2009). A glance beyond the quantum model. *Proceedings of the Royal Society A*, **466**:881–890.

Nielsen, M. A. (1999). Conditions for a class of entanglement transformations. *Physical Review Letters*, **83**(2):436.

Nielsen, M. A., and Chuang, I. L. (2000). Quantum computation and quantum information. Cambridge University Press. pp. 112–113.

Nielsen, M. A., and Chuang, I. L. (2011). *Quantum Computation and Quantum Information*, 10th anniversary edition. Cambridge: Cambridge University Press.

Non-Pan, J.-W. Bouwmeester, D., Weinfurter, H., and Zeilinger, A. (1998). Experimental entanglement swapping: Entangling photons that never interacted. *Physical Review Letters*, **80**:3891.

Pawlowski, M., Patarek, T., Kaszlikowski, D., Scarani, V., Winter, A., and Zukowski, M. (2009). A new physical principle: Information causality. *Nature*, 461:1101.

Pirandola, S., Andersen, U. L., Banchi, L., Berta, M., Bunandar, D., Colbeck, R., Englund, D., Gehring, T., Lupo, C., Ottaviani, C., Pereira, J. L., Razavi, M., Shamsul Shaari, J., Tomamichel, M., Usenko, V. C., Vallone, G., Villoresi, P., and Wallden, P. (2020). Advances in quantum cryptography. *Advances in Optics and Photonics*, **12**(4):1012–1236.

Plenio, M. B., and Virmani, S. (2007). An introduction to entanglement measures. *Quantum Information Computation*, **1**:1–51.

Ramanathan, R., Patarek, T., Kay, A., Kurzynski, P., and Kaszkilowski, D. (2010). Local realism of macroscopic correlations. *Physical Review Letters*, **107**:060405.

Renner, R., Gisin, N., and Kraus, B. (2005). An information-theoretic security proof for QKD protocols. *Physical Review A*, **72**:012332.

Ringbauer, M., Fedrizzi, A., Berry, D. W., and White, A. G. (2014). Information causality in the quantum and post-quantum regime. *Scientific Reports*, **4**:6955.

Rozatkar, G. (2018). *Demonstration of Quantum Entanglement*. OSF.

Sabin, C., Garcia-Ripoll, J. J., Solano, E., and Leon, J. (2010). Dynamics of entanglement via propagating microwave photons. *Physical Review B*, **81**(18):184501.

Sakurai, J. J., and Napolitano, J. J. (2010). *Modern Quantum Mechanics*, 2nd edition. Pearson, p. 68.

Schrödinger, E. (1935). Discussion of probability relations between separated systems. *Mathematical Proceedings of the Cambridge Philosophical Society*, **31**(4):555–563.

Schrödinger, E. (1936). Probability relations between separated systems. *Mathematical Proceedings of the Cambridge Philosophical Society*, **32**(3):446–452.

Schumacher, B. (1995). Quantum coding. *Physical Review A*, **51**:2738–2747.

Shahinpoor, M. (1987). *Speakable and Unspeakable in Quantum Mechanics*. CERN.

Shahinpoor, M. (2003). A quantum computer needs only one universe. *Studies in History and Philosophy of Modern Physics*, **34**(3):469–478.

Shahinpoor, M. (2012). Unconditionally secure bit commitment by transmitting measurement outcomes. *Physical Review Letters*, **109**:130501.

Shahinpoor, M. (2021). Vibrating drumheads are entangled quantum mechanically. *Physics World*, May 17, 2021. Retrieved June 14, 2021.

Shannon, C. E., and Weaver, W. (1949). *The Mathematical Theory of Communication*. Urbana: University of Illinois Press.

Siegel, E. (2023). No, we still can't use quantum entanglement to communicate faster than light. *Forbes*. Retrieved January 6, 2023.

Simon, R. (2000). Peres–Horodecki separability criterion for continuous variable systems. *Physical Review Letters*, **84**(12):2726–2729.

Skrzypczyk, P., Brunner, N., and Popescu, S. (2009). Emergence of quantum correlations from nonlocality swapping. *Physical Review Letters*, **102**:110402.

Steane, A. M. (1998). Quantum computing. *Reports on Progress in Physics*, **61**:117–173.

Steward, E. G. (2008). *Quantum Mechanics: Its Early Development and the Road to Entanglement*. Imperial College Press.

Swain, S. N., Bhaskara, V. S., and Panigrahi, P. K. (2022). Generalized entanglement measure for continuous-variable systems. *Physical Review A*, **105**(5):052441.

Swingle, B., and Van Raamsdonk, M. (2014). *Universality of Gravity from Entanglement Theory*. New York: Oxford University Press.

Thomas, R. A., Parniak, M., Østfeldt, C., *Møller, C.* B., Bærentsen, C., Tsaturyan, Y., Schliesser, A., Appel, J., Zeuthen, E., and Polzik, E. S. (2020). Entanglement between distant macroscopic mechanical and spin systems. *Nature Physics*, **17**(2):228–233.

Timpson, C. G. (2013). *Quantum Information Theory and the Foundations of Quantum Mechanics*. Oxford: Oxford University Press.

Van Dam, W. (2013). Implausible consequences of superstrong nonlocality. *Natural Computing*, **12**(1):9–12.

Van Fraassen, B. (1982). The Charybdis of realism: Epistemological implications of Bell's inequality. *Synthese*, **52**:25–38.

Van Raamsdonk, M. (2010). Building up spacetime with quantum entanglement. *General Relativity and Gravitation*, **42**(10):2323–2329.

Vértesi, T., and Brunner, N. (2014). Disproving the Peres conjecture by showing Bell nonlocality from bound entanglement. *Nature Communications*, **5**(1):5297.

Vilenkin, A. (1995). Predictions from quantum cosmology. *Physical Review Letters*, **74**:846.

Walborn, S., Taketani, B., Salles, A., Toscano, F., and de Matos Filho, R. (2009). Entropic entanglement criteria for continuous variables. *Physical Review Letters*, **103**(16):160505.

Weatherall, J. O. (2013). The scope and generality of Bell's theorem. *Foundations of Physics*, **43**(9):1153–1169.

Werner, R. F., and Wolf, M. M. (2001). Bound entangled Gaussian states. *Physical Review Letters*, **86**(16):3658–3661.

Wineland, D. J., Bollinger, J. J., Itano, W. M., Moore, F. L., and Heinzen, D. J. (1992). Spin squeezing and reduced quantum noise in spectroscopy. *Physical Review A*, **46**(11).

Wiseman, H. M., Jones, S. J., and Doherty, A. C. (2007). Steering, entanglement, nonlocality, and the Einstein–Podolsky–Rosen paradox. *Physical Review Letters*, **98**(14):140402.

Wong, B. (2019). Existence of tachyons and their detection: Research & reviews. *Journal of Physics*, **8**(2):23–26.

Wootters, W. K., and Zurek, W. H. (1982). A single quantum cannot be cloned. *Nature*, **299**:802–803.

Yin, J., Cao, Y., Li, Y.-H., Liao, S.-K., Zhang, L., Ren, J.-G., Cai, W.-Q., Liu, W.-Y., Li, B., Dai, H., Li, G.-B., Lu, Q.-M., Gong, Y.-H., Xu, Y., Li, S.-L., Li, F.-Z., Yin, Y.-Y., Jiang, Z.-Q., Li, M., Jia, J.-J., Ren, G., He, D., Zhou, Y.-L., Zhang, X.-X., Wang, N., Chang, X., Zhu, Z.-C., Liu, N.-L., Chen, Y.-A., Lu, C.-Y., Shu, R., Peng, C.-Z., Wang, J.-Y., and Pan, J.-W. (2017). Satellite-based entanglement distribution over 1200 kilometers. *Science*, **356**(6343):1140–1144.

Yin, J., Cao, Y., Yong, H.-L., Ren, J.-G., Liang, H., Liao, S.-K., Zhou, F., Liu, C., Wu, Y.-P., Pan, G.-S., Zhang, Q., Peng, C.-Z., and Pan, J.-W. (2013). Bounding the speed of 'spooky action at a distance'. *Physical Review Letters*, **110**(26):260407.

Yin, J., Li, Y. H., Liao, S. K., Yang, M., Cao, Y., Zhang, L., Ren, J. G., Cai, W. Q., Liu, W. Y., Li, S. L., Shu, R., Huang, Y. M., Deng, L., Li, L., Zhang, Q., Liu, N. L., Chen, Y. A., Lu, C. Y., Wang, X. B., Xu, F., Wang, J. Y., Peng, C. Z., Ekert, A. K., and Pan, J. W. (2020). Entanglement-based secure quantum cryptography over 1,120 kilometers. *Nature*, **582**(7813):501–505.

Zeilinger, A. (2018). Quantum teleportation, onwards and upwards. *Nature Physics*, **14**:3–4.

Chapter 11

Development and Promotion of Artificial Intelligence (AI) Software and Hardware for Advanced Computers

This chapter discusses to develop energy, matter, intelligence, life, and consciousness (EMILC) toward the evolution of universal consciousness. Advanced software has been developed to understand IA consciousness, which will then be assigned to selected volunteers to transfer their identity-vita-assigned (IVA) consciousness to an intelligent (AI-based) computer.

Tim Palmer of the Institute of Art and Ideas (IAI) is the Royal Society Research Professor in the Department of Physics at the University of Oxford (Palmer, 2022). He has questioned *whether computers and intelligent machines will ever gain true understanding, become conscious, or even develop a feeling of sentience.* Palmer states that the lack of understanding is not the only thing we think separates us from computers. Most of us viscerally feel that whatever we do, we could have done otherwise. Even for those of us who believe that the laws of physics are ultimately deterministic, and hence that it makes no sense to say that we could have done otherwise, it is simply impossible to avoid thinking about counterfactual worlds from time to time.

Biomimetic Humanoid Robots with Human Consciousness
Mohsen Shahinpoor

ISBN 978-981-5129-87-8 (Hardcover), 978-1-003-71373-9 (eBook)
www.jennystanford.com

DOI: 10.1201/9781003713739-11

The mystery of consciousness is that if we had answered the interview question differently, we would now have our dream job. I would not have hit the ball out of bounds if I had not rushed my golf swing. We just would not be human if we did not have such thoughts. But from where do they originate? One can always consider Guiliu Tononi's Integrated Information Theory in connection with consciousness emergence and activation. In our brain, there are some 10 billion neurons, and collectively they generate the feeling of consciousness when they are at work. Thus, receiving information from 10 billion neurons is the miracle of consciousness because we can never do that by ourselves.

We all feel we are conscious beings. What is consciousness? It describes a visceral belief that, although we interact with the rest of the Universe, we retain some inherent independence from the world around us. For example, right now, one feels strongly that one is independent of the books on a bookshelf. Perhaps this perception arises from remembering past occasions in a different location than the bookcase. But then, a robot can have the same awareness of remembering its past. Does that mean that the robot is conscious? Making sense of these three human qualities—understanding, free will, and consciousness—involves appealing to counterfactual worlds. For example, Euclid's theorem is a hypothetical counterfactual world where Euclid added the number 2 to the product of primes and perhaps tore his hair out in frustration because the proof did not work. In the case of free will, it is a counterfactual world where one did not rush the swing, and the ball did not go out of bounds. In consciousness, it is a counterfactual world where one has a different relationship with one's books than the one you have right now.

Libraries, the Internet, or simply memories of our past interactions with the real world are possible sources of information for creating counterfactual worlds—quantum computing beyond the Many Worlds Interpretation (Tim Palmer, WolframMathwork).

Our theory of physics on small scales is quantum computing, in which certain computations, such as factoring composite numbers into primes, can be performed exponentially faster on a quantum computer than on a classical computer. From where does the extra processing power come? One could say the extra power is encoded in the mathematics of quantum mechanics. But that merely begs the question: What is the underlying physics encoded in the mathematics of quantum mechanics that gives quantum computers their power? One answer to this question, favored by one of the pioneers of quantum computing, David Deutsch, is "quantum parallelism." David believes in the so-called Many Worlds Interpretation of quantum mechanics, proposed by Hugh Everett in the 1950s.

The key idea in the Many Worlds Interpretation is that when we measure a quantum system, the Universe somehow branches into multiple copies, corresponding to each of the possible outcomes of the measurement. According to Deutsch, a quantum computer allows useful tasks to be performed in collaboration between these copies of the Universe. The quantum computer's processing power comes from outsourcing work in which calculations take place in other universes. Entangled quantum particles function as communication paths between universes, sharing information and gathering results.

Jim Baggott thinks Deutsch is right that the resource explaining quantum computation's power lies in these parallel worlds. However, we do not buy into Everett's Many Worlds Interpretation at a technical level.

In the Invariant Set Theory, nearby counterfactual worlds that lie on the cosmological fractal attractor contribute to the quantum parallelism needed to account for the speed of quantum computers. By contrast, hypothetical counterfactual worlds in fractal gaps in the attractor do not contribute to this parallelism.

According to Michael S. A. Graziano (TED-ED, Oct 28, 2019), (GPT-3 On Transferring Consciousness onto a Computer), it is possible to transfer our consciousness (Mind Uploading) to an AI computer. Note that when one dies, his or her consciousness ceases to exist. However, the transferred consciousness, with all the memories and experiences, will be a copy of the original. The copy will have all the experiences and memories of the original but will not be the original person due to a possible lack of sentience. Nonetheless, the digital consciousness will remain in the computer, rendering the person immortal. Here, immortality means living forever, while indefinite life means living indefinitely.

As suggested by Tim Palmer (2024), in *The Primacy of Doubt,* the concept of a cosmological fractal attractor is holistic. It is as much top-down as it is bottom-up. Technical mathematical results show that a fractal attractor is an example of what is known as "non-computational geometry," a geometry that cannot be described completely by using algorithms.

For example, there is no algorithm for determining whether a putative counterfactual world lies on the Universe's fractal attractor or in a gap. This is relevant because Nobel Laureate Roger Penrose has argued strongly about human understanding.

He says our brains, as quantum computers, want to suggest that our brains are quantum computers in the sense of having a cognitive awareness of nearby counterfactual worlds on the cosmological fractal attractor. But hang on, you may complain; I have a hard enough job factoring the number 30 into primes, never mind some humungous number that a quantum computer might one day factor to break an encryption code. Well, he never said that your quantum brain could factor in large numbers. That would not be possible, not least because the warm, noisy environment of the brain would prevent entangled quantum superpositions from lasting long enough to do serious quantum computational calculations (indeed, he believes this same noise is a necessary element in accounting for human creativity). But that does not mean there are not some vestiges of quantum parallelism in our cognitive capabilities.

But why should our brains ever make use of quantum physics in the first place? Here, Roger Penrose believes the primal answer is energy efficiency. Energy is a precious resource.

A classical computer squanders this energy, needing megawatts of power to process petabytes of data. The brain does the same with six orders of magnitude less power. How could this be? I believe it is by taking advantage of quantum physics. For example, there is good evidence that pumping ions through channels in the walls of axon membranes, needed to amplify spike signals as they propagate along more than the 80 billion axons in the brain, could not be achieved with 20 W of power if the pumping was done using classical physics. With quantum physics, it can be done within the brain's very limited energy budget.

Could it be that the extra information needed to understand something, or to give us the visceral feelings of free will and consciousness, ultimately arises from a weak cognition of nearby counterfactual worlds on the cosmological fractal attractor, arising from manifestations of quantum parallelism in the brain? An analogy is when someone shows you photos on their smartphone, and one of the static photos is unexpectedly preceded by a very short movie sequence.

Moreover, one suspects that quantum parallelism is the missing ingredient that connects many holistically to the world around us.

Perhaps it is the physical component that leads to deep spiritual feelings about our place in the Universe and the sense that both artists and mathematicians have that they are not creators but mere discoverers of pre-existing knowledge and information (something many conventional scientists dismiss as new-age mumbo-jumbo).

Hence, if quantum parallelism taps into the geometry of the cosmological fractal attractor, and our cognition uses quantum parallelism, then our brains are tapping into the non-computability of the fractal attractor, consistent with Penrose's claim that we humans do not think algorithmically.

Does this mean that quantum computers will be capable of understanding, have free will, and be conscious? Penrose supposes that present-day quantum computers have any of these attributes, though conceivably, they have some precursors of these attributes. However, he thinks that quantum technology is necessary to one day create artificial intelligence on a par with humans.

He does not suppose creating such an AI will be easy or that we are close to achieving this goal, should we indeed desire such a goal (be careful what you ask for). However, if we do, it will be achieved by a judicious hybrid of classical and quantum computing elements).

Hartmut Neven, the founder and lead of Google Quantum AI, says quantum computers obtain superpowers by tapping into parallel universes. He explains how this emerging tech can surpass traditional computers by relying on quantum physics rather than binary logic and shares a roadmap to build the ultimate quantum computer.

We define consciousness and then answer the question of whether AI machines are capable of being conscious. How would we recognize it if it happened? Wikipedia defines consciousness as awareness of internal and external existence. *Scientific American* defines it as everything you experience.

In 1950, English mathematician Alan Turing proposed a way to determine whether a machine can actually think and whether it has a mind, called the Turing test in his honor, but was originally called the imitation game. In this test, a human judge holds a text conversation with a human being and a computer.

If he cannot reliably tell which of the two entities is artificial, then the artificial machine must be considered to have a mind. In March 2024, Stanford University researchers reported that the latest version of ChatGPT, GPT4, had passed a rigorous version of the Turing test. The problem with the Turing test is that while it can show that a machine can simulate human conversation, it does not prove that the machine has a mind, or is aware.

According to Arvin Hash, while a computer may perfectly simulate the workings of a coffee machine, it does not make anything that we can drink. This is why it is called a large language model (LLM). When you ask it something, it pieces together words that fit best with the question and context based on patterns that it recognizes from all the material it was trained on.

LLMs are nothing but algorithms trained to synthesize results based on human-produced data. They will not lead to new thoughts or discoveries. However, the argument against this is that if only humans or biological animals can be conscious, there is something unique about a biological brain that can never be replicated artificially.

What is the uniqueness of the human or animal brain? Some people believe consciousness does not arise from within the brain but from elsewhere and that the brain acts like a radio receiver. But there is no evidence of this.

Most cognitive scientists believe consciousness is an emergent phenomenon within the brain. It means that you would not find consciousness in individual neurons or other isolated brain structures but arising from the interconnections and chemical and electrical interactions of billions of neurons.

On the other hand, one can recite the vision of the Godfathers of AI "John Hopfield and Geoffrey Hinton, who believe that machines will eventually also have consciousness in time."[1]

Incidentally, the 2024 Nobel Prize in Physics for discoveries and inventions that enable machine learning within artificial neural networks was awarded to Geoffrey Hinton, a British Canadian computer scientist at the University of Toronto, and John Hopfield of Princeton University (Fig. 11.1).

[1]https://www.youtube.com/watch?v=qrvK_KuIeJk

The development of machine learning has expanded over the past 20 years and benefits from artificial neural networks (ANNs), which are modeled based on the dynamics and reconfiguration of 10 billion neurons in the human brain. Nowadays, when we talk about *artificial intelligence*, an ANN is often the type of technology we mean. Figure 11.2 shows an example of an ANN.

Figure 11.1 Professor John Hopfield, left, of Princeton University, and Professor Geoffrey Hinton, right, of the University of Toronto, won the 2024 Nobel Prize in Physics.

We elaborate on the evolution of consciousness in the Universe, starting with the Big Bang some 13.7 billion years ago. A recent book by Popa and Shahinpoor entitled *Energy, Mass, Intelligence, and Life* (EMIL, 2000) fully describes and maintains that after the Big Bang, the released energy started to convert to mass, which subsequently got converted to intelligent molecular structures such as DNA (deoxyribonucleic acid) and RNA (ribonucleic acid). RNA differs from DNA chemically because the nucleotides in RNA are ribonucleotides and contain ribose (hence the name ribonucleic acid). RNA contains the bases adenine (A), guanine (G), and cytosine (C); it contains the base uracil (U) instead of the thymine (T) in DNA.

Figure 11.2 An example of an ANN (with permission from Johan Jarnestad/ The Royal Swedish Academy of Sciences). © The Royal Swedish Academy of Sciences.

References and Further Readings

Akopian, N. (2006). Entangled photon pairs from semiconductor quantum dots. *Physical Review Letters*, **96**(2):130501.

Aspect, A., Grangier, P., and Roger, G. (1982). Experimental test of Bell's inequalities using time-varying analyzers. *Physical Review Letters*, **49**:1804–1807.

Augusiak, R., Demianowicz, M., Tura, J., and Acín, A. (2015). Entanglement and nonlocality are inequivalent for any number of parties. *Physical Review Letters*, **115**(3):030404.

Beiser, A. (1995). *Concepts of Modern Physics*, 5th edition. McGraw-Hill.

Bell, J. S. (1964). On the Einstein–Podolsky–Rosen paradox. *Physics*, **1**, 195.

Bengtsson, I., and Życzkowski, K. (2006). *Geometry of Quantum States. An Introduction to Quantum Entanglement.* Cambridge: Cambridge University Press.

Bernstein, J. (2013). *A Palette of Particles*. Harvard University Press.

Bhaskara, V. S., and Panigrahi, P. K. (2017). Generalized concurrence measure for faithful multiparticle pure state entanglement quantification using Lagrange's identity and wedge product. *Quantum Information Processing*, **16**(5):118.

Boette, A., Rossignoli, R., Gigena, N., and Cerezo, M. (2016). System–time entanglement in a discrete-time model. *Physical Review A*, **93**(6):062127.

Bokulich, A., and Jaeger, G. (2010). *Philosophy of Quantum Information and Entanglement*. Cambridge University Press.

Bub, J. (2019). *Quantum Entanglement and Information*. Stanford, California: Stanford University.

Clauser, J. F., Horne, M. A., Shimony, A., and Holt, R. A. (1969). Proposed experiment to test local hidden-variable theories. *Physical Review Letters*, **23**, 880.

Cramer, J. G. (2015). *The Quantum Handshake: Entanglement, Nonlocality and Transactions*. Springer Verlag.

Dickson, M. (1930). Quantum chance and non-locality: Probability and non-dirac PAM. In: *The Principles of Quantum Mechanics*. Oxford University Press.

Duarte, F. J. (2019). *Fundamentals of Quantum Entanglement*. Bristol, UK: Institute of Physics.

Dube, S. (1993). Undecidable problems in fractal geometry. *Complex Systems*, **7**:423–444.

Duncan, A. (2012). *The Conceptual Framework of Quantum Field Theory*. OUP Oxford.

Einstein, A., Podolsky, B., and Rosen, N. (1935). Can quantum-mechanical description of physical reality be considered complete? *Physical Review*, **47**:777–780.

Francis, M. (2012). Quantum entanglement shows that reality can't be local. *Ars Technica*. Retrieved from https://arstechnica.com/science/2012/10/quantum-entanglement-shows-that-reality-cant-be-local.

Freedman, S. J., and Clauser, J. F. (1972). Experimental test of local hidden-variable theories. *Physical Review Letters*, **28**, 938.

Friis, N., Vitagliano, G., Malik, M., and Huber, M. (2019). Entanglement certification from theory to experiment. *Nature Reviews Physics*, **1**:72–87.

Georgiev, D. D., and Gudder, S. P. (2022). Sensitivity of entanglement measures in bipartite pure quantum states. *Modern Physics Letters B*, **36**(22):22501012250255.

Georgiev, D., and Cohen, E. (2022). Entanglement measures for two-particle quantum histories. *Physical Review A*, **106**(6):062437.

Gharibian, S. (2010). Strong NP-hardness of the quantum separability problem. *Quantum Information and Computation*, **10**(3&4):343–360.

Gibney, E. (2014). Entangled photons make a picture from a paradox. *Nature*, doi:10.1038/nature.2014.15781.S2CID 124976589.

Gour, G., and Wallach, N. R. (2013). Classification of multipartite entanglement of all finite dimensionality. *Physical Review Letters*, **111**(6):060502.

Grassl, M., Rötteler, M., and Beth, T. (1998). Computing local invariants of quantum-bit systems. *Physical Review A*, **58**(3):1833–1839.

Gühne, O. (2004). Characterizing entanglement via uncertainty relations. *Physical Review Letters*, **92**(11):117903.

Gühne, O., and Lewenstein, M. (2004). Entropic uncertainty relations and entanglement. *Physical Review A*, **70**(2):022316.

Gühne, O., and Tóth, G. (2009). Entanglement detection. *Physics Reports*, **474**(1–6):1–75.

Gurvits, L. (2003). Classical deterministic complexity of Edmonds' problem and quantum entanglement. *Proceedings of the Thirty-Fifth Annual ACM Symposium on Theory of Computing*, p. 10. ACM Press, New York, 2003.

Hardy, L. (1992). Quantum mechanics, local realistic theories, and Lorentz-invariant realistic theories. *Physical Review Letters*, **68**(20):2981–2984.

Hesketh, G. (2016). *The Particle Zoo: The Search for the Fundamental Nature of Reality.* United Kingdom: Quercus.

Hillery, M., and Zubairy, M. S. (2006). Entanglement conditions for two-mode states. *Physical Review Letters*, **96**(5):050503.

Hofmann, H. F., and Takeuchi, S. (2003). Violation of local uncertainty relations as a signature of entanglement. *Physical Review A*, **68**(3):032103.

Holland, M. J., and Burnett, K. (1993). Interferometric detection of optical phase shifts at the Heisenberg limit. *Physical Review Letters*, **71**(9):1355–1358.

Hopfield, J., and Hinton, G. share the 2024 Nobel Prize for Physics, 08 Oct 2024.

Horodecki, M., Horodecki, P., and Horodecki, R. (1998). Mixed-state entanglement and distillation: Is there a bound entanglement in nature? *Physical Review Letters*, **80**(1998):5239–5242.

Horodecki, R., Horodecki, P., Horodecki, M., and Horodecki, K. (2009). Quantum entanglement. *Reviews of Modern Physics*, **81**(2):865–942.

Huang, Y. (2010). Entanglement criteria via concave-function uncertainty relations. *Physical Review A*, **82**(1):012335.

Huang, Y. (2013). Entanglement detection: Complexity and Shannon entropic criteria. *IEEE Transactions on Information Theory*, **59**(10):6774.

Jaeger, G. (2009). *Entanglement, Information, and the Interpretation of Quantum Mechanics*. Heildelberg: Springer.

Jozsa, R., and Linden, N. (2002). On the role of entanglement in quantum computational speed-up. *Proceedings of the Royal Society A: Mathematical, Physical and Engineering Sciences*, **459**(2036):2011–2032.

Kitagawa, M., and Ueda, M. (1993). Squeezed spin states. *Physical Review A*, **47**(6):5138–5143.

Kocher, C. A. (1971). Time correlations in the detection of successively emitted photons. *Annals of Physics*, **65**(1):1–18.

Kotler, S., Peterson, G. A., Shojaee, E., Lecocq, F., Cicak, K., Kwiatkowski, A., Geller, S., Glancy, S., Knill, E., Simmonds, R. W., Aumentado, J., and Teufel, J. D. (2021). Direct observation of deterministic macroscopic entanglement. *Science*, **372**(6542):622–625.

Lami, L., and Regula, B. (2023). No second law of entanglement manipulation after all. *Nature Physics*, **19**(2):184–189.

Leinaas, J. M., Myrheim, J., and Ovrum, E. (2006). Geometrical aspects of entanglement. *Physical Review A*, **74**(1):012313.

Lo Franco, R., and Compagno, G. (2018). Indistinguishability of elementary systems as a resource for quantum information processing. *Physical Review Letters*, **120**(24):240403.

Ma, X.-S., Zotter, S., Kofler, J., Ursin, R., Jennewein, T., Brukner, Č., and Zeilinger, A. (2012). Experimental delayed-choice entanglement swapping. *Nature Physics*, **8**(6):480485.

Markoff, J. (2015). Sorry, Einstein. Quantum study suggests 'spooky action' is real. *The New York Times*. Retrieved October 21, 2015.

Marletto, C., Coles, D. M., Farrow, T., and Vedral, V. (2018). Entanglement between living bacteria and quantized light witnessed by Rabi splitting. *Journal of Physics Communications*, **2**(10):101001.

Merzbacher, E. (1996). *Quantum Mechanics*, 2nd edition. New York: John Wiley.

Modinos, A. (1996). *Quantum Theory of Matter: A Novel Introduction*. John Wiley & Sons.

Moreva, E. (2014). Time from quantum entanglement: An experimental illustration. *Physical Review A*, **89**(5):052122.

Nielsen, M. A. (1999). Conditions for a class of entanglement transformations. *Physical Review Letters*, **83**(2):436.

Nielsen, M. A., and Chuang, I. L. (2000). *Quantum Computation and Quantum Information*. Cambridge University Press, pp. 112–113.

Palmer, T. (2022). *The Primacy of Doubt: From Climate Change to Quantum Physics, how the Science of Uncertainty Can Help Predict and Understand Our Chaotic World*. Oxford University Press.

Pan, J. W., Bouwmeester, D., Weinfurter, H., and Zeilinger, A. (1998). Experimental entanglement swapping: Entangling photons that never interacted. *Physical Review Letters*, **80**:3891.

Penrose, R. (1989). *The Emperor's New Mind*. Oxford University Press.

Penrose, R. (1994). *Shadows of the Mind: A Search for the Missing Science of Consciousness.* Oxford University Press.

Pirandola, S., Andersen, U. L., Banchi, L., Berta, M., Bunandar, D., Colbeck, R., Englund, D., Gehring, T., Lupo, C., Ottaviani, C., Pereira, J. L., Razavi, M., Shamsul Shaari, J., Tomamichel, M., Usenko, V. C., Vallone, G., Villoresi, P., and Wallden, P. (2020). Advances in quantum cryptography. *Advances in Optics and Photonics*, **12**(4):1012–1236.

Plenio, M. B., and Virmani, S. (2007). An introduction to entanglement measures. *Quantum Information & Computation*, **1**:1–51.

Popa, S. and Shahinpoor, M. (2000). *Energy, Matter, Intelligence and Life (EMIL)*, ECDM Press, Abq, NM.

Renner, R., Gisin, N., and Kraus, B. (2005). An information-theoretic security proof for QKD protocols. *Physical Review A*, **72**:012332.

Rozatkar, G. (2018). Demonstration of quantum entanglement. *OSF.*

Sabin, C., Garcia-Ripoll, J. J., Solano, E., and Leon, J. (2010). Dynamics of entanglement via propagating microwave photons. *Physical Review B*, **81**:184501.

Sakurai, J. J., and Napolitano, J. J. (2010). *Modern Quantum Mechanics*, 2nd edition. Pearson, p.68.

Schrödinger, E. (1935). Discussion of probability relations between separated systems. *Mathematical Proceedings of the Cambridge Philosophical Society*, **31**(4):555–563.

Schrödinger, E. (1936). Probability relations between separated systems. *Mathematical Proceedings of the Cambridge Philosophical Society*, **32**(3):446–452.

Shadbolt, P. J., Verde, M. R., Peruzzo, A., Politi, A., Laing, A., Lobino, M., Matthews, J. C. F., Thompson, M. G., and O'Brien, J. L. (2012). Generating, manipulating and measuring entanglement and mixture with a reconfigurable photonic circuit. *Nature Photonics*, **6**(1):45–59.

Simon, R. (2000). Peres–Horodecki separability criterion for continuous variable systems. *Physical Review Letters*, **84**(12):2726–2729.

Steward, E. G. (2008). *Quantum Mechanics: Its Early Development and the Road to Entanglement*. Imperial College Press.

Summhammer, J., Sulyok, G., and Bernroider, G. (2018). Quantum dynamics and non-local effects behind ion transition states during permeation in membrane channel proteins. *Entropy*, **20**:558.

Swain, S. N., Bhaskara, V. S., and Panigrahi, P. K. (2022). Generalized entanglement measure for continuous-variable systems. *Physical Review A*, **105**(5):052441.

Swingle, B., and Van Raamsdonk, M. (2014). Universality of gravity from entanglement. https://arxiv.org/abs/1405.2933v1.

Thomas, R. A., Parniak, M., Østfeldt, C., Møller, C. B., Bærentsen, C., Tsaturyan, Y., Schliesser, A., Appel, J., Zeuthen, E., and Polzik, E. S. (2020). Entanglement between distant macroscopic mechanical and spin systems. *Nature Physics*, **17**(2):228–233.

Van Raamsdonk, M. (2010). Building up spacetime with quantum entanglement. *General Relativity and Gravitation*, **42**(10):2323–2329.

Vértesi, T., and Brunner, N. (2014). Disproving the Peres conjecture by showing Bell nonlocality from bound entanglement. *Nature Communications*, **5**(1):5297.

Vilenkin, A. (1995). Predictions from quantum cosmology. *Physical Review Letters*, **74**:846–849.

Walborn, S., Taketani, B., Salles, A., Toscano, F., and de Matos Filho, R. (2009). Entropic entanglement criteria for continuous variables. *Physical Review Letters*, **103**(16):160505.

Weatherall, J. O. (2013). The scope and generality of Bell's theorem. *Foundations of Physics*, **43**(9):1153–1169.

Werner, R. F., and Wolf, M. M. (2001). Bound entangled Gaussian states. *Physical Review Letters*, **86**(16):3658–3661.

Wineland, D. J., Bollinger, J. J., Itano, W. M., Moore, F. L., and Heinzen, D. J. (1992). Spin squeezing and reduced quantum noise in spectroscopy. *Physical Review A*, **46**(11):R6797–R6800.

Wiseman, H. M., Jones, S. J., and Doherty, A. C. (2007). Steering, entanglement, nonlocality, and the Einstein–Podolsky–Rosen paradox. *Physical Review Letters*, **98**(14):140402.

Wong, B. (2019). Existence of tachyons and their detection. *Research & Reviews: Journal of Physics*, **8**(2):23–26.

Wong, B. (2019). On quantum entanglement. *International Journal of Automatic Control System*, **5**(2):1–7.

Yin, J., Cao, Y., Li, Y.-H., Liao, S.-K., Zhang, L., Ren, J.-G., Cai, W.-Q., Liu, W.-Y., Li, B., Dai, H., Li, G.-B., Lu, Q.-M., Gong, Y.-H., Xu, Y., Li, S.-L., Li, F.-Z., Yin, Y.-Y., Jiang, Z.-Q., Li, M., Jia, J.-J., Ren, G., He, D., Zhou, Y.-L., Zhang, X.-X., Wang, N., Chang, X., Zhu, Z.-C., Liu, N.-L., Chen, Y.-A., Lu, C.-Y., Shu, R., Peng, C.-Z., Wang, J.-Y., and Pan, J.-W. (2017). Satellite-based entanglement distribution over 1200 kilometers. *Science*, **356**(6343):1140–1144.

Yin, J., Cao, Y., Yong, H.-L., Ren, J.-G., Liang, H., Liao, S.-K., Zhou, F., Liu, C., Wu, Y.-P., Pan, G.-S., Zhang, Q., Peng, C.-Z., and Pan, J.-W. (2013). Bounding the speed of 'spooky action at a distance'. *Physical Review Letters*, **110**(26):260407.

Yin, J., Li, Y.-H., Liao, S.-K., Yang, M., Cao, Y., Zhang, L., Ren, J.-G., Cai, W.-Q., Liu, W.-Y., Li, S.-L., Shu, R., Huang, Y.-M., Deng, L., Li, L., Zhang, Q., Liu, N.-L., Chen, Y.-A., Lu, C.-Y., Wang, X.-B., Xu, F., Wang, J.-Y., Peng, C.-Z., Ekert, A. K., and Pan, J.-W. (2020). Entanglement-based secure quantum cryptography over 1,120 kilometers. *Nature*, **582**(7813):501–505.

Chapter 12

Development of Advanced Software to Understand IA Consciousness

This chapter describes the development of methodologies, strategies, and paradigms to prepare individuals as they gradually complete their human lives while benefitting from the companionship/friendship of their corresponding biomimetic humanoid robots with partial human consciousness. These individuals are transferred to a conversion unit to conclude their human lives and continue living as biomimetic humanoid robots with their identity-vita-assigned consciousness (IVA-consciousness).

Advanced software was developed to understand IVA-consciousness. The software was then transferred to selected volunteers so that their IA consciousness could be transferred to an intelligent (AI-based) computer. Note that one can recite the vision of the winners of the 2024 Nobel Prize for Physics, or Godfathers of AI, "John Hopfield and Geoffrey Hinton, who believe that machines will eventually also have consciousness in time."[1]

The human masters will continuously teach their humanoid robots about consciousness, especially the complex consciousness of love, like, hate, jealousy, anger, regrets, music enjoyment, sex enjoyment, vengeance/retaliation, worry, anxiety, etc. Thus, the

[1]https://www.youtube.com/watch?v=qrvK_KuleJk

Biomimetic Humanoid Robots with Human Consciousness
Mohsen Shahinpoor

ISBN 978-981-5129-87-8 (Hardcover), 978-1-003-71373-9 (eBook)
www.jennystanford.com

DOI: 10.1201/9781003713739-12

humanoid robots will eventually acquire partial consciousness from the master humans and develop normal communication skills. Here, the biomimetic humanoid robots with human consciousness start to live independently but under the human masters' identity and IVA-consciousness.

Essentially, the transfer of consciousness to humanoid robots starts with identifying the transferring consciousness. In other words, as discussed in Chapters 1 and 2, this was designed and created with an onboard set of microprocessors, computing instructions, storage, and onboard intelligent computers, which may also be AI computers. Having programmed the humanoid robots, say Captain Kirk's humanoid robot, to identify itself as Captain Kirk's humanoid will enable the human Master (Captain Kirk) to scan, transfer all the consciousness issues and knowledge gradually and upload IVA Consciousness to the onboard AI computers. The human master and the humanoid will then treat each other as companions and close friends and communicate about the human master's consciousness for several years.

Research has been proposed in the book on how to transfer IVA-consciousness to biomimetic humanoid robots. They will interact regarding the transferred consciousness, as described in the book. When the time arrives, the corresponding human master of a humanoid robot needs to exit or complete his or her life (due to old age or sickness) and move toward cremation or burial. Then, the humanoid robot with almost human consciousness will live immortally in place of its human master and can travel in deep space without needing air, water, food, normal temperature, or whatever is needed on the Earth during normal life. However, it will have a long-lasting nuclear diamond battery that has energy for a long time before being charged or replaced.

Research on machine consciousness, which is entirely non-organic, also clearly shows that humanoids could go non-organic and follow a silicone-based life. Discussing the preservation of humanity through machine consciousness seems doable, and creating immortality in humanoids is possible and is a philosophical issue.

It is important to note that humans will not become obsolete in this scenario. They will continue to live for as long as possible, maintaining interaction and companionship with their humanoid robot, which now houses the transferred consciousness. While a human's life will eventually come to an end, the humanoid robot will persist, enriched by the transferred and improved human IVA-consciousness.

We are always exploring these capabilities in ourselves and sometimes need help from a council. A robot does not know what kind of robot it is and what it can do. Robot inverse kinematics and inverse dynamics software can instruct it to move in certain ways or configurations, perform complicated maneuvers and motions, and perform stimuli-responsive reactions (see the Atlas 1 robot's unbelievable maneuvers and flipping from Boston Dynamics).

The human IVA-consciousness recorded in the embedded consciousness computer will be transferred to the robot's memory bank as IVA-consciousness. After the transfer, the human and the humanoid robot start to interact and communicate with each other and become companions and friends. Enhance mind uploading of consciousness and try to interact to teach the humanoid robot regarding the IVA-consciousness software to communicate with the humanoid robot to teach further the humanoid content of the transferred IVA-consciousness software. In this final interaction between the human and the humanoid robot, the human consciousness can be transferred to the humanoid robot by cognition, logical explanations, and analysis.

The book proposes this interaction as an *oral cognitive consciousness transfer* from a human to a humanoid robot. The humanoid robot will not reproduce itself because it has its identity and personality. These humanoids do not need to reproduce themselves because they are unique, but they can design and create baby humanoid robots to be trained and allowed to grow up. You can also develop enjoyment when creating baby humanoid robots or artwork, creativity, and intellectual properties (IP).

The humanoid robots will live on immortally and can travel to other planets and deep space on interplanetary ships, similar to the Enterprise in the Star Trek episodes.

References and Further Readings

Akopian, N. (2006). Entangled photon pairs from semiconductor quantum dots. *Physical Review Letters*, **96**(2):130501.

Aspect, A., Grangier, P., and Roger, G. (1982). Experimental test of Bell's inequalities using time-varying analyzers. *Physical Review Letters*, **49**:1804–1807.

Augusiak, R., Demianowicz, M., Tura, J., and Acín, A. (2015). Entanglement and nonlocality are inequivalent for any number of parties. *Physical Review Letters*, **115**(3):030404.

Bell, J. S. (1964). On the Einstein–Podolsky–Rosen paradox. *Physics*, **1**:195.

Bengtsson, I., and Życzkowski, K. (2006). *Geometry of Quantum States: An Introduction to Quantum Entanglement.* Cambridge: Cambridge University Press.

Bhaskara, V. S., and Panigrahi, P. K. (2017). Generalized concurrence measure for faithful quantification of multiparticle pure state entanglement using Lagrange's identity and wedge product. *Quantum Information Processing*, **16**(5):118.

Boette, A., Rossignoli, R., Gigena, N., and Cerezo, M. (2016). System–time entanglement in a discrete-time model. *Physical Review A*, **93**(6):062127.

Bokulich, A., and Jaeger, G. (2010). *Philosophy of Quantum Information and Entanglement.* Cambridge University Press, p. xv.

Bub, J. (2019). *Quantum Entanglement and Information. Stanford Encyclopedia of Philosophy*. Stanford, California: Stanford University.

Clauser, J. F., Horne, M. A., Shimony, A., and Holt, R. A. (1969). Proposed experiment to test local hidden-variable theories. *Physical Review Letters*, **23**:880.

Cramer, J. G. (2015). *The Quantum Handshake: Entanglement, Nonlocality and Transactions*. Springer Verlag.

Duarte, F. J. (2019). *Fundamentals of Quantum Entanglement.* Bristol, UK: Institute of Physics.

Einstein, A., Podolsky, B., and Rosen, N. (1935). Can quantum-mechanical description of physical reality be considered complete? *Physical Review*, **47**:777–780.

Francis, M. (2012). Quantum entanglement shows that reality can't be local. *Ars Technica*. Retrieved from https://arstechnica.com/science/2012/10/quantum-entanglement-shows-that-reality-cant-be-local.

Freedman, S. J., and Clauser, J. F. (1972). Experimental test of local hidden-variable theories. *Physical Review Letters*, **28**, 938.

Friis, N., Vitagliano, G., Malik, M., and Huber, M. (2019). Entanglement certification from theory to experiment. *Nature Reviews Physics*, **1**:72–87.

Georgiev, D. D., and Gudder, S. P. (2022). Sensitivity of entanglement measures in bipartite pure quantum states. *Modern Physics Letters B*, **36**(22):22501012250255.

Georgiev, D., and Cohen, E. (2022). Entanglement measures for two-particle quantum histories. *Physical Review A*, **106**(6):062437.

Gharibian, S. (2010). Strong NP-hardness of the quantum separability problem. *Quantum Information and Computation*, **10**(3&4):343–360.

Gibney, E. (2014). Entangled photons make a picture from a paradox. *Nature*, doi:10.1038/nature.2014.15781.S2CID 124976589.

Gour, G., and Wallach, N. R. (2013). Classification of multipartite entanglement of all finite dimensionality. *Physical Review Letters*, **111**(6):060502.

Grassl, M., Rötteler, M., and Beth, T. (1998). Computing local invariants of quantum-bit systems. *Physical Review A*, **58**(3):1833–1839.

Gühne, O. (2004). Characterizing entanglement via uncertainty relations. *Physical Review Letters*, **92**(11):117903.

Gühne, O., and Lewenstein, M. (2004). Entropic uncertainty relations and entanglement. *Physical Review A*, **70**(2):022316.

Gühne, O., and Tóth, G. (2009). Entanglement detection. *Physics Reports*, **474**(1–6):1–75.

Gurvits, L. (2003). Classical deterministic complexity of Edmonds' problem and quantum entanglement, in *Proceedings of the 35th ACM Symposium on Theory of Computing*, ACM Press, New York.

Hardy, L. (1992). Quantum mechanics, local realistic theories, and Lorentz-invariant realistic theories. *Physical Review Letters*, **68**(20):2981–2984.

Hillery, M., and Zubairy, M. S. (2006). Entanglement conditions for two-mode states. *Physical Review Letters*, **96**(5):050503.

Hofmann, H. F., and Takeuchi, S. (2003). Violation of local uncertainty relations as a signature of entanglement. *Physical Review A*, **68**(3):032103.

Holland, M. J., and Burnett, K. (1993). Interferometric detection of optical phase shifts at the Heisenberg limit. *Physical Review Letters*, **71**(9):1355–1358.

Horodecki, M., Horodecki, P., and Horodecki, R. (1998). Mixed-state entanglement and distillation: Is there a bound entanglement in nature? *Physical Review Letters*, **80**(1998):5239–5242.

Horodecki, R., Horodecki, P., Horodecki, M., and Horodecki, K. (2009). Quantum entanglement. *Reviews of Modern Physics*, **81**(2):865–942.

Huang, Y. (2010). Entanglement criteria via concave-function uncertainty relations. *Physical Review A*, **82**(1):012335.

Huang, Y. (2013). Entanglement detection: Complexity and Shannon entropic criteria. *IEEE Transactions on Information Theory*, **59**(10):6774.

Jaeger, G. (2009). *Entanglement, Information, and the Interpretation of Quantum Mechanics*. Heildelberg: Springer.

Jozsa, R., and Linden, N. (2002). On the role of entanglement in quantum computational speed-up. *Proceedings of the Royal Society A: Mathematical, Physical and Engineering Sciences*, **459**(2036):2011–2032.

Kitagawa, M., and Ueda, M. (1993). Squeezed spin states. *Physical Review A*, **47**(6):5138–5143.

Kocher, C. A. (1971). Time correlations in the detection of successively emitted photons. *Annals of Physics*, **65**(1):1–18.

Kotler, S., Peterson, G. A., Shojaee, E., Lecocq, F., Cicak, K., Kwiatkowski, A., Geller, S., Glancy, S., Knill, E., Simmonds, R. W., Aumentado, J., and Teufel, J. D. (2021). Direct observation of deterministic macroscopic entanglement. *Science*, **372**(6542):622–625.

Lami, L., and Regula, B. (2023). No second law of entanglement manipulation after all. *Nature Physics*, **19**(2):184–189.

Leinaas, J. M., Myrheim, J., and Ovrum, E. (2006). Geometrical aspects of entanglement. *Physical Review A*, **74**(1):012313.

Lo Franco, R., and Compagno, G. (2018). Indistinguishability of elementary systems as a resource for quantum information processing. *Physical Review Letters*, **120**(24):240403.

Ma, X.-S., Zotter, S., Kofler, J., Ursin, R., Jennewein, T., Brukner, Č., and Zeilinger, A. (2012). Experimental delayed-choice entanglement swapping. *Nature Physics*, **8**(6):480485.

Markoff, J. (2015). Sorry, Einstein. Quantum study suggests 'spooky action' is real. *The New York Times*. Retrieved 21 October 2015.

Marletto, C., Coles, D. M., Farrow, T., and Vedral, V. (2018). Entanglement between living bacteria and quantized light witnessed by Rabi splitting. *Journal of Physics Communications*, **2**(10):101001.

Moreva, E. (2014). Time from quantum entanglement: An experimental illustration. *Physical Review A*, **89**(5):052122.

Niels Bohr Institute. (2020). Quantum entanglement realized between distant large objects. Retrieved on October 9, 2020, from https://nbi.ku.dk/english/news/news20/quantum-entanglement-realized-between-distant-large-objects.

Nielsen, M. A. (1999). Conditions for a class of entanglement transformations. *Physical Review Letters*, **83**(2):436.

Nielsen, M. A., and Chuang, I. L. (2000). *Quantum Computation and Quantum Information*. Cambridge University Press, pp. 112–113.

Pan, J. W., Bouwmeester, D., Weinfurter, H., and Zeilinger, A. (1998). Experimental entanglement swapping: Entangling photons that never interacted. *Physical Review Letters*, **80**:3891.

Pirandola, S., Andersen, U. L., Banchi, L., Berta, M., Bunandar, D., Colbeck, R., Englund, D., Gehring, T., Lupo, C., Ottaviani, C., Pereira, J. L., Razavi, M., Shamsul Shaari, J., Tomamichel, M., Usenko, V. C., Vallone, G., Villoresi, P., and Wallden, P. (2020). Advances in quantum cryptography. *Advances in Optics and Photonics*, **12**(4):1012–1236.

Plenio, M. B., and Virmani, S. (2007). An introduction to entanglement measures. *Quantum Information & Computation*, **1**:1–51.

Renner, R., Gisin, N., and Kraus, B. (2005). An information-theoretic security proof for QKD protocols. *Physical Review A*, **72**:012332.

Rozatkar, G. (2018). Demonstration of quantum entanglement. *OSF*.

Sakurai, J. J., and Napolitano, J. J. (2010). *Modern Quantum Mechanics*, 2nd edition. Pearson, p.68.

Schrödinger, E. (1935). Discussion of probability relations between separated systems. *Mathematical Proceedings of the Cambridge Philosophical Society*, **31**(4):555–563.

Schrödinger, E. (1936). Probability relations between separated systems. *Mathematical Proceedings of the Cambridge Philosophical Society*, **32**(3):446452.

Shadbolt, P. J., Verde, M. R., Peruzzo, A., Politi, A., Laing, A., Lobino, M., Matthews, J. C. F., Thompson, M. G., and O'Brien, J. L. (2012). Generating, manipulating and measuring entanglement and mixture with a reconfigurable photonic circuit. *Nature Photonics*, **6**(1):45–59.

Simon, R. (2000). Peres–Horodecki separability criterion for continuous variable systems. *Physical Review Letters*, **84**(12):2726–2729.

Steward, E. G. (2008). *Quantum Mechanics: Its Early Development and the Road to Entanglement*. Imperial College Press.

Swain, S. N., Bhaskara, V. S., and Panigrahi, P. K. (2022). Generalized entanglement measure for continuous-variable systems. *Physical Review A*, **105**(5):052441.

Swingle, B., and Van Raamsdonk, M. (2014). Universality of gravity from entanglement. https://arxiv.org/abs/1405.2933v1.

Thomas, R. A., Parniak, M., Østfeldt, C., Møller, C. B., Bærentsen, C., Tsaturyan, Y., Schliesser, A., Appel, J., Zeuthen, E., and Polzik, E. S. (2020). Entanglement between distant macroscopic mechanical and spin systems. *Nature Physics*, **17**(2):228–233.

Van Raamsdonk, M. (2010). Building up spacetime with quantum entanglement. *General Relativity and Gravitation*, **42**(10):2323–2329.

Vértesi, T., and Brunner, N. (2014). Disproving the Peres conjecture by showing Bell nonlocality from bound entanglement. *Nature Communications*, **5**(1): 5297.

Walborn, S., Taketani, B., Salles, A., Toscano, F., and de Matos Filho, R. (2009). Entropic entanglement criteria for continuous variables. *Physical Review Letters*, **103**(16):160505.

Werner, R. F., and Wolf, M. M. (2001). Bound entangled Gaussian states. *Physical Review Letters*, **86**(16):3658–3661.

Wineland, D. J., Bollinger, J. J., Itano, W. M., Moore, F. L., and Heinzen, D. J. (1992). Spin squeezing and reduced quantum noise in spectroscopy. *Physical Review A*, **46**(11).

Wiseman, H. M., Jones, S. J., and Doherty, A. C. (2007). Steering, entanglement, nonlocality, and the Einstein–Podolsky–Rosen paradox. *Physical Review Letters*, **98**(14):140402.

Wogan, T. (2021). Vibrating drumheads are entangled quantum mechanically. *Physics World*, May 17, 2021.

Yin, J., Cao, Y., Li, Y.-H., Liao, S.-K., Zhang, L., Ren, J.-G., Cai, W.-Q., Liu, W.-Y., Li, B., Dai, H., Li, G.-B., Lu, Q.-M., Gong, Y.-H., Xu, Y., Li, S.-L., Li, F.-Z., Yin, Y.-Y., Jiang, Z.-Q., Li, M., Jia, J.-J., Ren, G., He, D., Zhou, Y.-L., Zhang, X.-X., Wang, N., Chang, X., Zhu, Z.-C., Liu, N.-L., Chen, Y.-A., Lu, C.-Y., Shu, R., Peng, C.-Z., Wang, J.-Y., and Pan, J.-W. (2017). Satellite-based entanglement distribution over 1200 kilometers. *Science*, 356(6343): 1140–1144.

Yin, J., Cao, Y., Yong, H.-L., Ren, J.-G., Liang, H., Liao, S.-K., Zhou, F., Liu, C., Wu, Y.-P., Pan, G.-S., Zhang, Q., Peng, C.-Z., and Pan, J.-W. (2013). Bounding the speed of 'spooky action at a distance.' *Physical Review Letters*, **110**(26):260407.

Yin, J., Li, Y.-H., Liao, S.-K., Yang, M., Cao, Y., Zhang, L., Ren, J.-G., Cai, W.-Q., Liu, W.-Y., Li, S.-L., Shu, R., Huang, Y.-M., Deng, L., Li, L., Zhang, Q., Liu, N.-L., Chen, Y.-A., Lu, C.-Y., Wang, X.-B., Xu, F., Wang, J.-Y., Peng, C.-Z., Ekert, A. K., and Pan, J.-W. (2020). Entanglement-based secure quantum cryptography over 1,120 kilometers. *Nature*, **582**(7813):501–505.

Chapter 13

Emergence of Machine Consciousness to Replace or Mimic Human Consciousness

13.1 Introduction

This chapter discusses the emergence of machine consciousness to replace or mimic human consciousness. Artificial consciousness (also known as machine consciousness, synthetic consciousness, or identity-vita-assigned (IVA)-consciousness) refers to a non-biological, human-created machine that is aware of its existence (being) as well as the resume or vita of its human master. Machine consciousness will help the humanoid robot's design, development, fabrication, software transfer, and operation in moving capabilities (walking, running, flying, jumping, skiing, swimming, jetting, etc.) of biomimetic humanoid robots with human consciousness. Here, the book covers robotic fundamentals such as homogeneous transformations, Denavit–Hartenberg transformations, and direct and inverse kinematics (Shahinpoor and Gheshmi, 2015). Ways to provide moving and dynamic capabilities to humanoids with IVA-consciousness have also been discussed.

The basic strategy to transfer consciousness to human beings starts after the human being is born as an individual and grows up. It is later embedded with an AI-based, advanced computer. The embedded AI smart computer observes and records all events as

Biomimetic Humanoid Robots with Human Consciousness
Mohsen Shahinpoor

ISBN 978-981-5129-87-8 (Hardcover), 978-1-003-71373-9 (eBook)
www.jennystanford.com

DOI: 10.1201/9781003713739-13

the individual grows, observes, and reacts to them. As the individual grows, the embedded computer using IVA-consciousness will record and may recall everything observed, heard, or experienced. The humanoid robot is then fabricated and becomes a *life companion* of the human master for several years, as the human master gradually transfers and describes his or her consciousness to the humanoid robot to remember and be aware of. There will be laboratory research facilities for the individuals ready to design, develop, fabricate, and make operational the humanoid biomimetic robot and transfer consciousness cognitively and life vita (resume) from the humans to become a biomimetic humanoid robot with consciousness to serve in the future. When the transferred individuals are ready to exit for whatever reason (sickness or old age), they will exit and be accordingly cremated or buried. At the same time, their corresponding biomimetic humanoid robot will emerge to lead a new life. These laboratory chambers can also convert animals into biomimetic robots with consciousness and sentience. The only catch is how to teach or describe the emotional effects and feelings, such as love, hate, like, dislike, jealousy, anger, regrets, music enjoyment, sex enjoyment, vengeance/retaliation, worry, and anxiety. The present book also discusses these topics in detail.

The design and development of moving capabilities (walking, running, flying, jumping, skiing, swimming, jetting, other sports activities, etc.) were covered in Chapter 6, which discusses the kinematics and dynamics of humanoid robots and their inverse kinematics and inverse dynamics.

The basic strategy to transfer consciousness to human beings starts after the human being grows up to be a young or middle-aged individual. It is later embedded with an AI-based, advanced computer. The embedded AI smart computer observes and records all events as the individual observes and reacts to them. As the individual grows, the embedded computer using IVA-consciousness will record and may recall everything observed, heard, or experienced. There will be laboratory research facilities for the individuals ready to participate in designing, developing, fabricating, and operationalizing the humanoid biomimetic robots. The humanoid robot is further assigned the identity of a human master to remember and be self-aware of, as well as assigning and transferring the human master's entire resume (vita) to the AI memory of resident computers.

Further, it transfers consciousness and awareness to resident AI computers from humans to become biomimetic humanoid robots with machine consciousness to serve in the future. The concept of being on and waiting silently should also be taught cognitively to the humanoid robot.

When the transferred individuals are ready to leave for whatever reason (sickness or old age), they will be cremated or buried accordingly. At the same time, their corresponding biomimetic humanoid robot will emerge to continue replacing them, leading to a new life and possibly immortality.

Artificial consciousness implies sentience and self-awareness. It could be used in a voice assistant or humanoid robot designed with interactivity. Some argue that consciousness is complex and non-binary and that a machine is either conscious or not. Others, such as Ned Block, on the other hand, believe that consciousness is a mongrel concept and that there are several different types of consciousness.

On a similar line of thought, Marco Marinelli argues for "states of consciousness." In explaining consciousness, Marinelli uses a computer analogy wherein the brain represents our computer hardware, and the states of consciousness represent its operating programs.

In a book titled *Architects of Intelligence*, writer and futurist Martin ford interviews a number of prominent people working in AI, asking the question of when there will be at least 50% chance of artificial general intelligence (AGI)—not even artificial consciousness—being built. Some others, such as Rodney Brooks (cofounder of iRobot), were less optimistic.

Futurist Ray Kurzweil (1990) predicts that by this point, humans will be a hybrid of biological and non-biological intelligence that will become increasingly dominated by the non-biological (artificial) component. AI will reach human-level intelligence by 2029, and that humanity will merge with technology, becoming "superhuman" by around 2045, a concept he calls the "Singularity." Kurzweil suggests that "AI is not an intelligent invasion from Mars. These are brain extenders that we have created to expand our mental reach. They are part of our civilization. They are part of who we are."

Once a two-way "brain to technology" interface has been developed, augmented humans combining the best biological human intelligence, inspiration, and emotion with artificial technological processing speed and storage capabilities could begin to make significant new technological developments. Past this point, the pace of change might grow exponentially.

Therefore, the development of artificial consciousness could become gradual, with the biological component of "intelligence" slowly diminishing as increasingly sophisticated technology does more of the work of "thought."

13.2 Can a Machine Be Conscious? What Is "Consciousness"?

There does not seem to be a consensus on what "consciousness" means when discussing artificial consciousness. There is still debate over its definition, with several different explanations put forth by neuroscientists and philosophers. The difficulty lies in that, unlike intelligence, consciousness involves subjective experience. David Chalmers coined this subjectivity as the "hard problem of consciousness."

The hard problem is the difficulty in explaining how subjective states can arise from objective physical systems. A subjective experience is, for example, what it is like to see the color red or feel pain. Our perception is subjective and involves sight, smell, touch, and emotion and has, by and large, several biochemical influences.

We see colors differently from a dog, which sees differently from an insect, and yet we are all "alive."

13.3 Types of Consciousness

While there are several different theories and papers written on consciousness, there is also a general understanding that consciousness involves both an objective and a subjective element.

Ned Block distinguishes between two types of consciousness: phenomenal consciousness and access consciousness. The former refers to the mind's ability to reason and guide behavior, while the latter relates to "experience"—"what it is like to be in that state."

This concept of "access consciousness" may be what most people mean when discussing artificial consciousness. Arguably, artificial phenomenal consciousness may have already been reached: self-driving cars can understand their environment and make decisions.

13.4 Understanding Consciousness is Needed First Before Realizing Artificial Consciousness

One of the difficulties in creating artificial consciousness is that to do so, we need to have a strong understanding of what consciousness is and how it arises in the brain—particularly from a scientific perspective. While the debate has been predominantly discussed from a philosophical standpoint, neuroscience has recently taken an interest in consciousness and seems determined to come up with an explanation of how it arises in the physical sense.

We know that consciousness is affected by neurons and has at its core a biochemical origin. For example, Margnelli cites the effect of LSD on the state of consciousness due to the chemical's direct impact on how neurons communicate. He claims the study on the effects of LSD in the brain "suddenly disclosed extraordinary connections between the neuronal hardware and the mental software, thus suggesting that consciousness is somehow a product of the activity of neurons and of chemical relations set up among them."

Neuroscience suggests that whatever consciousness is, it must arise physically through the brain and nervous system. The idea is that if something has its origins in the physical, science can replicate it. Science has already replicated a human heart, so why would it not be able to replicate the brain in the form of artificial consciousness?

13.5 Identifying Artificial Consciousness

Philosopher Nick Bostrom has said that, given our problems with understanding "consciousness," we must accept the possibility that true self-aware artificial consciousness could arise long before machines reach human-level intellect (or beyond). Bostrom suggests that humanity could, in the future, unwittingly cause the suffering of an artificial consciousness.

13.5.1 What Does It Mean for a Machine to Act Intelligently?

There is no one definition of intelligence or test for measuring machine intelligence. We assume that basic intelligence is the ability to survive and proliferate.

As with consciousness, there are several different interpretations. In fact, Legg and Hutter produced an entire report reviewing over 70 different definitions of intelligence, highlighting the numerous interpretations depending on the field and subject matter.

Nonetheless, when discussing AI and artificial consciousness, the "gold standard" is to human beings and, therefore, natural intelligence. Much in the same way that human intelligence is measured by testing problem-solving, a machine is considered intelligent if it can solve problems. The more complex these problems are, the more intelligent the machine can be considered.

If a machine can solve specific problems better than a human, it can be considered more intelligent in that field, but that does not mean that they are intelligent in all measures of intelligence. Perhaps the existing definition of intelligence is too narrow and needs to be reconsidered.

13.5.2 The Turing Test

In 1950, Alan Turing proposed "The Imitation Game," now known as the "Turing Test," which tests a machine's ability to exhibit intelligent behavior. It is based on the notion that if a machine acts in a way that is indistinguishable from a person, then it is considered to be intelligent. In this game, a human evaluator must decide between A and B, which is the machine and which is the human, based solely on their answers. If the evaluator cannot correctly distinguish the human from the machine, the machine would be considered intelligent.

Machine intelligence has come a long way since 1950, and scientists have already created robots that surpass human intelligence—for example at chess, data mining, search theorem, and others. As such, the Turing Test has been criticized for having limited applicability in this new age of intelligence.

13.5.3 The Chinese Room Argument

In a seminal article published in 1980, philosopher John Searle put forth "one of the best-known arguments" against strong AI: The Chinese Room Argument. In his argument, Searle imagines himself in a room where he receives Chinese characters that have been slipped under the door. Searle knows no Chinese but is following a program for manipulating symbols and numerals much like a computer does. Then, he sends back the appropriate Chinese characters under the door from those instructions. Because he successfully followed the program, people on the other side of the door would suppose there was a Chinese speaker on the other end—when, in fact, there is not. Searle's point that artificial intelligence is and can never be strong lies in the fact that AI uses syntactic rules but does not understand meaning or semantics.

13.6 Are Human and Machine Intelligence the Same?

Machine intelligence is inherently different from human intelligence, not only because of the differences in hardware (one analogous and one digital) but also because machine intelligence tends to be highly specialized. To build conscious machines, focus on general intelligence: a framework for the assessment of consciousness in biological and artificial systems.

In a paper on machine consciousness, Shevlin et al. argue there is a difference between specialized and general intelligence (Shevlin, Vold Crosby, and Malin, 2019). They argue that when it comes to machine consciousness, "it is general intelligence that matters." They cite three criteria for assessing general intelligence (and, therefore, the possibility of consciousness): robustness, flexibility, and whole-system integration.

A specialized intelligent machine—for example, a toaster that knows when your toast is made the way you like it—is intelligent when measured in that way. But it cannot tell you the weather outside, tie shoelaces, or aspire to be anything other than a smart toaster.

13.7 Philosophy of Artificial Intelligence and Artificial Consciousness

There are some deep philosophical questions about what it means to be alive and so the degree to which this is (or could be) reproducible in technology.

13.7.1 Can a Machine Have Emotions?

Whether machines can have artificial emotions is the same as answering whether they could have artificial consciousness. We do not know. We do not yet know how to artificially create emotion because we do not know how exactly it arises in the brain.

Robots have been created that can imitate emotions and *appear* to have emotions. These "emotional robots" are simply doing as programmed, though, and are lightyears away from possessing any intelligence or artificial consciousness. In this study, emotional robots were programmed to appear as if they had feelings by saying, "Please don't switch me off" and "I'm afraid of the dark." This, in turn, affected how people interacted with them.

However, AI has been developed to read emotions in humans. Humans and animals, as social creatures, rely on emotions to interact with and understand each other. Body language, tone, and intonation all express our feelings and emotions and are usually spontaneous and automatic. Understanding these signals is called emotional intelligence and has been described as "critical to the success of human interactions." These robots are being developed to learn and interpret human emotion by interpreting tone, voice, and body language cues, such as facial expressions. However, there still are not any robots that can replicate this and "feel" emotions in the same way.

Perhaps one of the reasons developments of artificial consciousness have not yet reached a point where robots can feel emotions is because there do not seem to be many reasons we would want robots to feel emotions. There is a strong argument that robots are more efficient without artificial emotion or artificial consciousness, especially when considering them within the workplace, which would be counterproductive. If robots can "feel" tired or emotional and get distracted from their core duties, would there be any advantage over human workers?

However, there are other industries where robots would be taking care of patients, where artificial consciousness and emotions might be beneficial. In care homes today, for instance, some AI is being used to care for the elderly or the infirm, and the more human they appear, the more they can foster "relationships" with those they care for—thus improving their function.

Thus, this book proposes that keeping humanoid robots as companions of their human masters for several years may be one way to semi-cognitively transfer consciousness, self-awareness, emotions, and similar sensations to humanoid robots.

13.7.2 Can a Machine Be Self-Aware?

Among the numerous definitions of consciousness, it has been helpful to many scientists to categorize different levels or stages of consciousness. Some scientists argued there are three levels and that self-awareness emerges in the third level, "C2," and is "commonly called introspection, or what psychologists call meta-cognition." There has been little evidence of humanoid robots developing this level of consciousness or self-awareness, but according to the 2024 Nobel laureates Hinton and Hopfield, we will eventually develop machine consciousness in time.

13.7.3 Can a Machine Be Original or Creative?

AI is creative in several tasks, from songwriting to painting and even rapping. However, in these studies involving machine learning, where machines produce content that might be deemed art, it is difficult to argue with any conviction that creativity is involved. This is because all the AI does is extrapolate from a data set and reproduce within a predefined amount of random error.

13.7.4 Can a Machine Be Benevolent or Hostile?

Benevolence and malevolence are largely related to emotions. We know that AI cannot feel emotions at the moment and is, for the most part, highly predictable. Nonetheless, there is much out there about the dangers of AI, and plenty of science fiction novels and TV series premised on the idea that artificially intelligent machines will one day turn on us.

James Barrat, author of *Our Final Invention: Artificial Intelligence and the End of the Human Era*, predicts that AI in the future will not necessarily be friendly or benevolent and may turn on humans. Elon Musk has also mentioned several times that once artificial intelligence surpasses human intelligence, we will not be able to control it. That may be beneficial or detrimental; there are no ways of predicting that outcome.

However, the ability to feel or not might not be the cause for hostility. Musk gives an example that humans when building a road may destroy an ant nest, not because we are inherently evil or dislike the ants, but because our goal is to build a road.

He argues that a machine, for example, programmed to fix a problem might consider humans and the human race to be the problem. One solution may be to destroy humans.

We, as humans, would, of course, view this as hostile, but it is a kind of hostility that does not necessarily relate to emotions. As such, the concept of hostility is highly subjective.

13.8 Creating Artificial Consciousness: Could You Give a Robot a Soul?

Scientists have already found consciousness difficult to define—let alone a "soul," which has an inherently theological aspect. Vladimir Havlik, a philosopher at the Czech Academy of Sciences, suggests we define a soul as a "coherent identity" that stands the test of time. If we consider consciousness a soul, the answer remains: we do not know.

However, some argue that true artificial consciousness will never be achieved. This is what the dualists in philosophy argue; they argue that there is a difference between the brain and the mind.

One might be able to be replicated, but the other might not. The materialists, conversely, argue that neuroscience can explain everything, even if it does not yet have the answers.

13.9 Ethics of Exploiting Artificial Consciousness

The problem with using the word "conscious" to describe AGI is that it brings up certain connotations of humanity. If machines were ever to be deemed conscious, several ethical and perhaps legal considerations would come into play.

13.9.1 Robot Slaves

As mentioned earlier, there is the possibility that artificial consciousness might exist long before we can identify and, as such, humanity might ignorantly enslave a new life. In fact, the creation of a humanoid robotic world may be one answer to this survival in the universe.

The idea of "robot rights" has been discussed often before. It stands to reason that should we succeed in creating a conscious machine, there is a compelling argument for it to enjoy rights and legal protections. Humans do not prevent those with a lower IQ from being afforded the same protection and rights. They are enjoyed by all simply because of being human. If future machines are truly intelligent and possess an artificial consciousness, at what point would they acquire rights?

In a paper by Joanna Bryson,[1] she argues that robots should be considered slaves because they would be servants and that it would be wrong to consider their place on our planet alongside humanity. Bryson argues that we do, in fact, own robots, and everything about them, from their appearance to their intelligence, is either directly or indirectly designed by humans. She argues that exploiting human empathy for AI can be potentially dangerous. Of course, we disagree with this notion because humans generate other human beings.

It is becoming clear that with all the brain and consciousness theories out there, the proof will be in the pudding. This means that any particular theory can create a human adult-level conscious machine. The bet is on the late Gerald Edelman's Extended Theory of Neuronal Group Selection (TNGS). Based on this theory, the lead group in robotics is the Neurorobotics Lab at UC Irvine. Dr. Edelman

[1]Robots should be slaves, Joanna Bryson, Academia.edu, 2010

distinguished between primary consciousness, which came first in evolution and that humans share with other conscious animals, and higher-order consciousness, which came only to humans with language acquisition. A machine with primary consciousness will probably have to come first.

What is found special about the TNGS is the Darwin series of automata created at the Neurosciences Institute by Dr. Edelman and his colleagues in the 1990s and 2000s. These machines perform in the real world, not in a restricted simulated world, and display convincing physical behavior indicative of higher psychological functions necessary for consciousness, such as perceptual categorization, memory, and learning. They are based on realistic models of the parts of the biological brain that the theory claims subserve these functions. The extended TNGS allows for the emergence of consciousness based only on the further evolutionary development of the brain areas responsible for these functions in a parsimonious way. No other research I have encountered is anywhere near as convincing.

One wonders because in almost every video and article about the brain and consciousness encountered, the attitude is that we still know next to nothing about how the brain and consciousness work and that there is a lot of data but no unifying theory. The extended TNGS is that theory. The motivation to write this book is to keep that theory in front of the public. And obviously, one considers it the route to a truly conscious machine, primary and higher order.

Good advice to people who want to create a conscious machine is to ground themselves in the extended TNGS and the Darwin automata first and possibly apply it to Jeff Krichmar's lab (Krichmar, 2018) at UC Irvine. Dr. Edelman's roadmap to a conscious machine can be found at https://arxiv.org/abs/2105.10461.

References and Further Readings

Akopian, N. (2006). Entangled photon pairs from semiconductor quantum dots. *Physical Review Letters*, **96**(2):130501.

Aspect, A., Grangier, P., and Roger, G. (1982). Experimental test of Bell's inequalities using time-varying analyzers. *Physical Review Letters*, **49**:1804–1807.

Augusiak, R., Demianowicz, M., Tura, J., and Acín, A. (2015). Entanglement and nonlocality are inequivalent for any number of parties. *Physical Review Letters*, **115**(3):030404.

Bell, J. S. (1964). On the Einstein–Podolsky–Rosen paradox. *Physics*, **1**, 195.

Bengtsson, I., and Życzkowski, K. (2006). *Geometry of Quantum States. An Introduction to Quantum Entanglement.* Cambridge: Cambridge University Press.

Bhaskara, V. S., and Panigrahi, P. K. (2017). Generalized concurrence measure for faithful multiparticle pure state entanglement quantification using Lagrange's identity and wedge product. *Quantum Information Processing*, **16**(5):118.

Boette, A., Rossignoli, R., Gigena, N., and Cerezo, M. (2016). System–time entanglement in a discrete-time model. *Physical Review A*, **93**(6):062127.

Bokulich, A., and Jaeger, G. (2010). *Philosophy of Quantum Information and Entanglement.* Cambridge University Press.

Bub, J. (2019). *Quantum Entanglement and Information.* Stanford, California: Stanford University.

Clauser, J. F., Horne, M. A., Shimony, A., and Holt, R. A. (1969). Proposed experiment to test local hidden-variable theories. *Physical Review Letters*, **23**, 880.

Cramer, J. G. (2015). *The Quantum Handshake: Entanglement, Nonlocality and Transactions.* Springer Verlag.

Duarte, F. J. (2019). *Fundamentals of Quantum Entanglement.* Bristol, UK: Institute of Physics.

Edelman, G. M. (1987). *Neural Darwinism: The Theory of Neuronal Group Selection.* New York: Basic Books.

Einstein, A., Podolsky, B., and Rosen, N. (1935). Can quantum–mechanical description of physical reality be considered complete? *Physical Review*, **47**:777–780.

Francis, M. (2012). Quantum entanglement shows that reality can't be local. *Ars Technica.* Retrieved from https://arstechnica.com/science/2012/10/quantum-entanglement-shows-that-reality-cant-be-local.

Freedman, S. J., and Clauser, J. F. (1972). Experimental test of local hidden-variable theories. *Physical Review Letters*, **28**, 938.

Friis, N., Vitagliano, G., Malik, M., and Huber, M. (2019). Entanglement certification from theory to experiment. *Nature Reviews Physics*, **1**:72–87.

Georgiev, D. D., and Gudder, S. P. (2022). Sensitivity of entanglement measures in bipartite pure quantum states. *Modern Physics Letters B*, **36**(22):22501012250255.

Georgiev, D., and Cohen, E. (2022). Entanglement measures for two-particle quantum histories. *Physical Review A*, **106**(6):062437.

Gharibian, S. (2010). Strong NP-hardness of the quantum separability problem. *Quantum Information and Computation*, **10**(3&4):343–360.

Gibney, E. (2014). Entangled photons make a picture from a paradox. *Nature*, doi:10.1038/nature.2014.15781.S2CID 124976589.

Gour, G., and Wallach, N. R. (2013). Classification of multipartite entanglement of all finite dimensionality. *Physical Review Letters*, **111**(6):060502.

Grassl, M., Rötteler, M., and Beth, T. (1998). Computing local invariants of quantum-bit systems. *Physical Review A*, **58**(3):1833–1839.

Gühne, O. (2004). Characterizing entanglement via uncertainty relations. *Physical Review Letters*, **92**(11):117903.

Gühne, O., and Lewenstein, M. (2004). Entropic uncertainty relations and entanglement. *Physical Review A*, **70**(2):022316.

Gühne, O., and Tóth, G. (2009). Entanglement detection. *Physics Reports*, **474**(1–6):1–75.

Gurvits, L. (2003). Classical deterministic complexity of Edmonds' problem and quantum entanglement. *Proceedings of the Thirty-Fifth Annual ACM Symposium on Theory of Computing*, p. 10. ACM Press, New York, 2003.

Hardy, L. (1992). Quantum mechanics, local realistic theories, and Lorentz-invariant realistic theories. *Physical Review Letters*, **68**(20):2981–2984.

Hillery, M., and Zubairy, M. S. (2006). Entanglement conditions for two-mode states. *Physical Review Letters*, **96**(5):050503.

Hofmann, H. F., and Takeuchi, S. (2003). Violation of local uncertainty relations as a signature of entanglement. *Physical Review A*, **68**(3):032103.

Holland, M. J., and Burnett, K. (1993). Interferometric detection of optical phase shifts at the Heisenberg limit. *Physical Review Letters*, **71**(9):1355–1358.

Horodecki, M., Horodecki, P., and Horodecki, R. (1998). Mixed-state entanglement and distillation: Is there a bound entanglement in nature? *Physical Review Letters*, **80**(1998):5239–5242.

Huang, Y. (2010). Entanglement criteria via concave-function uncertainty relations. *Physical Review A*, **82**(1):012335.

Huang, Y. (2013). Entanglement detection: Complexity and Shannon entropic criteria. *IEEE Transactions on Information Theory*, **59**(10):6774.

Hwu, T., Wang, A. Y., Oros, N., and Krichmar, J. L. (2018). Adaptive robot path planning using a spiking neuron algorithm with axonal delays. *IEEE Transactions on Cognitive and Developmental Systems*, **10**:126–137.

Jaeger, G. (2009). *Entanglement, Information, and the Interpretation of Quantum Mechanics*. Heildelberg: Springer.

Jozsa, R., and Linden, N. (2002). On the role of entanglement in quantum computational speed-up. *Proceedings of the Royal Society A: Mathematical, Physical and Engineering Sciences*, **459**(2036):2011–2032.

Kitagawa, M., and Ueda, M. (1993). Squeezed spin states. *Physical Review A*, **47**(6):5138–5143.

Kocher, C. A. (1971). Time correlations in the detection of successively emitted photons. *Annals of Physics*, **65**(1):1–18.

Kotler, S., Peterson, G. A., Shojaee, E., Lecocq, F., Cicak, K., Kwiatkowski, A., Geller, S., Glancy, S., Knill, E., Simmonds, R. W., Aumentado, J., and Teufel, J. D. (2021). Direct observation of deterministic macroscopic entanglement. *Science*, **372**(6542):622–625.

Krichmar, J. L. (2018). Neurorobotics: A thriving community and a promising pathway toward intelligent cognitive robots. *Frontiers in Neurorobotics*, **12**, 2018.

Lami, L., and Regula, B. (2023). No second law of entanglement manipulation after all. *Nature Physics*, **19**(2):184–189.

Leinaas, J. M., Myrheim, J., and Ovrum, E. (2006). Geometrical aspects of entanglement. *Physical Review A*, **74**(1):012313.

Lo Franco, R., and Compagno, G. (2018). Indistinguishability of elementary systems as a resource for quantum information processing. *Physical Review Letters*, **120**(24):240403.

Ma, X.-S., Zotter, S., Kofler, J., Ursin, R., Jennewein, T., Brukner, Č., and Zeilinger, A. (2012). Experimental delayed-choice entanglement swapping. *Nature Physics*, **8**(6):480485.

Markoff, J. (2015). Sorry, Einstein. Quantum study suggests 'spooky action' is real. *The New York Times*. Retrieved October 21, 2015.

Marletto, C., Coles, D. M., Farrow, T., and Vedral, V. (2018). Entanglement between living bacteria and quantized light witnessed by Rabi splitting. *Journal of Physics Communications*, **2**(10):101001.

Moreva, E. (2014). Time from quantum entanglement: An experimental illustration. *Physical Review A*, **89**(5):052122.

Nielsen, M. A. (1999). Conditions for a class of entanglement transformations. *Physical Review Letters*, **83**(2):436.

Nielsen, M. A., and Chuang, I. L. (2000). *Quantum Computation and Quantum Information*. Cambridge University Press, pp. 112–113.

Pan, J. W., Bouwmeester, D., Weinfurter, H., and Zeilinger, A. (1998). Experimental entanglement swapping: Entangling photons that never interacted. *Physical Review Letters*, **80**:3891.

Pirandola, S., Andersen, U. L., Banchi, L., Berta, M., Bunandar, D., Colbeck, R., Englund, D., Gehring, T., Lupo, C., Ottaviani, C., Pereira, J. L., Razavi, M., Shamsul Shaari, J., Tomamichel, M., Usenko, V. C., Vallone, G., Villoresi, P., and Wallden, P. (2020). Advances in quantum cryptography. *Advances in Optics and Photonics*, **12**(4):1012–1236.

Plenio, M. B., and Virmani, S. (2007). An introduction to entanglement measures. *Quantum Information & Computation*, **1**:1–51.

Renner, R., Gisin, N., and Kraus, B. (2005). An information-theoretic security proof for QKD protocols. *Physical Review A*, **72**:012332.

Rozatkar, G. (2018). Demonstration of quantum entanglement. *OSF*.

Sakurai, J. J., and Napolitano, J. J. (2010). *Modern Quantum Mechanics*, 2nd edition. Pearson, p.68.

Schrödinger, E. (1935). Discussion of probability relations between separated systems. *Mathematical Proceedings of the Cambridge Philosophical Society*, **31**(4):555–563.

Schrödinger, E. (1936). Probability relations between separated systems. *Mathematical Proceedings of the Cambridge Philosophical Society*, **32**(3):446–452.

Shadbolt, P. J., Verde, M. R., Peruzzo, A., Politi, A., Laing, A., Lobino, M., Matthews, J. C. F., Thompson, M. G., and O'Brien, J. L. (2012). Generating, manipulating and measuring entanglement and mixture with a reconfigurable photonic circuit. *Nature Photonics*, **6**(1):45–59.

Shahinpoor, M. (2016). *Ionic Polymer Metal Composites (IPMCs): Smart Multi-Functional Materials and Artificial Muscles*, Vol. I. Royal Society of Chemistry Publishers.

Shahinpoor, M. (2016). *Ionic Polymer Metal Composites (IPMCs): Smart Multi-Functional Materials and Artificial Muscles*, Vol. II. Royal Society of Chemistry Publishers.

Shahinpoor, M. (2020). *Fundamentals of Smart Materials*. Royal Society of Chemistry Publishers.

Shahinpoor, M. (2022). *Artificial Muscles: Advanced Polymeric Nano Composites*, 2nd edition. London: CRC Press, Taylor & Francis Group.

Shahinpoor, M., and Gheshmi, S. (2015). *Robotic Surgery*. Singapore: Jenny Stanford Publishing.

Shahinpoor, M., and Oh, I. (Eds). (2014). Selected papers from the 7th. International Conference on Biomimetics, Artificial Muscles and Nano-Bio (BAMN2013), Jeju Island, South Korea, August 26–30, 2013. *Smart Materials and Structures*, **23**(7): 070301.

Shahinpoor, M., Soltanpour, D., and Shahinpoor, P. (2024). *Engineering Ophthalmology*. Singapore: Jenny Stanford Publishing.

Shevlin, H., Vold, K., Crosby, M., and Halina, M. (2019). The limits of machine intelligence: Despite progress in machine intelligence, artificial general intelligence is still a major challenge. *EMBO Reports*, **20**(10):e49177.

Siegel, E. (2023). No, we still can't use quantum entanglement to communicate faster than light. *Forbes*. Retrieved January 6, 2023.

Simon, R. (2000). Peres–Horodecki separability criterion for continuous variable systems. *Physical Review Letters*, **84**(12):2726–2729.

Steward, E. G. (2008). *Quantum Mechanics: Its Early Development and the Road to Entanglement*. Imperial College Press.

Swain, S. N., Bhaskara, V. S., and Panigrahi, P. K. (2022). Generalized entanglement measure for continuous-variable systems. *Physical Review A*, **105**(5):052441.

Swingle, B., and Van Raamsdonk, M. (2014). Universality of gravity from entanglement. https://arxiv.org/abs/1405.2933v1.

Thomas, R. A., Parniak, M., Østfeldt, C., Møller, C. B., Bærentsen, C., Tsaturyan, Y., Schliesser, A., Appel, J., Zeuthen, E., and Polzik, E. S. (2020). Entanglement between distant macroscopic mechanical and spin systems. *Nature Physics*, **17**(2):228–233.

Van Raamsdonk, M. (2010). Building up spacetime with quantum entanglement. *General Relativity and Gravitation*, **42**(10):2323–2329.

Vértesi, T., and Brunner, N. (2014). Disproving the Peres conjecture by showing Bell nonlocality from bound entanglement. *Nature Communications*, **5**(1):5297.

Walborn, S., Taketani, B., Salles, A., Toscano, F., and de Matos Filho, R. (2009). Entropic entanglement criteria for continuous variables. *Physical Review Letters*, **103**(16):160505.

Werner, R. F., and Wolf, M. M. (2001). Bound entangled Gaussian states. *Physical Review Letters*, **86**(16):3658–3661.

Wineland, D. J., Bollinger, J. J., Itano, W. M., Moore, F. L., and Heinzen, D. J. (1992). Spin squeezing and reduced quantum noise in spectroscopy. *Physical Review A*, **46**(11):R6797–R6800.

Wiseman, H. M., Jones, S. J., and Doherty, A. C. (2007). Steering, entanglement, nonlocality, and the Einstein–Podolsky–Rosen paradox. *Physical Review Letters*, **98**(14):140402.

Wogan, T. (2021). Vibrating drumheads are entangled quantum mechanically. *Physics World*, May 17, 2021. Retrieved June 14, 2021.

Yin, J., Cao, Y., Li, Y.-H., Liao, S.-K., Zhang, L., Ren, J.-G., Cai, W.-Q., Liu, W.-Y., Li, B., Dai, H., Li, G.-B., Lu, Q.-M., Gong, Y.-H., Xu, Y., Li, S.-L., Li, F.-Z., Yin, Y.-Y., Jiang, Z.-Q., Li, M., Jia, J.-J., Ren, G., He, D., Zhou, Y.-L., Zhang, X.-X., Wang, N., Chang, X., Zhu, Z.-C., Liu, N.-L., Chen, Y.-A., Lu, C.-Y., Shu, R., Peng, C.-Z., Wang, J.-Y., and Pan, J.-W. (2017). Satellite-based entanglement distribution over 1200 kilometers. *Science*, **356**(6343):1140–1144.

Yin, J., Cao, Y., Yong, H.-L., Ren, J.-G., Liang, H., Liao, S.-K., Zhou, F., Liu, C., Wu, Y.-P., Pan, G.-S., Zhang, Q., Peng, C.-Z., and Pan, J.-W. (2013). Bounding the speed of 'spooky action at a distance'. *Physical Review Letters*, **110**(26):260407.

Yin, J., Li, Y.-H., Liao, S.-K., Yang, M., Cao, Y., Zhang, L., Ren, J.-G., Cai, W.-Q., Liu, W.-Y., Li, S.-L., Shu, R., Huang, Y.-M., Deng, L., Li, L., Zhang, Q., Liu, N.-L., Chen, Y.-A., Lu, C.-Y., Wang, X.-B., Xu, F., Wang, J.-Y., Peng, C.-Z., Ekert, A. K., and Pan, J.-W. (2020). Entanglement-based secure quantum cryptography over 1,120 kilometers. *Nature*, **582**(7813):501–505.

Chapter 14

Concluding Remarks

14.1 Introduction

This book presents a non-fiction possibility for human beings to develop intelligent biomimetic humanoid robots that could represent them after they leave human life to live in the universe immortally and continue representing their human master forever, as long as they have enough energy to do so. But they can have long-lasting nuclear batteries. Thus, this could be the beginning of biomimetic humanoid robots for all human beings to stay on and be able to live immortally and travel in space to other planes as space aliens from Earth. This chapter maintains that humanity should move toward creating silicon-enabled or lithium-enabled intelligent humanoid robots that are away from organic life and have comparable human consciousness and self-awareness. Earth will not allow humanity to survive in time due to many factors such as melting polar caps and icebergs, rising water and flooding, climatical pressures, and the rise of the sun's temperature. There is no difficulty in designing, developing, fabricating, and operating humanoid robots, but one also needs to equip them with some human consciousness. They are embedded with an intelligent AI computer, which continuously observes senses and records all events as the individual observes and reacts to them.

Biomimetic Humanoid Robots with Human Consciousness
Mohsen Shahinpoor

ISBN 978-981-5129-87-8 (Hardcover), 978-1-003-71373-9 (eBook)
www.jennystanford.com

DOI: 10.1201/9781003713739-14

Human beings are born as individuals. As the individual grows, the embedded computer, using identity-vita-assigned consciousness (IVA-consciousness), records and may recall everything observed, heard, sensed, or experienced. There will be a laboratory facility for the individuals ready to fabricate their humanoid biomimetic robots and transfer consciousness. The first thing to do is to instruct a humanoid robot that it has a master human with an identity, say Captain Kirk's humanoid. Thus, the humanoid robot will have what we have described as IVA-consciousness, the humanoid AI computer's initial memory, and knowledge transfer. This will be the beginning of consciousness for the humanoid robot to be instructed that it is Captain Kirk's humanoid, which is its identity and vita. It must always be aware when it is turned on and operating. Once a humanoid robot is chosen, the long period of companionship starts, and the human consciousness is gradually described or transferred to the robot. When the humans are ready to exit human life for whatever reason (sickness or old age), they will exit and be accordingly cremated or buried. At the same time, their biomimetic humanoid robots will emerge to lead a new life, such as Captain Kirk's humanoid robot with almost Kirk's consciousness. In the Star Trek series, Captain Kirk's robot travels in a spaceship, like the old U.S.S. Enterprise, and moves to other planets as it does not need air, water, or food, and needs only a long-lasting nuclear battery, which is also replaceable. Thus, human beings will be able to survive in this vast universe. Laboratory facilities can also design, develop, fabricate, and operate animaloid robots with consciousness and sentience.

The ultimate goal of this book is to describe a realistic future, and not science fiction, about how humanity and life can survive immortally by creating humanoid robots with the consciousness of humans who would serve as companions and learn everything about humans. The humanoid will take over once human life is close to being over (due to age or sickness). It can stay alive if it has the necessary energy to live on and even travel through space and other planets. It can live there forever and help the local entities. These humanoids can benefit from *quantum entanglement* to immediately move through universal space to any cosmic destination. This book describes the essential steps to get there in Chapter 10. Interestingly, the vision here is that humanoids can become space aliens, visiting other planets using quantum entanglement, which means traveling faster than light (photons) from one part of the universe to another.

Another exciting possibility is that with the presented technology of designing and developing humanoid robots, it is possible to make giant robots with human consciousness, especially for space travel and special needs. The humanoid robots could be quite massive and strong.

The only catch is that emotions such as love, hate, like, dislike, jealousy, anger, regrets, music enjoyment, sex enjoyment, and vengeance/retaliation are included. This book discusses these topics in detail. As discussed in Chapters 1, 2, 4, and 5, there will be years of companionship between the human master and his or her humanoid robot. Through semi-cognitive interaction and knowledge transfer, these emotions will be gradually taught to the humanoid robot for all future interactions.

Another exciting notion is that once our humanoid robots can travel through space, using quantum entanglement capabilities, to other planets, the humanoid individuals will be similar to aliens visiting other planets, and possibly living ones, to help them in any way they can. This is exciting, and we look forward to becoming space aliens in the universe.

14.2 Steven Dick: Why Aren't Aliens Already Here?

It seems absurd that we are the only intelligent life in a universe with more than 100 billion galaxies, each with billions of stars and planets. So where are all the others? This is the famous "Fermi Paradox" asked by Nobel Laureate Enrico Fermi. By any reasonable calculation, we should see evidence of other civilizations all over the universe, but we have seen nothing but us. Steven J. Dick is an American astronomer, author, and historian of science, most noted for his work in the field of astrobiology. Dick served as the Chief Historian for the National Aeronautics and Space Administration from 2003 to 2009.

Let us describe Captain Kirk's futuristic love affair with a humanoid robot. In a world where technology blurs the lines between reality and science fiction, Kirk's humanoid stands at the forefront, pushing the boundaries of innovation. However, Kirk's personal life takes a revolutionary turn as he embraces companionship with a beautiful and highly advanced female humanoid robot. Recall that companionship with humanoid robots has been fully discussed as another way to transfer the consciousness of a human master to a humanoid robot. This relationship is not just a mere experiment but a profound exploration of companionship, intelligence, and the potential of AI in our daily lives. We explore the ethical and societal questions that arise from such a relationship, addressing the benefits and potential challenges.

Of course, the humanoid must be maintained in terms of its electromechanical sensors and actuator systems, as well as any other biomimetic or physical structures or body muscles. Regular and timely maintenance is necessary. The humanoid will also need enough resources to be left behind by its human master; it must have continuous energy or long-lasting batteries for its dynamics and motions. The knowledge and technology available to create look-alike smart functioning robots are currently very advanced [see Boston Dynamics' Atlases I and II, Hyundai Robotics in Korea, US Companies, Sophia (David Hanson), US Universities, Japanese entities, Asimov, Grace, Nadine, AI-DA, Jia Jia, Chinese entities, Navigator-Alpha, Jia Jia, French entities, Aldebaran's NAO, Pepper, Romeo and Plato, British humanoids, AMECO, Germany, BMW automation robot, Italy, automation robot RO-BEE, and also other European countries humanoids, for example]. The book hopes to describe how humanity can survive the universe despite the biological–medical and time limitations and that our humanoids are left behind to carry us forward, serve us, and explore space and become space aliens for other planets.

References and Further Readings

Alahbakhshi, M., Fallahi, A., Mohajerani, E., Fathollahi, M. R., Afshar Taromi, F., and Shahinpoor, M. (2017). High-performance bi-stage process in reduction of graphene oxide for transparent conductive electrodes. *Optical Materials*, **64**:366–375.

Armstrong, D., Najafi, B., and Shahinpoor, M. (2017). Potential applications of smart multi-functional wearable materials to gerontology. *Gerontology Journal*, **63**:287–298.

Asaka, K., Kim, K., Oguro, K., and Shahinpoor, M. (2016). *IPMCs as EAPs: Fundamentals. Electromechanically Active Polymers, Polymers, and Polymeric Composites: A Reference Series*, F. Carpi (Ed.). Springer International Publishing Switzerland.

Asanuma, H., Asaka, K., Su, J., Poubel, L., and Shahinpoor, M. (2016). Smart contact oscillations by IPMCs. *Smart Materials and Structures International Journal*, **25**(2):15015–15022.

Bakhtiarpour, P., Parvizi, A., Muller, M., Shahinpoor, M., Marti, O., and Amirkhani, M. (2016). An external disturbance sensor for ionic polymer metal composite actuator. *Smart Materials and Structures International Journal*, **25**(1):15008–15014.

Bloom, J., Tabatabaie, S. E., Shahinpoor, M., and Hejrati, B. (2020). An investigation of multimodal sensing capabilities of ionic polymer-metal composites. *Journal of Smart Materials and Structures*, **29**(4):045031.

Chella, A. (Ed). *Book Series: Series on Machine Consciousness*. University of Palermo, Italy & ICAR-CNR Palermo, Italy.

Glaser, R., Caccese, V., and Shahinpoor, M. (2018). Comparative finite element and experimental analysis of quasi-static inflation of a thin deployable membrane space structure. *Journal of Finite Elements in Analysis and Design*, **138**:48–65.

Igor, A., and Morton, H. (2006). Phenomenology in computational models of consciousness. *International Journal of Pattern Recognition and Artificial Intelligence*, **20**(6): 785–796.

Kim, K. J., and Shahinpoor, M. (2007). Special Issue: Biomimetics, Artificial Muscles, and Nano-Bio 2004. *Journal of Intelligent Material Systems and Structures*, **18**:101.

Michopoulos, J. G., Shahinpoor, M., and Iliopoulos, A. (2016). *Multiphysics Modeling of Nonlinear Ionic Polymer Metal Composite Plates. RSC Smart Materials Series*, 18. Royal Society of Chemistry Publishers, pp. 285–310.

Michopoulos, J. G., Shahinpoor, M., and Iliopoulos, A. (2016). *Multiphysics Theory for Electroactive Polymers and Ionic Polymer Metal Composites. RSC Smart Materials Series*, 18. Royal Society of Chemistry Publishers, pp. 257–284.

Noonan, C., Tajvidi, M., Tayeb, A., Shahinpoor, M., and Tabatabaie, E. (2019). Structure–property relationships in hybrid cellulose nanofibrils/nafion-based ionic polymer-metal composites. *Materials (Basel)*, **12**(4):23–28.

Schneider, H.-J., and Shahinpoor, M. (Eds). *Smart Materials*, Book Series. Cambridge: Royal Society of Chemistry Publishers.

Shahinpoor, M. (2016). *Ionic Polymer Metal Composites (IPMCs) Optimal Manufacturing. RSC Smart Materials Series,* 17. Cambridge: Royal Society of Chemistry Publishers, pp. 61–147.

Shahinpoor, M. (2016). *Ionic Polymer Metal Composites (IPMCs): Smart Multi-Functional Materials and Artificial Muscles*, Vol. II. Cambridge: Royal Society of Chemistry Publishers.

Shahinpoor, M. (2016). *Ionic Polymer Metal Composites (IPMCs): Smart Multi-Functional Materials and Artificial Muscles*, Vol. I. Cambridge: Royal Society of Chemistry Publishers.

Shahinpoor, M. (2016). *Ionic Polymer Metal Composites as Dexterous Manipulators and Haptic Feedback/Tactile Sensors for Minimally Invasive Robotic Surgery. RSC Smart Materials Series*, 18. Cambridge: Royal Society of Chemistry Publishers, pp. 311–340.

Shahinpoor, M. (2016). *Ionic Polymer Metal Composites as Soft Biomimetic Robotic Artificial Muscles. RSC Smart Materials Series*, 18. Cambridge: Royal Society of Chemistry Publishers, pp. 341–363.

Shahinpoor, M. (2020). *Fundamentals of Smart Materials*. Cambridge: Royal Society of Chemistry Publishers.

Shahinpoor, M. (2022). *Artificial Muscles: Advanced Polymeric Nano Composites*, 2nd edition. London: CRC Press, Taylor & Francis Group.

Shahinpoor, M., and Gheshmi, S. (2014). *Robotic Surgery: With Smart Materials, Robotic Structures, and Artificial Muscles*. Singapore: Jenny Stanford Publishing.

Shahinpoor, M., and Oh, I. (Eds). (2014). Selected papers from the 7th. International Conference on Biomimetics, Artificial Muscles and Nano-Bio (BAMN2013), Jeju Island, South Korea, August 26–30, 2013. *Smart Materials and Structures International Journal*, **23**(7):070301.

Shahinpoor, M., Kim, K. J., and Mojarrad, M. (2007). *Artificial Muscles: Applications of Advanced Polymeric Nano Composites*, 1st edition. London: CRC Press, Taylor & Francis Group.

Shahinpoor, M., Soltanpour, D., and Shahinpoor, P. (2024). *Engineering Ophthalmology*. Singapore: Jenny Stanford Publishing.

Tabatabaie, S. E., and Shahinpoor, M. (2018). Novel configurations of slit tubular soft robotic actuators and sensors made with ionic polymer metal composites (IPMCs). *Robotics and Automation Engineering Journal*, **3**(4):1–10.

Tabatabaie, S. E., and Shahinpoor, M. (2018). Soft biomimetic robotic looped haptic feedback sensors. *Journal of Robotic Engineering & Automation Technology*, **2018**(1):1–10.

Tabatabaie, S. E., and Shahinpoor, M. (2019). Artificial soft robotic elephant trunk made with ionic polymer-metal nanocomposites (IPMCs). *International Robotics and Automation Journal*, **5**(4):138–142.

Bibliography

Ciofu, I. (1994). *Numarul de Aur. Matrice a Evolutiei?* (*Golden Number: Matrix of Evolution?*). Coresi: Bucharest, Romania.

Einstein, A. (1920). *Ether and the Theory of Relativity*. University of Leyden.

Einstein, A. (1921). *Geometry and Experience*. Prussian Academy of Sciences.

Einstein, A. (1996). *Cum Vad Eu Lumea. Teoria Relativitatii pe Intelesul Tuturor* (*How Do I See the World? Theory of Relativity on Everybody's Understanding*). Humanitas: Bucharest, Romania.

Freeman, W. J. (1991). The physiology of perception. *Scientific American*, **264**(2):78–85.

Frolov, A. V. (1995). *Matter as Process*. St. Petersburg, Russia.

Greco, D. (1998). *Ether and Field Theories*. Massachusetts Institute of Technology.

Haldane, J. B. S. (1929). The origin of life. *Rationalist Annual*, **148**:3–10.

Lindemann, P. A. (1994). Thermodynamics and Free Energy. *Borderlands Magazine*. Retrieved from https://www.borderlandresearch.com/thermodynamics-free-energy.

Lusted, H. S., and Benjamin, K. R. (1996). Controlling computers with neural signals. *Scientific American*, **10**.

Nicu, M. D. (1975). *Biotehnologia* (*Biotechnology*). EDP: Bucharest, Romania.

Popa, S. G., and Nicu, M. D. (1989). *Unele consideratii asupra efectului de piramida* (*Some Considerations Regarding the Effect of the Pyramid*). Session of Scientific Communications, Politehnica University of Bucharest.

Popa, S. G., Pop, V., and Serban, I. (1994). Probleme privind abordarea sistemica a relatiei SNC-psihism (Problems regarding the systemic approach of the relationship Central Nervous System: Psychism). *Studies and Research on Biotechnology*, **26**.

Roland-Mieszkowski, M. (1998). *Life on Earth: Flow of Energy and Entropy*. Digital Recordings.

Shahinpoor, M. (1996). Intelligent materials and structures revisited. *Proc. SPIE 1996 North American Conference on Smart Structures and Materials*, February 27–29, 1996, San Diego, California, vol. 2716, paper no. 33.

Shahinpoor, M. (1997). *Intelligent Civil Engineering Materials and Structures Revisited Intelligent Civil Engineering Materials & Structures*, ed. A. K. Maji. Engineering Mechanics Division/ASCE.

Shahinpoor, M., and Thompson, M. S. (1995). The Venus flytrap as a model for biomimetic material with built-in sensors and actuators. *Journal of Materials Science & Engineering*, **C2**:229–233.

Shahinpoor, M., and Wang, G. (1995). Electro-thermo-mechanics of SMA fiber bundles embedded in an elastic medium. *Proceedings of SPIE 2427, Active Materials and Smart Structures*, pp. 272–382.

Shahinpoor, M., Bar-Cohen, Y., Simpson, J., and Smith, J. (1998). Ionic polymer-metal composites (IPMCs) as biomimetic sensors, actuators and artificial muscles: A review. *Smart Materials & Structures*, **7**:R15–R30.

Shannon, C. E. (1949). *A Mathematical Theory of Communication*. University of Illinois Press.

Wang, G., and Shahinpoor, M. (1997). A new design for a rotatory joint actuator made with shape memory alloy contractile wire. *Journal of Intelligent Materials Systems & Structures*, **8**(3):191–279.

Wang, G., and Shahinpoor, M. (1997). Design for shape memory alloy rotatory joint actuators using shape memory effect and pseudoelastic effect. *Proceedings of SPIE 3040, Smart Materials Technologies*, pp. 23–30.

Wang, G., and Shahinpoor, M. (1997). Design, prototyping and computer simulation of a novel large bending actuator made with a shape memory alloy contractile wire. *Smart Materials and Structures Journal*, **6**(2):214–221.

Zadeh, L. A. (1973). Outline of a new approach to the analysis of complex systems and decision processes. *IEEE Transactions on Systems, Man, and Cybernetics*, **3**:28–44.

Appendix A

Complete List of References

Aleksander, I., and Morton, H. B. (2012). *Aristotle's Laptop: The Discovery of our Informational Mind:* 1 (Series on Machine Consciousness). World Scientific Publishing Co Pte Ltd.

Argenziano, M., Oz, M. C., DeRose, J. J. Jr, Ashton, R. C. Jr, Beck, J., Wang, F., Chitwood, W. R., Nifong, L. W., Dimitui, J., Rose, E. A., and Smith, C. R. Jr. (2002). Totally endoscopic atrial septal defect repair with robotic assistance. *The Heart Surgery Forum*, **5(3)**:294–300.

Armstrong, D., Najafi, B., and Shahinpoor, M. (2017). Potential applications of smart multi-functional wearable materials to gerontology. *Gerontology Journal*, **63**:287–298.

Asahi Chemical Industry Co., Ltd. (1995). Aciphex formula. Public release.

Asaka, K., and Oguro, K. (2000). Bending of polyelectrolyte membrane platinum composites by electric stimuli. Part II. Response kinetics. *Journal of Electroanalytical Chemistry*, **480**:186–198.

Asaka, K., Kim, K., Oguro, K., and Shahinpoor, M. (2016). *IPMCs as EAPs: Fundamentals. Electromechanically Active Polymers, Polymers, and Polymeric Composites: A Reference Series*, ed. F. Carpi. Springer International Publishing Switzerland.

Asaka, K., Oguro, K., and Takenaka, H. (1994). Bending response of polyelectrolyte membrane-Pt composite. In *Preprints Sapporo Symposium on Intelligent Polymer Gels*, October 6–8, Sapporo, Japan, 87–88.

Asaka, K., Oguro, K., Nishimura, Y., Misuhata, M., and Takenaka, H. (1995). Bending of polyelectrolyte membrane-platinum composites by electric stimuli. I. Response characteristics to various waveforms. *Polymer Journal*, **27**:436–440.

Asanuma, H., Asaka, K., Su, J., Poubel, L., and Shahinpoor, M. (2016). Smart contact oscillations by IPMCs. *Smart Materials and Structures International Journal*, **25**(2):15015–15022.

Ashton-Miller, J. A., and Pandy, M. G. (1990). Issues in modeling and control of biomechanical systems. In *Proceedings of the Winter Annual Meeting of the American Society of Mechanical Engineers*, November 25–30, Dallas, TX. ASME Publications, DSC-Vol. 25.

Asimov, I. Retrieved from http://www.used-robots.com/robot-education.php?page=asimov, November 07, 2012, 2:20 pm EST.

Asimov, I., and Frenkel, K. (1985). *Robots: Machines in Man's Image*. New York: Harmony Books, p. 19.

Aspect, A., Grangier, P., and Roger, G. (1982). Experimental tests of Bell's inequalities using time-varying analyzers. *Physical Review Letters*, **49**:1804–1807.

Atkins, P. W. (1982). *Physical Chemistry*, 2nd edition. London: Oxford University Press.

Augusiak, R., Demianowicz, M., Tura, J., and Acín, A. (2015). Entanglement and nonlocality are inequivalent for any number of parties. *Physical Review Letters*, **115**(3):030404.

Aviram, A. (1978). Mechanophotochemistry. *Macromolecules*, **11**:1275.

Bakhtiarpour, P., Parvizi, A., Muller, M., Shahinpoor, M., Marti, O., and Amirkhani, M. (2016). An external disturbance sensor for ionic polymer metal composite actuator. *Smart Materials and Structures International Journal*, **25**(1):15008–15014.

Bann, S., Khan, M., Hernandez, J., Munz, Y., Moorthy, K., Datta, V., Rockall, T., and Darzi, A. (2003). Robotics in surgery. *Journal of the American College of Surgeons*, **196**(5):784–795.

Bann, S., Khan, M., Hernandez, J., Munz, Y., Moorthy, K., Datta, V., Rockall, T., and Darzi, A. (2003). Robotics in surgery. *Journal of the American College of Surgeons*, **196**(5): 784–795.

Bar-Cohen, Y., Leary, S. P., Shahinpoor, M., Simpson, J. O., and Smith, J. (1999a). Flexible low-mass devices and mechanisms actuated by electro-active polymers. In *Electroactive Polymers SPIE*, publication no. 3669-38, 51–56.

Bar-Cohen, Y., Leary, S. P., Shahinpoor, M., Simpson, J. O., and Smith, J. (1999b). Electro-active polymer (EAP) actuators for planetary applications. In *Electroactive Polymers SPIE*, publication no. 3669-05, 57–63.

Bar-Cohen, Y., Xue, T., Joffe, B., Lih, S.-S., Shahinpoor, M., Simpson, J., Smith, J., and Willis, P. (1997a). Electroactive polymers (IPMC) low-mass muscle actuators. In *Proceedings of (1997) SPIE Conference on Smart Materials and Structures*, March 5, San Diego, CA.

Bar-Cohen, Y., Xue, T., Joffe, B., Lih, S.-S., Willis, P., Simpson, J., Smith, J., and Shahinpoor, M. (1997b). Electroactive polymers (EAP) low-mass muscle actuators. In *Proceedings of SPIE 3041, Smart Structures and Materials (1997): Smart Structures and Integrated Systems*, ed. M. E. Regelbrugge. Bellingham, WA: SPIE, 697–701. ISBN 0-8194-2454-4.

Bar-Cohen, Y., Xue, T., Shahinpoor, M., Salehpoor, K., Simpson, J., Smith, J., and Willis, P. (1998a). Low-mass muscle actuators using electroactive polymers (EAP). In *Proceedings of SPIE Smart Materials and Structures Conference*, March 3–5, San Diego, CA, SPIE publication no. 3324-32.

Bar-Cohen, Y., Xue, T., Shahinpoor, M., Simpson, J., and Smith, J. (1998b). Flexible low-mass robotic arm actuated by electroactive polymers (EAP). In *Proceedings of SPIE Smart Materials and Structures Conference*, March 3–5, San Diego, CA, SPIE publication no. 3329-07.

Bar-Cohen, Y., Xue, T., Shahinpoor, M., Simpson, J., and Smith, J. (1998c). Flexible, low-mass robotic arm actuated by electroactive polymers and operated equivalently to a human arm and hand. In *Proceedings of the Space '98-Robotics '98 Conference, Third International Conference Exposition on Robotics for Challenging Environment*, eds. L. A. Demsetz, R. H. Byrne, and J. P. Weyzel. April 26–30, Albuquerque, NM: American Society of Civil Engineers.

Barrett, J. (2007). Information processing in generalized probabilistic theories. *Physical Review A*, **75**:032304.

Barrett, J., Hardy, L., and Kent, A. (2005). No signaling and quantum key distribution. *Physical Review Letters*, **95**:010503.

Baughman, R. H. (1996). Conducting polymer artificial muscles. *Synthetic Metals*, **78**:339–353.

Baughman, R. H., Cui, C., Zakhidov, A. A., Iqbal, Z., Basrisci, J. N., Spinks, G. M., Wallace, G. G., Mazzoldi, A., de Rossi, D., Rinzier, A. G., Jaschinski, O., Roth, S., and Kertesz, M. (1999). Carbon nanotube actuators. *Science*, **284**:1340–1344.

Baughman, R. H., Shacklette, L. W., Elsenbaumer, R. L., Plichta, E. J., and Becht, C. (1991). Microelectromechanical actuators based on conducting polymers. In *Molecular Electronics*, ed. P. I. Lazarev. Dordrecht: Kluwer Academic Publishers.

Beatty, M. F. (1987). Topics in finite elasticity: Hyperelasticity of rubber, elastomers, and biological tissues—With examples. *Applied Mechanics Review*, **40**:1699–1733.

Bedini, S. A. (1962). The compartmented cylindrical clepsydra. *Technology and Culture*, **3**(2):115–141.

Bejczy, A. K., and Salisbury, J. K. (1983). Controlling remote manipulators through kinesthetic coupling. *Computers in Mechanical Engineering*, **2**(1).

Bell, J. S. (1964). On the Einstein–Podolsky–Rosen paradox. *Physics*, **1**:195–200.

Bengtsson, I., and Życzkowski, K. (2006). *Geometry of Quantum States. An Introduction to Quantum Entanglement.* Cambridge: Cambridge University Press.

Bennet, M., and Leo, D. J. (2003). Manufacture and characterization of ionic polymer transducers with non-precious metal electrodes. *Smart Materials and Structures*, **12**(3):424–436.

Bennett, C. H., and Di Vincenzo, B. D. (2000). Quantum information and computation. *Nature*, **404**:247–255.

Bennett, C. H., Brassard, G., Crepeau, C., Jozsa, R., Peres, A., and Wotters, W. K. (1993). Teleporting an unknown quantum state via dual classical and Einstein–Podolsky–Rosen channels. *Physical Review Letters*, **70**:1895–1899.

Benveniste, J. (1998). From water memory effects to digital biology. *DigiBio*.

Bernardi, D. M., and Verbugge, M. W. (1992). A mathematical model of a solid polymer electrolyte fuel cell. *Journal of the Electrochemical Society*, **139**(9):2477–2491.

Bernardi, P., D'Inzeo, G., and Pisa, S. (1994). A generalized ionic model of the neuronal membrane electrical activity. *IEEE Transactions on Biomedical Engineering*, **41**(2):125–133.

Bhaskara, V. S., and Panigrahi, P. K. (2017). Generalized concurrence measure for faithful multiparticle pure state entanglement quantification using Lagrange's identity and wedge product. *Quantum Information Processing*, **16**(5):118.

Biggers. (1986). Design of the UTAH/M.I.T. dexterous hand. In *IEEE International Conference on Robotics and Automation*, April, San Francisco.

Bloom, J., Tabatabaie, S. E., Shahinpoor, M., and Hejrati, B. (2020). An investigation of multimodal sensing capabilities of ionic polymer-metal composites. *Journal of Smart Materials and Structures*, **29**(4):045031.

Bochkarev, V., Ringley, C. D., and Oleynikov, D. (2005). Robotic-assisted operative techniques in general surgery. *Operative Techniques in General Surgery*, **7**(4):188–200.

Bochkarev, V., Ringley, C. D., and Oleynikov, D. (2005). Robotic-assisted operative techniques in general surgery. *Operative Techniques in General Surgery*, **7**(4):153–210.

Boette, A., Rossignoli, R., Gigena, N., and Cerezo, M. (2016). System-time entanglement in a discrete-time model. *Physical Review A*, **93**(6):062127.

Bohr, N. (1935). Can quantum-mechanical description of physical reality be complete? *Physical Review*, **38**:696–702.

Bone, Q., and Marshall, N. B. (1982). *Biology of Fishes*. London: Blackie & Son.

Born, M. (Ed.) (1992). *The Born-Einstein Letters*. Dordrecht: Reidel.

Bourla D. H., Hubschman, J. P., Culjat, M., Tsirbas, A., Gupta, A., and Schwartz, S. D. (2008). Feasibility study of intraocular robotic surgery with the da Vinci surgical system. *Retina*, **28**(1):154–158.

Brand, H. R., and Finkelmann, H. (1998). Physical properties of liquid crystalline elastomers. In *Handbook of Liquid Crystals, Vol. 3: High Molecular Weight Liquid Crystals*, eds. D. Demus, J. Goodby, G. W. Gray, H.-W. Spiess, and V. Vill. Wiley-VCH Verlag GmbH.

Brand, P. W., and Hollister, A. (1993). *Clinical Mechanics of the Hand*, 2nd edition. Mosby Year Book.

Brandt, G., Radermacher, K., Zimolong, A., Rau, G., Merloz, P., Klos, T. V., Robb, J., and Staudte, H. W. (2000). CRIGOS: Development of a compact robot for image-guided orthopedic surgery. *Orthopade*, **29**(7):645–649.

Brandt, H. R., and Pleiner, H. (1994). Electrohydrodynamics of nematic liquid crystalline elastomers. *Physica A*, **208**:359.

Brassard, G. (2005). Is information the key? *Nature Physics*, **1**:2–4.

Brock, D. (1991a). *Artificial Muscle Research Review*. Cambridge, MA: MIT Artificial Intelligence Lab. (1991b). *Design and Control of an Artificial Muscle*. Cambridge, MA: MIT Artificial Intelligence Lab. (1991c). *Review of Artificial Muscle Based on Contractile Polymers*. MIT Artificial Intelligence Lab. AI Memo No. 1330.

Brock, D., Lee, W., Segalman, D., and Witkowski, W. (1994a). A dynamic model of a linear actuator based on polymer hydrogel. In *Proceedings of the International Conference on Intelligent Materials*, 210–222. (1994b). A dynamic model of a linear actuator based on polymer hydrogel. *Journal of Intelligent Material Systems and Structures*, **5**(6):764–771.

Brooks, M. (2022). Roger Penrose: "Consciousness must be beyond computable physics." *NewScientist*, 14 November 2022.

Bub, J. (2006). Quantum information and computation. In *Philosophy of Physics (Handbook of Philosophy of Science)*, eds. J. Earman and J. Butterfield. Amsterdam: North Holland, 555–660.

Bub, J. (2019). *Quantum Entanglement and Information. Stanford Encyclopedia of Philosophy*. Stanford, California: Stanford University.

Bub, T., and Bub, J. (2018). *Totally Random: Why Nobody Understands Quantum Mechanics (A Serious Comic on Entanglement)*. Princeton: Princeton University Press.

Burgmayer, P., and Murray, R. W. (1982). An ion gate membrane: Electrochemical control of ion permeability through a membrane with an embedded electrode. *Journal of the American Chemical Society*, **104**:6139.

Butner, S. E., and Ghodoussi, M. (2003). Transforming a surgical robot for human telesurgery. *IEEE Transactions on Robotics and Automation*, **19**(5):818–824.

Cadeddu, J. A., Bzostek, A., Schreiner, S., Barnes, A. C., Roberts, W. W., Anderson, J. H., Taylor, R. H., and Kavoussi, L. R. (1997). A robotic system for percutaneous renal access. *Journal of Urology*, **158**:1589.

Cadiere, G., Himpens, J., Vertruyen, M., and Favretti, F. (1999). The world's first obesity surgery performed by a surgeon at a distance. *Obesity Surgery*, **9**:206–209.

Caldwell, D. (1993). Natural and artificial muscle elements as robot actuators. *Mechatronics*, **3**(3):269–283.

Caldwell, D. G., and Taylor, P. M. (1989). An artificial muscle actuator for robots. In *Advanced Robotics*, eds. K. J. Waldron. Springer, Berlin, Heidelberg.

Caldwell, D., and Taylor, P. (1990). Chemically stimulated pseudo-muscular actuation. *International Journal of Engineering Science*, **28**(8):797–808.

Cao, Y., Smith, P., and Heeger, A. J. (1991). Mechanical and electrical properties of polyacetylene films oriented by tensile drawing. *Polymer*, **32**:1210.

Carlson, J. D. (1999a). Low-cost MR fluid sponge devices. *Journal of Intelligent Material Systems and Structures*, **10**:589–594. (1999b). Magnetorheological fluid actuators. In *Adaptronics and Smart Materials*, ed. H. Janocha. Berlin: Springer-Verlag, 180–195.

Carlson, J. D., and Weiss, K. D. (1994). A growing attraction to magnetic fluids. *MACH Design*, **8**:61–66.

Carman, G. P., and Garcia, E. (1994a). Micro-electro-mechanics of ionic polymeric gels as electrically controllable artificial muscles. In *Proceedings of the International Conference on Intelligent Materials*, 1095–1104. (1994b). Electro-mechanics of resilient contractile fiber bundles with applications to ionic polymeric gel and SMA robotic actuators. In *Proceedings (1994) IEEE International Conference on Robotics & Automation*, San Diego, CA, Vol. 2, 1502–1508.

Carpentier, A., Loulmet, D., Aupecle, B., Kieffer, J. P., Tournay, D., Guibourt, P., Fiemeyer, A., Méléard, D., Richomme, P., and Cardon, C. (1998). Computer-assisted open heart surgery: First case operated on with success. *Comptes Rendus de l'Académie des Sciences III*, **321**:437–442.

Carroll, M. M., and Hayes, M. A. (1996). *Nonlinear Effects in Fluids and Solids*. New York, NY: Plenum Press, 16–112.

Casale, P., and Kojima, Y. (2009). Robotic-assisted laparoscopic surgery in pediatric urology: An update. *Scandinavian Journal of Surgery*, **98**:110–119.

Cassilly, R., Diodato, M. D., Bottros, M., and Damiano, R. J. Jr. (2004). Optimizing motion scaling and magnification in robotic surgery. *Surgery*, **136**(2):291–294.

Castle, S. L., and Kernstine, K. H. (2008). Robotic-assisted thymectomy. *Seminars in Thoracic and Cardiovascular Surgery*, **20**(4):326–331.

CERN. (1987). Speakable and Unspeakable in Quantum Mechanics (PDF). CERN. ISBN 0521334950. Archived from the original (PDF) on 12 April 2015, retrieved 14 June 2014.

Chalmers, D. (2010). *The Character of Consciousness, Philosophy of Mind*, Oxford University Press.

Chan, F., Kassim, I., Lo, C., Ho, C. L., Low, D., Ang, B. T., and Ng, I. (2009). Image-guided robotic neurosurgery: An in vitro and in vivo point accuracy evaluation experimental study. *Advanced Robotic Applications Such as Surgical Neurology*, **71**:640–648.

Chella, A. (2023). *Computational Approaches to Conscious Artificial Intelligence*: 5 (Series on Machine Consciousness). World Scientific Publishing Co Pte Ltd.

Chen, W., Fu, G., Gong, J., He, Y., and Dong, S. (2002). A new design conception for large-span deployable flat grid structures. *International Journal of Space Structures*, **17**(4):293–299.

Chen, Z., Tan, X., and Shahinpoor, M. (2005). Quasistatic positioning of ionic polymer–metal composite (IPMC) actuators. *IEEE/ASME International Conference on Advanced Intelligent Mechatronics*, AIM. 1. 60–65.

Chiang, C. K., Druy, A. A., Gau, S. C., Heeger, A. J., Shirakawa, H., Louis, E. J., Gau, S. C., Mac Diarmid, A. G., and Park, W. (1978). Synthesis of highly conducting films of derivatives of polyacetylene, (CH)x. *Journal of the American Chemical Society*, **10**:1013.

Chiang, C. K., Fischer, C. R., Park, Y. W., Heeger, A. J., Shirakawa, H., Louis, E. J., Gau, S. C., and Mac Diarmid, A. G. (1977). Electrical conductivity in doped polyacetylene. *Physical Review Letters*, **39**:1098.

Chiarelli, P., and De Rossi, D. (1988). Determination of mechanical parameters related to swelling kinetics in an electrically activated contractile gel. *Progress in Colloid and Polymer Science*, **78**:4–8.

Chiarelli, P., De Rossi, D., and Umezawa, K. (1989). Progress in the design of an artificial urethral sphincter. In *Proceedings of the Third Vienna International Workshop on Functional Electrostimulation*, September, Vienna, Austria.

Chiarelli, P., Della Santa, A., De Rossi, D., and Mazzoldi, A. (1994). Actuation properties of electrochemically driven polypyrrole free-standing films. In *Proceedings of the International Conference on Intelligent Materials*, Vol. ICIM-3, June 1996, Lyon, France, 352–360.

Chiarelli, P., Umezawa, K., and Rossi, D. D. (1991). A polymer composite showing electrocontractile response. *Polymer Gels*, 195–201.

Chiribella, G., and Spekkens, R. (2016). *Quantum Theory: Informational Foundations and Foils*. New York: Springer.

Choi, K., Kim, K. J., Kim, D., Manford, C., Heo, S., and Shahinpoor, M. (2006). Performance characteristics of electrochemically driven polyacrylonitrile fiber bundle actuators. *Journal of Intelligent Material Systems and Structures*, **17**(7):563–576.

Ciofu, I. (1994). *Numarul de Aur. Matrice a Evolutiei?* (*Golden Number: Matrix of Evolution?*), ed. Coresi. Bucharest, Romania.

Clauser, J. F., Horne, M. A., Shimony, A., and Holt, R. A. (1969). Proposed experiment to test local hidden-variable theories. *Physical Review Letters*, **23**:880.

Cramer, J. G. (2015). *The Quantum Handshake: Entanglement, Nonlocality and Transactions*. Springer Verlag.

Crowson, A. (1996). Smart materials technologies and biomimetics. In *Proceedings of the SPIE Smart Structures and Materials Conference*, February, San Diego, CA.

Crowson, A., and Bailey, J. A. (1993a). *U.S. Army Research Office Publications*, 78–89. (1993b). Microelectro-mechanics of ionic polymeric gels as artificial muscles for robotic applications. In *Proceedings (1993) IEEE International Conference on Robotics & Automation*, May, Atlanta, GA, Vol. 2, 380–385. (1993c). Current-voltage curves of bipolar membranes. *Journal of Applied Physics*, **72**(1):259–264.

Dautzenberg, H., Jaeger, W., Kotz, J., Philipp, B., Seidel, C., and Stscherbina, D. (1994). *Polyelectrolytes, Formulation, Characterization, and Application*. Munich: Hanser Publishers.

Davies, B. L., Hibberd, R. D., Coptcoat, M. J., and Wickham, J. E. (1989). A surgeon robot prostatectomy: A laboratory evaluation. *Journal of Medical Engineering and Technology*, **13**:273–277.

Davis, T. A., Genders, J. D., and Pletcher, D. (1997). *A First Course in Ion Permeable Membranes*. Romsey: Electrochemical Consultancy.

De Gennes, P. G., Okumura, K., Shahinpoor, M., and Kim, K. J. (2000). Mechanoelectric effects in ionic gels. *Europhysics Letters*, **50**(4): 513–518.

De Gennes, P. G., Hebert, M., and Kant, R. (1997). Artificial muscles based on nematic gels. *Macromolecular Symposia*, **113**:39.

De Rossi, D., Charelli, P., Buzzigoli, G., Domenici, C., and Lazzeri, L. (1986). Contractile behavior of electrically activated mechanochemical polymer actuators. *Transactions of the American Society for Artificial Internal Organs*, **XXXII**:157–162.

De Rossi, D., Domenici, C., and Charelli, P. (1988). Analogs of biological tissues for mechanotransduction: Tactile sensors and muscle-like actuators. In *Sensors and Sensory Systems for Advanced Robots (NATO ASI Serie)*, Vol. F43, 201–218.

De Rossi, D., Parrini, D., Chiarelli, P., and Buzzigoli, G. (1985). Electrically induced contractile phenomena in charged polymer networks: Preliminary study on the feasibility of muscle-like structures. *Transactions of the American Society for Artificial Internal Organs*, **XXXI**:60–65.

De Rossi, D., Suzuki, M., Osada, Y., and Morasso, P. (1992). Pseudomuscular gel actuators for advanced robotics. *Journal of Intelligent Material Systems and Structures*, **3**:75–95.

De, S. K., Aluru, N. R., Johnson, B., Crone, W. C., Beebe, D. J., and Moore, J. (2002). Equilibrium swelling and kinetics of pH-responsive hydrogel: Models, experiments, and simulation. *Journal of Microelectromechanical Systems*, **11**(5):544–555.

Degueldre, M., Vandromme, J., Huong, P. T., and Cadiere, G. B. (2000). Robotically assisted laparoscopic micro advanced tubal anastomosis: A feasibility study. *Fertility and Sterility*, **74**:1020–1023.

Del Grosso, A. E., and Basso, P. (2010). Adaptive building skin structures. *Smart Materials and Structures*, **19**(12):124011.

Della Santa, A., De Rossi, D., and Mazzoldi, A. (1997). Characterization and modeling of a conducting polymer muscle-like linear actuator. *Smart Materials and Structure*, **6**:23–24.

Deole, U., Lumia, R., and Shahinpoor, M. (2004). Characterization of impedance properties of ionic polymer metal composite actuators. In *Proceedings of the Second World Congress on Biomimetics and Artificial Muscle (Biomimetics and Nano-bio 2004)*, December 5–8, Albuquerque, NM.

Deole, U., Lumia, R., Shahinpoor, M., and Bermudez, M. (2008). Design and test of IPMC artificial muscle microgripper. *Journal of Micro-Nano Mechatronics*, **4**:95–102.

Deutsch, D. (1985). Quantum theory, the Church–Turing principle and the universal quantum computer. *Proceedings of the Royal Society (London)*, **A400**:97–117.

Diaz-Arrastia, C., Jurnalov, C., Gomez, G., and Townsend, C. Jr. (2002). Laparoscopic hysterectomy using a computer-enhanced advanced robot. *Surgical Endoscopy*, **16**:1271–1273.

Dieks, D. (1982). Communication by EPR Devices. *Physics Letters A*, **92**:271–272.

Diodato, M., Prasad, S., Klingensmith, M. E., and Damiano, R. J. Jr. (2004). Robotics in surgery. *Current Problems in Surgery*, **41**:752–810.

Diolaiti, N. (2010). Minimally invasive advanced systems. U.S. Patent No. 7,725,214.

Doi, M., Matsumoto, M., and Hirose, Y. (1992). Deformation of ionic polymer gels by electric fields. *Macromolecules*, **25**:5504–5511.

Dorfner, K. (1972). *Ion Exchangers Properties and Applications*, 3rd edition. Ann Arbor, MI: Ann Arbor Science Publishers, Inc.

Drasin, T., Dutson, E., and Gracia, C. (2004). Use of a robotic system as advanced first assistant in advanced laparoscopic surgery. *Journal of the American College of Surgeons*, **199**(3):368–373.

Duarte, F. J. (2019). *Fundamentals of Quantum Entanglement*. Bristol, UK: Institute of Physics.

Dukhin, S. S., and Shilov, V. N. (1974). *Dielectric Phenomena and the Double Layer in Disperse Systems and Polyelectrolytes*. Jerusalem: Keter Publishing House Ltd.

Dunai, T. J., and Finlay, S. M. (2009). Reporting of cosmogenic nuclide data for exposure age and erosion rate determinations. *Quaternary Geochronology*, **4**(6):437–440.

Dusek, K. (ed.) (1993). *Advances in Polymer Science*, vols. 109 and 110, *Responsive Gels, Transitions I and II*. Berlin: Springer-Verlag.

Dwyer-Joyce, R. S., Bullough, W. A., and Lingard, S. (1996). Elastohydrodynamic performance of unexcited electro-rheological fluids. *International Journal of Modern Physics B*, **10**(23–24):3181–3189.

Eckerle, J. S., Andeen, G. B., and Kornbluh, R. D. (1992). I am exploring artificial muscles as robot actuators. *Rob. Int. Soc. Manuf. Eng.* **5**(1):1–4.

Eguchi, M. (1925). Piezoelectric polymers. *Philosophical Magazine*, **49**.

Einstein A., Podolsky, B., and Rosen, N. (1935). Can quantum-mechanical description of physical reality be considered complete? *Physical Review*, **47**, 777–780.

Einstein, A. (1996). *Cum Vad Eu Lumea. Teoria Relativitatii pe Intelesul Tuturor* (How Do I See the World. Theory of Relativity on Everybody's Understanding), Ed. Humanitas, Bucharest, Romania.

Eisenberg, A., and Bailey, F. E. (Eds.) (1986). *Coulombic Interactions in Macromolecular Systems*, Vol. 302. ACS Symposium Series.

Eisenberg, A., and King, M. (1977). *Ion-Containing Polymers*. New York, NY: Academic Press.

Eisenberg, A., and Yeager, H. L. (Eds.) (1982). *Perfluorinated Ionomer Membranes*, Vol. 180. Washington, DC: American Chemical Society.

Ekert, A. (1991). Quantum cryptography based on Bell's theorem. *Physical Review Letters*, **67**:661–663.

Ekert, A., and Renner, R. (2014). The ultimate physical limits of privacy. *Nature*, **507**:443–447.

Ellington, C. P., and Pedley, T. J. (1995). Biological fluid dynamics. In *Proceedings of Symposia of the Society for Experimental Biology*, **XLIX**, Society for Experimental Biology.

Engdahl, G., and Mayergoyz, I. D. (2000). *Handbook of Giant Magnetostrictive Materials*, 1st edition. New York, NY: Academic Press.

Erhard, M., Krenn, M., and Zeilinger, A. (2020). Advances in high-dimensional quantum entanglement. *Nature Review Physics*, **2**:365–381.

Escoubes, M., and Pineri, M. (1982). *Perfluorinated Ionomer Membranes*, eds. A. Eisenberg and H. L. Yeager. Washington, DC: American Chemical Society.

Evans, R. B., and Thompson, D. E. (1993). The application of force to the healing tendon. *Journal of Hand Therapy*, 266–284.

Everett, H. (1957). "Relative state" formulation of quantum mechanics. *Reviews of Modern Physics*, **29**:454–462.

Fankhauser, H., Glauser, D., Flury, P., Piguet, Y., Epitaux, M., Favre, J., and Meuli, R. A. (1994). Robot for CT-guided stereotactic neurosurgery. *Stereotactic and Functional Neurosurgery*, **63**(1–4):93–98.

Ferrara, L., Shahinpoor, M., Kim, K. J., Schreyer, B., Keshavarzi, A., Benzel, E., and Lantz, J. (1999). Use of ionic polymer–metal composites (IPMCs) as a pressure transducer in the human spine. In *Electroactive Polymers*, SPIE publication no. 3669-45, 394–401.

Ferrara, L., Shahinpoor, M., Kim, K. J., Schreyer, H. B., Keshavarzi, A., Benzel, E., and Lantz, J. W. (1999). Use ionic polymer–metal composites (IPMCs) as a pressure transducer in the human spine. In *Proceedings of SPIE 3669, Smart Structures and Materials 1999: Electroactive Polymer Actuators and Devices* (May 28, 1999). https://doi.org/10.1117/12.349704.

Fest, E., Shea, K., Domer, B., and Smith, I. F. C. (2003). Adjustable tensegrity structures. *Journal of Structural Engineering*, **129**(4):515–526.

Feynman, R. (1996). *Feynman Lectures on Computation*, eds. J. G. Hey and R. W. Allen. Reading, MA: Addison-Wesley Publishing Company.

Finkelmann, H., and Brand, H. R. (1994). Liquid crystalline elastomers: A class of materials with novel properties. *Trends in Polymer Science*, **2**:222.

Finkelmann, H., and Shahinpoor, M. (2002). Electrically controllable liquid crystal elastomer–graphite composite artificial muscles. In *Proceedings of SPIE 9th Annual International Symposium on Smart Structures and Materials*, March, San Diego, CA, 4695–4653.

Finkelmann, H., Kock, H. J., and Rehage, G. (1981). Investigations on liquid crystalline siloxanes: 3. Liquid crystalline elastomer—A new type of liquid crystalline material. *Die Makromolekulare Chemie, Rapid Communications*, **2**:317–323.

Firoozbakhsh, K., and Shahinpoor, M. (1998). Mathematical modeling of ionic interactions and deformation in ionic polymeric metal composite artificial muscles. In *Proceedings of SPIE Smart Materials and Structures Conference*, March 3–5, San Diego, CA, publication no. SPIE 3323-66.

Flory, P. J. (1941). Thermodynamics of high polymer solutions. *Journal of Chemical Physics*, **9**(8):660.

Flory, P. J. (1953a). *Principles of Polymer Chemistry*. Ithaca, NY: Cornell University Press. (1953b). *Statistical Mechanics of Swelling Network Structures*. Ithaca, NY: Cornell University Press; 1969. *Statistical Mechanics of Polymer Chains*. New York, NY: Interscience Publishers.

Fragala, A., Enos, J., LaConti, A., and Boyack, J. (1972). Electrochemical activation of synthetic artificial muscle membrane. *Electrochemica Acta*, **17**:1507–1522.

Francis, M. (2012). Quantum entanglement shows that reality can't be local. *Ars Technica.* Retrieved from https://arstechnica.com/science/2012/10/quantum-entanglement-shows-that-reality-cant-be-local.

Freedman, S. J., and Clauser, J. F. (1972). Experimental test of local hidden-variable theories. *Physical Review Letters*, **28**:938.

Freeman, W. J. (1991). The physiology of perception. *Scientific American*, **264**(2):78–85.

Fries, N., Vitagliano, G., Malik, M., and Huber, M. (2019). Entanglement certification from theory to experiment. *Nature Review Physics*, **1**:72–87.

Froes, M. M., Correia, A. H. P., Garcia-Abreu, J., Spray, D. C., Campos De Carvalho, A. C., and Neto, V. M. (1999). Gap-junctional coupling between neurons and astrocytes in primary central nervous system cultures. *Proceedings of the National Academy of Sciences*, **96**(13):7541–7546.

Frolov, A. V. (1995). *Matter as Process*. St. Petersburg, Russia.

Fuchs, C. A. (2014). An introduction to QBism with an application to the locality of quantum mechanics. *American Journal of Physics*, **82**:749–754.

Full, R. J., and Meijer, K. (2001). Metrics of natural muscle. In *Electroactive Polymers (EAP), Such as Artificial Muscles, Reality Potential, and Challenges*, ed. Y. Bar-Cohen. SPIE & William Andrew/Noyes Publications, 67–83.

Full, R. J., Kubow, T., Schmitt, J., Holmes, P., and Koditschek, D. (2002). I am quantifying dynamic stability and maneuverability in legged locomotion. *Integrative and Comparative Biology*, **42**:149–157.

Furukawa, T., and Seo, N. (1990). Electrostriction is the origin of piezoelectricity in ferroelectric polymers. *Japanese Journal of Applied Physics*, **29**(4):675–680.

Furusha, J., and Sakaguchi, M. S. (1999). New actuators using ER fluids and their applications to force display devices in virtual reality and medical treatment. *International Journal of Modern Physics B*, **13**(14–16):2051–2059.

Gamow, G. (1946). Expanding universe and the origin of elements. *Physical Review*, **70**:572.

Gandhi, M. R., Murray, P., Spinks, G. M., and Wallace, G. G. (1995). Mechanisms of electromechanical actuation in polypyrrole. *Synthetic Metals*, **75**:247–256.

Gandhi, M. V., Thompson, B. S., and Choi, S.-B. (1989a). A new generation of innovative ultra-intelligent composite materials featuring electro-rheological: An experimental investigation. *Journal of Composite Materials*, **23**:1232–1255.

Gandhi, M. V., Thompson, B. S., Choi, S.-B., and Shakair, S. (1989b). Electro-rheological fluid-based articulating robotic systems. *Journal of Mechanisms, Transmissions, and Automation*, **111**:328–336.

Gantes, C. J., and Konitopoulou, E. (2004). Geometric design of arbitrarily curved bistable deployable arches with discrete joint size. *International Journal of Solids and Structures*, **41**(20):5517–5540.

Gebel, G., Aldebert, P., and Pineri, M. (1987). Structure and related properties of solution-case perfluorosulfonate ionomer films. *Macromolecules*, **20**:1425–1428.

Genuini, G., Casalino, G., Chiarelli, P., and De Rossi, D. (1990). *Pseudomuscular Linear Actuators: Modeling and Simulation Experiences in the Motion of Articulated Chains.* Maratea, Italy: NATO ACI Science.

Georgiev, D. D., and Gudder, S. P. (2022). Sensitivity of entanglement measures in bipartite pure quantum states. *Modern Physics Letters B*, **36**(22):2250101–2250255.

Georgiev, D., and Cohen, E. (2022). Entanglement measures for two-particle quantum histories. *Physical Review A*, **106**(6):062437.

Gharibian, S. (2010). Strong NP-hardness of the quantum separability problem. *Quantum Information and Computation*, **10**(3&4):343–360.

Gibney, E. (2014). Entangled photons make a picture from a paradox. *Nature*, doi:10.1038/nature.2014.15781.S2CID 124976589.

Gierke, T. D., and Hsu, W. Y. (1982). The cluster-network model of ion clustering in perfluoro sulfonate membranes. In *Perfluorinated Ionomer Membranes*, eds. A. Eisenberg and H. L. Yeager. Washington, DC: ACS, 283–307.

Gierke, T. D., Munn, G. E., and Wilson, F. C. (1982). Morphology of perfluorosulfonated membrane products: Wide-angle and small-angle x-ray studies. *ACS Symposium Series*, **180**:195–216.

Giorgi, C., Sala, R., Riva, D., Cossu, A., and Eisenberg, H. (2000). Robotics in child neurosurgery. *Child's Nervous System*, **16**(10–11):832–834.

Glaser, R., Caccese, V., and Shahinpoor, M. (2018). Comparative finite element and experimental analysis of quasi-static inflation of a thin deployable membrane space structure. *Journal of Finite Elements in Analysis and Design*, **138**:48–65.

Gobin, P. F., and Tatibouet, J. (Eds.) (1996). *Proceedings of the Third International Conference on Intelligent Materials*, Vol. 2779, The International Society for Optical Engineering.

Gomes, P. (2011). Surgical robotics: Reviewing the past, analyzing the present, imagining the future. *Robotics and Computer-Integrated Manufacturing*, **27**(2):261–266.

Gong, J. P., and Osada, Y. (1994). Modeling and simulation of ionic polymer network. In *Preprints of the Sapporo Symposium on Intelligent Polymer Gels*, October 6–8, Sapporo, Japan, 21–22.

Gong, J. P., Nitta, T., and Osada, Y. (1994a). Electrokinetic modeling of the contractile phenomena of polymeric-truly gels: One-dimensional capillary model. *Journal of Physical Chemistry*, **98**:9583–9587.

Gour, G., and Wallach, N. R. (2013). Classification of multipartite entanglement of all finite dimensionality. *Physical Review Letters*, **111**(6), 060502.

Grassl, M., Rötteler, M., and Beth, T. (1998). Computing local invariants of quantum-bit systems. *Physical Review A*, **58**(3):1833–1839.

Greco, D. (1998). *Ether and Field Theories*. MIT.

Grimshaw, P. E., Nussbaum, J. H., Grodzinsky, A. J., and Yarmush, M. L. (1990a). Kinetics of electrically and chemically induced swelling in polyelectrolyte gels. *Journal of Chemical Physics*, **93**(6):4462–4472.

Grimshaw, P. E., Nussbaum, J. H., Yarmush, M. L., and Eisenberg, S. R. (1989). Dynamic membranes for protein transport: Chemical electrical control. *Chem. Eng. Sci.* **44**(4):827–840.

Grodzinsky, A. J. (1974). *Electromechanics of Deformable Polyelectrolyte Membranes*. Sc.D. dissertation. MIT, Cambridge, MA.

Grodzinsky, A. J. (1975). Fields, forces, and flows in biological tissues and membranes. Lecture notes.

Grodzinsky, A. J., and Melcher, J. R. (1974). Electromechanics of deformable, charged polyelectrolyte membranes. In *Proceedings of the 27th Annual Conference on Engineering in Medicine and Biology*, 16, paper 53.2. (1976). Electromechanical transduction with charged polyelectrolyte membranes. *IEEE Transactions on Biomedical Engineering*, **23**(6):421–433.

Gühne, O. (2004). Characterizing entanglement via uncertainty relations. *Physical Review Letters*, **92**(11):117903.

Gühne, O., and Lewenstein, M. (2004). Entropic uncertainty relations and entanglement. *Physical Review A*. **70**(2), 022316.

Gühne, O., and Tóth, G. (2009). Entanglement detection. *Physics Reports*, **474**(1–6):1–75.

Guillonneau, B., Jayet, C., Tewari, A., and Vallancien, G. (2001). Robot-assisted laparoscopic nephrectomy. *Journal of Urology*, **166**:200–201.

Guo, S., Fukuda, T., Kosuge, K., Arai, F., Oguro, K., and Negoro, M. (1994). *Micro Catheter System with Active Guide Wire Structure, Experimental Results, and Characteristic Evaluation of Active Guide Wire Catheter Using ICPF Actuator*. Osaka: Osaka National Research Institute, 191–197. (1995). *Micro Catheter System with Active Guide Wire*. Preprint, Osaka, Japan.

Gurvits, L. (2003). Classical deterministic complexity of Edmonds' problem and quantum entanglement. In: *Proceedings of the Thirty-Fifth Annual ACM Symposium on Theory of Computing*. New York: ACM Press, p.10.

Guth, A. H. (1981). Cosmic inflation. *Physical Review D*, **23**, 347.

Haber, G. P., Crouzet, S., and Gill, I. S. (2008). Laparoscopic and robotic assisted radical cystectomy for bladder cancer: A critical analysis. *European Urology*, **54**(2008):54–64.

Haidegger, T., and Benyo, Z. (2008). Advanced robotic support for long duration space missions. *Acta Astronautica*, **63**(2008):996–1005.

Haikonen, P. (2011). XCR-1: An experimental cognitive robot based on an associative neural architecture. *Cognitive Computation*, **3**(2):360–366.

Haikonen, P. O. (2012). *Consciousness and Robot Sentience*: 2 (Series on Machine Consciousness). World Scientific Publishing Co Pte Ltd.

Haikonen, P. O. (2019). *Consciousness and Robot Sentience*: 4 (Series on Machine Consciousness), 2nd edition. World Scientific Publishing Co Pte Ltd.

Haldane, J. B. S. (1929). The origin of life. *Rationalist Annual*, **148**:3–10.

Hales, C. G. (2014). *The Revolutions of Scientific Structure*: 3 (Series on Machine Consciousness). World Scientific Publishing Co Pte Ltd.

Halpert, G., and Landgrebe, A. R. (Eds.) (1995). *The Electrochemical Society Proceedings Series*. Pennington, NJ: PV 95–23, p. 193.

Hameroff, S. R. (1994). Quantum coherence in microtubules: A neural basis for emergent consciousness. *Journal of Consciousness Studies*, **1**:91–118.

Hameroff, S. R. (2006). The entwined mysteries of anesthesia and consciousness: Is there a common underlying mechanism? *Anesthesiology*, **105**:400–412.

Hameroff, S. R. (2021). "Orch OR" is the most complete, and most easily falsifiable theory of consciousness. *Cognitive Neuroscience*, **12**(2):74–76.

Hameroff, S. R. (2022). Consciousness, cognition and the neuronal cytoskeleton: A new paradigm needed in neuroscience. *Frontiers in Molecular Neuroscience*, **15**:869935.

Hamlen, R. P., Kent, C. E., and Shafer, S. N. (1965). Electrolytically active polymers. *Nature*, **206**:1149–1150.

Happel, J., and Brenner, H. (1973). *Low Reynolds Number Hydrodynamics*. Englewood Cliffs, NJ: Prentice Hall.

Hardy, L. (1992). Quantum mechanics, local realistic theories, and Lorentz-invariant realistic theories. *Physical Review Letters*, **68**(20):2981–2984.

Hawkins, G. F., O'Brien, M. J., and Creasy, T. S. (2004). Nastic materials using internally generated pressure. In *International Conference on Adaptive Structures and Technologies*, CAST 2004, October, Bar Harbor, ME.

He, M., Wang, M., and Wang, Z. (2022). The new-type batteries with ultimate energy density. *Journal of Physics: Conference Series*, **2247**:012013.

Hebert, M. R. K., and de Gennes, P. G. (1997). Dynamics and thermodynamics of artificial muscles based on nematic gels. *Journal of Physics I France*, **7**:909–918.

Heeger, A. J. (2001). Semiconducting and metallic polymers: The fourth generation of polymeric materials. The Noble Prize 2000 lecture. *Current Applied Physics*, **1**:247–267.

Heitner-Wirguin, C. (1996). Recent advances in perfluorinated ionomer membranes: Structure, properties and applications. *Journal of Membrane Science*, **120**(1):1–33.

Helfferich, F. (1995). *Ion Exchange*. New York, NY: Dover Publications, Inc.

Hemal, A. K., and Menon, M. (2004). Robotics in urology. *Current Opinion in Urology*, **14**(2):89–93.

Henderson, B., Lane, S., Shahinpoor, M., Kim, K., and Leo, D. (2001). Evaluation of ionic polymer-metal composites for use as near-DC mechanical sensors. In *AIAA Space 2001— Conference and Exposition*, Albuquerque, NM, AIAA paper 2001–4600.

Herbst, T., Scheidl, T., Fink, M., Handsteiner, J., Wittmann, B., Ursin, R., and Zeilinger, A. (2015). Teleportation of entanglement over 143 km. *Proceedings of the National Academy of Sciences of the United States of America*, **112**:14202–14205.

Hess, C., and Li, L. (1989). Smart hands for EVA retriever. In *NASA Conference on Space Telerobotics*, January, Pasadena, CA.

Higa, M., and Kira, A. (1994). A new equation of ion flux in a membrane: Inclusion of frictional force generated by the electric field. *Journal of Physical Chemistry*, **98**(25):6339–6342.

Hillery, M., and Zubairy, M. S. (2006). Entanglement conditions for two-mode states. *Physical Review Letters*, **96**(5):050503.

Himpens, J., Leman, G., and Cadiere, G. B. (1998). Teleadvanced laparoscopic cholecystectomy. *Surgical Endoscopy*, **12**:091.

Hirai, M., Hirai, T., Sukumoda, A., Nemoto, H., Amemiya, Y., Kobayashi, K., and Ueki, T. (1995). Electrically induced reversible structural change of a highly swollen polymer gel network. *Journal of the Chemical Society Faraday Transactions*, **91**:473–477.

Hirai, T., Zheng, J., and Watanabe, M. (1999). Solvent-drag bending motion of polymer gel induced by an electric field. In *Proceedings of the SPIE 6th Annual International Symposium on Smart Structures and Materials*, Vol. 3669, ed. Y. Bar-Cohen, 209–217.

Hirokawa, Y., and Tanaka, T. (1984). Volume transition in nonionic gel. *Journal of Chemical Physics*, **81**:6379.

Hirotsu, S., Hirokawa, Y., and Tanaka, T. (1987). Volume-phase transitions of ionized n-isopropylacrylamide gels. *Journal of Chemical Physics*, **87**(2):1392–1395.

Hoberman, C. (1990). Reversibly expandable doubly-curved truss structure. U.S. Patent 4,942,700.

Hoberman, C. (1991). Radial expansion/retraction truss structures. U.S. Patent 5,024,031.

Hoberman, C. (2007). Unfolding Structures. (http://www.hoberman.com).

Hofmann, H. F., and Takeuchi, S. (2003). Violation of local uncertainty relations as a signature of entanglement. *Physical Review A*, **68**(3):032103.

Holevo, A. S. (1973). Statistical problems in quantum physics. In *Proceedings of the Second Japan-USSR Symposium on Probability Theory*, eds. G. Murayama and J. V. Prokhorov. Berlin: Springer, 104–109.

Holland, M. J., and Burnett, K. (1993). Interferometric detection of optical phase shifts at the Heisenberg limit. *Physical Review Letters*, **71**(9):1355–1358.

Horgan, S., and Vanuno, D. (2001). Robots in laparoscopic surgery. *Journal of Laparoendoscopic & Advanced Techniques*, **11**(6).

Horodecki, M., Horodecki, P., and Horodecki, R. (1998). Mixed-state entanglement and distillation: Is there a bound entanglement in nature? *Physical Review Letters*, **80**(1998):5239–5242.

Horodecki, R., Horodecki, P., Horodecki, M., and Horodecki, K. (2009). Quantum entanglement. *Reviews of Modern Physics*, **81**(2):865–942.

Hoznek, A., Zaki, S. K., Samadi, D. B., Salomon, L., Lobontiu, A., Lang, P., and Abbou, C. C. (2002). Robotic-assisted kidney transplantation: An initial experience. *Journal of Urology*, **167**:1604–1606.

Hsu, W. Y., and Gierke, T. D. (1982). Ion clustering and transport in Nafion perfluorinated membranes. *Journal of the Electrochemical Society*, **129**(3):C121–C129.

Hu, X. (1996). Molecular structure of polyacrylonitrile fibers. *Journal of Applied Polymer Science*, **62**:1925–1932.

Huang, J. P., Karttunen, M., Yu, K. W., and Dong, L. (2003). Dielectrophoresis of charged colloidal suspensions. *Physical Review E*, **67**:021403.

Huang, Y. (2010). Entanglement criteria via concave-function uncertainty relations. *Physical Review A*, **82**(1):012335.

Huang, Y. (2013). Entanglement detection: Complexity and Shannon entropic criteria. *IEEE Transactions on Information Theory*, **59**(10):6774–6779.

Hubble, E. (1929). Extra-galactic nebulae. *Proceedings of the National Academy of Sciences*, **15**(3):168–173.

Huggins, M. L. (1941). Solutions of long chain compounds. *Journal of Chemical Physics*, **9**(15):440.

Huxley, A. F. (1957). Muscle structure and theories of contraction. *Progress in Biophysics and Biophysical Chemistry*, **7**:255–264.

Ichijo, H., Hirasa, O., Kishi, R., Oowada, M., Sahara, K., Kokufuta, E., and Kohno, S. (1995). Thermo-responsive gels. *Radiation Physics and Chemistry*, **46**(2):185–190.

Iordachita, I., Kapoor, A., Mitchell, B., Kazanzides, P., Hager, G., Handa, J., and Taylor, R. (2006). *Steady-Hand Manipulator for Retinal Surgery*. The Johns Hopkins University.

Ito, S. (1989). Phase transition of an aqueous solution of poly (N-alkyl acrylamide) derivatives: Effects of side chain structure. *Kobunsha*, **46**(7):437.

Itoh, Y., Okui, N., Matsumura, T., Umemoto, S., and Sakai, T. (1987). Contraction/elongation mechanism of acrylonitrile gel fibers. *Polymer Preprints*, **36**(9):2897–2899.

Jacob, F. (1988). *The Statue Within: An Autobiography*. Basic Books.

Jacobsen, S. C. (1989). The state of the art in dexterous robotics. In *Conference Dinner, Speaker, IEEE International Conference on Robotics and Automation*, May, Scottsdale, AZ.

Jacobsen, S. C., Iverson, E. K., Knutti, D. F., Johnson, R. T., and Biggers, K. B. (1986). Design of the UTAH/M.I.T. dexterous hand. In *IEEE International Conference on Robotics and Automation*, April, San Francisco.

Jaeger, G. (2009). *Entanglement, Information, and the Interpretation of Quantum Mechanics*. Heidelberg: Springer.

Jakopec, M., Harris, S. J., Rodriguez y Baena, F., Gomes, P., Cobb, J., and Davies, B. L. (2001). The first clinical application of a "hands-on" robotic knee surgery system. *Computer Aided Surgery*, **6**:329–339.

Jamshidi, M., Lu, J.Y.S., and Shahinpoor, M. (1986). *Recent Trends in Robotics: Modeling, Control and Education*, North-Holland Publishing Corp., New York, and Amsterdam.

Jamshidi, M., Lumia, R., Mullins, J., and Shahinpoor, M. (1993). *Robotics and Manufacturing: Recent Trends in Research, Education, and Applications*, ASME Press Series, New York, vol. 4, pp. 11–12.

Jang, B. Z., and Zhang, Z. J. (1994). Thermally and phase transformation-induced volume changes of polymers for actuator applications. *Journal of Intelligent Material Systems and Structures*, **5**:758–763.

Jolly, M. E., Carlson, J. D., and Muñoz, B. C. (1996). A model of the behavior of magnetorheological materials. *Smart Materials and Structures*, **5**:607–614.

Jolly, M. R., and Carlson, J. D. (2000). Composites with field responsive rheology. In *Comprehensive Composite Materials*, Vol. 5. New York, NY: Elsevier Science Ltd., Chapter 27, 86.

Jozsa, R., and Linden, N. (2002). On the role of entanglement in quantum computational speed-up. *Proceedings of the Royal Society A: Mathematical, Physical and Engineering Sciences*, **459**(2036):2011–2032.

Kaga, Y., Okuzaki, H., Yasunaga, H., and Osada, Y. (1994). Electrically controlled insulin release from polyelectrolyte gel. In *Proceedings of the International Conference on Intelligent Materials*, 711–718.

Kagami, Y., Matsuda, A., Yasunaga, H., and Osada, Y. (1994). Order–disorder transition of hydrogel with n-alkyl acrylate and shape memory function as a smart diaphragm. In *Preprints of the Sapporo Symposium on Intelligent Polymer Gels*, October 6–8, Sapporo, Japan, 129–130.

Kaiser, W. A., Fischer, H., Vagner, J., and Selig, M. (2000). Robotic system for biopsy and therapy of breast lesions in a high-field whole-body magnetic resonance tomography unit. *Investigative Radiology*, **35**:513–519.

Kajiwara, K., and Ross-Murphy, S. B. (1992). Synthetic gels on the move. *Nature*, **355**(6357):208–209.

Kajiyama, T., Oishi, Y., Takahara, A., and He, X. (1994). Higher order structures and thermoresponsive properties of polymeric gel with stearyl acrylate. In *Preprints of the Sapporo Symposium on Intelligent Poly-Gels*, October 6–8, Sapporo, Japan, 27–30.

Kaneto, K., Kaneko, M., Min, Y., and MacDiarmid, A. G. (1995). Artificial muscle: Electromechanical actuators using polyaniline films. *Synthetic Metals*, **71**:2211.

Kanno, R., Hattori, M., Tadokoro, S., Takamori, T., and Oguro, K. (1994). *Modeling of Electric Characteristics of ICPF Actuator*. Kobe: Kobe University Preprint.

Kanno, R., Kurata, A., Hattori, M., Tadokoro, S., Takamori, T., and Oguro, K. (1994a). Characteristics and modeling of ICPF actuators. In *Proceedings of Japan–USA Symposium on Flexible Automation*, Vol. 2, 692–698.

Kanno, R., Tadokoro, S., Takamori, T., and Hattori, M. (1996). Linear approximate dynamic model of ICPF actuator. In *Proceedings of the IEEE International Conference on Robotics and Automation*, 219–225.

Kassabian, P., You, Z., and Pellegrino, S. (1999). Retractable roof structures. *Proceedings Institution of Civil Engineers Structures and Buildings*, **134**:45–56.

Katchalsky, A. (1949). Rapid swelling and deswelling of reversible gels of polymeric acids by ionization. *Experientia*, **V**:319–320.

Kent, A. (1999). Unconditionally secure bit commitment. *Physical Review Letters*, **83**:1447–1450.

Keshavarzi, A., Shahinpoor, M., Kim, K. J., and Lantz, J. (1999). Using ionic polymer-metal composite sensors, blood pressure, pulse rate, and rhythm measurement. In *Electroactive Polymers*, SPIE publication no. 3669-36, 369 -376.

Kim, D., and Kim, K. J. (2005). Self-oscillatory behavior of ionic polymer–metal composite (IPMC): A new finding. In *SPIE Smart Materials and Structures Conference*, March, #5759-7.

Kim, J., Kim, J.-Y., and Choe, S.-J. (2000). Electro-active paper: Its possibility as actuators. In *Proceedings of the SPIE EAPAD Conference, Part of the 7th Annual International Symposium on Smart Structures and Materials, SPIE Proceedings*, Vol. 3987, ed. Y. Bar-Cohen, 203–209.

Kim, K. J., and Shahinpoor, M. (1999). Effect of the surface-electrode resistance on the actuation of the ionic polymer–metal composite (IPMC) artificial muscles. In *Electroactive Polymers*, SPIE publication no. 3669-43, 308–319.

Kim, K. J., and Shahinpoor, M. (2001a). Development of three-dimensional polymeric artificial muscles. In *Proceedings of SPIE 8th annual international symposium on smart structures and materials*, March, Newport Beach, CA, 4329–(58). (2001b-2003a). Ionic polymer–metal composites—II. Manufacturing techniques, smart materials, and structures (SMS). *Inst. Phys. Publ.* **12**(1):65–79. (2003b). Effective diffusivity of nanoscale ion–water clusters within ion-exchange membranes determined by a novel mechano-electrical technique. *International Journal of Hydrogen Energy*, **28**(1):99–104.

Kim, K. J., and Shahinpoor, M. (2002). A novel method of manufacturing three-dimensional ionic polymer-metal composites (IPMC's) biomimetic sensors, actuators and artificial muscle. *Polymer*, **43**(3):797–802.

Kim, K. J., and Shahinpoor, M. (2007). Special issue: Biomimetics, artificial muscles, and Nano-Bio 2004. *Journal of Intelligent Material Systems and Structures*, **18**:101.

Kim, K. J., Caligiuri, J., and Shahinpoor, M. (2003). Contraction/elongation behavior of cation-modified poly-acrylonitrile fibers. In *Proceedings of SPIE 10th Annual International Symposium on Smart Structures and Materials*, March 2–6, San Diego, CA, SPIE publication no. 5051-23, 207–213.

Kim, K. J., Caligiuri, J., Choi, K., Shahinpoor, M., Norris, I. D., and Mattes, B. R. (2002). Polyacrylonitrile nanofibers as artificial nano-muscles. In *Proceedings of the First World Congress on Biomimetics and Artificial Muscle (Biomimetics 2002)*, December 9–11, Albuquerque, NM.

Kim, K. J., Shahinpoor, M., and Razani, R. (1998). Solid polymer fuel cells for the next century. *International Journal of Environmentally Conscious Design and Manufacturing*, **7**(3):17–46. (1999). Electro-active polymer materials for solid polymer fuel cells. In *Electroactive Polymers*, SPIE publication no. 3669-42, 385–393. (2000a). Preparation of IPMCs for fuel cells, electrolysis, and hydrogen sensors. In *SPIE Smart Materials and Structures*, SPIE publication no. 3987-41, 311–320. (2000b). Preparation of IPMCs for fuel cells, electrolysis, and hydrogen sensors. In *Proceedings of SPIE 7th International Symposium on Smart Structures and Materials*, Vol. 3687, 110–120.

Kim, K., Detweiler, J., Lloyd, G., Shahinpoor, M., and Razani, A. (2002). Experimental and theoretical investigation of a metal hydride artificial muscle. In *Proceedings of the First World Congress on Biomimetics and Artificial Muscle (Biomimetics 2002)*, December 9–11, Albuquerque, NM.

Kishi, R., Hasebe, M., Hara, M., and Osada, Y. (1990). Mechanism and process of chemomechanical contraction of polyelectrolyte gels under electric field. *Polymers of Advanced Technologies*, **1**:19–25.

Kishi, R., Ichijo, H., and Hirasa, O. (1993). Thermo-responsive devices using poly(vinyl methyl ether) hydrogels. *Journal of Intelligent Material Systems and Structures*, **4**:533–537.

Kitagawa, M., and Ueda, M. (1993). Squeezed Spin States. *Physical Review A*, **47**(6):5138–5143.

Kocher, C. A. (1971). Time correlations in the detection of successively emitted photons. *Annals of Physics*, **65**(1):1–18.

Kohno. (1995). Thermo-responsive gels. *Radiation Physics and Chemistry*, **46**:185–190.

Kolde, J. A., Bahar, B., Wilson, M. S., and Zawodzinski, T. A. (1995). In *Proton Conducting Membrane Fuel Cells I*, eds. S. Gottesfeld, G. Halpert, and A. Landgrebe. Pennington, NJ: The Electrochemical Society, PV 95–23, p.193.

Kolosov, O., Suzuki, M., and Yamanaka, K. (1993). Microscale evaluation of the viscoelastic properties of polymer gel for artificial muscles using transmission acoustic microscopy. *Journal of Applied Physics*, **74**(10):6407–6412.

Komoroski, R. A., and Mauritz, K. A. (1982). Nuclear magnetic resonance studies and the theory of ion pairing in perfluorinated ionomers. In *ACS Symposium Series*, Vol. 180. Washington, DC: The American Chemical Society.

Koren, Y. (1985). *Robotics for Engineers*. McGraw & Hill.

Kotler, S., Peterson, G. A., Shojaee, E., Lecocq, F., Cicak, K., Kwiatkowski, A., Geller, S., Glancy, S., Knill, E., Simmonds, R. W., Aumentado, J., and Teufel, J. D. (2021). Direct observation of deterministic macroscopic entanglement. *Science*, **372**(6542):622–625.

Kottke, E. A., Partridge, L. D., and Shahinpoor, M. (2004). Bio-potential neural activation of artificial muscles. In *Proceedings of the Second World Congress on Biomimetics and Artificial Muscle (Biomimetics and Nano-Bio 2004)*, December 5–8, Albuquerque, NM. (2007). Bio-potential activation of artificial muscles. *Journal of Intelligent Material Systems and Structures*, **18**(2).

Kuhn, W. (1949). Dehnung und Kontraktion bei Anderung der Ionisation eines Netzwerks Polyvalenter Fadenmolekulionen. *Experientia* **V**:318–319.

Kuhn, W., and Hargitay, B. (1951). Muskelahnliche Kontraktion und Dehnung von Netzwerken Polyvalenter Fadenmolekulionen. *Experientia* **VII**:1–11.

Kuhn, W., Hargitay, B., Katchalsky, A., and Eisenberg, H. (1950). Reversible dilation and contraction by changing the ionization state of high-polymer acid networks. *Nature*, **165**:514–516.

Kuhn, W., Kunzle, O., and Katchalsky, A. (1948). Verhalten polyvalenter fademolekelionen in losung. *Helvetica Chemica Acta*, **31**:1994–2037.

Kuntz, W. H., Larter, R., and Uhegbu, C. E. (1987). Enhancement of membrane transport of ions by spatially nonuniform electric fields. *Journal of the American Chemical Society*, **109**(9):2582–2585.

Kwoh, Y. S., Hou, J., Jonckheere, E. A., and Hayati, S. (1988). A robot with improved absolute positioning accuracy for CT-guided stereotactic brain surgery. *IEEE Transactions on Biomedical Engineering*, **35**:153–160.

Lami, L., and Regula, B. (2023). No second law of entanglement manipulation after all. *Nature Physics*, **19**(2):184–189.

Larkin, D. Q., and Shafer, D. C. (2011). Robotic surgery system including position sensors using fiber Bragg gratings. U.S. Patent No. 7,930,065.

Laverack, M. S. (1985). Physiological adaptations of marine animals. In *Symposia of the Society for Experimental Biology. No. XIX*, Society for Experimental Biology.

Lavrov, A. N., Komiya, S., and Ando, Y. (2002). Antiferromagnets: Magnetic shape-memory effects in a crystal. *Nature*, **418**:385–386.

Le Roux, P. D., Das, H., Esquenazi, S., and Kelly, P. J. (2001). Robot-assisted microsurgery: A feasibility study in the rat. *Neurosurgery*, **48**:584–589.

Leinaas, J. M., Myrheim, J., and Ovrum, E. (2006). Geometrical aspects of entanglement. *Physical Review A*, **74**(1):012313.

Leo, D. J., and Cuppoletti, J. (2004). High-energy density actuation based on biological transport mechanisms. In *International Conference on Adaptive Structures and Technologies (CAST 2004)*, October, Bar Harbor, ME.

Li, F. K., Zhu, W., Zhang, X., Zhao, C. T., and Xu, M. (1999). Shape memory effect of ethylene-vinyl acetate copolymers. *Journal of Applied Polymer Science*, **71**(7):1063–1070.

Li, J. Y., and Nemat-Nasser, S. (2000). Micromechanical analysis of ionic clustering in Nafion perfluorinated membrane. *Mechanics of Materials*, **32**(5):303–314.

Li, Y., and Tanaka, T. (1989). Study of the universality class of the gel network system. *Journal of Chemical Physics*, **90**(9):5161–5166.

Liang, C., and Rogers, C. A. (1990). One-dimensional thermomechanical constitutive relations for shape-memory materials. *Journal of Intelligent Material Systems and Structures*, **1**(2):54–59. (1992). Design of shape memory alloy actuators. *ASME Journal of Mechanical Design*, **114**:223–230.

Liang, C., Rogers, C. A., and Malafeew, E. (1991). Preliminary investigation of shape memory polymers and their hybrid composites. In *ASME Conference on Smart Structures and Materials*, Vol. 123, 97–105. (1997). Investigation of shape memory polymers and their hybrid composites. *Journal of Intelligent Material Systems and Structures*, **8**:380.

Lifson, S., and Katchalsky, A. (1954). The electrostatic free energy of polyelectrolyte solutions—II. Fully stretched macromolecules. *Journal of Polymer Science*, **13**:43–55.

Lindemann, P. A. (2011). *Thermodynamics & Free Energy*. Borderlands.

Liu, Z., and Calvert, P. (2000). Multilayer hydrogens and muscle-like actuators. *Advanced Materials*, **12**(4):288–291.

Lloyd, L. G., Kim, K. J., Razani, A., and Shahinpoor, M. (2002). Investigation of a solar-thermal biomimetic metal hydride actuator. In *ASME Solar 2002: International Solar Energy Conference*, June 15–20, 2002, Reno, Nevada, USA, 301–308.

Lo Franco, R., and Compagno, G. (2018). Indistinguishability of elementary systems as a resource for quantum information processing. *Physical Review Letters*, **120**(24):240403.

Lo, H.-K., and Chau, H. F. (1997). Is quantum bit commitment possible? *Physical Review Letters*, **78**:3410–3413.

Lo, H.-K., Popescu, S., and Spiller, T. (1998). *Introduction to Quantum Computation and Information*. Singapore: World Scientific.

Lum, M. J. H., Rosen, J., Lendvay, T. S., Wright, A. S., Sinanan, M. N., and Hannaford, B. (2008). TeleRobotic fundamentals of laparoscopic surgery (FLS): Effects of time delay—Pilot study. *30th Annual International IEEE EMBS Conference 2008*.

Lumia, R., and Shahinpoor, M. (1999). Microgripper design using electro-active polymers. In *Electroactive Polymer*, SPIE publication no. 3669-30, 322–329. (2002). Artificial muscle micro-gripper. In *Proceedings of the First World Congress on Biomimetics and Artificial Muscle (Biomimetics 2002)*, December 9–11, Albuquerque, NM.

Lusted, H. S., and Knapp, R. B. (1996). Controlling computers with neural signals. *Scientific American*, **275**(4):82–87.

Ma, J., and Berkelman, P. (2007). Task evaluations of a compact laparoscopic advanced robot system. *IEEE/RSJ International Conference on Intelligent Robots and Systems*, IROS 2007, October 29–November 2, 2007.

Ma, X.-S., Zotter, S., Kofler, J., Ursin, R., Jennewein, T., Brukner, Č., and Zeilinger, A. (2012). Experimental delayed-choice entanglement swapping. *Nature Physics*, **8**(6):480485.

MacDiarmid, A. G. (2001). Synthetic metals: A novel role for organic polymers. The Noble Prize 2000 lecture. *Current Applied Physics*, **1**:269–279.

Maddock, L., Bone, Q., and Rayner, J. M. V. (1994). *Mechanics and Physiology of Animal Swimming*. Cambridge: Cambridge University Press.

Maden, F., Korkmaza, K., and Akgünb, Y. (2011). A review of planar scissor structural mechanisms: Geometric principles and design methods. *Architectural Science Review*, **54**(3):246–257.

Mallavarapu, K., and Leo, D. J. (2001). Feedback control of the bending response of ionic polymer actuators. *Journal of Intelligent Material Systems and Structures*, **12**:143–155.

Malone, R. (1978). *The Robot Book*. New York: Push Pin Press, p. 26.

Mao, S. P., Lai, H. C., Chang, F. W., Yu, M. H., and Chang, C. C. (2007). Laparoscopy-assisted robotic myomectomy using the da Vinci system. *Taiwanese Journal of Obstetrics and Gynecology*, **46**(2):174–176.

Marescaux, J., Smith, M., Fölscher, D., Jamali, F., Malassagne, B., and Leroy, J. (2001). Telerobotic laparoscopic cholecystectomy: Initial experience with 25 patients. *Annals of Surgery*, **234**:1–7.

Margolis, J. M. (1989). *Conductive Polymers and Plastics*. London: Chapman & Hall.

Margossian, H., Garcia-Ruiz, A., Falcone, T., Goldberg, J. M., Attaran, M., and Gagner, M. (1998). Robotically assisted laparoscopic micro advanced uterine horn anastomosis. *Fertility and Sterility*, **70**:530–534.

Marieb, E. N. (1992). *Human Anatomy and Physiology*, 2nd edition. Redwood City, CA: Benjamin/Cummings Publishing.

Markoff, J. (2015). Sorry, Einstein. Quantum study suggests 'spooky action' is real. *The New York Times*. Retrieved October 21, 2015.

Marletto, C., Coles, D. M., Farrow, T., and Vedral, V. (2018). Entanglement between living bacteria and quantized light witnessed by Rabi splitting. *Journal of Physics Communications*, **2**(10):101001.

Martinez, B. D., and Wiegand, C. S. (2004). Robotics in vascular surgery. *The American Journal of Surgery*, **188**:57S–62S.

Matsui, H., and Kobayashi, K. (1983a). Biomechanics VIII-A. International series on biomechanics. In *Proceedings of the 8th International Congress of Biomechanics*, Vol. 4A. Nagoya: Human Kinetics Publishers, Inc. (1983b). Biomechanics VIII-B. International series on biomechanics. In *Proceedings of the 8th International Congress of Biomechanics*, Vol. 4B. Nagoya: Human Kinetics Publishers, Inc.

Matsukata, M., Aoki, T., Sanui, K., Ogata, N., Kikuchi, A., Sakurai, Y., and Okano, M. (1994). New temperature-responsive biosystems by IPAA-modified enzymes. In *Preprints of the Sapporo Symposium on Intelligent Polymer Gels*, October 6–8, Sapporo, Japan, 37–38.

Matsuo, E. S., and Tanaka, T. (1988). Kinetics of discontinuous volume-phase transition of gels. *The Journal of Chemical Physics*, **89**(3):1695–1703.

Mayers, D. (1997). Unconditionally secure quantum bit commitment is impossible. *Physical Review Letters*, **78**:3414–3417.

McGehee, M. D., Miller, E. K., Moses, D., and Heeger, A. J. (1999). Twenty years of conductive polymers: From fundamental science to applications. In *Advances in Synthetic Metals: Twenty Years of Progress in Science and Technology*, eds. P. Bamier, S. Lefrant, and Bidan, G. New York, NY: Elsevier, 98–203.

Meaning, H. C. M., Hendrix, R., Rosielle, P. C. J. N., Steinbuch, M., Nijmeijer, H., and de Smet, M. C. (2010). A master-μslave robot for vitreo-retinal eye surgery. *Proceedings of the Euspen International Conference – Delft*, June 2010.

Meghdari, A., Jafarian, M., Mojarrad, M., and Shahinpoor, M. (1993). Exploring artificial muscles as actuators for artificial hands. In *Intelligent Structures, Materials, and Vibrations*, ASME publication DE-Vol. 58, eds. M. Shahinpoor and Tzou, H. S., 21–26.

Merleau-Ponty, M. (1945). *Phénoménologie de la perception, 1945 (French), 1962 (English)*, English translation from French by Colin Smith (1st English translation), Donald Landes (2nd English translation), Éditions Gallimard, Routledge & Kegan Paul, 1945, English translation (1962), 466 (1965 Routledge edition), ISBN, 978-0415834339 (2012 Routledge edition).

Micali, S., Virgili, G., Vannozzi, E., Grassi, N., Jarrett, T. W., Bauer, J. J., Vespasiani, G., and Kavoussi, L. R. (2000). Feasibility of telementoring between Baltimore (USA) and Rome (Italy): The first five cases. *Journal of Endourology*, **14**:493–496.

Michopolous, J. G., and Shahinpoor, M. (2002a). Continuous electrodynamic estimation of impedance associated with multi-dimensional ionic polymeric artificial muscles. In *Proceedings of the First World Congress on Biomimetics and Artificial Muscles (Biomimetics 2002)*, December 9–11, Albuquerque, NM. (2002b). Towards a multiphysics formulation of electroactive large deflection plates made from ionic polymeric artificial muscles. In *Proceedings of the First World Congress on Biomimetics and Artificial Muscle (Biomimetics 2002)*, December 9–11, Albuquerque, NM. (2004). Experimental calibration of non-linear continuum multi-field ionic polymer plate modeling. In *Proceedings of the Second World Congress on Biomimetics and Artificial Muscle (Biomimetics and Nano-Bio 2004)*, December 5–8, Albuquerque, NM.

Michopoulos, J. G., Shahinpoor, M., and Iliopoulos, A. (2016). *Multiphysics Modeling of Nonlinear Ionic Polymer Metal Composite Plates. RSC Smart Materials Series*, 18. Royal Society of Chemistry Publishers, 285–310.

Michopoulos, J. G., Shahinpoor, M., and Iliopoulos, A. (2016). *Multiphysics Theory for Electroactive Polymers and Ionic Polymer Metal Composites. RSC Smart Materials Series*, 18. Royal Society of Chemistry Publishers, 257–284.

Millet, P., Pinneri, M., and Durand, R. (1989). New solid polymer electrolyte composites for water electrolysis. *Journal of Applied Electrochemistry*, **19**:162–166.

Mirbagheri, A., Farahmand, F., Meghdari, A., and Karimian, F. (2011). Design and development of an effective low-cost robotic cameraman for laparoscopic surgery: RoboLens. *Scientia Iranica*, **18**(1):105–114.

Mitchell, B., Koo, J., Iordachita, I., Kazanzides, P., Kapoor, A., Handa, J., Hager, G., and Taylor, R. (2007). Development and application of a new steady-hand manipulator for retinal surgery. *IEEE International Conference on Robotics and Automation*, Roma, Italy, 10–14 April 2007.

Mohr, F. W., Falk, V., Ziegler, A., and Autschback, R. (1999). Computer-enhanced coronary artery bypass surgery. *The Journal of Thoracic and Cardiovascular Surgery*, **117**:1212–1214.

Mojarrad, M. (1997). Autonomous robotic swimming vehicle employing artificial muscle fin mimicking fish propulsion. In *AUSI Conference on Unmanned Untethered Submersible Technology*, September 7–10, Durham, NH. (1999). Design of composite artificial muscle (CAM) fin for aquatic vehicle propulsion. In *AUSI Conference on Unmanned Untethered Submersible Technology*, August 23–25, Durham, NH.

Mojarrad, M. (2001). Study of ionic polymeric gels as smart materials and artificial muscles for biomimetic swimming robotic applications. Ph.D. thesis. Department of Mechanical Engineering, University of New Mexico, Albuquerque, NM.

Mojarrad, M., and Shahinpoor, M. (1996a). Noiseless propulsion for swimming robotic structures using polyelectrolyte ion-exchange membranes. In *Proceedings of SPIE 1996 North American Conference on Smart Structures and Materials*, February 26–29, San Diego, CA, 2716, paper no. 27, 183–192. (1996b). Ion exchange membrane-platinum composites as electrically controllable artificial muscles. In *Proceedings of the Third International Conference on Intelligent Materials*, June 3–5, Lyon, France, 1012–1016. (1997a). Ion-exchange-metal composite sensor films. In *Proceedings of SPIE Conference on Intelligent Structures and Materials*, March 3–6, San Diego, CA. (1997b). Ion-exchange-metal composite artificial muscle actuator load characterization and modeling. In *Proceedings of SPIE Conference on Intelligent Structures and Materials*, March 3–6, San Diego, CA. (1997c). Biomimetic robotic propulsion using polymeric artificial muscles. In *Proceedings of (1997) IEEE Robotics and Automation Conference*, April 20–25, Albuquerque, NM.

Mojarrad, M., and Wilson, D. (2000). Electroactive polymeric composite fin design for propulsion of autonomous aquatic vehicles. In *Proceedings of the Fourth International Conference and Exposition/Demonstration on Robotics for Challenging Situations and Environments*, February 27–March 2.

Moneim, M. S., Keikhosrow, F., Mustapha, A.-A., Larsen, K., and Shahinpoor, M. (2002). Flexor tendon repair using shape memory alloy suture: A biomechanical evaluation. *Clinical Orthopaedics and Related Research*, (402):251–259.

Monod, J. (1971). *Chance and Necessity: An Essay on the Natural Philosophy of Modern Biology*. New York: Harper Collins.

Monod, J., and Bornek, E. (Eds.) (1971). *Of Microbes and Life*. New York: Columbia University Press.

Monod, J. (2010). The Nobel Prize in Physiology or Medicine 1965, François Jacob, André Lwoff. *Nobelprize.org*. Retrieved June 30, 2010.

Moor, R. B., Cable, K. M., and Croley, T. L. (1992). Barriers to flow in semicrystalline ionomer: A procedure for preparing melt-processes perfluorosulfonate ionomer films and membranes. *Journal of Membrane Science*, **75**:7–14.

Moor, W. (1972). *Physical Chemistry*, 4th edition. Englewood Cliffs, NJ: Prentice-Hall.

Moradi Dalvand, M., and Shirinzadeh, B. (2013). Motion control analysis of a parallel robot-assisted minimally invasive surgery/microsurgery system (PRAMiSS). *Robotics and Computer-Integrated Manufacturing*, **29**(2):318–327.

Moreva, E. (2014). Time from quantum entanglement: An experimental illustration. *Physical Review A*, **89**(5):052122.

Motamedi, A. R., Blevins, F. T., Willis, M. C., McNally, T. P., and Shahinpoor, M. (2000). Biomechanics of the coracoclavicular ligament complex and augmentations used in its repair and reconstruction. *The American Journal of Sports Medicine*, **28**(3):380–384.

Munz, Y., Moorthy, K., Kudchadkar, R., Hernandez, J. D., Martin, S., Darzi, A., and Rockall, T. (2004). Robotic-assisted rectopexy. *The American Journal of Surgery*, **187**:88–92.

Nagasawa, M. (1988). Molecular conformation and dynamics of macromolecules in condensed systems. In *Studies in Polymer Science*. New York, NY: Elsevier.

Nagatake, and Tsuchiya, K. (1992). Theoretical analysis of an electrostatic linear actuator developed as a biomimicking skeletal muscle. *JSME International Journal, Series III*, **35**(3):400–405.

Narita, T. M., Gong, J. P., and Osada, Y. (1998). Kinetic study of surfactant binding into polymer gel—Experimental and theoretical analyses. *Journal of Physical Chemistry B*, **102**:4566–4572.

Naumann, H. (1987). Conjugated polymers. In *Electronic Properties of Conjugated Polymers*, eds. H. Kuzmany, M. Mehring, and S. Roth. New York, NY: Springer-Verlag.

Navascues, M., and Wunderlich, H. (2009). A glance beyond the quantum model. *Proceedings of the Royal Society A*, **466**:881–890.

Nemat-Nasser, S. (2002). Micro-mechanics of actuation of ionic polymer–metal composites (IPMCs). *Journal of Applied Physics*, **92**(5):2899–2915.

Nemat-Nasser, S., and Li, J. Y. (2000). Electromechanical response of ionic polymer–metal composites. *Journal of Applied Physics*, **87**(7):3321–3331.

Nemat-Nasser, S., and Wu, Y. (2003). Comparative experimental study of ionic polymer–metal composites with different backbone ionomers and in various cation forms. *Journal of Applied Physics*, **93**:5255–5267.

Newbury, K. M. (2002). Characterization, modeling, and control of ionic polymer transducers. Ph.D. dissertation. Virginia Tech.

Newbury, K. M., and Leo, D. J. (2002). Electrically induced permanent strain in ionic polymer–metal composite actuators. In *Proceedings of SPIE (2002) North American Conference on Smart Structures and Materials*, March, San Diego, CA, Vol. 4695, 67–77.

Ng, W. S., Davies, B. L., Hibberd, R. D., and Timoney, A. G. (1993). A first-hand experience in transurethral resection of the prostate. *IEEE EMBS Journal*, 123–125.

Nicoli, D., Young, C., Tanaka, T., Pollak, A., and Whitesides, G. (1983). Chemical modification of acrylamide gels: Verification of the role of ionization in phase transitions. *Macromolecules* **16**:887–891.

Nicu, M. D. *Biotehnologia* (Biotechnology). Bucharest: EDP.

Nielsen, M. A. (1999). Conditions for a class of entanglement transformations. *Physical Review Letters*, **83**(2):436.

Nielsen, M. A., and Chuang, I. L. (2000). *Quantum Computation and Quantum Information*. Cambridge University Press, 112–113.

Nielsen, M. A., and Chuang, I. L. (2011). *Quantum Computation and Quantum Information*, 10th anniversary edition. Cambridge: Cambridge University Press.

Nitta, T., Akama, K., Gong, J. P., and Osada, Y. (1994). Ionic conduction and water transport in the charged polymer networks. In *Preprints of the Sapporo Symposium on Intelligent Polymer Gels*, October 6–8, Sapporo, Japan, 119–120.

Noonan, C., Tajvidi, M., Tayeb, A., Shahinpoor, M., and Tabatabaie, E. (2019). Structure–property relationships in hybrid cellulose nanofibrils/nafion-based ionic polymer-metal composites. *Materials Journal*, **12**(4):23–28.

Nowlin, W. C., Mohr, P. W., Schena, B. M., Larkin, D. Q., and Guthart, G. (2011). Software center and highly configurable robotic systems for surgery and other uses. U.S. Patent No. 8,004,229.

O'Handley, R. C. (1998). Model for strain and magnetostriction in magnetic shape memory alloys. *Journal of Applied Physics*, **83**:3263–3271.

O'Handley, R. C., Ullakko, K., Huang, J. K., and Kantner, C. (1996). Large magnetic-field-induced strains in Ni_2MnGa single crystals. *Applied Physics Letter*, **69**:1966–1971.

Ogston, A. G., Preston, B. N., and Wells, J. D. (1973). On the transport of compact particles through solutions of chain-polymers. *Proceedings of the Royal Society of London*, **333**:297.

Oguro, K., Asaka, K., and Takenaka, H. (1993). Polymer film actuator is driven by low voltage. In *Proceedings of the 4th International Symposium of Machines and Human Science*, Nagoya, Japan, 39–40.

Oguro, K., Fujiwara, N., Asaka, K., Onishi, K., and Sewa, S. (1999). Polymer electrolyte actuator with gold electrodes. In *Proceedings of the SPIE 6th Annual International Symposium on Smart Structures and Materials*, SPIE Proceedings 3, Vol. 669, 64–71.

Oguro, K., Kawami, Y., and Takenaka, H. (1992). Bending of an ion-conducting polymer film-electrode composite by an electric stimulus at low voltage. *Transactions of Journal of Micromachine Society*, **5**:27–30.

Oguztoreli, M. N., and Stein, R. B. (1983). Optimal control of antagonistic muscles. *Biological Cybernetics*, **48**:1–99.

Ohmine, I., and Tanaka, T. (1982). Salt effects on the phase transitions of polymer gels. *The Journal of Chemical Physics*, **77**:5725.

Okabayashi, K., Goto, F., Abe, K., and Yoshida, T. (1987). Electrochemical studies of polyaniline and its applications. *Synthetic Metals*, **18**:365.

Okuzaki, H., and Osada, Y. (1994a). Chemomechanical polymer gel with electrically driven motility. In *Proceedings of the International Conference on Intelligent Materials*, 960–970. (1994b). Effects of hydrophobic interaction on the cooperative binding of surfactant to a polymer network. *Macromolecules*, **27**:502–506. (1994c). Electro-driven chemomechanical polymer gel as an intelligent soft material. *Journal of Biomaterials Science, Polymer Edition*, **5**(5):485–496.

Okuzaki, H., Katsuyama, Y., and Osada, Y. (1994). Electrically driven chemomechanical polymer gel based on molecular assembly reaction. In *Preprints of the Sapporo Symposium on Intelligent Polymer Gels*, October 6–8, Sapporo, Japan, 115–116.

Olsen, L. H. (2006). Robotics in pediatric urology. *Journal of Pediatric Urology*, **2**:40e45.

Onishi, K., Sewa, S., Asaka, K., Fujiwara, N., and Oguro, K. (2000). Bending response of polymer electrolyte actuator. In *Proceedings of Smart Structures and Materials 2001: Electroactive Polymer Actuators and Devices*.

Onnasch, J. F., Schneider, F., Falk, V., Mierzwa, M., Bucerius, J., and Mohr, F. W. (2002). Five years of less invasive minimal surgery: From experimental to routine. *Heart Surgery Forum*, **5**:132–135.

Onoda, J., Fu, D.-Y., and Minesugi, K. (1996). Two-dimensional deployable hexapod truss. *Journal of Spacecraft and Rockets*, **33**:416–421.

Osada, Y. (1991). Chemical valves and gel actuators. *Advanced Materials*, **3**(2):107–108. (1992a). A chemomechanical polymer gel with electrically driven motility. In *Proceedings of the Conference on Recent Advances in Adaptive and Sensory Materials and Their Applications*,

783–790. (1992b). Electro-stimulated chemomechanical system using polymer gels (an approach to an intelligent artificial muscle system). In *Proceedings of the International Conference on Intelligent Materials*, 155–161.

Osada, Y., and Hasebe, M. (1985). Electrically activated mechanochemical devices using polyelectrolyte gels. *Chemistry Letters*, **4**:1285–1288.

Osada, Y., and Kishi, R. (1989). Reversible volume change of microparticles in an electric field. *Journal of the Chemical Society*, **85**:655–662.

Osada, Y., and Matsuda, A. (1995). Shape memory in hydrogels. *Nature*, **376**:219.

Osada, Y., and Ross-Murphy, S. B. (1993). Intelligent gels. *Scientific American*, **268**:82–87.

Osada, Y., Okuzaki, H., and Hori, H. (1992). A polymer gel with electrically driven motility. *Nature*, **355**:242–244.

Osada, Y., Okuzaki, H., Gong, J. P., and Nitta, T. (1994). Electro-driven gel motility on the base of cooperative molecular assembly reaction. *Polymer Science*, **36**:340–351.

Oster, G., and Auslander, D. (1971). Topological representations of thermodynamic systems—II. Some elements are subunits for irreversible thermodynamics. *The Journal of the Franklin Institute*, **292**:77–92.

Otake, M., Inaba, M., and Inoue, H. (1999). Development of gel robots made of electro-active polymer PAMPS gel. In *Proceedings of IEEE International Conference on Systems, Man and Cybernetics*, WA20-2, CDROM (1999).

Otake, M., Kagami, Y., Inaba, M., and Inoue, H. (2000b). The behavior of a mollusk-type robot made of electro-active polymer gel under spatially varying electric fields. In *Intelligent Autonomous Systems*, Vol. 6, eds. E. Pagello et al. IOS Press, 686–691.

Otake, M., Kagami, Y., Inaba, M., and Inoue, H. (2002b). Motion design of a starfish-shaped gel robot made of electro-active polymer gel. *Robotics and Autonomous Systems*, **40**:185–191. (2002c). Starfish-shaped gel robots made of EAP. *WW-EAP Newsletter*, **4**(2):7–8.

Otero, T. F. (1997). Artificial muscles, electrode solution, and REDOX processes in conducting polymers. In *Handbook of Organic Conductive Molecules and Polymers*, ed. H. S. Nalwa. New York, NY: John Wiley & Sons Ltd.

Otero, T. F., and Rodríguez, J. (1992). Electrochemomechanical and electro-chemopositioning devices: Artificial muscles. In *Intrinsically Conducting Polymers: An Emerging Technology*, ed. M. Aldissi. The Netherlands: Kluwer Academic Publishers, 40.

Otero, T. F., and Sansifiena, J. M. (1998). Soft and wet conducting polymers for artificial muscles. *Advanced Materials*, **10**(6):491– 494.

Otero, T. F., and Sansinena, J. M. (1995). Artificial muscles based on conducting polymers. *Bioelectrochemistry and Bioenergetics*, **38**:411–414.

Otero, T. F., Angulo, E., Rodríguez, J., and Santamaría, C. (1992). Electrochemomechanical properties from a bilayer: Polypyrrole/ non-conducting and flexible material—artificial muscle. *Journal of Electroanalytical Chemistry*, **341**:369–375.

Otero, T. F., Grande, H., and Rodriguez, J. (1995). A new model for electrochemical oxidation of polypyrrole under conformational relaxation control. *Journal of Electroanalytical Chemistry*, **394**:211–216. (1996a). Reversible electrochemical reactions in conducting polymers: A molecular approach to artificial muscles. *Journal of Physical Organic Chemistry*, **9**:381. (1996b). Influence of the counterion size on the rate of electrochemical relaxation in polypyrrole. *Synthetic Metals*, **9**:285.

Otero, T. F., Rodríguez, J., and Santamaría, C. (1994). Conductive polymers. *Materials Research Society Symposium Proceedings*, **330**:333.

Otero, T. F., Rodriguez, J., Angulo, E., and Santamaria, C. (1993). Artificial muscles from bilayer structures. *Synthetic Metals*, **55–57**:3713–3717.

Pan, J. W., Bouwmeester, D., Weinfurter, H., and Zeilinger, A. (1998). Experimental entanglement swapping: Entangling photons that never interacted. *Physical Review Letters*, **80**:3891.

Paquette, J., and Kim, K. J. (2002). An electric circuit model for ionic polymer-metal composites. In *Proceedings of the First World Congress on Biomimetics and Artificial Muscles*, December 9–11, Albuquerque, NM.

Park, I.-S., Kim, K. J., and Kim, D. (2006). Multi-fields responsive ionic polymer–metal composites. In *Proceedings of SPIE Smart Materials and Structures Conference*, March, 6168–6136.

Park, Y. H., and Han, M. H. (1992). Preparation of conducting polyacrylonitrile/polypyrrole composite films by electrochemical synthesis and their electrical properties. *Journal of Applied Polymer Science*, **45**:1973–1982.

Patel, K. (2008). Robotics the future of surgery. *International Journal of Surgery*, **6**:441–442.

Patel, M. N., Menon, M., and Rogers, C. G. (2010). Robotic partial nephrectomy: A comparison to current techniques. *Urologic Oncology: Seminars and Original Investigations*, **28**:74–76.

Pawlowski, M., Patarek, T., Kaszlikowski, D., Scarani, V., Winter, A., and Zukowski, M. (2009). A new physical principle: Information causality. *Nature*, **461**:1101.

Peace, G. S. (1993). *Taguchi Methods: Hands-on Approach*. New York, NY: Addison–Wesley Publishing Company, Inc.

Pei, Q., and Inganäs, O. (1993a). Electrochemical muscles: Bending strips built from conjugated polymers. *Synthetic Metals*, **55–57**:3718–3723. (1993b). Electrochemical applications of the bending beam method. 2. Electroshrinking and slow relaxation in polypyrrole. *The Journal of Physical Chemistry*, **97**:6034.

Pei, Q., Inganas, O., and Lundstrom, I. (1993). Bending bilayer strips built from polyaniline for artificial electrochemical muscles. *Smart Materials and Structures*, **2**(1):1–5.

Pellegrino, S., and Calladine, C. R. (1986). Matrix analysis of statically and kinematically indeterminate frameworks. *International Journal of Solids and Structures*, **22**:409–402.

Penrose, R. (1989). *The Emperor's New Mind: Concerning Computers, Minds, and the Laws of Physics*. Oxford: Oxford University Press.

Penrose, R. (1996). On gravity's role in quantum state reduction. *General Relativity and Gravitation*, **28**:581–600.

Penrose, R. (2022). New physics for the Orch OR consciousness proposal. In *Consciousness and Quantum Mechanics*, ed. S. Gao. Oxford: Oxford University Press.

Penrose, R., and Hameroff, S. (1995). What gaps? Reply to Grush and Churchland. *Journal of Consciousness Studies*, **2**(2):98–112.

Perline, R., Kornbluh, R., and Joseph, J. P. (1998). Electrostriction of polymer dielectrics with compliant electrodes as a means of actuation. *Sensors and Actuators*, **64**:77– 85.

Perline, R., Kornbluh, R., Pei, Q., and Joseph, J. (2000). High-speed electrically actuated elastomers with strain greater than 100%. *Science*, **287**:836–839.

Phadke, M. S. (1989). *Quality Engineering Using Robust Design*. Englewood Cliffs, NJ: Prentice Hall.

Pinero, E. P. (1961). Project for a mobile theatre. *Architectural Design*, **12**:570.

Pirandola, S., Andersen, U. L., Banchi, L., Berta, M., Bunandar, D., Colbeck, R., Englund, D., Gehring, T., Lupo, C., Ottaviani, C., Pereira, J. L., Razavi, M., Shamsul Shaari, J., Tomamichel, M., Usenko, V. C., Vallone, G., Villoresi, P., and Wallden, P. (2020). Advances in quantum cryptography. *Advances in Optics and Photonics*, **12**(4):1012–1236.

Pires, N. J. (2000). Using actual industrial robot manipulators with construction tasks. *Proceedings of the 17th ISARC (2000)*, Taipei, Taiwan, 1–5.

Plenio, M. B., and Virmani, S. (2007). An introduction to entanglement measures. *Quantum Information Computation*, **1**:1–51.

Pollack, G. H. (2001). *Cells, Gels and the Engines of Life*. Seattle, WA: Ebner and Sons.

Popa, S. G., and Nicu, M. D. (1989). Unele consideratii asupra efectului de piramida (Some considerations regarding the effect of the pyramid), *Session of Scientific Communications*, Politehnica University of Bucharest.

Popa, S. G., Pop, V., and Serban, I. (1994). Probleme privind abordarea sistemica a related SNC-psychism (Problems regarding the systemic approach of the relationship Central Nervous System—Psychism). *Studies and Research on Biotechnology*, **26**.

Prasad, S. M., Maniar, H. S., Soper, N. J., Damiano, R. J. Jr., and Klingensmith, M. E. (2002). The effect of robotic assistance on learning curves for basic laparoscopic skills. *The American Journal of Surgery*, **183**:702–707.

Prasad, S. M., Prasad, S. M., Maniar, H. S., Chu, C., Schuessler, R. B., and Damiano, R. J. Jr. (2004). Surgical robotics: Impact of motion scaling on task performance. *Journal of the American College of Surgeons*, **199**(6):863–868.

Price, W. E., and Wallace, G. G. (1994). Conducting polymer membranes as intelligent separation systems. In *Proceedings of the International Conference on Intelligent Materials*, 994–1002.

Prigogine, I. (1973). Irreversibility as a symmetry-breaking process. *Nature*, **246**:67–71.

Ramanathan, R., Patarek, T., Kay, A., Kurzynski, P., and Kaszkilowski, D. (2010). Local realism of macroscopic correlations. *Physical Review Letters*, **107**:060405.

Ramirez, P., Rapp, H. J., Reichle, S., Strathmann, H., and Mafe, S. (1992). Current–voltage curves of bipolar membranes. *Journal of Applied Physics*, **72**(1):259–264.

Rashid, T., and Shahinpoor, M. (1999). Force optimization of ionic polymeric platinum composite artificial muscles using an orthogonal array manufacturing method. In *Electroactive Polymers*, SPIE publication no. 3669-28, 289–298.

Rasmussen, S., Karampurwala, H., Vaidyanath, R., Jensen, K. S., and Hameroff, S. (1990). Computational connectionism within neurons: A model of cytoskeletal automata subserving neural networks. *Physica D Nonlinear Phenomena*, **42**, 428–449.

Ratna, B. R., Selinger, J. V., and Jeon, H. G. (2002). Isotropic-nematic transition in liquid-crystalline elastomers. *Physical Review Letters*, **89**:225701.

Renner, R., Gisin, N., and Kraus, B. (2005). An information-theoretic security proof for QKD protocols. *Physical Review A*, **72**:012332.

Rieder, W. G., and Busby, H. R. (1990). *Introductory Engineering Modeling Emphasizing Differential Models and Computer Simulations*. Malabar, FL: Robert E. Krieger Publishing Company.

Ringbauer, M., Fedrizzi, A., Berry, D. W., and White, A. G. (2014). Information causality in the quantum and post-quantum regime. *Scientific Reports*, **4**:6955.

Rohen, I. W., Yokochi, C., and Lutjen-Drecoll, E. (2006). *Color Atlas of Anatomy: A Photographic Study of the Human Body*, 5th edition. Philadelphia, PA: Lippincott Williams & Wilkins, 208–209.

Roland-Mieszkowski, M. (1998). *Life on Earth: Flow of Energy and Entropy*, Digital Recordings.

Röntgen, W. C. (1880). About the changes in shape and volume of dielectrics caused by electricity. *Ann. Phys. Chem.* **I**(1):771–786.

Rosen, M. W. (1959). Water flows about a swimming fish. Master's thesis. U.S. Naval Ordinance Test Station.

Rosheim, M. E. (1994). *Robot Evolution: The Development of Anthrobotics*. John Wiley and Sons, Inc., p. 2.

Rozatkar, G. (2018). *Demonstration of Quantum Entanglement*. OSF.

Sabharwal, A., Pradhan, S., and Kumar, A. (2006). Current role of robotics in urology. *Apollo Medicine*, **3**(4):365–370.

Sacerdote, M. P. (1899). Strains in polymers due to electricity. *Journal of Physics*, **3**:31.

Sadeghipour, K., Salomon, R., and Neogi, S. (1992). Development of a novel electrochemically active membrane and "smart" material-based vibration sensor/damper. *Smart Materials and Structures*, **1**:172–179.

Sakurada, I., Nakajima, A., and Fujiwara, H. (1959). Vapor pressures of polymer solutions. II. Vapor pressure of the poly(vinyl alcohol)-water system. *Journal of Polymer Science*, **35**:497–505.

Sakurai, J. J., and Napolitano, J. J. (2010). *Modern Quantum Mechanics*, 2nd edition. Pearson, p. 68.

Salisbury, J. K. (1984). Design and control of an articulated hand. In *International Symposium of Design Synthesis*, July, Tokyo.

Samec, Z., Trojanek, A., and Samcova, E. (1994). Evaluation of ion transport parameters in a Nafion membrane from ion-exchange measurements. *The Journal of Physical Chemistry*, **98**(25):6352–6358.

Schmitz, K. S. (1994). Macro-ion characterization from dilute solutions to complex fluids. In *ACS Symposium Series 548*. New York, NY: American Chemical Society.

Schneider, H.-J., and Shahinpoor, M. (Eds). *Smart Materials*, Book Series. Cambridge: Royal Society of Chemistry Publishers.

Schreyer, H. B., Gebhart, N., Kim, K. J., and Shahinpoor, M. (2000). Electric activation of artificial muscles containing polyacrylonitrile gel fibers. *Biomacromolecules Journal*, **1**:42–647.

Schreyer, H. B., Shahinpoor, M., and Kim, K. J. (1999). Electrical activation of PAN-Pt artificial muscles. In *Proceedings of SPIE/Smart Structures and Materials/Electroactive Polymer Actuators and Devices*, March, Newport.

Schrödinger, E. (1935). Discussion of probability relations between separated systems. *Mathematical Proceedings of the Cambridge Philosophical Society*, **31**(4):555–563.

Schrödinger, E. (1936). Probability relations between separated systems. *Mathematical Proceedings of the Cambridge Philosophical Society*, **32**(3):446–452.

Schumacher, B. (1995). Quantum coding. *Physical Review A*, **51**:2738–2747.

Segalman, D. J., and Witkowski, W. R. (1994). Two-dimensional finite element analysis of a polymer gel drug delivery system. In *Proceedings of the International Conference on Intelligent Materials*, 1055–1066.

Segalman, D., Witkowski, W., Adolf, D., and Shahinpoor, M. (1991). Electrically controlled polymeric gels as active materials in adaptive structures. In *Proceedings of the ADPA/AIAA/ASME/SPIE Conference on Active Materials and Adaptive Structures*, 335–345. (1992a). Theory of electrically controlled polymeric muscles as active materials in adaptive structures. *International Journal of Smart Materials and Structures*, **1**(1):44–54. (1992b). Numerical simulation of dynamic behavior of polymeric gels. In *Proceedings of the 1st International Conference on Intelligent Materials, ICIM'92*, July, Tsukube, Japan, Technomic Publishing Co., 310–313. (1992c). Theory and application of electrically controlled polymeric gels. *Smart Materials and Structures*, **1**:95–100.

Segalman, D., Witkowski, W., Rao, R., Adolf, D., and Shahinpoor, M. (1993). Finite element simulation of the 2D collapse of a polyelectrolyte gel disk. In *Proceedings (1993) of SPIE North American Conference on Smart Structures and Materials*, February, Albuquerque, NM, Vol. 1916, 14–22.

Sen, A., Scheinbeim, J. I., and Newman, B. A. (1984). The effect of plasticizer on the polarization of poly(vinylidene fluoride) films. *Journal of Applied Physics*, **56**(9):2433–2439.

Senador, A. E., Shaw, M. T., and Mather, P. T. (2001). *MRS Symposium Proceedings*. Warrendale, PA: Materials Research Society, 661, KK5.9.1.

Sessler, G. M., and Hillenbrand, J. (1999). Novel polymer electrets. *Electroactive Polymers (EAP): MRS Symposium Proceedings*, **600**:143–158.

Shadbolt, P. J., Verde, M. R., Peruzzo, A., Politi, A., Laing, A., Lobino, M., Matthews, J. C. F., Thompson, M. G., and O'Brien, J. L. (2012). Generating, manipulating and measuring entanglement and mixture with a reconfigurable photonic circuit. *Nature Photonics*, **6**(1):45–59.

Shahinpoor, M. (1987). *A Robot Engineering Text Book*, Harper and Row Publishers, New York and London.

Shahinpoor, M. (1990). *Kypc Robototexhnkny* (Kypc Robot Technology), in Russian, MIR Publishers, Moscow, Former Soviet Union, Russian Translation of *A Robot Engineering Text Book*, Harper and Row, New York (1987).

Shahinpoor, M. (1991). Conceptual design, kinematics and dynamics of swimming robotic structures using active polymer gels. In *Proceedings of ADPA/AIAA/ASME/SPIE Conference on Active Materials & Adaptive Structures*, November, Alexandria, VA.

Shahinpoor, M. (1995a). The Venus flytrap as a model for biomimetic material with built-in sensors and actuators. *Journal of Material Science and Engineering*, **2**(4):229–233.

Shahinpoor, M. (1995b). Micro-electro-mechanics of ionic polymeric gels as electrically controllable artificial muscles. *International Journal of Intelligent Materials System*, **6**(3):307–314.

Shahinpoor, M. (1996a). Intelligent materials and structures revisited. *Proc. SPIE 1996 North American Conference on. Smart Structures and Materials*. February, 25–29, 1996.

Shahinpoor, M. (1996b). Multifingered grabbers as smart structures for robotic applications. *Proceedings of SPIE 2779*, April 1996.

Shahinpoor, M. (1997). *Intelligent Civil Engineering Materials and Structures Revisited*. Engineering Mechanics Division/ASCE.

Shahinpoor, M. (2000a). Electromechanical modeling of ionic polymer-conductive composite (IPCC) artificial muscles. *Proc. SPIE 3984, Smart Structures and Materials 2000: Mathematics and Control in Smart Structures*, publication no. 3984-37, 310–320.

Shahinpoor, M. (2000b). Ion-exchange membrane-metal composite as biomimetic sensors and actuators. In *Polymer Sensors and Actuators*, eds. Y. Osada and D. De Rossi. Springer-Verlag-Heidelberg, 325–359.

Shahinpoor, M. (2002). Artificial muscles. In *Encyclopedia of Biomaterials and Biomedical Engineering*, eds. G. Wnek and G. Bowlin. New York: Marcel Dekker Publishers, 43–52.

Shahinpoor, M. (2003). Ionic polymer-conductor composites as biomimetic sensors, robotic actuators and artificial muscles: A review. *Electrochimica Acta*, **48**(14–16):2343–2353.

Shahinpoor, M. (2005). Soft plastic robots and artificial muscles. *International Journal of Advanced Robotic Systems*, **2**(2):161–174.

Shahinpoor, M. (2008). Ionic polymeric conductor nanocomposites (IPCMCs) as distributed nanosensors and nanoactuators. *Advances in Science and Technology*, **54**:70–81.

Shahinpoor, M. (2009a). Biomimetics nanosensors and nanoactuators. In *Biomimetics and Bioinspired Nanomaterials*, eds. S. S. Challa and R. Kumar. Weinheim: John Wiley and Sons, 1–26.

Shahinpoor, M. (2009b). Recent advances in ionic polymer metal nanocomposites as distributed biomimetic nanosensors, nanoactuators and artificial muscles. *Journal of Physics: Conference Series*, **127**.

Shahinpoor, M. (2011). *Intelligent Robotic Systems: Modeling & Simulation*, 2nd edition. Albuquerque, New Mexico: ERI Press.

Shahinpoor, M. (2024). Immortal biomimetic humanoid robots with a human consciousness. *International Journal of Robotics and Automation*, **10**(3), 70–71.

Shahinpoor, M., Ahghar, M., Kim, K. J., and Sillerud, L. O. 2002. Industrial and medical applications of ionic polymer–metal composites as biomimetic sensors, actuators, and artificial muscles. In *Proceedings of SPIE 9th Annual International Symposium on Smart Structures and Materials*, March, San Diego, CA, publication no. 4695-43.

Shahinpoor, M., and Ahghar, M. (2002). Modeling of electrochemical deformation in polyacrylonitrile (PAN) artificial muscles. In *Proceedings of the First World Congress on Biomimetics and Artificial Muscle (Biomimetics 2002)*, December 9–11, Albuquerque, NM.

Shahinpoor, M., and Alvarez, R. (2002). Simulation and control of iono-elastic beam dynamic deformation model. In *Proceedings of SPIE 9th Annual International Symposium on Smart Structures and Materials*, March, San Diego, CA, publication no. 4695-40.

Shahinpoor, M., and Gheshmi, S. (2012). Space-saving laparoscopic advanced slave robot. U.S. Provisional Patent Application No. 61718822, November 2012.

Shahinpoor, M., and Guran, A. (2003). Ionic polymer-conductor composites (IPCCs) as biomimetic sensors, actuators, and artificial muscles. In *Selected Topics in Structronics and Mechatronic Systems*, eds. A. Belyaev and A. Guran. London: World Scientific Publishers, 417–436.

Shahinpoor, M., and Kim, K. J. (2000a). The effect of surface-electrode resistance on the performance of ionic polymer–metal composite (IPMC) artificial muscles. *Smart Materials and Structures*, **9**:543–551. (2000b). Artificial sarcomere and muscle are made with conductive polyacrylonitrile (C-PAN) fiber bundles. In *SPIE Smart Materials and Structures*, publication no. 3987-34, 243–251.

Shahinpoor, M., and Kim, K. J. (2002). A solid-state soft actuator exhibiting large electromechanical effect. *Applied Physics Letters (APL)*, **80**(18):3445–3447.

Shahinpoor, M., and Kim, K. J. (2005). Ionic polymer-metal composites–IV. Industrial and medical applications (Review Paper). *Smart Materials and Structures*, **14**(1):197–214.

Shahinpoor, M., and Mojarrad, M. (1994). Active musculoskeletal structures equipped with a circulatory system and a network of ionic polymeric gel muscles. In *Proceedings of the International Conference on Intelligent Materials*, 1079–1085.

Shahinpoor, M., and Mojarrad, M. (1997a). Biomimetic robotic propulsion using ion-exchange membrane metal composite artificial muscles, In *Proceedings of IEEE Robotic Automation Conference*, April 1997, Albuquerque, NM, USA.

Shahinpoor, M., and Mojarrad, M. (1997b). Ion-exchange-metal composite sensor films, In *Proceedings of SPIE Smart Materials and Structures Conference*, March 1997, San Diego, CA, publication no. 3042-10.

Shahinpoor, M., and Mojarrad, M. (1997c). Ion-exchange-metal composite artificial muscle actuator load characterization and modeling, *Smart Mater. Technol.* 3040: 294–301.

Shahinpoor, M., and Mojarrad, M. (1997d). Electrically induced large amplitude vibration and resonance characteristics of ionic polymeric membrane-metal composites. In *Proceedings of SPIE Conference on Intelligent Structures and Materials*, March 3–6, San Diego, CA.

Shahinpoor, M., and Osada, Y. (1995a). Electrically induced dynamic contraction of ionic polymeric gels. In *Preprints of the Sapporo Symposium on Intelligent Polymer Gels*, October 6–8, 1994, Sapporo, Japan. Also in *Proceedings of SPIE Conference on Smart Materials and Structures*, February 28–March 2, San Diego, CA. (1995b). Heart tissue replacement with ionic polymeric gels. In *Proceedings (1996) of ASME Winter Annual Meeting*, November 12–18, San Francisco.

Shahinpoor, M., and Popa, S. G. (2002). Recent technology development in contactless monitoring of the electromagnetic activities of the human heart and brain. In *Proceedings of SPIE 9th Annual International Symposium on Smart Structures and Materials*, March, San Diego, CA, publication no. 4694-44.

Shahinpoor, M., and Schneider, H. J. (2008). *Intelligent Materials*, 1st edition. Royal Society of Chemistry (RSC) Publishers.

Shahinpoor, M., and Thompson, M. S. (1994). The Venus fly trap and the waterwheel plant as smart carnivorous botanical structures with built-in sensors and actuators. In *Proceedings (1994) of the International Conference on Intelligent Materials*, ICIM '94, June, Williamsburg, VA, 1086–1094.

Shahinpoor, M., and Thompson, M. S. (1995). The Venus flytrap as a model for biomimetic material with built-in sensors and actuators. *Journal of Material Sciences and Engineering*, **C2**, 229–233.

Shahinpoor, M., and Tzou, H. S. (1993). Intelligent structures, materials, and vibrations. In *Proceedings of the 14th Biennial Conference on Mechanical Vibration and Noise*, September 19–22. Albuquerque, NM: ASME Publications.

Shahinpoor, M., and Wang, G. (1995). Design, modeling and performance evaluation of a novel large motion shape memory alloy actuator. In *Proceedings of SPIE (1995) North American Conference on Smart Structures and Materials*, February 28–March 2, San Diego, CA, paper no. 31, 2447.

Shahinpoor, M., and Wang, G. (1995). Electro-thermo-mechanics of SMA fiber bundles embedded in an elastic medium, in *Proceedings of SPIE 2427, Active Materials and Smart Structures*, vol. 2427, 272–382.

Shahinpoor, M., Bar-Cohen, Y., Simpson, J., and Smith, J. (1998a). Ionic polymer–metal composites (IPMCs) as biomimetic sensors, actuators and artificial muscles—A review. *Smart Materials and Structures*, **7**:R15–R30. (1999). Ionic polymer–metal composites (IPMCs) as biomimetic sensors and actuators. In *Field-Responsive Polymers*, eds. I. M. Khan and J. S. Harrison. American Chemical Society Publication, ACS-FRP, ACS Symposium Series 726. Oxford: Oxford University Press, 25–50.

Shahinpoor, M., Bar-Cohen, Y., Xue, T., Simpson, J., and Smith, J. (1998b). Some experimental results on ion-exchange polymer–metal composites as biomimetic sensors and actuators. In *Proceedings of SPIE Smart Materials and Structures Conference*, March 3–5, San Diego, CA, publication no. 3324-37.

Shahinpoor, M., Gheshmi, S., and Soltanpour, D. (2012). Intraocular robotic surgical system. US provisional patent application no. 61716718.

Shahinpoor, M., Kim, K. J., and Leo, D. (2003). Ionic polymer–metal composites as multifunctional materials. *Polymer Composites*, **24**(1):24–33.

Shahinpoor, M., Kim, K. J., and Mojarrad, M. (2007). *Artificial Muscles: Applications of Advanced Polymeric Nano-Composites*. London and New York: CRC Press, Taylor and Francis Publishers.

Shahinpoor, M., Kim, K. J., and Mojarrad, M. (2005). *Ionic Polymeric Conductor Composite Artificial Muscles*, 2nd edition. Albuquerque, NM: ERI/AMRI Press.

Shahinpoor, M., Kim, K. J., Griffin, S., and Leo, D. (2001). Sensing capabilities of ionic polymer–metal composites. In *Proceedings of SPIE 8th Annual International Symposium on Smart Structures and Materials*, March, Newport Beach, CA, publication no. 4329-28.

Shahinpoor, M., Kim, K. J., Sillerud, L. O., Norris, I. D., and Mattes, B. R. (2002). Electroactive polyacrylonitrile nanofibers as artificial nano muscles. In *Proceedings of SPIE 8th Annual International Symposium on Smart Structures and Materials*, March, San Diego, CA, publication no. 4695-42.

Shahinpoor, M., Norris, I. D., Mattes, B. R., Kim, K. J., and Sillerud, L. O. (2002). Electroactive polyacrylonitrile nanofibers as artificial nano-muscles. In *Proceedings of the 2002 SPIE Conference on Smart Materials and Structures*, March, San Diego, CA, publication no. 4695-42, 169–173.

Shahinpoor, M., Sillerud, L. O., and Popa, S. G. (2002). Smart fiber optic magnetometer. In *Proceedings of the First World Congress on Biomimetics and Artificial Muscle (Biomimetics 2002)*, December 9–11, Albuquerque, NM.

Shahinpoor, M., Wang, G., and Mojarrad, M. (1994). Electro-thermo-mechanics of spring-loaded contractile fiber bundles with applications to ionic polymeric gel and SMA actuators. In *Proceedings of the international conference on intelligent materials*, 1105–1116.

Shannon, C. E., and Weaver, W. (1949). *The Mathematical Theory of Communication*. Urbana: University of Illinois Press.

Shew, S. B., Ostlie, D. J., and Holcomb III, G. W. (2003). Robotic telescopic assistance in pediatric laparoscopic surgery. *Pediatric Endosurgery & Innovative Techniques*, **7**(4).

Shiga, T. 1997. Deformation and viscoelastic behavior of polymer gels in electric fields. *Advances in Polymer Science*, **134**:131–163.

Shiga, T., and Karachi, T. (1990). Deformation of polyelectrolyte gels under the influence of electric field. *Journal of Applied Polymer Science*, **39**:2305–2320.

Shiga, T., Hirose, Y., Okada, A., and Kurauchi, T. (1993). Bending of ionic polymer gel caused by swelling under sinusoidally varying electric fields. *Journal of Applied Polymer Science*, **47**:113–119.

Shinohara, S., Tajima, N., and Yanagisawa, K. (1994). Photo fabrication for small polymer gels and their properties. In *Preprints of the Sapporo Symposium on Intelligent Polymer Gels*, October 6–8, Sapporo, Japan, 91–92.

Shirakawa, H. (2001). The discovery of polyacetylene films—The dawning of an era of conductive polymers. The Noble Prize 2000 lecture. *Current Applied Physics*, **1**:281–286.

Shirakawa, H., Louis, E. J., MacDiarmid, A., Chiang, C. K., and Heeger, A. J. (1977). Synthesis of electrically conducting organic polymers: Halogen derivatives of polyacetylene, (CH)x. *Journal of the Chemical Society, Chemical Communications*, **285**:578.

Siegel, E. (2023). No, we still can't use quantum entanglement to communicate faster than light. *Forbes*. Retrieved January 6, 2023.

Simon, R. (2000). Peres–Horodecki separability criterion for continuous variable systems. *Physical Review Letters*, **84**(12):2726–2729.

Singh, D., Lu, D. M., and Djilali, N. (1999). A two-dimensional analysis of mass transport in proton exchange membrane fuel cells. *International Journal of Engineering Science*, **37**:431–452.

Siwek, L. G., and Reynolds, B. (2007). Totally robotic mitral valve repair. *Operative Techniques in Thoracic and Cardiovascular Surgery: A Comparative Atlas*, **12**(4):235–249.

Skalak, R., and Chien, S. (1987). *Handbook of Bioengineering*. New York, NY: McGraw-Hill.

Skrzypczyk, P., Brunner, N., and Popescu, S. (2009). Emergence of quantum correlations from nonlocality swapping. *Physical Review Letters*, **102**:110402.

Smela, E., and Gadegaard, N. (2001). Volume change in polypyrrole studied by atomic force microscopy. *The Journal of Physical Chemistry B*, **105**:9395.

Smela, E., Inganäs, O., and Lundström, I. (1995). Controlled folding of micrometer-size structures. *Science*, **268**:1735–1738.

Smela, E., Inganäs, O., Pei, Q., and Lundström, I. (1993). Electrochemical muscles: Micromachining fingers and corkscrews. *Advanced Materials*, **5**(9):630–632.

Sofla, A., Elzey, D., and Wadley, H. (2009). Shape morphing hinged truss structures. *Smart Materials and Structures*, **18**:065012.

Soltanpour, D., and Shahinpoor, M. (2002). Development of a synthetic-muscle-based miniature diaphragm pump for medical applications. In *Proceedings of the First World Congress on Biomimetics and Artificial Muscle (Biomimetics 2002)*, December 9–11, Albuquerque, NM.

Soltanpour, D., Shahinpoor, P., and Shahinpoor, M. (2002). Development of an artificial muscle-based smart band to correct refractive errors of the human eye. In *Proceedings of the First World Congress on Biomolecular-Metrics and Artificial Muscle (Biomimetics 2002)*, December 9–11, Albuquerque, NM.

Springer, T. E., Wilson, M. S., and Gottesfeld, S. (1993). Modeling and experimental diagnostics in polymer electrolyte fuel cells. *Journal of the Electrochemical Society*, **140**(12).

Springer, T. E., Zawodzinski, T. A., and Gottesfeld, S. (1991). Polymer electrolyte fuel cell model. *Journal of the Electrochemical Society*, **138**(8).

Steane, A. M. (1998). Quantum computing. *Reports on Progress in Physics*, **61**:117–173.

Stein, J. L., Ashton-Miller, J. A., and Pandy, M. G. (1989). Issues in modeling and control of biomechanical systems. In *Proceedings of the Winter Annual Meeting of the American Society of Mechanical Engineers*, December 10–15. San Francisco, CA: ASME Publications, DSC-Vol. 17.

Steinberg, I. Z., Oplatka, A., and Katchalsky, A. (1966). Mechanochemical engines. *Nature*, **210**:568–571.

Steinmetz, C. G., and Larter, R. (1988). Electrostatic model for enhancement of membrane transport by a nonuniform electric field. *The Journal of Physical Chemistry*, **92**(21):6113–6120.

Steward, E. G. (2008). *Quantum Mechanics: Its Early Development and the Road to Entanglement*. Imperial College Press.

Stone, R. J., and Stone, J. A. (1990). *Atlas of the Skeletal Muscles*. Dubuque, IA: Wm. C. Brown Publishers.

Strobel, M., Lyons, C. S., and Mittal, K. L. (1994). *Plasma Surface Modification of Polymers: Relevance to Adhesion*. Utrecht: VSP Publication.

Sutherland, G. R., Louw, D. F., McBeth, P. B., Fielding, T., and Gregoris, D. J. (2006). Microadvanced robot system. U.S. Patent No. 7155316, December 26, 2006.

Sutherland, G. R., Louw, D. F., McBeth, P. B., Fielding, T., and Gregoris, D. J. (2012). U.S. Patent No. 8170717, May 1, 2012.

Swain, S. N., Bhaskara, V. S., and Panigrahi, P. K. (2022). Generalized entanglement measure for continuous-variable systems. *Physical Review A*, **105**(5):052441.

Sweeney, T., and Rattner, D. W. (2002). Robotically assisted minimally invasive biliary surgery in a porcine model. *Surgical Endoscopy*, **16**:138–141.

Swingle, B., and Van Raamsdonk, M. (2014). *Universality of Gravity from Entanglement Theory*. New York: Oxford University Press.

Tabatabaie, S. E., and Shahinpoor, M. (2018). Novel configurations of slit tubular soft robotic actuators and sensors made with ionic polymer metal composites (IPMCs). *Robotics and Automation Engineering Journal*, **3**(4):1–10.

Tabatabaie, S. E., and Shahinpoor, M. (2018). Soft biomimetic robotic looped haptic feedback sensors. *Journal of Robotic Engineering & Automation Technology*, **2018**(1):1–10.

Tabatabaie, S. E., and Shahinpoor, M. (2019). Artificial soft robotic elephant trunk made with ionic polymer-metal nanocomposites (IPMCs). *International Robotics and Automation Journal*, **5**(4):138–142.

Tadokoro, S. (2000). An actuator model of ICPF for robotic applications on the basis of physicochemical hypotheses. In *Proceedings of the IEEE*, ICRA, 1340–1346.

Tadokoro, S., Takamori, T., and Oguro, K. (2001). Application of the Nafion–platinum composite actuator. In *Proceedings of the SPIE*, Vol. 4329, 28–42.

Tadokoro, S., Yamagami, S., Takamori, T., and Oguro, K. (2000). Modeling of Nafion-Pt composite actuators (ICPF) by ionic motion. In *Proceedings of the SPIE*, Vol. 3987, 92–102.

Takenaka, H., Torikai, E., Kawami, Y., and Wakabayshi, N. (1982). Solid polymer electrolyte water electrolysis. *International Journal of Hydrogen Energy*, **7**:397–403.

Tal, J. (1994). *Step-by-Step Design of Motion Control Systems*. Ontario: Electromate Industries Publication.

Tanaka, T. (1978). Collapse of gels and the critical endpoint. *Physical Review Letters*, **40**:820.

Tanaka, T., Fillmore, D., Sun, S. T., Nishio, I., Swislow, G., and Shah, A. (1980). Phase transitions in ionic gels. *Physical Review Letters*, **45**, 1636.

Tanaka, T., Nishio, I., and Sun, S. T. (1982). Collapse of gels in an electric field. *Science*, **218**:467–469.

Tanaka, T., Sun, S., Hirokawa, Y., Katayama, S., Kucera, J. P., Hirose, Y., and Amiya, T. (1987). Mechanical instability of gels at the phase transition. *Nature*, **325**(6107):796–798.

Taylor, R. H. (2003). *Medical Robotics in Computer-Integrated Surgery. IEEE Transactions on Robotics and Automation*, **19**(5).

Tchartchian, G., Dietzel, J., Bojahr, B., Hackethal, A., and De Wilde, R. (2011). Decreasing strain on the surgeon in gynecologic minimally invasive surgery by using semi-active robotics. *International Journal of Gynecology and Obstetrics*, **112**:72–75.

Terris, D. J., and Amin, S. H. (2008). Robotic and endoscopic surgery in the neck. *Operative Techniques in Otolaryngology-Head and Neck Surgery*, **19**(1):36–41.

Tesla, N. (1898). Method of and apparatus for controlling mechanism of moving vessels of vehicles. U.S. Patent No. 613809, November 8, 1898.

Tewari, A., Peabody, J., Sarle, R., Balakrishnan, G., Hemal, A., Shrivastava, A., and Menon, M. (2002). The technique of da Vinci robot-assisted anatomic radical prostatectomy. *Urology*, **60**:569–572.

Thomas, R. A., Parniak, M., Østfeldt, C., Møller, C. B., Bærentsen, C., Tsaturyan, Y., Schliesser, A., Appel, J., Zeuthen, E., and Polzik, E. S. (2020). Entanglement between distant macroscopic mechanical and spin systems. *Nature Physics*, **17**(2):228–233.

Timpson, C. G. (2013). *Quantum Information Theory and the Foundations of Quantum Mechanics*. Oxford: Oxford University Press.

Tobushi, H., Hayashi, S., and Kojima, S. (1992). Mechanical properties of shape memory polymer of polyurethane series. *JSAE International Journal, Series 1*, **35**(3):296–302.

Tononi, G. (2015). Integrated information theory. *Scholarpedia*, **10**(1):4164.

Tononi, G., and Koch, C. (2015). Consciousness: Here, there and everywhere? *Philosophical Transactions of the Royal Society*, **370**(1668).

Torraca, L., Ismeno, G., Quarti, A., and Alfieri, O. (2002). Totally endoscopic atrial septal defect closure with a robotic system: Experience with seven cases. *Heart Surge Forum*, **5**:125–127.

Torresi, R. (1995). Ionic exchanges in dodecylbenzenesulfonate doped polypyrrole. I—Optical beam deflection studies. *Synthetic Metals*, **72**:59–64.

Tortora, G., and Grabowski, S. R. (1993). *Principles of Anatomy and Physiology*, 7th edition. New York, NY: Harper-Collins College Publishers.

Tourillon, G., and Garnier, F. (1984). Structural effect on the electrochemical properties of polythiophene and derivatives. *Journal of Electroanalytical Chemistry*, **161**:51. (1994). Effect of dopant on conjugated polymers. *Journal of Polymer Science, Polymer Physics Edition*, **22**:33.

Tozzi, P., Shahinpoor, M., Hayoz, D., and L. von Segesser. (2004). Electroactive polymers to assist failing heart: The future is now. In *Proceedings of the Second World Congress on Biomimetics and Artificial Muscle (Biomimetics and Nano-Bio 2004)*, December 5–8, Albuquerque, NM.

Triantafyllou, M. S., and Triantafyllou, G. S. (1995). An efficient swimming machine. *Scientific American*, 64–70.

Truesdell, C. A., and Noll, W. (1965). The non-linear field theories of mechanics. In *The Non-Linear Field Theories of Mechanics/Die Nicht-Linearen Feldtheorien der Mechanik. Encyclopedia of Physics/ Handbuch der Physik*, vol. 2/3/3. Berlin, Heidelberg: Springer.

Tsirbas, A., Mango, C., and Dutson, E. (2007). Use of robotics for intraocular surgery. *British Journal of Ophthalmol*, **91**(1):18–21.

Tsui, I., Tsirbas, A., Mango, C. W., Schwartz, S. D., and Hubschman, J. P. (2010). *Robotic Surgery in Ophthalmology*, ed. S. H. Baik. InTech.

Tsutomu, K., and Tokai, H. (1997). Cable scissors arch-marionettes structure. Structural morphology, towards the new millennium. *Proceedings of International Conference of IASS*, University of Nottingham, 107–116.

Turchetti, G., Palla, I., Pierotti, F., and Cuschieri, A. (2012). Economic evaluation of da Vinci–assisted robotic surgery: A systematic review. *Surgical Endoscopy Volume*, **26**(3):598–606.

Tyldesley, B., and Grieve, J. I. (1989). *Muscles, Nerves, and Movement*. Glasgow: Blackwell Scientific Publications.

Tyson, J., Schmidt, T., Galanulis, K., and Shahinpoor, M. (2002). Full-field deformation and strain measurement in biomechanics and biomimetics. In *Proceedings of the First World Congress on Biomimetics and Artificial Muscle (Biomimetics 2002)*, December 9–11, Albuquerque, NM.

Tyson, J., Schmidt, T., and Galanulis, K. (2003). Biomechanics deformation and strain measurements with 3D image correlation photogrammetry. *Experimental Techniques*, **27**(4):32–46.

Tzou, H. S., and Fukuda, T. (1992). *Precision Sensors, Actuators and Systems*. Dordrecht: Kluwer Academic Publishers.

Ueoka, Y., Isogai, N., and Nitta, T. (1994). Eel-like gel actuator with biomimetic movement. In *Preprints of the Sapporo Symposium on Intelligent Polymer Gels*, October 6–8, Sapporo, Japan, 117–118.

Ueta, T., Yamaguchi, Y., Shirakawa, Y., Nakano, T., Ideta, R., Noda, Y., Morita, A., Mochizuki, R., Sugita, N., Mitsuishi, M., and Tamaki, Y. (2009). Robot-assisted vitreoretinal surgery: Development of a prototype and feasibility studies in an animal model. *Ophthalmology*, **116**(8):1538–1543.

Ugural, A. C., and Fenster, S. K. (1987). *Advanced Strength and Applied Elasticity*. New York, NY: Elsevier.

Ullakko, K. (1996). Magnetically controlled shape memory alloys: A new class of actuator materials. *Journal of Materials Engineering and Performance*, **5**:405–409.

Umemoto, S., Okui, N., and Sakai, T. (1991). Contraction behavior of poly(acrylonitrile) gel fibers. In *Polymer Gels*, eds. D. DeRossi, K. Kajiwara, Y. Osada, and A. Yamauchi. New York, NY: Plenum Press, 257–270.

Urayama, K., Takaigawa, T., Masuda, T., and Kohjiya, S. (1994). Stress relaxation and creep of polymer gels in a solvent under various deformation modes. In *Preprints of the Sapporo Symposium on Intelligent Poly-Gels*, October 6–8, Sapporo, Japan, 89–90.

Van dam, W. (2013). Implausible consequences of superstrong nonlocality. *Natural Computing*, **12**(1):9–12.

Van der Brug, W. P., De Bliek, H. L. T., and Gerritsen, F. A. (1999). Image-guided surgery system. U.S. Patent No. 6,006,127.

Van der Veen, G., and Prins, W. (1971). Photomechanics directs the bending of a polymer film by light. *Physical Science*, **230**:70.

Van der, A. J., Sherman, J. H., and Luciano, D. S. (1985). *Human Physiology: The Mechanism of Body Function*, 4th edition. New York, NY: McGraw-Hill, 255–298.

Van Fraassen, B. (1982). The Charybdis of realism: Epistemological implications of Bell's inequality. *Synthese*, **52**:25–38.

Van Raamsdonk, M. (2010). Building up spacetime with quantum entanglement. *General Relativity and Gravitation*, **42**(10):2323–2329.

Veltink, P. H., Chizeck, H. J., Crago, P. E., and El-Bialy, A. (1992). Nonlinear joint angle control for artificially stimulated muscle. *IEEE Transactions on Biomedical Engineering*, **39**(4):368–380.

Verbrugge, M. W., and Hill, R. F. (1993). Ion and solvent transport in ion-exchange membranes. *Journal of the Electrochemical Society*, **140**(5):1218–1225.

Vértesi, T., and Brunner, N. (2014). Disproving the Peres conjecture by showing Bell nonlocality from bound entanglement. *Nature Communications*, **5**(1):5297.

Walborn, S., Taketani, B., Salles, A., Toscano, F., and de Matos Filho, R. (2009). Entropic entanglement criteria for continuous variables. *Physical Review Letters*, **103**(16):160505.

Wang, G. (1998). A general design of bias force shape memory alloy (BFSMA) actuators and an electrically controlled SMA knee and leg muscle exerciser for paraplegics and quadriplegics. Ph.D. dissertation. Department of Mechanical Engineering, University of New Mexico, Albuquerque.

Wang, G., and Shahinpoor, M. (1997a). A new design for a rotatory joint actuator made with shape memory alloy contractile wire. *Journal of Intelligent Material Systems and Structures*, **8**(3), 191–279.

Wang, G., and Shahinpoor, M. (1997b). Design for shape memory alloy rotatory joint actuators using shape memory effect and pseudoelastic effect. *Smart Materials Technologies*, **3040**, 23–30.

Wang, G., and Shahinpoor, M. (1997c). Design, prototyping and computer simulation of a novel large bending actuator made with a shape memory alloy contractile wire. *Smart Materials and Structures*, **6**(2), 214–221.

Wang, G., and Shahinpoor, M. (1998). Design of a knee and leg muscle exerciser using a shape memory alloy rotary actuator. In *Proceedings of SPIE Smart Materials and Structures Conference*, March 3–5, San Diego, CA, publication no. 3324-29.

Wang, Q., Du, X., Xu, B., and Cross, L. E. (1999). Electromechanical coupling and output efficiency of piezoelectric bending actuators. *IEEE Transactions on Ultrasonics, Ferroelectrics, and Frequency Control*, **46**(3):638–646.

Wang, T. T., Herbert, J. M., and Glass, A. M. (Eds.) 1988. *The Applications of Ferroelectric Polymers*. New York, NY: Chapman & Hall.

Weatherall, J. O. (2013). The scope and generality of Bell's theorem. *Foundations of Physics*, **43**(9):1153–1169.

Webb, P. W., and Weihs, D. (1983). *Fish Biomechanics*. New York, NY: Praeger.

Weiss, K. D., Carlson, J. D., and Nixon, D. A. (1994). Viscoelastic properties of magneto- and electro-rheological fluids. *Journal of Intelligent Material Systems and Structures*, **5**:772–775.

Werner, R. F., and Wolf, M. M. (2001). Bound entangled Gaussian states. *Physical Review Letters*, **86**(16):3658–3661.

White, M. A., Haber, G. P., Autorino, R., Khanna, R., Forest, S., Yang, B., Altunrende, F., Stein, R. J., and Kaouk, J. H. (2010). Robotic laparoendoscopic single-site radical prostatectomy: Technique and early outcomes. *European Urology*, **58**:544–550.

Whiting, C. J., Voice, A. M., Olmsted, P. D., and McLeish, T. C. B. (2001). Shear modulus of polyelectrolyte gels under electric field. *Journal of Physics: Condensed Matter*, **13**:1381–1393.

Williams, W., and Bannister, D. (1989). *Gray's Anatomy*, 37th edition. Edinburgh: Churchill Livingstone, 614–616.

Wineland, D. J., Bollinger, J. J., Itano, W. M., Moore, F. L., and Heinzen, D. J. (1992). Spin squeezing and reduced quantum noise in spectroscopy. *Physical Review A*, **46**(11):R6797–R6800.

Winter, D. A. (1990). *Biomechanics and Motor Control of Human Movement*. New York, NY: Wiley-Interscience.

Winter, D., Norman, R. W., Wells, R. P., Hayes, K. C., and Patla, A. E. (1985a). Biomechanics IX—A, international series on biomechanics. In *Proceedings of the Ninth International Congress of Biomechanics*, Vol. 5A. Waterloo: Human Kinetics Publishers, Inc. (1985b). Biomechanics IX—B, international series on biomechanics. In *Proceedings of Ninth International Congress of Biomechanics*, Vol. 5B. Waterloo: Human Kinetics Publishers, Inc.

Wiseman, H. M., Jones, S. J., and Doherty, A. C. (2007). Steering, entanglement, nonlocality, and the Einstein–Podolsky–Rosen paradox. *Physical Review Letters*, **98**(14):140402.

Wisselink, W., Cuesta, M. A., Gracia, C., and Rauwerda, J. A. (2002). Robot-assisted laparoscopic aortabifemoral bypass for aortoiliac occlusive disease: A report of two cases. *Journal of Vascular Surgery*, **36**:1079–1082.

Wong, B. (2019). On quantum entanglement. *International Journal of Automatic Control System*, **5**(2):1–7p.

Wood, J. E., Meek, S. G., and Jacobsen, S. C. (1989a). Quantitation of human shoulder anatomy for prosthetic arm control I. Surface modeling. *Journal of Biomechanics*, **22**(3):273–292. (1989b). Quantitation of human shoulder anatomy for prosthetic arm control II. Anatomy matrices. *Journal of Biomechanics*, **22**(4):309–325.

Woojin, L. (1996). Polymer gel-based actuator: Dynamic model of gel for real-time control. Ph.D. thesis. Massachusetts Institute of Technology.

Wootters, W. K., and Zurek, W. H. (1982). A single quantum cannot be cloned. *Nature*, **299**:802–803.

Wu, Y. T., Brokaw, C. J., and Brennen, C. (1975). *Swimming and Flying in Nature*, Vols. I and II. New York, NY: Plenum Press.

Yamada, H. (1970). *Strength of Biological Materials*. Baltimore, MD: The Williams & Wilkins Company.

Yannas, I. V., and Grodzinsky, A. J. (1973). Electromechanical energy conversion with collagen fibers in an aqueous medium. *Journal of Mechanochemistry & Cell Motility*, **2**:113–125.

Yasuda, K., Gong, P., Katsuwama, Y., Nakavama, A., Tanabe, Y., Kondo, E., Ueno, M., and Osada, Y. (2005). Biomechanical properties of high-toughness double network hydrogels. *Biomaterials Journal*, **26**(21):4468–4475.

Yeager, H. L. (1982). Perfluorinated ionomer membranes. In *Perfluorinated Ionomer Membranes*, eds. A. Eisenberg and H. L. Yeager. American Chemical Society Symposium Series, 180.

Yen, C. C., and Chang, T. C. (1989). Preparation of electric-conducting film from polyacrylonitrile-silver nitrate complex. *Journal of Applied Polymer Science*, **40**:267–277.

Yildrim, Y. (2010). *Cytoreductive Surgery in Gynecologic Oncology: A Multidisciplinary Approach*. Kerala: Transworld Research Network, 213–232.

Yin, J., Cao, Y., Li, Y.-H., Liao, S.-K., Zhang, L., Ren, J.-G., Cai, W.-Q., Liu, W.-Y., Li, B., Dai, H., Li, G.-B., Lu, Q.-M., Gong, Y.-H., Xu, Y., Li, S.-L., Li, F.-Z., Yin, Y.-Y., Jiang, Z.-Q., Li, M., Jia, J.-J., Ren, G., He, D., Zhou, Y.-L., Zhang, X.-X., Wang, N., Chang, X., Zhu, Z.-C., Liu, N.-L., Chen, Y.-A., Lu, C.-Y., Shu, R., Peng, C.-Z., Wang, J.-Y., and Pan, J.-W. (2017). Satellite-based entanglement distribution over 1200 kilometers. *Science*, **356**(6343):1140–1144.

Yin, J., Cao, Y., Yong, H.-L., Ren, J.-G., Liang, H., Liao, S.-K., Zhou, F., Liu, C., Wu, Y.-P., Pan, G.-S., Zhang, Q., Peng, C.-Z., and Pan, J.-W. (2013). Bounding the speed of 'spooky action at a distance'. *Physical Review Letters*, **110**(26):260407.

Yin, J., Li, Y.-H., Liao, S.-K., Yang, M., Cao, Y., Zhang, L., Ren, J.-G., Cai, W.-Q., Liu, W.-Y., Li, S.-L., Shu, R., Huang, Y.-M., Deng, L., Li, L., Zhang, Q., Liu, N.-L., Chen, Y.-A., Lu, C.-Y., Wang, X.-B., Xu, F., Wang, J.-Y., Peng, C.-Z., Ekert, A. K., and Pan, J.-W. (2020). Entanglement-based secure quantum cryptography over 1,120 kilometers. *Nature*, **582**(7813):501–505.

Yoshida, H., and Miura, Y. (1992). The behavior of water in perfluorinated ionomer membranes having various monovalent cations. *Journal of Membrane Science*, **68**:1–10.

Yoshida, R., Yamaguchi, T., and Ichijo, H. (1996). Novel oscillation, swelling-deswelling dynamic behavior for pH-polymer gels. *Materials Science and Engineering C*, **4**:107–113.

Young, R. J., and Lovell, P. A. (1991). *Introduction to Polymers*, 2nd edition. London: Chapman & Hall, 353.

Yu, H., Madden, J. D., Madden, P. G., Swager, T. M., and Hunter, I. W. (2002). Thiophene-based conducting polymers' molecular actuation. In *Smart Structures and Materials EAPAD Symposium Proceedings*, SPIE, 4695.

Yuh, J. (1994). Underwater robotic vehicle: Design and control. In *NSF Workshop on Future Research Directions in Underwater Robotics*, Maui, HI.

Zadeh, L. A. (1973). Outline of a new approach to the analysis of complex systems and decision processes. *IEEE Transactions on Systems, Man, & Cybernetics*, **3**(1):28–44.

Zeilinger, A. (2018). Quantum teleportation, onwards and upwards. *Nature Physics*, **14**:3–4.

Zhang, Q. M., Bharti, V., and Zhao, X. (1998). Giant electrostriction and relaxor ferroelectric behavior in electron-irradiated poly(vinylidene fluoride-tetrafluoroethylene) copolymer. *Science*, **280**:2101–2104.

Zhang, Q. M., Furukawa, T., Bar-Cohen, Y., and Scheinbeim, J. (Eds.) (1999). *Proceedings of the Fall MRS Symposium on Electroactive Polymers (EAP)*, Vol. 600. Warrendale, PA: Materials Research Society, 1–336.

Zrinyi, M., Barsi, L., Szabo, D., and Kilian, H. G. (1997). Direct observation of abrupt shape transition in ferrogels induced by a nonuniform magnetic field. *Journal of Chemical Physics*, **106**(13):5685–5692.

Zrinyi, M., Szabo, D., and Feher, J. (1999). Comparative studies of electro- and magnetic field-sensitive polymer gels. In *Proceedings of SPIE 6th Annual International Symposium of Smart Structures and Materials*, EAPAD, Vol. 3669, ed. Y. Bar-Cohen. 406–413.

Index

actuation 81, 145, 151, 194, 198, 201–202, 322–324, 328–330, 335
  linear 207
  soft 320–321
  thermal 199
actuator 15–16, 94, 108, 151, 153–154, 159–160, 198–201, 206, 273, 320, 329
  electromechanical 297
  joint 202, 282
  linear 337
  moving 4, 103
  pneumatic 263
  soft biomimetic surface 320–321
  spring-biased SMA 202
acupuncture 50
adaptability 61, 147, 157
adaptation 28, 40, 44, 58, 81, 148, 158, 172
  geometric 171
advanced software 373, 387–388
aerolites 168–169
AGI *see* artificial general intelligence
AI *see* artificial intelligence
algorithm 18, 29, 177, 312, 375–376, 378
aluminum 150, 154, 157–158, 170
anesthesia 112
anxiety 2, 16, 49, 78, 94–95, 102, 387, 398
application 150–151, 153–154, 156, 159–160, 199, 202, 204–206, 208–209, 211, 216–217, 302, 304, 307–308, 336
  advanced robotic 254, 261, 286, 330, 336–337, 345–346, 348
  biomaterial 209–210
  biomedical 209–210
  geometrical 185
  medical 150
  military 159
  piezoelectric 151
  real-world 259
  robotic 254, 259, 322, 337, 346
  robotic force feedback 255, 339, 348
  smart sensor 208
  terrestrial 300
approximation 111, 172, 175–176
artificial general intelligence (AGI) 399, 407
artificial intelligence (AI) 3, 13–14, 16, 94–95, 97, 101–102, 148, 273–276, 311–312, 316, 373–380, 387–388, 397–399, 402–407, 415–416, 418
awareness 2, 17–18, 94–95, 98, 100, 311, 374, 377, 399

battery 300–302, 305–308
  atomic 300–306
  chemical 300
  diamond 301–302, 305
  nuclear 13, 98, 297–300, 302–309, 415–416
  traditional 304
Bayes' rule 129
behavior 30–32, 41–43, 79, 113, 152, 216
  chemomechanical 199
  electrorheological 153
  human 260, 312

intelligent 402
physical 408
bending 200, 320–321, 324, 328, 330–331, 338–340, 345–347
bending force 337, 339–340
Big Bang 1, 4, 20, 33, 145–146, 161–162, 164–165, 379
biological field 48–53, 55–56, 58–60, 70, 164
biomimetic 13–14, 16–17, 93–98, 100–104, 107, 191–218, 253, 255, 297–308, 311, 319–348, 387–388, 397–399, 415–416, 418
biorhythm 34, 59
biosensing 209–210
biosystem 17, 24, 26, 28, 96–97
brain 73–76, 79, 100, 102, 112–115, 311–315, 374, 376–378, 399, 401, 404, 406–408
animal 378
biological 378, 408
human 3, 77, 101, 113, 313, 379
immature 77
neural 14, 16, 94–95, 102
universal robot 316
brain microtubules 100, 312–313
brain neurons 100, 311, 314

calibration 255, 339–340, 348
capability 50, 78, 80, 99, 101, 156, 260, 322, 389
activation 319
cognitive 376
dynamic 397
energy-harvesting 323
informational 69
information-processing 355
load-bearing 322
sensing 15–16, 94–95, 102, 328–330
transduction 332
visual 261
Captain Kirk 16, 101, 191, 193, 388, 416–417
cation 200, 207, 211–212, 322–323, 327
causal power 110, 123, 125, 128–129, 131–132
cause–effect power 109, 111, 114, 117–129, 131–132, 134
CCD *see* charge-coupled device
chaos 21, 41, 66
charge-coupled device (CCD) 195
chemical reaction 29, 32, 57–58, 199, 302
cognition 94, 100, 102, 377, 389
collagen 148, 213–214
communication 37, 45, 50–51, 56, 60, 62–63, 67, 72–73, 164, 260, 360–361
biological 63
continuous 73
intercellular 70
speech 45
ultrasound 45
community 43, 45–46
computer 13–14, 94–97, 101–102, 260, 311–312, 314, 316, 373, 375, 377–378, 387–388, 398–399, 415–416
classical 374, 376
embedded consciousness 15–16, 95–96, 98–99, 389
intelligent 14–16, 94–97, 101–102, 108, 191, 388
quantum 313, 353, 360, 374–377
resident 398
traditional 377
universal 313
conception vessel (CV) 51
conditions 23–24, 39–40, 43, 47, 55–57, 60, 74–75, 78, 145, 149, 164, 170

abnormal cerebral 77
altered cerebral 77
background 120, 123, 126
critical 75
dynamic 28, 171
hypothesized 23
isothermal 216
mental 51
molecular 65, 362
natural 43
normal 47, 204
pathological 118
physical/mental 79
static 328
steady state 329
windy 159
conductive polymer (CP) 194–195, 198, 201
configuration 38, 99, 155, 170–172, 320–321, 327, 333, 336, 344–346, 389
connection 27, 51, 58, 133, 135, 144, 168, 178, 353, 355, 360
conscience 31–32, 68–69
consciousness 1–82, 93–103, 107–136, 144, 148, 171–185, 191–193, 253, 297–298, 311, 313–316, 351, 353, 373–379, 387–389, 397–403, 405–406, 408, 416
artificial 397, 399–402, 404–407
human 17, 25, 76, 96–98, 100, 103, 191, 193, 387–389, 397, 415–417
Kirk's 416
machine 97–98, 388, 397, 399, 403, 405
oral transfer of 15–16, 96
universal 4, 25, 143, 178, 373
cosmic body 21, 168–170
cosmological fractal attractor 375–377
CP *see* conductive polymer
CV *see* conception vessel

Darcy permeability 328
decay 299–301, 303–304
deformation 101, 151–152, 194, 197, 206, 208, 213–215, 319–324, 329, 340, 345
dendrite 14, 16, 94–95, 101–102, 311–312
device 47–48, 62, 68–69, 80, 160, 168, 176, 208, 286, 304–306, 358
antientropic 28
energy storage 23
informational 68–69
intelligent 46–47
low-energy 304
low-energy electronic 308
multilevel feedback 65
nuclear-powered 302
remotely controlled 258
smart sensing 160
specialized 26, 29, 37, 44, 77, 259
dilution 120, 129–130, 132
discovery 3, 47, 62, 75, 193, 209, 300–301, 378
DNA 4, 24, 26, 33, 52–53, 146, 148, 156, 312, 314, 379
dualism 37, 57, 69–70, 108, 151, 169

EAP *see* electroactive polymer
Einstein-Podolsk-Rosen paradox (EPR paradox) 82–83, 101, 355, 363–364
electric field 149, 151–154, 193, 196–198, 200–201, 203–204, 208, 213–214, 217–218, 322–324, 328–329, 331–332
electricity 62, 202, 211, 216, 302, 304–305, 307
electroactive polymer (EAP) 193–209, 331
electrode 159, 197–198, 200–201, 212, 215–217, 263, 321, 323, 328, 335

electrorheological fluid (ERF) 203–205
emotion 2, 7, 15–17, 30, 49, 94–96, 102, 314–315, 400, 404–406, 417
emotional effects 16, 94–95, 102, 398
end-effector 272, 279, 282, 336–337, 345–346
energy 4, 18–19, 21–23, 27–30, 32–33, 35, 53, 56–62, 66–67, 161–164, 176, 297, 299–300, 302–307, 315, 354–355, 376, 379, 415–416
  carbon-free 57, 300
  chemical 57, 207, 215
  continuous 418
  dissociation 181
  elastic 203
  electrical 56, 152
  free 155, 214
  kinetic 56
  laser light 203
  latent 67
  magnetic 206
  mechanical 150, 152, 193, 216
  non-visible dark 147
  nuclear 57, 301, 305, 307
  photon 162
  potential 56–57, 354
  static 57
  thermal 56, 150–151, 161, 163, 299
  wind 56
entanglement 83, 101, 351–353, 355–356, 360–364
  quantum 96, 351–356, 358–364, 416–417
entropy 22–23, 28, 39, 63–65, 161, 164–165, 361–362
environment 17, 19, 26–29, 31–32, 37, 39–43, 45, 47, 68, 71–74, 81–82, 147–148, 157, 171–173, 259–260
  alkaline 199
  aqueous 36
  biomedical 331
  dynamic 148, 157, 172
  electrocautery 337
  noisy 376
  nuclear reactor 261
  quasistatic 180
  static 157
  sterile 348
  wet human body 255, 337, 339, 348
EPR paradox *see* Einstein-Podolsk-Rosen paradox
equilibrium 28, 39, 42, 50, 57–59, 63, 67, 149, 171, 215
ERF *see* electrorheological fluid
ether 53–55, 58
Euler's formula 185
evolution 21–26, 31–34, 36–41, 44, 52–53, 56, 58–59, 72–74, 80–81, 143, 147–148, 163–165, 169–170, 173, 177
  artificial 80
  continuous 50
  dynamic 173
  human 36
  intelligent 20, 24–25, 60, 165
  interdependent 171
  matter's 41
  natural 36
  nonorganic 148
  oxygen 212
  social 45, 79
  subsystem's 67
  system's dynamical 131
  voluntary 78
expansion 20, 120, 129–130, 132, 161, 199, 207, 213, 218, 346
experience 25, 30, 32, 42–43, 56, 58, 108–121, 124, 136, 172, 314–315, 375, 377

fabrication 15–16, 93, 320, 397
facial expressions 257, 319–320, 348, 404
feedback 15, 28, 41, 94–96, 102, 205, 336
  kinesthetic force 254–255, 336–337, 339–348
feelings 15–17, 30, 32, 35, 49–50, 94–96, 102, 113, 119, 373–374, 398, 404
  conscious 16, 96
  human master's 14
  spiritual 377
  visceral 376
feelings and emotions 15, 94–96, 102, 404
Fibonacci numbers 143, 188
Fibonacci sequence 187–188
Fibonacci series 177–178, 188
forces 50, 52, 57–58, 154, 199, 201, 205, 207, 214, 217–218, 313, 336–337, 339, 344–345, 347–348
  blocking 337
  conjugate 328
  electromagnetic 164
  electrophoretic 218
  electrostatic 198
  gravitational 1, 25
  isometric 213
  kinesthetic 255, 336–338, 345–346
  magnetic 209
  physical 58
  repulsive 211
  supernatural 36
  surface mask feedback 320–321
free will 374, 376–377
functionality 28–29, 32, 34, 41, 287

galaxy 1, 25–26, 33, 147, 165, 168, 178, 417
gel 149, 194, 196, 199–200, 204, 207, 211, 214–218
  activated 195
  actuator 200
  charged 211
  chitosan 331
  elastic 200
  electrolyte 207
  electrolytic 214
  fibrous 331
  hydrolyzed acrylamide 214
  ionic polymeric 148–149, 217
  magnetic 196, 331
  nonionic 200
  polymer 199–200, 211–212, 215–216
  polymeric acid 211
  rod-shaped 215
giant magnetostrictive material (GMM) 206
GMM *see* giant magnetostrictive material
golden number 33, 177
golden ratio 143, 182, 187–188
golden triangle 182, 185–186
grasping forceps 336, 345–346
Great Pyramid 159, 183–185

Han the Robot 7
helium 19, 146, 161, 170
Higgs field 20, 144
humanity 19, 96–98, 351, 388, 399, 401, 407, 415–416, 418
human master 14, 16, 93, 95–99, 191–193, 253, 387–388, 397–398, 405, 415, 417–418
humanoid 4–5, 7–8, 10–11, 13–17, 93–100, 102–104, 191–193, 253–256, 258–259, 297–298, 307–308, 319–321, 330–331, 339–341, 348, 351, 387–389, 397–399, 405, 415–418
hydrogel 196, 208–210
hydrogen 1, 18–19, 21, 23, 25, 161, 163, 165, 168, 170, 203, 212

identity-vita-assigned consciousness (IVA-consciousness) 14–16, 94–100, 102–103, 191, 297, 311, 373, 387–389, 397–398, 416
instinct 30, 42–43, 46
intelligence 4, 21–22, 25–26, 30, 40–44, 46–47, 51–53, 58–59, 68–69, 73, 80–82, 146, 148, 150, 155–157, 159, 163–164, 171–185, 399–400, 402
- adaptive 82–83
- basic 47, 402
- emotional 404
- geometric 176
- human 72, 173, 402–403, 406
- human-level 399
- inherited 44
- natural 402
- non-biological 399
- primordial 42
- social 43, 45
- system's 41, 81

interactions 7, 14, 27–28, 51–52, 55, 57, 98, 100, 102, 257, 261, 314–315, 355
- chemical 32
- collaborative 311
- dynamic 28
- electrical 378
- electrochemical 214
- energetic 54
- environmental 57, 210
- human 320, 404
- informational 32
- ion 218
- kinesthetic 346
- microtubule 102
- pairwise 135
- physical 355
- reciprocal 24, 82
- semi-cognitive 417

interplanetary ship 100, 389
intrinsicality 109, 114, 117, 119–120, 122, 130–132
intrinsic information 117, 121, 123, 127–128, 130–131, 134–135
inverse kinematics 253–254, 263, 265, 276, 279–280, 284, 397–398
ionic polymer–metal composite (IPMC) 101, 200, 255, 319–333, 335–337, 339–341, 344–346, 348
ionic polymer–metal nanocomposite (IPMNC) 194, 202, 332–333
ions 149, 201, 217–218, 327
IPMC *see* ionic polymer–metal composite
IPMC strip 322–324, 332, 335, 338–339, 343, 345–347
IPMNC *see* ionic polymer–metal nanocomposite
isotope 170, 299, 304, 306, 308
IVA-consciousness *see* identity-vita-assigned consciousness

Jia Jia 11, 14, 256–257, 418
joystick 336–337, 346

laparoscopic surgery 254–255, 337, 339
large language model (LLM) 378
law 22, 25, 62, 120, 172, 177, 259
- evolutionary 25
- higher-order 259
- indefinite integration 41
- universal 67

Laws of Robotics 259
LCE *see* liquid crystal elastomer
life 4, 17–19, 21–27, 29–30, 32–33, 36–37, 40–43, 47–49, 55–56, 58–59, 62, 79–80, 97–98, 103, 171–185, 388, 398–399, 416
- animal's 43

artificial 69
human 44, 80, 103, 389, 415–416
human master's 94
indefinite 375
intelligent 417
organic 415
organic-based 96
silicone-based 98, 388
system's 30
liquid crystal elastomer (LCE) 198–199
living bodies 22–23, 48, 51
living cells 21–22, 26
living organisms 23–24, 26, 36, 70, 215
LLM *see* large language model
logarithmic abundance 166–167

machine 3, 7, 72, 97, 108, 257, 260, 377–378, 387, 399–402, 404–408
artificial 378
coffee 378
conscious 102, 403, 407–408
human-created 397
intelligent 373, 403, 406
self-moving 258
machine learning 3, 11, 99, 378–379, 405
magnetic field 54, 152–154, 195–196, 204–206, 209
magnetorheological fluid (MRF) 204–205
manipulation 111, 117, 211, 262, 320–321
material 53–54, 81–82, 146–151, 153–155, 157–159, 170–171, 193–194, 197–199, 205–210, 212, 216, 299, 301, 328, 330–332
active 202, 205
artificial muscle 202
ceramic 151
dielectric 196, 208
electronic EAP 194
electrorheological 152–154
electrostrictive 154, 208
ferrogel 196
giant magnetoresistive 209
hazardous 259, 302
hybrid 210
intelligent 17, 81, 145, 148, 154, 157, 191, 193, 204
intelligent wearable 97
magnetorheological 148, 153–154
magnetostrictive 154, 160, 196, 206
mechanochromic 210
meteoritic 171
multifunctional 330–331
nanocomposite 210
noncentrosymmetric 196
nonliving 71, 148
piezoceramic 331
piezoelectric 151–152, 154, 197
polarized 197
radioactive 298
semiconductor 154
smart 15–16, 145, 149, 152, 193, 201, 203, 208, 210, 330–331, 339
spherical 171
stimuli-responsive 297
viscoelastic 204
material intelligence quotient (MIQ) 81, 146–147, 149
material smartness quotient (MSQ) 81, 146–147, 149
mathematical modeling 71, 328
matter 20–22, 24–30, 32–35, 40–42, 47–48, 50–53, 61–62, 71, 73–74, 145, 147, 149, 160–165, 171–173, 315
dark 147
evolution of 21, 25, 55, 59, 80, 164, 168–169, 171–185

exchange of 27–28
inorganic 24
intelligent form of 24, 52
living 22–23, 34, 40, 56, 147, 157
nonliving 22, 51, 71, 74, 80–81
organization of 34, 41, 75
physical 29
primordial 164
pure 150
matter formation 20, 28, 35, 59, 161
maximal existence 124–126, 130, 134–135
Maxwell stress 198
mechanism 37, 40–41, 44–45, 74–75, 79, 120–121, 125, 194, 199, 201, 205
activation 194
correction 65–66
intelligent 74
super-specialized 73
memory 11, 15–16, 29–30, 68, 71, 94–96, 100, 312, 314, 374–375, 398
mental processes 41, 57–58
metal 150, 152, 195, 200, 203, 207, 209–210
meteorites 168, 171
microprocessor 15, 96, 148, 253, 388
microRNA 146–147
microtubule 100, 311–313, 315
mind 17, 25, 50, 57–58, 75, 77–78, 108, 165, 172, 376–378, 406
minimal existence 123, 126, 134
minimum partition (MIP) 123, 126–127, 134–135
Minkowski spaces 174
MIP *see* minimum partition
MIQ *see* material intelligence quotient
model 18–19, 33–34, 36–37, 53–54, 64, 66, 156, 163, 172, 177, 213, 218, 312–313
causal 109, 124, 128
communication 64
continuum 214
general 115
informational 33–35
large language 378
linear irreversible thermodynamic 201
mathematical 36, 39, 52, 55, 63, 66, 71, 315
natural 159
realistic 408
theoretical 174, 217
universal 33
motion 51, 55, 58, 97, 99, 205, 214, 218, 262–263, 273, 276
MRF *see* magnetorheological fluid
MSQ *see* material smartness quotient
muscle 159, 201, 211–212, 215–216, 319–321
artificial 15, 101, 191, 193, 201–204, 207, 212, 216, 319, 330–332, 341
electroactive 212
facial 320–321
pH-sensitive 212

nanogel 208–210
NDE *see* near-death experience
near-death experience (NDE) 56
negentropy 22, 28
Neumann entropy 357, 362
neurons 14, 16, 31, 73, 94–95, 101–102, 311–312, 314–315, 374, 378–379, 401
neutrons 20, 145, 161–162, 299
nickel 149, 168–169, 209, 299
nitrogen 23, 59, 170
noise 45, 132, 136, 376
nuclear fission 300–301
nuclei 20, 53, 145–146, 161, 163

ocean 11, 18, 45–46, 160
organ 22, 31, 34, 73–74, 76, 79, 254–255, 337, 341, 345–346, 348
organism 23–26, 29–32, 34, 40–41, 46, 50, 52, 59, 62, 73–74, 76–80, 155
conscious 74
unicellular 312
organization 21–22, 26, 28, 33–34, 37, 39, 42, 44, 58, 149, 156
energetic 52
hierarchic 24
intelligent 41, 79, 156
intelligent informational 35
social 45
oxygen 19, 23–24, 26, 59, 78, 146, 163, 165, 168, 170, 180

paradox 82–83, 360–361, 363
path 37, 64, 68, 73, 287
perception 2, 17, 56, 72–73, 76, 374, 400
perpetuation 30, 32, 41, 44, 55, 164
phenomena 35, 48, 50, 59, 61–62, 68, 72, 75, 77, 196, 200, 203, 360–361
electro-osmosis 213
mechanical 360
mind-boggling 353
physical 176
social 79
unexplained 55
philosopher 315, 400, 406
photons 161–162, 357, 361, 417
physical existence 109, 117–119, 121
piezoelectric effect 151, 197
piezoelectricity 196–197
piezoresistive effect 151–152, 208
piezoresistivity 207–208
planet 18–19, 21–23, 25, 59, 97, 100, 168, 176, 178–179, 407, 416–418
Planck constant 144–145, 162
Poisson–Nernst–Planck phenomena 322
polyelectrolyte 149, 213–214, 216
polymer 148, 150–151, 153, 193–198, 201, 211–212, 214, 216
conductive 194, 201
electronic 194
ion-containing 326–327
ionic gel 199
ionized 210
photonic 195
piezoelectric 159, 193, 197
sensitive 216
stimulated 194, 202
stimuli-responsive 203
positrons 161, 300–301
postulates 108–109, 111, 114–115, 118–119, 121–123, 125, 130–131, 315
power source 298, 303–304, 307, 322
betavoltaic 305
radioisotope 307
power supply 304, 306, 320–321
pressure 46, 149, 152, 159, 211
probability 24, 63–65, 110, 122, 129–131, 133–134, 357, 363
conditional 120, 122, 128–129
equal 128, 357
forward 129
marginal 128
unconstrained 128
probability distribution 120, 127, 131–132, 356–357, 362
process
causal 113
continuous 73
decision-making 312
divergent 176
dual 73
dynamic 164
electrodialysis 212

endothermic 203
evolutionary 67
freezing 76
intelligent 72
interactive 69
metabolic 23
quantum 100, 312
reverse 199–200
scanning 353
semiconductor fabrication 155
stochastic 64
telepathic 61
protein 23, 34, 147–148, 155, 214, 313
protocol 359–360
protons 20–21, 145, 161–162, 299
protozoa 31, 41
pyramid 59, 159, 183–185, 187, 267–269, 271

quantum computing 352, 374–375
quantum formalism 83, 101, 360, 364
quantum parallelism 375–377
quantum teleportation 353, 356
quantum wave function 311, 353–354
quarks 20, 144–145
qubits 312–313, 356–357, 363

radiation 36, 46, 60, 307
radioactive decay 299, 305, 307
radioisotope 300, 302, 304, 307
RNA 4, 146, 148, 379
robot 7, 9, 11, 13–14, 16–17, 94–99, 191–192, 258–262, 319–320, 348, 374, 388–389, 402, 404–407, 416
animaloid 416
emotional 404
four-legged 316
giant 417
industrial 259
programmable 260
service 260
slave 262, 348
surgical 259, 286
robotic arm 261–262, 273–274, 276–277, 279–280, 282–286, 348
robotic hand 159, 285–287
robotic manipulator 259, 262–264, 272, 277, 279–282, 285–287, 297
robotics 12, 15, 157, 204, 253–286, 316, 320, 330, 348, 407
robotic surgery 15, 254–255, 280, 330–331, 336–337, 340, 345–346, 348
rock 19, 45–47, 71

self-awareness 94, 97, 102, 191, 399, 405, 415
self-organization 28, 37–39, 65, 148
semiconductor 152, 195, 207–208, 298–299, 302–303
sensing 16, 81–82, 151, 160, 194, 201–202, 319–323, 328–330, 335, 345, 348
sensing signal 255, 339, 343, 346, 348
sensor 4, 94, 104, 153–154, 159–160, 200, 208–209, 216, 320–323, 346, 348
electromechanical 15, 418
IPMC 320, 336, 340, 347
stimuli-responsive 16
shape-memory alloy (SMA) 71, 101, 148–150, 160, 202, 319, 322, 331
shape-memory material (SMM) 202–203, 205–206
shape-memory polymer (SMP) 150, 202–203, 331
siderolites 168–169
silicon 150, 154, 170

SIQ *see* structural intelligence quotient
sleep 76–79, 112
SMA *see* shape-memory alloy
SMM *see* shape-memory material
SMP *see* shape-memory polymer
solar system 18–19, 166, 259
Sophia 6–8, 257–258, 418
species 22, 30–33, 36–37, 41, 43–46, 56, 67, 76, 79–80, 113
specificity 110, 119, 131–132
spectrum 60, 79, 162–163, 259
Sphinx 159
SSQ *see* structural smartness quotient
state 18, 64–66, 68–69, 73, 75–80, 108, 110, 115, 117, 119–124, 126–133, 150–151, 353–357, 361–363, 400
  alpha state 77–79
  binary 312
  cause–effect 117–118, 121, 123–125, 127–134
  chaotic 20
  classical 357
  conscious 77, 112
  emotional 50
  entangled 355–356, 358, 362
  eternal 101
  hydrated 214
  interface 76
  latent 75
  microscopic 64, 362
  natural 353
  physical 30
  polarization 357
  quantum 355–357, 360
  qubit 357
  raw 207
  solid 47
  spin-squeezed 363
  stationary 354
  theta 78
  unconscious 112
  wakening 77
stimuli
  chemical 72
  electrochemical 149
  environmental 40
  mechanical 152
strain 194, 196–197, 200, 202, 205–208
  deformation 149
  electrostrictive 196–197
  plastic deformation 149
stress 80, 153–154, 197, 202, 204, 207–208, 215
  critical 215
  shear 204
structural intelligence quotient (SIQ) 81, 146
structural smartness quotient (SSQ) 81, 146
structure 26, 31, 34–35, 56–58, 67, 109–113, 118–119, 121, 136, 146–147, 149–151, 155–157, 159–161, 185, 313–314
  anatomic 31
  artificial 156
  asymmetric 23
  bacteriophage 155
  cause–effect 109–111, 114–115, 121, 124–125
  cerebral 73
  complex 156
  crystalline 196
  electro-magneto-mechanical 15, 96
  energetic 50, 52
  etheric 55
  evolutionary 174
  geometric 57
  Heusler 205
  hierarchical 35, 38, 65, 81, 148, 155, 170
  intelligent 24–25, 33, 37, 69, 72, 75, 80, 150, 155–157, 159, 164
  ionic polymeric gel 148

isolated brain 378
living 26, 48, 155
material 31, 33, 35–36, 58, 67, 81, 146, 149, 181
multilevel control 80
octahedral 169
organic 25
organized 203
periodic 180
phenomenal 116
physical 418
polyelectrolyte 214
polymer 150
robotic 101, 262, 319, 330
smart 164
solid crystalline 197
universal 20, 25, 35
substrate 108–112, 114–115, 117–118, 121–122, 125–126, 135–136
consciousness 118
hypothetical 122
integrated 110
maximal 114, 119, 121, 124, 127, 135
neural 119
universal 110, 124
substrate of consciousness 109, 114, 117–118, 121, 124, 135
subsystem 27, 31, 34, 37, 40, 79, 164, 362
sun 1–3, 18–19, 25–26, 163, 178–179, 184
surgeon 254, 262, 330, 336–337, 340, 345–346, 348
surgery 254–255, 262, 332, 337, 339, 345–346, 348
survival 17, 19, 24, 31–32, 37–38, 40, 43–44, 46, 50, 56, 66, 96
survival strategy 24, 27, 37, 44, 58, 79, 81–82, 145, 147, 152, 154–155, 170, 172
synapse 14, 16, 94–95, 101–102, 311–312
system 21–22, 25–32, 34–41, 43–44, 46–47, 50–52, 60, 62–72, 79, 81–82, 108–109, 111, 119–124, 126–135, 148, 163, 174, 216–217, 354–356, 362–363
active 75
actuator 322, 418
aqueous medium 216
artificial 111, 216, 403
artificial muscle 203
battery 304
bio 22
biological 4, 26, 28–31, 51, 80, 215
chaotic 41
chemomechanical 216
classical 355, 357
closed 22, 163–164
colloidal 59
communication 63
complex 23, 31, 38
composite 356
conscious 81
conservative energetic 164
continuous 66
coordinate 272–273, 275–277, 282, 284
decarbonizing electricity 300
decoding communication 56
deterministic 130
dissipative 66
dynamic 1, 39, 61, 82, 148, 163, 172–173
electronic 260
energy storage 322
hierarchical 27, 37, 67, 169, 174
higher-organized 30
informational 28, 35, 64–66, 82
intelligent 22, 29, 43, 61, 65, 72
interdependent 67
living 2, 24, 26–29, 32–37, 39–42, 45–46, 48, 51–53, 55–56, 59–62, 67–69, 71–72, 74, 76, 79–80, 155

magnocellular 32
material 27, 34, 82
measuring 185
mechanical 94
multidimensional 172
nervous 31–32, 35, 52, 68–69, 75, 78, 160, 401
nervous parasympathetic 78
non-biological 28
nonliving 27–30, 33, 45–46, 55, 59, 61, 71, 82
open 27–28, 32, 40, 45, 51, 60, 69, 82, 122, 148, 163
organ 22
organized 25
physical 83, 108, 356–357, 361, 400
plant's 69
quantum 353–355, 357–358, 363, 375
qutrit 363
realistic 111–112
robotic 262, 287
self-organizing 25
stochastic 122
super-intelligent 34
surgical 254, 261, 337
synergetic 43
truck seat 205
two-phase 326
vegetative 32
visual-servo-controlled 261
warning 45

telepathy 53, 55, 61–62, 75, 187
Terfenol-D 160, 206
tetrahedron 82–83, 172–173, 186
tissue 22, 34, 209–210, 254–255, 337, 341, 345
tonus 73–74
total productive maintenance (TPM) 111, 126–128, 133–134
TPM *see* total productive maintenance
transformation 21–22, 203, 206, 265, 268–270, 273, 275–276, 279
Denavit–Hartenberg 263, 272–274, 397
homogeneous 263, 265, 267–269, 271–272, 286, 397
transition 24, 116, 150, 254–255, 337, 339
tritium 162, 304, 307–308
Turing test 377–378, 402

universal intelligence 33, 42–43, 56, 58, 67, 80, 163, 165, 176

vector 208–209, 263, 265–267, 269, 271, 273–274
position 265, 272–273

wavefunction 353–354
waves 45, 47, 60, 76–77, 176, 261, 361
alpha 77–78
beta 77, 79
brain 76–79
delta 77–79
electromagnetic 53, 60, 154

For Product Safety Concerns and Information please contact our EU representative GPSR@taylorandfrancis.com Taylor & Francis Verlag GmbH, Kaufingerstraße 24, 80331 München, Germany

Batch number: 10726507

Printed by Printforce, the Netherlands